HOLMAN TOPICAL CONCORDANCE

An Index to the Bible arranged by subjects in alphabetical order

A. J. HOLMAN COMPANY
DIVISION OF J. B. LIPPINCOTT COMPANY
Philadelphia/New York

U. S. Library of Congress Cataloging in Publication Data

Main entry under title:

Holman topical concordance.

1. Bible—Indexes, Topical.   I. Holman (A. J.)
Company, Philadelphia.
BS432.H63   220.2   73-7656
ISBN-0-87981-019-X

Preface

The *Holman Topical Concordance* provides one of the indispensable tools of Bible study. Unlike a standard concordance of Scripture words, this work covers subjects, themes, and doctrines.

Both trained and unschooled students of Scripture will find it a key to a better understanding of Holy Scripture. It takes its place beside the Bible itself, the standard concordance, and the Bible dictionary.

Grouped together under alphabetized subjects and themes are thousands of Bible verses on topics ranging from idolatry to redemption.

The *Holman Topical Concordance* is a compact, invaluable handbook for every serious student of the Bible.

HOLMAN
TOPICAL
CONCORDANCE

A

ABILITY
From God.   1 P 4:11.
Giving according to.   Ezr 2:69. Ac 11:29.
Greater, promised.   Jn 14:12.
Limited only by faith.   Mk 9:23.
Measured by one's readiness.   2 Co 8:12.
Of Jesus, through the Father.   Jn 5:19.
Of Paul, through Christ.   Php 4:13.
Of the woman who anointed Jesus.   Mk 14:8.
Spiritual, assigned by God.   Ro 12:3–8.
Spiritual, inspired by the Spirit.   1 Co 12:4–11.
Talents given according to.   Mt 25:15.
To build the Tabernacle.   Ex 36:2.
To make the priests' garments.   Ex 28:3.

ABSENCE
From the body means presence with the Lord. Php 1:20–23.
Of body, presence in spirit.   1 Co 5:3.
Of Christ necessary.   Jn 16:7.
Or presence under the Lord.   2 Co 5:9.

ABUNDANCE
Of blessings promised the righteous.   Pr 28:20.
Of divine grace.   Ro 5:20. 2 Co 8:7.
Of divine mercy.   Ps 86:5.
Of entrance into the kingdom.   2 P 1:11.
Of harvest promised Israel.   Lv 26:5. Dt 30:9.
Of the heart, source of our words.   Mt 12:34.
Of human life commanded.   Gn 1:28.
Of joy with the Lord.   Ps 16:11.
Of life at the creation.   Gn 1:20.
Of life in Christ.   Jn 10:10.
Of spiritual riches.   Php 4:18–19.

ACCEPTANCE
By the grace of God.   Ro 5:17. Ep 1:6.
Of prayers.   Gn 19:21.
Of sacrifices.   Ps 119:108.
Of sinners.   Ezk 20:40–41; 36:23–29.

ACCESS TO GOD
Blessedness of.   Pss 16:11; 65:4; 73:28.
Follows upon reconciliation to God.   Cl 1:21, 22.
In his temple.   Pss 15:1; 27:4; 43:3; 65:4.
In prayer.   Dt 4:7. Mt 6:6. 1 P 1:17. (See Prayer.)
Is a privilege of saints.   Dt 4:7. Pss 15; 23:6; 24:3–4.
Is by Christ.   Jn 10:7, 9; 14:6. Ro 5:2. Ep 2:13; 3:12. He 7:19, 25; 10:19. 1 P 3:18.
Is by the Holy Ghost.   Ep 2:18.
Is of God.   Ps 65:4.
Obtained through faith.   Ac 14:27 Ro 5:2. Ep 3:12. He 11:6.
Promises connected with.   Ps 145:18. Is 55:3. Mt 6:6. Ja 4:8.
Saints earnestly seek.   Pss 27:4; 42:1–2; 43:3; 84:1, 2.
Saints have, with confidence.   Ep 3:12. He 4:16; 10:19, 22.
To obtain mercy and grace.   He 4:16.
Urge others to seek.   Is 2:3. Jr 31:6.
Typified.   Lv 16:12–15, with He 10:19–22.
Vouchsafed to repenting sinners.   Ho 14:2. Jl 2:12. See also Repentance.
Wicked commanded to seek.   Is 55:6. Ja 4:8.

ACCOMPLISHMENT
Cost of.   Lk 14:28.
Of all things.   Rv 16:17.
Of the Christian race.   1 Co 9:24–27.
Of collection for Paul.   2 Co 8:11.
Of creation   Gn 1:31.
Of entry into the promised land.   Jsh 3:1–17.
Of idol destruction   2 Ch 34:7.
Of Israel's warfare.   Is 40:2.
Of Jesus, source of.   Jn 5:19–20.

ACCUSATION
Against Jesus.   Mt 27:13. Lk 23:2.
Against Stephen.   Ac 6:11.
Against the woman taken in adultery.   Jn 8:4, 10.
Answered.   Ro 8:1. 1 Jn 3:21.
False, and restitution.   Lk 19:8.

False, forbidden. Lk 3:14.
Of Adam and Eve. Gn 3:12–13.
Of Satan against Job. Jb 1:9–11; 2:4–5.

ACHIEVEMENT
See Accomplishment.

ADOPTION
Being gathered together in one by Christ. Jn 11:52.
Confers a new name. Nu 6:27. Is 62:2. Ac 15:17. *See also* Titles of Saints.
Entitles to an inheritance. Mt 13:43. Ro 8:17. Gl 3:29; 4:7. Ep 3:6.
Evidenced by being led by the Spirit. Ro 8:14.
Explained. 2 Co 6:18.
God is long-suffering and merciful toward the partakers of. Jr 31:1, 9, 20.
Holy Spirit a witness of. Ro 8:16.
ILLUSTRATED BY
Esther. Es 2:7.
Joseph's sons. Gn. 48:5, 14, 16, 22.
Moses. Ex 2:10.
Is according to promise. Ro 9:8. Gl 3:29.
Is a privilege of saints. Jn 1:12. 1 Jn 3:1.
Is by faith. Gl 3:7, 26.
Is of God's grace. Ezk 16:3–6. Ro 4:16, 17. Ep 1:5, 6, 11.
Is through Christ. Jn 1:12. Gl 4:4, 5. Ep 1:5. He 2:10, 13.
New birth connected with. Jn 1:12–13.
Of Gentiles, predicted. Ho 2:23. Ro 9:24–26. Ep 3:6.
Safety of those who receive. Pr 14:26.
Saints become brethren of Christ by. Jn 20:17. He 2:11–12.
Saints predestined unto. Ro 8:29. Ep 1:5, 11.
Saints receive the Spirit of. Ro 8:15. Gl 4:6.
Saints wait for the final consummation of. Ro 8:19, 23. 1 Jn 3:2.
Should lead to holiness. 2 Co 6:17–18, with 2 Co 7:1. Php 2:15. 1 Jn 3:2–3.
SHOULD PRODUCE
An avoidance of ostentation. Mt 6:1–4, 6, 18.
A desire for God's glory. Mt 5:16.
A forgiving spirit. Mt 6:14.
A love of peace. Mt 5:9.
A merciful spirit. Lk 6:35–36.
A spirit of prayer. Mt 7:7–11.
Childlike confidence in God. Mt 6:25–34.
Likeness to God. Mt 5:44–45, 48. Ep 5:1.

Subjects saints to the fatherly discipline of God. Dt 8:5. 2 S 7:14. Pr 3:11–12. He 12:5–11.
To be pleaded in prayer. Is 63:16. Mt 6:9.
Typified. Israel. Ex 4:22. Ho 11:1. Ro 9:4.

ADORATION
Observed by Isaiah. Is 6:1–3.
Of God, commanded.1 Ch 16:29. Pss 95:6; 96:1; 99:9; 100:1–2; 107:1; 112:1; 113:1; 117.
Of Jesus. Mt 8:2; 9:18; 14:33; 18:26; 28:16–17. Mk 5:6. Jn 20:28. Php 2:10. He 1:6.
Of the wise men. Mt 2:2.
To God, ascribed. Jde 1:25. Rv 4:8.

ADVENT OF CHRIST
Attested in the Lord's Supper. 1 Co 11:26.
Celebrated. Mt 21:5, 9.
Coming again. Lk 21:27. Ac 1:11. Rv 1:7.
Meaning for Christians. 2 P 3:10–12. Rv 22:12–14.
Prophesied. Is 52:13—53:12. Mi 4:1–8; 5:2. Ml 4:2.

ADVOCATE
THE HOLY SPIRIT
Another Comforter. Jn 14:16.
Christ to send. Jn 16:7.
Will teach us all things. Jn 14:26.
Will testify of Christ. Jn 15:26.
JESUS
Our advocate with the Father. 1 Jn 2:1.
See also Comforter.

AFFECTIONS
Blessedness of making God the object of. Ps 91:14.
Carnal, crucified in saints. Ro 6:6. Gl 5:24.
Carnal, should be mortified. Ro 8:13; 13:14. 1 Co 9:27. Cl 3:5 1 Th 4:5.
Christ claims the first place in. Mt 10:37. Lk 14:26.
Enkindled by communion with Christ. Lk 24:32.
False teachers seek to captivate. Gl 1:10; 4:17. 2 Tm 3:6. 2 P 2:3, 18. Rv 2:14, 20.
Of saints, supremely set on God. Pss 42:1; 73; 25; 119:10.
Of the wicked, not sincerely set on God. Is 58:1–2. Ezk 33:31–32. Lk 8:13.
Of the wicked, unnatural and perverted. Ro 1:31. 2 Tm 3:3. 2 P 2:10.

SHOULD BE SET.
Upon the commandments of God. Pss 19:8–10; 119:20, 97, 103, 167.
Upon God supremely. Dt 6:5. 12:30.
Upon heavenly things. Cl 3:1–2.
Upon the house and worship of God. 1 Ch 29:3. Pss 26:8; 27:4; 84:1–2.
Upon the people of God. Ps 16:3. Ro 12:10. 2 Co 7:13–15. 1 Th 2:8.
Should be zealously engaged for God. Pss 69:9; 119:139. Gl 4:18.
Should not grow cold. Ps 106:12–13. Mt 24:12. Gl 4:15. Rv 2:4.

AFFLICTED, DUTY TOWARD THE
To bear them in mind. He 13:3.
To comfort them. Jb 16:5; 29:25. 2 Co 1:4. 1 Th 4:18.
To pity them. Jb 6:14.
To pray for them. Ac 12:5. Ph 1:16, 19. Ja 5:14–16.
To protect them. Ps 82:3. Pr 22:22; 31:5.
To relieve them. Jb 31:19–20. Is 58:10 Php 4:14.
To sympathize with them. Ro 12:15. Gl 6:2.
To visit them. Ja 1:27.

AFFLICTED SAINTS
CHRIST
Comforts. Is 61:2. Mt 11:28–30. Lk 7:13. Jn 14:1; 16:33.
Delivers. Rv 3:10.
Is with. Jn 14:18.
Preserves. Is 63:9. Lk 21:18.
Supports. 2 Tm 4:17. He 2:18.
GOD
Comforts. Is 49:13. Jr 31:13. Mt 5:4. 2 Co 1:4–5; 7:6.
Delivers. Ps 34:4, 19. Pr 12:13. Jr 39:17–18.
Is a refuge and strength to. Ps 27:5–6. Is 25:4.
Is with. Ps 46:5, 7. Is 43:2.
Preserves. Ps 34:20.
SHOULD
Acknowledge the justice of their chastisements. Ne 9:33. Jb 2:10. Is 64:5–7. Lm 3:39. Mi 7:9.
Avoid sin. Jb 34:31–32. Jn 5:14. 1 P 2:12.
Be frequent in prayer. Pss 50:15; 55:16–17. *See also* Affliction, Prayer Under.

Be patient. Lk 21:19. Ro 12:12. 2 Th 1:4. Ja 1:4. 1 P 2:20.
Be resigned. 1 S 3:18. 2 K 20:19. Jb 1:21. Ps 39:9.
Imitate Christ. He 12:1–3. 1 P 2:21–23.
Imitate the prophets. Ja 5:10.
Keep the pious resolutions made during affliction. Ps 66:13–15.
Not despise chastening. Jb 5:17. Pr 3:11. He 12:5.
Praise God. Pss 13:5–6; 56:8–10; 57:6–7; 71:20–23.
Take encouragement from former mercies. Ps 27:9. 2 Co 1:10.
Trust in the goodness of God. Jb 13:15. Ps 71:20. 1 Co 1:9.
Turn and devote themselves to God. Ps 116:7–9. Jr 50:3–4. Jsh 6:1.

AFFLICTION, CONSOLATION UNDER
By ministers of the gospel. Is 40:1–2. 1 Co 14:3. 2 Co 1:4, 6.
Christ the Author and Giver of. Is 61:2. Jn 14:18. 2 Co 1:5.
God the Author and Giver of. Ps 23:4. Ro 15:5.
Holy Ghost the Author and Giver of. Jn 14:16–17; 15:26; 16:7. Ac 9:31.
In prospect of death. Jb 19:25–26. Ps 23:4 Jn 14:2. 2 Co 5:1. 1 Th 4:14. He 4:9. Rv 7:14–17; 14:13.
Is
Abundant. Ps 71:21. Is 66:11.
A Cause of praise. Is 12:1; 49:13.
Everlasting. 2 Th 2:16.
Sought in vain from the world. Ps 69:20. Ec 4:1. Lm 1:2.
Strong. He 6:18.
Pray for. Ps 119:82.
Promised. Is 51:3, 12; 66:13. Ezk 14:22–23. Ho 2:14. Zc 1:17.
Saints should administer to each other. 1 Th 4:18; 5:11, 14.
Through scriptures. Ps 119:50, 76. Ro 15:4.
To the persecuted. Dt 33:27.
To the poor. Pss 10:14; 34:6, 9–10.
To the sick. Ps 41:3.
To the tempted. Ro 16:20. 1 Co 10:13. 2 Co 12:9. Ja 1:12; 4:7. 2 P 2:9. Rv 2:10.
To the troubled in mind. Pss 42:5; 94:19. Jn 14:1, 27; 16:20, 22.
To those deserted by friends. Pss 27:10; 41:9–12. Jn 14:18; 15:18–19.

To those who mourn for sin.   Ps 51:17. Is
1:18; 40:1–2; 61:1.   Mi 7:18–19.   Lk 4:18.
Under the infirmities of age.   Ps 71:9, 18.

AFFLICTION, PRAYER UNDER
Exhortation to.   Ja 5:13.
For deliverance.   Pss 25:17, 22; 39:10.   Is
64:9–12.   Jr 17:14.
For divine comfort.   Pss 4:6; 119:76.
For divine teaching and direction.   Jb 34:32.
Pss 27:11; 143:10.
For increase of faith.   Mk 9:24.
For mercy.   Ps 6:2.   Hk 3:2.
For mitigation of troubles.   Ps 39:12–13.
For pardon and deliverance from sin.   Pss
39:8; 51:1; 79:8.
For the presence and support of God.   Pss
10:1; 102:2.
For protection and preservation from enemies.
2 K 19:19.   2 Ch 20:12   Ps 17:8–9.
For restoration to joy.   Pss 51:8, 12; 69:29;
90:14–15.
That God would consider our trouble.   2 K
19:16.   Ne 9:32.   Ps 9:13.   Lm 5:1.
That the Holy Spirit may not be withdrawn.
Ps 51:11.
That we may be quickened.   Ps 143:11.
That we may be taught the uncertainty of life.
Ps 39:4.
That we may be turned to God.   Pss 80:7;
85:4–6.   Jr 31:18.
That we may know the causes of our trouble.
Jb 6:24; 10:2; 13:23–24.

AFFLICTIONS
Always less than we deserve.   Ezr 9:13. Ps
103:10.
Consequent upon the fall.   Gn 3:16–19.
Exhibit the love and faithfulness of God.   Dt
8:5.   Ps 119:75.   Pr 3:12.   1 Co 11:32.   He
12:6–7.   Rv. 3:19.
Frequently terminate in good.   Gn 50:20.   Ex
1:11–12.   Dt   8:15–16.   Jr   24:5–6.   Ezk
20:37.
God appoints.   2 K 6:33.   Jb 5:6, 17.   Ps
66:11.   Am 3:6.   Mi 6:9.
God determines the continuance of.   Gn
15:13–14.   Nu 14:33.   Is 10:25.   Jr 29:10.
God dispenses, as he will.   Jb 11:10.   Is 10:15;
45:7.
God does not willingly send.   Lm 3:33.
God regulates the measure of.   Ps 80:5.   Is
9:1.   Jr 46:28.
Man is born to.   Jb 5:6–7; 14:1.

Of saints, but temporary.   Pss 30:5; 103:9.   Is
54:7–8.   Jn 16:20.   1 P 1:6; 5:10.
Of saints, comparatively light.   Ac 20:23–24.
Ro 8:18.   2 Co 4:17.
Of saints, end in joy and blessedness.   Ps
126:5–6.   Is 61:2–3.   Mt 5:4.   1 P 4:13–14.
Often arise from the profession of the gospel.
Mt 24:9.   Jn 15:21.   2 Tm 3:11–12.
Often severe.   Jb 16:7–16.   Pss 42:7; 66:12.
Jnh 2:3.   Rv 7:14.
Saints appointed to.   1 Th 3:3.
Saints are to expect.   Jn 16:33.   Ac 14:22.
Saints have joy under.   Jb 5:17.   Ja 5:11.
Sin produces.   Jb 4:8; 20:11.   Pr 1:31.
Sin visited with.   2 S 12:14.   Ps 89:30–32.   Is
57:17.   Ac 13:10–11.
Tempered   with   mercy.   Pss   78:38–39;
106:43–46.   Is   30:18–21.   Lm   3:32.   Mi
7:7–9.   Na 1:12.

AFFLICTIONS MADE BENEFICIAL
In convincing us of sin.   Jb 36:8–9.   Ps
119:67.   Lk 15:16–18.
In exercising our patience   Ps 40:1.   Ro 5:3.
Ja 1:3.   1 P 2:20.
In exhibiting the power and faithfulness of
God.   Ps 34:19–20.   2 Co 4:8–11.
In   furthering   the   gospel.   Ac   8:3,   4;
11:19–21.   Php.   1:12.   2   Tm   2:9–10;
4:16–17.
In humbling us.   Dt 8:3, 16.   2 Ch 7:13–14.
Lm 3:19, 20.   2 Co 12:7
In keeping us from again departing from God.
Jb 34:31–32.   Is 10:20.   Ezk 14:10–11.
In leading us to confession of sin.   Nu 21:7.
Pss 32:5; 51:3, 5.
In leading us to seek God in prayer.   Jg 4:3.
Jr 31:18.   Lm 2:17–19.   Ho 5:14–15.   Jnh
2:1.
In promoting the glory of God.   Jn 9:1–3;
11:3–4; 21:18–19.
In purifying us.   Ec 7:2–3.   Is 1:25–26; 48:10.
Jr 9:6–7.   Zc 13:9.   Ml 3:2–3.
In rendering us fruitful in good works.   Jn
15:2.   He 12:10–11.
In teaching us the will of God.   Ps 119:71.   Is
26:9.   Mi 6:9.
In testing and exhibiting our sincerity.   Jb
23:10.   Ps 66:10.   Pr 17:3.
In trying our faith and obedience.   Gn
22:1–2, with He 11:17.   Ex 15:23–25.   Dt
8:2, 16.   1 P 1:7.   Rv 2:10.
In turning us to God.   Dt 4:30–31.   Ne
1:8–9.   Ps 78:34.   Is 10:20–21.   Ho 2:6–7.

AFFLICTIONS OF THE WICKED
Are continual. Jb 15:20. Ec 2:23. Is 32:10.
Are for examples to others. Ps 64:7–9. Zp 3:6–7. 1 Co 10:5–11. 2 P 2:6.
Are ineffectual of themselves, for their conversion. Ex 9:30. Is 9:13. Jr 2:30. Hg 2:17.
Are multiplied. Dt 31:17. Jb 20:12–18. Ps 32:10.
Are often judicially sent. Jb 21:17. Ps 107:17. Jr 30:15.
Are often sudden. Ps 73:19. Pr 6:15. Is 30:13. Rv 18:10.
Frequently harden. Ne 9:28–29. Jr 5:3.
God glorified in. Ex 14:4. Ezk 38:22–23.
God holds in derision. Ps 37:12. Pr 1:26–27.
Impenitence a cause of. Pr 1:30, 31. Ezk 24:13. Am 4:6–12. Zc 7:11–12. Rv 2:21–22.
Produce slavish fear. Jb 15:24. Ps 73:19. Jr 49:3, 5.
Saints should not be alarmed at. Pr 3:25–26.
Sometimes humble them. 1 K 21:27.
Their persecution of saints, a cause of. Dt 30:7. Ps 55:19. Zc 2:9. 2 Th 1:6.

AGRICULTURE
BEASTS USED IN
   Ass. Dt 22:10.
   Horse. Is 28:28.
   Ox. Dt 25:4.
Climate of Canaan favorable to. Gn 13:10. Dt 8:7–9.
Contributes to the support of all. Ec 5:9.
Cultivates the earth. Gn 3:23.
Diligence in, recompensed. Pr 12:11; 13:23; 28:19. He 6:7.
ENACTMENTS TO PROTECT
   Against injuring the produce of. Ex 22:6.
   Against the trespass of cattle. Ex 22:5.
   Not to covet the fields of another. Dt 5:21.
   Not to cut down crops of another. Dt 23:25.
   Not to move landmarks. Dt 19:14. Pr 22:28.
Grief occasioned by the failure of the fruits of. Jl 1:ll. Am 5:16–17.
ILLUSTRATIVE OF
   The culture of the church. 1 Co 3:9.
   The culture of the heart. Jr 4:3. Ho 10:12.
IMPLEMENTS OF
   Ax. 1 S 13:20.
   Cart. 1 S 6:7. Is 28:27–28.

   Fan. Is 30:24. Mt 3:12.
   Flail. Is 28:27.
   Fork. 1 S 13:21.
   Harrow. 2 S 12:31.
   Mattock. 1 S 13:20.
   Plow. 1 S 13:20.
   Pruning hook. Is 18:5. Jl 3:10.
   Shovel. Is 30:24.
   Sickle. Dt 16:9; 23:25.
   Sieve. Am 9:9.
   Teethed threshing instrument. Is 41:15.
The Jews loved and followed. Jg 6:11. 1 K 19:19. 2 Ch 26:10.
Labor of, supposedly lessened by Noah. Gn 5:29. with 9:20.
Man doomed to labor in, after the fall. Gn 3:23.
Man's occupation, before the fall. Gn 2:15.
Not to be engaged in during the sabbatical year. Ex 23:10–11.
Often performed by hirelings. 1 Ch 27:26. 2 Ch 26:10. Mt 20:8. Lk 17:7.
OPERATIONS IN
   Binding. Gn 37:7. Mt 13:30.
   Digging. Is 5:6. Lk 13:8; 16:3.
   Gathering out the stones. Is 5:2.
   Gleaning. Lv 19:9. Ru 2:3.
   Grafting. Ro 11:17–19, 24.
   Harrowing. Jb 39:10. Is 28:24.
   Hedging. Is 5:2, 5. Ho 2:6.
   Manuring. Is 25:10. Lk 14:34–35.
   Mowing. Ps 129:7. Am 7:1.
   Planting. Pr 31:16. Is 44:14. Jr 31:5.
   Plowing. Jb 1:14.
   Pruning. Lv 25:3. Is 5:6. Jn 15:2.
   Reaping. Is 17:5.
   Sowing. Ec. 11:4. Is 32:20. Mt 13:3.
   Stacking. Ex 22:6.
   Storing in barns. Mt 6:26; 13:30.
   Threshing. Dt 25:4. Jg 6:11.
   Watering Dt 11:10. 1 Co 3:6–8.
   Weeding. Mt 13:28.
   Winnowing. Ru 3:2. Mt 3:12.
Patriarchs engaged in. Gn 4:2; 9:20.
Peace favorable to. Is 2:4. Jr 31:24.
PERSONS ENGAGED IN, CALLED
   Husbandmen. 2 Ch 26:10.
   Laborers. Mt 9:37; 20:1.
   Tillers of the ground. Gn 4:2.
PRODUCE OF
   Acknowledges providence of God. Jr 5:24. Ho 2:8.
   Exported. 1 K 5:11. Ezk 27:17.
   Given as rent for land. Mt 21:33–34.

Often blasted because of sin. Is ,10; 7:23.
Jr 12:13. Jl 1:10–11.
PROMOTED AMONG THE JEWS BY
Allotments to each family. Nu 36:7–9.
Prohibition against usury. Ex 22:25.
Promises of God's blessing. Lv 26:4. Dt
7:13; 11:14–15.
Right of redemption. Lv 25:23–28.
Separation from other nations. Ex 33:16.
Rendered laborious by the curse on the earth.
Gn 3:17–19.
REQUIRES
Diligence. Pr 27:23–27. Ec 11:6
Patience Ja 5:7.
Toil. 2 Tm 2:6.
Wisdom. Is 28:26.
Soil of Canaan suited to. Gn 13:10. Dt
8:7–9.
War destructive to. Jr 50:16; 51:23

ALLIANCE WITH THE ENEMIES OF GOD

Blessedness of avoiding. Ps 1:1.
Blessedness of forsaking. Ezk 9:12. Pr 9:6. 2
Co 6:17–18.
A call to come out from. Nu 16:26. Ezr
10:11. Jr 51:6, 45. 2 Co 6:17. 2 Th 3:6.
Rv 18:4.
Children who enter into, bring shame upon
their parents. Pr 28:7.
Evil consequences of. Pr 28:19. Jr 51:7.
Exhortations to hate and avoid. Pr 14:7. Ro
16:17. 1 Co 5:9–11. Ep 5:6–7. 1 Tm 6:5.
2 Tm 3:5.
Exhortations to shun all inducements to. Pr
1:10–15; 4:14–15. 2 P 3:17.
Forbidden Ex 23:32; 34:12. Dt 7:2–3; 13:6,
8. Jsh 23:6–7. Jg 2:2. Ezr 9:12. Pr 1:10,
15. 2 Co 6:14–17. Ep 5:11.
Has led to murder and human sacrifice. Ps
106:37–38.
Is
Defiling. Ezr 9:1–2.
Degrading. Is 1:23.
Enslaving 2 P 2:18–19.
Ensnaring. Ex 23:33. Nu 25:18. Dt
12:30; 13:6. Ps 106:36
Proof of folly. Pr 12:11.
Ruinous to moral character. 1 Co 15:33.
Ruinous to spiritual interests. Pr 29:24.
He 12:14–15. 2 P 3:17.
Leads to idolatry. Ex 34:15–16. Nu 25:1–8.
Dt. 7:4. Jg 3:5–7. Rv 2:20.

Means of preservation from. Pr 2:10–20;
19:27.
Persons in authority should denounce. Ezr
10:9–11. Ne 13:23–27.
Pious parents prohibit, to their children. Gn
28:1.
Provokes the anger of God. Dt 7:4;
31:16–17. 2 Ch 19:2. Ezr 9:13–14. Ps
106:29, 40. Is 2:6.
Provokes God to leave men to reap the fruits of
them. Jsh 23:12–13. Jg 2:1–3.
Punishment of. Nu 33:56. Dt 7:4. Jsh
23:13. Jg 2:3; 3:5–8. Ezr 9:7, 14. Ps
106:41–42. Rv 2:16, 22–23.
SAINTS
Are separate from. Ex 33:16. Ezr 6:21.
Are tempted by the wicked to. Ne 6:2–4.
Deprecate. Gn 49:6. Pss 6:8; 15:4; 101:4,
7; 119:115; 139:19.
Grieve to meet with. Pss 57:4; 120:5–6. 2
P 2:7–8.
Grieve to witness in their brethren. Gn
26:35. Ezr 9:3; 10:6.
Hate and avoid. Pss 26:4–5; 31:6; 101:7.
Rv 2:2.
Should be circumspect when undesignedly
thrown into. Mt 10:16. Co 4:5. 1 P
2:12.
Sin of, to be confessed, deeply repented of, and
forsaken. Ezr 10.
Unbecoming in those called saints. 2 Ch
19:2. 2 Co 6:14–16. Php 2:15.
The wicked are prone to. Ps 50:18. Jr 2:25.

ALTARS

Afforded no protection to murderers. Ex
21:14. 1 K 2:18–34.
Designed for sacrifice. Ex 20:24.
For burnt offering. Ex 27:1–8.
For idolatrous worship, often erected on roofs
of houses. 2 K 23:12. Jr 19:13; 32:29.
For idolatrous worship, to be destroyed. Ex
34:13. Dt 7:5.
For incense. Ex 30:1–6.
Idolaters planted groves near. Jg 6:30. 1 K
16:32–33. 2 K 21:3.
The Jews not to plant groves near. Dt 16:21.
Natural rocks sometimes used as. Jg 6:19–21;
13:19–20.
Not to have steps up to them. Ex 20:26.
Of brick, hateful to God. Is 65:3.
Probable origin of inscriptions on. Dt 27:8.
Protection afforded by. 1 K 1:50–51.

Should be made of earth, or unhewn stone.
Ex 20:24–25. Dt 27:5–6.
THOSE OF, MENTIONED
  Abraham. Gn 12:7–8; 13:18; 22:9.
  Ahaz. 2 K 16:10–12.
  Athenians. Ac 17:23.
  Balaam. Nu 23:1, 14, 29.
  David. 2 S 24:21, 25.
  Gideon. Jg 6:26–27.
  Isaac. Gn 26:25.
  Jacob. Gn 33:20; 35:1, 3, 7.
  Jeroboam at Bethel. 1 K 12:33.
  Joshua. Jsh 8:30–31.
  Moses. Ex 17:15; 24:4.
  Noah. Gn 8:20.
  People of Israel. Jg 21:4.
  Reubenites, etc. Jsh 22:10.
  Samuel. 1 S 7:17.
  Second temple. Ezr 3:2–3.
  Temple of Solomon. 2 Ch 4:1, 19.

ALTAR OF BURNT OFFERING
Ahaz removed and profaned. 2 K 16:10–16.
All gifts to be presented at. Mt 5:23–24.
All its vessels of brass. Ex 27:3; 38:3.
All sacrifices to be offered on. Ex 29:38–42. Is 56:7.
Anointed and sanctified with holy oil. Ex 40:10. Lv 8:10–11.
The blood of sacrifices put on the horns and poured at the foot of. Ex 29:12. Lv 4:7, 18, 25; 8:15.
CALLED
  Altar of God. Ps 43:4.
  Altar of the Lord. Ml 2:13.
  Bronze altar. Ex 39:39. 1 K 8:64.
Cleansed and purified with blood. Ex 29:36–37.
Covered with brass. Ex 27:2.
Dimensions, etc., of. Ex 27:1 38:1.
Furnished with rings and staves. Ex 27:6–7; 38:5–7.
Horns on the corners of. Ex 27:2; 38:2.
ITS FIRE
  Came from before the Lord. Lv 9:24.
  Consumed the sacrifices. Lv 1:8–9.
  Was continually burning. Lv 6:13.
The Jews condemned for swearing lightly by. Mt 23:18–19.
Made after a divine pattern. Ex 27:8.
Network grate of brass placed in. Ex 27:4–5; 38:4.

Nothing polluted or defective to be offered on. Lv 22:22. Ml 1:7–8.
Offering at the dedication of. Nu 7.
Placed in the court before the door of the tabernacle. Ex 40:6, 29.
PRIESTS
  Alone to serve. Nu 18:3, 7.
  Derived support from. 1 Co 9:13.
Sacrifices bound to the horns of. Ps 118:27.
Sanctified by God. Ex 29:44.
Sanctified whatever touched it. Ex 29:37.
A type of Christ. He 13:10.
Was most holy. Ex 40:10.

ALTAR OF INCENSE
Anointed with holy oil. Ex 30:26–27.
Atonement made for, by the high priest once every year. Ex 30:10. Lv 16:18–19.
Blood of all sin offerings put on the horns of. Lv 4:7, 18.
Called the golden altar. Ex 39:38.
Covered by the priests before removal from the sanctuary. Nu 4:11.
Covered with gold. Ex 30:3; 37:26.
Dimensions, etc., of. Ex 30:1, 2; 37:25.
Had four rings of gold under crown for staves. Ex 30:4; 37:27.
Incense burned on, every morning and evening. Ex 30:7–8.
No strange incense nor any sacrifice to be offered on. Ex 30:9.
Placed before the veil in the outer sanctuary. Ex 30:6; 40:5, 26.
PUNISHMENT FOR
  Offering strange fire on. Lv 10:1, 2.
  Unauthorized offering on. 2 Ch 26:16–19.
Said to be before the Lord. Lv 4:7 1 K 9:25.
Staves of, covered with gold. Ex 30:5.
Top of, surrounded with a crown of gold. Ex 30:3; 37:26.
A type of Christ. Rv 8:3; 9:3.

AMBASSADOR
SENT TO
  Congratulate. 1 K 5:1. 2 S 8:10.
  Make alliance. Jsh 9:4.
  Negotiate. 2 K 18:17—19:8.
  Protest injustice. Jg 11:12.
  Seek favors. Nu 20:14.
SPIRITUAL
  For Christ. 2 Co 5:20.
  In chains. Ep 6:20.
  Suffering imprisonment. Phm 1:9.

AMBITION
And covetousness. Hk 2:8–9.
And cruelty. Hk 2:12.
And pride. Hk 2:5.
Condemned by Christ. Mt 18:1, 3–4; 20:25–26; 23:11–12.
Condemned by God. Gn 11:7. Is 5:8.
Leads to strife and contention. Ja 4:1–2.
Punishment of. Pr 17:19. Is 14:12–15. Ezk 31:10–11. Ob 1:3–4.
Saints avoid. Ps 131:1–2.
Vanity of. Jb 20:5–9; 24:24. Ps 49:11–20.

AMEN
Affirms a malediction or oath. Nu 5:22 Dt 27:15 ff.
Christ as. Rv 3:14.
Concludes a benediction or prayer. Mt 6:13. Gl 6:18.
Expresses agreement with a statement of praise or benediction. Pss 41:13; 72:19. 1 Ch 16:36. Ro 16:24.
Uttered through Christ. 2 Co 1:20.

AMUSEMENTS AND PLEASURES, EVIL
Abstinence from, seems strange to the wicked. 1 P 4:4.
Are all vanity. Ec 2:11.
Are transitory. Jb 21:12–13. He 11:25.
Belong to the works of the flesh. Gl 5:19, 21.
Choke the word of God in the heart. Lk 8:14.
Denounced by God. Is 5:11–12.
Formed a part of idolatrous worship. Ex 32:4, 6, 19, with 1 Co 10:7. Jg 16:23–25.
INDULGENCE IN
  An abuse of riches. Ja 5:1, 5.
  A characteristic of the wicked. Is 47:8. Ep 4:17, 19. 2 Tm 3:4. Ti 3:3. 1 P 4:3.
  A proof of folly. Ec 7:4.
  A proof of spiritual death. 1 Tm 5:6.
LEAD TO
  Disregard of the judgments and works of God. Is 5:12. Am 6:1–6.
  Poverty. Pr 21:17.
  Rejection of God. Jb 21:14–15.
May lead to greater evil. Jb 1:5. Mt 14:6–8.
Punishment of. Ec 11:9. 2 P 2, 13.
Shunned by the primitive saints. 1 P 4:3.
Terminate in sorrow. Pr 14:13.
Wisdom of abstaining from Ec 7:2–3.

ANARCHY
In man's final rebellion. 2 Tm 4:3.
When violence reigns. Jr 51:46.
Without law or government. Jg 2:19; 21:25.
Without self-discipline. Pr 25:28.

ANGELS
ANNOUNCED THE
  Ascension and second coming of Christ. Ac 1:11.
  Birth of Christ. Lk 2:10–12.
  Conception of Christ. Mt 1:20–21. Lk 1:31.
  Conception of John the Baptist. Lk 1:13, 36.
  Resurrection of Christ. Mt 28:5–7. Lk 24:23.
ARE
  Elect. 1 Tm 5:21.
  Examples of meekness. 2 P 2:11. Jde 9.
  Holy. Mt 25:31.
  Innumerable. Jb 25:3. He 12:22.
  Mighty. Ps 103:20.
  Ministering spirits. 1 K 19:5. Pss 68:17; 104:4. Lk 16:22. Ac 12:7–11; 27:23, He 1:7, 14.
  Not to be worshiped. Cl 2:18. Rv 19:10; 22:9.
  Of different orders. Is 6:2. 1 Th 4:16. 1 P 3:22. Jde 9. Rv 12:7.
  Subject to Christ. Ep 1:21. Cl 1:16; 2:10. 1 P 3:22.
  Wise. 2 S 14:20.
Celebrate the praises of God. Jb 38:7. Ps 148:2. Is 6:3. Lk 2:13–14. Rv 5:11–12; 7:11–12.
Communicate the will of God and Christ. Dn 8:16–17; 9:21–23; 10:11; 12:6–7. Mt 2:13, 20. Lk 1:19, 28. Ac 5:20; 8:26; 10:5, 27:23. Rv 1:1.
Execute the judgments of God. 2 S 24:16. 2 K 19:35. Ps 35:6–6. Ac 12:23. Rv 16:1.
Execute the purposes of God. Nu 22:22. Ps 103:21. Mt 13:39–42; 28:2. Jn 5:4. Rv 5:2.
Have charge over the children of God. Pss 34:7; 91:11–12. Dn 6:22. Mt 18:10.
Know and delight in the gospel of Christ. Ep 3:9–10. 1 Tm 3:16. 1 P 1:12.
The law given by the ministration of. Ps 68:17. Ac 7:53. He 2:2.
Minister to Christ. Mt 4:11. Lk 22:43. Jn 1:51.
Ministration of, obtained by prayer. Mt 26:53. Ac 12:5, 7.

Obey the will of God. Ps 103:20. Mt 6:10.

Rejoice over every repentant sinner. Lk 15:7, 10.

Shall attend Christ at his second coming. Mt 16:27; 25:31. Mk 8:38. 2 Th 1:7.

Shall execute the purposes of Christ. Mt 13:41; 24:31.

Were created by God and Christ. Ne 9:6. Cl 1:16.

Worship God and Christ. Ne 9:6. Php 2:9–11. He 1:6.

ANGER

Avoid those given to. Gn 49:6. Pr 22:24.

Be slow to. Pr 15:18; 16:32; 19:11. Ti 1:7. Ja 1:19.

Brings its own punishment. Jb 5:2. Pr 19:19; 25:28.

A characteristic of fools. Pr 12:16; 14:29; 27:3. Ec 7:9.

Children should not be provoked to. Ep 6:4. Cl 3:21.

CONNECTED WITH

Clamor and evil-speaking. Ep 4:31.

Cruelty. Gn 49:7. Pr 27:3-4.

Malice and blasphemy. Cl 3:8.

Pride. Pr 21:24.

Strife and contention. Pr 21:19; 29:22; 30:33.

Forbidden. Ec 7:9. Mt 5:22. Ro 12:19.

Grievous words stir up. Jg 12:4. 2 S 19:43. Pr 15:1.

In prayer be free from. 1 Tm 2:8.

May be averted by wisdom. Pr 29:8.

Meekness pacifies. Pr 15:1. Ec 10:4.

Should not betray us into sin. Ps 37:8. Ep 4:26.

A work of the flesh. Gl 5:20.

ANGER OF GOD

AGAINST

Apostasy. He 10:26–27.

Idolatry. Dt 29:20, 27–28; 32:19–20, 22. Jsh 23:16. 2 K 22:17. Ps 78:58–59. Jr 44:3.

Impenitence. Ps 7:12. Pr 1:30–31. Is 9:13–14. Ro 2:5.

Sin, in saints. Pss 89:30–32; 90:7–9; 99:8; 102:9–10. Is 47:6.

Those who forsake him. Ezr 8:22. Is 1:4.

Those who oppose the gospel, extreme. Ps 2:2–3, 5. 1 Th 2:16.

Unbelief. Ps 78:21–22. He 3:18–19. Jn 3:36.

The wicked. Pss 7:11; 21:8–9. Is 3:8; 13:9. Na 1:2–3. Ro 1:18; 2:8. Ep 5:6. Cl 3:6.

Aggravated by continual provocation. Nu 32:14.

AVERTED

By Christ. Lk 2:11, 14. Ro 5:9. 2 Co 5:18–19. Ep 2:14, 17. Cl 1:20. 1 Th 1:10.

From them that believe. Jn 3:14–18. Ro 3:25; 5:1.

Upon confession of sin and repentance. Jb 33:27–28. Ps 106:43–45. Jr 3:12–13; 18:7–8; 31:18–20. Jl 2:12–14. Lk 15:18–20.

Cannot be resisted. Jb 9:13; 14:13. Ps 76:7. Na 1:6.

Folly of provoking. Jr 7:19. 1 Co 10:22.

Justice of, not to be questioned. Ro 9:18, 20, 22.

Manifested in judgments and afflictions. Jb 21:17. Pss 78:49–51; 90:7. Is 9:19. Jr 7:20. Ezk 7:19. He 3:17.

Manifested in terrors. Ex 14:24. Ps 76:6–8. Jr 10:10. Lm 2:20–22.

Removal of, should be prayed for. Pss 39:10; 79:5; 80:4. Dn 9:16. Hk 3:2.

Righteous. Ps 58:10–11. Lm 1:18. Ro 2:6, 8; 3:5–6. Rv 16:6–7.

Should lead to repentance. Is 42:24–25. Jr 4:8.

Slow. Ps 103:8. Is 48:9. Jnh 4:2. Na 1:3.

Specially reserved for the day of wrath. Zp 1:14–18. Mt 25:41. Ro 2:5, 8. 2 Th 1:8. Rv 6:17; 11:18; 19:15.

Tempered with mercy to saints. Ps 30:5. Is 26:20; 54:8; 57:15–16. Jr 30:11. Mi 7:11.

To be borne with submission. 2 S 24:17. Lm 3:39, 43. Mi 7:9.

To be deprecated. Ex 32:11. Pss 6:1; 38:1; 74:1–2. Is 64:9.

To be dreaded. Pss 2:12; 76:7; 90:11. Mt 10:28.

ANOINTING

APPLIED TO

Eyes. Rv 3:18.

Face. Ps 104:15.

Feet. Lk 7:38–39. Jn 12:3.

Head. Ps 23:5. Ec 9:8.

Deprivation of, threatened as a punishment. Dt 28:40. Mi 6:15.

The Jews very fond of. Pr 27:9. Am 6:6.

Neglect of, to guests, a mark of disrespect.
Lk 7:46.
Neglected in times of affliction. 2 S 12:20;
14:2. Dn 10:3.

OINTMENT FOR
An article of commerce. Ezk 27:17. Rv
18:13.
Most expensive. 2 K 20:13. Am 6:6. Jn
12:3, 5.
Prepared by the apothecary. Ec 10:1.
Richly perfumed. S S 4:10. Jn 12:3.
Recommended by Christ in times of fasting.
Mt 6:17–18.

USED FOR
Curing the sick. Mk 6:13. Ja 5:14.
Decorating the person. Ru 3:3.
Healing wounds. Is 1:6. Lk 10:34.
Preparing the dead for burial. Mt 26:12.
Mk 16:1, with Lk 23:56.
Preparing weapons for war. Is 21:5.
Purifying the body. Es 2:12. Is 57:9.
Refreshing the body. 2 Ch 28:15.
With oil. Ps 92:10.
With ointment. Jn 11:2.

ANOINTING OF THE HOLY GHOST
Abiding in saints. 1 Jn 2:27.
From God. 2 Co 1:21.
God preserves those who receive. Pss 18:50;
20:6; 89:20–23.
Guides into all truth. 1 Jn 2:27.
Saints receive. Is 61:3. 1 Jn 2:20.

THAT CHRIST SHOULD RECEIVE
Foretold. Ps 45:7. Is 61:1. Dn 9:24.
Fulfilled. Lk 4:18, 21. Ac 4:27; 10:38.
He 1:9.
Types. Ex 40:13–15. Lv 8:12. 1 S 16:13. 1
K 19:16.

ANOINTING, SACRED
Antiquity of. Gn 28:18; 35:14.
Consecrates to God's service. Ex 30:29.

OIL OR OINTMENT FOR
Compounded by priests. 1 Ch 9:30.
Divinely prescribed. Ex 30:23–25.
Holy forever. Ex 30:25, 31.
The Jews condemned for imitating. Ezk
23:41.
Not to be imitated. Ex 30:32.
To be put on no stranger. Ex 30:33.

PERSONS WHO RECEIVED
Kings. Jg 9:8. 1 S 9:16. 1 K 1:34.
Priests. Ex 40:13–15.
Prophets 1 K 19:16. Is 61:1.

THINGS WHICH RECEIVED
Bronze altar. Ex 29:36; 40:10.
Bronze laver. Ex 40:11.
Tabernacle, etc. Ex 30:26–27; 40:9.

THOSE WHO PARTOOK OF
Not to be injured or insulted. 1 S 24:6;
26:9. 2 S 1:14–15; 19:21.
Protected by God. 1 Ch 16:22. Ps
105:15.

ANTICHRIST
Deceit characteristic of. 2 Jn 7.
Denies Father and Son. 1 Jn 2:22.
Denies incarnation of Christ. 1 Jn 4:3. 2 Jn 7.
Spirit prevalent in apostolic times. 1 Jn 2:18.

ANXIETY
Articulated. Ps 38:6.
Makes the word of God unfruitful. Mk 4:19.
Overcome. Ps 23:4.
Prevented. Ps 121:4. 1 P 5:7.
Prohibited. Mt 6:34.

APOSTATES
Cautions against becoming. He 3:12. 2 P
3:17.
Described. Dt 13:13. He 3:12.
Guilt and punishment of. Zp 1:4–6. He
10:25–31, 39. 2 P 2:17, 20–22.
Impossible to restore. He 6:4–6.
Made by persecution. Mt 24:9, 10. Lk 8:13.
Made by a worldly spirit. 2 Tm 4:10.
Never belonged to Christ. 1 Jn 2:19.
Saints do not become. Ps 41:18–19. He 6:9;
10:39.
Shall abound in the latter days. Mt 24:12. 2
Th 2:3. 1 Tm 4:1–3.

APOSTLES
CALLED BY
Christ. Mt 10:1. Mk 3:13. Ac 20:24. Ro
1:5.
God. 1 Co 1:1; 12:28. Gl 1:1, 15–16.
The Holy Ghost. Ac 13:2, 4.
Christ always present with. Mt 28:20.
Christ as preeminent. He 3:1.
Empowered to work miracles. Mt 10:1, 8.
Mk 16:20. Lk 9:1. Ac 2:43.
Equal authority given to each of. Mt 16:19,
with 18:18. 2 Co 11:5.
Guided by the Spirit into all truth. Jn 14:26;
15:26; 16:13.
The Holy Ghost given to. Jn 20:22. Ac
2:1–4; 9:17.

Humility urged upon. Mt 20:26–27. Mk 9:33–37. Lk 22:24–30.

Instructed by the Spirit to answer adversaries. Mt 10:19–20. Lk 12:11–12.

Mutual love urged upon. Jn 15:17.

Ordained by Christ. Mk 3:14. Jn 15:16.

Persecutions and sufferings of. Mt 10:16, 18. Lk 21:16. Jn 15:20; 16:2.

Received their title from Christ. Lk 6:13.

Saw Christ in the flesh. Lk 1:2. Ac 1:22. 1 Co 9:1. 1 Jn 1:1.

Selected from obscure stations. Mt 4:18.

Self-denial urged upon. Mt 10:37–39.

Sent first to the house of Israel. Mt 10:5–6. Lk 24:47. Ac 13:46.

Sent to preach the gospel to all nations. Mt 28:19–20. Mk 16:15. 2 Tm 1:11.

Specially devoted to the office of the ministry. Ac 6:4; 20:27.

Warned against a timid profession of Christ. Mt 10:27–33.

Were hated by the world. Mt 10:22; 24:9. Jn 15:18.

Were not of the world. Jn 15:19; 17:16.

Were unlearned men. Ac 4:13.

Witnesses of the resurrection and ascension of Christ. Lk 24:33–41, 51. Ac 1:2–9; 10:40–41. 1 Co 15:8.

ARK, NOAH'S

Building commanded. Gn 6:14.

Exhibited Noah's faith and righteousness. 1 P 3:20. He 11:7.

Set forth surrounding unrighteousness. Lk 17:26–27.

Specifications. Gn 6:15 ff.

Successful test. Gn 7—9.

ARK OF THE COVENANT

Anointed with sacred oil. Ex 30:26.

At Kirjath-jearim twenty years. 1 S 7:1–2.

Brought by Solomon into the temple with great solemnity. 1 K 8:1–6. 2 Ch 5:2–9.

Brought into the city of David. 2 S 6:12–15. 1 Ch 15:25–28.

CALLED THE

Ark of the covenant of the Lord. Nu 10:33.

Ark of God. 1 S 3:3.

Ark of God's strength. 2 Ch 6:41. Ps 132:8.

Ark of the testimony. Ex 30:6. Nu 7:89.

Captured by the Philistines. 1 S 4:11.

CARRIED

Before the Israelites in their journeys. Nu 10:33. Jsh 3:6.

By priests or Levites alone. Dt 10:8. Jsh 3:14. 2 S 15:24. 1 Ch 15:2.

Sometimes to the camp in war. 1 S 4:4–5.

A copy of the law laid in the side of. Dt 31:26.

Covered with the veil by the priests before removal. Nu 4:5-6.

David made a tent for. 2 S 6:17. 1 Ch 15:1.

Dimensions, etc., of. Ex 25:10; 37:1.

Entirely covered with gold. Ex 25:11; 37:2.

Esteemed the glory of Israel. 1 S 4:21–22.

Furnished with rings and staves. Ex 25:12–15; 37:3–5.

The Israelites inquired of the Lord before. Jsh 7:6–9. Jg 20:27. 1 Ch 13:3.

Mercy seat laid upon. Ex 25:21; 26:34.

MIRACLES CONNECTED WITH

Fall of Dagon. 1 S 5:1–4.

Fall of the walls of Jericho. Jsh 6:6–20.

Jordan divided. Jsh 4:7.

Manner of its restoration. 1 S 6:1–18.

Philistines plagued. 1 S 5:6–12.

Placed in the Holy of Holies. Ex 26:33; 40:21. He 9:3–4.

Pot of manna and Aaron's rod laid up before. He 9:4, with Ex 16:33–34. Nu 17:10.

Profanation of, punished. Nu 4:5, 15. 1 S 6:19. 1 Ch 15:13.

Protecting of, rewarded. 1 Ch 13:14.

Removed from Kirjath-jearim to the house of Obed-edom. 2 S 6:1–11.

Sanctified its resting place. 2 Ch 8:11.

Surrounded with a crown of gold. Ex 25:11.

Symbol of the presence and glory of God. Nu 14:43–44. Jsh 7:6. 1 S 14:18–19. Ps 132:8.

Tables of testimony alone placed in. Ex 25:16, 21.

A type of Christ. Ps 40:8. Rv 11:19.

Was holy. 2 Ch 35:3.

ARMIES

Accompanied by beasts of burden and wagons for baggage. Jg 7:12. 2 K 7:7. Ezk 23:2.

Ancient, often numerous. Jsh 11:4. 1 S 13:5.

Antiquity of. Gn 14:1–8.

Began their campaigns in the spring. 2 S 11:1.

Brought their idols with them. 1 Ch 14:12.

CALLED THE

Bands. 2 K 24:2. 1 Ch 7:4.

Hosts. Jsh 10:5. Jg 8:10.
Power of kings. 2 Ch 32:9.
Wings of a nation. Is 8:8. Jr 48:40.
Commenced their battles with a shout. 1 S 17:20. 2 Ch 13:15. Jr 51:14.

COMPARED TO
Caterpillars. Jr 51:14, 27.
Clouds. Ezk 38:9–16.
Flies. Is 7:18–19.
Grasshoppers. Jg 6:3–5; 7:12.
Locusts. Is 33:4. Rv 9:3, 7.
Overflowing torrents. Is 28:2. Dn 11:10, 26.
Waters of a river. Is 8:7.
Whirlwinds. Jr 25:32.

COMPOSED OF
Bowmen and slingers. 1 Ch 12:2. Jr 4:29.
Cavalry. Ex 14:9. 1 K 20:20.
Spearmen or heavy troops. Ps 68:30. Ac 23:23.
War chariots. Jsh 17:16. Jg 4:3.
Devastation occasioned by. Is 37:18. Jr 5:17.
Divided the spoil. Ex 15:9. Zc 14:1.

EMPLOYED IN
Assaulting cities. Jsh 7:3–4.
Beseiging cities. Dt 20:12. Is 29:3.
Fighting battles. 1 S 17:2–3. 1 Ch 19:17.

ENCAMPED
Before cities. Jsh 10:5. 1 S 11:1.
In the open fields. 2 S 11:11. 1 Ch 11:15.
Exercised savage cruelties on the vanquished. Jr 50:42. Lm 5:11–13. Am 1:13.
Fear occasioned by. Nu 22:3. Jr 6:25.
Frequently the instrument of God's vengeance. Is 10:5–6; 13:5.
Furnished with standards. S S 6:4. Is 10:18. Jr 4:21.
Generally in three divisions. Gn 14:15. Jb 1:17.

ILLUSTRATIVE OF
The church. Dn 8:10–13. S S 6:4, 10.
Multitudes of angels. 1 K 22:19. Ps 148:2. Dn 4:35. Mt 26:53.
Numerous and heavy afflictions. Jb 19:12.
In latter ages received pay. Lk 3:14. 1 Co 9:7.

LED BY
Experienced captains. 2 K 18:17, 24.
Kings in person. 2 K 18:13; 25:1.

MARCHED
Often in open line. Hk 1:6, 8.
With noise and tumult. Is 17:12–13. Jl 2:5.

With order and precision. Is 5:27. Jl 2:7–8.
With rapidity. Jr 48:40. Hk 1:8.
Of different nations often confederated. Jsh 9:2; 10:5. Jg 3:13. 1 K 20:1.
Often consisted of the whole effective strength of nations. Nu 21:23. 1 S 29:1.

OFTEN DESTROYED BY
Supernatural means. Jsh 10:11. 2 K 19:35.
Their enemies. Ex 17:13. Jsh 10:10, 20. Jg 11:33. 2 S 18:7. 1 K 20:21.
Themselves through divine intervention. Jg 7:22. 1 S 14:15–16. 2 Ch 20:23.
Often surprised their enemies. Jsh 8:2. 2 Ch 13:13. Jr 51:12.
Often went on foreign service. Jr. 5:15; 50:3.
Sent out foraging parties. 2 K 5:2.
Toil and fatigue often endured by. Ezk 29:18.
Troops often hired for. 1 Ch 19:7. 2 Ch 25:6.

ARMIES OF ISRAEL
Ark of God frequently brought with. Jsh 6:6–7. 1 S 4:4–5. 2 S 11:11; 15:24.
Attended by priests with trumpets. Nu 10:9; 31:6. 2 Ch 13:13–14.

BEFORE GOING TO WAR
Consulted the Lord. Jg 1:1; 20:27–28.
Were encouraged by their commanders. 2 Ch 20:20.
Were numbered and reviewed. 2 S 18:1–2, 4. 1 K 10:15, 27.
Were required to keep from iniquity. Dt. 23:9.
Bravery and fidelity in, rewarded. Jsh 15:16. 1 S 17:25; 18:17. 2 S 18:11. 1 Ch 11:6.

CALLED
The armies of the living God. 1 S 17:26.
The host. Dt 23:9. 1 S 28:19.

COLLECTED BY
Extraordinary means. Jg 19:29 with 20:1. 1 S 11:7.
Sound of trumpets. Jg 3:27; 6:34.
Special messengers. Jg 6:35. 2 S 20:14.
Commanded by the captain of the host. 2 S 2:8; 17:25; 20:23.
Composed of infantry. Nu 11:21. Jg 5:15.
Congratulated on returning victorious. 1 S 18:6–7, with Ex 15:1–21.
Directed in their movements by God. Jsh 8:1–2. Jg 1:2. 2 S 5:25. 1 Ch 14:16.
Disbanded after war. 1 S 13:2. 1 K 22:36.

DIVIDED INTO

Companies of thousands, etc.   Nu 31:14.
2 K 1:9, 11. 1 Ch 13:1, 27:1.

Three divisions.   Jg 7:16. 1 S 11:11.

Van and rear.   Jsh 6:9.

Educated in the art of war.   Is 2:4. Mi 4:3.

Enrolled by the chief scribe.   2 K 25:19.

Fearful ones allowed to leave.   Dt 20:8. Jg 7:3.

First mention of.   Ex 7:4.

Horsemen and chariots introduced into, after David's reign.   1 K 1:5; 4:26.

INFERIOR OFFICERS OF, APPOINTED BY

The captain of the host.   2 S 18:11. 2 K 4:13.

The king.   2 S 18:1. 2 Ch 25:5.

The shoterim or chief officers.   Dt 20:9.

Men selected from, for difficult enterprises.
Ex 17:9. Nu 31:5–6. Jsh 7:4; 8:3. Jg 7:5–6.
2 S 17:1.

MODE OF PROVISIONING

Food brought by themselves.   Jsh 1:11.

Food sent by their families.   1 S 17:17.

Levies.   Jg 8:5. 1 S 25:4–8.

Presents.   2 S 17:27–29.

Often led by the king in person.   1 S 8:20;
15:4–5. 2 S 12:29. 1 K 22.

Often supplied with arms from public armories.   2 Ch 11:12; 26:14.

Part of, retained in times of peace by the kings.
1 S 13:1–2. 1 Ch 27:1–15.

PERSONS EXEMPTED FROM SERVING IN

Who had built a house.   Dt 20:5.

Who had planted a vineyard.   Dt 20:6.

Who were lately betrothed.   Dt 20:7.

Who were newly married.   Dt 24:5.

Persons liable to serve in.   Nu 1:2–3.

Praises of God often sung before.   2 Ch 20:21–22.

Purified on returning from war.   Nu 31:19–25.

Refusal to join, often punished.   Jg 21:5, 8–11. L S 11:7.

Refusal to join, stigmatized.   Jg 5:15–17.

Sometimes consisted of the whole nation.   Jg 20:11. 1 S 11:7.

Strict discipline observed in.   Jsh 7:16–21. 1 S 14:24–44.

With the aid of God, all powerful.   Lv 26:3, 7–8. Dt 7:24; 32:30. Jsh 1:5.

Without God, easily overcome.   Lv 26:17. Nu 14:22, 45.

ARMS, MILITARY

Armories built for.   2 K 20:13. S S 4:4.

BEFORE USING

Anointed.   Is 21:5.

Burnished.   Jr 46:4. Ezk 21:9–11, 28.

Tried and proved.   1 S 17:39.

DEFENSIVE

Buckler.   1 Ch 5:18. Ezk 26:8.

Called armor.   Lk 11:22.

Called harness.   1 K 22:34.

Coat of mail, breastplate, habergeon, or brigandine.   1 S 17:5, 38. Ex 28:32. Jr 46:4. Rv 9:9.

Girdle.   1 S 18:4. 2 S 18:11.

Greaves.   1 S 17:6.

Helmet.   1 S 17:5, 38. 2 Ch 26:14.

Shield.   1 K 10:16–17; 14:26–27.

Target.   1 S 17:6.

FOR SIEGES

Battering rams.   2 S 20:15.. Exk 4:2.

Engines for casting stones, etc.   2 Ch 26:15.

Great stores of, prepared.   2 Ch 32:5.

Hung on the walls of cities.   Ezk 27:10–11.

ILLUSTRATIVE OF

Judgments of God.   Is 13:5. Jr 50:25.

Spiritual armor.   Ro 13:12. 2 Co 6:7. Ep 6:11–14. 1 Th 5:8.

Spiritual weapons.   2 Co 10:4. Ep 6:17.

Inferior to wisdom.   Ec 9:18.

Made of iron, steel, or brass.   Jb 20:24. 1 S 17:5–6.

Not worn in ordinary.   1 S 21:8.

OFFENSIVE

Battleax.   Ezk 26:9. Jr 51:20.

Bow and arrows.   Gn 48:22. 1 K 22:34.

Called instruments of death.   Ps 7:13.

Called instruments of war.   1 Ch 12:33, 37.

Called weapons of war.   2 S 1:27.

Dagger.   Jg 3:16, 21–22.

Dart or javelin.   1 S 18:10–11. 2 S 18:14.

Handstaff.   Mt 26:47.

Sling.   1 S 17:50. 2 K 3:25.

Spear or lance.   1 S 26:7. Jr 50:42.

Sword.   Jg 20:15. Ezk 32:27.

Two-edged sword.   Ps 149:6. Pr 5:4.

Of conquered nations taken away to prevent rebellion.   Jg 5:8. 1 S 13:19–22.

OF THE VANQUISHED

Sometimes burned.   Ezk 39:9–10.

Sometimes kept as trophies.   1 S 17:54.

Taken off them.   2 S 2:21. Lk 11:22.

Often given as presents.   1 K 10:25.
Part of, borne by armor bearers.   Jg 9:54. 1 S 14:1; 16:21.
Put on at the first alarm.   Is 8:9. Jr 46:3–4.
WERE PROVIDED
  By individuals themselves.   1 Ch 12:33, 37.
  From the public arsenals.   2 Ch 11:12; 26:14.

ARROWS

The ancients divined by.   Ezk 21:21.
Bright and polished.   Is 49:2. Jr 51:11.
Called shafts.   Is 49:2.
Carried in a quiver.   Gn 27:3. Is 49:2. Jr 5:16. Lm 3:13.
Deadly and destructive weapons.   Pr 26:18.
DISCHARGED
  Against enemies.   2 K 19:32. Jr 50:14.
  At the beasts of the earth.   Gn 27:3.
  At a mark for amusement.   1 S 20:20–22.
  From a bow.   Ps 11:2. Is 7:24.
  From engines.   2 Ch 26:15.
  With great force.   Nu 24:8. 2 K 9:24.
Fleetness of, alluded to.   Zc 9:14.
ILLUSTRATIVE OF
  Bitter words.   Ps 64:3.
  Christ.   Is 49:2.
  Destruction of power (when broken).   Ps 76:3.
  Devices of the wicked.   Ps 11:2.
  False witnesses.   Pr 25:18.
  God's judgment.   Dt 32:23–42. Pss 7:13; 21:12; 64:7. Ezk 5:16.
  Lightnings.   Ps 77:17–18. Hk 3:11.
  Paralyzing power (when falling from the hand).   Ezk 39:3.
  Severe afflictions.   Jb 6:4. Ps 38:2.
  Slanderous tongues.   Jr 9:8.
  Word of Christ.   Ps 45:5.
  Young children.   Ps 127:4.
Sharp.   Ps 120:4. Is 5:28.
Sometimes poisoned.   Jb 6:4.

ARTS

Apothecary or perfumer.   Ex 30:25, 35.
Armorer.   1 S 8:12.
Baker.   Gn 40:1. 1 S 8:13.
Blacksmith.   Gn 4:22. 1 S 13:19.
Brazier.   Gn 4:22. 2 Tm 4:14.
Brickmaker.   Gn 11:3. Ex 5:7–8, 18.
Calker.   Ezk 27:8, 27.
Carpenter.   2 S 5:11. Mk 6:3.
Carver.   Ex 31:5. 1 K 6:18.

Confectioner.   1 S 8:13.
Dyer.   Ex 25:5.
Embalmer.   Gn 50:2–3, 26.
Embroiderer.   Ex 35:35; 38:23.
Engraver.   Ex 28:11. Is 49:16. 2 Co 3:7.
Founder.   Jg 17:4. Jr 10:9.
Fuller.   2 K 18:17. Mk 9:3.
Gardener.   Jr 29:5. Jn 20:15.
Goldsmith.   Is 40:19.
Husbandman.   Gn 4:2; 9:20.
Mariner.   Ezk 27:8–9.
Mason.   2 S 5:11. 2 Ch 24:12.
Musician.   1 S 18:6. 1 Ch 15:16.
Potter.   Is 64:8. Jr 18:3. Lm 4:2. Zc 11:13.
Refiner of metals.   1 Ch 28:18. Ml 3:2–3.
Ropemaker.   Jg 16:11.
Shipbuilder.   1 K 9:26.
Silversmith.   Ac 19:24.
Smelter of metals.   Jb 28:2.
Spinner.   Ex 35:25. Pr 31:19.
Stonecutter.   Ex 20:25. 1 Ch 22:15.
Tailor.   Ex 28:3.
Tanner.   Ac 9:43; 10:6.
Tentmaker.   Gn 4:20. Ac 18:3.
Weaver.   Ex 35:35. Jn 19:23.
Winemaker.   Ne 13:15. Is 63:3.
Writer.   Jg 5:14.

ASCENSION OF CHRIST

As the forerunner of his people.   He 6:20.
Compared to his second coming.   Ac 1:10–11.
Described.   Ac 1:9.
Foretold by himself.   Jn 6:62; 7:33; 14:28; 16:5; 20:17.
Forty days after his resurrection.   Ac 1:3.
From Mount Olivet.   Lk 24:50, with Mk 11:1. Ac 1:12.
Prophecies respecting.   Pss 24:7; 68:18, with Ep 4:7, 8.
To intercede.   Ro 8:34. He 9:24.
To prepare a place for his people.   Jn 14:2.
To receive gifts for men.   Ps 68:18, with Ep 4:8, 11.
To send the Holy Ghost.   Jn 16:7. Ac 2:33.
Typified.   Lv 16:15, with He 6:20. He 9:7, 9, 12.
Was to supreme power and dignity.   Lk 24:26. Ep 1:20–21. 1 P 3:22.
Was triumphant.   Ps 68:18.
When he had atoned for sin.   He 9:12; 10:12.
While blessing his disciples.   Lk 24:50.

ASSURANCE

Abundant in the understanding of the gospel. Co 2:2. 1 Th 1:5.

Confident hope in God restores. Ps 42:11.

Confirmed by love. 1 Jn 3:14, 19; 4:18.

Give diligence to attain. 2 P 1:10–11.

Made full by hope. He 6:11, 19.

Need to maintain. He 3:14, 18.

Produced by faith. Ep 3:12. 2 Tm 1:12. He 10:22.

Results from righteousness. Is 32:17.

SAINTS PRIVILEGED TO HAVE, OF

Answers to prayer. 1 Jn 3:22; 5:14–15.

Comfort in affliction. Ps 73:26. Lk 4:18–19. 2 Co 4:8–10, 16–18.

Continuance in grace. Php 1:6.

Crown. 2 Tm 4:7, 8.

Eternal life. 1 Jn 5:13.

Glorious resurrection. Jb 19:26. Ps 17:15. Php 3:21. 1 Jn 3:2.

Kingdom. He 12:28. Rv 5:10.

Peace with God by Christ. Ro 5:1.

Preservation. Pss 3:6, 8; 27:3–5; 46:1–3.

Support in death. Ps 23:4.

Their adoption. Ro 8:16. 1 Jn 3:2.

Their election. Ps 4:3. 1 Th 1:4.

Their redemption. Jb 19:25.

Their salvation. Is 12:2.

Unalienable love of God. Ro 8:38–39.

Union with God and Christ. 1 Co 6:15. 2 Co 13:5. Ep 5:30. 1 Jn 2:5; 4:13.

ASSYRIA

Antiquity and origin of. Gn 10:8–11.

Armies of, described. Is 5:26–29.

AS A POWER, WAS

An instrument of God's vengeance. Is 7:18–19; 10:5–6.

Cruel and destructive. Is 10:7.

Intolerant and oppressive. Na 3:19.

Most formidable. Is 28:2.

Proud and haughty. 2 K 19:22–24. Is 10:8.

Selfish and reserved. Ho 8:9.

Unfaithful, etc. 2 Ch 28:20–21.

CALLED

Asshur. Ho 14:3.

Land of Nimrod. Mi 5:6.

Shinar. Gn 11:2; 14:1.

CELEBRATED FOR

Extensive commerce. Ezk 27:23–24.

Extent of conquests. 2 K 18:33–35; 19:11–13.

Fertility. 2 K 18:32. Is 36:17.

Chief men of, described. Ezk 23:6, 12, 23.

Condemned for oppressing God's people. Is 52:4.

Governed by kings. 2 K 15:19, 29.

Greatness, extent, duration, and fall of, illustrated. Ezk 31:3–17.

Idolatry, the religion of. 2 K 19:37.

Idolatry brought into Samaria. 2 K 17:29.

Israel condemned for trusting to. Ho 5:13; 7:11; 8:9.

The Jews condemned for following the idolatries of. Ezk 16:28; 23:5, 7, etc.

Judah condemned for trusting to. Jr 2:18, 36.

Manasseh taken captive to. 2 Ch 33:11.

Nineveh, chief city of. Gn 10:11. 2 K 19:36.

PREDICTIONS RESPECTING

Conquest and captivity of Israel by. Is 8:4. Ho 9:3; 10:6; 11:5.

Conquest of the Kenites by. Nu 24:22.

Conquest of Syria by. Is 8:4.

Destruction of. Is 10:19–19; 14:24–25; 30:31–33; 31:8–9. Zc 10:11.

Invasion of Judah by. Is 5:26; 7:17–20; 8:8; 10:5–6, 12.

Participation in the blessings of the gospel. Is 19:23–25. Mi 7–12.

Restoration of Israel from. Is 27:12–13. Ho 11:11. Zc 10:10.

PUL, KING OF

Bought off by Menahem. 2 K 15:19–20.

Invaded Israel. 2 K 15:19.

Repeopling of Samaria from, completed by Asnapper. Ezr 4:10.

SENNACHERIB, KING OF

Assassinated by his sons. 2 K 19:37.

Blasphemed the Lord. 2 K 18:33–35.

Bought off by Hezekiah. 2 K 18:14–16.

His army destroyed by God. 2 K 19:35.

Insulted and threatened Judah. 2 K 18:17–32; 19:10–13.

Invaded Judah. 2 K 18:13.

Prayed against by Hezekiah. 2 K 19:14–19.

Reproved for pride and blasphemy. 2 K 12:20–34. Is 37:21–29.

SHALMANESER, KING OF

Carried Israel captive. 2 K 17:5–6.

Imprisoned Hoshea. 2 K 17:4.

Reduced Israel to tribute. 2 K 17:3.

Repeopled Samaria from Assyria. 2 K 17:24.

Was conspired against by Hoshea. 2 K 17:4.

Situated beyond the Euphrates. Is 7:20.

TIGLATH-PILESER, KING OF

Asked to aid Ahaz against Syria. 2 K 16:7–8.

Conquered Syria. 2 K 16:9.

Ravaged Israel. 2 K 15:29.

Took money from Ahaz, but strengthened him not. 2 Ch 28:20–21.

Watered by the Tigris. Gn 2:14.

ATONEMENT

Acceptable to God. Ep 5:2.

Access to God by. He 10:19–20.

Commemorated in the Lord's Supper. Mt 26:26–28. 1 Co 11:23–26.

Effected by Christ alone. Jn 1:29, 36. Ac 4:10, 12. 1 Th 1:10. 1 Tm 2:5–6. He 2:9. 1 P 2:24.

EXHIBITS THE

Grace and mercy of God. Ro 8:32. Ep 2:4–5, 7. 1 Tm 2:4. He 2:9.

Love of Christ. Jn 15:13. Gl 2:20. Ep 5:2, 25. Rv 1:5.

Love of God. Ro 5:8. 1 Jn 4:9–10.

Explained. Ro 5:8–11. 2 Co 5:18–19. Gl 4. 1 Jn 2:2; 4:10.

Faith in, indispensable. Ro 3:25. Gl 3:13–14.

Foreordained. 1 P 1:11, 20. Rv 13:8.

Foretold. Is 53:4–6, 8–12. Dn 9:24–27. Zc 13:1, 7. Jn 11:50–51.

HAS DELIVERED SAINTS FROM THE

Power of the devil. Cl 2:15. He 2:14–15.

Power of sin. Ro 8:3. 1 P 1:18–19.

Power of the world. Gl 1:4; 6:14.

Justification by. Ro 5:9. 2 Co 5:21.

Made but once. He 7:27; 9:24–28; 10:10, 12, 14. 1 P 3:18.

Ministers should fully set forth. Ac 5:29–31, 42. 1 Co 15:3. 2 Co 5:18–21.

Necessity for. Is 59:16. Lk 19:10. He 9:22.

Reconciles the justice and mercy of God. Is 45:21. Ro 3:25–26.

Reconciliation to God effected by. Ro 5:10. 2 Co 5:18–20. Ep 2:13–16. Cl 1:20–22. He 2:17. 1 P 3:18.

Redemption by. Mt 20:28. Ac 20:28. 1 Tm 2:6. He 9:12. Rv 5:9.

Remission of sins by. Jn 1:29. Ro 3:25. Ep 1:7. 1 Jn 1:7. Rv 1:5.

Saints glorify God for. 1 Co 6:20. Gl 2:20. Php 1:20–21.

Saints praise God for. Rv 5:9–13.

Saints rejoice in God for. Ro 5:11.

Sanctification by. 2 Co 5:15. Ep 5:26–27. Ti 2:14. He 10:10; 13:12.

Typified. Gn 4:4, with He 11:4. Gn 22:2, with He 11:17, 19. Ex 12:5, 11, 14, with 1 Co 5:7. Ex 24:8, with He 9:20. Lv 16:30, 34, with He 9:7, 12, 28. Lv 17:11, with He 9:22.

Was voluntary. Ps 40:6–8, with He 10:5–9. Jn 10:11, 15, 17–18.

ATONEMENT, DAY OF

ATONEMENT MADE ON, FOR THE

High priest. Lv 16:11. He 9:7.

Holy place. Ex 30:10. Lv 16:15–16.

Whole congregation. Lv 16:17, 24; 23:28. He 9:7.

For humiliation. Lv 16:29, 31; 23:27.

High priest entered into the holy place on. Lv 16:2–3. He 9:7.

Observed as a sabbath. Lv 23:28, 32.

Offerings to be made on. Lv 16:3, 5–15.

Punishment for not observing. Lv 23:29–30.

Tenth day of seventh month. Lv 23:26–27.

Typical. He 9:8, 24.

Year of Jubilee commenced on. Lv 25:9.

ATONEMENT, UNDER THE LAW

By priests alone. 1 Ch 6:49. 2 Ch 29:24.

Extraordinary cases of. Ex 32:30–34. Nu 16:47; 25:10–13.

Made by sacrifice. Lv 1:4, 5.

NECESSARY FOR

Propitiating God. Ex 32:30. Lv 23:27–28. 2 S 21:3.

Purifying. Ex 29:36.

Ransoming. Ex 30:15–16. Jb 33:24.

OFFERED FOR

Altar. Ex 29:36–37. Lv 16:18–19.

Congregation. Nu 15:25. 2 Ch 29:24.

Healed Lepers. Lv 14:18.

Holy place. Lv 16:16–17.

Leprous house healed. Lv 14:53.

Persons sinning ignorantly. Lv 4:20, etc.

Persons sinning willfully. Lv 6:7.

Persons swearing rashly. Lv 5:4, 6.

Persons unclean. Lv 5:2–3, 6.

Persons withholding evidence. Lv 5:1, 6.

Priests. Ex 29:31–33. Lv 8:34.

Women after childbirth. Lv 12:8.

Typical of Christ's atonement. Ro 5:6–11.

ATTAINMENT

Of divine knowledge, beyond man.   Ps 139:6.
Of perfection, disclaimed by Paul.   Php 3:12–14.
Of the resurrection, desired by Paul.   Php 3:11.
Of wisdom, through understanding.   Pr 1:5.
Of the world at the cost of loss of one's soul.   Mt 16:26.
See also Accomplishment.

AUTHORITY

Given to the disciples.   Lk 9:1.
In the family.   Ep 5:22; 6:1–4. 1 Co 11:3. 1 Tm 2:12; 3:4, 12. 1 P 3:1–6.
Of Christ's power over spirits.   Mk 1:27.
Of Christ's teaching.   Mt 7:29.
Of God.   Ps 29:10. Dn 4:34–35.
Of government.   Pr 29:2. Ro 13:1–7.
Of rulers, prayer for.   1 Tm 2:1, 2.
Promised to believers.   Lk 19:17. Rv 2:26.
Submission to.   He 13:17. Ro 13:7.

B

BABYLON

Ambassadors of, sent to Hezekiah. 2 K 20:12.

Armies of, described. Hk 1:7-9.

As a Power Was

An instrument of God's vengeance on other nations. Is 47:6. Jr 51:7.

Arrogant. Is 14:13-14. Jr 50:29, 31-32.

Covetous. Jr 51:13.

Cruel and destructive. Is 14:17; 47:6. Jr 51:25. Hk 1:6-7.

Grand and stately. Is 47:1, 5.

Oppressive. Is 14:4.

Secure and self-confident. Is 47:7-8.

Babylon the chief province of. Dn 3:1.

Capital of

Antiquity of. Gn 11:4, 9.

Called Babylon the great. Dn 4:30.

Called beauty of Chaldees, etc. Is 13:19.

Called the city of merchants. Ezk 17:4.

Called the glory of kingdoms. Is 13:19.

Called the golden city. Is 14:4.

Enlarged by Nebuchadnezzar. Dn 4:30.

Surrounded with a great wall and fortified. Jr 51:53, 58.

Composed of many nations. Dn 3:4, 29.

Destroyed by the Medes. Dn 5:30-31.

Formerly a part of Mesopotamia. Ac 7:2.

Founded by the Assyrians, and part of their empire. 2 K 17:24, with Is 23:13.

Gospel preached in. 1 P 5:13.

Grief of the Jews in. Ps 137:1-6.

Inhabitants of

Addicted to magic. Is 47:9, 12-13. Dn 2:1-2.

Idolatrous. Jr 50:38. Dn 3:18.

Profane and sacrilegious. Dn 5:1-3.

Wicked. Is 47:10.

The Jews exhorted to be subject to, and settle in. Jr 27:17; 29:1-7.

Languages spoken in. Dn 1:4; 2:4.

Nebuchadnezzar, King of

Besieged and took Jerusalem. 2 K 24:10-11; 25:1-4.

Burned Jerusalem, etc. 2 K 25:9-10.

Made Jehoiakim tributary. 2 K 24:1.

Made Zedekiah king. 2 K 24:17.

Rebelled against by Zedekiah. 2 K 24:20.

Spoiled and burned the temple. 2 K 24:13; 25:9, 13-17. 2 Ch 36:18-19.

Took Jehoiachin, etc., captive to Babylon. 2 K 24:12, 14-16. 2 Ch 36:10.

Took Zedekiah, etc., captive to Babylon. 2 K 25:7, 11, 18-21. 2 Ch 36:20.

Origin of. Gn 10:10.

Origin of name. Gn 11:8-9.

Predictions Respecting

Captivity of the Jews by. Jr 20:4-6; 22:20-26; 25:9-11. Mi 4:10.

Conquests by. Jr 21:3-10; 27:2-6; 49:28-33. Ezk 21:19-32; 29:18-20.

Destruction of. Is 13; 14:4-22; 21:1-10; 47. Jr 25:12; 50; 51.

Perpetual desolation of. Is 13:19-22; 14:22-23. Jr 50:13,39; 51:37.

Preaching of the gospel in. Ps 87:4.

Restoration of the Jews from. Is 14:1-4; 44:28; 48:20. Jr 29:10; 50:4, 8, 19.

Presidents placed over. Dn 2:48; 6:1.

Remarkable for

Antiquity. Jr 5:15.

Commerce. Ezk 17:4.

Manufacture of garments. Jsh 7:21.

Military power. Jr 5:16; 50:23.

National greatness. Is 13:19. Jr 51:41.

Naval power. Is 43:14.

Wealth. Jr 50:37; 51:13.

Represented by a

Great eagle. Ezk 17:3.

Head of gold. Dn 2:32, 37-38.

Lion with eagle's wings. Dn 7:4.

Restoration of the Jews from. 2 Ch 36:23. Ezr 1; 2:1-67.

Revolt of the Jews from, and their punishment illustrated. Ezk 17.

Treatment of the Jews in. 2 K 25:27-30. Dn 1:3-7.

A type of antichrist. Rv 16:19; 17:5.

Was Called

Desert of the sea. Is 21:1, 9.

Lady of kingdoms. Is 47:5.

Land of Merathaim. Jr 50:21.

Land of Shinar. Dn 1:2. Zc 5:11.
Land of the Chaldeans. Ezk 12:13,
Sheshach. Jr 25:12, 26.
Watered by the rivers Euphrates and Tigris.
Ps 137:1. Jr 51:13.
With Media and Persia, divided by Darius into
120 provinces. Dn 6:1.

BACKSLIDING
Afflictions sent to heal. Ho 5:15.
Blessedness of those who keep from. Pr
28:14. Is 26:3–4. Cl 1:21–23.
Brings its own punishment. Pr 14:14. Jr
2:19.
Endeavor to bring back those guilty of. Gl
6:1. Ja 5:10, 20.
Exhortations to return from. 2 Ch 30:6. Is
31:6. Jr 3:12, 14, 22. Ho 6:1.
God is displeased at. Ps 78:57, 59.
Guilt and consequences of. Nu 14:43. Ps
125:5. Is 59:2, 9–11. Jr 5:6; 8:5, 13; 15:6.
Lk 9:62.
Hateful to saints. Ps 101:3.
A haughty spirit leads to. Pr 16:18.
Healing of, promised. Jr 3:22. Ho 14:4.
Is
    Departing from the simplicity of the gospel.
    2 Co 11:3. Gl 3:1–3; 5:4, 7.
    Leaving the first love. Rv 2:4.
    Turning from God. 1 K 11:9.
Likely to continue and increase. Jr 8:5; 14:7.
Not hopeless. Ps 37:24. Pr 24:16.
Pardon of, promised. 2 Ch 7:14. Jr 3:12;
31:20; 36:3.
Pray to be restored from. Pss 80:3; 85:4. Lm
5:21.
Proneness to. Pr 24:16. Ho 11:7.
Punishment of tempting others to the sin of.
Pr 28:10. Mt 18:6.
Sin of, to be confessed. Is 59:12–14. Jr
3:13–14; 14:7–9.
Warnings against. Ps 85:8. 1 Co 10:12.

BALM
Anointing the king. Ps 89:20.
Healing the Lord's people. Jr 51:8.
Producing joy. Is 61:3.
Restoring sight. Rv 3:18.
Sought. Jr 8:22.

BAPTISM
ADMINISTERED TO
    Households. Ac 16:15. 1 Co 1:16.
    Individuals. Ac 8:38; 9:16.

Adopted by Christ. Jn 3:22; 4:1–2.
Appointed an ordinance of the Christian
church. Mt 28:19–20. Mk 16:15–16.
As administered by John. Mt 3:5–12. Jn
3:23. Ac 13:24; 19:4.
Confession of sin necessary to. Mt 3:6.
Emblematic of the influences of the Holy
Ghost. Mt 3:11. Ti 3:5.
Faith necessary to. Ac 8:37; 18:8.
Regeneration, the inward and spiritual grace
of. Jn 3:3, 5–6. Ro 6:3–4, 11.
Remission of sins, signified by. Ac 2:38;
22:16.
Repentance necessary to. Ac 2:38.
Sanctioned, by Christ's submission to it. Mt
3:13–15. Lk 3:21.
There is but one. Ep 4:5.
To be administered in the name of the Father,
the Son, and the Holy Ghost. Mt 28:19.
Typified. 1 Co 10:2. 1 P 3:20, 21.
Unity of the church effected by. 1 Co 12:13.
Gl 3:27–28.
Water, the outward and visible sign in. Ac
8:36; 10:47.
See also Purification.

BAPTISM WITH THE HOLY SPIRIT
All saints partake of. 1 Co 12:13.
Christ administered. Mt 3:11. Jn 1:33.
Foretold. Ezk 36:25.
Is through Christ. Ti 3:6.
Necessity for. Jn 3:5. Ac 19:2–6.
Promised to saints. Ac 1:5; 2:38–39; 11:16.
Renews and cleanses the soul. Ti 3:5. 1 P
3:20–21.
Typified. Ac 2:1–4.
Word of God instrumental to. Ac 10:44. Ep
5:26.

BEASTS
Belong to God. Ps 50:10.
CLEAN
    Chamois. Dt 14:5.
    Fallow deer. Dt 14:5.
    Goat. Dt 14:4.
    Hart. Dt 14:5, with 2 S 2:18.
    Ox. Ex 21:28, with Dt 14:4.
    Pygarg. Dt 14:5.
    Roebuck Dt 14:5, with 2 S 2:18.
    Sheep. Dt 7:13, with 14:4.
    Wild goat. Dt 14:5.
    Wild ox. Dt 14:5.
Created by God. Gn 1:24–25; 2:19.
Creation of, exhibits God's power. Jr 27:5.

DESCRIBED AS
  Being four-footed. Ac 10:12.
  By nature wild, etc. Ps 50:11. Mk 1:13.
  Capable of being tamed. Ja 3:7.
  Devoid of immortality. Ps 49:12–15.
  Devoid of speech. 2 P 2:16.
  Devoid of understanding. Pss 32:9; 73:22.
  Possessed of instinct. Is 1:3.
Differ in flesh from birds and fishes. 1 Co 15:39.
DOMESTIC
  Not to be cruelly used. Nu 22:27–32. Pr 12:10.
  To be taken care of. Lv 25:7. Dt 25:4.
  To enjoy the sabbath. Ex 20:10. Dt 5:14.
Early differentiated as clean or unclean. Gn 7:2.
FOUND IN
  Deserts. Is 13:21.
  Fields. Dt 7:22. Jl 2:22.
  Forests. Is 56:9. Mi 5:8.
  Mountains. S S 4:8.
Frequently suffered on account of the sins of men. Jl 1:18, 20. Hg 1:11.
Given to man for food after the flood. Gn 9:3.
HABITATIONS OF
  Dens and caves. Jb 37:8; 38:40.
  Deserted cities. Is 13:21–22. Zp 2:15.
  Under spreading trees. Dn 4:12.
Herb of the field given to, for food. Gn 1:30.
History of, written by Solomon. 1 K 4:33.
ILLUSTRATIVE OF
  Antichrist. Rv 13:2; 20:4.
  Kingdoms. Dn 7:11, 17; 8:4.
  People of different nations. Dn 4:12, 21–22.
  Persecutors. 1 Co 15:32. 2 Tm 4:17.
  Ungodly professors. 2 P 2:12. Jde 1:10.
  Wicked men. Ps 49:20. Ti 1:12.
Instinctively fear man. Gn 9:2.
Lessons of wisdom to be learned from. Jb 12:7.
Liable to diseases. Ex 9:3.
Made for the praise and glory of God. Ps 148:10.
Man by nature no better than. Ec 3:18–19.
Many kinds of, domestic. Gn 36:6; 45:17.
Many kinds of, noisome and destructive. Lv 26:6. Ezk 5:17.
Named by Adam. Gn 2:19–20.
No likeness of, to be worshiped. Dt 4:17.
Not to be eaten alive or with blood. Gn 9:4. Dt 12:16, 23.

Often cut off for the sins of men. Gn 6:7, with 7:23. Ex 11:5. Ho 4:3.
Often used as instruments of punishment. Lv 26:22. Dt 32:24. Jr 15:3. Ezk 5:17.
Power over, given to man. Gn 1:26, 28. Ps 8:7.
Representations of, worshiped by the heathen. Ro 1:23.
Subjects of God's care. Pss 36:6; 104:10–11.
Supply clothing to man. Gn 3:21. Jb 31:20.
That died naturally or were torn, not to be eaten. Ex 22:31. Lv 17:15; 22:8.
THOSE CLEAN
  First-born of, not redeemed. Nu 18:17.
  How distinguished. Lv 11:3. Dt 14:6.
  Used for food. Lv 11:2. Dt 12:15.
  Used for sacrifice. Gn 8:20.
THOSE UNCLEAN
  Caused uncleanness when dead. Lv 5:2.
  First-born of, redeemed. Nu 18:15.
  How distinguished. Lv 11:26.
  Not eaten. Lv 11:4–8. Dt 1:7–8.
  Not offered in sacrifice. Lv 27:11.
UNCLEAN
  Ape. 1 K 10:22.
  Ass. Gn 22:3. Mt 21:2.
  Badger. Ex 25:5. Ezk 16:10.
  Bear. 2 S 17:8.
  Behemoth. Jb 40:15.
  Camel. Gn 24:64, with Lv 11:4.
  Coney. Lv 11:5. Ps 104:18.
  Dog. Ex 22:31. Lk 16:2.
  Dromedary. 1 K 4:28. Es 8:10.
  Ferret. Lv 11:30.
  Fox. Ps 63:10. S S 2:5.
  Hare. Lv 11:6. Dt 14:7.
  Horse. Jb 39:19–25.
  Leopard. S S 4:8.
  Lion. Jg 14:5, 6.
  Mole. Lv 11:30. Is 2:20.
  Mouse. Lv 11:29. Is 66:17.
  Mule. 2 S 13:29. 1 K 10:25.
  Swine. Lv 11:7. Is 66:17.
  Unicorn. Nu 23:22.
  Weasel. Lv 11:29.
  Wild ass. Jb 6:5; 39:5–8.
  Wolf. Gn 49:27. Jn 10:12.

BEAUTY
Emptiness of. Pr 11:22; 31:30. Ezk 16:15.
Of the church. Ep 5:27. Rv 21:2.
Of holiness. 1 Ch 16:29. 2 Ch 20:21. Pss 29:2; 96:9.
Of the Lord. Pss 27:4; 90:17. Is 33:17.

Of the temple. Ps 96:6.
Of Zion. Pss 48:2; 50:2.

BEGINNING
Christ as. Rv 1:8.
Of creation. Gn 1:1. He 1:10.
Of eternity. Jn 1:1.
Of the gospel. Mk 1:1.
Of life on earth. Gn 1:11.
Of light. Gn 1:3.
Of man. Gn 1:26.
Of the new creation. Cl 1:18.
Of wisdom. Ps 111:10.

BELIEF
In Christ. Jn 3:16; 14:1; 20:31. Ac 8:37.
In God required. 2 Ch 20:20.
Making all things possible. Mk 9:23.
Of devils. Ja 2:19.
Producing healing. Mt 9:22.

BIBLE
See Inspiration of the Bible; Scriptures.

BIRDS
Are hostile to strange kinds. Jr 12:9.
Blood of, not to be eaten. Lv 7:26.
CALLED
 Birds of the air. Mt 8:20.
 Feathered fowl. Ezk 39:17.
 Fowls of the air. Gn 7:3.
 Fowls of heaven. Jb 35:11.
 Winged fowl. Dt 4:17.
Can all be tamed. Ja 3:7.
CLEAN
 Cock and hen. Mt 23:37; 26:34, 74.
 Crane. Is 38:14. Jr 8:7.
 Dove. Gn 8:8.
 Partridge. 1 S 26:20. Jr 17:11.
 Pigeon. Lv 1:14; 12:6.
 Quail. Ex 16:12–13. Nu 11:31–32.
 Sparrow. Mt 10:29–31.
 Swallow. Ps 84:3. Is 38:14.
 Turtledove. Lv 14:22. S S 2:12.
Confinement in cages of, alluded to. Jr 5:27.
Created by God. Gn 1:20–21; 2:19.
Created for the glory of God. Ps 148:10.
Differ in flesh from beasts and fishes. 1 Co 15:39.
Early differentiated as clean or unclean. Gn 8:20.
Fly above the earth. Gn 1:20.
Furnished with claws. Dn 4:33.
Given as food to man. Gn 9:2–3.

God provides for. Ps 104:10–12. Mt 6:26. Lk 12:23–24.
Have each their peculiar note or song. Ps 104:12. Ec 12:4. S S 2:12.
Herb of the field given as food to. Gn 1:30.
ILLUSTRATIVE OF
 Cruel and rapacious kings. Is 46:11.
 Death (when snared). Ec 9:12.
 Designs of the wicked (when snared). Ps 124:7. Pr 1:10-17; 7:23.
 The devil and his spirits. Mt 13:4, 19.
 Hostile nations. Jr 12:9.
 People of different countries. Ezk 31:6. Mt 13:32.
 Unsettled persons, etc. Pr 27:8. Is 16:2.
INHABIT
 Deserted cities. Is 34:11, 14-15.
 Deserts. Ps 102:6.
 Marshes. Is 14:23.
 Mountains. Ps 50:11.
Instinct of, inferior to man's reason. Jb 35:11.
Instinctively fear man. Gn 9:2.
Lessons of wisdom to be learned from. Jb 12:7.
Make and dwell in nests. Mt 8:20.
MAKE THEIR NESTS
 In clefts of rocks. Nu 24:21. Jr 48:28.
 In trees. Ps 104:17. Ezk 31:6.
 On the ground. Dt 22:6.
MANY KINDS OF
 Carnivorous. Gn 15:11, 40:19. Dt 28:26.
 Granivorous. Mt 13:4.
 Migratory. Jr 8:7.
Named by Adam. Gn 2:19-20.
No likeness of, to be made for worship. Dt 4:17.
Not to be eaten, when unclean. Lv 11:13, 17. Dt 14:12; 22:6-7.
Often leave places suffering calamities. Jr 4:25; 9:10.
Often suffered for man's sins. Gn 6:7. Jr 12:4. Ezk 38:20. Ho 4:3.
Often worshiped by idolaters. Ro 1:23.
Power over, given to man. Gn 1:26. Ps 8:8.
Propagated by eggs. Dt 22:6. Jr 17:11.
Property of God. Ps 50:11.
Rapid flight of, alluded to. Is 31:5. Ho 9:11, 11:11.
Rest in trees. Dn 4:12. Mt 13:32.
Solomon wrote the history of. 1 K 4:33.
Taken in snares or nets. Pr 1:17.
To be eaten, when clean. Dt 14:11, 20.

To be offered in sacrifice, when clean. Gn 8:20. Lv 1:14.

UNCLEAN

Bat. Lv 11:19. Is 2:20.

Bittern. Is 14:23; 34:11.

Cormorant. Lv 11:17. Is 34:11.

Cuckoo. Lv 11:16.

Eagle. Lv 11:13. Jb 39:27.

Gier eagle. Lv 11:18.

Glede. Dt 14:13.

Great owl. Lv 11:17.

Hawk. Lv 11:16. Jb 39:26.

Heron. Lv 11:19.

Kite. Lv 11:14.

Lapwing. Lv 11:19.

Little owl. Lv 11:17.

Night hawk. Lv 11:16.

Osprey. Lv 11:13.

Ossifrage. Lv 11:13.

Ostrich. Lb 39:13, 18.

Owl. Lv 11:16. Jb 30:29.

Peacock. 1 K 10:22. Jb 39:13.

Pelican. Lv 11:18. Ps 102:6.

Raven. Lv 11:15. Jb 38:41.

Stork. Lv 11:19. Ps 104:17.

Swan. Lv 11:18.

Vulture. Lv 11:14. Jb 28:7. Is 34:15.

BIRTH

Act of God. Ac 17:25.

From above. Jn 1:13; 3:5. 1 P 1:23.

Into trouble. Jb 5:7.

OF CHRIST

First-born of many brethren. Ro 8:29.

Joy from. Lk 1:14.

Narrated. Mt 1:18—2:23. Lk 1:26—2:20.

Prophesied. Is 9:6.

Purpose. Jn 18:37.

A time for. Ec 3:2.

BIRTHRIGHT

Coveted. Gn 25:31.

Defined. Dt 21:17.

Despised. Gn 25:32, 34. He 12:16.

Loss mourned. Gn 27:36.

BITTERNESS

Against wives proscribed. Cl 3:19.

Christians must put away. Ep 4:31. He 12:15.

Known in the heart. Pr 14:10.

Of the harlot. Pr 5:4.

Of the militaristic Chaldeans. Hk 1:6.

Of the prophet Jeremiah. Lm 3:15.

Of the wicked. Ps 140:3. Ro 3:14.

BLASPHEMY

Against the Holy Ghost, unpardonable. Mt 12:31–32.

Charged upon Christ. Mt 9:2. 3; 26:64–65. Jn 10:33, 36.

Charged upon saints. Ac 6:11, 13.

Christ assailed with. Mt 10:25. Lk 22:64–65. 1 P 4:14.

Connected with folly and pride. 2 K 19:22. Ps 74:18.

Forbidden. Ex 20:7. Cl 3:8.

Give no occasion for. 2 S 12:14. 1 Tm 6:1.

Hypocrisy counted as. Rv 2:9.

Idolatry counted as. Is 65:7. Ezk 20:27–28.

Proceeds from the heart. Mt 15:19.

Punishment of. Lv 24:16. Is 65:7. Ezk 20:27–33; 35:11–12.

Saints grieved to hear. Pss 44:15–16; 74:10, 18, 22.

The wicked addicted to. Ps 74:18. Is 52:5. 2 Tm 3:2. Rv 16:11, 21.

THE BLESSED

The bountiful. Dt 15:10. Ps 41:1. Pr 22:9. Lk 14:13–14.

The children of the just. Pr 20:7.

The faithful. Pr 28:20.

The generation of the upright. Ps 112:2.

Holy mourners. Mt 5:4. Lk 6:21.

The just. Ps 106:3. Pr 10:6.

The meek. Mt 5:5.

The merciful. Mt 5:7.

The peacemakers. Mt 5:9.

The poor in spirit. Mt 5:3.

The pure in heart. Mt 5:8.

The righteous. Ps 5:12.

Saints at the judgment day. Mt 25:34.

To whom God imputes righteousness without works. Ro 4:6–9.

The undefiled. Ps 119:1.

Who are not offended at Christ. Mt 11:6.

Who avoid the wicked. Ps 1:1.

Who believe. Lk 1:45. Gl 3:9.

Who delight in the commandments of God. Ps 112:1.

Who die in the Lord. Rv 14:13.

Who endure temptation. Ja 1:12.

Who favor saints. Gn 12:3. Ru 2:10.

Who fear God. Pss 112:1; 128:1, 4.

Who frequent the house of God. Pss 65:4; 84:4.

Who have the Lord for their God. Ps 144:15.

Who have part in the first resurrection. Rv 20:6.

Who hear and keep the word of God. Ps 119:2. Ja 1:25. Mt 13:16 Lk 11:28. Rv 1:3; 22:7.

Who hunger and thirst after righteousness. Mt 5:6.

Who keep the commandments of God. Rv 22:14.

Who know Christ. Mt 16:16–17.

Who know the gospel. Ps 89:15.

Who rebuke sinners. Pr 24:25.

Who shall eat bread in the kingdom of God. Lk 14:15. Rv 19:9.

Who suffer for Christ. Lk 6:22.

Who trust in God. Pss 2:12; 34:8; 40:4; 84:12. Jr 17:7.

Who wait for the Lord. Is 30:18.

Who watch against sin. Rv 16:15.

Who watch for the Lord. Lk 12:37.

Whom God calls. Is 51:2. Rv 19:9.

Whom God chastens. Jb 5:17. Ps 94:12.

Whom God chooses. Ps 65:4. Ep 1:3–4.

Whose sins are forgiven. Ps 32:1, 2. Ro 4:7.

Whose strength is in the Lord. Ps 84:5.

BLINDNESS, SPIRITUAL

Christ appointed to remove. Is 42:7. Lk 4:18. Jn 8:12;

Christ's ministers are lights to remove. Mt 5:14. Ac 26:18.

The effect of sin. Is 29:10. Mt 6:23. Jn 3:19–20.

Explained. Jn 1:5. 1 Co 2:14.

Is inconsistent with communion with God. 1 Jn 1:6–7.

Judicially inflicted. Ps 69:23. Is 29:10; 44:18. Mt 13:13–14. Jn 12:40.

Leads to all evil. Ep 4:17–19.

Of ministers, fatal to themselves and to the people. Mt 15:14.

Pray for the removal of. Pss 13:3; 119:18.

Removal of, illustrated. Jn 9:7, 11, 25. Ac 9:18. Rv 3:18.

Saints delivered from. Jn 8:12. Ep 5:8. Cl 1:13. 1 Th 5:4–5. 1 P 2:9.

The self-righteous are in. Mt 23:19, 26. Rv 3:17.

Unbelief the effect of. Ro 11:8. 2 Co 4:3–4.

Uncharitableness, a proof of. 1 Jn 2:9, 11.

The wicked are in. Ps 82:5. Jr 5:21.

The wicked willfully guilty of. Is 26:11. Ro 1:19–21.

A work of the devil. 2 Co 4:4.

BLOOD

Beasts of prey delight in. Nu 23:24. Ps 68:23.

Birds of prey delight in. Jb 39:30.

EATING OF, FORBIDDEN TO

Early Christians. Ac 15:20, 29.

Israelites under the law. Lv 3:17; 17:10, 12.

Man after the flood. Gn 9:4.

Fluid. Dt 12:16.

Idolaters made drink offerings of. Ps 16:4.

ILLUSTRATIVE OF

Guilt, when on one's head. Lv 20:9. 2 S 1:16. Ezk 18:13.

Oppression and cruelty, when building with. Hk 2:12.

Ripening for destruction, when preparing unto. Ezk 35:6.

Severe judgments, when given to drink. Ezk 16:38. Rv 16:6.

Victories, when washing the feet in. Pss 58:10; 68:23.

The Jews often guilty of eating. 1 S 14:32–33. Ezk 33:25.

The life of animals. Gn 9:4. Lv 17:11, 14.

Of all men the same. Ac 17:26.

Of animals slain for food to be poured on the earth and covered. Lv 17:13. Dt 12:16, 24.

OF LEGAL SACRIFICES

For atonement. Ex 30:10. Lv 17:11.

For purification. He 9:13, 19–22.

How disposed of. Ex 29:12. Lv 4:7.

Ineffectual to remove sin. He 10:4.

Not offered with leaven. Ex 23:18; 34:25.

Price of, not to be consecrated. Mt 27:6.

Red. 2 K 3:22. Jl 2:31.

SHEDDING OF HUMAN

Always punished. Gn 9:6.

Defiling to the land. Ps 106:38.

Defiling to the person. Is 59:3.

Forbidden. Gn 9:5.

Hateful to God. Pr 6:16–17.

Jews often guilty of. Jr 22:17. Ezk 22:4.

Mode of clearing those accused of. Dt 21:1–9.

Water turned into, as a sign. Ex 4:9, 30.

Waters of Egypt turned into, as a judgment. Ex 7:17–21.

BOASTING
About the Christians of Corinth. 2 Co 8:24; 9:3.
In the last days. 2 Tm 3:2.
In the Lord. Pss 34:2; 44:8. Jr 9:23–24. 2 Co 10:13; 10:17. Gl 6:14.
Of the man of perdition. 2 Th 2:3–4.
Of the wicked. Pss 10:3; 12:3; 17:10; 52:1; 94:4.
Warned against. Dt 8:17; 32:27. Pr 27:1.

BOLDNESS, HOLY
A characteristic of saints. Pr 28:1.
Christ set an example of. Jn 7:26.
Exhortations to. Jsh 1:17. 2 Ch 19:11. Jr 1:8. Ezk 3:9.
Express your trust in God with. He 13:6.
Have, in prayer. Ep 3:12. He 4:16.
MINISTERS SHOULD EXHIBIT IN
The face of opposition. Ac 13:46. 1 Th 2:2.
Faithfulness to their people. 2 Co 7:4; 10:1.
Preaching. Ac 4:31. Php 1:14.
Reproving sin. Is 58:1. Mi 3:8.
Pray for. Ac 4:29. Ep 6:19–20.
PRODUCED BY
Faithfulness to God. 1 Tm 3:13.
Fear of God. Ac 4:19; 5:29.
Trust in God. Is 50:7.
Saints shall have, in judgment. 1 Jn 4:17.
Through faith in Christ. Ep 3:12. He 10:19.

BONDAGE, SPIRITUAL
Christ delivers from. Lk 4:18, 21. Jn 8:36. Ro 7:24–25. Ep 4:8.
Deliverance from, illustrated. Dt 4:20.
Deliverance from, promised. Is 42:6–7.
The gospel as instrument of deliverance from. Jn 8:32. Ro 8:2.
Saints are delivered from. Ro 6:18, 22.
To the devil. 1 Tm 3:7. 2 Tm 2:26.
To the fear of death. He 2:14–15.
To sin. Jn 8:34. Ac 8:23. Ro 6:16; 7:23. Gl 4:3. 2 P 2:19.

BOOKS
The ancients fond of making. Ec 12:12.
Divine communications recorded in. Ex 17:14. Is 30:8. Jr 36:2. Rv 1:19.
Erasures in, alluded to. Ex 32:33. Nu 5:23.
ILLUSTRATIVE OF
Memorials of conversation and conduct of men. Dn 7:10. Ml 3:16. Rv 20:12.

Memorials of God's providence. Pss 56:8; 139:16.
Record of the church of Christ. Dn 12:1. He 12:23. Rv 20:12, 15; 22:19.
Important events recorded in. Ezr 4:15; 6:1–2. Es 2:23.
In a roll. Is 34:4. Jr 36:2. Ezk 2:9.
MADE OF
Papyrus or paper reed. Is 19:7.
Parchment. 2 Tm 4:13.
NOT EXTANT, BUT MENTIONED IN SCRIPTURE
Acts of Solomon. 1 K 11:41.
Ahijah the Shilonite. 2 Ch 9:29.
Chronicles of David. 1 Ch 27:24.
Gad the seer. 1 Ch 29:29.
History of the kings. I Ch 9:1.
Jasher. Jsh 10:13. 2 S 1:18.
Jehu the son of Hanani. 2 Ch 20:34.
Nathan. 1 Ch 29:29. 2 Ch 9:29.
Natural history by Solomon. 1 K 4:32–33.
Samuel concerning the kingdom. 1 S 10:25.
Samuel the seer. 1 Ch 29:29.
Sayings of the seers. 2 Ch 33:19.
Shemaiah. 2 Ch 12:15.
Visions of Iddo. 2 Ch 9:29; 12:15.
Wars of the Lord. Nu 21:14.
Numerous and most expensive. Ac 19:19.
Often dedicated to persons of distinction. Lk 1:3. Ac 1:1.
Often sealed. Is 29:11. Dn 12:4. Rv 5:1.
Often written on both sides. Ezk 2:10.
Probable origin of. Jb 19:23–24.
Written with pen and ink. Jr 36:18. 3 Jn 13.

BOTTLES
The ancients often drank from. Hk 2:15.
First mention of, in scripture. Gn 21:14.
ILLUSTRATIVE OF
The afflicted, when dried up. Ps 119:83.
The clouds. Jb 38:37.
God's remembrance. Ps 56:8.
The impatient, when ready to burst. Jb 32:19.
Severe judgments, when broken. Is 30:14. Jr 19:10; 48:12.
Sinners ripe for judgment. Jr 13:12–14.
MADE OF SKINS
Marred by age and use. Jsh 9:4, 13.
Shriveled and dried by smoke. Ps 119:83.
Sometimes probably of large dimensions. 1 S 25:18. 2 S 16:1.
When old, unfit for holding new wine. Mt 9:17. Mk 2:22.

Some, made of earthenware. Jr 19:1.
USED FOR HOLDING
   Milk. Jg 4:19.
   Water. Gn 21:14–15, 19.
   Wine. 1 S 1:24; 16:20.

BOW
Called the battle bow. Zc 9:10; 10:4.
Drawn with full force. 2 K 9:24.
For shooting arrows. 1 Ch 12:2.
Given as a token of friendship. 1 S 18:4.
Held in the left hand. Ezk 39:3.
An instrument of war. Gn 48:22. Is 7:24.
ILLUSTRATIVE OF
   The hypocrite, when deceitful. Ps 78:57.
     Ho 7:16.
   The overthrow of power, when broken. 1
     S 2:4. Jr 49:35. Ho 1:5; 2:18.
   Strength and power. Jb 29:20.
   The tongue of the wicked. Ps 11:2. Jr 9:3.
The Jews taught to use. 2 S 1:18.
Of the vanquished, broken and burned. Ps
   37:15. Ezk 39:9.
Often furnished by the state. 2 Ch 26:14.
Sometimes used in hunting. Gn 27:3.
THOSE WHO USE, CALLED
   Archers. 1 S 31:3. Jr 51:3.
   Bowmen, Jr 4:29.
USED EXPERTLY BY
   Benjamites. 1 Ch 12:2. 2 Ch 14:8.
   Elamites. Jr 49:35.
   Lydians. Jr 46:9.
   Philistines. 1 S 31:2–3.
   Sons of Reuben, Gad, and Manasseh. 1
     Ch 5:18.
Usually of steel. 2 S 22:35. Jb 20:24.

BRASS OR COPPER
Antiquity of working in. Gn 4:22.
Canaan abounded in. Dt 8:9; 33:25.
CHARACTERIZED BY
   Fusibility. Ezk 22:18, 20.
   Hardness. Lv 26:19.
   Sonorousness. 1 Co 13:1.
   Strength. Jb 40:18.
   Yellow color. Ezr 8:27.
Coined for money. Mt 10:9. Mk 12:41.
Collected by David for the temple. 1 Ch
   22:3, 14, 16; 29:2.
Dug out of the mountains. Dt 8:9.
Extensive commerce in. Ezk 27:13. Rv
   18:12.
ILLUSTRATIVE OF
   Decrees of God. Zc 6:1

Earth made barren. Lv 26:19.
Extreme drought. Dt 28:23.
Macedonian empire. Dn 2:39.
Obstinate sinners. Is 48:4. Jr 6:28.
Strength and firmness of Christ. Dn 10:6.
   Rv 1:15.
Strength given to saints. Jr 15:20. Mi
   4:13.
Inferior in value to gold and silver. Is 60:17.
   Dn 2:32, 39.
MADE INTO
   Altars. Ex 27:2; 39:39.
   Bars for gates. 1 K 4:13.
   Fetters. Jg 16:21. 2 K 25:7.
   Gates. Ps 107:16. Is 45:2.
   Greaves for the legs. 1 S 17:6.
   Helmets. 1 S 17:5.
   Household vessels. Mk 7:4.
   Idols Dn 5:4. Rv 9:20.
   Instruments of music. 1 Ch 15:19.
   Lavers. Ex 30:18. 1 K 7:38.
   Mirrors. Ex 38:8.
   Pillars. 1 K 7:15–16.
   Sacred vessels. Ex 27:3. 1 K 7:45.
   Shields. 1 K 14:27. 2 Ch 12:10.
   Sockets for pillars. Ex 38:10–11, 17.
Moses made the serpent of. Nu 21:9. 2 K
   18:4.
OFFERINGS OF
   For the tabernacle. Ex 38:29.
   For the temple. 1 Ch 29:6–7.
Purified by smelting. Jb 28:2.
TAKEN IN WAR
   Cleansed by fire. Nu 31:21–23.
   Generally consecrated to God. Jsh 6:19,
     24. 2 S 8:10–11.
   Often in great quantities. Jsh 22:8. 2 S
     8:8. 2 K 25:13–16.
Takes a high polish. 2 Ch 4:16. Ezk 1:7.
Working in, a trade. Gn 4:22. 1 K 7:14. 2
   Ch 24:12. 2 Tm 4:14.

BREAD
BAKED
   In ovens. Lv 26:26. Ho 7:4–7.
   On coals of fire. Is 44:19. Jn 21:9.
   On hearths. Gn 18:6.
Broken for use. Lm 4:4. Mt 14:19.
Corn ground for making. Is 28:28.
Crumb of, used to wipe the fingers, thrown
   under the table. Mt 15:27. Lk 16:21.
First fruit of, offered to God. Nu 15:19–20.
FORMED INTO
   Cakes. 2 S 6:19. 1 K 17:13.

Loaves. 1 S 10:3, 4. Mt 14:17
Wafers. Ex 16:31; 29:23.
Given by God. Ru 1:6. Mt 6:11.
ILLUSTRATIVE OF
Abundance, when plentiful. Dt 8:9. Ezk 16:49.
Affliction (——— of adversity). Is 30:20.
Christ. Jn 6:33–35.
Communion of saints, when partaking of. Ac 2:46. 1 Co 10:17.
Death of Christ, when broken. Mt 26:26, with 1 Co 11:23–24.
Oppression (——— of wickedness). Pr 4:17.
Poverty, when in want of. 1 S 2:36. Ps 37:25. Pr 12:9. Is 3:7. Lm 1:11.
Sloth (——— of idleness). Pr 31:27.
Sorrow (——— of tears). Ps 80:5.
Unlawful gain (——— of deceit). Pr 20:17.
In times of scarcity, sold by weight. Lv 26:26. Ezk 4:16.
Kept in baskets. Gn 40:16. Ex 29:32.
MADE OF
Barley. Jg 7:13. Jn 6:9.
Beans, millet, etc. Ezk 4:9.
Manna (in the wilderness). Nu 11:8.
Wheat. Ex 29:2. Ps 81:16.
Making of, a trade. Gn 40:2. Jr 37:21.
Multitudes miraculously fed by Christ with. Mt 14:19–21; 15:34–37.
Nutritious and strengthening. Ps 104:15.
Offered with sacrifices. Ex 29:2, 23. Nu 28:2.
Often given as a present. 1 S 25:18. 2 S 16:2. 1 Ch 12:40.
Often put for the whole sustenance of man. Gn 3:19; 39:6. Mt 6:11.
Ordinary, called common. 1 S 21:4.
Placed on table of showbread. Ex 25:30.
Plenty of, promised to the obedient. Lv 26:5.
Principal food of the ancients. Gn 18:5; 21:14, 27:17. Jg 19:5.
Publicly sold. Mt 14:15; 15:33.
Sacred, called hallowed. 1 S 21:4, 6.
Scarceness of, sent as a punishment. Ps 105:16. Is 3:1. Ezk 4:16.
Served after funerals. Ezk 24:17–22.
Sometimes unleavened. Ex 12:18. 1 Co 5:8.
Troughs used for kneading. Ex 12:34.
Usually leavened. Lv 23:17. Mt 13:33.
Was kneaded. Gn 18:6. Jr 7:18. Ho 7:4.
When old, dry and moldy. Jsh 9:5, 12.

With water, the food of prisons. 1 K 22:27.
Yielded by the earth. Jb 28:5. Is 55:10.

BRIBES
Characterize the wicked. Ps 26:10. Am 5:12.
Create injustice. Dt 16:19.
Forbidden by God. Ex 23:8. Lv 19:13.
Punishment for. JB 15:34.

BROTHERHOOD
Basis for peace in. Gn 13:8.
Betrayal of. Gn 4:1–16; 37:1–36. Ja 2:1–5.
Blessings of. Ps 133:1. Pr 17:17.
Danger of offending brethren. Ro 14:21. 1 Co 8:11.
Responsibility of. Gn 4:9. Dt 15:11. Ro 12:10.
Test of. 1 Jn 2:9; 3:14; 4:20.

BROTHERLY LOVE
Demonstrates Christian faith. 1 Jn 2:9–11.
Enjoined upon Christians. Ro 12:10. Jn 13:34.
Is to continue. He 13:1.
Should increase. 1 Th 4:9–10.
Should supplement godliness and love. 2 P 1:7.

BURDENS
Relief of. Ps 55:22. Mt 11:28–30.
Sharing of. Gl 6:2.
Weight of. 1 K 12:9. Jb 7:20. Ps 119:28.

BURIAL
Antiquity of coffins for. Gn 50:26.
Antiquity of purchasing places for. Gn 23:7–16.
ATTENDED BY
Family of the dead. Gn 50:5–6, 8. Mt 8:21.
Female friends. Mk 15:47. Lk 7:13.
Great lamentation at. Gn 50:10–11. 2 S 3:31–32.
Hired mourners. Jr 9:17–18.
Numbers of friends, etc. Gn 50:7, 9. 2 S 3:31. Lk 7:13.
THE BODY WAS
Anointed for. Mt 26:12.
Carried on a bier to. 2 S 3:31. Lk 7:14.
Preserved with spices. Jn 19:39–40.
Sometimes burned before. 1 S 31:12.
Washed before. Ac 9:37.
Wound in linen for. Jn 11:44; 19:40.

Design of. Gn 23:3–4.

Followed by a feast. 2 S 3:35, Jr 16:7–8, Ho 9:4.

Ignominious, compared to the burial of an ass. Jr 22:10.

Illustrative of regeneration. Ro 6:4. Cl 2:12.

Jews anxious to be interred in their family places of. Gn 47:29–31; 49:29–30; 50:25, 2 S 19:37.

Of enemies, sometimes performed by the conquerors. 1 K 11:15. Ezk 39:11–14.

Of the friendless, a kind act. 2 S 2:5.

Of persons embalmed, deferred for seventy days. Gn 50:3–4.

Of persons hanged, always on the days of execution. Dt 21:23. Jn 19:31.

Often took place immediately after death. Jn 11:17, 39, with Ac 5:6, 10.

Orations sometimes made at. 2 S 3:33–34.

Perfumes burned at. 2 Ch 16:14. Jr 34:5.

PLACES OF

For criminals, marked by heaps. Jsh 7:26.

Frequently prepared and pointed out during life. Gn 50:5. 2 Ch 16:14. Mt 27:60.

Held in high veneration. Ne 2:3, 5.

Members of a family interred in the same. Gn 25:10; 49:31. 2 S 2:32.

Often desecrated by idolatry. Is 65:3–4.

Pillars erected on. Gn 35:20.

Provided for aliens and strangers. Mt 27:7.

Provided for the common people. Jr 26:23.

Sometimes had inscriptions. 2 K 23:17.

Sometimes not apparent. Lk 11:44.

Tombs erected over. Mt 23:27–29.

Visited by sorrowing friends. Jn 11:31.

Were ceremonially unclean. Nu 19:16, 18.

PLACES USED FOR

City of David for the kings of Judah. 1 K 2:10. 2 Ch 21:20; 24:16.

Caves hewn out of rocks. Is 22:16. Mt 27:60.

Gardens. 2 K 21:18, 26. Jn 19:41.

Houses of the deceased. 1 S 25:1. 1 K 2:34.

Natural caves. Gn 23:19. Jn 11:38.

Tops of the hills. Jsh 24:33. 2 K 23:16.

Under trees. Gn 35:8. 1 S 31:13.

PRIVATION OF

Considered a calamity. Ec 6:3.

Threatened as a punishment. 2 K 9:10. Jr 8:2; 16:4.

Probable origin of. Gn 4:9–10.

Right of all nations. Jg 16:31. Jn 19:38.

BURNT OFFERING

Abraham tried by the command to offer Isaac as. Gn 22.

Ashes of, collected at foot of altar and carried outside the camp. Lv 6:11.

An atonement for sin. Lv 9:7.

Blood of, sprinkled round about upon the altar. Lv 1:5, 11.

Fat, etc., of all peace offerings laid on and consumed with the daily. Lv 3:5; 6:12.

Guilt of offering, except in the place appointed. Lv 17:8–9.

Guilt of unauthorized persons offering. 1 S 13:12–13.

Guilt transferred to, by imposition of hands. Lv 1:4. Nu 8:12.

If a bird, blood wrung out at side of altar. Lv 1:15.

Incapable of removing sin and reconciling to God. Pss 40:6; 50:8. He 10:6.

Knowledge of God better than. Ho 6:6.

Love of God better than. Mk 12:33.

Most ancient of all sacrifices. Gn 4:4, with 8:20; 22:2, 13. Jb 1:5.

Most costly, no adequate tribute to God. Is 40:16, with Ps 50:9–13.

Obedience better than. 1 S 15:22. Jr 7:21–23.

Of human victims execrated. Dt 12:31. 2 K 3:27. Jr 7:31; 19:5.

Of the wicked, not accepted by God. Is 1:10–11. Jr 6:19–20. Am 5:22.

OFFERED

After great mercies. 1 S 6:14. 2 S 24:22, 25.

At consecration of kings. 1 Ch 29:21–23.

At consecration of Levites. Nu 8:12.

At consecration of priests. Lv 9:2, 12–14.

At dedication of sacred places. Nu 7:15, etc. 1 K 8:64.

At purification of women. Lv 12:6.

Before going to war. 1 S 7:9.

By the Jews before the law. Ex 10:25; 24:5.

Every morning and evening. Ex 29:38–42.

Every sabbath day. Nu 28:9–10.

For the healed leper. Lv 14:13, 19–20.

For Nazarites after defilement, or at expiration of their vow. Nu 6:11, 14.

On atonement day. Lv 16:3, 5. Nu 29:8.

On the first day of every month. Nu 28:11.

Seven days of unleavened bread. Nu 28:19, 24.

With sound of trumpets at feasts. Nu 10:10.

REQUIRED TO BE

A male without blemish. Lv 1:3; 22:19.

Entirely burned. Lv 1:8, 9, 12–13; 6:9.

For the people at large, killed and prepared by the Levites. Ezk 44:11.

Killed, if a beast, by the person who brought it. Lv 1:5, 11.

Killed, if a bird, by the priest. Lv 1:15.

Offered by priests only. Lv 1:9. Ezk 44:15.

Offered in righteousness. Ps 51:19.

Presented at the door of the tabernacle. Lv 1:3. Dt 12:6, 11, 14.

Voluntary. Lv 1:3; 22:18–19.

Skin of, given to the priests for clothing. Lv 7:8. (See Gn 3:21.)

Specially acceptable. Gn 8:21. Lv 1:9, 13, 17.

To be offered only to the Lord. Jg 13:16.

TO BE TAKEN FROM

The flock or herd. Lv 1:2.

The fowls. Lv 1:14.

C

CALL OF GOD
Addressed to all. Is 45:22. Mt 20:16.
Blessedness of receiving. Rv 19:9.
By Christ. Is 55:5. Ro 1:6.
By his gospel. 2 Th 2:14.
By his ministers. Jr 35:15. 2 Co 5:20.
By his Spirit. Rv 22:17.
By his works. Ps 19:2–3. Ro 1:20.
Effectual to saints. Ps 110:3. Ac 2:47; 13:48.
1 Co 1:21.
Illustrated. Pr 9:3–4. Mt 23:3–9.
Is from darkness. 1 P 2:9.
ITS REJECTION LEADS TO
Condemnation. Jn12:48. He2:1–3;12:25.
Delusion. Is 66:4. 2 Th 2:10–11.
Destruction. Pr 29:1. Mt 22:3–7.
Judicial blindness. Is 6:9; with Ac
28:24–27. Ro 11:8–10.
Rejection by God. Pr 1:24–32. Jr 6:19, 30.
Temporal judgments. Is 28:12. Jr 6:16,
19; 35:17. Zc 7:12–14.
Withdrawal of the means of grace. Jr
26:4–6. Ac 13:46; 18:6. Rv 2:5.
Most reject. Pr 1:24. Mt 20:16.
Partakers of, justified. Ro 8:30.
Praise God for. 1 P 2:9.
TO MAN IS
According to the purpose of God. Ro
8:28; 9:11, 23–24.
Heavenly. He 3:1.
High. Php 3:14.
Holy. 1 Tm 1:19.
Of grace. Gl 1:15. 2 Tm 1:9.
To the eternal glory of Christ. 2 Th 2:14.
1 P 5:10.
To eternal life. 1 Tm 6:12.
To fellowship with Christ. 1 Co 1:9.
To glory and virtue. 2 P 1:3.
To holiness. 1 Th 4:7.
To liberty. Gl 5:13.
To peace. 1 Co 7:15. Cl 3:15.
Walk worthy of. Ep 4:1.

CAPTIVITY
Hope in. Ezr 9:9. Zp 2:7.
Lessons of. Ex 13:3. Is 5:13. Lm 1:3.

Of sin. Ro 7:23.
Of thoughts. 2 Co 10:5.
Redemption from. Dt 30:3. Jb 42:10. Ps
14:7. Jr 29:14.

CARE, GOD'S
Affirmed in faith. Ps 23.
Assured through trust. Ps 55:22.
Illustrated in the church. 1 Co 12:25.
Promised. 1 P 5:7.

CARE, OVERMUCH
About earthly things, forbidden. Mt 6:25.
Lk 12:22, 29. Jn 6:27.
Be without. 1 Co 7:32. Php 4:6.
God's promises should keep us from. He
13:5.
God's providential goodness should keep us
from. Mt 6:26, 28, 30. Lk 22:35.
Inutility of. Mt 6:27. Lk 12:25–
26.
Obstructs the gospel. Mt 13:22. Lk 8:14;
14:18–20.
Sent as a punishment to the wicked. Ezk
4:16; 12:19.
Should be cast on God. Pss 37:5; 55:22. Pr
16:3. 1 P 5:7.
Trust in God should free us from. Jr 17:7–8.
Dn 3:16.
Unbecoming in saints. 2 Tm 2:4.
Vanity of. Ps 39:6. Ec 4:8.
Warning against. Lk 21:34.

CAREER
Assigned by God. 1 Co 7:17. Ex 31:1–
11.
Dedication in. Ps 119:32.
Diversity of. Ep 4:11. Ro 12:6–
8.
Faithfulness in. 1 Co 7:24.
Reward of. 2 Tm 2:6.

CARELESSNESS
Admonition against. He 2:1.
Danger of. Ezk 39:6. Mt 12:36.
Folly of. Pr 14:16. Mt 7:26–27.

Warning against. Is 47:8. Lk 8:15. Dt 8:11.

CERTAINTY
Of faith. He 10:22. Jn 6:69.
Of hope. He 6:11.
Of judgment for sin. Nu 32:23. He 9:27.
Of reward for righteousness. Pr 11:18.
Of salvation. 2 P 1:10.
Of truth. Pr 22:21.

CHARITY
Enjoined. Cl 3:14. *(See* Love to Man.)
Explained. 1 Co 13:4-7.

CHASTITY
Advantages of. 1 P 3:1, 2.
Breach of, punished. 1 Co 3:16-17. Ep 5:5-6. He 13:4. Rv 22:15.
Commanded. Ex 20:14. Pr 31:3. Ac 15:20. Ro 13:13. Cl 3:5. 1 Th 4:3.
Consequences of associating with those devoid of. Pr 5:3-11; 7:25-27; 22:14.
Drunkenness destructive to. Pr 23:31-33.
Keep the body in. 1 Co 6:13, 15-18.
Motives for. 1 Co 6:19. 1 Th 4:7.
Preserved by wisdom. Pr 2:10-11, 16; 7:1-5.
Required in heart. Pr 6:25.
Required in look. Jb 31:1. Mt 5:28.
Required in speech. Ep 5:3.
Saints are kept in. Ec 7:26.
Shun those devoid of. 1 Co 5:11. 1 P 4:3.
Temptation to deviate from, dangerous. 2 S 11:2-4.
Want of, excludes from heaven. Gl 5:19-21.
The wicked are devoid of. Ro 1:29. Ep 4:19. 2 P 2:14. Jde 1:8.

CHEERFULNESS
And charity. Ro 12:8.
And praise. Ja 5:13.
And redemption. Is 52:9. Zc 8:19.
And sharing. Phm 1:20.
And stewardship. 2 Co 9:7.
Value of. Pr 15:15; 17:22.

CHERUBIM
Animated by the Spirit of God. Ezk 1:12, 20.
Called the cherubim of glory. He 9:5.
Engaged in accomplishing the purposes of God. Ezk 1:15, 21; 10:9-11, 16-17.
Form and appearance of. Ezk 1:5-11, 13-14.
Glory of God exhibited upon. Ezk 1:22, 26-28; 10:4, 18, 20.

Of Gold
Formed out of, and at each end of the mercy seat. Ex 25:18-20.
God's presence manifested between. 2 S 6:2. 2 K 19:15. Pss 80:1; 99:1.
Oracles or answers of God delivered from between. Ex 25:22. Nu 7:89.
Placed over the ark of the covenant. 1 S 4:4. 1 K 8:6-7. 2 Ch 5:7-8.
Placed at the entrance of Eden. Gn 3:24.
Representations of, Made on the
Bases of bronze lavers. 1 K 7:28, 36.
Curtains of the tabernacle. Ex 26:1, 31.
Doors of the temple. 1 K 6:32, 35.
Veil of the tabernacle. Ex 26:31.
Veil of the temple. 2 Ch 3:14.
Walls of the temple. 2 Ch 3:7.
Riding on, illustrative of majesty and power of God. 2 S 22:11. Ps 18:10.
Sound of their wings was as the voice of God. Ezk 1:24; 10:5.

CHILDISHNESS
As instability and folly. Ep 4:14. Pr 22:15.
Of thought rebuked. 1 Co 14:20.
Versus freedom. Gl 4:3.
Versus spiritual maturity. 1 Co 13:11.

CHILDLIKENESS
And growth. 1 P 2:2. 1 Co 14:20.
And the kingdom. Mt 10:14.
And obedience. 1 P 1:14.
As saving faith. Mt 18:3. Mk 10:15.
As trust. Ps 131:1-2.

CHILDREN
Amusements of. Zc 8:5. Mt 11:16-17.
Anxiety of the Jews for. Gn 30:1. 1 S 1:5, 8.
Capable of glorifying God. Gn 33:5. Ps 127:3.
Casting out of weak, etc., alluded to. Ezk 16:5.
Christ an example to. Lk 2:51. Jn 19:26-27.
Circumcised on the eighth day. Php 3:5.
Could demand their portion during their father's life. Lk 15:12.
Destruction of, a punishment. Lv 26:22. Ezk 9:6. Lk 19:44.
Female
Inherited property in default of sons. Nu 27:1-8. Jsh 17:1-6.
Taken care of by nurses. Gn 35:8.
Usefully employed. Gn 24:13. Ex 2:16.
Fondness and care of mothers for. Ex

2:2–10. 1 S 2:19. 1 K 3:27. Is 49:15, 1 Th 2:7–8.

Frequently bore the curse of parents. Ex 20:5. Ps 109:9–10.

Gifts from God. Gn 33:5. Ps 127:3.

Grief occasioned by loss of. Gn 37:35; 44:27–29. 2 S 13:37. Jr 6:26; 31:15.

Heritage from the Lord. Pss 113:9; 127:3.

ILLEGITIMATE

Despised by their brethren. Jg 11:2.

Excluded from the congregation. Dt 23:2.

Had no inheritance. Gn 21:10, 14. Gl 4:30.

Not cared for by the father. He 12:8.

Sometimes sent away with gifts. Gn 25:6.

Inhuman practice of offering to idols. 2 K 17:31. 2 Ch 28:3, 33:6.

MALE

Birth of, announced to the father by a messenger. Jr 20:15.

If first-born, belonged to God and were redeemed. Ex 13:12–13, 15.

Inherited the possessions of their father. Dt 21:16–17. Lk 12:13–14.

Received the blessing of their father before his death. Gn 27:1–4; 48:15; 49.

Under the care of tutors, till they came of age. 2 K 10:1. Gl 4:1–2.

Usefully employed. 1 S 9:3; 17:15.

Mode of giving public instruction to. Lk 2:46. Ac 22:3.

Mostly nursed by the mothers. 1 S 1:22. 1 K 3:21. Ps 22:9. S S 8:1.

Named at circumcision. Lk 1:59; 2:21.

NOT TO HAVE

A reproach in Israel. 1 S 1:6–7. Lk 1:25.

Considered an affliction. Gn 15:2–3. Jr 22:30.

Numerous, considered an especial blessing. Pss 115:14; 127:4–5.

Of God's people, holy. Ezr 9:2. 1 Co 7:14.

Of God's people, interested in the promises. Dt 29:29. Ac 2:39.

Often given in answer to prayer. Gn 25:21. 1 S 1:27. Lk 1:13.

Often numerous. 2 K 10:1. 1 Ch 4:27.

Often prayed for. 1 S 1:10–11. Lk 1:13.

Often wicked and rebellious. 2 K 2:23.

Power of parents over, during patriarchal age. Gn 9:24–25; 21:14; 38:24.

Prosperity of, greatly depended on obeying parents. Dt 4:40; 12:25, 28. Ps 128:1–3.

Rebellious, punished by the civil power. Ex 21:15–17. Dt 21:18–21.

Resignation manifested at loss of. Lv 10:19–20. 2 S 12:18–23. Jb 1:19–21.

SHOULD

Attend to parental teaching. Pr 1:8–9.

Fear God. Pr 24:21.

Fear parents. Lv 19:3.

Honor parents. Ex 20:12. He 19:9.

Honor the aged. Lv 19:32. 1 P 5:5.

Not imitate bad parents. Ezk 20:18.

Obey God. Dt 30:2.

Obey parents. Pr 6:20. Ep 6:1.

Remember God. Ec 12:1.

Take care of parents. 1 Tm 5:4.

SHOULD BE

Brought early to the house of God. 1 S 1:21.

Brought to Christ. Mk 10:13–16.

Instructed in the ways of God. Dt 31:12–13. Pr 22:6.

Judiciously trained. Pr 22:15; 29:17, Ep 6:4.

Sometimes born when parents were old. Gn 15:3, 6; 17:17. Lk 1:18.

Sometimes devoted their property to God to avoid supporting parents. Mt 15:5. Mk 7:11–12.

Treatment of, after birth, noticed. Ezk 16:4.

Weaning of, a time of joy and feasting. Gn 21:8. 1 S 1:24.

WERE NAMED

After relatives. Lk 1:59, 61.

From circumstances connected with their birth. Gn 25:25–26; 35:18. 1 Ch 4:9.

From remarkable events. Gn 21:3, 6, with 18:13. Ex 2:10; 18:3–4.

Often by God. Is 8:3. Ho 1:4, 6, 9.

WERE REQUIRED

To attend to instruction. Dt 4:9; 11:19.

To honor their parents. Ex 20:12.

To respect the aged. Lv 19:32.

To submit to discipline. Pr. 29:17. He 12:9.

CHILDREN, GOOD

Adduced as a motive for submission to God. He 12:9.

Attend to parental teaching. Pr 13:1.

Honor the aged. Jb 32:6–7.

Illustrative of a teachable spirit. Mt 18:4.

Know the scriptures. 2 Tm 3:15.

The Lord is with. 1 S 3:19.

Make their parents' hearts glad. Pr 10:1; 29:17.

Obey parents. Gn 28:7; 47:30.

Observe the law of God. Pr 28:7.
Partake of the promises of God. Ac 2:39.
Shall be blessed. Pr 3:1–4. Ep 6:2–3.
Show love to parents. Gn 46:29.
Spirit of, a requisite for the kingdom of heaven. Mt 18:3.
Take care of parents. Gn 45:9, 11; 47:12.
Their obedience to parents is well pleasing to God. Cl 3:20.

CHILDREN, WICKED
Are proud. Is 3:5.
Are void of understanding. Pr 7:7.
Despise their elders. Jb 19:18.
Know not God. 1 S 2:12.
PUNISHED FOR
Cursing parents. Ex 21:15, with Mk 7:10.
Disobeying parents. Dt 21:21.
Gluttony and drunkenness. Dt 21:20–21.
Mocking a prophet. 2 K 2:23–24.
Mocking parents. Pr 30:17.
Setting light by parents. Dt 27:16.
Smiting parents. Ex 21:15.
WITH REGARD TO PARENTS
Are a calamity to them. Pr 19:13.
Are a grief to them. Pr 17:25.
Bring reproach on them. Pr 19:26.
Curse them. Pr 30:11.
Despise them. Pr 15:5, 20. Ezk 22:7.
Hearken not to them. 1 S 2:25.
Rob them. Pr 28:24.

CHOICE
And wisdom. 1 K 3:9.
By God. Ps 65:4. Ja 2:5. Cl 3:12.
Of life or death. Dt 30:19.
Of a master. Jsh 24:15.

CHOSEN OF GOD
By grace. Dt 7:7. Ep 2:1–10.
In Christ. Jn 15:16. Ro 1:6. Gl 1:1.
Separated for service. 1 P 2:9.
Through the Spirit. 1 P 1:2.
Unto holiness. Nu 16:7. Ep 1:4.

CHRIST, CHARACTER OF
Altogether lovely. S S 5:16.
Benevolent. Mt 4:23–24. Ac 10:38.
Compassionate. Is 40:11. Lk 19:41.
Faithful. Is 11:5. 1 Th 5:24.
Forgiving. Lk 23:34.
Good. Mt 19:16.
Guileless. Is 53:9. 1 P 2:22.
Harmless. He 7:26.

Holy. Lk 1:35. Ac 4:27. Rv 3:7.
Humble. Lk 22:27. Phm 2:8.
Innocent. Mt 27:4.
Just. Zc 9:9. Jn 5:30. Ac 22:14.
Long-suffering. 1 Tm 1:16.
Loving. Jn 13:1; 15:13.
Lowly in heart. Mt 11:29.
Meek. Is 53:7. Zc 9:9. Mt 11:29.
Merciful. He 2:17.
Obedient to God the Father. Ps 40:8. Jn 4:34; 15:10.
Patient. Is 53:7. Mt 27:14.
Resigned. Lk 22:42.
Resisting temptation. Mt 4:1–10.
Righteous. Is 53:11. He 1:9.
Saints are conformed to. Ro 8:29.
Self-denying. Mt 8:20. 2 Co 8:9.
Sinless. Jn 8:46. 2 Co 5:21.
Spotless. 1 P 1:19.
Subject to his parents. Lk 2:51.
True. Jn 1:14; 7:18. 1 Jn 5:20.
Zealous. Lk 2:49. Jn 2:17; 8:29.
See also Titles and Names of Christ.

CHRIST, GLORY OF
As the Blessed of God. Ps 45:2.
As Creator. Jn 1:3. Cl 1:17. He 1:2.
As the First begotten. He 1:6.
As the First-born. Cl 1:15, 18.
As the foundation of the church. Is 28:16.
As God. Jn 1:1–5. Php 2:6, 9–10.
As Head of the church. Ep 1:22.
As the image of God. Cl 1:15. He 1:3.
As incarnate. Jn 1:14.
As Judge. Mt 16:27. Mt 25:31, 33.
As King. Is 6:1–5, with Jn 12:41.
As the life. Jn 11:25. Cl 3:4. 1 Jn 5:11.
As Lord of lords, etc. Rv 17:14.
As Mediator. 1 Tm 2:5. He 8:6.
As one with the Father. Jn 10:30, 38.
As Priest. Ps 110:4. He 4:15.
As Prophet. Dt 18:15–16, with Ac 3:22.
As Shepherd. Is 40:10–11. Jn 10:11, 14.
As the Son of God. Mt 3:17. He 1:6, 8.
As the true Light. Lk 1:78–79. Jn 1:4, 9.
As the truth. 1 Jn 5:20. Rv 3:7.
As the way. Jn 14:6. He 10:19–20.
Celebrated by the redeemed. Rv 5:8–14; 7:9–12.
Followed his resurrection. 1 P 1:21.
Followed his sufferings. 1 P 1:10–11.
Imparted to saints. Jn 17:22. 2 Co 3:18.
In the calling of the Gentiles. Ps 72:17. Jn 12:21, 23.

In the fullness of his grace and truth. Ps 45:2, with Jn 1:14.

In his exaltation. Ac 7:55–56. Ep 1:21.

In his sinless perfection. He 7:26–28.

In his transfiguration. Mt 17:2, with 2 P 1:16–18.

In his triumph. Is 63:1–3, with Rv 19:11, 16.

In his words. Lk 4:22. Jn 7:46.

In his works. Mt 13:54. Jn 2:11.

In the restoration of the Jews. Ps 102:16.

Is incomparable. S S 5:10. Php 2:9.

Is unchangeable. He 1:10–12.

Revealed in the gospel. Is 40:5.

Saints shall behold, in heaven. Jn 17:24.

Saints shall rejoice at the revelation of. 1 P 4:13.

CHRIST IS GOD

Acknowledged by his apostles. Jn 20:28.

Acknowledged by Old Testament saints. Gn 17:1, with 48:15, 16. Gn 32:24–30, with Ho 12:3–5. Jg 6:22–24; 13:21–22. Jb 19:25–27.

As creator of all things. Is 40:28. Jn 1:3. Cl 1:16. He 1:2.

As discerning the thoughts of the heart. 1 K 8:39, with Lk 5:22. Ezk 11:5, with Jn 2:24–25. Rv 2:23.

As Emmanuel. Is 7:14, with Mt 1:23.

As entitled to equal honor with the Father. Jn 5:23.

As eternal. Is 9:6. Mi 5:2. Jn 1:1. Cl 1:17. He 1:8–10. Rv 1:8.

As the Eternal God and Creator. Ps 102:24–27, with He 1:8, 10–12.

As giver of pastors to the church. Jr 3:15, with Ep 4:11–13.

As God, he presents the church to himself. Ep 5:27, with Jde 24–25.

As God, he redeems and purifies the church unto himself. Rv 5:9, with Ti 2:14.

As God over all. Ps 45:6–7. Ro 9:5.

As God the Judge. Ec 12:14, with 1 Co 4:5. 2 Co 5:10. 2 Tm 4:1.

As God the Word. Jn 1:1.

As the Great God and Savior. Ho 1:7, with Ti 2:13.

As having power to forgive sins. Cl 3:13, with Mk 2:7, 10.

As the Holy One. 1 S 2:2, with Ac 3:14.

As husband of the church. Is 54:5, with Ep 5:25–32. Is 62:5, with Rv 21:2, 9.

As Jehovah. Is 40:3, with Mt 3:3.

As Jehovah above all. Ps 97:9, with Jn 3:31.

As Jehovah the first and the last. Is 44:6, with Rv 1:17. Is 48:12–16, with Rv 22:13.

As Jehovah for whose glory all things were created. Pr 16:4, with Cl 1:16.

As Jehovah (invoked). Jl 2:32, with Ac 2:21 and 1 Co 1:2.

As Jehovah the messenger of the covenant. Ml 3:1, with Mk 1:2 and Lk 2:27.

As Jehovah of glory. Ps 24:7, 10, with 1 Co 2:8. Ja 2:1.

As Jehovah of Hosts. Is 6:1–3, with Jn 12:41. Is 8:13–14, with 1 P 2:8.

As Jehovah our Righteousness. Jr 23:5–6, with 1 Co 1:30.

As Jehovah the Shepherd. Is 40:11. He 13:20.

As Jehovah's fellow and equal. Zc 13:7. Php 2:6.

As King of kings and Lord of lords. Dn 10:17, with Rv 1:5. Rv 17:14.

As the Lord from heaven. 1 Co 15:47.

As Lord of all. Ac 10:36. Ro 10:11–13.

As Lord of the sabbath. Gn 2:3, with Mt 12:8.

As the mighty God. Is 9:6.

As the object of divine worship. Ac 7:59. 2 Co 12:8–9. He 1:6. Rv 5:12.

As the object of faith. Ps 2:12. with 1 P 2:6. Jr 17:5, 7, with Jn 14:1.

As omnipotent. Ps 45:3. Php 3:21. Rv 1:8.

As omnipresent. Mt 18:20; 28:30. Jn 3:13.

As omniscient. Jn 16:30; 21:17.

As one with the Father. Jn 10:30, 38; 12:45; 14:7–10; 17:10.

As the only begotten Son of the Father. Jn 1:14, 18; 3:16, 18. 1 Jn 4:9.

As owner of all things equally with the Father. Jn 16:15.

As possessed of the fullness of the Godhead. Cl 2:9. He 1:3.

As raising the dead. Jn 5:21, 6:40, 54.

As raising himself from the dead. Jn 2:19, 21; 10:18.

As sending the Spirit equally with the Father. Jn 14:16, with 15:26.

As Son of God. Mt 26:63–67.

As the source of grace equally with the Father. 1 Th 3:11. 2 Th 2:16–17.

As supporter and preserver of all things. Ne 9:6, with Cl 1:17. He 1:3.

As the true God. Jr 10:10, with 1 Jn 5:20.

As unchangeable. Ml 3:6, with He 1:12. He 13:8.

As unrestricted by the law of the sabbath, equally with the Father. Jn 5:17.

As unsearchable, equally with the Father. 1 Th 3:11. 2 Th 2:16–17.

Saints live unto him as. Ro 6:11. Gl 2:19, with 2 Co 5:15.

CHRIST, THE HEAD OF THE CHURCH

Appointed by God. Ep 1:22.

As his mystical body. Ep 4:12, 15; 5:23,

Commissioned his apostles. Mt 10:1, 7; 28:19. Jn 20:21.

Declared by himself. Mt 21:42.

Has the preeminence in all things. 1 Co 11:3. Ep 1:22. Cl 1:18.

Imparts gifts. Ps 68:18, with Ep 4:8.

Instituted the sacraments. Mt 28:19. Lk 22:19–20.

Perverters of the truth do not hold. Cl 2:18–19.

Predicted. Ps 118:22, with Mt 21:42.

Saints are complete in. Cl 2:10.

CHRIST, THE HIGH PRIEST

After the order of Melchizedek. Ps 110:4, with He 5:6. He 6:20; 7:15, 17.

Appointed and called by God. He 3:1, 2; 5:4, 5.

Appointment of, and encouragement to stead-fastness. He 4:14.

Blesses. Nu 6:23–26, with Ac 3:26.

Consecrated with an oath. He 7:20, 21.

Entered into heaven. He 4:14; 10:12.

Faithful. He 3:2.

Has an unchangeable priesthood. He 7:23, 28.

His sacrifice superior to all others. He 9:13–14, 23.

Intercedes. He 7:25; 9:24.

Is of unblemished purity. He 7:26, 28.

Made reconciliation. He 2:17.

Needed no sacrifice for himself. He 7:27,

Obtained redemption for us. He 9:12.

Offered himself a sacrifice. He 9:14, 26.

Offered sacrifice but once. He 7:27; 9:25–26.

On his throne. Zc 6:13.

Superior to Aaron and the Levitical priests. He 7:11, 16, 22; 8:1, 2, 6.

Sympathizes with those who are tempted. He 2:18; 4:15.

CHRIST, THE KING

ACKNOWLEDGED BY

His followers. Lk 19:38. Jn 12:13.

Nathanael. Jn 1:49.

The wise men from the East. Mt 2:2.

Declared by himself. Mt 25:34. Jn 18:37.

Foretold. Nu 24:17. Pss 2:6; 45. Is 9:7. Jr 23:5. Mi 5:2.

Glorious. Ps 24:7–10. 1 Co 2:8. Ja 2:1.

Has an everlasting kingdom. Dn 2:44; 7:14. Lk 1:33.

Has a righteous kingdom. Ps 45:6, with He 1:8–9. Is 32:1. Jr 23:5.

Has an universal kingdom. Pss 2:8; 72:8. Zc 14:9. Rv 11:15.

His kingdom not of this world. Jn 18:36.

In the throne of God. Rv 3:21.

The Jews shall seek unto. Ho 3:5.

King of Zion. Ps 2:6. Is 52:7. Zc 9:9. Mt 21:5. Jn 12:12–15.

Kings shall do homage to. Ps 72:10. Is 49:7.

On the throne of David. Is 9:7. Ezk 27:24–25. Lk 1:32. Ac 2:30.

Saints, the subjects of. Cl 1:13. Rv 15:3.

Saints receive a kingdom from. Lk 22:29–30. He 12:28.

Saints shall behold. Is 33:17. Rv 22:3–4.

Shall overcome all his enemies. Ps 110:1. Mk 12:36. 1 Co 15:25. Rv 17:14.

Supreme. Ps 89:27. Rv 1:5; 19:16.

Written on his cross. Jn 19:19.

CHRIST, THE LORD

Accepted. Jn 6:68.

Confessed. Php 2:11.

Named. Lk 2:11.

Seen. Jn 20:25.

Sovereign. 1 Tm 6:15. Mt 12:8.

CHRIST, THE MEDIATOR

In virtue of his atonement. Ep 2:13–18. He 9:15; 12:24.

Of the gospel covenant. He 8:6; 12:24.

The only one between God and man. 1 Tm 2:5.

CHRIST, THE PROPHET

Abounds in wisdom. Lk 2:40, 47, 52. Cl 2:3.

Alone knows and reveals God. Mt 11:27. Jn 3:2, 13, 34; 17:6, 14, 26. He 1:1–2.

Anointed with the Holy Ghost. Is 61:1, with Lk 4:18. Jn 3:34.

Declared his doctrine to be that of the Father. Jn 8:26, 28; 12:49–50; 14:10, 24; 15:15; 17:8, 16.

Faithful to his trust. Lk 4:32. Jn 17:8. He 3:2. Rv 1:5; 3:14.

Foretold. Dt 18:15, 18. Is 52:7. Na 1:15.

Foretold things to come. Mt 24:3–35. Lk 19:41, 44.

God commands us to hear. Dt 18:15. Mt 17:25. Ac 3:22; 7:37.

God will severely visit our neglect of. Dt 18:19. Ac 3:23. He 2:3.

Meek and unostentatious in his teaching. Is 42:2. Mt 12:17–20.

Mighty in deed and word. Mt 13:54. Mk 1:27. Lk 4:32. Jn 7:46.

Preached the gospel and worked miracles. Mt 4:23; 11:5. Lk 4:43.

CHRIST, THE SAVIOR
Announced at his birth. Mt 1:21. Lk 2:11.
Our healer. Ac 9:34.
Our liberator. Is 61:1. Ro 8:2.
Our redemption. 1 Co 1:30. 2 Co 5:21.
Our sin bearer. Jn 1:29.
Preached by disciples. Ac 2:21; 3:6; 8:4.
Proclaimed by himself. Mt 20:28.

CHRIST, THE SHEPHERD
As chief. 1 P 5:4.
As good. Jn 10:11, 14.
As great. Mi 5:4. He 13:20.
Foretold. Gn 49:24. Is 40:11. Ezk 34:23; 37:24.
His Sheep
He calls. Jn 10:3.
He cherishes tenderly. Is 40:11.
He feeds. Ps 23:1-2. Jn 10:9.
He gathers. Is 40:11. Jn 10:16.
He gives eternal life to. Jn 10:28.
He guides. Ps 23:3. Jn 10:3–4.
He knows. Jn 10:14, 27.
He laid down his life for. Zc 13:7. Mt 26:31. Jn 10:11, 15. Ac 20:28.
He protects and preserves. Jr 31:10. Ezk 34:10. Zc 9:16. Jn 10:28.

CHRISTIANS
Almost persuaded. Ac 26:28.
Daily life. Mt 5:46–48. Ep 4:17.
First named. Ac 11:26.
Under suffering. 1 P 4:16.

THE CHURCH
As body of Christ. Ep 1:23. Cl 1:24.
Believers continually added by the Lord. Ac 2:47; 5:14; 11:24.
Belongs to God. 1 Tm 3:15.
Christ, the foundation stone of. 1 Co 3:11. Ep 2:20. 1 P 2:4, 6.
Christ, the head of. Ep 1:22; 5:23.
Clothed in righteousness. Rv 19:8.
Defiling of, will be punished. 1 Co 3:17.
Displays the wisdom of God. Ep 3:10.
Elect. 1 P 5:13.
Extent of, predicted. Is 2:2. Ezk 17:22–24. Dn 2:34–35. Hk 2:14.
Glorious. Ps 45:13. Ep 5:27.
Glory to be ascribed to God by. Ep 3:21.
God defends. Ps 89:18. Is 4:5; 49:25. Mt 16:18.
God provides ministers for. Jr 3:15. Ep 4:11–12.
Is edified by the word. 1 Co 14:4, 13. Ep 4:15–16.
Loved by Christ. S S 7:10. Ep 5:25.
Ministers commanded to feed. Ac 20:28.
Not to be despised. 1 Co 11:22.
Object of the grace of God. Is 27:3. 2 Co 8:1.
Persecuted by the wicked. Ac 8:1–3. 1 Th 2:14–15.
Purchased by the blood of Christ. Ac 20:28. Ep 5:25. He 9:12.
Saints baptized into, by one Spirit. 1 Co 12:13.
Sanctified and cleansed by Christ. 1 Co 6:11. Ep 5:26–27.
Shows forth the praises of God. Is 60:6.
Subject to Christ. Ro 7:4. Ep 5:24.
Unity of. Ro 12:5. 1 Co 10:17; 12:12. Gl 3:28.

CHURCH, GLORY OF THE
Augmented by increase of its members. Is 49:18; 60:4–14.
Consist in Its
Being the body of Christ. Ep 1:22–23.
Being the bride of Christ. Ps 45:13–14. Rv 19:7–8; 21:2.
Being established. Ps 48:8. Is 33:20.
Being the seat of God's worship. Ps 96:6.
Being the temple of God. 1 Co 3:16–17. Ep 2:21–22.
Eminent position. Ps 48:2. Is 2:2.
Graces of character. S S 2:14.

Members being righteous. Is 60:21. Rv 19:8.
Perfection of beauty. Ps 50:2.
Sanctification. Ep 5:26–27.
Strength and defense. Ps 48:12–13.
Derived from Christ. Is 60:1. Lk 2:34.
Derived from God. Is 28:5.
God delights in. Ps 45:11. Is 62:3–5.
Is abundant. Is 66:11.
Result from the favor of God. Is 43:4.
Saints delight in. Is 66:11.
Sin obscures. Lm 2:14–15.

CHURCH OF ISRAEL
Admission into, by circumcision. Gn 17:10–14.
All Israelites members of. Ro 9:4.
Attachment of the Jews to. Jn $:28–29. Ac 6:11.
CALLED THE
Congregation of Israel. Ex 12:47. Lv 4:13.
Congregation of the Lord. Nu 27:17; 31:16.
Depository of holy writ. Ro 3:2.
Established by God. Dt 4:5–14. Dt 26:18, with Ac 7:35, 38.
HAD
Appointed feasts. Lv 23:2. Is 1:14.
Appointed ordinances. Ex 18:20. He 9:1, 10.
An appointed place of worship. Dt 12:5.
The divine presence manifested in it. Ex 29:45–46. Lv 26:11–12. 1 K 8:10, 11.
An ordained ministry. Ex 29:9. Dt 10:8.
A spiritual church within it. Ro 9:6–8; 11:2–7.
In covenant with God. Dt 4:13, 23. Ac 3:25.
MEMBERS OF
Excommunicated for heavy offenses. Nu 15:30–31; 19:20.
Required to attend its worship. Ex 23:17.
Required to keep its statutes. Dt 16:12.
Required to know its statutes. Lv 10:11.
Separated from, while unclean. Lv 13:46; 15:31. Nu 5:2–4.
Persons excluded from. Ex 12:48. Dt 23:1–4. Ezk 44:7, 9.
Privileges of. Ro 9:4.
Proselytes admitted into. Nu 9:14; 15:15, 29.
Supported by the people. Ex 34:20. Dt 16:17.
A type of the church of Christ. Gl 4:24–26. He 12:23.

Was relatively holy. Ex 31:13. Nu 16:3.
WORSHIP OF, CONSISTED IN
Praise. 2 Ch 5:13; 30:21.
Prayer. Ex 24:1. Pss 5:7; 95:6.
Preaching, Ne 8:4, 7.
Reading God's word. Ex 24:7. Dt 31:11.
Sacrifice. Ex 10:25. Lv 1:2. He 10:1.

CIRCUMCISION
Abolished by the gospel. Ep 2:11, 15. Cl 3:11.
Accompanied with naming the child. Gn 21:3–4. Lk 1:59; 2:21.
A painful and bloody rite. Ex 4:26. Jsh 5:8.
A seal of the covenant. Gn 17:11. Ro 4:11.
CALLED THE
Circumcision in the flesh. Ep 2:11.
Concision. Php 3:2.
Covenant of circumcision. Ac 7:8.
Described. Gn 17:11. Ex 4:25.
Enforced by the law. Lv 12:3, with Jn 7:22.
First performed on Abraham and his family. Gn 17:24–27.
ILLUSTRATIVE OF
Purity of heart. Dt 10:16; 30:6.
Purity of speech. Ex 6:12.
Readiness to hear and obey. Jr 6:10.
Instituted by God. Gn 17:9–10.
Introductory Jewish sacrament. Gl 5:3.
Inward grace of. Ro 2:29.
THE JEWS
Denominated by. Ac 10:45. Gl 2:9.
Despised as unclean those not of the. 1 S 14:6; 17:26. Mt 15:26–27. Ep 2:11.
Held it unlawful to intermarry with those not of the. Gn 34:14. Jg 14:3.
Held no intercourse with those not of the. Ac 10:28; 11:3. Gl 2:12.
Necessary to enjoying the privileges of the Jewish church. Ex 11:48. Ezk 44:7.
Necessity of, asserted by false teachers. Ac 15:24. Gl 6:12. Ti 1:10.
Necessity of, denied by Paul. Gl 2:3–5.
Not performed in the wilderness. Jsh 5:5.
Outward sign of. Ro 2:28.
Paul denounced for opposing. Ac 21:21.
Performed by Joshua at Gilgal. Jsh 5:2, 7.
Performed on Timothy as a matter of expediency because of the Jews. Ac 16:3.
Promises to Abraham previous to. Ro 4:9, 13.
Punishment for neglecting. Gn 17:14. Ex 4:24, 26.
Saints the true spiritual. Php 3:3. Cl 2:11.

Sometimes performed on slain enemies. 1 S 18:25–27. 2 S 3:14.

Trusting to, a denial of Christ. Gl 3:3–4, with 5:3, 4.

WAS PERFORMED

By the heads of families. Gn 17:23. Ex 4:25.

By persons in authority. Jsh 5:3.

Even on the sabbath day. Jn 7:22, 23.

In the presence of the family, etc. Lk 1:58–61.

On the eighth day. Gn 17:12. Lv 12:3.

On males home-born and bought. Gn 17:12, 13.

With knives of flint. Ex 4:25. Jsh 5:3.

Without faith, vain. Ro 3:30. Gl 5:6.

Without obedience, vain. Ro 2:25. 1 Co 7:19.

CITIES

Afforded refuge in times of danger. Jr 8:14–16.

Arranged in streets and lanes. Zc 8:5. Lk 14:21.

BUILT

Beside rivers. Pss 46:4; 137:1.

In desert places. 2 Ch 8:4. Ps 107:35–36.

In pleasant situations. 2 K 2:19. Ps 48:2.

In plains. Gn 11:2, 4; 13:12.

Of brick and mortar. Ex 1:11, 14.

Of brick and slime. Gn 11:3.

Of stone and wood. Ps 102:14. Ezk 26:12.

Often of a square form. Rv 21:16.

On hills. Mt 5:14. Lk 4:29. Rv 17:9.

On solid foundations. Ezr 6:3. Rv 21:14.

With compactness. Ps 122:3.

CALLED AFTER THE

Country in which built. Dn 4:29–30.

Family of the founder. Gn 4:17. Jg 18:29.

Proprietor of the land. 1 K 16:24.

Densely inhabited. Jnh 4:11. Na 3:8.

Designed for habitations. Ps 107:7, 36.

DIFFERENT KINDS OF

Chariot. 2 Ch 1:14; 9:25.

Commercial. Is 23:11. Ezk 27:3.

Fenced. Jsh 10:20. Is 36:1.

Levitical. Lv 25:32–33. Nu 35:7–8.

Refuge. Nu 35:6.

Royal. Nu 21:26. Jsh 10:2. 2 S 12:26.

Store. 2 Ch 8:4, 6.

Treasure. Ex 1:11.

Difficulty of taking, alluded to. Pr 18:19. Jr 1:18–19.

Entered through gates. Gn 34:24. Ne 13:19, 22.

First mentioned Gn 4:17.

Furnished with stores. 2 Ch 11:11–12.

Garrisoned in war. 2 Ch 17:2, 19.

A great defense to a country. 2 Ch 11:5.

ILLUSTRATIVE OF

Apostasy. Rv 16:10; 17:18.

Church triumphant. Rv 21:2; 22:19.

Heavenly inheritance. He 11:16.

Riches. Pr 10:15.

Saints. Mt 5:14.

Visible church. S S 3:2–3. Rv 11:2.

Infested by dogs. 1 K 14:11. Ps 59:6, 14.

Inhabitants of, called citizens. Ac 21:13.

Numerous. Jsh 15:21. 1 Ch 2:22. Jr 2:28.

Often built to perpetuate a name. Gn 11:4.

Often deserted on the approach of an enemy. 1 S 31:7. Jr 4:29.

Often fortified by art. 2 Ch 11:5–10, 23. Ps 48:12–13. Jr 4:5. Dn 11:15.

Often fortified by nature. Ps 125:2. Is 33:16.

Often founded and enlarged by blood and rapine. Mi 3:10. Hk 2:12.

Often great and goodly. Gn 10:12. Dt 6:10. Dn 4:30. Jnh 3:3.

Often had citadels. Jg 9:51.

Often insignificant. Gn 19:20. Ec 9:14.

Often of great antiquity. Gn 10:11–12.

Perishable nature of. He 13:14.

Prosperity of, increased by commerce. Gn 49:13, with Dt 33:18–19. Ezk 28:5.

Protected at night by watchmen. Ps 127:1. S S 5:7. Is 21:11.

Provided with judges. Dt 16:18. 2 Ch 19:5.

Sometimes had suburbs. Nu 35:2. Jsh 21:3.

Surrounded by walls. Dt 1:28; 3:5.

Under governors. 2 Ch 33:14. 2 Co 11:32.

Water supplied artificially to. 2 K 18:17; 20:20.

WERE FREQUENTLY

Besieged. Dt 28:52. 2 K 19:24–25.

Burned. Jg 20:38, 40. Is 1:7.

Depopulated. Is 17:9. Ezk 26:19.

Made heaps of ruins. Is 25:2.

Pillaged. Is 13:16. Jr 20:5.

Razed and sown with salt. Jg 9:45.

Stormed. Jsh 8:3–7. Jg 9:44.

Wasted by famine. Jr 52:6. Am 4:6.

Wasted by pestilence. 1 S 5:11.

CITIES OF REFUGE

Afforded no asylum to murderers. Ex 21:14. Nu 35:16–21.

Design of. Ex 21:13. Nu 35:11. Jsh 20:3.
ILLUSTRATIVE OF
Christ. Ps 91:2. Is 25:4.
The hope of the gospel. He 6:18.
The way to Christ. Is 35:8. Jn 14:16.
Names, etc., of. Dt 4:41–43. Jsh 20:7–8.
REQUIRED TO BE
Easy of access. Dt 19:3. Is 62:10.
Open to all manslayers. Jsh 20:4.
Strangers might take advantage of. Nu
35:15.
THOSE ADMITTED TO
Not protected outside of. Nu 35:26–27.
Obliged to remain in, until the high priest's
death. Nu 35:25, 28.
Put on their trial. Nu 35:12, 24.

CLOUD FORMATIONS
Are the garment of the sea. Jb 38:9.
CALLED THE
Bottles of heaven. Jb 38:37.
Chambers of God. Ps 104:3, 13.
Clouds of heaven. Dn 7:13. Mt 24:30.
Dust of God's feet. Na 1:3.
Waters above the firmament. Gn 1:7.
Windows of heaven. Gn 7:11. Is 24:18,
DIFFERENT KINDS OF, MENTIONED
Black. 1 K 18:45
Bright. Jb 37:11. Zc 10:1.
Great. Ezk 1:4.
Small. 1 K 18:44.
Swift. Is 19:1.
Thick. Jb 22:14; 37:11.
White. Rv 14:14.
Formed from the sea. 1 K 18:44. Am 9:6.
Frequently the instruments of God's judg-
ments. Gn 7:11–12. Jb 37:13. Ps 77:17.
From the west, bring rain. Lk 12:54.
GOD
Balanced in the air. Jb 37:16.
Binds up. Jb 26:8.
Brings over the earth. Gn 9:14.
Disposed in order. Jb 37:15.
Established. Pr 8:28.
Scatters. Jb 37:11.
Spreads out. Jb 26:9.
ILLUSTRATIVE OF
False teachers. 2 P 2:17. Jde 1:12.
The favor of good rulers. Pr 16:15.
The fraudulent. Pr 25:14.
Goodness of prosperity of hypocrites. Ho
6:4; 13:3.
Hostile armies. Jr 4:13. Ezk 38:9, 16.

Judgments of God. Lm 2:1. Ezk 30:3;
34:12. Jl 2:2.
Multitudes of persons. Is 60:8. He 12:1.
The power and greatness of God. Ps
104:3. Is 19:1.
Sins of men. Is 44:22.
Unsearchableness of God. 2 S 22:12. Ps
97:2. Ezk 1:4.
Wise rulers. 2 S 23:3–4.
Made for the glory of God. Ps 148:4.
MAN
Cannot cause to rain. Jb 38:34.
Cannot number. Jb 38:37.
Cannot say. Jb 38:37.
Ignorant of the balancing of. Jb 37:16.
Ignorant of the disposing of. Jb 37:15.
Ignorant of the spreading of. Jb 36:29.
Often cover the heavéns. Ps 147:8.
Often dispersed by the wind. Ho 13:3.
Often obscure the sun, etc. Jb 36:32. Ezk
32:7.
Power and wisdom of God exhibited in con-
densing. Jb 36:27–28; 37:10–11. Pr 3:20.
Power and wisdom of God exhibited in form-
ing. Pss 135:6–7; 147:5, 8. Jr 10:13;
51:16.
The rainbow appears in. Gn 9:13–14.
Though small, often bring much rain. 1 K
18:44–45.
Thunder and lightning come from. Ps
77:17–18.
USES OF
To give rain. Jg 5:4. Ps 104:13–14.
To moderate heat. Is 25:5.
To supply dew. Pr 3:20. Is 18:4.

CLOUD OF GLORY
CALLED
The cloud. Ex 34:5.
Cloud of the Lord. Nu 10:34.
Cloudy pillar. Ex 33:9–10.
Pillar of cloud and pillar of fire. Ex 13:22,
The presence of God. Ex 33:14–15.
Continued during the journeyings of Israel.
Ex 13:22; 40:38.
First manifestation of. Ex 13:20–21.
God came down in. Ex 34:5. Nu 11:25.
God spoke from. Ex 24:16. Ps 99:7.
God's glory manifested in. Ex 16:10; 40:35.
ILLUSTRATIVE OF
The glory of Christ. Rv 10:1.
The protection of the church. Is 4:5.
Manifested in the temple of Solomon. 1 K
8:10–11. 2 Ch 5:13. Ezk 10:4.

Our Lord shall make his second appearance in. Lk 21:27. Ac 1:11.

SPECIAL APPEARANCES OF

At Christ's ascension. Ac 1:9.

At Christ's transfiguration. Mt 17:5.

At giving of the law. Ex 19:9, 16; 24:16–18.

At the murmuring for bread. Ex 16:10.

At the murmuring of Israel on account of Korah's death. Nu 16:42.

At the murmuring of Israel on report of the spies. Nu 14:10.

At the rebellion of Korah, etc. Nu 16:19.

At sedition of Aaron and Miriam. Nu 12:5.

Was dark to the enemies of Israel. Ex 14:20.

WAS DESIGNED TO

Cover the tabernacle. Ex 40:34. Nu 9:15.

Defend Israel. Ex 14:19. Ps 105:39.

Guide Israel. Ex 13:21. Ne 9:19.

Regulate the movements of Israel. Ex 40:36–37. Nu 9:17–25.

Show light to Israel. Pss 78:14; 105:39.

Was the Shekinah over the mercy seat. Lv 16:2.

COMFORT

According to the word. Ps 119:76.

False. Jb 16:2.

From God. Is 40:1; 61:1–2. Ps 86:17.

Promised. Mt 5:4.

Through Christ. 2 Co 1:5.

True. Jb 35:10. Ps 23:4.

COMFORTER

Abides forever. Jn 14:16.

Guides into truth. Jn 16:13.

Reproves the world. Jn 16:8.

Teaches all things. Jn 14:26.

Witnesses to Christ. Jn 15:26.

See also Advocate.

COMING OF CHRIST

See Second Coming of Christ.

COMMANDMENTS, TEN

Enumerated. Ex 20:3–17.

Law of, is spiritual. Mt 5:28. Ro 7:14.

Spoken by God. Ex 20:1. Dt 5:4, 22.

Summed up by Christ. Mt 22:35–40.

Written by God. Ex 32:16; 34:1, 28. Dt 4:13; 10:4.

See also Law of God.

COMMUNION OF SAINTS

According to the prayer of Christ. Jn 17:20–21.

Christ is present in. Mt 18:20.

Delight of. Pss 16:3; 42:4; 133:1–3. Ro 15:32.

Exhortation to. Ep 4:1–3.

God marks, with his approval. Ml 3:16.

In exhortation. Cl 3:16. He 10:25.

In holy conversation. Ml 3:16.

In the Lord's supper. 1 Co 10:17.

In mutual comfort and edification. 1 Th 4:18; 5:11.

In mutual sympathy and kindness. Ro 12:15. Ep 4:32.

In prayer for each other. 2 Co 1:11. Ep 6:18.

In public and social worship. Pss 34:3; 55:14. Ac 1:14. He 10:25.

IS WITH

Each other. Gl 2:9. 1 Jn 1:3, 7.

God. 1 Jn 1:3.

Saints in heaven. He 12:22–24.

Opposed to communion with the wicked. 2 Co 6:14–17. Ep 5:11.

COMMUNION OF THE LORD'S SUPPER

Both bread and wine are necessary to be received in. Mt 26:27. 1 Co 11:26.

Continually partaken of, by the primitive church. Ac 2:42; 20:7.

Instituted. Mt 26:26. 1 Co 11:23.

Is the communion of the body and blood of Christ. 1 Co 10:16.

Newness of heart and life necessary to the worthy partaking of. 1 Co 5:7–8.

Object of. Lk 22:19. 1 Co 11:24, 26.

Partakers of, should be wholly separate unto God. 1 Co 10:21.

Prefigured. Ex 12:21–28. 1 Co 5:7–8.

Self-examination commanded before partaking of. 1 Co 11:28, 31.

UNWORTHY PARTAKERS OF

Are guilty of the body and blood of Christ. 1 Co 11:27.

Are visited with judgments. 1 Co 11:30.

Discern not the Lord's body. 1 Co 11:29.

COMMUNION WITH GOD

Holiness essential to. 2 Co 6:14–16.

Is communion with the Father. 1 Jn 1:3.

Is communion with the Holy Ghost. 1 Co 12:13. 2 Co 13:14. Php 2:1.

Is communion with the Son. 1 Co 1:9. 1 Jn 1:3. Rv 3:20.
Promised to the obedient. Jn 14:23.
Reconciliation must precede. Am 3:3.
SAINTS
Desire. Ps 42:1. Php 1:23.
Have, in the Lord's supper. 1 Co 10:16.
Have, in meditation. Ps 63:5–6.
Have, in prayer. Php 4:6. He 4:16.
Should always enjoy. Ps 16:8. Jn 14:16–18.

COMPANIONSHIP
With the disciples. Gl 2:9. Ac 2:44–47. 1 Jn 1:7.
With God. Co 13:14. 1 Jn 1:3.
With the righteous. Ps 119:63.
With the unrighteous. Ps 1:1.

COMPASSION AND SYMPATHY
Christ set an example of. Lk 19:41–42.
EXERCISE TOWARD
The afflicted. Jb 6:14. He 13:3.
The chastened. Is 22:4. Jr 9:1
Enemies. Ps 35:13.
The poor. Pr 19:17.
Saints. 1 Co 12:25, 26.
The weak. 2 Co 11:29. Gl 6:2.
Exhortation to. Ro 12:15. 1 P 3:8.
Inseparable from love to God. 1 Jn 3:17; 4:20.
MOTIVES TO
The compassion of God. Mt 13:27, 33.
The sense of our infirmities. He 5:2.
Promise to those who show. Pr 19:17. Mt 10:42.
The wicked made to feel, for saints. Ps 106:46.

COMPASSION AND SYMPATHY OF CHRIST
An encouragement to prayer. He 4:15.
MANIFESTED FOR THE
Afflicted. Lk 7:13. Jn 11:33, 35.
Diseased. Mt 14:14. Mk 1:41.
Perishing sinners. Mt 9:36. Lk 19:41. Jn 3:16.
Poor. Mk 8:2.
Tempted. He 2:18.
Weak in faith. Is 40:11; 42:3, with Mt 12:20.
Weary and heavy-laden. Mt 11:28–30.
Necessary to his priestly office. He 5:2, 7.

CONDEMNATION
According to men's deserts. Mt 12:37. 2 Co 11:15.
Apostates ordained unto. Jde 1:4.
Chastisements are designed to rescue us from. Ps 94:12–13. 1 Co 11:32.
Conscience testifies to the justice of. Jb 9:20. Ro 2:1. Ti 3:11.
INCREASED BY
Hypocrisy. Mt 23:14.
Impenitence. Mt 11:20–24.
Oppression. Ja 5:1–5.
Pride. 1 Tm 3:6.
Unbelief. Jn 3:18–19.
Inseparable consequence of sin. Pr 12:2. Ro 6:23.
The law is the ministration of. 2 Co 3:9.
The law testifies to the justice of. Ro 3:19.
Of the wicked, an example. 2 P 2:6. Jde 1:7.
Saints are delivered from, by Christ. Jn 3:18; 5:24. Ro 8:1, 33–34.
The sentence of God against sin. Mt 25:41.
Unbelievers remain under. Jn 3:18, 36.
Universal, caused by the offense of Adam. Ro 5:12, 16, 18.

CONDUCT, CHRISTIAN
Abounding in the work of the Lord. 1 Co 15:58. 2 Co 8:7. 1 Th 4:1.
Abstaining from all appearance of evil. 1 Th 5:22.
Adorning the gospel. Mt 5:16. Ti 2:10.
Being contented. Php 4:11. He 13:5.
Being liberal to others. Ac 20:35. Ro 12:13.
Believing God. Mk 11:22. Jn 14:11–12.
Believing in Christ. Jn 6:29. 1 Jn 3:23.
Controlling the body. 1 Co 9:27. Cl 3:5.
Doing as we would be done by. Mt 7:12. Lk 6:31.
Fearing God. Ec 12:13. 1 P 2:17.
Following after that which is good. Php 4:8. 1 Th 5:15. 1 Tm 6:11.
Following the example of Christ. Jn 13:15. 1 P 2:21–24.
Following God. Ep 5:1. 1 P 1:15–16.
Forgiving injuries. Mt 6:14. Ro 12:20.
Fulfilling domestic duties. Ep 6:1–8. 1 P 3:1–7.
Hating defilement. Jde 1:23.
Honoring others. Ps 15:4. Ro 12:10.
LIVING
Soberly, righteously, and godly. Ti 2:12.
To Christ. Ro 14:8. 2 Co 5:15.

Unto righteousness. Mi 6:8. Ro 6:18. 1 P 2:24.

Living peaceably with all. Ro 12:18. He 12:14.

Loving Christ. Jn 21:15. 1 P 1:7–8.

Loving God. Dt 6:5. Mt 22:37.

Loving one another. Jn 15:12. Ro 12:10. 1 Co 13. Ep 5:2. He 13:1.

Obeying Christ. Jn 14:21; 15:14.

Obeying God. Lk 1:6. 1 Jn 5:3.

Overcoming the world. 1 Jn 5:4–5.

Perfecting holiness. Mt 5:48. 2 Co 7:1. 2 Tm 3:17.

Putting away all sin. 1 Co 5:7. He 12:1.

Rejoicing in Christ. Php 3:1; 4:4.

Rejoicing in God. Ps 33:1. Hk 3:18.

Showing a good example. 1 Tm 4:12. 1 P 2:12. Ti 2:7.

Shunning the wicked. Ps 1:1. 2 Th 3:6.

Striving for the faith. Php 1:27. Jde 1:3.

Subduing the temper. Ep 4:26. Ja 1:19.

Submitting to authorities. Ro 13:1–7.

Submitting to injuries. Mt 5:39–41. 1 Co 6:7.

Sympathizing with others. Gl 6:2. 1 Th 5:14.

Visiting the afflicted. Mt 25:36. Ja 1:27.

WALKING

After the Spirit. Ro 8:1.

As children of light. Ep 5:8.

Honestly. 1 Th 4:12.

In newness of life. Ro 6:4.

In the Spirit. Gl 5:25.

Worthy of God. 1 Th 2:12.

Worthy of the Lord. Cl 1:10.

Worthy of our vocation. Ep 4:1.

Worth of maintaining. Pss 1:1–3; 19:9–11; 50:23. Mt 5:3–12. Jn 7:17; 15:10.

CONFESSING CHRIST

As evidence of union with God. 1 Jn 4:15.

As test of being saints. 1 Jn 2:23; 4:2–3.

Consequences of not. Mt 10:33.

Ensures his confessing us. Mt 10:32.

Fear of man prevents. Jn 7:13; 12:42–43.

Influences of the Holy Spirit necessary to. 1 Co 12:3. 1 Jn 4:2.

Must be connected with faith. Ro 10:9.

Necessary to salvation. Ro 10:9–10.

Persecution should not prevent us from. Mk 8:35. 2 Tm 2:12.

CONFESSION OF SIN

Exhortation to. Jsh 7:19. Jr 3:13. Ja 5:16.

Followed by pardon. Ps 32:5. 1 Jn 1:9.

God regards. Jb 33:27, 28. Dn 9:20, etc.

God requires. Lv 5:5. Ho 5:15.

Illustrated. Lk 15:21; 18:13.

Promises to. Lv 26:40–42. Pr 28:13.

SHOULD BE ACCOMPANIED WITH

Forsaking sin. Pr 28:13.

Godly sorrow. Ps 38:18. Lm 1:20.

Prayer for forgiveness. 2 S 24:10. Pss 25:11; 51:1. Jr 14:7–9, 20.

Restitution. Nu 5:6–7.

Self-abasement. Is 64:5–6. Jr 3:25.

Submission to punishment. Lv 26:41. Ne 9:33. Ezr 9:13.

Should be full and unreserved. Pss 32:5; 51:3; 106:6.

CONFIDENCE

Before God. 1 Jn 3:21.

Foolish. Ps 49:13. Php 3:3.

For the judgment. 1 Jn 4:17.

In the Lord. Ps 118:8–9. Gl 5:10. 2 Th 3:4.

In the Lord's people. Php 1:21.

Producing results. Mt 17:20. Mk 9:23.

Sustaining. He 3:14.

Wise (in the Lord). Ps 118:8.

CONSCIENCE

Accuses of sin. Gn 42:21. 2 S 24:10. Mt 27.3. Ac 2:37.

Blood of Christ alone can purify. He 9:14; 10:2–10, 22.

Keep the faith in purity of. 1 Tm 1:19; 3:9.

Ministers should commend themselves to that of their people. 2 Co 4:2; 5:11.

Of others, not to be offended. Ro 14:21. 1 Co 10:28–32.

Of saints, pure and good. He 13:18. 1 P 3:16, 21.

Of the wicked, defiled. Ti 1:15.

Of the wicked, seared. 1 Tm 4:2.

Submit to authority for. Ro 13:5.

Suffer patiently for. 1 P 2:19.

Testimony of, a source of joy. 2 Co 1:12. 1 Jn 3:21.

We should have the approval of. Jb 27:6. Ac 24:16. Ro 9:1, 14:22.

Without spiritual illumination, a false guide. Ac 23:1, with 26:9.

Witnesses in man. Pr 20:27. Ro 2:15.

CONTEMPT

Causes saints to cry unto God. Ne 4:4. Ps 123:3.

A characteristic of the wicked. Pr 18:3. Is 5:24. 2 Tm 3:3.

Folly of. Pr 11:12.

FORBIDDEN TOWARD
Believing masters. 1 Tm 6:2.
Christ's little ones. Mt 18:10.
Parents. Pr 23:22.
The poor. Ja 2:1–3.
Weak brethren. Ro 14:3.
Young ministers. 1 Co 16:11.

Ministers should give no occasion for. 1 Tm 4:12.

Of ministers, is a despising of God. Lk 10:16. 1 Th 4:8.

Pride and prosperity prompt to. Ps 123:4.

Saints sometimes guilty of. Ja 2:6.

Self-righteousness prompts to. Is 65:5. Lk 18:9, 11.

Sin of. Jb 31:13, 14. Pr 14:21.

THE WICKED EXHIBIT TOWARD
The afflicted. Jb 19:18.
Authorities. 2 P 2:10. Jde 1:8.
Christ. Ps 22:6. Is 53:3. Mt 27:29.
Parents. Pr 15:5, 20.
The poor. Ps 14:6. Ec 9:16.
Saints. Ps 119:111.

TOWARD THE CHURCH
Often punished. Ezk 28:26.
Often turned into respect. Is 60:14.

CONTENTMENT

God's promises should lead to. He 13:5.

SAINTS SHOULD EXHIBIT
In their respective callings. 1 Co 7:20.
With appointed wages. Lk 3:14.
With food and raiment. 1 Tm 6:8.
With what things they have. He 13:5.

The wicked want. Is 5:8. Ec 5:10.

With godliness is great gain. Ps 37:16. 1 Tm 6:6.

CONVERSION

By Christ. Ac 3:26. Ro 15:18.

By God. 1 K 18:37. Jn 6:44. Ac 21:19.

By the power of the Holy Ghost. Pr 1:23.

Commanded. Jb 36:10.

Danger of neglecting. Ps 7:12. Jr 44:5, 11. Ezk. 3:19.

Duty of leading sinners to. Ps 51:13.

Encouragement for leading sinners to. Dn 12:3. Ja 5:19–20.

Exhortations to. Pr 1:23. Is 31:6; 55:7. Jr 3:7. Ezk 33:11.

Follows repentance. Ac 3:19; 26:20.

Is accompanied by confession of sin, and prayer. 1 K 8:35.

Is necessary. Mt 18:3.

Is of grace. Ac 11:21, with v. 23.

Is the result of faith. Ac 11:21.

Of Gentiles, predicted. Is 2:2; 11:10; 60:5; 66:12.

Of Israel, predicted. Ezk 36:25–27.

OF SINNERS, A CAUSE OF JOY
To God. Ezk 18:23. Lk 15:32.
To saints. Ac 15:3. Gl 1:23–24.

Pray for. Pss 80:7; 85:4. Jr 31:18. Lm 5:21.

Promises connected with. Ne 1:9. Is 1:27. Jr 3:11. Ezk 18:27.

THROUGH THE INSTRUMENTALITY OF
Affliction. Ps 78:34.
Ministers. Ac 26:18. 1 Th 1:9.
Scripture. Ps 19:7.
Self-examination. Ps 119:59. Lm 3:40.

CORRECTION

As discipline. Ps 39:11.

For righteousness of life. He 12:11.

From government. 1 P 2:14.

From scripture. 2 Tm 3:16.

In love. He 12:5–7.

Of children. Pr 13:24; 19:15.

COUNSELS AND PURPOSES OF GOD

ARE
Eternal. Ep 3:11.
Faithfulness and truth. Is 25:1.
Great. Jr 32:19.
Immutable. Ps 33:11. Pr 19:21. Jr 4:28. Ro 9:11. He 6:17.
Sovereign. Is 40:13–14. Dn 4:35.
Wonderful. Is 28:29.

Attend to. Jr 49:20; 50:45.

None can disannul. Is 14:27.

Saints called and saved according to. Ro 8:28. 2 Tm 1:9.

Secret not to be searched into. Dt 29:29. Mt 24:36. Ac 1:7.

Shall be performed. Is 14:24; 46:11.

Should be declared by ministers. Ac 20:27.

Sufferings and death of Christ were according to. Ac 2:23; 4:28.

Union of all saints in Christ is according to. Ep 1:9–10.

THE WICKED
Despise. Is 5:19.

Reject. Lk 7:30.
Understand not. Mi 4:12.
Works of God are according to. Ep 1:11.

COURAGE
Despite enemies. Php 1:28.
Enjoined. Dt. 31:6. Jsh 1:7. Is 41:10.
From the Lord. He 13:6.

COURTS OF JUSTICE
THE ACCUSED
Evidence of two or more witnesses required
  in. Dt 17:6; 19:15. Jn 8:17. 2 Co 13:1.
Examined on oath. Lv 5:1. Mt 26:63.
Exhorted to confess. Jsh 7:19.
Might have advocates. Pr 31:8–9. Is 1:17.
Permitted to plead their own cause. 1 K
  3:22. Ac 24:10; 26:1.
Sometimes examined by torture. Ac
  22:24, 29.
Sometimes treated with insult. Mt 26:67.
  Jn 18:22–23. Ac 23:2–3.
Stood before the judge. Nu 35:12. Mt
  27:11.
Witnesses sometimes laid their hands on
  the criminal's head before punishment.
  Lv 24:14.
Both the accusers and accused required to ap-
  pear before. Dt 25:1. Ac 25:16.
CAUSES IN, WERE OPENED BY
Advocate. Ac 24:1.
Complainant. 1 K 3:17–21. Ac 16:19–21.
Corruption and bribery often practiced in. Is
  10:1. Am 5:12; 8:6.
False witnesses in to receive the punishment of
  the accused. Dt 19:19.
Generally held in the morning. Jr 21:12. Mt
  27:1. Lk 22:66. Ac 5:21.
Have authority from God. Ro 13:1–5.
INFERIOR
All minor cases decided by. Ex 18:26. 2 S
  15:4.
All transfers of property made before. Gn
  23:17–20. Ru 4:1–2.
Held at the gates. Gn 34:20. Dt 16:18;
  21:19. Jb 5:4.
In all cities. Dt 16:18. 2 Ch 19:5–7.
Judges of, appointed by the governor. Ex
  18:21, 25. Dt 1:9–15. 2 S 15:3.
JUDGES OF
Called elders. Dt 25:7. 1 S 16:4.
Called magistrates. Lk 12:58.
Conferred together before giving judgment.
  Ac 5:34–40; 25:12; 26:30–31.

Examined the parties. Ac 24:8.
Not to take bribes. Ex 23:8. Dt 16:19.
Pronounced the judgment of the court.
  Mt 26:65–66. Lk 23:24. Ac 5:40.
Rode often on white asses. Jg 5:10.
Sat on the judgment seat while hearing
  causes. Ex 18:13. Jg 5:10. Is 28:6. Mt
  27:19.
To decide according to law. Ezk 44:24.
To judge as for God. 2 Ch 19:6–7, 9.
To investigate every case. Dt 19:18.
To judge righteously. Lv 19:15. Dt 1:16
To judge without respect of persons. Ex
  23:3, 6. Lv 19:15. Dt 1:17. Pr 22:22.
To promote peace. Zc 8:16.
JUDGMENT OF
Alluded to. Jb 5:4. Ps 127:5. Mt 5:22.
Illustrative of the last judgment. Mt
  19:28. Ro 14:10. 1 Co 6:2.
Immediately executed. Dt 25:2. Jsh 7:25.
  Mk 15:15–20.
Not given till accused was heard. Jn 7:51.
Recorded in writing. Is 10:1.
Witnesses first to execute. Dt 17:7. Ac
  7:58.
OF THE ROMANS IN JUDEA
Appeals from, made to the emperor. Ac
  25:11; 26:32; 28:19.
Could alone award death. Jn 18:31.
Never examined their own citizens by tor-
  ture. Ac 22:25–29.
Never interfered in any dispute about minor
  matters or about religion. Ac 18:14–15.
Place of, called the hall of judgment. Jn
  18:28, 33; 19:9.
Presided over by the governor or deputy.
  Mt 27:2, 11. Ac 18:12.
PROVIDED WITH
Judges. Dt 16:18.
Officers. Dt 16:18. Mt 5:25.
Tormentors or executioners. Mt 18:34.
Reestablished by Ezra. Ezr 7:25.
Reestablished by Jehoshaphat. 2 Ch 19:5–10.
SANHEDRIN OR COURT OF THE SEVENTY
Consisted of chief priests, etc. Mt 26:57,
  59.
Mentioned in the latter part of sacred his-
  tory. Lk 22:66. Jn 11:47. Ac 5:27.
Presided over by high priest. Mt
  26:62–66.
Probably derived from the seventy elders
  appointed by Moses. Ex 24:9. Nu
  11:16–17, 24–30.
Sat in high priest's palace. Mt 26:57–58.

Sometimes held in synagogues. Mt 10:17. Ac 22:19; 26:11.

SUPERIOR

Consisted of priests and Levites. Dt 17:9, with Ml 2:7.

Decided on all appeals and difficult cases. Ex 18:26. Dt 1:17; 17:8–9.

Decisions of, conclusive. Dt 17:10–11.

Held at the seat of government. Dt 17:8.

Held first by Moses alone in the wilderness. Ex 18:13–20.

Presided over by the governor or the high priest. Dt 17:12. Jg 4:4–5.

COVENANT

An agreement between two parties. Gn 26:28. Dn 11:6.

CONDITIONS OF

Clearly specified. 1 S 11:1–2.

Confirmed by oath. Gn 21:23, 31; 26:31.

Witnessed. Gn 23:17–18. Ru 4:9–11.

Written and sealed. Ne 9:38; 10:1.

DESIGNED FOR

Establishing friendship. 1 S 18:8.

Establishing peace. Jsh 9:15–16.

Mutual protection. Gn 26:28–29; 31:50–52.

Procuring assistance in war. 1 K 15:18–19.

Promoting commerce. 1 K 5:6–11

Selling land. Gn 23:14–16.

Followed by a feast. Gn 26:30; 31:54.

God often called to witness. Gn 31:50, 53.

ILLUSTRATIVE OF

Carnal security (with death and hell). Is 28:15, 18.

God's promises to man. Gn 9:9–11. Ep 2:12.

Good resolutions. Jb 31:1.

Marriage contract. Ml 2:14.

Peace and prosperity (with stones and beasts of the earth). Jb 5:23. Ho 2:18.

The united determination of a people to serve God. 2 K 11:17. 2 Ch 15:12. Ne 10:29.

THE JEWS

Condemned for making with idolatrous nations. Is 30:2–5. Ho 12:1.

Forbidden to make with the nations of Canaan. Ex 23:32. Dt 7:2.

Frequently made with other nations. 1 K 5:12. 2 K 17:4.

Regarded as sacred. Jsh 9:16–19. Ps 15:4.

Made by passing between the pieces of the

divided sacrifices. Gn 15:9–17. Jr 34:18–19.

Names given to places where made. Gn 21:31; 31:47–49.

Pillars raised in token of. Gn 31:45–46.

Presents given as tokens of. Gn 21:27–30. 1 S 18:3–4.

Ratified by joining hands. Pr 11:21. Ezk 17:18.

Salt a sign of perpetuity in. Nu 18:19. 2 Ch 13:5.

Violated by the wicked. Ro 1:31. 2 Tm 3:3.

When confirmed, unalterable. Gl 3:15.

THE COVENANT

All saints interested in. Pss 25:14; 89:29–37. He 8:10.

Be mindful of. 1 Ch 16:15.

Blessings connected with. Is 56:4–7. He 8:10–12.

Caution against forgetting. Dt 4:23.

Christ the mediator of. He 8:6; 9:15; 12:24.

Christ the messenger of. Ml 3:1.

Christ the substance of. Is 42:6; 49:8.

Confirmed in Christ. Gl 3:17.

Everlasting. Ps 111:9. Is 55:3; 61:8. Ezk 16:60–63. He 13:20.

Fulfilled in Christ. Lk 1:68–79.

God is ever mindful of. Pss 105:8; 111:5. Lk 1:72.

God is faithful to. Dt 7:9. 1 K 8:23. Ne 1:5. Dn 9:4.

MADE WITH

Abraham. Gn 15:7–18; 17:2–14. Lk 1:72–75. Ac 3:25. Gl 3:16.

David. 2 S 23:5. Ps 89:3–4.

Isaac. Gn 17:19, 21; 26:3–4.

Israel. Ex 6:4. Ac 3:25.

Jacob. Gn 28:13–14, with 1 Ch 16:16–17.

One of peace. Is 54:9–10. Ezk 34:25; 37:26.

Plead, in prayer. Ps 74:20. Jr 14:21.

Punishment for despising. He 10:29–30.

Ratified by the blood of Christ. He 9:11–14, 16–23.

Renewed under the gospel. Jr 31:31–33. Ro 11:27. He 8:8–10, 13.

Unalterable. Ps 89:34. Is 54:10; 59:21. Gl 3:17.

The wicked have no interest in. Ep 2:12.

COVETOUSNESS

Abhorred by God. Ps 10:3.

Avoid those guilty of. 1 Co 5:11.

Beware of. Lk 12:15.

A characteristic of the slothful. Pr 21:26.
A characteristic of the wicked. Ro 1:29.
Comes from the heart. Mk 7:22–23.
Commended by the wicked alone. Ps 10:3.
Engrosses the heart. Ezk 33:31. 2 P 2:14.
Excludes from heaven. 1 Co 6:10. Ep 5:5.
Forbidden. Ex 20:17.
Hated by saints. Ex 18:21. Ac 20:33.
Is
  Idolatry. Ep 5:5. Cl 3:5.
  Never satisfied. Ec 5:10. Hk 2:5.
  The root of all evil. 1 Tm 6:10.
  Vanity. Ps 39:6. Ec 4:8.
Is INCONSISTENT
  In ministers. 1 Tm 3:3.
  In saints. Ep 5:3. He 13:5.
LEADS TO
  Departure from the faith. 1 Tm 6:10.
  Domestic affliction. Pr 15:27.
  Foolish and hurtful lusts. 1 Tm 6:9.
  Injustice and oppression. Pr 28:20. Mi 2:2.
  Lying. 2 K 5:22–25.
  Misery. 1 Tm 6:10.
  Murder. Pr 1:18–19. Ezk 22:12.
  Poverty. Pr 28:22.
  Theft. Jsh 7:21.
Pray against. Ps 119:36.
Punishment of. Jb 20:15. Is 57:17. Jr 22:17–19. Mi 2:2–3.
Reward of those who hate. Pr 28:16.
Shall abound in the last days. 2 Tm 3:2. 2 P 2:1–3.
To be mortified by saints. Cl 3:5.
Woe denounced against. Is 5:8. Hk 2:9.

CREATION
Approved of by God. Gn 1:31.
By faith we believe, to be God's work. He 11:3.
EFFECTED
  According to God's purpose. Ps 135:6.
  By Christ. Jn 1:3, 10. Cl 1:16.
  By the command of God. Ps 33:9. He 11:3.
  By God. Gn 1:1; 2:4–5. Pr 26:10.
  By the Holy Ghost. Jb 26:13. Ps 104:30.
  For Christ. Cl 1:16.
  For God's pleasure. Pr 16:4. Rv 4:11.
  In the beginning. Ex 20:11; 31:17.
  In six days. Ex 20:11; 31:17.
EXHIBITS
  The deity of God. Ro 1:20.
  The glory and handiwork of God. Ps 19:1.

God as the sole object of worship. Is 45:16, 18. Ac 17:24, 27.
The goodness of God. Ps 33:5.
The power of God. Is 40:26, 28. Ro 1:20.
The wisdom of God. Ps 104:24; 136:5.
Formation of things which had no previous existence. Ro 4:17, with He 11:3.
Glorifies God. Pss 145:10; 148:5.
God rested from, on the seventh day. Gn 2:2–3.
God to be praised for. Ne 9:6. Ps 136:3–9.
Groaneth because of sin. Ro 8:22.
ILLUSTRATIVE OF
  Daily renewal of saints. Ps 51:40. Ep 4:24.
  New birth. 2 Co 5:17. Ep 2:10.
  Renewal of the earth. Is 65:17. 2 P 3:11, 13.
Insignificance of man seen from. Ps 9:3–4. Is 40:12, 17.
Leads to confidence. Pss 124:8; 146:5–6.
ORDER OF
  First day, making light and dividing it from darkness. Gn 1:3–5. 2 Co 4:6.
  Second day, making the firmament or atmosphere, and separating the waters. Gn 1:6–8.
  Third day, separating the land from the water, and making it fruitful. Gn 1:9–13.
  Fourth day, placing the sun, moon, and stars to give light, etc. Gn 1:14–19.
  Fifth day, making birds, insects, and fishes. Gn 1:20–23.
  Sixth day, making beasts of the earth, and man. Gn 1:24, 28.
A subject of joy to angels. Jb 38:7.

CREDITORS
Defined. Phm 1:18.
ILLUSTRATIVE OF
  The demands of the law. Gl 5:3.
  God's claim upon men. Mt 5:25–26, with 18:23, 35. Lk 7:41, 47.
MIGHT DEMAND
  Bills or promissory notes. Lk 16:6–7.
  Mortgages on property. Ne 5:3.
  Pledges. Dt 24:10–11. Pr 22:27.
  Security of others. Pr 6:1; 22:26.
Might take interest from strangers. Dt 23:20.
Often cruel in exacting debts. Ne 5:7–9. Jb 24:3–9. Mt 18:28–30.
OFTEN EXACTED DEBTS
  By imprisonment. Mt 5:25–26. Mt 18:34.

By selling the debtor or taking him for a servant. Mt 18:25, with Ex 21:2.

By selling the debtor's family. 2 K 4:1. Jb 24:9. Mt 18:25.

By selling the debtor's property. Mt 18:25.

From the sureties. Pr 11:15; 22:26–27.

PROHIBITED FROM

Exacting debts from brethren during sabbatical year. Dt 15:2–3.

Exacting usury from brethren. Ex 22:25. Lv 25:36–37.

Taking millstones in pledge. Dt 24:6.

Violently selecting pledges. Dt 24:10

Sometimes entirely remitted debts. Ne 5:10–12. Mt 18:27. Lk 7:42.

To return before sunset, garments taken in pledge. Ex 22:26–27. Dt 24:12–13. Ezk 18:7, 12.

Were often defrauded. 1 S 22:2. Lk 16:5–7.

CRIME

Craftiness of criminals. Pr 1:11, 15, 18.

Rebuked. Is 1:16–17. Jnh 3:8.

Results of bloodshed. Gn 9:6. Mt 26:52.

Significance of. Jn 3:19. 1 Co 6:10.

Source. Mt 15:19–20.

Totality of disorder. Jr 7:9. Ezk 7:23.

D

DAILY SACRIFICE
Abolition of, foretold. Dn 9:26–27; 11:31.
Doubled on the sabbath. Nu 28:9–10.
ILLUSTRATIVE OF
Acceptable prayer. Ps 141:2.
Christ. Jn 1:29, 36. 1 P 1:19.
A lamb as a burnt offering morning and evening. Ex 29:38–39. Nu 28:3–4.
Ordained in Mount Sinai. Nu 28:6.
Peculiarly acceptable. Nu 28:8. Ps 141:2.
REQUIRED TO BE
Perpetually observed. Ex 29:42. Nu 28:3, 6.
Slowly and entirely consumed. Lv 6:9–12.
With a meat and drink offering. Ex 29:40–41. Nu 28:5–8.
Restored after the captivity. Ezr 3:3.
Secured God's presence and favor. Ex 29:43–44.
Times of offering were seasons of prayer. Ezr 9:5. Dn 9:20–21, with Ac 3:1.

DARKNESS
Called night. Gn 1:5.
Called the swaddling band of the sea. Jb 38:9.
Cannot hide us from God. Ps 139:11–12.
Caused by setting of the sun. Gn 15:17. Jn 6:17.
Created by God. Ps 104:20. Is 45:7.
DEGREES OF, MENTIONED
Great. Gn 15:12.
Gross. Jr 13:16.
Outer or extreme. Mt 8:12.
That may be felt. Ex 10:21.
Thick. nDt 5:22. Jl 2:2.
EFFECTS OF
Causes us to go astray. Jn 12:35, 1 Jn 2:11.
Causes us to stumble. Is 59:10.
Keeps us from seeing objects. Ex 10:23.
Exhibits God's power and greatness. Jb 38:8–9.
ILLUSTRATIVE OF
Abstruse and deep subjects. Jb 28:3.
Anything hateful. Jb 3:4–9.
A course of sin. Pr 2:13. Ep 5:11.
The grave. 1 S 2:9. Jb 10:21–22.
The greatness and unsearchableness of God. Ex 20:21. 2 S 22:10, 12. 1 K 8:12. Ps 97:2.
Heavy afflictions. Jb 23:17. Ps 112:4. Ec 5–17. Is 5:30; 8:22; 59:9.
Ignorance and error. Jb 37:19. Is 60:2. Jn 1:5; 3:19; 12:35. Ac 26:18.
The power of Satan. Ep 6:12. Cl 1:13.
The punishment of devils and wicked men. Mt 22:13. 2 P 2:4, 17. Jde 1:6, 13.
Secrecy. Is 45:19. Mt 10:27.
Inexplicable nature of. Jb 38:19–20.
MIRACULOUS
At the death of Christ. Mt 27:45.
Before the destruction of Jerusalem. Mt 24:29.
On Mount Sinai. Ex 19:16, with He 12:18.
Over the land of Egypt. Ex 10:21–22.
Often put for night. Ps 91:6.
Originally covered the earth. Gn 1:2.
Separated from the light. Gn 1:4.
THE WICKED
Are children of. 1 Th 5:5.
Are full of. Mt 6:23.
Live in. Ps 107:10.
Perpetrate their designs in. Jb 24:16.
Walk in. Ps 82:5.

DAY
ARTIFICIAL, DIVIDED INTO
Break of. Gn 32:24, 26. S S 2:17.
Morning. Ex 29:39. 2 S 23:4.
Noon. Gn 43:16. Ps 55:17.
Decline of. Jg 19:8–9. Lk 9:12; 24:29.
Evening. Gn 8:11. Ps 104:23. Jr 6:4.
Artificial, the time of the sun's continuance above the horizon. Gn 31:39–40. Ne 4:21–22.
Divided into four parts. Ne 9:3.
ILLUSTRATIVE OF
The path of the just. Pr 4:18.
Spiritual light. 1 Th 5:5, 8. 2 P 1:19.
Time of judgment. 1 Co 3:13, with 4:3.

Latterly subdivided into twleve hours. Mt 20:3, 5–6. Jn 11:9

The light first called. Gn 1:5.

Made for the glory of God. Ps 74:16.

Natural, from evening to evening. Gn 1:5, etc. Lv 23:32.

Proclaims the glory of God. Ps 19:2.

Prophetical, a year. Ezk 4:6. Dn 12:12.

Succession, of, secured by covenant. Gn 8:22.

Time ascertained by the dial. 2 K 20:11.

Time for labor. Ps 104:23. Jn 9:4.

A TIME OF FESTIVITY CALLED A

Day of gladness. Nu 10:10.

Day of good tidings. 2 K 7:9.

Day which the Lord has made. Ps 118:24.

Good day. Es 8:17; 9:19.

Solemn day. Nu 10:10. Ho 9:5.

A TIME OF JUDGMENT CALLED A DAY OF

Adversity. Pr 24:10.

Anger. Lm 2:21.

Calamity. Dt 32:35. Jr 18:17.

Darkness. Jl 2:2. Zp 1:15.

Destruction. Jb 21:30.

Evil. Jr 17:17. Am 6:3. Ep 6:13.

The Lord. Is 2:12; 13:6. Zp 1:14.

Slaughter. Is 30:25. Jr 12:3.

Trouble. Ps 102:2.

Vengeance. Pr 6:34. Is 61:2.

Visitation. Mi 7:4.

Wrath. Jb 20:28. Zp 1:15, 18. Ro 2:5.

A TIME OF MERCY CALLED A DAY OF

God's power. Ps 110:3.

Redemption. Ep 4:30.

Salvation. 2 Co 6:2.

Visitation. Jr 27:22. 1 P 2:12.

Under the control of God. Am 5:8; 8:9.

Wild beasts hide during. Ps 104:22.

THE DEAD

All offerings to, forbidden. Dt 26:14.

CHARACTERIZED BY

Absence of all human passions. Ec 9:6.

Being incapable of motion. Mt 28:4. Rv 1:17.

Being without the Spirit. Ja 2:26.

Ignorance of all human affairs. Ec 9:5.

Inability to glorify God. Ps 115:17.

Even bones of, caused uncleanness. Nu 19:16. (See also 2 Ch 34:5.)

Eyes of, closed by nearest of kin. Gn 46:4.

Heathenish expressions of grief for, forbidden. Lv 19:28. Dt 14:1–2.

High priest in no case to mourn for. Lv 21:10–11.

IDOLATERS

Consecrated part of their crops to. Dt 26:14.

Invoked and consulted. 1 S 28:7–8.

Offered sacrifices for. Ps 106:28.

Tore themselves for. Jr 16:7.

ILLUSTRATIVE OF

Diviners, etc. Is 8:19.

Faith without works. 1 Tm 5:6. Ja 2:17, 26.

Freedom from the law. Ro 7:4.

Freedom from the power of sin. Ro 6:2, 8, 11. Cl 3:3.

Impotence. Gn 20:3. Ro 4:19.

Man's state by nature. 2 Co 5:4. Ep 2:1, 5.

A state of deep affliction, etc. Pss 88:5–6; 143:3. Is 59:10.

In a house, rendered it unclean. Nu 19:14–15.

Instances of, restored by Christ, etc. Mt 9:25. Lk 7:15. Jn 11:44. Ac 9:40; 20:12.

Instances of, restored to life before Christ. 1 K 17:22. 2 K 4:34–36; 13:21.

The Jews looked for a resurrection from. Is 26:19. Ac 24:15.

MOURNING FOR, OFTEN

By hired mourners. Jr 9:17–18. Am 5:16.

Lasted many days. Gn 37:34; 50:3, 10.

Loud and clamorous. Jr 16:6. Mk 5:38.

Testified by change of apparel. 2 S 14:2.

Testified by covering the head. 2 S 19:4.

Testified by rending the garments. Gn 37:34. 2 S 3:31.

Testified by tearing the hair. Jr 16:7.

Very great. Gn 37:35. Jr 31:15. Mt 2:18. Jn 11:33.

With plaintive music. Jr 48:36. Mt 9:23.

Nazarites not to touch or mourn for. Nu 6:6–7.

Priests not to mourn for, except when near of kin. Lv 21:1–3. Ezk 44:25.

Regard often shown to the memory of. Ru 1:8.

Return not to this life. Jb 7:9–10; 14:10, 14.

TERMS USED TO EXPRESS

Carcasses. Nu 14:29, 32–33. 1 K 13:24.

Corpses. 2 K 19:35. Na 3:3

Deceased. Is 26:14. Mt 22:25.

They who have departed this life. Gn 23:2; 25:8. Jb 1:19.

Those defiled by, removed from the camp. Nu 5:2.

Those who are not.   Mt 2:18.
Too soon forgotten.   Ps 31:12. Ec 9:5.
Touching of, caused uncleanness.   Nu 9:6–7;
    19:11, 13, 16.
Uncleanness contracted from, removed by the
    water of separation.   Nu 19:12, 18.
Were washed and laid out.   Ac 9:37.
Were wrapped in linen with spices.   Jn 19:40.

DEATH, ETERNAL
CALLED
Damnation of hell.   Mt 23:33.
Destruction.   To 9:22. 2 Th 1:9.
Everlasting punishment.   Mt 25:46.
Perishing.   2 P 2:12.
A resurrection to damnation.   Jn 5:29.
A resurrection to shame, etc.   Dn 12:2.
The second death.   Rv 2:11.
The wrath to come.   1 Th 1:10.
Christ the only way of escape from.   Jn 3:16;
    8:51. Ac 4:12.
DESCRIBED AS
Banishment from God.   2 Th 1:9.
Indignation, wrath, etc.   Ro 2:8–9.
A lake of fire.   Rv 19:20; 21:8.
A mist of darkness forever.   2 P 2:17.
Outer darkness. Mt 25:30.
Society with the devil, etc.   Mt 25:41.
The worm that dieth not.   Mk 9:44.
God alone can inflict.   Mt 10:28. Ja 4:12.
The necessary consequence of sin.   Ro 6:16,
    21; 8:13. Ja 1:15.
The portion of the wicked.   Mt 25:41, 46.
    Ro 1:32.
Saints shall escape.   Rv 2:11; 20:6.
Self-righteousness leads to.   Pr 14:12.
Shall be inflicted by Christ.   Mt 25:31, 41. 2
    Th 1:7–8.
Strive to preserve others from.   Ja 5:20.
The wages of sin.   Ro 6:23.
The way to, described.   Ps 9:17. Mt 7:13.

DEATH, NATURAL
Abolished by Christ.   2 Tm 1:10.
All shall be raised from.   Ac 24:15.
By Adam.   Gn 3:19. 1 Co 15:21–22.
Christ delivers from the fear of.   He 2:15.
Conquered by Christ.   Ro 6:9. Rv 1:18.
Consequence of sin.   Gn 2:17. Ro 5:12.
Consideration of, a motive to diligence.   Ec
    9:10. Jn 9:4.
DESCRIBED AS
Being cut down.   Jb 14:2.

Departing.   Php 1:23.
The earthly house of this tabernacle being
    dissolved.   2 Co 5:1.
Fleeing as a shadow.   Jb 14:2.
Gathering to our people.   Gn 49:33.
God requiring the soul.   Lk 12:20.
Going down into silence.   Ps 115:17.
Going the way whence there is no return.
    Jb 16:22.
Putting off this tabernacle.   2 P 1:14.
Returning to dust.   Gn 3:19. Ps 104:29.
A sleep.   Dt 31:16. Jn 11:11.
Yielding up the ghost.   Ac 5:10.
Enoch and Elijah exempted from.   Gn 5:24,
    with He 11:5. 2 K 2:11.
Illustrates the change produced in conversion.
    Ro 6:2. Cl 2:20.
Levels all ranks.   Jb 3:17–19.
Lot of all.   Ec 8:8. He 9:27.
None subject to, in heaven.   Lk 20:36. Rv
    21:4.
Ordered by God.   Dt 32:39. Jb 14:5.
Pray to be prepared for.   Pss 39:4, 13; 90:12.
Prepare for.   2 K 20:1.
Puts an end to earthly projects.   Ec 9:10.
Regard as at hand.   Jb 14:1–2. Pss 39:4–5;
    90:9. 1 P 1:24.
Shall finally be destroyed by Christ.   Ho
    13:14. 1 Co 15:26.
Strips of earthly possessions.   Jb 1:21. 1 Tm
    6:7.
When averted for a season, a motive to
    increased   devotedness.   Pss 56:12–13;
    118:17. Is 38:18, 20.

DEATH, SPIRITUAL
Alienation from God.   Ep 4:18.
A call to arise from.   Ep 5:14.
Carnal-mindedness.   Ro 8:6.
A consequence of the fall.   Ro 5:15.
Deliverance from is through Christ.   Jn
    5:24–25. Ep 2:5. 1 Jn 5:12.
The fruits of, dead works.   He 6:1; 9:14.
Hypocrisy.   Rv 3:1–2.
Illustrated.   Ezk 37:2–3. Lk 15:24.
Living in pleasure.   1 Tm 5:6.
Love of the brethren, a proof of being raised
    from.   1 Jn 3:14.
Saints are raised from.   Ro 6:13.
Spiritual ignorance.   Is 9:2. Mt 4:16. Lk
    1:79. Ep 4:18.
The state of all men by nature.   Ro 6:13; 8:6.
Unbelief.   Jn 3:36. 1 Jn 5:12.

Walking in trespasses and sins. Ep 2:1. Cl 2:13.

DEATH OF CHRIST
Acceptable, as a sacrifice to God. Mt 20:28. Ep 5:2. 1 Th 5:10.
Accompanied by preternatural signs. Mt 27:45, 51–53.
Appointed by God. Is 53:6, 10. Ac 2:23.
Commemorated in the sacrament of the Lord's Supper. Lk 22:19–20. 1 Co 11:26–29.
Demanded by the Jews. Mt 27:22–23.
Emblematical of the death unto sin. Ro 6:3–8. Gl 2:20.
Foretold. Is 53:8. Dn 9:26. Zc 13:7.
Inflicted by the Gentiles. Mt 27:26–35.
In the company of malefactors. Is 53:12, with Mt 27:38.
MODE OF
    Accursed. Gl 3:13.
    Exhibited his humility. Php 2:8.
    Foolishness to Gentiles. 1 Co 1:18, 23.
    Foretold by Christ. Mt 20:18–19. Jn 12:32–33.
    Ignominious. He 12:2.
    Prefigured. Nu 21:8, with Jn 3:14.
    A stumbling block to Jews. 1 Co 1:23.
Necessary for the redemption of man. Lk 24:46. Ac 17:3.
Undeserved. Is 53:9.
Voluntary. Is 53:12. Mt 26:53. Jn 10:17–18.

DEATH OF SAINTS
Blessed. Rv 14:13.
Disregarded by the wicked. Is 57:1.
God is with them in. Ps 23:4.
IS FULL OF
    Faith. He 11:13.
    Hope. Pr 14:32.
    Peace. Is 57:2.
Is gain. Php 1:21.
LEADS TO
    Christ's presence. 2 Co 5:8. Php 1:23.
    Comfort. Lk 16:25.
    A crown of life. 2 Tm 4:8. Rv 2:10.
    A joyful resurrection. Is 26:19. Dn 12:2.
    Rest. Jb 3:17. 2 Th 1:7.
Met with resignation. Gn 50:24. Jsh 23:14. 1 K 2:2.
Met without fear. 1 Co 15:55.
Precious in God's sight. Ps 116:15.
Preserved unto by God. Ps 48:14.

Removes from coming evil. 2 K 22:20. Is 57:1.
A sleep in Christ. 1 Co 15:18. 1 Th 4:14.
Sometimes desired. Lk 2:29.
Survivors consoled for. 1 Th 4:13–18.
Waited for. Jb 14:14.
The wicked wish theirs to resemble. Nu 23:10.

DEATH OF THE WICKED
Frequently marked by terror. Jb 18:11–15; 27:19–21. Ps 73:19.
Frequently sudden and unexpected. Jb 21:13, 23; 27:21. Pr 29:1.
God has no pleasure in. Ezk 18:23, 32.
Illustrated. Lk 12:20; 16:22–23.
In their sins. Ezk 3:19. Jn 8:21.
Like the death of beasts. Ps 49:14.
Punishment follows. Is 14:9. Ac 1:25.
The remembrance of them perishes in. Jb 18:17. Ps 34:16. Pr 10:7.
Sometimes without fear. Jr 34:5, with 2 Ch 36:11–13.
Without hope. Pr 11:7.

DEBTS
MATERIAL
    Excessive interest prohibited. Ex 22:25.
    Necessity of paying promptly. Dt 24:14–15. Pr 3:27. Ro 13:8.
    Parables about. Lk 7:41–42. Mt 18:23–25.
    Protection of borrowers. Dt 24:6, 17.
SPIRITUAL
    Condition of forgiveness. Mt 6:12, 14–15; 18:23–25.
    Deliverance through Christ. Ro 6:20–23.
    God's claim. Mt 25—26. Lk 7:41, 47; 16:5.
    Our responsibility. Ro 1:14–15; 13:8.

DECEIT
Abhorred by God. Ps 5:6.
Blessedness of being free from. Pss 24:4–5; 32:2.
A characteristic of antichrist. 2 Jn 1:7.
A characteristic of the apostasy. 2 Th 2:10.
Characteristic of the heart. Jr 17:9.
Christ was perfectly free from. Is 53:9, with 1 P 2:22.
Comes from the heart. Mk 7:22.
EVIL OF
    Keeps from knowledge of God. Jr 9:6.
    Keeps from turning to God. Jr 8:5.

Leads to lying.   Pr 14:25.
Leads to pride and oppression.   Jr 5:27–28.
Falsehood.   Ps 119:118.
FALSE TEACHERS
Are workers of.   2 Co 11:13.
Impose on others by.   Ro 16:18. Ep 4:14.
Preach.   Jr 14:14; 23:26.
Sport themselves with.   2 P 2:13.
False witnesses use.   Pr 12:17; 14:5.
The folly of fools.   Pr 14:8.
Forbidden.   Pr 24:28. 1 P 3:10.
Hatred often concealed by.   Pr 26:24–28.
Hypocrites devise.   Jb 15:35.
Hypocrites practice.   Ho 11:12.
The kisses of an enemy.   Pr 27:6.
Ministers should lay aside.   2 Co 4:2. 1 Th
2:3.
Often accompanied by fraud and injustice.
Pss 10:7; 43:1.
Punishment of.   Ps 55:23. Jr 9:7–9.
SAINTS
Are free from.   Ps 24:4. Zp 3:13. Rv 14:5.
Are delivered from those who use.   Ps
72:14.
Avoid.   Jb 31:5.
Pray for deliverance from those who use.
Pss 43:1; 120:2.
Purpose against.   Jb 27:4.
Should beware of those who teach.   Ep
5:6. Cl 2:8.
Should lay aside, in seeking truth.   1 P 2:1.
Shun those addicted to.   Ps 101:7.
Tongue as the instrument of.   Ro 3:13.
THE WICKED
Are full of.   Ro 1:29.
Delight in.   Pr 20:17.
Devise.   Pss 35:20; 38:12. Pr 12:5.
Increase in.   2 Tm 3:13.
Use to each other.   Jr 9:5.
Use to themselves.   Jr 37:9. Ob 1:3, 7.
Utter.   Pss 10:7; 36:3.
Work.   Pr 11:18.

DECISION
Blessedness of.   Jsh 1:7.
EXHIBITED IN
Being on the Lord's side.   Ex 32:26.
Following God fully.   Nu 14:24; 32:12.
Jsh 14:8.
Keeping the commandments of God.   Ne
10:29.
Loving God perfectly.   Dt 6:5.
Seeking God with the heart.   2 Ch 15:12.
Serving God.   Is 56:6.

Exhortations to.   Jsh 24:14–15.
Necessary to the service of God.   Lk 9:62.
OPPOSED TO
A divided service.   Mt 6:24.
Double-mindedness.   Ja 1:8.
Halting between two opinions.   1 K 18:21.
Not setting the heart aright.   Ps 78:8, 37.
Turning to the right or left.   Dt 5:32.

DEDICATION
Consecration of a place of worhip.   2 Ch 2:4.
Devoting anything to sacred uses.   1 Ch
28:12.
Illustrative of devotedness to God.   Ps
119:38.
Of idolaters in setting up idols.   Dn 3:2–3.
Of property, often perverted.   Mk 7:9–13.
Solemn confirmation of a covenant.   He 9:18.
SUBJECTS OF
Houses when built.   Dt 20:5. Ps 30.
Persons.   Ex 22:29. 1 S 1:11.
Property.   Lv 27:28. Mt 15:5.
Second temple.   Ezr 6:16–17.
Spoils of war.   2 S 8:11. 1 Ch 18:11.
Tabernacle.   Nu 7.
Temple of Solomon.   1 K 8:1–63. 2 Ch
7:5.
Tribute from foreigners.   2 S 8:10–11.
Walls of cities.   Ne 12:27.
THINGS DEDICATED TO GOD
Applied to the repair and maintenance of
the temple.   2 K 12:4–5. 1 Ch 26:27.
Esteemed holy.   Lv 27:28. 2 K 12:18.
For support of priests.   Nu 18:14. Ezk
44:29.
Given to propitiate enemies.   2 K
12:17–18.
Law respecting the release of.   Lv 27.
Levites placed over.   1 Ch 26:20, 26. 2 Ch
31:12.
Placed with the treasures of the Lord's
house.   1 K 7:51. 2 Ch 5:1.
Special chambers prepared for.   2 Ch
31:11–12.

DEDICATION, FEAST OF
To commemorate the cleansing of the temple
after its defilement by Antiochus.   Dn
11:31.
Held in the winter month, Chislev.   Jn 10:22.

DEEDS
Judgment according to.   Ro 2:5–6. Rv 20:12.
Of a child, significance of.   Pr 20:11.

Of Christians. Lk 6:46. Cl 3:17. Mt 5:16.
Of evil men. Jn 3:19.
Of God, glory of. Ex 15:11. 1 S 12:7. Ps 9:1, 11.
Of Jesus, good. Lk 24:19. Mt 11:5.
Of love, required. 1 Jn 3:18.
Of the old nature. Cl 3:9.

DEFILEMENT

Causes of, improperly enlarged by tradition. Mk 7:2, with Mt 15:20.
Ceremonial, abolished under the gospel. Ac 10:15. Ro 14:14. Cl 2:20–22.
CEREMONIAL, CAUSED BY
Being alone with a dead body. Nu 19:14.
Burning the red heifer. Nu 19:8.
Childbearing. Lv 12:2.
Eating things that died. Lv 17:15.
Eating unclean things. Lv 11:8. Ac 10:11, 14.
Gathering ashes of the red heifer. Nu 19:10.
Going into a leprous house. Lv 14:46.
Having an issue, etc. Lv 15:2. Nu 5:2.
Having a leprosy. Lv 13:3, 11. Nu 5:2–3.
Mourning for the dead. Lv 21:1–3.
Sacrificing the red heifer. Nu 19:7.
Touching a dead beast. Lv 5:2; 11:24–28.
Touching a dead body or a bone. Nu 9:6–7; 19:11, 16.
Touching a grave. Nu 19:16.
Touching an unclean person. Nu 19:22.
Touching anything defiled by an issue, etc. Lv 15:5–11.
Cleansed by legal ablutions. Nu 19:18–19. He 9:13.
Forbidden to the Jews. Lv 11:44–45.
ILLUSTRATIVE OF
Sin. Mt 15:11, 18. Jde 1:8.
Unholy doctrines. 1 Co 3:16–17.
MORAL, CAUSED BY
Following the sins of the heathen. Lv 18:24.
Giving children to Molech. Lv 20:3.
Making and serving idols. Ezk 20:17–18; 22:3–4; 23:7.
Seeking after wizards. Lv 19:31.
Shedding blood. Is 59:3.
Moral, punished. Lv 18:24–25, 28–29.
Neglecting purification from, punished by cutting off. Nu 19:13, 20.
PRIESTS
Not to eat holy things while under. Lv 22:2, 4–6.

Punished for eating of the holy things while under. Lv 22:3.
Specially required to avoid. Lv 21:1–6, 11–12.
To decide in all cases. of. Lv 10:10; 13:3.
THINGS LIABLE TO CEREMONIAL
Furniture, etc. Lv 15:9–10. Nu 19:14–15
Garments. Lv 13:59.
Houses. Lv 14:44.
The land. Lv 18:25. Dt 21:23.
The person. Lv 5:3.
The sanctuary. Lv 20:3. Zp 3:4.
Those under, removed from the camp. Nu 5:3–4. Dt 23:14.

DELIGHTING IN GOD

Commanded. Ps 37:4.
HYPOCRITES
Blessedness of. Ps 112:1.
In heart despise. Jb 27:10. Jr 6:10.
Pretend to. Is 58:2.
Promises to. Ps 37:4.
Observing the sabbath leads to. Is 58:13–14.
Reconciliation leads to. Jb 22:21, 26.
SAINTS' EXPERIENCE IN
The comforts of God. Ps 94:19.
Communion with God. S S 2:3.
The goodness of God. Ne 9:25.
The law of God. Pss 1:2; 119:24, 35.

DENIAL OF CHRIST

A characteristic of false teachers. 2 P 2:1. Jde 1:4.
Christ will deny those guilty of. Mt 10:33. 2 Tm 2:12.
In doctrine. Mk 8:38. 2 Tm 1:8.
In practice. Php 3:18–19. Ti 1:16.
Is the spirit of antichrist. 1 Jn 2:22–23; 4:3.
Leads to destruction. 2 P 2:1. Jde 1:4, 15.

DESERT, JOURNEY OF ISRAEL THROUGH THE

By a circuitous route. Ex 13: 17–18.
Caused universal terror and dismay. Ex 15:14–16. Nu 22:3–4.
Circumcision omitted during. Jsh 5:5.
Commenced in haste. Ex 12:39.
Conducted with regularity. Ex 13:18.
Constant goodness and mercy of God to them during. Pss 106:10, 43–46; 107:6, 13.
CONTINUED FORTY YEARS
As a punishment. Nu 14:33–34.
To prove and humble them, etc. Dt 8:2.

To teach them to live on God's word. Dt 8:3.

Date of its commencement. Ex 12:41–42.

Difficulty and danger of. Dt 8:15.

Illustrative of the pilgrimage of the church. S S 8:5. 1 P 1:17.

Justice administered during. Ex 18:13, 26.

Marked by constant murmurings and rebellions. Pss 78:40; 95:10; 106:7–39.

A mixed multitude accompanied them in. Ex 12:38. Nu 11:4.

Obstructed, etc., by the surrounding nations. Ex 17:8. Nu 20:21.

Order of encamping during. Nu 2.

Order of marching during. Nu 10:14–28.

Territory acquired during. Dt 29:7–8.

Their clothing preserved during. Dt 8:4; 29:5. Ne 9:21.

Their healthy state commencing. Ps 105:37.

Their number commencing. Ex 12:37.

Under God's guidance. Ex 13:21–22; 15:13. Ne 9:12. Ps 78:52. Is 63:11–14.

Under God's protection. Ex 14:19–20, with Ps 105:39. Ex 23:20, with Ps 78:53.

Under Moses as leader. Ex 3:10–12, with Ac 7:36, 38.

With miraculous provision. Ex 16:35. Dt 8:3.

Worship of God celebrated during. Ex 24:5–8; 29:38–42; 40:24–29.

COMMENCED FROM RAMESES IN EGYPT. Ex 12:37.

To SUCCOTH. Ex 12:37. Nu 33:5.

To ETHAM. Ex 13:20. Nu 33:6.

BETWEEN BAALZEPHON AND PIHAHIROTH. Ex 14:2. Nu 33:7.

Overtaken by Pharaoh. Ex 14:9.

Exhorted to look to God. Ex 14:13–14.

The cloud removed to the rear. Ex 14:19–20.

The Red Sea divided. Ex 14:16, 21.

THROUGH THE RED SEA. Ex 14:22, 29.

Faith exhibited in passing. He 11:29.

Pharaoh and his host destroyed. Ex 14:23–28. Ps 106:11.

Israel's song of praise. Ex 15:1–21. Ps 106:12.

THROUGH THE WILDERNESS OF SHUR OR ETHAM. Ex 15:22. Nu 33:8.

To MARAH. Ex 15:23. Nu 33:8.

Murmuring of the people on account of bitter water. Ex 15:24.

Water sweetened. Ex 15:25.

To ELIM. Ex 15:27. Nu 33:9.

BY THE RED SEA. Nu 33:10.

THROUGH THE WILDERNESS OF SIN. Ex 16:1. Nu 33:11.

Murmuring for bread. Ex 16:2–3.

Quails given for one night. Ex 16:8, 12–13.

Manna sent. Ex 16:14, 8, 16–31.

To DOPHKAH. Nu 33:12.

To ALUSH. Nu 33:13.

To REPHIDIM. Ex 17:1. Nu 33:14.

Murmuring for water. Ex 17:2–3.

Water brought from the rock. Ex 17:5–6.

Called Massah and Meribah. Ex 17:7.

Amalek opposes Israel. Ex 17:8.

Amalek overcome. Ex 17:9–13.

To MOUNT SINAI. Ex 19:1–2. Nu 33:15.

Jethro's visit. Ex 18:1–6.

Judges appointed. Ex 18:14–26. Dt 1:9–15.

Moral law given. Ex 19:3; 20.

Covenant made. Ex 24:3–8.

Moral law written on tables. Ex 31:18.

Order for making the tabernacle, etc. Ex 24—27.

Tribe of Levi taken instead of the first-born. Nu 3:11–13.

Aaron and his sons selected for priesthood. Ex 28—29. Nu 3:1–3, 10.

Levites set apart. Nu 3:5–9.

Golden calf made. Ex 32:1, 4.

Tables of testimony broken. Ex 32:19.

People punished for idolatry. Ex 32:25–29, 35.

God's glory shown to Moses. Ex 33:18–23; 34:5–8.

The tables of testimony renewed. Ex 34:1–4, 27–29. Dt 10:1–5.

Tabernacle first set up. Ex 40.

Nadab and Abihu destroyed for offering strange fire. Lv 10:1–2. Nu 3:4.

Passover first commemorated. Nu 9:1–5.

Second numbering of the people. Nu 1:1–46, with Ex 38:25–26.

To KIBROTH-HATTAAVAH. Nu 33:16.

Complaining punished by fire. Nu 11:1–3.

Called Taberah. Nu 11:3.

Murmuring of the mixed multitude and of Israel, for flesh. Nu 11:4–9.

Flesh promised. Nu 11:10–15, 18–23.

Seventy elders appointed to assist Moses. Nu 11:16, 17, 24–30.

Quails sent for a month. Nu 11:19–20, 31–32.

Their murmuring punished. Nu 11:23.
Ps 78:30–31.

Why called Kibroth-hattaavah. Nu 11:34.

To HAZEROTH. Nu 11:35; 33:17.

Aaron and Miriam envy Moses. Nu 12:1–2.

Miriam punished by leprosy. Nu 12:10.

Delayed seven days for Miriam. Nu 12:14–15.

To KADESH-BARNEA IN WILDERNESS OF RITH-MAH OR PARAN. Dt 1:19, and Nu 32:8 with 12:16 and 33:18.

The people anxious to have the land of Canaan searched. Dt 1:22.

Moses commanded to send spies. Nu 13:1–2.

Persons selected as spies. Nu 13:3–16.

Spies sent. Jsh 14:7, with Nu 13:17–20.

Spies bring back evil report. Nu 13:26–33.

The people terrified and rebel. Nu 14:1–4.

Punishment for rebellion. Nu 14:26, 35; 32: 11–13. Dt 1:35–36, 40.

Guilty spies slain by plague. Nu 14:36–37.

People smitten by Amalek for going up without the Lord. Nu 14:40–45. Dt 1:41–44.

RETURNED BY THE WAY OF THE RED SEA. Nu 14:25. Dt 1:40; 2:1.

Sabbath breaker stoned. Nu 15:32–36.

Rebellion of Korah. Nu 16:1–19.

Korah, etc., punished. Nu 16:30–35.

Plague sent. Nu 16:41–46.

Plague stayed. Nu 16:47–50.

God's choice of Aaron confirmed. Nu 17.

To RIMMON-PAREZ. Nu 33:19.

To LIBNAH OR LABAN. Nu 33:20. Dt 1:1.

To RISSAH. Nu 33:21.

To KEHELATHAH. Nu 33:22.

To MOUNT SHAPHER. Nu 33:23.

To HARADAH. Nu 33:24.

To MAKHELOTH. Nu 33:25.

To TAHATH. Nu 33:26.

To TARAH. Nu 33:27.

To MITHCAH. Nu 33:28.

To HASHMONAH. Nu 33:29.

To MOSEROTH OR MOSERA. Nu 33:30.

To BENE-JAAKAN. Nu 33:31.

To HORHAGIDGAD OR GUDGODAH. Nu 33:32. Dt 10:7.

To JOTBATHAH OR LAND OF RIVERS. Nu 33:33. Dt 10:7.

Several of these stations probably revisited. Dt 10:6–7, with Nu 33:30–32.

To EBRONAH. Nu 33:34.

To EZION-GABER. Nu 33:35.

To KADESH IN THE WILDERNESS OF ZIN. Nu 20:1, 33:36. Jg 11:16.

Miriam dies and is buried. Nu 20:1.

Second murmuring for water. Nu 20:2–6.

Moses striking the rock instead of speaking to it, disobeys God. Nu 20:7–11.

Moses and Aaron punished. Nu 20:12.

Called Meribah to commemorate the murmuring. Nu 20:13; 27:14.

Orders given respecting Edom. Dt 2:3–6.

The king of Edom refuses a passage. Nu 20:14–21. Jg 11:17.

To MOUNT HOR. Nu 20:22; 33:37.

Aaron dies. Nu 20:28–29; 33:38–39.

Arad conquered. Nu 21:1–3; 33:40.

Called Hormah. Nu 21:2–3.

To ZALMONAH. Nu 33:41.

Murmuring of the people. Nu 21:4–5.

Fiery serpents sent. Nu 21:6.

Bronze serpent raised up. Nu 21:7–9.

To PUNON. Nu 33:42.

To OBOTH. Nu 21:10; 33:43.

To IJE-ABARIM BEFORE MOAB. Nu 21:11; 33:44.

Orders given respecting Moab. Dt 2:8–9.

To ZARED OR DIBON-GAD. Nu 21:12; 33:45.

To ALMON-DIBLATHAIM. Nu 33:46.

ACROSS THE BROOK ZERED. Dt 2:13.

Time occupied in going from Kadesh-barnea to this station. Dt 2:14.

Order to pass through Ar. Dt 2:18.

Orders given respecting Ammon. Dt 2:19.

ACROSS THE ARNON. Nu 21:13–15. Dt 2:24.

To BEER OR THE WELL. Nu 21:16.

To MATTANAH. Nu 21:18.

To NAHALIEL. Nu 21:19.

To BAMOTH. Nu 21:19.

To THE MOUNTAINS OF ABARIM. Nu 21:20; 33:47.

The Amorites refuse a passage to Israel. Nu 21:21–23. Dt 2:26–30.

Sihon conquered. Nu 21:23–32. Dt 2:32–36.

Og conquered. Nu 21:33–35. Dt 3:1–11.

Reubenites, etc., obtained the land taken from the Amorites. Nu 32. Dt 3:12–17.

RETURN TO THE PLAINS OF MOAB. Nu 22:1; 33:48–49.

Balak sends for Balaam. Nu 22:5–6; 15–17.

Balaam not permitted to curse Israel. Nu 22:9–41; 23—24.

Israel seduced to idolatry, etc., by advice of Balaam. Nu 25:1–3. Rv 2:14.

Israel punished. Nu 25:5, 9.

Third numbering. Nu 26:1–62.

All formerly numbered over twenty years old, except Caleb and Joshua, dead. Nu 26:63–65, with 14:29.

The law of female inheritance settled. Nu 27:1–11, with 36:1–9.

Appointment of Joshua. Nu 27:15–23.

Midianites destroyed and Balaam slain. Nu 31 with 25:17–18.

The law rehearsed. Dt 1:3.

The law written by Moses. Dt 31:9.

Moses beholds Canaan. Dt 34:1–4.

Moses dies and is buried. Dt 34:5–6.

Joshua ordered to cross Jordan. Jsh 1:2.

Two spies sent to Jericho. Jsh 2:1.

ACROSS THE RIVER JORDAN. Jsh 2:1.

DESERTS

Danger of traveling in. Ex 14:3. 2 Co 11:26.

DESCRIBED AS -

Desolate. Ezk 6:14.

Dry and without water. Ex 17:1. Dt 8:15.

Great and terrible. Dt 1:19.

Trackless. Is 43:19.

Uncultivated. Nu 20:5. Jr 2:2.

Uninhabited and lonesome. Jr 2:6.

Waste and howling. Dt 32:10.

The disaffected fled to. 1 S 22:2. Ac 21:38.

Guides required in. Nu 10:31. Dt 32:10.

Heath often found in. Jr 17:6.

ILLUSTRATIVE OF

Barrenness. Pss 106:9; 107:33, 35.

Desolation by armies. Jr 12:10–13; 50:12.

The Gentiles. Is 35:1, 6; 41:19.

Those deprived of all blessings. Ho 2:3.

What affords no support. Jr 2:31.

The world. S S 3:6; 8:5.

INFESTED WITH

Robbers. Jr 3:2. Lm 4:19.

Serpents. Dt 8:15.

Wild beasts. Is 13:21. Mk 1:13.

Inhabited by wandering tribes. Gn 21:20–21. Ps 72:9. Jr 25:24.

MENTIONED IN SCRIPTURE

Arabian or great desert. Ex 23:31.

Beersheba. Gn 21:14. 1 K 19:3–4.

Bethaven. Jsh 18:12.

Damascus. 1 K 19:15.

Edom. 2 K 3:8.

Engedi. 1 S 24:1.

Gibeon. 2 S 2:24.

Jeruel. 2 Ch 20:16.

Judea. Mt 3:1.

Kadesh. Ps 29:8.

Kedemoth. Dt 2:26.

Maon. 1 S 23:24–25.

Near Gaza. Ac 8:26.

Of the Red Sea. Ex 13:18.

Paran. Gn 21:21. Nu 10:12.

Shur. Gn 16:7. Ex 15:22.

Sin. Ex 16:1.

Sinai. Ex 19:1–2. Nu 33:16.

Zin. Nu 20:1; 27:14.

Ziph. 1 S 23:14–15.

Parts of, afforded pasture. Gn 36:24. Ex 3:1.

The persecuted fled to. 1 S 23:14. He 11:38.

PHENOMENA OF, ALLUDED TO

Clouds of sand and dust. Dt 28:24. Jr 4:12–13.

Mirage or deceptive appearance of water. Jr 15:18.

Simoon or deadly wind. 2 K 19:7. Jr 4:11.

Tornadoes or whirlwinds. Is 21:1.

Uninhabited places. Mt 14:15. Mk 6:31.

Vast barren plains. Ex 5:3. Jn 6:13.

DESPAIR

LEADS TO

Blasphemy. Is 8:21. Rv 16:10–11.

Continuing in sin. Jr 2:25; 18:12.

Produced in the wicked by divine judgments. Dt 28:34, 67. Rv 9:6; 16:10.

Saints enabled to overcome. 2 Co 4:8–9.

Saints sometimes tempted to. Jb 7:6. Lm 3:18.

Shall seize upon the wicked at the appearing of Christ. Rv 6:16.

Trust in God a preservative against. Ps 42:5, 11.

THE DEVIL

The apostasy is of. 2 Th 2:9. 1 Tm 4:1.

Assumes the form of an angel of light. 2 Co 11:14.

Author of the fall. Gn 3:1, 6, 14, 24.

Cast down to hell. 2 P 2:4. Jde 1:6.

Cast out of heaven. Lk 10:18.

CHARACTER OF

Cowardly. Ja 4:7.

Deceitful. 2 Co 11:14. Ep 6:11.

Fierce and cruel. Lk 8:29; 9:39, 42. 1 P 5:8.

Malignant. Jb 1:9; 2:4.

Powerful. Ep 2:2; 6:12.
Presumptuous. Jb 1:6. Mt 4:5–6.
Proud. 1 Tm 3:6.
Subtle. Gn 3:1, with 2 Co 11:3.
Wicked. 1 Jn 2:13.
COMPARED TO
    A fowler. Ps 91:3.
    Fowls. Mt 13:4.
    A roaring lion. 1 P 5:8.
    A serpent. Rv 12:9; 20:2.
    A sower of tares. Mt 13:25, 28.
    A wolf. Jn 10:12.
Everlasting fire is prepared for. Mt 25:41.
Hinders the gospel. Mt 13:19. 2 Co 4:4.
Opposes God's work. Zc 3:1. 1 Th 2:18.
Perverts the scriptures. Mt 4:6, with Ps
    91:11–12.
SAINTS
    Are afflicted by, only as God permits. Jb
        1:12; 2:4–7.
    Are sifted by. Lk 22:31.
    Are tempted by. 1 Ch 21:1. 1 Th 3:5.
    Overcome. 1 Jn 2:13. Rv 12:10–11.
    Shall finally triumph over. Ro 16:20.
    Should be armed against. Ep 6:11–16.
    Should be watchful against. 2 Co 2:11.
    Should resist. Ja 4:7. 1 P 5:9.
Shall be condemned at the judgment. Jde
    1:6. Rv 20:10.
Sinned against God. 2 P 2:4. 1 Jn 3:8.
Tempted Christ. Mt 4:3–10.
TRIUMPH OVER, BY CHRIST
    Completed by his death. Cl 2:15. He
        2:14.
    Illustrated. Lk 11:21–22.
    In casting out the spirits of. Lk 11:20;
        13:32.
    In destroying the works of. 1 Jn 3:8.
    In empowering his disciples to cast out.
        Mt 10:1. Mk 16:17.
    In resisting his temptations. Mt 4:11.
    Predicted. Gn 3:15.
THE WICKED
    Are blinded by. 2 Co 4:4.
    Are the children of. Mt 13:38. Ac 13:10.
        1 Jn 3:10.
    Are deceived by. 1 K 22:21–22. Rv
        20:7–8.
    Are ensnared by. 1 Tm 3:7. 2 Tm 2:26.
    Are possessed by. Lk 22:3. Ac 5:3. Ep
        2:2.
    Are punished, together with. Mt 25:41.
    Are troubled by. 1 S 16:14.
    Do the lusts of. Jn 8:44.

Turn aside after. 1 Tm 5:15.
Works lying wonders. 2 Th 2:9. Rv 16:14.

DEVOTEDNESS TO GOD
A characteristic of saints. Jb 23:12.
Christ an example of. Jn 4:34; 17:4.
GROUNDED UPON
    The call of God. 1 Th 2:12.
    The death of Christ. 2 Co 5:15.
    The goodness of God. 1 S 12:24.
    The mercies of God. Ro 12:1.
    Our creation. Ps 86:9.
    Our preservation. Is 46:4.
    Our redemption. 1 Co 6:19–20.
SHOULD BE
    Abounding. 1 Th 4:1.
    In life and death. Ro 14:8. Php 1:20.
    Persevering. Lk 1:74–75; 9:62.
    Unreserved. Mt 6:24. Lk 14:33.
    With our bodies. Ro 12:1. 1 Co 6:20.
    With our members. Ro 6:12, 13. 1 P 4:2.
    With our spirit. 1 Co 6:20. 1 P 4:6.
    With our substance. Ex 22:29. Pr 3:9.
SHOULD BE EXHIBITED
    Bearing the cross. Mk 8:34.
    Doing all to God's glory. 1 Co 10:31.
    Giving up all for Christ. Mt 19:21, 28–29.
    Living to Christ. 2 Co 5:15.
    Loving God. Dt 6:5. Lk 10:27.
    Self-denial. Mk 8:34.
    Serving God. 1 S 12:24. Ro 12:11.
    Walking worthy of God. 1 Th 2:12.
Want of, condemned. Rv 3:16.

DIET OF THE JEWS
ARTICLES USED FOR
    Bread. Gn 18:5. 1 S 17:17.
    Butter. Dt 32:14. 2 S 17:29.
    Cheese. 1 S 17:18. Jb 10:10.
    Dried fruit. 1 S 25:18; 30:12.
    Fish. Mt 7:10. Lk 24:42.
    Flesh. 2 S 6:19. Pr 9:2.
    Fruit. 2 S 16:2.
    Herbs. Pr 15:17. Ro 14:2. He 6:7.
    Honey. S S 5:1. Is 7:15.
    Milk. Gn 49:12. Pr 27:27.
    Oil. Dt 12:17. Pr 21:17. Ezk 16:13.
    Parched corn. Ru 2:14. 1 S 17:17.
    Vinegar. Nu 6:3. Ru 2:14.
    Water. Gn 21:14. Mt 10:42.
    Wine. 2 S 6:19. Jn 2:3, 10.
Expressed by bread and water. 1 K 13:9, 16.
Generally prepared by females. Gn 27:9. 1 S
    8:13. Pr 31:15.

A hymn sung after.   Mt 26:30.
In Egypt.   Ex 16:3. Nu 11:5.
In patriarchal age.   Gn 18:7–8; 27:4.
In the wilderness.   Ex 16:4–12.
Items of, often sent as presents.   1 S 17:18; 25:18, 27. 2 S 16:1–2.
Men and women did not partake of, together. Gn 18:8–9. Es 1:3, 9.
Of the poor, frugal.   Ru 2:14. Pr 15:17.
Of the rich, luxurious.   Pr 23:1–3. Lm 4:5. Am 6:4–5. Lk 16:19.
Purification before.   2 K 3:11. Mt 15:2.
Thanks given before.   Mk 8:6. Ac 27:35.
WAS TAKEN
    At noon.   Gn 43:16. Jn 4:6, 8.
    In the evening.   Gn 24:11, 33. Lk 24:29–30.
    In the morning, sparingly.   Jg 19:5, with Ec 10:16–17.
    Often reclining.   Am 6:4. Jn 13:23.
    Often sitting.   Gn 27:19; 43:33.
    With the hand.   Mt 26:23, with Lk 22:21.

DIFFICULTIES
God and.   Gn 18:14. Jr 32:17.
Of the true way.   Mt 7:14.
Overcoming.   Php 1:19.
Power over.   Php 4:13.
Reality of.   Ps 137:15.

DILIGENCE
Christ an example.   Mk 1:35. Lk 2:49.
God rewards.   Dt 11:14. He 11:6.
Illustrated.   Pr 6:6–8.
IN THE SERVICE OF GOD
    Is not in vain.   1 Co 15:58.
    Leads to assured hope.   He 6:11.
    Preserves from evil.   Ex 15:26.
    Should be persevered in.   Gl 6:9.
IN TEMPORAL MATTERS, LEADS TO
    Favor.   Pr 11:27.
    Honor.   Pr 12:24; 22:29.
    Prosperity.   Pr 10:4; 13:4.
REQUIRED BY GOD IN
    Cultivating Christian graces.   2 P 1:5.
    Discharging official duties.   Dt 19:18.
    Following every good work.   1 Tm 5:10.
    Guarding against defilement.   He 12:15.
    Hearkening to him.   Is 55:2.
    Instructing children.   Dt 6:7; 11:19.
    Keeping the heart.   Pr 4:23.
    Keeping the soul.   Dt 4:9.
    Labors of love.   He 6:10–12.
    Lawful business.   Pr 27:23. Ec 9:10.

Making our calling, etc., sure.   2 P 1:10.
Obeying him.   Dt 6:17; 11:13.
Seeking him.   1 Ch 22:19. He 11:6.
Seeking to be found spotless.   2 P 3:14.
Self-examination.   Ps 77:6.
Striving after perfection.   Php 3:13–14.
Teaching religion.   2 Tm 4:2. Jde 1:3.
Saints should abound in.   2 Co 8:7.

DIRECTION
Affirmation of.   Ps 23.
By an angel.   Ac 10:22.
Of the Lord.   Dt 32:12. Ex 13:21.
Prayer for.   Pss 31:3; 43:3.
Promise of.   Ps 32:8. Pr 3:6.
Through Christ.   Jn 10:3.
Toward the highest.   2 Th 3:5.

DISAPPOINTMENT
Examples of.   Lv 26:16. 1 Ch 22:7. Ac 16:7.
Judgment and.   He 6:10–12.
One reason for.   Pr 15:22.
Victory over.   Hk 3:17–19. Ro 8:28.

DISCIPLINE OF THE CHURCH
CONSISTS IN
    Maintaining sound doctrine.   1 Tm 1:3. Ti 1:13.
    Ordering its affairs.   1 Co 11:34. Ti 1:5.
    Rebuking offenders.   1 Tm 5:20. 2 Tm 4:2.
    Removing obstinate offenders.   1 Co 5:3:5, 13. 1 Tm 1:20.
Decency and order, the objects of.   1 Co 14:40.
Exercise, in a spirit of charity.   2 Co 2:6–8.
Ministers authorized to establish.   Mt 16:19; 18:18.
Prohibits women preaching.   1 Co 14:34. 1 Tm 2:12.
Should be submitted to.   He 13:17.

DISCOURAGEMENT
Conquering.   Hk 3:17–19. Hg 1:2–14. Ac 28:15. 2 Co 12:9.
Danger of causing.   Cl 3:21. 1 Th 5:19.
Illustrated.   1 K 19:4. Ne 4:10. Ps 43:3. Is 49:14. Lk 5:5; 24:24.
Reasons for.   Pr 13:12. 2 Co 12:7.

DISEASES
Art of curing, defective.   Jb 13:4. Mk 5:26.
Children subject to.   2 S 12:15. 1 K 17:17.

FREQUENTLY
Complicated. Dt 28:60–61. Ac 28:8.
Incurable. 2 Ch 21:18. Jr 14:19.
Loathsome. Pss 38:7; 41:8.
Painful. 2 Ch 21:15. Jb 33:19.
Tedious. Dt 28:59. Jn 5:5. Lk 13:16.
God often entreated to cure. 2 S 12:16. 2 K 20:1–3. Ps 6:2. Ja 5:14.
Illustrates sin. Is 1:5.
Intemperance a cause of. Ho 7:5.
Medicine used for curing. Pr 17:22. Is 1:6.
MENTIONED IN SCRIPTURE
Abscess. 2 K 20:7.
Ague. Lv 26:16.
Atrophy. Jb 16:8.
Blindness. Jb 29:15. Mt 9:27.
Boils and blains. Ex 9:10.
Consumption. Lv 26:16. Dt 28:22.
Deafness. Ps 38:13. Mk 7:32.
Debility. Ps 102:23. Ezk 7:17.
Demoniacal possession. Mt 15:22. Mk 5:15.
Dropsy. Lk 14:2.
Dumbness. Pr 31:8. Mt 9:32.
Dysentery. 2 Ch 21:12–19. Ac 28:8.
Emerods. Dt 28:27. 1 S 5:6, 12.
Fever. Dt 28:22. Mt 8:14.
Impediment speech. Mk 7:32.
Inflammation. Dt 28:22.
Itch. Dt 28:27.
Issue of blood. Mt 9:20.
Lameness. 2 S 4:4. 2 Ch 16:12.
Leprosy. Lv 13:2. 2 K 5:1.
Loss of appetite. Jb 33:20. Ps 107:18.
Lunacy. Mt 4:24; 17:15.
Melancholy. 1 S 16:14.
Palsy. Mt 8:6; 9:2.
Plague. Nu 11:33. 2 S 24:15, 21, 25.
Scab. Dt 28:27.
Sunstroke. 2 K 4:18–20. Is 49:10.
Ulcers. Is 1:6. Lk 16:20.
Worms. Ac 12:23.
Not looking to God in, condemned. 2 Ch 16:12.
Overexcitement a cause of. Dn 8:27.
Physicians undertook the cure of. Jr 8:22. Mt 9:12. Lk 4:23.
Regarded as visitations. Jb 2:7–10. Ps 38:2, 7.
SENT
As punishment. Dt 28:21. Jn 5:14.
Through Satan. 1 S 16:14–16. Jb 2:7.
Sins of youth a cause of. Jb 20:11.

THOSE AFFLICTED WITH
Anointed. Mk 6:13. Ja 5:14.
Laid in the streets to receive advice from passers-by. Mk 6:56. Ac 5:15.
Often divinely cured. 2 K 20:5. Ja 5:15.
Often divinely supported. Ps 41:3.
Were many and divers. Mt 4:24.

DISOBEDIENCE TO GOD
Acknowledge the punishment of, to be just. Ne 9:32–33. Dn 9:10–11, 14.
Bitter results of, illustrated. Jr 9:13, 15.
Brings a curse. Dt 11:28; 28:15, etc.
A characteristic of the wicked. Ep 2:2. Ti 1:16; 3:3.
Forfeits his favor. 1 S 13:14.
Forfeits his promised blessings. Jsh 5:6. 1 S 2:30. Jr 18:10.
Heinousness of, illustrated. Jr 35:14, etc.
Men prone to excuse. Gn 3:12–13.
Provokes his anger. Ps 78:10, 40. Is 3:8.
Shall be punished. Is 42:24–25. He 2:2.
Warnings against. 1 S 12:15. Jr 12:17.
The wicked persevere in. Jr 22:21.

DIVINATION
An abominable practice. 1 S 15:23.
All who practiced it, abominable. Dt 18:12.
Books of, numerous and expensive. Ac 19:19.
Connected with idolatry. 2 Ch 33:5–6.
Could not injure the Lord's people. Nu 23:23.
EFFECTED THROUGH
Cups. Gn 44:2, 5.
Dreams. Jr 29:8. Zc 10:2.
Enchantments. Ex 7:11. Nu 24:1.
The flight of arrows. Ezk 21:21–22.
Inspecting the inside of beasts. Ezk 21:21.
Observing heavenly bodies. Is 37:13.
Observing times. 2 K 21:6.
Raising the dead. 1 S 28:11–12.
Rods. Ho 4:12.
Sorcery. Is 47:12. Ac 8:11.
Frustrated by God. Is 44:25.
The Jews prone to. 2 K 17:17. Is 2:6.
THE LAW
Forbade its practice for Israelites. Lv 19:26. Dt 18:10–11.
Forbade seeking to. Lv 19:31. Dt 18:14.
Punished those who sought to. Lv 20:6.
Punished with death those who used. Ex 22:18. Lv 20:27.

A lucrative employment. Nu 22:7. Ac 16:16.

PRACTICED BY

Astrologers. Is 47:13. Dn 4:7.

Charmers. Dt 18:11.

Consulters of familiar spirits. Dt 18:11.

Diviners. Dt 18:14.

Enchanters. Dt 18:10. Jr 27:9.

False prophets. Jr 14:14. Ezk 13:3, 6.

Magicians. Gn 41:8. Dn 4:7.

Necromancers. Dt 18:11.

Soothsayers. Is 2:6. Dn 2:27.

Sorcerers. Jr 27:9. Ac 13:6, 8.

Witches. Ex 22:18. Dt 18:10.

Wizards. Dt 18:11. 1 S 28:3.

A system of fraud. Ezk 13:6–7. Jr 29:8.

THOSE WHO PRACTICED

Consulted in difficulties. Dn 2:2; 4:6–7.

Regarded as wise men. Dn 2:12, 27.

Regarded with awe. Ac 8:9, 11.

Used mysterious words and gestures. Is 8:19.

See also Magic.

DIVISIONS

ARE CONTRARY TO THE

Desire of Christ. Jn 17:21–23.

Purpose of Christ. Jn 10:16.

Spirit of the primitive church. 1 Co 11:16.

Unity of Christ. 1 Co 1:13; 12:12.

Are proof of a carnal spirit. 1 Co 3:3.

Avoid those who cause. Ro 16:17.

Condemned in the church. 1 Co 1:11–13; 11:18.

Evil of, illustrated. Mt 12:25.

Forbidden in the church. 1 Co 1:10.

Unbecoming in the church. 1 Co 12:24–25.

DIVORCE

Forbidden by Christ except for adultery. Mt 5:32; 19:9.

Forced on those who had idolatrous wives. Ezr 10:2–17.

Illustrative of God's casting off of the Jewish church. Is 50:1. Jr 3:8.

The Jews condemned for love of. Ml 2:14–16.

Law of marriage against. Gn 2:24. Mt 19:6.

Not allowed to those who falsely accused their wives. Dt 22:18–19.

Of captives, regulated by law. Dt 21:13–14.

Of servants, regulated by law. Ex 21:7, 11.

Often sought by the Jews. Mi 2:9. Ml 2:14.

PERMITTED

By Mosaic law. Dt 24:1.

On account of hardness of heart. Mt 19:8.

Priests not to marry women after. Lv 21:14.

Prohibition of, offended the Jews. Mt 19:10.

Sought on slight grounds. Mt 5:31; 19:3.

WOMEN

Afflicted by. Is 54:4, 6.

Could obtain. Pr 2:17, with Mk 10:12.

Could remarry. Dt 24:2.

Remarried, could not return to first husband. Dt 24:3–4. Jr 3:1.

Responsible for vows after. Nu 30:9.

DOCTRINES, FALSE

Curse on those who teach. Gl 1:8–9.

Destructive to faith. 2 Tm 2:18.

Hateful to God. Rv 2:14–15.

Punishment of those who teach. Mi 3:6–7. 2 P 2:1, 3.

SHOULD BE AVOIDED BY

All men. Jr 23:16; 29:3.

Ministers. 1 Tm 1:4; 6:20.

Saints. Ep 4:14. Cl 2:8.

TEACHERS OF

Attract many. 2 P 2:2.

Bring reproach on religion. 2 P 2:2.

Deceive many. Mt 24:5.

Not to be countenanced. 2 Jn 10.

Pervert the gospel of Christ. Gl 1:6–7.

Shall abound in the latter days. 1 Tm 4:1.

Shall be exposed. 2 Tm 3:9.

Should be avoided. Ro 16:17–18.

Speak perverse things. Ac 20:30.

TEACHERS OF, DESCRIBED AS

Corrupt and reprobate. 2 Tm 3:8.

Covetous. Ti 1:11. 2 P 2:3.

Cruel. Ac 20:29.

Deceitful. 2 Co 11:13.

Proud and ignorant. 1 Tm 6:3–4.

Ungodly. Jde 1:4, 8.

Try, by scripture. Is 8:20. 1 Jn 4:1.

Unprofitable and vain. Ti 3:9. He 13:9.

The wicked given up to believe. 2 Th 2:11.

The wicked love. 2 Tm 4:3–4.

DOCTRINES OF THE GOSPEL

Are from God. Jn 7:16. Ac 13:12.

Are godly. 1 Tm 6:3. Ti 1:1.

Are taught by scripture. 2 Tm 3:16.

Bring no reproach on. 1 Tm 6:1. Ti 2:5.

A faithful walk adorns. Ti 2:10.

Immorality condemned by. 1 Tm 1:9–11.

Lead to fellowship with the Father and with the Son. 1 Jn 1:3. 2 Jn 9.
Lead to holiness. Ro 6:17–22. Ti 2:12.

MINISTERS SHOULD
Attend to. 1 Tm 4:13, 16.
Be nourished up in. 1 Tm 4:6.
Continue in. 1 Tm 4:16.
Hold in sincerity. 2 Co 2:17. Ti 2:7.
Hold steadfastly. 2 Tm 1:13. Ti 1:9.
Speak things which become. Ti 2:1.
Not endured by the wicked. 2 Tm 4:3.
Obedience of saints leads to surer knowledge of. Jn 7:17.
Saints abide in. Ac 2:42.
Saints obey, from the heart. Ro 6:17.

THOSE WHO OPPOSE ARE
Doting about questions, etc. 1 Tm 6:4.
Ignorant. 1 Tm 6:4.
Not to be received. 2 Jn 10.
Proud. 1 Tm 6:3–4.
To be avoided. Ro 16:17.

DOG

DESCRIBED AS
Carnivorous. 1 K 14:11. 2 K 9:35–36.
Dangerous and destructive. Ps 22:16.
Fond of blood. 1 K 21:19; 22:38.
Impatient of injury. Pr 26:17.
Unclean. Lk 16:21. 2 P 2:22.
Despised by the Jews. 2 S 3:8.

ILLUSTRATIVE OF
Apostates. 2 P 2:22.
Covetous ministers. Is 56:11.
False teachers. Php 3:2.
Fools. Pr 26:11.
Gentiles. Mt 15:22, 26.
The mean (when dead). 1 S 24:14. 2 S 9:8.
Obstinate sinners. Mt 7:6. Rv 22:15.
Persecutors. Ps 22:16, 20.
Unfaithful ministers (when dumb). Is 56:10.
Infested cities by night. Ps 59:14–15.
Manner of drinking alluded to. Jg 7:5.
Nothing holy to be given to. Mt 7:6; 15:26.
Price of, not to be consecrated. Dt 23:18.
Sacrificing of, an abomination. Is 66:3.
Things torn by beasts given to. Ex 22:31.

WHEN DOMESTICATED
Employed in watching flocks. Jb 30:1.
Fed with the crumbs, etc. Mt 15:27.

DOVE

CHARACTERIZED BY
Comeliness of countenance. S S 2:14.

Richness of plumage. Ps 68:13.
Simplicity. Mt 10:16.
Softness of eyes. S S 1:15.
Sweetness of voice. S S 2:14.
Clean and used as food. Dt 14:11.
Dwells in rocks. S S 2:14. Jr 48:28.
Frequents streams and rivers. S S 5:12.
The harbinger of spring. S S 2:12.

ILLUSTRATIVE OF
The church. S S 2:14; 5:2.
Converts to the church. Is 60:8.
The Holy Ghost. Mt 3:16. Jn 1:32.
The meekness of Christ. S S 5:12.
Mourners. Is 38:14; 59:11.
The return of Israel from captivity (in its flight). Ho 11:11.
Impiously sold in the court of the temple. Mt 21:12. Jn 2:16.
Mournful tabering of, alluded to. Na 2:7.
Offered in sacrifice. Gn 15:9. Lv 1:14.
Sent from the ark by Noah. Gn 8:8, 10, 12.
Why considered the emblem of peace. Gn 8:11.

DRAGON

DESCRIBED AS
Of a mournful voice. Mi 1:8.
Of solitary habits. Jb 30:29.
Often of a red color. Rv 12:3.
Poisonous. Dt 32:33.
Powerful. Rv 12:4.
Snuffing up the air. Jr. 14:6.
Swallowing its prey. Jr 51:34.
Wailing. Mi 1:8.

FOUND IN
Deserted cities. Is 13:22. Jr 9:11.
Dry places. Is 34:13; 43:20.
Rivers (a species). Ps 74:13. Is 27:1.
The wilderness. Ml 1:3.

ILLUSTRATIVE OF
Cruel and persecuting kings. Is 27:1; 51:9. Ezk 29:3.
The devil. Rv 13:2; 20:2, 7.
Enemies of the church. Ps 91:13.
Wicked men. Ps 44:19.
Wine (poison of). Dt 32:33.

DREAMS

THE ANCIENTS
Anxious to have explained. Gn 40:8. Dn 2:3.
Consulted magicians on. Gn 41:8. Dn 2:2–4.
Often perplexed by. Gn 40:6; 41:8. Jb 7:14. Dn 2:1; 4:5.

Put great faith in.   Jg 7:15.

Excess of business frequently leads to.   Ec 5:3.

FALSE PROPHETS

Condemned for pretending to.   Jr 23:32.
Not to be regarded in.   Dt 13:1–3. Jr 27:9.
Pretended to.   Jr 23:25–28; 29:8.

God the only interpreter of.   Gn 40:8; 41:16. Dn 2:27–30; 7:16.

God's will often revealed in.   Nu 12:6. Jb 33:15.

ILLUSTRATIVE OF

Enemies of the church.   Is 29:7–8.
Impure imaginations.   Jde 1:8.
Prosperity of sinners.   Jb 20:5–8. Ps 73:19–20.

MENTIONED IN SCRIPTURE, OF

Abimelech.   Gn 20:3–7.
Daniel.   Dn 7.
Jacob.   Gn 28:12; 31:10.
Joseph.   Gn 37:5–9. Mt 1:20–21; 2:13, 19–20.
Laban.   Gn 31:24.
Midianite.   Jg 7:13–15.
Nebuchadnezzar.   Dn 2:1, 31; 4:5, 8.
Pharaoh.   Gn 41:1–7.
Pharaoh's butler and baker.   Gn 40:5–19.
Pilate's wife.   Mt 27:19.
Solomon.   1 K 3:5–15.
Wise men.   Mt 2:11–12.

Often but imaginary.   Jb 20:8. Is 29:8.
Vanity of trusting to natural.   Ec 5:7.
Visions in sleep.   Jb 33:15. Dn 2:28.

DRINK OFFERING

Antiquity of.   Gn 35:14.

For public sacrifices, provided by the state.   Ezr 7:17. Ezk 45:17.

Idolaters often used blood for.   Ps 16:4.

IDOLATROUS JEWS

Offered to the queen of heaven.   Jr 7:18; 44:17–19.
Reproved for offering to idols.   Is 57:5–6; 65:11. Jr 19:13. Ezk 20:28.

ILLUSTRATIVE OF

Devotedness of ministers.   Php 2:17.
Offering of Christ.   Is 53:12.

Pouring out of the Spirit.   Jl 2:28.

Not poured on the altar of incense.   Ex 30:9.

Omission of, caused by bad vintage.   Jl 1:9, 13.

Quantity appointed to be used for each kind of sacrifice.   Nu 15:3–10.

Sacrifices accompanied by.   Ex 29:40. Lv 23:13.

Vanity of offering, to idols.   Dt 32:37–38.

DRUNKENNESS

Avoid those given to.   Pr 23:20. 1 Co 5:11.

Caution against.   Lk 21:34.

Debases.   Is 28:8.

DENUNCIATIONS AGAINST

Those given to.   Is 5:11, 12; 28:1–3.
Those who encourage.   Hk 2:15.

Excludes from heaven.   1 Co 6:10. Gl 5:21.

False teachers often addicted to.   Is 56:12.

Folly of yielding to.   Pr 20:1.

Forbidden.   Ep 5:18.

Inflames.   Is 5:11.

LEADS TO

Contempt of God's works.   Is 5:12.
Error.   Is 28:7.
Poverty.   Pr 21:17; 23:21.
Rioting and wantonness.   Ro 13:13.
Scorning.   Ho 7:5.
Strife.   Pr 23:29–30.
Woe and sorrow.   Pr 29–30.

Overcharges the heart.   Lk 21:34.

Punishment of.   Dt 21:20–21. Jl 1:5–6. Am 6:6–7. Mt 24:49–51.

Takes away the heart.   Ho 4:11.

The wicked addicted to.   Dn 5:1–4.

A work of the flesh.   Gl 5:21.

DUTY

And stagnation.   Dt 1:6.

Before God.   Dt 6:18. 1 Ch 16:29. Ec 12:13.

Summarized in love.   Ro 13:9.

Toward children.   Ep 6:4.

Toward Christian brethren.   Ro 15:1. 1 Co 8:11.

Toward government.   Lk 20:25. 1 P 2:17.

Toward men.   Pr 3:27. Ro 13:7. 1 Jn 4:11.

E 🎋

EAGLE
A bird of prey. Jb 9:26. Mt 24:28.
Called the eagle of the heavens. Lm 4:19.
Delights in the lofty cedars. Ezk 17:3–4.

DESCRIBED AS
Long-sighted. Jb 39:29.
Soaring to heaven. Pr 23:5.
Swift. 2 S 1:23.
Different kinds of. Lv 11:13, 18. Ezk 17:3.
Dwells in the high rocks. Jb 39:27–28.
Feeds her young with blood. Jb 39:29–30.
Greatness of its wings alluded to. Ezk 17:3, 7.

ILLUSTRATIVE OF
Calamities, in its increased baldness in the molting season. Mi 1:16.
The fancied but fatal security of the wicked, in the height and security of its dwelling. Jr 49:16. Ob 1:4.
God's care of his church, in its mode of teaching the young to fly. Ex 19:4. Dt 32:11.
Great and powerful kings. Ezk 17:3. Ho 8:1.
The melting away of riches, in its swiftness. Pr 23:5.
Protection afforded to the church, by its wings. Rv 12:14.
Renewal of saints, in its renewed strength and beauty. Ps 103:5.
The saint's rapid progress toward heaven, in its upward flight. Is 40:31.
The swiftness of hostile armies, in its swiftness. Dt 28:49. Jr 4:13; 48:40. Lm 4:19.
The swiftness of man's days, in hasting to the prey. Jb 9:26.
Wisdom and zeal of God's ministers. Ezk 1:10. Rv 4:7.
Peculiarity of its flight alluded to. Pr 30:19.
Strength of its feathers alluded to. Dn 4:33.
Unclean. Lv 11:13. Dt 14:12.
Was the standard of the Roman armies. Mt 24:15, with 28.

EAR
BLOOD PUT ON THE RIGHT EAR OF
The healed leper in cleansing him. Lv 14:14.
Priests at consecration. Ex 29:20. Lv 8:23.
Capable of trying and distinguishing words. Jb 12:11.
Christ opens. Is 35:5; 43:8, 10.
GOD
Judicially closes. Is 6:10, with Mt 13:15.
Made. Pr 20:12.
Opens. Jb 33:16; 36:10.
Planted. Ps 94:9.
Instruction received through. Is 30:21.
Not satisfied with earthly things. Ec 1:8.
Not to be stopped at cry of the poor. Pr 21:13.
Of servants who refused to leave their masters, bored to the door. Ex 21:6. Dt 15:17.
Often adorned with rings. Ezk 16:12. Ho 2:13.
OF THE WICKED
Itching. 2 Tm 4:3.
Not inclined to hear God. Jr 7:24; 35:15.
Stopped against God's word. Ps 58:4. Zc 7:11.
Turned away from God's law. Pr 28:9.
Uncircumcised. Jr 6:10. Ac 7:51.
Organ of hearing. Jb 13:1; 29:11.
SHOULD
Be bowed down to instructions. Pr 5:1.
Be given to the law of God. Is 1:10.
Be inclined to wisdom. Pr 2:2.
Hear and obey reproof. Pr 15:31; 25:12.
Receive the word of God. Jr 9:20.
Seek knowledge. Pr 18:15.
That hears and receives the word of God, blessed. Ex 15:26. Mt 13:16.

EARNESTNESS
In all things. Cl 3:23.
In awaiting redemption. Ro 8:19. 2 Co 5:2.
In obedience. Jsh 22:5. Ep 6:6.
In prayer. 2 Ch 6:12–42. Ac 12:5.
In seeking God. Ac 16:30–34.

In spiritual perseverance. He 2:1; 12:15.
In the work of the church. 2 Co 8:16–22.

EARTH
Corrupted by sin. Gn 6:11–12. Is 24:5.
Created to be inhabited. Is 45:18.
DESCRIBED AS
    Burning at God's presence. Na 1:5.
    Full of God's glory. Nu 14:21. Is 6:3.
    Full of God's goodness. Ps 33:5.
    Full of God's mercy. Ps 119:64.
    Full of God's riches. Ps 104:24.
    God's footstool. Is 66:1. Mt 5:35.
    Melting at God's voice. Ps 46:6.
    Shining with God's glory. Ezk 43:2.
    Trembling before God. Ps 68:8. Jr 10:10.
Diversified by hills and mountains. Hk 3:6.
The dry land as divided from waters. Gn
    1:10.
First division of. Gn 10:25.
Full of minerals. Dt 8:9. Jb 28:1–5, 15–19.
GOD
    Created. Gn 1:1. Ne 9:6.
    Enlightens. Gn 1:14–16. Jr 33:25.
    Establishes. Ps 78:69; 119:90.
    Formed. Ps 90:2.
    Governs supremely. Jb 34:13. Ps 135:6.
    Inspects. Zc 4:10.
    Laid the foundation of. Jb 38:4. Ps
        102:25.
    Makes fruitful. Gn 1:11; 27:28.
    Reigns in. Ex 8:22. Ps 97:1.
    Shall be exalted in. Ps 46:10.
    Spread abroad. Is 42:5; 44:24.
    Supports. Ps 75:3.
    Suspended in space. Jb 26:7.
    Waters. Pss 65:9; 147:8.
Ideas of the ancients respecting the form of.
    Jb 11:9; 38:18. Pr 25:3.
Is the Lord's. Ex 9:29. 1 Co 10:26.
Made barren by sin. Dt 28:23. Ps 107:34.
Made to mourn and languish by sin. Is 24:4.
    Jr 4:28; 12:4. Ho 4:3.
MAN
    Brought a curse on. Gn 3:17.
    By nature is of. 1 Co 15:47–48.
    By nature minds the things of. Php 3:19.
    Formed out of. Gn 2:7. Ps 103:14.
    Given dominion over. Gn 1:26. Ps
        115:16.
    Shall return to. Gn 3:19. Ps 146:4.
Not to be again inundated. Gn 9:11. 2 P
    3:6–7.
Once inundated. Gn 7:17–24.

Saints shall inherit. Ps 25:13. Mt 5:5.
Satan goes to and fro in. Jb 1:7. 1 P 5:8.
Shall be filled with the knowledge of God. Is
    11:9. Hk 2:14.
Subject to God's judgments. Ps 46:8. Is
    11:4.
To be dissolved by fire. 2 P 3:7, 10, 12.
To be renewed. Is 65:17. 2 P 3:13.
The world in general. Gn 1:2.

EARTHQUAKES
ARE VISIBLE TOKENS OF
    God's anger. Pss 18:7; 60:2. Is 13:13.
    God's power. Jb 9:6. He 12:26.
    God's presence. Pss 68:7–8; 114:7.
At Christ's second coming, predicted. Zc
    14:4.
Before destruction of Jerusalem, predicted.
    Mt 24:7. Lk 21:11.
FREQUENTLY ACCOMPANIED BY
    Convulsion and receding of the sea. 2 S
        22:8, 16. Pss 18:7, 15; 46:3.
    Opening of the earth. Nu 16:31–32.
    Overturning of mountains. Ps 46:2. Zc
        14:4.
    Rending of rocks. Mt 27:51.
    Volcanic eruptions. Ps 104:32. Na 1:5.
ILLUSTRATIVE OF
    The judgments of God. Is 24:19–20; 29:6.
        Jr 4:24. Rv 8:5.
    The overthrow of kingdoms. Hg 2:6, 22.
        Rv 6:12–13; 16:18–19.
Islands and mountainous districts liable to.
    Ps 114:4, 6. Rv 6:14; 16:18, 20.
Men always terrified by. Nu 16:34. Zc 14:5.
    Mt 27:54. Rv 11:13.
MENTIONED IN SCRIPTURE
    At Mount Sinai. Ex 19:18.
    At our Lord's death. Mt 27:51.
    At our Lord's resurrection. Mt 28:2.
    At Philippi. Ac 16:26.
    In strongholds of Philistines. 1 S 14:15.
    In Uzziah's reign. Am 1:1. Zc 14:5.
    In the wilderness. Nu 16:31–32.
    When Elijah fled from Jezebel. 1 K 19:11.

EDIFICATION
All to be done to. 2 Co 12:19. Ep 4:29.
Described. Ep 4:12–16.
Exhortation to. Jde 1:20–21.
Foolish questions opposed to. 1 Tm 1:4.
Gospel as the instrument of. Ac 20:32.
IS THE OBJECT OF
    Ministerial authority. 2 Co 10:8; 13:10.

Ministerial gifts. 1 Co 14:3–5, 12.
The church's union in Christ. Ep 4:16.
The ministerial office. Ep 4:11–12.
Love leads to. 1 Co 8:1.
Mutual, commanded. Ro 14:19. 1 Th 5:11.
Peace of the church favors. Ac 9:31.
Use self-denial to promote, in others. 1 Co 10:23, 33.

EDUCATION
From life. Is 28:10. Pr 6:6.
From personal experience. Ps 78:1–8.
In the pastoral ministry. 1 Tm 4:11.
In the prophetic ministry. Is 28:10.
Of children in God's Word. Dt 6:7. Ep 6:4. 2 Tm 3:15–16.

EGYPT
ARMIES OF
Assistance of, sought by Judah against the Chaldees. Ezk 17:15, with Jr 37:5, 7.
Beseiged and plundered Jerusalem in Rehoboam's time. 1 K 14:25–26.
Captured and burned Gezer. 1 K 9:16.
Deposed Jehoahaz and made Judea tributary. 2 K 23:31–35.
Described. Ex 14:7–9.
Destroyed in the Red Sea. Ex 14:23–28.
Invaded Assyria and killed Josiah who assisted it. 2 K 23:29.
AS A POWER WAS
Ambitious of conquests. Jr 46:8.
Mighty. Is 30:2–3.
Pompous. Ezk 32:12.
Proud and arrogant. Ezk 29:3; 30:6.
Treacherous. Is 36:6. Ezk 29:6–7.
Boundaries of. Ezk 29:10.
CALLED
House of bondmen. Ex 13:3, 14. Dt 7:8.
Land of Ham. Pss 105:23; 106:22.
Rahab. Pss 87:4; 89:10.
Sihor. Is 23:3.
The South. Jr 13:19. Dn 11:14, 25.
CELEBRATED FOR
Commerce. Gn 41:57. Ezk 27:7.
Fertility. Gn 13:10; 45:18.
Fine horses. 1 K 10:28–29.
Fine linen, etc. Pr 7:16. Is 19:9.
Literature. 1 K 4:30. Ac 7:22.
Wealth. He 11:26.
Diet used in. Nu 11:5.
Dry climate of. Dt 11:10–11.
Had princes and counselors. Gn 12:15. Is 19:11.

HISTORY OF ISRAEL IN
Their sojourn there, foretold. Gn 15:13.
Joseph sold into. Gn 37:28; 39:1.
Potiphar blessed for Joseph's sake. Gn 39:2–6.
Joseph unjustly cast into prison. Gn 39:7–20.
Joseph interprets the chief baker's and the chief butler's dreams. Gn 40:5–19.
Joseph interprets Pharaoh's dreams. Gn 41:14–32.
Joseph counsels Pharaoh. Gn 41:33–36.
Joseph made governor. Gn 41:41–44.
Joseph successfully provides against the years of famine. Gn 41:46–56.
Joseph's ten brethren arrive. Gn 42:1–6.
Joseph recognizes his brethren. Gn 42:7–8.
Benjamin brought. Gn 43:15.
Joseph makes himself known to his brethren. Gn 45:1–8.
Joseph sends for his father. Gn 45:9–11.
Pharaoh invites Jacob into. Gn 45:16–20.
Jacob's journey. Gn 46:5–7.
Jacob, etc., presented to Pharaoh. Gn 47:1–10.
Israel placed in the land of Goshen. Gn 46:34; 47:11, 27.
Joseph enriches the king. Gn 47:13–26.
Jacob's death and burial. Gn 49:33; 50:1–13.
Israel increase and are oppressed. Ex 1:1–14.
Male children destroyed. Ex 1:15–22.
Moses born and hid for three months. Ex 2:2.
Moses exposed on the Nile. Ex 2:3–4.
Moses adopted and brought up by Pharaoh's daughter. Ex 2:5–10.
Moses slays an Egyptian. Ex 2:11–12.
Moses flees to Midian. Ex 2:15.
Moses sent to Pharaoh. Ex 3:2–10.
Pharaoh increases their affliction. Ex 5.
Moses proves his divine mission by miracles. Ex 4:29–31; 7:10.
Egypt is plagued for Pharaoh's obstinacy. Ex 7:14—10.
The passover instituted. Ex 12:1–28.
Destruction of the first-born. Ex 12:29–30.
Israel despoils the Egyptians. Ex 12:35–36.
Israel driven out of. Ex 12:31–33.
Date of the exodus. Ex 12:41. He 11:27.

Pharaoh pursues Israel and is miraculously destroyed. Ex 14:5–25.

Idolatry of, followed by Israel. Ex 32:4, with Ezk 20:8, 19.

INHABITANTS OF

Abhorred shepherds. Gn 46:34.

Abhorred the sacrifice of oxen, etc. Ex 8:26.

Hospitable. Gn 47:5–6. 1 K 11:18.

Might be received into the congregation in third generation. Dt 23:8.

Not to be abhorred by Israel. Dt 23:7.

Often intermarried with strangers. Gn 21:21. 1 K 3:1; 11:19. 1 Ch 2:34–35.

Superstitious. Is 19:3.

Inundations of, alluded to. Am 8:8.

Magic practiced in. Ex 7:11–12, 22; 8:7.

Mode of embalming in. Gn 50:3.

Mode of entertaining in. Gn 43:32–34.

Often a refuge to strangers. Gn 12:10; 47:4.

Peopled by Mizraim's posterity. Gn 10:6, 13–14.

PROPHECIES RESPECTING

Allies to share its misfortunes. Ezk 30:4, 6.

Armies destroyed by Babylon. Jr 46:2–12.

Captivity of its people. Is 20:4. Jr 46:19, 24, 26. Ezk 30:4.

Christ to be called out of. Ho 11:1. Mt 2:15.

Civil war and domestic strife. Is 19:2.

Conversion of. Is 19:18–20.

Destruction of its cities. Ezk 30:14–18.

Destruction of its idols. Jr 43:12–13; 46:25. Ezk 30:13.

Destruction of its power. Ezk 30:24–25.

Dismay of its inhabitants. Is 19:1, 16–17.

Ever to be a base kingdom. Ezk 29:15.

Failure of internal resources. Is 19:5–10.

Infatuation of its princes. Is 19:3, 11–14.

Invasion by Babylon. Jr 46:2–12.

The Jews who practiced its idolatry to share its punishments. Jr 44:7–28.

Prophetic illustration of its destruction. Jr 43:9–10. Ezk 30:21–22; 32:4–6.

Spoil of, a reward to Babylon for services against Tyre. Ezk 29:18–20.

Terror occasioned by its fall. Ezk 32:9–10.

To be numbered and blessed along with Israel. Is 19:23–25.

Utter desolation of, for forty years. Ezk 29:8–12; 30:12; 32:15.

Religion of, idolatrous. Ex 12:12. Nu 33:4. Is 19:1. Ezk 29:7.

Ruled by kings who assumed the name of Pharaoh. Gn 12:14–15; 40:1–2. Ex 1:8, 22.

Sometimes visited by famine. Gn 41:30.

Subject to plague, etc. Dt 7:15; 28:27, 60.

Under a governor. Gn 41:41–44.

Watered by the Nile. Gn 41:1–3. Ex 1:22.

ELECTION

ENSURES TO SAINTS

Acceptance with God. Ro 11:7.

Belief in Christ. Ac 13:48.

Blessedness. Pss 33:12; 65:4.

Divine teaching. Jn 17:6.

Effectual calling. Ro 8:30.

The inheritance. Is 65:9. 1 P 1:4–5.

Protection. Mk 13:20.

Vindication of their wrongs. Lk 18:7.

Working of all things for good. Ro 8:28.

Of Christ, as Messiah. Is 42:1. 1 P 2:6.

Of churches. 1 P 5:13.

Of good angels. 1 Tm 5:21.

Of Israel. Dt 7:6. Is 45:4.

Of ministers. Lk 6:13. Ac 9:15.

OF SAINTS, Is

According to the foreknowledge of God. Ro 8:29. 1 P 1:2.

According to the purpose of God. Ro 9:11. Ep 1:11.

By Christ. Jn 13:18; 15:16.

Eternal. Ep 1:4.

For the glory of God. Ep 1:6.

In Christ. Ep 1:4.

Irrespective of merit. Ro 9:11.

Of God. 1 Th 1:4. Ti 1:1.

Of grace. Ro 11:5.

Personal. Mt 20:16, with Jn 6:44. Ac 22:14. 2 Jn 1:13.

Recorded in heaven. Lk 10:20.

Sovereign. Ro 9:15–16. 1 Co 1:27. Ep 1:11.

Through faith. 2 Th 2:13.

Through sanctification of the Spirit. 1 P 1:2.

To adoption. Ep 1:5.

To conformity with Christ. Ro 8:29.

To eternal glory. Ro 9:23.

To good works. Ep 2:10.

To salvation 2 Th 2:13.

To spiritual warfare. 2 Tm 2:4.

Saints may have assurance of. 1 Th 1:4.

Should be evidenced by diligence. 2 P 1:10.

Should lead to cultivation of graces. Cl 3:12.

EMBALMING
An attempt to defeat God's purpose. Gn 3:19.
How performed by the Jews. 2 Ch 16:14. Lk 23:56, with Jn 19:40.
Learned by the Jews in Egypt. Gn 50:2, 26.
Not always practiced by the Jews. Jn 11:39.
Time required for. Gn 50:3.
Unknown to early patriarchs. Gn 23:4.

EMPLOYMENT
Duties of employers. Lv 19:13. Lk 10:17. Cl 4:1.
Duties of workers. Ex 20:9. Ep 6:5. 2 Th 3:12.
Payment of wages. Dt 24:15. Ml 3:5. Ja 5:4.
Spiritual work. Mi 3:11. Mt 9:37–38. Jn 10:12. 1 Co 3:10.
Value of. Gn 2:15. 2 Th 3:7–12.

ENCOURAGEMENT
Exhorted. 1 Th 5:14. He 3:13. Ac 27:22.
Needed by all. Ne 4:17–23. Dn 6:18–23.
Needed by prophets. 1 K 19:1–19.
Through the brethren. Ac 28:15.
Through Christ's presence. Mt 14:27.
Through God's care. Mt 10:30.
Through God's help. Is 41:13.
Through salvation. Is 43:1.

ENEMIES
Be affectionately concerned for. Ps 35:13.
Christ prayed for his. Lk 23:34.
Curse them not. Jb 31:30.
Desire not the death of. 1 K 3:11.
Friendship of, deceitful. 2 S 20:9–10. Pr 26:26; 27:6. Mt 26:48–49.
God defends against. Pss 59:9; 61:3.
God delivers from. 1 S 12:11. Ezr 8:31. Ps 18:48.
Goods of, to be taken care of. Ex 23:4–5.
Lives of, to be spared. 1 S 24:10. 2 S 16:10–11.
Made to be at peace with saints. Pr 16:7.
Of saints, God will destroy. Ps 60:12.
Praise God for deliverance from. Ps 136:24.
Pray for deliverance from. 1 S 12:10. Pss 17:9; 59:1; 64:1.
Rejoice not at the failings of. Pr 24:17.
Rejoice not at the misfortunes of. Jb 31:29.
SHOULD BE
Assisted. Pr 25:21, with Ro 12:20.
Loved. Mt 5:44.

Overcome by kindness. 1 S 26:21.
Prayed for. Ac 7:60.

ENDURANCE
Needed in spiritual life. Ro 2:5–7. Cl 1:23.
Of Christians encouraged. 2 Tm 2:3. Mt 10:22.
Of love. 1 Co 13:4–8.
Of the things of God. He 12:27. Ps 52:1.
Rewards of. 2 Tm 3:11. Ja 1:12.

ENJOYMENT
Abundant. 1 Tm 6:17
Blessings of. Ps 112:1.
Despite temptations or tests. Ja 1:2.
Despite trouble. 2 Co 7:4.
Of all things. 1 Tm 6:17.
Sacrifices of. Ps 27:6.
Satisfying. Is 55:1–2.
Way to. 1 P 3:10–11.

ENTERTAINMENT
Anxiety to have many guests at, alluded to. Lk 14:22–23.
Began with thanksgiving. 1 S 9:13. Mk 8:6.
A choice portion reserved in, for principal guests. Gn 43:43. 1 S 1:5; 9:23–24.
Concluded with a hymn. Mk 14:26.
Custom of presenting the sop at, to one of the guests, alluded to. Jn 13:26.
Forwardness to take chief seats at, condemned. Mt. 23:6. Lk 14:7–8.
Given by the guests in return. Jb 1:4. Lk 14:2.
GIVEN ON OCCASIONS OF
Birthdays. Mk 6:21.
Coronations. 1 K 1:9, 18–19. 1 Ch 12:39–40. Ho 7:5.
Festivals. 1 S 20:5, 24–26.
Harvest home. Ru 3:2–7. Is 9:3.
Marriage. Mt 22:2.
National deliverance. Es 8:17; 9:17–19.
Offering voluntary sacrifice. Gn 31:54. Dt 12:6–7. 1 S 1:4–5, 9
Ratifying covenants. Gn 26:30; 31:54.
Return of friends. 2 S 12:4. Lk 15:23, etc.
Sheep shearing. 1 S 25:2, 36. 2 S 13:23.
Taking leave of friends. 1 K 19:21.
Vintage. Jg 9:27.
Weaning children. Gn 21:8.
GUESTS AT
Arranged according to rank. Gn 43:33. 1 S 9:22. Lk 14:10.
Had their feet washed when they came a distance. Gn 18:4; 43:24. Lk 7:38, 44.

Often ate from the same dish. Mt 26:23.
Often had separate dishes. Gn 43:34. 1 S 1:4.
Saluted by the master. Lk 7:45.
Usually anointed. Ps 23:5. Lk 7:46.
INVITATIONS TO
Often addressed to many. Lk 14:16.
Often by the master in person. 2 S 13:24. Es 5:4. Zp 1:7. Lk 7:36.
Often only to relatives and friends. 1 K 1:9. Lk 14:12.
Repeated through servants when all things were ready. Pr 9:1–5. Lk 14:17.
Should be sent to the poor, etc. Dt 14:29, with Lk 14:13.
KINDS OF, MENTIONED IN SCRIPTURE
Banquet of wine. Ex 5:6.
Dinner. Gn 43:16. Mt 22:4. Lk 14:12.
Supper. Lk 14:12. Jn 12:2.
Men and women did not usually meet at. Es 1:8–9. Mk 6:21, with Mt 14:11.
Music and dancing often introduced at. Am 6:5. Mk 6:22. Lk 15:25.
None admitted to, after the master had risen and shut the door. Lk 13:24–25.
None asked to eat or drink more than he liked at. Es 1:8.
Offense given by refusing to go to. Lk 14:18, 24.
OFTEN GIVEN IN
The air, beside fountains. 1 K 1:9.
The court of the house. Es 1:5–6. Lk 7:36–37.
The house. Lk 5:29.
The upper room or guest chamber. Mk 14:14–15.
Often great. Gn 21:8. Dn 5:1. Lk 5:29.
Often scenes of great intemperance. 1 S 25:36. Dn 5:3–4. Ho 7:5.
Portions of, often sent to the absent. 2 S 11:8. Ne 8:10. Es 9:19.
Preparations made for. Gn 18:6–7. Pr 9:2. Mt 22:4. Lk 15:23.
Served often by hired servants. Mt 22:13. Jn 2:5.
Served often by members of the family. Gn 18:8. Lk 10:40. Jn 12:2.
Under the direction of a symposiarch or master of the feast. Jn 2:8–9.

ENTHUSIASM
Commanded. Ro 12:8. Cl 3:23.
For God. Nu 25:13. 2 K 10:16. Jn 2:17.

In everything. Cl 3:23.
In work. Ne 4:6. Ec 9:10.
Of spirit. Ro 12:11.
Unfounded. Ro 10:2. Php 3:6.

ENVY
Excited by good deeds of others. Ec 4:4.
Forbidden. Pr 3:31. Ro 13:13.
Hinders growth in grace. 1 P 2:1–2.
Hurtful to the envious. Jb 5:2. Pr 14:30.
Inconsistent with the gospel. Ja 3:14.
Leads to every evil work. Ja 3:16.
None can stand before. Pr 27:4.
Produced by foolish disputations. 1 Tm 6:4.
A proof of carnal mindedness. 1 Co 3:1, 3.
Prosperity of the wicked should not excite. Pss 37:1, 35; 73:3, 17–20.
Punishment of. Is 26:11.
THE WICKED
Are full of. Ro 1:29.
Live in. Ti 3:3.
A work of the flesh. Gl 5:21. Ja 4:5.

EPHOD
Emblem of the priestly office. Ho 3:4.
FOR THE HIGH PRIEST
Breastplate of judgment inseparably united to. Ex 28:25–28; 39:20–21.
Commanded to be made. Ex 28:4.
Fastened on with its own girdle. Lv 8:7.
Had a girdle of curious work. Ex 28:8.
Made of gold, blue, purple, scarlet, etc. Ex 28:6; 29:2–3.
Made of offerings of the people. Ex 25:4, 7.
Shoulders joined by onyx stones engraved with names of the twelve tribes of Israel. Ex 28:7, 9:12, 39:4, 6–7.
Worn or held by him when consulted. 1 S 23:6, 9–12; 30:7–8.
Worn over the robe. Ex 28:31. Lv 8:7.
Generally of linen. 1 S 2:18. 2 S 6:14.
Israel deprived of, for sin. Ho 3:4.
Used by idolatrous priests. Jg 8:27; 17:5; 18:14.
WORN BY
The high priest. 1 S 2:28; 14:3.
Ordinary priests. 1 S 22:18.
Persons engaged in the service of God. 1 S 2:18. 2 S 6:14.

EQUALITY
Among brethren. Gn 13:8. Mt 23:8.
In Christ. Gl 3:28.

In justice.   Pr 24:23.
In salvation.   Jn 3:16. Ro 5:18–21.
In sin and guilt.   Ro 3:10–19; 5:12–21.
Under God.   Pr 22:2.

EUPHRATES RIVER
Assyria bounded by.   2 K 23:29. Is 7:20.
Babylon situated on.   Jr 51:13, 36.
A branch of the river of Eden.   Gn 2:14.
CALLED
   The flood.   Jsh 24:2.
   The great river.   Gn 15:18. Dt 1:7.
   The river.   Ex 23:31. Ne 2:7. Ps 72:8.
Captivity of Judah represented by the marring
   of Jeremiah's girdle in.   Jr 13:3–9.
Egyptian army destroyed at.   Jr 46–2, 6, 10.
Extreme eastern boundary of the promised
   land.   Gn 15:18. Dt 1:7; 11:24.
Frequented by the captive Jews.   Ps 137:1.
Often overflowed its banks.   Is 8:7–8.
Prophecies respecting Babylon thrown into, as
   a sign.   Jr 51:63.
Shall be the scene of future judgments.   Rv
   16:12.
Waters of, considered wholesome.   Jr 2:18.

EVANGELISM
Beauty of.   Is 52:7.
Commanded.   Mt 28:19–20. Mk 16:5. 2
   Tm 4:5.
EXEMPLIFIED
   Paul.   Ro 1:16.
   Peter.   Ac 2:14–42.
   Philip.   Ac 8:5; 21:8.
   Timothy.   2 Tm 4:5.
Glory of.   Dn 12:3.
Wisdom of.   Pr 11:30.
Work of God.   Ep 4:11

EVENING
All defiled persons unclean until.   Lv
   11:24–28; 15:5–7; 17:15. Nu 19:19.
CALLED
   Cool of the day.   Gn 3:8.
   Even.   Gn 19:1. Dt 28:67.
   Eventide.   Jsh 8:29. Ac 4:3.
Custom of sitting at the gates in.   Gn 19:1.
The day originally began with.   Gn 1:5, etc.
Golden candlestick lighted in.   Ex 27:21,
   with 30:8.
Humiliation often continued until.   Jsh 7:6.
   Jg 20:23, 26; 21:2. Ezr 9:4–5.
Man ceases from labor in.   Ru 2:17. Ps
   104:23.

The outgoings of, praise God.   Ps 65:8.
Part of the daily sacrifice offered in.   Ex
   29:41. Ps 141:2. Dn 9:21.
Paschal lamb killed in.   Ex 12:6, 18.
A SEASON FOR
   Exercise.   2 S 11:2
   Meditation.   Gn 24:63.
   Prayer.   Ps 55:17. Mt 14:15, 23.
   Taking food.   Mk 14:17–18. Lk 24:29–
      30.
The sky red in, a token of fair weather.   Mt
   16:2.
Stretches out its shadows.   Jr 6:4.
Wild beasts to come forth in.   Ps 59:6, 14. Jr
   5:6.

EXAMINATION
Of the heart.   Ps 139:23–24.
Of one's faith and life.   1 Co 11:28.
Of the scriptures.   Ac 17:11.
Wrong standard of.   2 Co 10:12.

EXAMPLE OF CHRIST
Conformity to, progressive.   2 Co 3:18.
CONFORMITY TO, REQUIRED IN
   Being guileless.   1 P 2:21–22.
   Being not of the world.   Jn 17:16.
   Benevolence.   Ac 20:35. 2 Co 8:7, 9.
   Forgiving injuries.   Cl 3:13.
   Holiness.   1 P 1:15–16, with Ro 1:6.
   Humility.   Lk 22:27. Php 2:5, 7.
   Love.   Jn 13:34. Ep 5:2. 1 Jn 3:16.
   Meekness.   Mt 11:29.
   Ministering to others.   Mt. 20:28. Jn
      13:14–15.
   Obedience.   Jn 15:10.
   Overcoming the world.   Jn 16:33, with 1
      Jn 5:4.
   Purity.   1 Jn 3:3.
   Righteousness.   1 Jn 2:6.
   Self-denial.   Mt 16:24. Ro 15:3.
   Suffering for righteousness.   He 12:3–4.
   Suffering wrongly.   1 P 2:21–22.
Is perfect.   He 7:26.
Saints predestinated to follow.   Ro 8:29.

EXPERIENCE, SPIRITUAL
Basis of confidence.   Jn 4:42. 2 P 1:16. 1 Jn
   1:1.
Basis of sharing.   2 Co 1:4.
Basis of witness.   Mk 5:19.
Educational.   Gn 30:27.
Slow growth of.   Mk 4:28.

EYE

ACTIONS OF, MENTIONED IN SCRIPTURE
Directing. Nu 10:31. Ps 32:8.
Seeing. Jb 7:8; 28:10.
Weeping. Jb 16:20. Ps 88:9. Lm 1:16.
Winking. Pr 10:10.
Consumed by grief. Ps 6:7; 31:9.
Consumed by sickness. Lv 26:16.
Frequently fair. 1 S 16:12.

GOD
Enlightens. Ezr 9:8. Ps 13:3.
Formed. Ps 94:9.
Made. Pr 20:12.
Opens. 2 K 6:17. Ps 146:8.
Grows dim by age. Gn 27:1. 1 S 3:2.
Grows dim by sorrow. Jb 17:7.
A guard to be set on. Jb 31:1. Pr 23:31.

ILLUSTRATIVE OF
Healing by the Spirit (when anointed with salve). Rv 3:18.
The mind. Mt 6:22–23.
Spiritual illumination (when open). Ps 119:18, 37.
Jewish women often painted. 2 K 9:30. Jr 4:30. Ezk 23:40.

THE JEWS
Cast on the ground, in humiliation. Lk 18:13.
Not to make baldness between Dt 14:1.
Raised up, in prayer. Pss 122:1; 123:1.
Wore their phylacteries between. Ex 13:16, with Mt 23:5.
Light of, rejoices the heart. Pr 15:30.
The light of the body. Mt 6:22. Lk 11:34.
Made red by wine. Gn 49:12. Pr 23:29.
No evil thing to be set before. Ps 101:3.
Not satisfied with riches. Ec 4:8.
Not satisfied with seeing. Pr 27:20. Ec 1:8.
Often put out as a punishment. Jg 16:21. 1 S 11:2. 2 K 25:7.

PARTS OF, MENTIONED IN SCRIPTURE
Apple or ball. Dt 32:10.
Lid. Jb 16:16.
Brow. Lv 14:9.
Punishment for injuring. Ex 21:24, 26. Lv 24:20. Mt. 5:38.
Sometimes blemished. Lv 21:20.
Sometimes tender. Gn 29:17.

F

FAIRNESS
Demanded by John. Lk 3:12–13,
Exemplified in God. 2 Ch 19:7. Ezk 18:29. Rv 15:3.
Expected of Christians. Lk 10:7, 1 Tm 5:21. Ja 2:4.
Required by God. Dt 1:17. Pr 11:1.
Through faith. He 10:38.
Through wisdom. Pr 8:15,

FAITH
All difficulties overcome by. Mt 17:20; 21:21. Mk 9:23.
All things should be done in. Ro 14:22.
By It, Saints
  Are supported. Ps 27:13. 1 Tm 4:10,
  Live. Gl 2:20.
  Obtain a good report. He 11:2.
  Overcome the devil. Ep 6:16.
  Overcome the world. 1 Jn 5:4–5.
  Resist the devil. 1 P 5:9.
  Stand. Ro 11:20. 2 Co 1:24.
  Walk. Ro 4:12. 2 Co 5:7.
Christ the author and finisher of. He 12:2,
Christ dwells in the heart by. Ep 3:17.
Christ precious to those having. 1 P 2:7.
Commanded. Mk 11:22. 1 Jn 3:23.
Essential to the profitable reception of the gospel. He 4:2.
Evidence of the new birth. 1 Jn 5:1.
Evidence of things not seen. He 11:1.
Examine whether you be in. 2 Co 13:5,
Excludes boasting. Ro 3:27.
Excludes self-justification. Ro 10:3–4.
A gift of the Holy Ghost. 1 Co 12:9.
The gospel effectual in those who have. 1 Th 2:13.
Impossible to please God without. He 11:6.
In Christ, Is
  Accompanied by repentance. Mk 1:15. Lk 24:47.
  Followed by conversion. Ac 11:21.
  Fruitful. 1 Th 1:3.
  The gift of God. Ro 12:3. Ep 2:8; 6:23. Php 1:29.
  Most holy. Jde 1:20,

Precious. 2 P 1:1,
  The work of God. Ac 11:21. 1 Co 2:5.
Its Protection Illustrative of a
  Breastplate. 1 Th 5:8.
  Shield. Ep 6:16.
Justification is by, to be of grace. Ro 4:16,
Necessary in prayer. Mt 21:22. Ja 1:6.
Necessary in the Christian warfare. 1 Tm 1:18–19; 6:12.
Objects of
  Christ. Jn 6:29. Ac 20:21.
  God. Jn 14:1.
  The Gospel. Mk 1:15.
  Promises of God. Ro 4:21. He 11:13.
  Writings of Moses. Jn 5:46. Ac 24:14.
  Writings of the prophets. 2 Ch 20:20. Ac 26:27.
Often tried by affliction. 1 P 1:6–7.
Preaching designed to produce. Jn 17:20. Ac 8:12. Ro 10:14–15, 17. 1 Co 3:5.
Produces
  Boldness in preaching. Ps 116:10, with 2 Co 4:13.
  Confidence. Is 28:16, with 1 P 2:6.
  Hope. Ro 5:2.
  Joy. Ac 16:34. 1 P 2:6.
  Peace. Ro 15:13.
Saints die in. He 11:13.
Saints Should
  Abound in. 2 Co 8:7.
  Be grounded and settled in. Cl 1:23,
  Be sincere in. 1 Tm 1:5. 2 Tm 1:5.
  Be strong in. Ro 4:20–24.
  Continue in. Ac 14:22. Cl 1:23.
  Have full assurance of. 2 Tm 1:12. He 10:22.
  Hold, with a good conscience. 1 Tm 1:19.
  Pray for the increase of. Lk 17:5.
  Stand fast in. 1 Co 16:13.
The scriptures designed to produce. Jn 20:31. 2 Tm 3:15.
The substance of things hoped for. He 11:1.
Those who are not Christ's have not. Jn 10:26–27.
Through It Is
  Access to God. Ro 5:2. Ep 3:12.

Adoption. Jn 1:12. Gl 3:26.
Edification. 1 Tm 1:4. Jde 1:20.
Eternal life. Jn 3:15–16; 6:40, 47.
The gift of the Holy Ghost. Ac 11:15–17.
Gl 3:14. Ep 1:13.
Inheritance of the promises. Gl 3:22. He
6:12.
Justification. Ac 13:39. Ro 3:21–22, 28,
30; 5:1. Gl 2:16.
Preservation. 1 P 1:5.
Remission of sins. Ac 10:43. Ro 3:25.
Rest in heaven. He 4:3.
Salvation. Mk 16:16. Ac 16:31.
Sanctification. Ac 15:9; 26:18.
Spiritual life. Jn 20:31. Gl 2:20.
Spiritual light. Jn 12:36, 46.
Trial of, works patience. Ja 1:3.
True, evidenced by its fruits. Ja 2:21–25.
Whatsoever is not of, is sin. Ro 14:23.
The wicked destitute of. Jn 10:25; 12:37. Ac
19:9. 2 Th 3:2.
The wicked often profess. Ac 8:13, 21.

FAITHFULNESS
Associate with those who exhibit. Ps 101:6.
Blessedness of. 1 S 26:23. Pr 28:20.
A characteristic of saints. Ep 1:1. Cl 1:2. 1
Tm 6:2. Rv 17:14.
Difficulty of finding. Pr 20:6.
ESPECIALLY REQUIRED IN
Children of ministers. Ti 1:6.
Ministers. 1 Co 4:2. 2 Tm 2:2.
Wives of ministers. 1 Tm 3:11.
EXHIBITED IN
All things. 1 Tm 3:11.
Bearing witness. Pr 14:5.
Care of dedicated things. 2 Ch 31:12.
Conveying messages. Pr 13:17; 25:13.
Declaring the word of God. Jr 23:28. 2
Co 2:17; 4:2.
Doing work. 2 Ch 34:12.
Helping the brethren. 3 Jn 1:5.
Keeping secrets. Pr 11:13.
Reproving others. Pr 27:6. Ps 141:5.
Service to God. Mt 24:45.
Situations of trust. 2 K 12:15. Ne 13:13.
Ac 6:1–3.
The smallest matters. Lk 16:10–12.
Should be unto death. Rv 2:10.
The wicked devoid of. Ps 5:9.

FAITHFULNESS OF GOD
DECLARED TO BE
Established. Ps 89:2.

Everlasting. Pss 119:90; 146:6.
Great. Lm 3:23.
Incomparable. Ps 89:8.
Infinite. Ps 36:5.
Unfailing. Ps 89:33. 2 Tm 2:13.
MANIFESTED
In afflicting his saints. Ps 119:75.
In executing his judgments. Jr 23:20;
51:29.
In forgiving sins. 1 Jn 1:9.
In fulfilling his promises. 1 K 8:20. Ps
132:11. Mi 7:20. He 10:23.
In his counsels. Is 25:1.
In his testimonies. Ps 119:138.
In keeping his covenant. Dt 7:9. Ps 111:5
To his saints. Ps 89:24. 2 Th 3:3.
Part of his character. Is 49:7. 1 Co 1:9. 1
Th 5:24.
Saints encouraged to depend on. 1 P 4:19.
SHOULD BE
Magnified. Pss 89:5; 92:2.
Pleaded in prayer. Ps 143:1.
Proclaimed. Pss 40:10; 89:1.

FALL OF MAN
All men partake of the effects of. 1 K 8:46.
Gl 3:22. 1 Jn 1:8; 5:19.
By the disobedience of Adam. Gn 3:6,
11–12, with Ro 5:12, 15, 19.
Cannot be remedied by man. Pr 20:9. Jr
2:22; 13:23.
Dead in sin. Ep 2:1. Cl 2:13.
MAN, IN CONSEQUENCE
Abominable. Jb 15:16. Ps 14:3.
Blinded in heart. Ep 4:18.
Born in sin. Jb 15:14; 25:4. Ps 51:5. Is
48:8. Jn 3:6.
A child of wrath. Ep 2:3
Conscious of guilt. Gn 3:7–8, 10.
Constant in evil. Ps 10:5. 2 P 2:14.
Corrupt and perverse in his ways. Gn
6:12. Ps 10:5. Ro 3:12–16.
Defiled in conscience. Ti 1:15. He 10:22.
Depraved in mind. Ro 8:5–7. Ep 4:17.
Cl 1:21. Ti 1:15.
Devoid of the fear of God. Ro 3:18.
Estranged from God. Gn 3:8. Ps 58:3.
Ep 4:18. Cl 1:21.
Evil in heart. Gn 6:5; 8:21. Jr 16:12. Mt
15:19.
In bondage to the devil. 2 Tm 2:26. He
2:14–15.
In bondage to sin. Ro 6:19; 7:5, 23. Gl
5:17. Ti 3:3.

Intractable. Jb 11:12.
Loves darkness. Jn 3:19.
Made in the image of Adam. Gn 5:3, with
1 Co 15:48–49.
Receives not the things of God. 1 Co
2:14.
Short of God's glory. Ro 3:23.
Totally depraved. Gn 6:5. Ro 7:18.
Turned to his own way. Is 53:6.
Unrighteous. Ec 7:20. Ro 3:10.
Without understanding. Ps 14:2–3, with
Ro 3:11. Ro 1:31.

PUNISHMENT CONSEQUENT UPON
Banishment from paradise. Gn 3:24.
Condemnation to labor and sorrow. Gn
3:16, 19. Jb 5:6–7.
Eternal death. Jb 21:30. Ro 5:18, 21;
6:23.
Temporal death. Gn 3:19. Ro 5:12. 1 Co
15:22.
Remedy for, provided by God. Gn 3:15. Jn
3:16.
Through temptation of the devil. Gn 3:1–5.
2 Co 11:3. 1 Tm 2:14.

FAMILIES
Deceivers and liars should be removed from.
Ps 101:7.
Of saints blessed. Ps 128:3–6.
Punishment of irreligious. Jr 10:25.
SHOULD
Be duly regulated. Pr 31:27. 1 Tm 3:4–5,
12.
Be taught the scriptures. Dt 4:9–10.
Live in mutual forbearance. Gn 50:17–21.
Mt 18:21–22.
Live in unity. Gn 45:24. Ps 133:1.
Rejoice together before God. Dt 14:26.
Worship God together. 1 Co 16:19.
Warning against departing from God. Dt
29:18.

FAMINE
CAUSED
Blackness of the skin. Lm 4:8; 5:10.
Burning and fever. Dt 32:24.
Death. 2 K 7:4. Jr 11:22.
Faintness. Gn 47:13.
Grief and mourning. Jl 1:11–13.
Wasting of the body. Lm 4:8. Ezk 4:17.
CAUSED BY
Blasting and mildew. Am 4:9. Hg 2:17.
Devastation by enemies. Dt 28:33, 51.

God's blessing withheld. Ho 2:8–9. Hg
1:6.
Rotting of the seed in the ground. Jl 1:17.
Swarms of insects. Dt 28:38, 42. Jl 1:4.
Want of seasonable rain. 1 K 17:1. Jr
14:1–4. Am 4:7.
EXPRESSED BY
Arrows of famine. Ezk 5:16.
Cleanness of teeth. Am 4:6.
Taking away the stay of bread. Is 3:1.
God provided for his people during. 1 K
17:4, 9. Jb 5:20. Pss 33:19; 37:19.
ILLUSTRATIVE OF
A dearth of the means of grace. Am
8:11–12.
Destruction of idols. Zp 2:11.
INSTANCES OF, IN SCRIPTURE
After the captivity. Ne 5:3.
Before destruction of Jerusalem. Mt 24:7.
During the siege of Jerusalem. 2 K 25:3.
During the siege of Samaria. 2 K 6:25.
In the days of Abraham. Gn 12:10.
In the days of Isaac. Gn 26:1.
In the days of Joseph. Gn 41:53–56.
In the days of the Judges. Ru 1:1.
In the reign of Ahab. 1 K 17:1; 18:5.
In the reign of Claudius Caesar. Ac 11:28.
In the reign of David. 2 S 21:1.
In the time of Elisha. 2 K 4:38.
In the time of Jeremiah. Jr 14:1.
Of seven years foretold by Elisha. 2 K 8:1.
The Jews in their restored state not to be
afflicted by. Ezk 36:29–30.
Often accompanied by war. Jr 14:15; 29:18.
Often followed by pestilence. Jr 42:17. Ezk
7:15. Mt 24:7.
Often long continued. Gn 41:27. 2 K 8:1–2.
Often on account of sin. Lv 26:21, 26. Lm
4:4–6.
Often severe. Gn 12:10. 1 K 18:2. Jr 52:6.
One of God's four sore judgments. Ezk
14:21.
Provisions sold by weight during. Ezk 4:16.
Sent by God. Ps 105:16.
Suffering of brute creation from. Jr 14:5–6.
THINGS EATEN DURING
Ass's flesh. 2 K 6:25.
Human flesh. Lv 26:29. 2 K 6:28–29.
Ordure. 2 K 6:25. Lm 4:5.
Wild herbs. 2 K 4:39–40.

FASTING
ACCOMPANIED BY
Confession of sin. 1 S 7:6. Ne 9:1–2.

Humiliation.   Dt 9:18. Ne 9:1.
Mourning.   Jl 2:12.
Prayer.   Ezr 8:23. Dn 9:3
For the chastening of the soul.   Ps 69:10.
For the humbling of the soul.   Ps 35:13.
Not to be made a subject of display.   Mt 6:16–18.
OBSERVED ON OCCASIONS OF
Afflictions.   Ps 35:13. Dn 6:18.
Afflictions of the church.   Lk 5:33–35.
Approaching danger.   Es 4:16.
Judgments of God.   Jl 1:14; 2:12.
Ordination of ministers.   Ac 13:3; 14:23.
Private afflictions.   2 S 12:16.
Public calamities.   2 S 1:12.
OF HYPOCRITES
Boasted of, before God.   Lk 18:12.
Described.   Is 58:4–5.
Ostentatious.   Mt 6:16.
Rejected.   Is 58:3. Jr 14:12.
Promises connected with.   Is 58:8–12. Mt 6:18.
Should be unto God.   Zc 7:5. Mt 6:18.
Spirit of, explained.   Is 58:6–7.

FATHER
GOD AS
Chose a son.   1 Ch 28:6.
Everlasting.   Is 9:6.
In heaven.   Mt 6:9; 23:9.
Love of.   1 Jn 3:1.
Of Jesus.   Lk 2:49. Jn 8:49; 15:1.
Of Spirits.   He 7:3.
NATURAL
Duties.   Ep 6:4.
Happiness of.   Pr 10:1.
Messiah to humanize.   Ml 4:6.
Not to be dishonored.   Pr 20:20.
To be honored.   Ex 20:12. Ep 6:2.
SPIRITUAL
Of all that believe.   Ro 4:11.
Of Onesimus.   Phm 1:10.
Only one.   1 Co 4:15.
To the poor.   Jb 29:16.

FATHERLESS
See Orphans.

FAVOR OF GOD
Christ the special object of.   Lk 2:52.
Disappointment of enemies an assured evidence of.   Ps 41:11.
Domestic blessings traced to.   Pr 18:22.
Given in answer to prayer.   Jb 33:26.

Mercy and truth lead to.   Pr 3:3–4.
Plead, in prayer.   Ex 33:13. Nu 11:15.
Pray for.   Pss 106:4; 119:58.
SAINTS
Encompassed by.   Ps 5:12.
Exalted in.   Ps 89:17.
Obtain.   Pr 12:2.
Preserved through.   Jb 10:12.
Sometimes tempted to doubt.   Ps 77:7.
Strengthened by.   Ps 30:7.
Victorious through.   Ps 44:3.
THE SOURCE OF
Mercy.   Is 60:10.
Spiritual life.   Ps 30:5.
Spiritual wisdom leads to.   Pr 8:35.
THE WICKED
Do not obtain.   Is 27:11. Jr 16:13.
Uninfluenced by.   Is 26:10.
To be acknowledged.   Ps 85:1.

FEAR, GODLY
Advantages   of.   Pr   15:16;   19:23. Ec 8:12–13.
A characteristic of saints.   Ml 3:16.
Commanded.   Dt 13:4. Ps 22:23. Ec 12:13. 1 P 2:17.
DESCRIBED AS
Filial and reverential.   He 12:9, 28.
A fountain of life.   Pr 14:27.
Hatred of evil.   Pr 8:13.
Sanctifying.   Ps 19:9.
A treasure to saints.   Pr 15:16. Is 33:6.
Wisdom.   Jb 28:28. Ps 111:10.
God the author of.   Jr 32:39–40.
God the object of.   Is 8:13.
MOTIVES TO
Forgiveness of God.   Ps 130:4.
Goodness of God.   1 S 12:24.
Greatness of God.   Dt 10:12, 17.
Holiness of God.   Rv 15:4.
Judgments of God.   Rv 14:7.
Wondrous works of God.   Jsh 4:23–24.
NECESSARY TO
Avoiding sin.   Ex 20:20.
Impartial administration of justice.   2 Ch 19:6–9.
Perfecting holiness.   2 Co 7:1.
Righteous government.   2 S 23:3.
The service of God.   Ps 2:11. He 12:28.
The worship of God.   Pss 5:7; 89:7.
Searching the scriptures gives understanding of.   Pr 2:3–5.
Should accompany the joy of saints.   Ps 2:11.

SHOULD BE
Constantly maintained. Dt 14:23. Jsh
4:24. Pr 23:17.
Exhibited in giving a reason for our hope.
1 P 3:15.
Exhibited in our callings. Cl 3:22.
Prayed for. Ps 86:11.
Taught to others. Ps 34:11.
THOSE WHO HAVE
Afford pleasure to God. Ps 147:11.
Are accepted of God. Ac 10:35.
Are blessed. Pss 112:1; 115:13.
Are pitied by God. Ps 103:13.
Confide in God. Ps 115:11. Pr 14:26.
Converse together of holy things. Ml
3:16.
Days of, prolonged. Pr 10:27.
Depart from evil. Pr 16:6.
Desires of, fulfilled by God. Ps 145:19.
Receive mercy from God. Ps 103:11, 17.
Lk 1:50.
Should not fear man. Is 8:12–13. Mt
10:28.
The wicked destitute of. Ps 36:1. Pr 1:29. Jr
2:19. Ro 3:18.

FEAR, UNHOLY
A characteristic of the wicked. Rv 21:8.
DESCRIBED AS
Consuming. Ps 73:19.
Fear of future punishment. He 10:27.
Fear of idols. 2 K 17:38.
Fear of judgments. Is 2:19. Lk 21:26. Rv
6:16–17.
Fear of man. 1 S 15:24. Jn 9:22.
Overwhelming. Ex 15:16. Jb 15:21, 24.
Exhortations against. Is 8:12. Jn 14:27.
God mocks. Pr 1:26.
A guilty conscience leads to. Gn 3:8, 10. Ps
53:5. Pr 28:1.
Saints delivered from. Pr 1:33. Is 14:3.
Saints sometimes tempted to. Ps 55:5.
Seizes the wicked. Jb 15:24; 18:11.
Shall be realized. Pr 1:27; 10:24.
Surprises the hypocrite. Is 33:14, 18.
Trust in God, a preservative from. Ps 27:1.
The wicked judicially filled with. Lv
26:16–17. Dt 28:65–67. Jr 49:5.

FEASTS, ANNIVERSARY
All males to attend. Ex 23:17; 34:23.
Children commenced attending, when twelve
years old. Lk 2:42.
Christ attended. Jn 5:1; 7:10.

Dangers and difficulties encountered in going
up to, alluded to. Ps 84:6–7.
Enumerated. Ex 23:15–16.
Females often attended. 1 S 1:3, 9. Lk 2:41.
Illustrative of general assembly of the church.
He 12:23.
Instituted by God. Ex 23:14.
THE JEWS
Attended gladly. Ps 122:1–2.
Dispersed in distant parts often attended.
Ac 2:5–11; 8:27.
Went up to, in large companies. Ps 42:4.
Lk 2:44.
Land divinely protected during. Ex 34:24.
Offerings to be made at. Ex 34:20. Dt
16:16–17.
Rendered unavailing by the impiety of the
Jews. Is 1:13–14. Am 5:21.
Ten tribes seduced by Jeroboam from attend-
ing. 1 K 12:27.
WERE CALLED
Appointed feasts. Is 1:14.
Feasts of the Lord. Lv 23:4.
Solemn feasts. 2 Ch 8:13. Lm 1:4.
Solemn meetings. Is 1:13.
Were eucharistic. Ps 122:4.
WERE SEASONS OF
Entertainments. 1 S 1:4, 9.
Joy and gladness. Ps 42:4. Is 30:29.
Sacrificing. 1 S 1:3. 1 K 9:25. 2 Ch 8:13.

FEET
Condemnation expressed by shaking the dust
from. Mt 10:14. Mk 6:11.
Early use of shoes for. Ex 12:11.
ILLUSTRATIVE OF
Abundance, when washed or dipped in oil.
Dt 33:24. Jb 29:6.
Complete destruction, when trod under.
Is 18:7. Lm 1:15.
Liberty, when set in a large place. Ps 31:8.
Stability, when set on a rock. Ps 40:2.
Victory, when dipped in blood. Ps 68:23.
Yielding to temptation, when sliding. Jb
12:5. Pss 17:5; 38:16; 94:18.
Necessary members of the body. 1 Co 15:15,
21.
Neglect of washing, disrespectful to guest.
Lk 7:44.
OF CRIMINALS
Bound with fetters. Ps 105:18.
Placed in stocks. Jb 13:27. Ac 16:24.
Of enemies, often maimed and cut off. Jg
1:6–7. 2 S 4:14.

OF SAINTS
At liberty. Pss 18:36; 31:8.
Established by God. Pss 66:9; 121:3.
Guided by Christ. Is 48:17. Lk 1:79.
Kept by God. 1 S 2:9. Ps 116:8.
Of strangers and travelers washed. Gn 18:4; 19:2; 24:32. 1 Tm 5:10.
Often swift. 2 S 2:18; 22:34.

OF THE JEWS
Bare in affliction. 2 S 15:30.
Neglected in affliction. 2 S 19:24. Ezk 24:17.
Washed frequently. 2 S 11:8. SS 5:3.

OF THE WICKED
Ensnared. Jb 18:8. Ps 9:15.
Swift to mischief. Pr 6:18.
Swift to shed blood. Pr 1:16. Ro 3:15.
Of women often adorned with tinkling ornaments. Is 3:16, 18.
Origin of uncovering in consecrated places. Ex 3:5. Jsh 5:15.

PARTS OF, MENTIONED
Heel. Pss 41:9; 49:5. Ho 12:3.
Sole. Dt 11:24. 1 K 5:3.
Toes. Ex 29:20. 2 S 21:20. Dn 2:41.
Path of, to be pondered. Pr 4:26.
Respect, exhibited by falling at. 1 S 25:24. 2 K 4:37. Es 8:3. Mk 5:22. Ac 10:25.
Reverence expressed by kissing. Lk 7:38, 45.
Sleep expressed by covering. 1 S 24:3.
Stamped on the ground in extreme joy or grief. Ezk 6:11; 25:6.
Subjection expressed by licking the dust of. Is 49:23.
Subjugation of enemies shown by placing on neck. Jsh 10:24. Ps 110:1.
To be directed by God's word. Ps 119:105.
To be guided by wisdom and discretion. Pr 3:21, 23, 26.
To be refrained from evil. Pr 1:15. He 12:13.
To be turned to God's testimonies. Ps 119:59.
Washing for others, a menial office. 1 S 25:41. Jn 13:5–14.

WERE LIABLE TO
Disease. 1 K 15:23.
Injury from stones, etc. Ps 91:12.
Swelling from walking. Dt 8:4.

FELLOWSHIP
Blessings of. 1 Jn 1:7.
In Christ. Mt 18:20. 1 Co 1:9. Rv 3:20.
In the Holy Spirit. 2 Co 13:14.
Kinds and results. Pr 13:20.
Responsibilities of. Gl 6:2.
With God's people. Pss 55:14; 119:63. Gl 3:28.

FIG TREE
ABOUNDED IN
Canaan. Nu 13:23. Dt 8:8.
Egypt. Ps 105:33.
Afforded a thick shade. Jn 1:48, 50.
Failure of, a great calamity. Hk 3:17.

FRUIT OF
Eaten dried in cakes. 1 S 30:12.
Eaten fresh from the tree. Mt 21:18–19.
First ripe esteemed. Jr 24:2. Ho 9:10.
Formed after winter. SS 2:11, 13.
Gathered and kept in baskets. Jr. 24:1.
Sent as presents. 1 S 25:18. 1 Ch 12:40.
Sold in the markets. Ne 13:15.
Used in the miraculous healing of Hezekiah. 2 K 20:7. Is 38:21.

ILLUSTRATIVE OF
Mere professors of religion (when barren). Mt 21:19. Lk 13:6–7.
Prosperity and peace (sitting under one's own). 1 K 4:25. Mi 4:4.

ITS FRUIT ILLUSTRATIVE OF
Fathers of the Jewish church (when first ripe). Ho 9:10.
Good works. Mt 7:16.
Saints. Jr 24:2–3.
Wicked men (when bad). Jr 24:2–8.
The wicked ripe for judgment (when untimely and dropping). Is 34:4. Na 3:12. Rv 6:13.

THE JEWS PUNISHED BY
Barking and eating of, by locusts, etc. Jl 1:4, 7, 12. Am 4:9.
Enemies devouring fruit of. Jr 5:17.
Failure of fruit on. Jr 8:13. Hg 2:19.
God's breaking down. Ho 2:12.
Leaves of, a sign of the approach of summer. Mt 24:32.
Leaves of, used by Adam for covering. Gn 3:7.
Not found in desert places. Nu 20:5.
Often unfruitful. Lk 13:7.
Produces a rich sweet fruit. Jg 9:11.
Propagated by the Jews. Am 4:9.
Reasonableness of expecting fruit upon, when full of leaves. Mk 11:13.
Required cultivation. Lk 13:8.
Sometimes planted in vineyards. Lk 13:6.

A species of, produced vile and worthless fruit. Jr 29:17.

FIRE
Can be increased in intensity. Dn 3:19, 22.

CHARACTERIZED AS
Bright. Ezk 1:13.
Consuming. Jg 15:4–5. Ps 46:9. Is 10:16–17.
Drying. Jb 15:30. Jl 1:20.
Enlightening. Pss 78:14; 105:39.
Heating. Mk 14:54.
Insatiable. Pr 30:16.
Melting. Ps 68:2. Is 64:2.
Purifying. Nu 31:23. 1 P 1:7. Rv 3:18.
Spreading. Ja 3:5.

Christ shall appear in. Dn 7:10. 2 Th 1:8.
Frequently employed as an instrument of divine vengeance. Ps 97:3. Is 47:14; 66:16.
God appeared in. Ex 3:2; 19:18.

ILLUSTRATIVE OF
Affliction. Is 43:2.
Christ as judge. Is 10:17. Ml 3:2.
God's enemies. Is 10:17. Ob 1:18.
God's protection. Nu 9:16. Zc 2:5.
God's vengeance. Dt 4:24. He 12:29.
The Holy Spirit. Is 4:4. Ac 2:3.
The hope of hypocrites. Is 50:11.
Judgments. Jr 48:45. Lm 1:13. Ezk 39:6.
Lust. Pr 6:27–28.
Persecution. Lk 12:49–53.
The self-righteous. Is 65:5.
The tongue. Pr 16:27. Ja 3:6.
Wickedness. Is 9:18.
The word of God. Jr 5:14; 23:29.
Zeal of angels. Ps 104:4. He 1:7.
Zeal of saints. Pss 39:3; 119:139.

IN HOUSES
Lighted in the winter. Jr 36:22.
Lighted on spring mornings. Jn 18:18.
Made of charcoal. Jn 18:18.
Made of wood. Ac 28:3.
Not to be lighted on the sabbath. Ex 35:3.

Injury from, to be made good by the person who kindled it. Ex 22:6.

MIRACULOUS
Angel ascended in. Jg 13:20.
Consumed the company of Korah. Nu 16:35.
Consumed the sacrifice of Elijah. 2 K 1:18, 38.
Consumed the sacrifice of Gideon. Jg 6:21.

Destroyed the enemies of Elijah. 2 K 1:10, 12.
Destroyed Nadab and Abihu. Lv 10:2.
Destroyed the people at Taberah. Nu 11:1.
Elijah taken up in a chariot of. 2 K 2:11.
In the burning bush. Ex 3:2.
Led the people of Israel in the desert. Ex 13:22; 40:38.
On Mount Sinai at giving of law. Dt 4:11, 36.
Plagued the Egyptians. Ex 9:23–24.

Punishment of the wicked shall be in. Mt 13:42; 25:41.

SACRED
All burnt offerings consumed by. Lv 6:9, 12.
Always burning on the altar. Lv 6:13.
Came from before the Lord. Lv 9:24.
Guilt of burning incense without. Lv 10:1.
Incense burned with. Lv 16:12. Nu 16:46.
Restored to the temple. 2 Ch 7:1–3.

THINGS CONNECTED WITH
Ashes. 1 K 13:3. 2 P 2:6.
Burning coals. Pr 26:21.
Flame. S S 8:6. Is 66:15.
Smoke. Is 34:10. Jl 2:30.
Sparks. Jb 18:5. Is 1:31.

Though small, kindles a great matter. Ja 3:5.

FIRST
IN THE BEGINNING
Chosen. Ep 1:4.
God. Gn 1:1.
The Word. Jn 1:1.

Jesus Christ. Cl 1:15. Rv 1:17; 3:14.

PRIORITIES
God's kingdom and righteousness. Mt 6:33.
Love. Mt 22:35–40.
What has been received. 1 Co 15:3.

FIRST-BORN
The beginning of strength and excellency of power. Gn 49:3. Dt 21:17.
Dedicated to commemorate the sparing of the first-born of Israel. Ex 13:15. Nu 3:13; 8:17.

ILLUSTRATIVE OF
The dignity, etc., of Christ. Ps 89:27. Ro 8:29. Cl 1:18.
The dignity, etc., of the church. He 12:23.

INSTANCES OF BEING SUPERSEDED.
Aaron. Ex 7:1–2, with Nu 12:2, 8.
Adonijah. 1 K 2:15, 22.
Cain. Gn 4:4–5.
David's brothers. 1 S 16:6–12.
Esau. Gn 25:23. Ro 9:12–13.
Ishmael. Gn 17:19–21.
Japheth. Gn 10:21.
Manasseh. Gn 48:15–20.
Reuben, etc. 1 Ch 5:1–2.
LAWS RESPECTING
Observed at Christ's birth. Lk 2:22–23.
Restored after the captivity. Ne 10:36.
Objects of special love. Gn 25:28. Jr 31:9, 20.
Of the ass to be redeemed with a lamb or its neck broken. Ex 13:13; 34:20.
OF CLEAN BEASTS.
Antiquity of offering. Gn 4:4.
Could not be a free-will offering. Lv 27:26.
Flesh of, the priests' portion. Nu 18:18.
Not shorn. Dt 15:19.
Not taken from the dam for seven days. Ex 22:30. Lv 22:27.
Not to labor. Dt 15:19.
Offered in sacrifice. Nu 18:17.
OF ISRAEL
Price of, given to the priests. Nu 3:48–51.
Price of redemption for. Nu 3:46–47.
To be redeemed. Ex 34:20. Nu 18:15.
Tribe of Levi taken for. Nu 3:12, 40–43; 8:18.
Of man and beast dedicated to God. Ex 13:2, 12; 22:29.
OF UNCLEAN BEASTS
Law of redemption for. Nu 18:16.
To be redeemed. Nu 18:15.
Precious and valuable. Mi 6:7. Zc 12:10.
PRIVILEGES OF
Authority over the younger children. Gn 27:29. 1 S 20:29.
A double portion of inheritance. Dt 21:17.
Could be forfeited by misconduct. Gn 49:3–4, 8. 1 Ch 5:1.
Could be sold. Gn 25:31, 33. He 12:16–17.
The father's title and power. 2 Ch 21:3.
In case of death the next brother to raise up seed to. Dt 25:5–6. Mt 22:24–28.
Not to be alienated by parents through caprice. Dt 21:15–16.
Precedence in the family. Gn 48:13–14.

Special blessing by the father. Gn 27:4, 35.

FIRST FRUITS
Allotted to the priests. Nu 18:12–13. Lv 23:20. Dt 18:3–5.
DIFFERENT KINDS OF
All agricultural produce. Dt 26:2.
Barley harvest. Lv 23:10–14.
Fruit of new trees in fourth year. Lv 19:23–24.
Honey. 2 Ch 31:5.
Wheat harvest. Ex 23:16. Lv 23:16–17.
Wine and oil. Dt 18:4.
Wood. Dt 18:4.
God honored by the offering of. Pr 3:9.
Holy to the Lord. Ezk 48:14.
ILLUSTRATIVE OF
Church of Christ. Ja 1:18. Rv 14:4.
Early Jewish church. Jr 2:3.
First converts in any place. Ro 16:5.
Resurrection of Christ. 1 Co 15:20, 23.
Law of, restored after the captivity. Ne 10:35, 37; 13:31.
Offering of, consecrated the whole. Ro 11:16.
To be best of their kind. Nu 18:12.
To be brought to God's house. Ex 34:26.
TO BE OFFERED
In a basket. Dt 26:2.
With thanksgiving. Dt 26:3–10.
Without delay. Ex 22:29.

FISH
Cannot live without water. Is 50:2.
Catching of, a trade. Mt 4:18. Lk 5:2.
Created by God. Gn 1:20–21. Ex 20:11.
Different in flesh from beasts, etc. 1 Co 15:39.
Distinction between clean and unclean. Lv 11:9–12. Dt 14:9–10.
ILLUSTRATIVE OF
Men ignorant of future events. Ec 9:12.
Mere professors (when bad). Mt 13:48–49.
Saints (when good). Mt 13:48–49.
Those ensnared by the wicked. Hk 1:14.
The visible church. Mt 13:48.
The whole population of Egypt. Ezk 29:45.
INHABIT
Ponds. S S 7:4. Is 19:10.
Rivers. Ex 7:18. Ezk 29:5.
Seas. Nu 11:22. Ezk 47:10.

Made for God's glory. Jb 12:8–9. Ps 69:34.
Man given dominion over. Gn 1:26, 28. Ps
8:8.
Man permitted to eat. Gn 9:2–3.
MENTIONED IN SCRIPTURE
Leviathan. Jb 41:1. Ps 74:14.
Whale. Gn 1:21. Mt 12:40.
MIRACLES CONNECTED WITH
Dressed on the shore. Jn 21:9.
Immense draughts of. Lk 5:6, 9. Jn 21:6,
11.
Multiplying a few. Mt 14:17–21; 15:34.
Procuring tribute money from. Mt 17:27.
Mode of cooking alluded to. Lk 24:42. Jn
21:9.
No likeness of, to be made for worship. Ex
20:4. Dt 4:18.
Number and variety of. Ps 104:25.
Sold near the fish gate at Jerusalem. 2 Ch
33:14. Zp 1:10.
Solomon wrote the history of. 1 K 4:33.
Suffered for man's sin. Ex 7:21. Ezk 38:20.
TAKEN WITH
Hooks. Am 4:2. Mt 17:27.
Nets. Lk 5:4–6. Jn 21:6–8.
Spears. Jb 41:7.
The Tyrians traded in. Ne 13:16.
USED AS FOOD
By the Egyptians. Nu 11:5.
By the Jews. Mt 7:10.

FLATTERY
Avoid those given to. Pr 20:19.
Danger of. Pr 7:21–23; 29:5.
False prophets and teachers use. Ezk 12:24,
with Ro 16:18.
HYPOCRITES USE, TO
God. Ps 78:36.
Those in authority. Dn 11:34.
Ministers should not use. 1 Th 2:5.
Punishment of. Jb 17:5. Ps 12:3.
Saints should not use. Jb 32:21–22.
Seldom gains respect. Pr 28:23.
THE WICKED USE, TO
Others. Pss 5:9; 12:2.
Themselves. Ps 36:2.
Wisdom a preservative against. Pr 4:5.
Worldly advantage obtained by. Dn
11:21–22.

FLOOD
Called the waters of Noah. Is 54:9.
Came suddenly and unexpectedly. Mt
24:38–39.

Causes of its abatement. Gn 8:1–2.
Complete destruction effected by. Gn 7:23.
Date of its commencement. Gn 7:11.
Date of its complete removal. Gn 8:13.
Decrease of, gradual. Gn 8:3, 5.
Extreme height of. Gn 7:19–20.
Face of the earth changed by. 2 P 3:5–6.
ILLUSTRATIVE OF
Baptism. 1 P 3:20–21.
The destruction of sinners. Ps 32:6. Is
28:2, 18.
Suddenness of Christ's coming (in its unex-
pectedness). Mt   24:36–39. Lk
17:26–30.
Increased gradually. Gn 7:17–18.
Long-suffering of God exhibited in deferring.
Gn 6:3, with 1 P 3:20.
Noah forewarned of. Gn 6:13. He 11:7.
Noah saved from. Gn 6:18–22; 7:13–14.
PRODUCED BY
Forty days' incessant rain. Gn 7:4, 12, 17.
Opening up of the fountains of the great
deep. Gn 7:11.
Sent as a punishment for the extreme wicked-
ness of man. Gn 6:5–7, 11–13, 17.
THAT IT SHALL NEVER AGAIN OCCUR
A pledge of God's faithfulness. Is
54:9–10.
Confirmed by covenant. Gn 9:9–11.
Promised. Gn 8:21–22.
The rainbow a token. Gn 9:12–17.
Time of its increase and prevailing. Gn 7:24.
Traditional notice of. Jb 22:15–17.
Wicked warned of. 1 P 3:19–20. 2 P 2:5.

FLOWERS
Appear in spring. S S 2:12.
Cultivated in gardens. S S 6:2–3.
DESCRIBED AS
Beautiful. Mt 6:29.
Evanescent. Ps 103:16. Is 40:8.
Sweet. S S 5:13.
Garlands of, used in worship of idols. Ac
14:13.
ILLUSTRATIVE OF
Glory of man. 1 P 1:24.
Graces of Christ. S S 5:13.
Kingdom of Israel. Is 28:1.
Rich men. Ja 1:10–11.
Shortness of man's life. Jb 14:2. Ps
103:15.
REPRESENTATIONS OF, ON THE
Golden candlestick. Ex 25:31, 33. 2 Ch
4:21.

Sea of brass. 1 K 7:26. 2 Ch 4:5.
Woodwork of the temple. 1 K 6:18, 29, 33, 35.
THOSE MENTIONED IN SCRIPTURE
Flower of grass. 1 P 1:24.
Lily. Ho 14:5. Mt 6:28.
Lily of the valley. S S 2:1.
Rose. Is 35:1.
Rose of Sharon. S S 2:1.
Wild in fields. Ps 103:15.

FOOLS

All men are, without the knowledge of God.
Ti 3:3.
ARE
Angry. Ec 7:9.
Contentious. Pr 18:6.
Corrupt and abominable. Ps 14:1.
Full of words. Ec 10:14.
Given to meddling. Pr 20:3.
A grief to parents. Pr 17:25; 19:13.
Liars. Pr 10:18.
Mere professors of religion. Mt 25:2–12.
Self-confident. Pr 14:16.
Self-deceivers. Pr 14:8.
Self-sufficient. Pr 12:15. Ro 1:22.
Slanderers. Pr 10:18.
Slothful. Ec 4:5.
To be avoided. Pr 9:6; 14:7.
Blaspheme God. Ps 74:18.
Cling to their folly. Pr 26:11; 27:22.
Come to shame. Pr 3:35.
Delight not in understanding. Pr 18:2.
Deny God. Pss 14:1; 53:1.
Depend upon their wealth. Lk 12:20.
Despise instruction. Pr 1:7; 15:5.
Destroy themselves by their speech. Pr 10:8, 14. Ecc 10:12.
Exhorted to seek wisdom. Pr 8:5.
God has no pleasure in. Ec 5:4.
Hate knowledge. Pr 1:22.
Hate to depart from evil. Pr 13:19.
Hear the gospel and obey it not. Mt 7:26.
Honor is unbecoming for. Pr 26:1, 8.
Make a mock at sin. Pr 14:9.
Punishment of. Ps 107:17. Pr 19:29; 26:10.
Reproach God. Ps 74:22.
Shall not stand in the presence of God. Ps 5:5.
Sport themselves in mischief. Pr 10:23.
Their company ruinous. Pr 13:20.
Their lips a snare to the soul. Pr 18:7.
Their mouths pour out folly. Pr 15:2.
Their worship hateful to God. Ec 5:1.

Trust to their own hearts. Pr 28:26.
Walk in darkness. Ec 2:14.
Worship idols. Jr 10:8. Ro 1:22–23.

FORESTS

Abounded with wild honey. 1 S 14:25–26.
Called on to rejoice at God's mercy. Is 44:23.
ILLUSTRATIVE OF
Destruction of the wicked (when destroyed by fire). Is 9:18; 10:17–18. Jr 21:14.
The Jews rejected by God (when fruitful fields turned into). Is 29:17; 32:15.
The unfruitful world. Is 32:19.
Infested by wild beasts. Pss 50:10; 104:20. Is 56:9. Jr 5:6. Mi 5:8.
Jotham built towers, etc., in. 2 Ch 27:4.
MENTIONED IN SCRIPTURE
Arabian. Is 21:13.
Bashan. Is 2:13. Ezk 27:6. Zc 11:2.
Carmel. 2 K 19:23. Is 37:24.
Ephraim. 2 S 18:6, 8.
Hareth. 1 S 22:5.
The king's. Ne 2:8.
Lebanon. 1 K 7:2; 10:17.
The south. Ezk 20:46–47.
Often afforded pasture. Mi 7:14.
Often destroyed by enemies. 2 K 19:23. Is 37:24.
Places of refuge. 1 S 22:5; 23:16.
Power of God extends over. Ps 29:9.
Supplied timber for building. 1 K 5:6–8.
Tracts of land covered with trees. Is 44:14.
Underbrush often in. Is 9:18.

FORGETTING GOD

Backsliders are guilty of. Jr 3:21–22.
Cautions against. Dt 6:12; 8:11.
A characteristic of the wicked. Pr 2:17, Is 65:11.
Encouraged by false teachers. Jr 23:27.
Exhortation to those guilty of. Ps 50:22.
IS FORGETTING HIS
Benefits. Pss 103:2; 106:7.
Covenant. Dt 4:23. 2 K 17:38.
Law. Ps 119:153, 176. Ho 4:6.
Past deliverance. Jg 8:34. Ps 78:42.
Power to deliver. Is 51:13–15.
Word. He 12:5. Ja 1:25.
Works. Pss 78:7, 11; 106:13.
Prosperity often leads to. Dt 8:12–14. Ho 13:6.
Punishment of. Jb 8:12–13. Ps 9:17. Is 17:10–11. Ezk 23:35. Ho 8:14.

Resolve against. Ps 119:16, 93.
Trials should not lead to. Ps 44:17–20.

FORGIVENESS OF INJURIES
A characteristic of saints. Ps 7:4.
Christ set an example of. Lk 23:34.
Commanded. Mk 11:25. Ro 12:19.
A glory to saints. Pr 19:11.
Illustrated. Mt 18:23–35.
MOTIVES TO
    Christ's forgiveness of us. Cl 3:13.
    God's forgiveness of us. Ep 4:32.
    The mercy of God. Lk 6:36.
    Our need of forgiveness. Mk 11:25.
No forgiveness without. Mt 6:15. Ja 2:13.
Promises to. Mt 6:14. Lk 6:37.
SHOULD BE ACCOMPANIED BY
    Blessing and prayer. Mt 5:44.
    Forbearance. Cl 3:13.
    Kindness. Gn 45:5–11. Ro 12:20.
To be unlimited. Mt 18:22. Lk 17:4.

FORGIVENESS OF SIN
Accomplished by the cross. Cl 1:14. He 9:22.
Based on God's grace. Lk 7:42.
Conditioned by attitude toward others. Mt 6:12. Mk 11:25.
Connected with repentance. Ac 2:38.
Found in God. Ps 130:4. Dn 9:9.
Granted by Christ. Lk 7:47. Mt 2:5.
Received through Christ. 1 Jn 2:12.

FORSAKING GOD
Backsliders guilty of. Jr 15:6.
Brings confusion. Jr 17:13.
Brings down his wrath. Ezr 8:22.
Curse pronounced upon. Jr 17:5.
Followed by remorse. Ezk 6:9.
Idolaters guilty of. 1 S 8:8. 1 K 11:33.
IS FORSAKING
    His commandments. Ezr 9:10.
    His covenant. Dt 29:25. 1 K 19:10. Jr 22:9. Dn 11:30.
    His house. 2 Ch 29:6.
    The right way. 2 P 2:15.
Leads men to follow their own devices. Jr 2:13.
Prosperity tempts to. Dt 31:20; 32:15.
Provokes God to forsake men. Jg 10:13. 2 Ch 15:2; 24:20, 24.
Punishment of. Dt 28:20. 2 K 22:16–17. Is 1:28. Jr 1:16; 5:19.
Resolve against. Jsh 24:16. Ne 10:29–30.

Sin of, to be confessed. Ezr 9:10.
Trusting in man is. Jr 17:5.
Unreasonableness and ingratitude of. Jr 2:5–6.
Warnings against. Jsh 24:20. 1 Ch 28:9.
The wicked guilty of. Dt 28:20.
Wickedness of. Jr 2:13; 5:7.

FOUNDATION
DESCRIBED AS
    Deep laid. Lk 6:48.
    Joined together by corner stones. Ezr 4:12, with 1 P 2:6 and Ep 2:20.
    Of stone. 1 K 5:17.
    Strongly laid. Ezr 6:3.
FIGURATIVELY APPLIED TO
    The earth. Jb 38:4. Ps 104:5.
    The heavens. 2 S 22:8.
    Kingdoms. Ex 9:18.
    The mountains. Dt 32:22.
    The ocean. Ps 104:8.
    The world. Ps 18:15. Mt 13:35.
ILLUSTRATIVE OF
    Christ. Is 28:16. 1 Co 3:11.
    Decrees and purposes of God. 2 Tm 2:19.
    Doctrines of the apostles, etc. Ep 2:20.
    First principles of the gospel. He 6:1–2.
    Hope of saints. Ps 87:1.
    Magistrates. Ps 82:5.
    The righteous. Pr 10:25.
    Security of saints' inheritance. He 11:10.
LAID FOR
    Cities. Jsh 6:26. 1 K 16:34.
    Houses. Lk 6:48.
    Temples. 1 K 6:37. Ezr 3:10.
    Towers. Lk 14:28–29.
    Walls. Ezr 4:12. Rv 21:14.
The lowest part of a building, on which it rests. Lk 14:29. Ac 16:26.
Security afforded by. Mt 7:25. Lk 6:48.

FOUNTAINS AND SPRINGS
Abound in Canaan. Dt 8:7. 1 K 18:5.
AFFORD
    Drink to the beasts. Ps 104:11.
    Fruitfulness to the earth. 1 K 18:5. Jl 3:18.
    Refreshment to the birds. Ps 104:12.
Came from the great deep. Gn 7:11. Jb 38:16.
CONSTANTLY FLOWING
    Could not be ceremonially defiled. Lv 11:36.
    Especially esteemed. Is 58:11.

Created by God.   Pss 74:15; 104:10.
Drying up of, a severe punishment.   Ps 107:33–34. Ho 13:15.
Found in hills and valleys.   Dt 8:7. Ps 104:10.
Frequented by travelers.   Gn 16:7.
God to be praised for.   Rv 14:7.
ILLUSTRATIVE OF
  Christ.   Zc 13:1.
  The church (when not failing).   Is 58:11.
  The church (when sealed up).   S S 4:12.
  Constant supplies of grace.   Ps 87:7.
  Eternal life.   Jn 4:14. Rv 21:6.
  God.   Ps 36:9. Jr 2:13; 17:13.
  Godly fear.   Pr 14:27.
  A good wife.   Pr 5:18.
  The Holy Ghost.   Jn 7:38–39.
  The law of the wise.   Pr 13:14.
  The means of grace.   Is 41:18. Jl 3:18.
  The natural heart (when corrupt).   Ja 3:11, with Mt 15:18–19.
  Numerous posterity.   Dt 33:28.
  Saints led astray (when troubled).   Pr 25:26.
  Spiritual wisdom.   Pr 16:22; 18:4.
  Unceasing wickedness of the Jews (when always flowing).   Jr 6:7.
MENTIONED IN SCRIPTURE
  Of Jezreel.   1 S 29:1.
  Of Pisgah.   Dt 4:49.
  Of the waters of Nephtoah.   Jsh 15:9.
  On the way to Shur.   Gn 16:7.
  Upper and nether springs.   Jsh 15:19. Jg 1:15.
Send forth each but one kind of water.   Ja 3:11.
Sometimes dried up.   Is 58:11.
Sometimes stopped or turned off to distress enemies.   2 Ch 32:3–4.

FRANKINCENSE
Burned in worship.   Lv 16:12–13.
A gift for the Christ Child.   Mt 2:11.
No substitute for true worship.   Is 60:3.
Symbolized devotion.   Ps 141:2.
Used to anoint priests.   Ex 30:34.
See also Incense.

FRANKNESS
Characterized Christ.   Jn 16:29.
Marked St. Paul.   1 Th 2:3.
Marks Christian love.   Ep 6:24.
Sought by Job.   Jb 33:3.

FREEDOM
Characterizes the good news of the gospel.   Is 61:1. Lk 4:18.
The Christian's law.   Ja 1:25; 2:12.
Granted believers.   Ps 119:45. Ro 8:21.
Our glorious heritage.   Jn 8:36. Gl 5:1.
Proclaimed by God.   Lv 25:10.
Responsibility of.   1 P 2:16.

FRIENDSHIP
Constancy of.   Pr 17:17.
Faithfulness of.   Pr 27:6.
Helpfulness of.   Ec 4:9–10.
Of the brethren.   Ac 28:15. 2 Co 2:13. 3 Jn 1:14.
Of Christ.   Lk 7:34. Jn 15:14.

FRUIT
CALLED THE
  Fruit of the earth.   Is 4:2.
  Fruit of the ground.   Gn 4:3. Jr 7:20.
  Increase of the land.   Ps 85:12.
DIVIDED INTO
  Evil or bad.   Mt 7:17.
  Goodly.   Jr 11:16.
  Hasty or precocious.   Is 28:4.
  New and old.   S S 7:13.
  Pleasant.   S S 4:16
  Precious.   Dt 33:14.
  Summer.   2 S 16:1.
First of, devoted to God.   Dt 26:2.
Given by God.   Ac 14:17.
ILLUSTRATIVE OF
  Conduct and conversation of evil men, when bad.   Mt 7:17; 12:33.
  Converts to the church.   Ps 72:16. Jn 4:36.
  Doctrines of Christ.   S S 2:3.
  Effects of industry.   Pr 31:16, 31.
  Effects of repentance.   Mt 3:8.
  Example, etc., of the godly.   Pr 11:30.
  Good works.   Mt 7:17–18. Php 4:17.
  A holy conversation.   Pr 12:14; 18:20.
  Praise.   He 13:15.
  The reward of saints.   Is 3:10.
  The reward of the wicked.   Jr 17:9–10.
  Works of the Spirit.   Gl 5:22–23. Ep 5:9.
OFTEN DESTROYED
  By blight.   Jl 1:12.
  By drought.   Hg 1:10
  By enemies.   Ezk 25:4.
  By locusts, etc.   Dt 28:38–39. Jl 1:4.
  In God's anger.   Jr 7:20.
Often sent as presents.   Gn 43:11.

Preserved to us by God. Ml 3:11.

The produce of corn, etc. Dt 22:9, Ps 107:37.

The produce of trees. Gn 1:29. Ec 2:5.

Produced in their due seasons. Mt 21:41.

REQUIRE

A fruitful land. Ps 107:34.

Influence of the sun and moon. Dt 33:14.

Rain from heaven. Ps 104:13. Ja 5:18.

To be waited for with patience. Ja 5:7.

FRUSTRATION

Of an apostle. 1 Th 2:18.

Of a builder. Lk 14:30.

Of the disciples. Lk 5:5.

Of a gardener. Lk 13:7.

Of an individual. Jb 17:11.

Of a nation. Is 37:3.

Overcoming. Is 42:4. Php 4:13. 2 Co 4:16–18.

G

GALILEE

CHRIST

Appeared in, to his disciples after his resurrection. Mt 26:32; 28:7.

Brought up in. Mt 2:22. Lk 2:39, 51.

Chose his apostles from. Mt 4:18, 21. Jn 1:43–44. Ac 1:11.

Despised as of. Mt 26:69, with Jn 7:52.

Followed by the people of. Mt 4:25.

Kindly received in. Jn 4:45.

Ministered to by women of. Mt 27:55. Mk 15:41. Lk 8:3.

Preached throughout. Mk 1:39. Lk 4:44.

Preaching in, predicted. Is 9:1–2. Mt 4:14–15.

Sought refuge in. Jn 4:1, 3.

Wrought many miracles in. Mt 4:23–24; 15:29–31.

Christian churches established in. Ac 9:31.

Conquered by the Assyrians. 2 K 15:29.

Conquered by the Syrians. 1 K 15:20.

INHABITANTS OF

Called Galileans. Ac 2:7.

Cruelly treated by Pilate. Lk 13:1.

Despised by the Jews. Jn 7:41, 52.

Opposed the Roman taxation. Ac 5:37.

Used a peculiar dialect. Mt 26:73. Mk 14:70.

Jurisdiction of, granted to Herod by the Romans. Lk 3:1; 23:6–7.

Kadesh the city of refuge for. Jsh 21:32.

Lake of Gennesaret called the sea of. Mt 15:29. Lk 5:1.

Separated from Judea by Samaria. Jn 4:3–4.

Supplied Tyre, etc., with provisions. Ac 12:20.

TOWNS OF

Accho or Ptolemais. Jg 1:31.

Bethsaida. Mk 6:45. Jn 1:44.

Cana. Jn 2:1; 21:2.

Capernaum. Mt 4:13.

Cesarea. Ac 9:30; 10:24.

Cesarea Philippi. Mt 16:13. Mk 8:27.

Chorazin. Mt 11:21.

Nain. Lk 7:11.

Nazareth. Mt 2:22–23. Lk 1:26.

Tiberias. Jn 6:23.

Twenty cities of, given to Hiram. 1 K 9:11.

Upper part called Galilee of the Gentiles. Is 9:1. Mt 4:15.

GARDENS

Blasting of, a punishment. Am 4:9.

ILLUSTRATIVE OF

The church. S S 5:1; 6:2, 11.

Pleasantness, fruitfulness, and security of the church (when enclosed). S S 4:12.

Spiritual prosperity of the church (when well watered). Is 58:11. Jr 31:12.

The wicked (when dried up). Is 1:30.

Jews ordered to plant, in Babylon. Jr 29:5, 28.

KINDS OF, MENTIONED

Cucumbers. Is 1:8.

Fruit trees. Ec 2:5–6.

Herbs. Dt 11:10. 1 K 21:2.

Spices, etc. S S 4:16; 6:2.

Lodges erected in. Is 1:8.

OF EDEN

Called the garden of God. Ezk 28:13.

Called the garden of the Lord. Gn 13:10.

Fertility of Canaan like. Gn 13:10. Jl 2:3.

Future state of the Jews shall be like. Is 51:3. Ezk 36:35.

Had every tree good for food. Gn 2:9.

Man placed in, to dress and keep. Gn 2:8, 15.

Man sent from, after the fall. Gn 3:23–24.

Planted by the Lord. Gn 2:8.

Watered by a river. Gn 2:10–14.

Often enclosed. S S 4:12.

Often made by the banks of rivers. Nu 24:6.

Often refreshed by fountains. S S 4:15.

Taken care of by gardeners. Jn 20:15.

USED ALSO FOR

Burial. 2 K 21:18, 26. Jn 19:41.

Entertainments. S S 5:1.

Idolatrous worship. Is 1:29; 65:3.

Retirement. Jn 18:1.

GARMENTS

CALLED

Clothes. Pr 6:27. Ezk 16:39.
Clothing. Jb 22:6; 31:19.
Raiment. Gn 28:20. Dt 8:4.
Vesture. Gn 41:42. Rv 19:16.

Cleansed by water from ceremonial uncleanness. Lv 11:32. Nu 31:20.

COLORS OF, MENTIONED

Blue. Ezk 23:6.
Purple. Ezk 7:27. Lk 16:19.
Scarlet. 2 S 1:24. Dn 5:7.
Variegated. Gn 37:3. 2 S 13:18.
White. Ec 9:8.

Girt up during employment. Lk 17:8. Jn 13:4.
Given as a token of covenants. 1 S 18:4.
Given as presents. Gn 45:22. 2 K 5:22.
Grew old and wore out. Jsh 9:5. Ps 102:26.

ILLUSTRATIVE OF

Abundance (washed in wine). Gn 49:11.
Righteousness (white). Mt 28:3. Rv 3:18.
Victory (rolled in blood). Is 9:5.

Liable to plague and leprosy. Lv 13:47–59.

MADE OF

Camel's hair. Mt 3:4.
Linen. Lv 6:10. Es 8:15.
Sackcloth. 2 S 3:31. 2 K 19:1.
Silk. Pr 31:22.
Skins. He 11:37.
Wool. Pr 27:26. Ezk 34:3.

MENTIONED IN SCRIPTURE

Bonnet or hat. Lv 8:13. Dn 3:21.
Burnoose or cloak. Lk 6:29. 2 Tm 4:13.
Girdle. 1 S 18:4. Ac 21:11.
Hyke or upper garment. Dt 24:13. Mt 21:8.
Shoe or sandal. Ex 3:5. Mk 6:9.
Tunic or coat. Jn 19:23; 21:7.
Veil. Gn 24:65.

Not to be made of mixed materials. Dt 22:11.
Of Israel preserved for forty years. Dt 8:4.
Often changed. Gn 35:2; 41:14.
Often fringed and bordered. Nu 15:38. Dt 22:12.
Often rent in affliction. 2 S 15:32. Ezr 9:3, 5.

OF THE POOR

Not to be retained in pledge. Dt 24:12–13.
Provided specially by God. Dt 10:18.
Used as a covering by night. Dt 24:13.
Vile. Ja 2:2.

OF THE RICH

Embroidered. Ps 45:14. Ezk 16:18.
Gay. Ja 2:2–3.
Gorgeous. Lk 7:25. Ac 12:21.
Multiplied and heaped up. Jb 27:16. Is 3:22.
Often motheaten. Jb 13:28. Ja 5:2.
Of the finest materials. Mt 11:8.
Perfumed. Ps 45:8. S S 4:11.

Of the sexes, not to be interchanged. Dt 22:5.
Of those slain with a sword not used. Is 14:19.
Origin of. Gn 3:7, 21.
Scribes and Pharisees condemned for making broad the borders of. Mt 23:5.
Worn long and flowing. Lk 20:46. Rv 1:13.

GATES

Carcass of sin offering burned outside of. Lv 4:12. He 13:11–13.
Criminals generally punished outside of. Lv 24:23. Jn 19:17, with He 13:12.
Design of. Is 62:10.
Fastened with bars of iron. Ps 107:16. Is 45:2.

ILLUSTRATIVE OF

Access to God (heaven). Gn 28:12–17.
Christ. Jn 10:9.
Death (the grave). Is 38:10.
The entrance to life, when strait. Mt 7:14.
The entrance to ruin, when wide. Mt 7:13.
Satan's power (hell). Mt 16:18.

MADE OF

Brass. Ps 107:16. Is 45:2.
Iron. Ac 12:10.

MADE TO

Camps. Ex 32:26.
Cities. 1 K 17:10.
Houses. Lk 16:20. Ac 12:14.
Palaces. Es 5:13.
Prisons. Ac 12:10.
Rivers. Na 2:6.
Temples. Ac 3:2.

OF CITIES

Battering rams used against. Ezk 21:22.
Chief places of concourse. Pr 1:21.
Chief points of attack in war. Jg 5:8. Is 22:7. Ezk 21:15.
Conferences held at. Gn 34:20. 2 S 3:27.
Councils of state held at. 2 Ch 18:9. Jr 39:3.

Courts of justice held at. Dt 16:19. 2 S
15:2. Pr 22:22–23.
Criminals punished at. Dt 17:5. Jr 20:2.
Custom of sitting at, in the evening, alluded
to. Gn 19:1.
Experienced officers placed over. 2 K
7:17.
Idolatrous rites performed at. Ac 14:13.
Land redeemed at. Ru 4:1.
Land sold at. Gn 23:10, 16.
Markets held at. 2 K 7:1, 18.
Often razed and burned. Ne 1:3. Lm 2:9.
Proclamations made at. Pr 1:21. Jr.
17:19.
Public censure passed at. Jb 5:4. Is 29:21.
Public commendation given at. Pr 31:23,
31.
Shut at nightfall. Jsh 2:5. Ne 13:19.
Troops reviewed at. 2 S 18:4.

OF JERUSALEM
Benjamin Gate. Jr 20:2; 37:13.
Corner Gate. 2 Ch 26:9.
Dung Gate. Ne 3:14; 12:31.
Fish Gate. 2 Ch 33:14. Ne 3:3.
Fountain Gate. Ne 2:14; 3:15.
Gate of Ephraim. Ne 12:39.
Gate of Miphkad. Ne 3:31.
Horse Gate. 2 Ch 23:15. Ne 3:28.
Old Gate. Ne 3:6; 12:39.
Sheep Gate. Ne 3:1. Jn 5:2.
Valley Gate. 2 Ch 26:29. Ne 2:13.
Water Gate. Ne 3:26; 8:3.

OF THE TEMPLE
Called gates of righteousness. Ps 118:19.
Called gates of the Lord. Ps 118:20.
Called gates of Zion. Lm 1:4.
Charge of, given by lot. 1 Ch 26:13–19.
Frequented by beggars. Ac 3:2.
Levites the porters of. 2 Ch 8:14; 23:4.
One specially beautiful. Ac 3:2.
Overlaid with gold. 2 K 18:16.
Pious Israelites delighted to enter. Pss
118:1–20; 100:4.
Treasury placed at. 2 Ch 24:8. Mk 12:41.

GENEALOGIES
Illustrative of the record of saints in the book
of life. Lk 10:20. He 12:23. Rv 3:5.
The Jews reckoned by. 1 Ch 9:1. 2 Ch
31:19.

OF CHRIST
Given. Mt 1:1–17. Lk 3:23–38.
Prove his descent from Judah. He 7:14.
Priests who could not prove their own, ex-

cluded from the priesthood. Ezr 2:62. Ne
7:64.
Public registers kept of. 2 Ch 12:15. Ne 7:5.
Subject of, to be avoided. 1 Tm 1:4. Ti 3:9.

GENEROSITY
Affirmed. 1 Ch 29:14.
Commanded. Dt 16:17. 2 Co 9:7.
Encouraged. Ac 20:35. 2 Co 8:7.
Of God. Ps 107:9. Ro 8:32. Ja 1:5.
Of Jesus. Ac 10:38. 2 Co 8:9.
Rewarded. Pr 19:17; 22:9; 28:27. Ec 11:1.
Toward Jesus. Lk 8:3.

GENTILES
All nations except the Jews. Ro 2:9; 3:9;
9:24.

CALLED
Greeks. Ro 1:16; 10:12.
Heathen. Ps 2:1. Gl 3:8.
Nations. Pss 9:20; 22:28. Is 9:1.
Strangers. Is 14:1; 60:10.
Uncircumcised. 1 S 14:6. Is 52:1. Ro
2:26.

CHARACTERIZED AS
Blasphemous and reproachful. Ne 5:9.
Constant to their false gods. Jr 2:11.
Depraved and wicked. Ro 1:28–32. Ep
4:19.
Idolatrous. Ro 1:23, 25. 1 Co 12:2.
Ignorant of God. Ro 1:21. 1 Th 4:5.
Refusing to know God. Ro 1:28.
Superstitious. Dt 18:14.
Without the law. Ro 2:14.
Chastised by God. Pss 9:5; 94:10.
Christ given as a light to. Is 42:6. Lk 2:32.
Conversion of, predicted. Is 2:2; 11:10.
Counsel of, brought to nought. Ps 33:10.
Excluded from Israel's privileges. Ep
2:11–12.
First general introduction of the gospel to.
Ac 13:48–49, 52; 15:12.
First special introduction of the gospel to.
Ac 10:34–45; 15:14.
Given to Christ as his inheritance. Ps 2:8.
The gospel not to be preached to, till preached
to the Jews. Mt 10:5. Lk 24:47. Ac
13:46.
Hated and despised the Jews. Es 9:1, 5. Pss
44:13–14; 123:3.
Israel rejected till the fullness of. Ro 11:25.
Jerusalem trodden down by, etc. Lk 21:24.
THE JEWS
Despised, as if dogs. Mt 15:26.

Dispersed among.   Jn 7:35.
Never associated with.   Ac 10:28; 11:2–3.
Not to follow the ways of.   Lv 18:3. Jr
10:2.
Not to intermarry with.   Dt.7:3.
Often corrupted by.   2 K 17:7–8.
Permitted to have, as servants.   Lv 25:44.
Not allowed to enter the temple.   Ac
21:28–29.
Often ravaged and defiled the holy land and
sanctuary.   Ps 79:1. Lm 1:10.
Outer court of temple for.   Ep 2:14. Rv 11:2.
Paul the apostle of.   Ac 9:15. Gl 2:7–8.
Ruled by God.   2 Ch 20:6. Ps 47:8.
United with the Jews against Christ.   Ac
4:27.

GENTLENESS
Exhorted.   Ep 4:32. 1 P 3:8; 5:5.
Fruit of the Spirit.   Gl 5:22.
Mark of divine wisdom.   Ja 3:17.
Of the Christ.   2 Co 10:1. Mt 18:2. Jn
13:23.
Of the Messiah.   Is 40:1; 42:3.

GIFT OF THE HOLY GHOST
Abundant.   Ps 68:9. Jn 7:38–39.
By the Father.   Ne 9:20. Lk 11:13.
By the Son.   Jn 20:22.
An earnest of the inheritance of the saints.   2
Co 1:22; 5:5. Ep 1:14.
Evidence of union with Christ.   1 Jn 3:24;
4:13.
Fructifying.   Is 32:15.
GIVEN
According to promise.   Ac 2:38–39.
For comfort of saints.   Jn 14:16.
For instruction.   Ne 9:20.
In answer to prayer.   Lk 11:13. Ep
1:16–17.
Through the intercession of Christ.   Jn
14:16.
To Christ without measure.   Jn 3:34.
To the Gentiles.   Ac 10:44–45; 11:17;
15:8.
To those who obey God.   Ac 5:32.
To those who repent and believe.   Ac 2:38.
Upon the exaltation of Christ.   Ps 68:18.
Jn 7:39.
Permanent.   Is 59:21. Hg 2:5. 1 P 4:14.
A pledge of the continued favor of God.   Ezk
39:29.
Received through faith.   Gl 3:14.

GIFTS OF GOD
All blessings.   Ja 1:17. 2 P 1:3.
Dispensed according to his will.   Ec 2:26.
Dn 2:21. Ro 12:6. 1 Co 7:7.
Free and abundant.   Nu 14:8. Ro 8:32.
Illustrated.   Mt 25:15–30.
SPIRITUAL
Acknowledge.   Pss 4:7; 21:2.
Are through Christ.   Ps 68:18, with Ep
4:7–8. Jn 6:27.
Christ the chief of.   Is 42:6; 55:4. Jn 3:16;
4:10; 6:32–33.
Eternal life.   Ro 6:23.
Faith.   Ep 2:8. Php 1:29.
Glory.   Ps 84:11. Jn 17:22.
Grace.   Ps 84:11. Ja 4:6.
The Holy Ghost.   Lk 11:3. Ac 8:20.
A new heart.   Ezk 11:19.
Not repented of by him.   Ro 11:29.
Peace.   Ps 29:11.
Pray for.   Mt 7:7, 11. Jn 16:23–24.
Repentance.   Ac 11:18.
Rest.   Mt 11:28. 2 Th 1:7.
Righteousness.   Ro 5:16–17.
Strength and power.   Ps 68:35.
To be used for mutual profit.   1 P 4:10.
Wisdom.   Pr 2:6. Ja 1:5.
TEMPORAL
All creatures partake of.   Pss 136:25;
145:15–16.
All good things.   Ps 34:10. 1 Tm 6:17.
Food and raiment.   Mt 6:25–33.
Life.   Is 42:5.
Peace.   Lv 26:6. 1 Ch 22:9.
Pray for.   Zc 10:1. Mt 6:11.
Rain and fruitful seasons.   Gn 27:28. Lv
26:4–5. Is 30:23.
Should cause us to remember God.   Dt
8:18.
To be used and enjoyed.   Ec 3:13;
5:19–20. 1 Tm 4:4–5.
Wisdom.   2 Ch 1:12.

GLADNESS
Gift of God.   Pss 4:7; 30:11.
Should mark Christians.   Mt 5:12. Rv 19:7.
Source of strength.   Ne 8:10.

GLORIFYING GOD
Acceptable through Christ.   Php 1:11. 1 P
4:11.
ACCOMPLISHED BY
Bringing forth fruits of righteousness.   Jn
15:8. Php 1:11.

Confessing Christ. Php 2:11.
Doing all to him. 1 Co 10:31.
Dying for him. Jn 21:19.
Faithfulness. 1 P 4:11.
Glorifying Christ. Ac 19:17. 2 Th 1:12.
Patience in affliction. Is 24:15.
Praising him. Ps 50:23.
Relying on his promises. Ro 4:20.
Suffering for Christ. 1 P 4:14, 16.
All by nature fail in. Ro 3:23.
Blessings of God lead to. Is 60:21; 61:3.
Christ an example of. Jn 17:4.
Commanded. 1 Ch 16:28. Ps 22:23. Is 42:12.
Due to him. 1 Ch 16:29.
FOR HIS
Deliverance. Ps 50:15.
Faithfulness and truth. Is 25:1.
Grace to others. Ac 11:18. 2 Co 9:13. Gl 1:24.
Holiness. Ps 99:9. Rv 15:4.
Judgments. Is 25:3. Ezk 28:22. Rv 14:7.
Mercy and truth. Ps 115:1. Ro 15:9.
Wondrous works. Mt 15:31. Ac 4:21.
Heavenly hosts engaged in. Rv 4:11.
Holy example of saints may lead others to. Mt 5:16. 1 P 2:12.
Obligation of saints to. 1 Co 6:20.
Punishment for not. Dn 5:23, 30. Ml 2:2. Ac 12:23. Ro 1:21.
Required in body and spirit. 1 Co 6:20.
SAINTS SHOULD
Persevere in. Ps 86:12.
Resolve on. Pss 69:30; 118:28.
Unite in. Ps 34:3. Ro 15:6.
Shall be universal. Ps 86:9. Rv 5:13.
The wicked averse to. Dn 5:23. Ro 1:21.

GLORY

Bodies of saints shall be raised in. 1 Co 15:43. Php 3:21.
Christ is, to his people. Is 60:1. Lk 2:32.
ETERNAL
Accompanies salvation by Christ. 2 Tm 2:10.
Enhanced by present afflictions. 2 Co 4:17.
Inherited by saints. 1 S 2:8. Ps 73:24. Pr 3:35. Cl 3:4. 1 P 5:10.
Present afflictions not worthy to be compared with. Ro 8:18.
Procured by the death of Christ. He 2:10.
Saints afore prepared unto. Ro 9:23.
Saints called to. 2 Th 2:14. 1 P 5:10.

God is, to his people. Ps 3:3. Zc 2:5.
Gospel ordained to be, to saints. 1 Co 2:7.
Joy of saints is full of. 1 P 1:8.
Of hypocrites turned to shame. Ho 4:7.
Of the church shall be rich and abundant. Is 60:11–13.
Of the gospel, exceeds that of the law. 2 Co 3:9–10.
OF THE WICKED
Ends in destruction. Is 5:14.
Is in their shame. Php 3:19.
Saints shall be, of their ministers. 1 Th 2:19–20.
Seek not, from man. Mt 6:2. 1 Th 2:6.
SPIRITUAL
Is given by Christ. Jn 17:22.
Is given by God. Ps 84:11.
Is the work of the Holy Ghost. 2 Co 3:18.
TEMPORAL
The devil tries to seduce by. Mt 4:8.
Is given by God. Dn 2:37.
Passeth away. 1 P 1:24.

GLORY OF GOD

DESCRIBED AS
Eternal. Ps 104:31.
Great. Ps 138:5.
Highly exalted. Pss 8:1; 113:4.
Rich. Ep 3:16.
Earth is full of. Is 6:3.
Enlightens the church. Is 60:1–2. Rv 21:11, 23.
Exhibited in Christ. Jn 1:14. 2 Co 4:6. He 1:3.
EXHIBITED IN HIS
Holiness. Ex 15:11.
Majesty. Jb 37:22. Pss 93:1; 104:1; 145:5, 12. Is 2:10.
Name. Dt 28:58. Ne 9:5.
Power. Ex 15:1, 6. Ro 6:4.
Works. Pss 19:1; 111:3.
EXHIBITED TO
His church. Dt 5:24. Ps 102:16.
Moses. Ex 34:5–7, with 33:18–23.
Stephen. Ac 7:55.
God jealous of. Is 42:8.
Knowledge of shall fill the earth. Hk 2:14.
PEOPLE TO
Declare. 1 Ch 16:24. Ps 145:5, 11.
Magnify. Ps 57:5.
Plead in prayer. Ps 79:9.
Reverence. Is 59:19.
Saints desire to behold. Pss 63:2; 90:16.

GLUTTONY

Caution against. Pr 23:2–3. Lk 21:34. Ro 13:13–14.

Christ falsely accused of. Mt 11:19.

Danger of, illustrated. Lk 12:45–46.

Inconsistent in saints. 1 P 4:3.

LEADS TO

Carnal security. Is 22:13, with 1 Co 15:32. Lk 12:19.

Poverty. Pr 23:21.

Of princes, ruinous to their people. Ec 10:16–17.

Pray against temptations to. Ps 141:4.

Punishment of. Nu 11:33–34, with Ps 78:31. Dt 21:21. Am 6:4, 7.

The wicked addicted to. Php 3:19. Jde 1:12.

GOD

DECLARED TO BE

Compassionate. 2 K 13:23.

A consuming fire. He 12:29.

Eternal. Dt 33:27. Ps 90:2. Rv 4:8–10.

Faithful. 1 Co 10:13. 1 P 4:19.

Glorious. Ex 15:11. Ps 145:5.

Good. Pss 25:8; 119:68.

Gracious. Ex 34:6. Ps 116:5.

Great. 2 Ch 2:5. Ps 86:10.

Holy. Ps 99:9. Is 5:16.

Immortal. 1 Tm 1:17; 6:16.

Immutable. Ps 102:26–27. Ja 1:17.

Incorruptible. Ro 1:23.

Invisible. Jb 23:8, 9. Jn 1:18; 5:37. Cl 1:15. 1 Tm 1:17.

Jealous. Jsh 24:19. Na 1:2.

Just. Dt 32:4. Is 45:21.

Light. Is 60:19. Ja 1:17. 1 Jn 1:5.

Long-suffering. Nu 14:18. Mi 7:1.

Love. 1 Jn 4:8, 16.

Merciful. Ex 34:6–7. Ps 86:5.

Most High. Ps 83:18. Ac 7:48.

Omnipotent. Gn 17:1. Ex 6:3.

Omnipresent. Ps 139:7. Jr 23:23.

Omniscient. Ps 139:1–6. Pr 5:21.

Only wise. Ro 16:27. 1 Tm 1:17.

Perfect. Mt 5:48.

Righteous. Ezr 9:15. Ps 145:17.

True. Jr 10:10. Jn 17:3.

Unsearchable. Jb 11:7; 37:23. Ps 145:3. Is 40:28. Ro 11:33.

Upright. Pss 25:8; 92:15.

Fills heaven and earth. 1 K 8:27. Jr 23:24.

None before him. Is 43:10.

None beside him. Dt 4:35. Is 44:6.

None good but he. Mt 19:17.

None like to him. Ex 9:14. Dt 33:26. 2 S 7:22. Is 46:5, 9. Jr 10:6.

Should be worshiped in spirit and in truth. Jn 4:24.

A spirit. Jn 4:24. 2 Co 3:17.

GODLESSNESS

Of idolators. Ezk 14:5.

Of the unrighteous. Pss 10:4; 53:1.

Of those without hope. Ep 2:12.

GODLINESS

Expected of Christians. 1 Tm 6:11. Ti 2:12. 2 P 1:5.

Honored by God. Pss 4:3; 97:11. 1 Tm 4:7–8.

May be distorted. 1 Tm 6:5.

Mystery of. 1 Tm 3:16.

Rewarded. Mt 5:6. 1 Tm 6:6.

Value of. 1 Tm 4:8. 2 P 2:9.

GOLD

ABOUNDED IN

Havilah. Gn 2:11.

Ophir. 1 K 9:28. Ps 45:9.

Parvaim. 2 Ch 3:6.

Sheba. Ps 72:15. Is 60:6.

Abundance of, in Solomon's reign. 2 Ch 1:15.

An article of commerce. Ezk 27:22.

Belongs to God. Jl 3:5. Hg 2:8.

DESCRIBED AS

Fusible. Ex 32:3–4. Pr 17:3.

Malleable. Ex 39:3. 1 K 10:16–17.

Precious. Ezr 8:27. Is 13:12.

Valuable. Jb 28:15–16.

Yellow. Ps 68:13.

Estimated by weight. 1 Ch 28:14.

Exacted as tribute. 1 K 20:3, 5. 2 K 23:33, 35.

Found in the earth. Jb 28:1, 6.

Given as presents. 1 K 15:19. Mt 2:11.

ILLUSTRATIVE OF

Babylonian empire. Dn 2:38.

The doctrines of grace. Rv 3:18.

Saints after affliction. Jb 23:10.

Tried faith. 1 P 1:7.

True converts. 1 Co 3:12.

Imported by Solomon. 1 K 9:11, 28; 10:11.

Jews condemned for multiplying. Is 2:7.

Kings of Israel not to multiply. Dt 17:17.

Likely to grow dim. Lm 4:1.

Most valuable when pure and fine. Jb 28:19. Pss 19:10; 21:3. Pr 3:14.

Offerings of, for tabernacle. Ex 35:22.
Offerings of, for temple. 1 Ch 22:14; 29:4, 7.
Patriarchs were rich in. Gn 13:2.
Priestly and royal garments adorned with. Ex 28:4–6. Ps 45:9, 13.
Refined and tried by fire. Zc 13:9. 1 P 1:7.
Rusted. Ja 5:3.
Taken in war, dedicated to God. Jsh 6:19. 2 S 8:11. 1 K 15:15.
Used as money. Mt 10:9. Ac 3:6.
USED FOR
Chains. Gn 41:42. Dn 5:29.
Couches. Es 1:6.
Crowns. 2 S 12:30. Ps 21:3.
Earrings. Jg 8:24, 26.
Footstools. 2 Ch 9:18.
Idols. Ex 20:23. Ps 115:4. Dn 5:4.
Mercy seat and cherubims. Ex 25:17–18.
Ornaments. Jr 4:30.
Overlaying cherubim in the temple. 2 Ch 3:10.
Overlaying the ark, etc. Ex 25:11–13.
Overlaying the floor of temple. 1 K 6:30.
Overlaying the tabernacle. Ex 36:34, 38.
Overlaying the temple. 1 K 6:21–22.
Overlaying the throne of Solomon. 1 K 10:18.
Rings. S S 5:14. Ja 2:2.
Sacred candlesticks. Ex 25:31. 2 Ch 4:7, 20.
Sacred utensils. Ex 25:29, 38. 2 Ch 4:19–22.
Scepters. Es 4:11.
Shields. 2 S 8:7. 1 K 10:16–17.
Vessels. 1 K 10:21. Es 1:7.
Vanity of heaping up. Ec 2:8, 11.
Working in, a trade. Ne 3:8. Is 40:19.

GOLDEN RULE
Is the law and prophets. Mt 7:12.
Stated by Christ. Lk 6:31.

GOODNESS
And others. Mt 7:12.
And prayer. Pr 15:29.
Need of. Ro 12:9. Gl 6:10.
Power of. Ro 12:21.

GOODNESS OF GOD
DECLARED TO BE
Abundant. Ex 34:6. Ps 33:5.
Enduring. Pss 23:6, 52:1.
Great. Ne 9:35. Zc 9:17.
Rich. Ps 104:24. Ro 2:4.

Satisfying. Ps 65:4. Jr 31:12, 14.
Universal. Ps 145:9. Mt 5:45.
Despise not. Ro 2:4.
Leads to repentance. Ro 2:4.
Magnify. Ps 107:8. Jr 33:11.
MANIFESTED
In doing good. Pss 119:68; 145:9.
In forgiving sins. 2 Ch 30:18. Ps 86:5.
In providing for the poor. Ps 68:10.
In supplying temporal wants. Ac 14:17.
To his church. Ps 31:19. Lm 3:25.
Part of his character. Ps 25:8. Na 1:7. Mt 19:17.
Pray for the manifestation of. 2 Th 1:11.
Recognize, in his dealings. Ezr 8:18. Ne 2:18.
Reverence. Jr 33:9. Ho 3:5.
Urge others to confide in. Ps 34:8.
The wicked disregard. Ne 9:35.

THE GOSPEL
Awful consequences of not obeying. 2 Th 1:8–9.
Be careful not to hinder. 1 Co 9:12.
Brings peace. Lk 2:10, 14. Ep 6:15.
CALLED THE
Dispensation of the grace of God. Ep 3:2.
Doctrine according to godliness. 1 Tm 6:3.
Form of sound words. 2 Tm 1:13.
Glorious gospel of Christ. 2 Co 4:4.
Gospel of Christ. Ro 1:9, 16. 2 Co 2:12. 1 Th 3:2.
Gospel of God. Ro 1:1. 1 Th 2:8. 1 P 4:17.
Gospel of the grace of God. Ac 20:24.
Gospel of the kingdom. Mt 24:14.
Gospel of peace. Ep 6:15.
Gospel of salvation. Ep 1:13.
Ministration of the Spirit. 2 Co 3:8.
Mystery of the gospel. Ep 6:19.
Preaching of Jesus Christ. Ro 16:25.
Word of Christ. Cl 3:16.
Word of faith. Ro 10:8.
Word of God. 1 Th 2:13.
Word of grace. Ac 14:3; 20:32.
Word of life. Php 2:16.
Word of reconciliation. 2 Co 5:19.
Word of salvation. Ac 13:26.
Word of truth. Ep 1:13. Ja 1:18.
Everlasting. 1 P 1:25. Rv 14:6.
Exhibits the grace of God. Ac 14:3; 20:32.
Foretold. Is 41:27; 52:7; 61:1–3. Mk 1:15.
Glorious. 2 Co 4:4.

Good tidings of great joy for all people. Lk 2:10–11, 31–32.

Hid to them that are lost. 2 Co 4:3.

Knowledge of the glory of God by. 2 Co 4:4, 6.

Let him who preaches another be accursed. Gl 1:8.

Life and immortality brought to light by Jesus through. 2 Tm 1:10.

Ministers have a dispensation to preach. 1 Co 9:17.

Must be believed. Mk 1:15. He 4:2.

The power of God unto salvation. Ro 1:16. 1 Co 1:18. 1 Th 1:5.

Preached by Christ. Mt 4:23. Mk 1:14.

PREACHED TO

Abraham. Gn 22:18, with Gl 3:8.

Every creature. Mk 16:15. He 4:2.

The Gentiles. Mk 13:10. Gl 2:2, 9.

The Jews. Lk 24:47. Ac 13:46.

The poor. Mt 11:5. Lk 4:18.

Preached under the old testament. He 4:2.

Produces hope. Cl 1:23.

Profession of, attended by afflictions. 2 Tm 3:12.

Promises to sufferers for. Mk 8:35; 10:30.

Rejection of, by many, foretold. Is 53:1, with Ro 10:15–16.

Rejection of, by the Jews, a blessing to the Gentiles. Ro 11:28.

Saints have fellowship in. Php 1:5.

Testifies to the final judgment. Ro 2:16.

There is fullness of blessing in. Ro 15:29.

THOSE WHO RECEIVE, SHOULD

Adhere to the truth of. Gl 1:6–7, 2:14. 2 Tm 1:13.

Earnestly contend for the faith of. Php 1:17, 27. Jde 1:3.

Have their conversation becoming. Php 1:27.

Live in subjection to. 2 Co 9:13.

Not be ashamed of. Ro 1:16. 2 Tm 1:8.

Sacrifice friends and property for. Mt 10:37.

Sacrifice life itself for. Mk 8:35.

GOVERNMENT

CHURCH

Christ the head. Ep 5:23. Cl 2:19.

Through apostles. Mt 10:1–4. Ac 6:1–2.

Through bishops. Php 1:1. 1 Tm 3:2.

Through church councils. Ac 15.

Through deacons. Ac 6:3–7.

Through elders. Ac 14:23. 1 Tm 5:17.

Through lot. Ac 1:26.

Through prayer. Ac 1:24.

Through prophets and evangelists. Ep 4:11.

Through teachers. Ac 13:1.

Through the people. Ac 6:5.

DIVINE

Through Christ. Is 9:6. Mt 29:18. Jn 3:35. 1 Co 15:24–25. Ep 1:22. Rv 11:15.

Through human government. 1 S 16:1. Jg 2:14–18.

Through providence. Jg 2:14–16. Ho 4:5. Ml 1:14.

Through special spokesmen. Ho 12:13. Jr 1:13–19.

Through the kingdom. Pss 22:28; 99:1. 1 Co 4:20. He 1:8. Rv 19:6.

HUMAN

By divinely appointed leaders. Ex 12:35. Jg 2:16.

By elders. Ex 12:21.

By governors. Ezr 6:7.

By judges. Ex 18:13–26. Dt 1:9–18.

By kings. 1 S 10:24.

Of the people. Jg 11:11.

To be obeyed when possible. Ro 13. Ti 3:1. 1 P 2:13.

To be subordinate to God, and therefore to be obeyed when consonant with his will. Ro 13:4. Ac 5:29. Dn 3. Jr 32:1–5.

GRACE

Antinomians abused. Jde 1:4.

Beware lest you fail of. He 12:15.

Came by Christ. Jn 1:17. Ro 5:15.

Christ spoke with. Ps 45:2, with Lk 4:22.

Christ was full of. Jn 1:14.

DESCRIBED AS

All-abundant. Ro 5:15, 17, 20.

All-sufficient. 2 Co 12:9.

Exceeding. 2 Co 9:14.

Glorious. Ep 1:6.

Great. Ac 4:33.

Manifold. 1 P 4:10.

Rich. Ep 1:7; 2:7.

Sovereign. Ro 5:21.

Foretold by the prophets. 1 P 1:10.

Given by Christ. 1 Co 1:4.

Glory of, exhibited in our acceptance in Christ. Ep 1:6.

God the Giver of. Ps 84:11. Ja 1:17.

God the God of all. 1 P 5:10.

God's throne, the throne of. He 4:16.

God's work completed in saints by. 2 Th 1:11–12.

The gospel a declaration of. Ac 20:24, 32.

Holy Ghost is the Spirit of. Zc 12:10. He 10:29.

Inheritance of the promises by. Ro 4:16.

Justification by, opposed to that by works. Ro 4:4–5; 11:6. Gl 5:4.

Manifestation of, in others, a cause of gladness. Ac 11:23. 3 Jn 1:3–4.

Necessary to the service of God. He 12:28.

Not to be abused. Ro 3:8; 6:1, 15.

Not to be received in vain. 2 Co 6:1.

PRAY FOR
For others. 2 Co 13:14. Ep 6:24.
For yourselves. He 4:16.

Riches of, exhibited in God's kindness through Christ. Ep 2:7.

SAINTS
Abound in gifts of. Ac 4:33. 2 Co 8:1; 9:8, 14.
Are heirs of. 1 P 3:7.
Are under. Ro 6:14.
Are what they are by. 1 Co 15:10. 2 Co 1:12.
Receive, from Christ. Jn 1:16.
Should be established in. He 13:9.
Should be strong in. 2 Tm 2:1.
Should grow in. 2 P 3:18.
Should speak with. Ep 4:29. Cl 4:6.

SOURCE OF
The call of God. Gl 1:15.
Consolation. 2 Th 2:16.
Election. Ro 11:5.
Faith. Ac 18:27.
Forgiveness of sins. Ep 1:7.
Hope. 2 Th 2:16.
Justification. Ro 3:24. Ti 3:7.
Salvation. Ac 15:11. Ep 2:5, 8.

SPECIALLY GIVEN
To ministers. Ro 12:3, 6; 15:15. 1 Co 3:10. Gl 2:9. Ep 3:7.
To the humble. Pr 3:24, with Ja 4:6.
To those who walk uprightly. Ps 84:11.

Special manifestation of, at the second coming of Christ. 1 P 1:13.

Success and completion of the work of God to be attributed to. Zc 4:7.

Was upon Christ. Lk 2:40. Jn 3:34.

GRASS
CALLED
Of the earth. Rv 9:4.

Of the field. Nu 22:4.

Cattle fed upon. Jb 6:5. Jr 50:11.

DESTROYED BY
Drought. 1 K 17:1, with 18:5.
Hail and lightning. Rv 8:7.
Locusts. Rv 9:4.

Failure of, a great calamity. Is 15:5–6.

GOD
Adorns and clothes. Mt 6:30.
Causes to grow. Pss 104:14; 147:8.
The giver of. Dt 11:15.
Originally created. Gn 1:11–12.

A green herb. Mk 6:39.

ILLUSTRATIVE OF
Prosperity of the wicked. Ps 92:7.
Saints refreshed by grace (when refreshed by dew and showers). Ps 72:6. Mi 5:7.
Shortness and uncertainty of life. Pss 90:5–6; 103:15. Is 40:6–7. 1 P 1:24.
The wicked (when on housetops). 2 K 19:26. Is 37:27.

Often grew on the tops of houses. Ps 129:6.

Ovens often heated with. Mt 6:30.

Refreshed by rain and dew. Dt 32:2. Pr 19:12.

Soft and tender when young. Pr 27:25.

Springs out of the earth. 2 S 23:4.

Sufferings of cattle from failure of, described. Jr 14:5–6.

GRIEF
Marked Christ. Is 53:3–10. Jn 11:35.

May mark the righteous. Ps 139:21. 1 P 2:19.

Of men, lifted by God. Is 61:3. 2 Co 1:5.

Of the Holy Spirit. Ep 4:30.

GROWTH
In grace. 2 P 3:18.

In spiritual knowledge. 2 P 3:18.

In spiritual things. Mk 4:28.

In the life of Jesus. Lk 12:40, 52.

Obstacles to. Ac 18:24–28. 1 Co 3:1–3.

Of Christians. Ep 4:14–15.

Of faith. 2 Th 1:3.

Of the kingdom. Mk 4:30–32.

Through God's word. 1 P 2:2.

GUIDANCE
Of believers. Ps 32:8. Jn 0:3.

Of Israel. Ex 15:13. Dt 32:12. Ne 9:19.

Through divine light. Ps 43:3.

Through the word of God. Is 30:21.

Through witnessing. Pr 3:6.
Unto love and endurance. 2 Th 3:5.
Unto repentance. Ro 2:4.
Unto satisfaction. Rv 7:17.

GUILT
See Conscience; Forgiveness of Injuries; Forgiveness of Sin; Grace; Redemption; Sacrifices; Salvation; Sin.

H

HAIR
Black, particularly esteemed. S S 5:11.
Color of, changed by leprosy. Lv 13:3, 10, 20.
Cut off in affliction. Jr 7:29.
GOD
  Numbers. Mt 10:30.
  Takes care of. Dn 3:27. Lk 21:18.
Growth of. Jg 16:22.
Innumerable. Pss 40:12, 69:4.
JUDGMENTS EXPRESSED BY
  Sending baldness for. Is 3:24. Jr 47:5.
  Shaving. Is 7:20.
Man cannot even change the color of. Mt 5:36.
Men condemned for wearing long. 1 Co 11:14.
Natural covering of the head. Ps 68:21.
OF NAZARITES
  Not to be cut or shorn during their vow.
    Nu 6:5. Jg 16:7, 19–20.
  Shorn after completion of vow. Nu 6:18.
Often expensively anointed. Ec 9:8.
Of the healed leper, to be shorn. Lv 14:9.
OF WOMEN
  Neglected in grief. Lk 7:38. Jn 12:3.
  Plaited and broidered. 1 Tm 2:9. 1 P 3:3.
  Well set and ornamented. Is 3:24.
  Worn long for a covering. 1 Co 11:15.
Plucked out in extreme grief. Ezr 9:3.
Plucking out of, a reproach. Ne 13:25. Is 50:6.
Sometimes worn long by men. 2 S 14:26.
WHITE OR GRAY
  An emblem of wisdom. Dn 7:9, with Jb 12:12.
  To be reverenced. Lv 19:32.
  A token of age. 1 S 12:2. Ps 71:18.
  A token of weakness and decay. Ho 7:9.
  With righteousness, a crown of glory. Pr 16:31.

HANDS
Clapped together in joy. 2 K 11:12. Ps 47:1.
CRIMINALS OFTEN
  Bound by. Mt 22:13.

Deprived of. Dt 25:12. 2 S 4:12.
Hung by. Lm 5:12.
Mutilated in. Jg 1:6–7.
DISTINGUISHED AS
  Left. Gn 14:15. Ac 21:3.
  Right. Ac 3:7.
God makes impotent. Jb 5:12.
God strengthens. Gn 49:24.
ILLUSTRATIVE OF
  Illiberality, when shut. Dt 15:7.
  Liberality, when opened. Dt 15:8. Ps 104:28.
  Power. 1 K 18:46. 2 K 13:5.
  Rebellion, when lifted up against another. 2 S 20:21.
Imposition of, a first principle of the doctrine of Christ. He 6:1–2.   X
IMPOSITION OF, USED IN
  Blessing. Gn 48:14. Mk 10:16.
  Conferring civil power. Nu 27:18. Dt 34:9.
  Imparting the gifts of the Holy Ghost. Ac 8:17; 19:6.
  Ordaining ministers. Ac 6:6. 1 Tm 4:14.
  Setting apart the Levites. Nu 8:10.
  Transferring guilt of sacrifices. Lv 1:4; 3:2; 16:21–22.
The Jews carried a staff in. Ex 12:11. 2 K 4:29.
The Jews ate with. Mt 26:23.
Kissed in idolatrous worship. Jb 31:27.
Many expert with both. 1 Ch 12:2.
Many with more command of the left. Jg 3:15, 21; 20:16.
Necessary members of the body. 1 Co 12:21.
Often spread out in prayer. Ps 68:31. Is 1:15.
OF THE WICKED, DESCRIBED AS
  Bloody. Is 1:15; 59:3.
  Ensnaring to themselves. Ps 9:16.
  Mischievous. Ps 26:10. Mi 7:3.
  Slothful. Pr 6:10; 21:25.
  Violent. Ps 58:2. Is 59:6.
PARTS OF, MENTIONED
  Fingers. 2 S 21:20. Dn 5:5.
  Palm. Is 49:16. Mt 26:67.

Thumb. Ex 29:20. Lv 14:14, 17.

Placed under the thigh of a person to whom an oath was made. Gn 24:2–3; 47:29–31.

RIGHT HAND

Accuser stood at, of the accused. Ps 109:6. Zc 3:1.

Given in token of friendship. Gl 2:9.

Of healed leper, touched with blood of his sacrifice. Lv 14:14, 17, 25.

Of healed leper, touched with oil. Lv 14:28.

Of priests, touched with blood of consecration-ram. Ex 29:20. Lv 8:23–24.

Place of honor. 1 K 2:19. Ps 45:9.

Place of power. Ps 110:1. Mk 14:62.

Signet worn on. Jr 22:24.

Sworn by. Is 62:8.

Used in embracing. 2 S 20:9. S S 2:6; 8:3.

RIGHT HAND, ILLUSTRATIVE OF

Corruption, when full of bribes. Ps 26:10.

Deceitfulness, when full of falsehood. Ps 144:8, 11. Is 44:20.

Extreme self-denial, when cutting off. Mt 5:30.

Protection, when standing at. Pss 16:8; 109:31; 110:5.

Strength and power. Ex 15:6. Ps 17:7.

Support, when holding by. Ps 73:23. Is 41:13.

Support withheld, when withdrawn. Ps 74:11.

Saints blessed in the work of. Dt 2:7; 30:9. Jb 1:10. Ps 90:17.

Servants directed by movements of. Ps 123:2.

Servants pour water on, by custom. 2 K 3:11.

SHOULD BE EMPLOYED IN

Acts of benevolence. Pr 3:27; 31:20.

God's service. Ne 2:18. Zc 8:9, 13.

Work. Ep 2:28. 1 Th 4:11.

Smitten together in extreme anger. Nu 24:10. Ezk 21:14, 17.

Stretched out in derision. Ho 7:5. Zp 2:15.

Suretyship entered into by striking. Jb 17:3. Pr 6:1, 17:18; 22:26.

Treaties made by joining. 2 K 10:15. Pr 11:21.

USES OF, MENTIONED

Feeling. Ps 115:7. 1 Jn 1:1.

Holding. Jg 7:20. Rv 10:2.

Making signs. Is 13:2. Ac 12:17.

Striking. Mk 14:65. Jn 19:3.

Taking. Gn 3:22. Ex 4:4.

Writing. Is 44:5. Gl 6:11.

Working. Pr 31:19. 1 Th 4:11.

WERE LIFTED UP IN

Blessing. Lv 9:22.

Praise. Ps 134:2.

Prayer. Ps 141:2. Lm 3:41.

Taking an oath. Gn 14:22. Rv 10:5.

WERE WASHED

After touching an unclean person. Lv 15:11.

Before eating. Mt 15:2. Mk 7:3.

In token of innocence. Dt 21:6–7. Mt 27:24.

The wicked recompensed for the work of. Ps 28:4. Pr 12:14. Is 3:11.

HAPPINESS OF SAINTS

Abundant and satisfying. Pss 36:8; 63:5.

DERIVED FROM

Divine chastening. Jb 5:17. Ja 5:11.

Fear of God. Ps 128:1–2. Pr 28:14.

Finding wisdom. Pr 3:13.

God being their help. Ps 146:5.

God being their Lord. Ps 144:15.

Having mercy on the poor. Pr 14:21.

Hope in the Lord. Ps 146:5.

Hope of glory. Ro 5:2.

Obedience to God. Ps 40:8. Jn 13:17.

Praising God. Ps 135:3.

Salvation. Dt 33:29. Is 12:2–3.

Suffering for Christ. 2 Co 12:10. 1 P 3:14; 4:13–14.

Their mutual love. Ps 133:1.

Trust in God. Pr 16:20. Php 4:6–7.

Words of Christ. Jn 17:13.

Described by Christ in the Beatitudes. Mt 5:3–12.

Found only in the ways of wisdom. Pr 3:17–18.

Is in God. Ps 73:25–26.

HAPPINESS OF THE WICKED

DERIVED FROM

Drunkenness. Is 5:11; 56:12.

Gluttony. Is 22:13. Hk 1:16.

Popular applause. Ac 12:22.

Successful oppression. Hk 1:15. Ja 5:6.

Their power. Jb 21:7. Ps 37:35.

Their wealth. Jb 21:13. Ps 52:7.

Their worldly prosperity. Pss 17:14; 73:3–4, 7.

Vain pleasure. Jb 21:12. Is 5:12.

Envy not. Ps 37:1.

Illustrated. Ps 37:35–36. Lk 12:16–20; 16:19–25.

Leads to recklessness. Is 22:13.
Leads to sorrow. Pr 14:13.
Limited to this life. Ps 17:14. Lk 16:25.
Marred by jealousy. Es 5:13.
Often interrupted by judgments. Nu 11:33, Jb 15:21. Ps 73:18–20. Jr 25:10, 11.
Saints often permitted to see the end of. Ps 73:17–20.
Short. Jb 20:5.
Sometimes a stumbling block to saints. Ps 73:3, 16. Jr. 12:1. Hk 1:13.
Uncertain. Lk 12:20. Ja 4:13–14.
Vain. Ec 2:1; 7:6.
Woe against. Am 6:1. Lk 6:25.

HARDSHIP
Of believers. Ps 137:4.
Of Christian workers. 2 Tm 2:3.
Of Christians. Jn 16:33. Ac 15:26.
Of Paul. 2 Co 11:23–27.
Of sinners. Pr 13:15.
Overcome. Jn 16:33. 2 Co 4:17; 12:10.

HARMONY
Blessing of. Ps 133:1.
Condition of. Am 3:3.
Desirability of. Ro 12:18. Ep 4:3.

HARVEST
CALLED THE
  Appointed weeks of harvest. Jr 5:24.
  Harvest time. 2 S 23:13. Jr 50:16.
FAILURE OF
  A cause of great grief. Is 16:9. Jl 1:11.
  Occasioned by drought. Am 4:7.
  Occasioned by locusts. Jl 1:4.
  A punishment for sin. Is 17:10–11.
  Sometimes continued for years. Gn 45:6.
Fields appeared white before. Jn 4:35.
Former and latter rain necessary to abundance of. Jr 5:24. Am 4:7.
ILLUSTRATIVE OF
  The end of the world. Mt 13:30, 39.
  God's protection, etc. (dew in). Is 18:4.
  Honor given to fools (rain in). Pr 26:1.
  A refreshing message (cold in). Pr 25:13.
  Ripeness for wrath. Jl 3;13. Rv 14:15.
  Seasons of grace. Jr 8:20.
  A time of judgment. Jr 51:33. Ho 6:11.
  A time when many are ready to receive the gospel. Mt 9:37–38. Jn 4:35.
Ingathering of fruits of the fields. Mk 4:29.
Legal provision for the poor during. Lv 19:9–10; 23:22. Dt 24:19.

Men and women engaged in. Ru 2:8–9.
Miraculous thunder, etc., in. 1 S 12:17–18.
Not to be commenced until the first fruits had been offered to God. Lv 23:10, 14.
Of barley at the passover. Lv 23:6, 10. Ru 1:22.
Of wheat at Pentecost. Ex 34:22. 1 S 12:17.
Omitted in the sabbatical year. Lv 25:5.
Omitted in year of jubilee. Lv 25:11–12.
Patience required in waiting for. Ja 5:7.
PERSONS ENGAGED IN
  Binders. Gn 37:7. Ps 129:7.
  Called harvestmen. Is 17:5.
  Called laborers. Mt 9;37.
  Fed by the husbandman during. Ru 2:14.
  Often defrauded of their wages. Ja 5:4.
  Reapers. Ru 2:4.
  Received wages. Jn 4:36.
The sabbath to be observed during. Ex 34:21.
Slothfulness during, ruinous. Pr 10:5.
Time of great joy. Ps 126:6. Is 9:3.
To continue without intermission. Gn 8:22.

HATRED
Christ experienced. Ps 35:19, with Jn 7:7. Jn 15:18, 24–25.
Embitters life. Pr 15:17.
Forbidden. Lv 19:17. Cl 3:8.
INCONSISTENT WITH
  The knowledge of God. 1 Jn 2:9, 11.
  The love of God. 1 Jn 4:20.
Is murder. 1 Jn 3:15.
Leads to deceit. Pr 26:24–25.
Liars prone to. Pr 26:28.
Often cloaked by deceit. Pr 10:18; 26:26.
Punishment of. Pss 34:21; 44:7; 89:23. Am 1:11.
SAINTS SHOULD
  Expect. Mt 10:22. Jn 15:8–19.
  Give no cause for. Pr 25:17.
  Not marvel at. 1 Jn 3:13.
  Not rejoice in the calamities of those who exhibit. Jb 31:29–30. Ps 35:13–14.
  Return good for. Ex 23:5. Mt 5:44.
Stirs up strife. Pr 10:12.
WE SHOULD EXHIBIT AGAINST
  Backsliding. Ps 101:3.
  Evil. Ps 97:10. Pr 8:13.
  False ways. Ps 119:104, 128.
  Hatred and opposition to God. Ps 139:21–22.
  Lying. Ps 119:163.

THE WICKED EXHIBIT TOWARD
Each other. Ti 3:3.
God. Ro 1:30.
Saints. Ps 25:19. Pr 29:10.

HATRED TO CHRIST
Illustrated. Lk 19:12–14, 17.
INVOLVES
Hatred to his Father. Jn 15:23–24.
Hatred to his people. Jn 15:18.
Is on account of his testimony against the world. Jn 7:7.
Is without cause. Ps 69:4, with Jn 15:25.
No escape for those who persevere in. 1 Co 15:25. He 10:29–31.
Punishment of. Pss 2:2, 9; 21:8.

HEAD
All the other members necessary to. 1 Co 12:21.
Body supported and supplied by. Ep 4:16.
BOWED DOWN
As a token of respect. Gn 43:28.
In worshiping God. Gn 24:26. Ex 4:31.
Derision expressed by shaking, etc. 2 K 19:21. Pss 22:7; 109:25. Mt 27:39.
ILLUSTRATIVE OF
The chief city of a kingdom. Is 7:8.
Chief men. Is 9:14–15.
Christ. 1 Co 11:3. Ep 1:22. Cl 2:19.
Defense and protection, when covered. Ps 140:7.
Exaltation, when lifted up. Gn 40:13. Ps 27:6.
God. 1 Co 11:3.
Heavy judgments, when made bald. Is 3:24; 15:2; 22:12. Mi 1:16.
Joy and confidence, when lifted up. Ps 3:3. Lk 21:28.
Joy and prosperity, when anointed. Pss 23:5; 92:10.
Pride, etc., when lifted up. Ps 83:2.
Rulers. 1 S 15:17. Dn 2:38.
Subjection, when covered. 1 Co 11:5, 10.
IN GRIEF
Covered up. 2 S 15:30. Es 6:12.
One's hands placed on. 2 S 13:19. Jr 2:37.
Shorn. Jb 1:20.
Sprinkled with dust. Jsh 7:6. Jb 2:12.
The Jews censured for swearing by. Mt 5:36.
LIABLE TO
Baldness. Lv 13:40–41. Is 15:2.
Internal disease. 2 K 4:19. Is 1:5.
Leprosy. Lv 13:42–44.

Scab. Is 3:17.
Nazarites forbidden to shave. Nu 6:5.
Of criminals often cut off. Mt 14:10.
Of enemies slain in war, often cut off. Jg 5:26. 1 S 17:51, 57; 31:9.
Often anointed. Ec 9:8. Mt 6:17.
Of the leper always uncovered. Lv 13:45.
Of women generally covered in public. Gn 24:65. 1 Co 11:5.
PARTS OF, MENTIONED
Crown. Gn 49:26. Is 3:17.
Face. Gn 48:12. 2 K 9:30.
Forehead. 1 S 17:49. Ezk 9:4.
Hair. Jg 16:22. Ps 40:12.
Scalp. Ps 68:21.
Skull. 2 K 9:35. Mt 27:33.
Temples. Jg 4:21–22. S S 4:3.
Priests forbidden to shave, etc. Lv 21:5, 10.
Put for the life. Dn 1:10. 1 S 28:2.
Put for the whole person. Gn 49:26. Pr 10:6.
Uppermost and chief member of the body. Is 1:6. 2 K 6:31.
When hoary with age to be respected. Lv 19:32.

HEALTH
Communicated through gifts. 1 Co 12:9.
Connected with spiritual health. 3 Jn 1:2. 1 Co 11:30.
Promise of. Ex 15:26. Dt 7:15. Jr 30:17.
Restoration of. Ps 147:3.
Restored through faith. Ja 5:15.
Through Christ. Mk 3:15. Lk 7:21–22. Ac 9:34.

HEART
Faith, the means of purifying. Ac 15:9.
GOD
Creates a new. Ps 51:10. Ezk 36:26.
Enlightens. 2 Co 4:6. Ep 1:18.
Establishes. Ps 112:8. 1 Th 3:13.
Influences. 1 S 10:26. Ezr 6:22; 7:27. Pr 21:1. Jr 20:9.
Knows. Ps 44:21. Jr 20:12.
Opens. Ac 16:14.
Ponders. Pr 21:2; 24:12.
Prepares. 1 Ch 29:18. Pr 16:1.
Searches. 1 Ch 28:9. Jr 17:10.
Strengthens. Ps 27:14.
Tries. 1 Ch 29:17. Jr 12:3.
Understands the thoughts of. 1 Ch 28:9. Ps 139:2.
Harden not, against God. Ps 95:8, with He 4:7.

Harden not against the poor. Dt 15:7.
He that trusteth in, is a fool. Pr 28:26.
Issues of life are out of. Pr 4:23.
Know the plague of. 1 K 8:38.
No man can cleanse. Pr 20:9.
PRAY THAT IT MAY BE
Cleansed. Ps 51:10.
Directed into the love of God. 2 Th 3:5.
Inclined to God's testimonies. Ps 119:36.
United to fear God. Ps 86:11.
The pure in, shall see God. Mt 5:8.
Regard not iniquity in. Ps 66:18.
Renewal of, promised under the gospel. Ezk
11:19; 36:26. He 3:10.
SHOULD BE
Applied unto wisdom. Ps 90:12. Pr 2:2.
Given to God. Pr 23:26.
Guided in the right way. Pr 23:19.
Kept with diligence. Pr 4:23.
Perfect with God. 1 K 8:61.
Prepared unto God. 1 S 7:3.
Purified. Ja 4:8.
Single. Ep 6:5. Cl 3:22.
Tender. Ep 4:32.
Take heed lest it be deceived. Dt 11:16.
WE SHOULD
Believe with the. Ac 8:37. Ro 10:10.
Do the will of God from the. Ep 6:6.
Keep God's statutes with all. Dt 26:16.
Love God with all. Mt 22:37.
Love one another with a pure. 1 P 1:22.
Return to God with all. Dt 30:2.
Sanctify God in the. 1 P 3:15.
Serve God with all. Dt 11:13.
Trust in God with all. Pr 3:5.
Walk before God with all. 1 K 2:4.
When broken and contrite, not despised by
God. Ps 51:17.

HEART, RENEWED
Awed by the word of God. Ps 119:161.
Broken, contrite. Pss 34:18; 51:17.
Circumcised. Dt 30:6. Ro 2:29.
Clean. Ps 73:1.
Confident in God. Ps 112:7.
Desirous of God. Ps 84:2.
Enlarged. Ps 119:32. 2 Co 6:11.
Faithful to God. Ne 9:8.
Filled with the fear of God. Jr 32:40.
Filled with the law of God. Pss 40:8; 119:11.
Fixed on God. Pss 57:7; 112:7.
Honest and good. Lk 8:15.
Inclined to obedience. Ps 119:112.
Joyful in God. 1 S 2:1. Zc 10:7.

Meditative. Pss 4:4; 77:6.
Obedient. Ps 119:112. Ro 6:17.
Perfect with God. 1 K 8:61. Ps 101:2.
Prayerful. 1 S 1:13. Ps 27:8.
Prepared to seek God. 2 Ch 19:3. Ezr 7:10.
Ps 10:17.
Pure. Ps 24:4. Mt 5:8
Single and sincere. Ac 2:46. He 10:22.
Sympathizing. Jr 4:19. Lm 3:51.
Tender. 1 S 24:5. 2 K 22:19.
A treasury of good. Mt 12:35.
Upright. Pss 97:11; 125:4.
Void of fear. Ps 27:3.
Wholly devoted to God. Pss 9:1; 199:10, 69,
145.
Wise. Pr 10:8; 14:33; 23:15.
Zealous. 2 Ch 17:6. Jr 20:9.

HEART, UNRENEWED
Blind. Ep 4:18.
Carnal. Ro 8:7.
Covetous. Jr 22:17. 2 P 2:14.
Darkened. Ro 1:21.
Deceitful. Jr 17:9.
Deceived. Is 44:20. Ja 1:26.
Desperately wicked. Jr 17:9.
Despiteful. Ezk 25:15.
Divided. Ho 10:2.
Double. 1 Ch 12:33. Ps 12:2.
Elated by prosperity. 2 Ch 26:16. Dn 5:20.
Elated by sensual indulgence. Ho 13:6.
Ensnaring. Ec 7:26.
Far from God. Is 29:13, with Mt 15:8.
Foolish. Pr 12:23; 22:15.
Fretful against the Lord. Pr 19:3.
Froward. Ps 101:4. Pr 6:14; 17:20.
Full of evil. Ec 9:3.
Full of evil imaginations. Gn 6:5; 8:21. Pr
6:18.
Full of vain thoughts. Jr 4:14.
Fully set to do evil. Ec 8:11.
Hard. Ezk 3:7. Mk 10:5. Ro 2:5.
Hateful to God. Pr 6:16, 18; 11:20.
Haughty. Pr 18:12. Jr 48:29.
Idolatrous. Ezk 14:3-4.
Impenitent. Ro 2:5.
Influenced by the devil. Jn 13:2.
Mad. Ec 9:3.
Michievous. Pss 28:3; 140:2.
Not perfect with God. 1 K 15:3. Ac 8:21.
Pr 6:18.
Not prepared to seek God. 2 Ch 12:14.
Of little worth. Pr 10:20.

Often judicially hardened. Ex 4:21. Jsh 11:20.
Often judicially stupefied. Is 6:10. Ac 28:26–27.
Perverse. Pr 12:8.
Prone to depart from God. Dt 29:18. Jr 17:5.
Prone to error. Ps 95:10.
Proud. Ps 101:5. Jr 49:16.
Rebellious. Jr. 5:23.
Stiff. Ezk 2:4.
Stony. Ezk 11:19; 36:26.
Stout. Is 10:12; 46:12.
Studieth destruction. Pr 24:2.
A treasury of evil. Mt 12:35. Mk 7:21.
Unbelieving. He 3:12.
Uncircumcised. Lv 26:41. Ac 7:51.

HEATHEN
Aid missions to. 2 Co 11:9. 3 Jn 1:6–7.
Are without God and Christ. Ep 2:12.
Baptism to be administered to. Mt 28:19.
Cautions against imitating. Jr 10:2. Mt 6:7.
The church shall be avenged of. Ps 149:7. Jr 10:25. Ob 1:15.
Conversion of, acceptable to God. Ac 10:35. Ro 15:16.
Danger of intercourse with. Ps 106:35.
Degradation of. Lv 25:44.
DESCRIBED AS
    Cruel. Ps 74:20. Ro 1:31.
    Filthy. Ezr 6:21. Ep 4:19; 5:12.
    Having no hope. Ep 2:12.
    Idolatrous. Ps 135:15. Ro 1:23, 25.
    Ignorant. 1 Co 1:21. Ep 4:18.
    Persecuting. Ps 2:1–2. 2 Co 11:26.
    Scoffing at saints. Ps 79:10.
    Strangers to the covenant of promise. Ep 2:12.
    Worshipers of the devil. 1 Co 10:20.
Employed to chastise the church. Lv 26:33. Jr 39:14. Lm 1:3. Ezk 7:24; 25:7. Dn 4:27. Hk 1:5–9.
Evil of imitating. 2 K 16:3. Ezk 11:12.
Given to Christ. Ps 2:8. Dn 7:14.
Glory of God to be declared among. 1 Ch 16:24. Ps 96:3.
GOD
    Brings to nought the counsels of. Ps 33:10.
    Punishes. Ps 44:2. Jl 3:11–13. Mi 5:15. Hk 3:12. Zc 14:18.
    Rules over. 2 Ch 20:6. Ps 47:8.
    Will be exalted among. Pss 46:10; 102:15.

Will finally judge. Ro 2:12–16.
Gospel received by. Ac 11:1; 13:48; 15:3, 23.
Gospel to be preached to. Mt 24:14; 28:19. Ro 16:26. Gl 1:16.
HAVE
    Evidence of the goodness of God. Ac 14:17.
    Evidence of the power of God. Ro 1:19–20. Ac 17:27.
    The testimony of conscience. Ro 2:14–15.
The Holy Ghost poured out upon. Ac 10:44–45; 15:8.
Necessity for preaching to. Ro 10:14.
Praise God for success of the gospel among. Ps 98:1–3. Ac 11:18.
Pray for. Ps 67:2–5.
Salvation of, foretold. Gn 12:3, with Gl 3:8. Is 2:2–4. 52:10; 60:1–8.
Salvation provided for. Ac 28:28. Ro 15:9–12.

HEAVEN
Angels are in. Mt 18:10; 24:36.
CHRIST
    As mediator, entered into. Ac 3:21. He 6:20; 9:12, 24.
    Is all-powerful in. Mt 28:18. 1 P 3:22.
Created by God. Gn 1:1. Rv 10:6.
Enoch and Elijah translated into. Gn 5:24, with He 11:5. 2 K 2:11.
Everlasting. Ps 89:29. 2 Co 5:1.
Flesh and blood cannot inherit. 1 Co 15:50.
GOD
    Answers his people from. 1 Ch 21:26. 2 Ch 7:14. Ne 9:27. Ps 20:6.
    Fills. 1 K 8:27. Jr 23:24.
    Is the Lord of. Dn 5:23. Mt 11:25.
    Reigns in. Pss 11:4; 135:6. Dn 4:35.
    Sends his judgments from. Gn 19:24. 1 S 2:10. Dn 4:13–14. Ro 1:18.
God's dwelling place. 1 K 8:30. Mt 6:9.
God's throne. Is 66:1, with Ac 7:49.
Happiness of, described. Rv 7:16–17.
High. Ps 103:11. Is 57:15.
Holy. Dt 26:15. Ps 20:6. Is 57:15.
Immeasurable. Jr 31:37.
IS CALLED
    The Father's house. Jn 14:2.
    A garner. Mt 3:12.
    A heavenly country. He 11:16.
    The kingdom of Christ and of God. Ep 5:5.
    Paradise. 2 Co 12:2, 4.

A rest. He 4:9.
Lay up treasure in. Mt 6:20. Lk 12:33.
Names of saints are written in. Lk 10:20. He 12:23.
Repentance occasions joy in. Lk 15:7.
Saints rewarded in. Mt 5:12. 1 P 1:4.
The wicked excluded from: Gl. 5:21, Ep. 5:5. Rv 22:15.

HEAVE OFFERING
CONSISTED OF
First fruits of bread. Nu 15:19–21.
Part of all gifts. Nu 18:29.
Part of spoil taken in war. Nu 31:26–47.
Part of the meat offering of all peace offerings. Lv 7:14.
Right shoulder of peace offerings. Lv 7:32.
Shoulder of the priest's consecration ram. Ex 29:27.
Given to the priests. Ex 29:28. Lv 7:34.
Sanctified the whole offering. Nu 18:27, 30.
TO BE
Best of their kind. Nu 18:29.
Brought to God's house. Dt 12:6.
Eaten in a clean place. Lv 10:12–15.
Heaved up by the priest. Ex 29:27.

HEEDFULNESS
Commanded. Ex 23:13. Pr 4:25–27.
NECESSARY
Against false Christs, and false prophets. Mt 24:4–5, 23–25.
Against false teachers. Php 3:2. Cl 2:8. 2 P 3:16–17.
Against idolatry. Dt 4:15–16.
Against presumption. 1 Co 10:12.
Against sin. He 12:15–16.
Against unbelief. He 3:12.
In conduct. Ep 5:15.
In giving judgment. 1 Ch 19:6–7.
In how we hear. Lk 8:18.
In keeping God's commandments. Jsh 22:5.
In speech. Pr 13:3. Ja 1:19.
In the care of the soul. Dt 4:9.
In the house and worship of God. Ec 5:1.
In what we hear. Mk 4:24.
In worldly company. Ps 39:1. Cl 4:5.
Promises to. 1 K 2:4. 1 Ch 22:13.

HELL
The beast, false prophets, and the devil shall be cast into. Rv 19:20; 20:10.

Body suffers in. Mt 5:29; 10:28.
DESCRIBED AS
Devouring fire. Is 33:14.
Everlasting burnings. Is 33:14.
Everlasting fire. Mt 25:41.
Everlasting punishment. Mt 25:46.
Fire and brimstone. Rv 14:10.
A furnace of fire. Mt 13:42, 50.
A lake of fire. Rv 20:15.
Unquenchable fire. Mt 3:12.
Devils are confined in, until the judgment day. 2 P 2:4. Jde 1:6.
Endeavor to keep others from. Pr 23:14. Jde 1:23.
Human power cannot preserve from. Ezk 32:27.
Illustrated. Is 30:33.
THE PLACE OF DISEMBODIED SPIRITS
And a place of torment. Lk 16:23.
Contains, a place of rest, Abraham's bosom. Lk 16:23.
Paradise. Lk 23:43.
Which Christ visited. Lk 23:43. Ac 2:31, 1 P 3:19.
THE PLACE OF FUTURE PUNISHMENT
Destruction from the presence of God. 2 Th 1:9.
Eternal. Is 33:14. Rv 20:10.
Powers of, cannot prevail against the church. Mt 16:18.
Prepared for the devil, etc. Mt 25:41.
Society of the wicked leads to. Pr 5:5; 9:18.
Soul suffers in. Mt 10:28.
The wicked shall be turned into. Ps 9:17.
The wise avoid. Pr 15:24.

HELP
EXEMPLIFIED BY
Christians. Ac 16:9.
Gamaliel. Ac 5:17–42.
Good Samaritan. Lk 10:25–37.
Moses' helpers. Ex 17:11–12.
Neighbors. Is 41:6.
Testimony of. Pss 86:17, 118:13, He 13:6.

HIGH PRIEST
Assisted by a deputy. 2 S 15:24. Lk 3:2.
CALLED
God's high priest. Ac 23:4.
The priest. Ex 29:30. Ne 7:65.
Ruler of the people. Ex 22:28, with Ac 23:5.
Consecrated to his office. Ex 40:13. Lv 8:12.

DEPUTY OF
Called the second priest.　2 K 25:18.
Had oversight of the Levites.　Nu 3:32.
Had oversight of the tabernacle.　Nu 4:16.
DUTIES OF
Appointing priests to offices.　1 S 2:36.
Bearing before the Lord the names of Israel for a memorial.　Ex 28:12, 29.
Blessing the people.　Lv 9:22–23.
Consecrating the Levites.　Nu 8:11–21.
Inquiring of God by Urim and Thummim. 1 S 23:9–12; 30:7–8.
Lighting the sacred lamps.　Ex 30:8. Nu 8:3.
Making atonement in the most holy place once a year.　Lv 16. He 9:7.
Offering gifts and sacrifices.　He 5:1.
Presiding in the superior court.　Mt 26:3, 57–62. Ac 5:21–28; 23:1–5.
Taking charge of money collected in the sacred treasury.　2 K 12:10; 22:4.
Taking the census of the people.　Nu 1:3.
Family of Eli degraded from office of, for bad conduct.　1 S 2:27–36.
Forbidden to mourn for any.　Lv 21:10–12.
INFERIOR TO CHRIST IN
Being made without an oath.　He 7:20–22.
Being of the order of Aaron.　He 6:20; 7:11–17; 8:4, 5, with 1, 2, 6.
Entering into holiest every year.　He 9:7, 12, 25.
Needing to make atonement for his own sins.　He 5:2–3; 7:26–28; 9:7.
Not being able to continue.　He 7:23–24.
Offering the same sacrifices.　He 9:25–26, 28; 10:11–12, 14.
Needed to sacrifice for himself.　He 5:1–3.
Next in rank to the king.　Lm 2:6.
OFFICE OF
Hereditary.　Ex 29:29.
Made annual by the Romans.　Jn 11:49–51, with Ac 4:6.
Promised to the posterity of Phinehas for his zeal.　Nu 25:12–13.
Often exercised chief civil power.　1 S 4:18.
Sometimes deposed by the kings.　1 K 2:27.
Sometimes enabled to prophesy.　Jn 11:49–52.
SPECIAL GARMENTS OF
Breastplate.　Ex 28:15–29.
Broidered coat.　Ex 28:4, 39.
Crown of gold, etc.　Ex 28:36–38.
Ephod.　Ex 28:6–7.
Girdle.　Ex 28:4, 39.

Linen mitre.　Ex 28:4, 39.
Made by divine wisdom given to Bezaleel, etc.　Ex 28:3; 36:1; 39:1.
Robe of the ephod.　Ex 28:31–35.
Went to his successors.　Ex 29:29.
Were for beauty and ornament.　Ex 28:2.
Worn at his consecration.　Lv 8:7, 9.
Worn seven days after consecration.　Ex 29:30.
Specially called of God.　Ex 28:1–2. He 5:4.
To be tender and compassionate.　He 5:2.
To marry a virgin of Aaron's family.　Lv 21:13–14.
TYPIFIED CHRIST IN
Alone entering into most holy place.　He 9:7, 12, 24, with 4:14.
Bearing the names of Israel upon his heart. Ex 28:29, with S S 8:6.
Being called of God.　He 5:4–5.
Being liable to temptation.　He 2:18.
Blessing.　Lv 9:22–23. Ac 3:26.
Compassion and sympathy for the weak and ignorant.　He 4:15; 5:1–2.
His appointment.　Is 61:1. Jn 1:32–34.
His title.　He 3:1.
Holiness of office.　Lv 21:15, with He 7:26.
Interceding.　Nu 16:43–48. He 7:25.
Making atonement.　Lv 16:33. He 2:17.
Marrying a virgin.　Lv 21:13–14. 2 Co 11:2.
Performing by himself all the services on day of atonement.　Lv 16, with He 1:3.
Splendid dress.　Ex 28:2, with Jn 1:14.
Wore the ordinary priest's garments when making atonement in the holy place.　Lv 16:4.

HIGHWAYS

All obstructions removed from, before persons of distinction.　Is 40:3–4, with Mt 3:3.
Beggars sat by sides of.　Mt 20:30. Mk 10:46.
Bypaths more secure in times of danger.　Jg 5:6.
Called the king's highway.　Nu 20:17.
Desolation of, threatened as a punishment. Lv 26:22. Is 33:8.
Generally broad.　Jg 20:32, 45. Mt 7:13.
Generally straight.　1 S 6:12. Is 40:3.
ILLUSTRATIVE OF
Christ.　Jn 14:6.
Facilities for the restoration of the Jews. Is 11:16; 62:10.
Facilities for the spread of the gospel, when made in the deserts.　Is 40:3; 43:19.

The way of holiness. Is 35:8.
The way to destruction, when broad. Mt 7:13.
The way to life, when narrow. Mt 7:14.
INFESTED WITH
Robbers. Jr 3:2. Lk 10:30–33.
Serpents. Gn 49:17.
Wild beasts. 1 K 13:24, with Is 35:9.
Made to all cities of refuge. Dt 19:2–3.
Marked out by heaps of stones. Jr 31:21.
Often made in deserts. Is 40:3.
Often obstructed. Jr 18:15.
Roads for public use. Nu 20:19. Dt 2:27.

HOLINESS
Becoming in the church. Ps 93:5.
Behavior of aged women should be as becomes. Ti 2:3.
Character of Christ, the standard of. Ro 8:29. 1 Jn 2:6. Php 2:5.
Character of God, the standard of. Lv 19:2, with 1 P 1:15–16. Ep 5:1.
Chastisements are intended to produce, in saints. He 12:10. Ja 1:2–3.
CHRIST
An example of. He 7:26. 1 P 2:21–22.
Desires for his people. Jn 17:17.
Effects in his people. Ep 5:25–27.
Church is the beauty of. 1 Ch 16:29. Ps 29:2.
Commanded. Lv 11:45; 20:7. Ep 5:8. Cl 3:12. Ro 12:1.
Gospel the way of. Is 35:8.
MINISTERS SHOULD
Avoid everything inconsistent with. Lv 21:6. Is 52:11.
Be examples of. 1 Tm 4:12.
Exhort to. He 12:14. 1 P 1:14–16.
Possess. Ti 1:8.
MOTIVES TO
The dissolution of all things. 2 P 3:11.
The glory of God. Jn 15:8. Php 1:11.
The love of Christ. 2 Co 5:14–15.
The mercies of God. Ro 12:1–2.
Necessary to God's worship. Ps 24:3–4.
None shall see God without. Ep 5:5. He 12:14.
Promised to the church. Is 35:8. Ob 1:17. Zc 14:20–21.
Promise to women to continue in. 1 Tm 2:15.
Required in prayer. 1 Tm 2:8.
RESULT OF
God's keeping. Jn 17:15.

The manifestation of God's grace. Ti 2:3, 11–12.
Subjection to God. Ro 6:22.
Union with Christ. Jn 15:4–5; 17:9.
SAINTS
Called to. 1 Th 4:7. 2 Tm 1:9.
Elected to. Ro 8:29. Ep 1:4.
Have their fruit unto. Ro 6:22.
New created in. Ep 4:24.
Possess. 1 Co 3:17. He 3:1.
Shall be presented to God in. Cl 1:22. 1 Th 3:13.
Shall continue in, forever. Rv 22:11.
Should continue in. Lk 1:75.
Should follow after. He 12:14.
Should have their conversation in. 1 P 1:15. 2 P 3:11.
Should present their bodies to God in. Ro 12:1.
Should seek perfection in. 2 Co 7:1.
Should serve God in. Lk 1:74–75.
Should yield their members as instruments of. Ro 6:13, 19.
Should lead to separation from the wicked. Nu 16:21, 26. 2 Co 6:17–18.
The wicked are without. 1 Tm 1:9. 2 Tm 3:2.
The word of God the means of producing. Jn 17:17. 2 Tm 3:16–17.

HOLINESS OF GOD
EXHIBITED IN HIS
Character. Ps 22:3. Jn 17:11.
Kingdom. Ps 47:8. Mt 13:41. Rv 21:27. 1 Co 6:9–10.
Name. Is 57:15. Lk 1:49.
Words. Ps 60:6. Jr 23:9.
Works. Ps 145:17.
Heavenly hosts adore. Is 6:3. Rv 4:8.
Incomparable. Ex 15:11. 1 S 2:2.
PLEDGED FOR THE FULFILLMENT OF HIS
Judgments. Am 4:2.
Promises. Ps 89:35.
Requires holy service. Jsh 24:19. Ps 93:5.
Saints are commanded to imitate. Lv 11:44, with 1 P 1:15–16.
Saints should praise. Ps 30:4.
Should be magnified. 1 Ch 16:10. Pss 48:1; 99:3, 5. Rv 15:4.
Should produce reverential fear. Rv 15:4.

HOLY LAND
Abounded in minerals. Dt 8:9; 33:25.
All inheritances in, inalienable. Lv 25:10, 23.

Allotment of, specified. Jsh 14—19.
Burial place of the patriarchs. Gn 49:29–31; 50:13, 25. Jsh 24:32.
CALLED
Glorious land. Dn 11:16.
Good land. Nu 14:7. Dt 3:25.
The land. Lv 26:42. Lk 4:25.
Land of Canaan. Gn 11:31. Lv 14:34.
Land of Immanuel. Is 8:8.
Land of Israel. 1 S 13:19. Mt 2:20–21.
Land of Judah. Is 26:1.
Land of promise. He 11:9.
Land of the Hebrews. Gn 40:15.
The Lord's land. Ho 9:3.
Palestina. Ex 15:14. Is 14:29, 31.
Pleasant land. Ps 106:24. Dn 8:9.
Conquered by Joshua. Jsh 6—12.
Divided by lot. Nu 34:16–29, with Jsh 13:7–14.
DIVIDED INTO
Four provinces by the Romans. Lk 3:1.
Twelve provinces by Solomon. 1 K 4:7–19.
Two kingdoms in the time of Rehoboam. 1 K 11:35–36; 12:19–20.
Extensive commerce of, in Solomon's reign. 1 K 9:26–28; 10:22–29.
EXTENT OF
As at first divided. Nu 34:1–12.
As promised. Gn 15:18. Dt 1:7. Jsh 1:4.
Under Solomon. 1 K 4:21, 24. 2 Ch 9:26.
Extremely fruitful. Ex 3:8. Nu 13:27. Dt 8:7–9; 11:10–12.
Given by covenant to Israel. Ex 6:4.
Inhabitants of, expelled for wickedness. Gn 15:16. Ex 23:23. Lv 18:25. Dt 18:12.
Numerous population of, in Solomon's reign. 1 K 3:8. 2 Ch 1:9.
Obedience the condition of continuing in. Lv 23:3, etc. Dt 5:33; 11:16–17, 22–25.
Original inhabitants of. Gn 10:15–20. Dt 7:1.
PROMISED TO
Abraham. Gn 12:7; 13:15; 17:8.
Isaac. Gn 26:3.
Jacob. Gn 28:13, 15; 35:12.
Prosperity of, in Solomon's reign. 1 K 4:20.
A sabbath of rest appointed for. Lv 25:2–5.
Twelve men sent to spy. Nu 13.
A type of the rest that remains for saints. He 4:1–2, 9. 1 P 1:4.

HOLY OF HOLIES
CALLED THE
Holiest of all. He 9:3.

Holy place. Ex 28:29. Lv 16:2–3.
Holy sanctuary. Lv 16:33.
Most holy place. Ex 26:31–33.
Oracle. 1 K 6:5, 16, 20.
Sanctuary. Lv 4:6. Ps 20:2.
CONTAINED
Aaron's rod. Nu 17:10. He 9:4.
Ark of testimony. Ex 26:33; 40:3, 21.
Cherubim. Ex 25:18–22. 1 K 6:23–28.
Golden censer. He 9:4.
Mercy seat. Ex 26:34.
Pot of manna. Ex 16:33. He 9:4.
A written copy of the divine law. Dt 31:26. 2 K 22:8.
Divided from the outward tabernacle by a veil. Ex 26:31–33.
God appeared in. Ex 25:22. Lv 16:2.
HIGH PRIEST
Alone to enter, once a year. He 9:7.
Entered, in ordinary priest's dress. Lv 16:4.
Entered, not without blood of atonement. Lv 16:14–15. He 9:7.
Made atonement for. Lv 16:15–16, 20, 33.
Not to enter, at all times. Lv 16:2.
Offered incense in. Lv 16:12.
Laid open to view at Christ's death. Mt 27:51.
Priests allowed to enter and prepare the holy things for removal. Nu 4:5.
Saints have boldness to enter the true. He 10:19.
A type of heaven. Ps 102:19. He 9:12–13, 24.

HOLY SPIRIT IS GOD
As appointing and sending ministers. Ac 13:2, 4, with Mt 9:38. Ac 20:28.
As author of the new birth. Jn 3:5–6, with 1 Jn 5:4.
As called God. Ac 5:3–4.
As Comforter of the church. Ac 9:31, with 2 Co 1:3.
As convincing of sin, righteousness, and judgment. Jn 16:8–11.
As Creator. Gn 1:26–27, with Jb 33:4.
As directing where the gospel should be preached. Ac 16:6–7, 10.
As dwelling in saints. Jn 14:17, with 1 Co 14:25. 1 Co 3:16, with 6:19.
As equal to, and one with the Father. Mt 28:19. 2 Co 13:14.
As eternal. He 9:14.

As inspiring scripture. 2 Tm 3:16, with 2 P 1:21.

As Jehovah. Ex 17:7, with He 3:7–9. Nu 12:6, with 2 P 1:21.

As Jehovah Most High. Ps 78:17, 21, with Ac 7:51.

As Jehovah of hosts. Is 6:3, 8–10, with Ac 28:25.

As joined with the Father and the Son in the baptismal formula. Mt 28:19.

As omnipotent. Lk 1:35. Ro 15:19.

As omnipresent. Ps 139:7–13.

As omniscient. 1 Co 2:10.

As raising Christ from the dead. Ac 2:24, with 1 P 3:18. He 13:20, with Ro 1:4.

As sanctifying the church. Ezk 37:28, with Ro 15:16.

As sovereign Disposer of all things. Dn 4:35, with 1 Co 12:6, 11.

As the source of miraculous power. Mt 12:28, with Lk 11:20. Ac 19:11, with Ro 15:19.

As the source of wisdom. 1 Co 12:8. Is 11:2. Jn 16:13; 14:26.

As the Spirit of glory and of God. 1 P 4:14.

As the Witness. He 10:15, with 1 Jn 5:9.

Being invoked as Jehovah. Lk 2:26–29. Ac 4:23–25, with 1:16, 20. 2 Th 3:5.

HOLY SPIRIT, PERSONALITY OF

He appoints and commissions ministers. Is 48:16. Ac 13:2; 20:28.

He can be grieved. Ep 4:30.

He can be resisted. Ac 7:51.

He can be tempted. Ac 5:9.

He can be vexed. Is 63:10.

He comforts. Ac 9:31.

He creates and gives life. Jb 33:4.

He directs ministers where not to preach. Ac 16:6–7.

He directs ministers where to preach. Ac 8:29; 10:19–20.

He dwells with saints. Jn 14:17.

He glorifies Christ. Jn 16:14.

He guides. Jn 16:13.

He has a power of his own. Ro 15:13.

He helps our infirmities. Ro 8:26.

He instructs ministers what to preach. 1 Co 2:13.

He reproves. Jn 16:8.

He sanctifies. Ro 15:16. 1 Co 6:11.

He searches all things. Ro 11:33–34, with 1 Co 2:10–11.

He spoke in, and by, the prophets. Ac 1:16. 1 P 1:11–12. 2 P 1:21.

He strives with sinners. Gn 6:3.

He teaches. Jn 14:26. 1 Co 12:3.

He testifies of Christ. Jn 15:26.

He works according to his own will. 1 Co 12:11.

HOLY SPIRIT, SYMBOLS OF

CLOVEN TONGUES

Of Galileans. Ac 2:3.

Understood by others. Ac 2:6–11.

A DOVE

Descending. Mt 3:16.

Gentle. Mt 10:16, with Gl 5:22.

FIRE

Baptizing. Mt 3:11.

Illuminating. Ex 13:21. Ps 78:14.

Purifying. Is 4:4. Ml 3:2–3.

Searching. Zp 1:12, with 1 Co 2:10.

OIL

Comforting. Is 61:3. He 1:9.

Consecrating. Ex 29:7; 30:30. Is 61:1.

Gladdening. Ps 45:7.

Healing. Lk 10:34. Rv 3:18.

Illuminating. Mt 25:3–4. 1 Jn 2:20, 27.

RAIN AND DEW

Abundant. Ps 133:3.

Fertilizing. Ezk 34:26–27. Ho 6:3; 10:12; 14:5.

Imperceptible. 2 S 17:12, with Mk 4:26–28.

Refreshing. Pss 68:9; 72:6. Is 18:4.

A SEAL

Authenticating. Jn 6:27. 2 Co 1:22.

For servants of God. Rv 7:2.

Securing. Ep 1:13–14. Ep 4:30.

A VOICE

Guiding. Is 30:21, with Jn 16:13.

Speaking. Mt 10:20.

Warning. He 3:7–11.

WATER

Abundant. Jn 7:37–38.

Believing. Jn 7:38.

Born of. Jn 3:5.

Cleansing. Ezk 16:9; 36:25. Ep 5:26. He 10:22.

Fertilizing. Ps 1:3. Is 27:3, 6; 44:3–4; 58:11.

Freely given. Is 55:1. Jn 4:14. Rv 22:17.

Refreshing. Ps 46:4. Is 41:17–18.

WIND

Independent. Jn 3:8. 1 Co 12:11.

Powerful. 1 K 19:11, with Ac 2:2.

Reviving. Ezk 37:9–10, 14.

Sensible in its effects. Jn 3:8.

HOLY SPIRIT, THE COMFORTER
As Such He

Abides forever with saints. Jn 14:16.
Communicates joy to saints. Ro 14:17. Gl 5:22. 1 Th 1:6.
Dwells with and in saints. Jn 14:17.
Edifies the church. Ac 9:31.
Imparts hope. Ro 15:13. Gl 5:5.
Imparts the love of God. Ro 5:3–5.
Is known by saints. Jn 14:17.
Proceeds from the Father. Jn 15:26.
Teaches saints. Jn 14:26.
Testifies of Christ. Jn 15:26.

Given

By Christ. Is 61:3.
By the Father. Jn 14:16.
Through Christ's intercession. Jn 14:16.
Sent in the name of Christ. Jn 14:26.
The world cannot receive. Jn 14:17.

HOLY SPIRIT, THE TEACHER
Attend to the instruction of. Rv 2:7, 11, 29.
As Such He

Brings the words of Christ to remembrance. Jn 14:26.
Directs in the way of godliness. Is 30:21. Ezk 36:27.
Directs the decisions of the Church. Ac 15:28.
Enables ministers to teach. 1 Co 12:8.
Guides into all truth. Jn 14:26; 16:13.
Reveals the future. Lk 2:26. Ac 21:11.
Reveals the things of Christ. Jn 16:14.
Reveals the things of God. 1 Co 2:10, 13.
Teaches saints to answer persecutors. Mk 13:11. Lk 12:12.

Given

In answer to prayer. Ep 1:16–17.
To saints. Ne 9:20. 1 Co 2:12–13.
Natural man will not receive the things of. 1 Co 2:14.
Necessity for. 1 Co 2:9–10.
Promised. Pr 1:23.
Spirit of wisdom. Is 11:2; 40:13–14.

HONESTY
Delights the Lord. Pr 12:22.
Demanded by God. Pr 11:18. Am 8:4–7.
Imperative for Christians. Ro 12:17; 13:13. 2 Co 4:2; 8:21. Ep 4:25. 1 P 2:12.
Important for fellowship. Zc 8:16.
Necessary in speaking. Pr 12:19; 17:20. Mt 5:33–37. 1 K 22:16. Ps 101:7. Rv 22:15.

Required in business. Dt 25:13. Pr 11:1. Lv 19:35.

HONEY
Abounded In

Assyria. 2 K 18:32.
Canaan. Ex 3:8. Lv 20:24. Dt 8:8.
Egypt. Nu 16:13.
Esteemed a wholesome food. Pr 24:13.
Exported from Canaan. Ezk 27:17.
First fruits of, offered to God. 2 Ch 31:5.

Found In

Carcasses of dead animals. Jg 14:8.
Rocks. Dt 32:13. Ps 81:16.
Woods. 1 S 14:25–26. Jr 41:8.
Gathered and prepared by bees. Jg 14:18.
God the giver of. Ps 81:16. Ezk 16:19.

Illustrative Of

Holy speech of saints. S S 4:11.
Lips of a strange woman. Pr 5:3.
Pleasant words. Pr 16:24.
Wisdom. Pr 24:13–14.
The word of God. Pss 19:10; 119:103.
In the comb sweetest and most valuable. Pr 16:24; 24:13.
Loathed by those who are full. Pr 27:7.
Moderation needful in the use of. Pr 25:16, 27.
Not to be offered with any sacrifice. Lv 2:11.
Often sent as a present. Gn 43:11. 1 K 14:3.
Sweetness of. Jg 14:18.

Was Eaten

Mixed with flour. Ex 16:31. Ezk 16:13.
Plain. 1 S 14:25–26, 29.
With butter. Is 7:15, 22.
With locusts. Mt 3:4. Mk 1:6.
With milk. S S 4:11.
With the comb. S S 5:1. Lk 24:42.

HONOR
Belongs to God. Ps 145:5. Rv 4:11.
Due the old. Lv 19:32. 1 Tm 5:1.
Due to parents. Ex 20:12. Mt 15:4.
Obtained by honoring God. Pr 15:33; 21:31.
Received from God. Es 8:16. Dn 5:18. Jn 12:26.

HOPE
Be ready to give an answer concerning. 1 P 3:15.
A better, brought in by Christ. He 7:19.
Connected with faith and love. 1 Co 13:13.

Described As

Blessed. Ti 2:13.

Gladdening. Pr 10:28.
Good. 2 Th 2:16.
Lively. 1 P 1:3.
Sure and steadfast. He 6:19.
Encouragement to Ho 2:15. Zc 9:12.
Encourage others to. Ps 130:7.
Encourages boldness in preaching. 2 Co 3:12.
Happiness of. Ps 146:5.
In Christ. 1 Co 15:19. 1 Tm 1:1.
In God. Ps 39:7. 1 P 1:21.
In God's promises. Ac 26:6–7. Ti 1:2.
In the mercy of God. Ps 33:18.
Leads to patience. Ro 8:25. 1 Th 1:3.
Leads to purity. 1 Jn 3:3.
Life is the season of. Ec 9:4. Is 38:18.
Makes not ashamed. Ro 5:5.

OBJECTS OF
Christ's glorious appearing. Ti 2:13.
Eternal life. Ti 1:2; 3:7.
Glory. Ro 5:2. Cl 1:27.
Righteousness. Gl 5:5.
A resurrection. Ac 23:6; 24:15.
Salvation. 1 Th 5:8.

OBTAINED THROUGH
Faith. Ro 5:1–2. Gl 5:5.
The gospel. Cl 1:5, 23.
Grace. 2 Th 2:16.
Patience and comfort of the scriptures. Ro 15:4.

OF THE WICKED
Is in their worldly possessions. Jb 31:24.
Shall be extinguished in death. Jb 27:8.
Shall make them ashamed. Is 20:5–6. Zc 9:5.
Shall perish. Jb 8:13; 11:20. Pr 10:28.
Results from experience. Ro 5:4.

SAINTS
Are called to. Ep 4:4.
Have all, the same. Ep 4:4.
Have, in death. Pr 14:32.
Rejoice in. Ro 5:2; 12:12.
Should abound in. Ro 15:3.
Should continue in. Ps 71:14. 1 P 1:13.
Should hold fast. He 3:6.
Should look for the object of. Ti 2:13.
Should not be ashamed of. Ps 119:116.
Should not be moved from. Cl 1:23.
Seek for full assurance of. He 6:11.
Triumphs over difficulties. Ro 4:18.
The wicked have no ground for. Ep 2:12.
The work of the Holy Ghost. Ro 15:13. Gl 5:5.

HORSE
Adorned with bells on the neck. Zc 14:20.

COLORS OF, MENTIONED
Bay. Zc 6:3, 7.
Black. Zc 6:2, 6. Rv 6:5.
Grisled. Zc 6:3, 6.
Pale or ash color. Rv 6:8.
Red. Zc 1:8; 6:2. Rv 6:4.
Speckled. Zc 1:8.
White. Zc 1:8; 6:3. Rv 6:2.
Dedicated to the sun by idolaters. 2 K 23:11.

DESCRIBED AS
Fearless. Jb 39:20, 22.
Fierce and impetuous. Jb 39:21, 24.
Strong. Pss 33:17; 147:10.
Sure-footed. Is 63:13.
Swift. Is 30:16. Jr 4:13. Hk 1:8.
Warlike in disposition. Jb 39:21. Jr 8:6.
Endowed with strength by God. Jb 39:19.
Fed on grain and herbs. 1 K 4:23; 18:5.
Governed by bit and bridle. Ps 32:9. Ja 3:3.
Hard hoofs of, alluded to. Is 5:28.

ILLUSTRATIVE OF
Beauty of the church. S S 1:9. Zc 10:3.
Dull headstrong disposition. Ps 32:9.
Glorious and triumphant deliverance of the church. Is 63:13.
Impetuosity of the wicked in sin. Jr 8:6.
In battle protected by armor. Jr 46:4.

THE JEWS
Brought back from Babylon. Ezr 2:66.
Condemned for multiplying. Is 2:7.
Condemned for trusting to. Is 30:16; 31:3.
Forbidden to multiply. Dt 17:16.
Imported from Egypt. 1 K 10:28–29.
Multiplied in Solomon's reign. 1 K 4:26.
Not to trust in. Ho 14:3.
Kings and princes rode on. Es 6:8–11. Ezk 23:23.
Loud snorting of, alluded to. Jr 8:16, with Jb 39:20.
Notice of early traffic in. Gn 47:17.
Numbers of, kept for war. Jr 51:27. Ezk 26:10.

OFTEN SUFFERED
From bites of serpents. Gn 49:17.
From blindness. Zc 12:4.
From murrain. Ex 9:3.
From plague. Zc 14:15.
In battle. Jr 51:21. Hg 2:22.
In the hoof from prancing. Jg 5:22.
Prepared and trained for war. Pr 21:31.

Sold in fairs and markets. Ezk 27:14. Rv 18:13.
Urged on by whips. Pr 26:3.
USED FOR
Bearing burdens. Ezr 2:66. Ne 7:68.
Conveying posts, etc. 2 K 9:17–19. Es 8:10.
Drawing chariots. Mi 1:13. Zc 6:2.
Hunting. Jb 39:18.
Mounting cavalry. Ex 14:9. 1 S 13:5.
Vanity of trusting to. Ps 33:17. Am 2:15.
Want of understanding in, alluded to. Ps 32:9.

HOSPITALITY
Commanded. Ro 12:13. 1 P 4:9.
Encouragement to. Lk 14:14. He 13:2.
Required in ministers. 1 Tm 3:2. Ti 1:8.
SPECIALLY TO BE SHOWN TO
Enemies. 2 K 6:22–23. Ro 12:20.
The poor. Is 58:7. Lk 14:13.
Strangers. He 13:2.
A test of Christian character. 1 Tm 5:10.

HUMANITY
Care in construction. Dt 22:8.
Concern for the needy. Dt 24:19. Mt 25:40.
Love for brethren. 1 P 2:17. 1 Jn 2:10.
Love for enemies. Mt 5:44.
Love for neighbors. Lv 19:18. Lk 10:27. Gl 5:14.
Regard for animals. Dt 22:6. Pr 12:10. Jb 5:23. Mt 18:12. Ex 23:5.

HUMAN NATURE OF CHRIST
Acknowledged by men. Mk 6:3. Jn 7:27; 19:5. Ac 2:22.
Attested by himself. Mt 8:20; 16:13.
Confession of, a test of belonging to God. Jn 4:2.
Denied by antichrist. 1 Jn 4:3. 2 Jn 1:7.
Genealogy of. Mt 1:1, etc. Lk 3:23, etc.
Like our own in all things except sin. Ac 3:22. Php 2:7–8. He 2:17.
Necessary to his mediatorial office. 1 Tm 2:5.
PROVED BY HIS
Being a man of sorrows. Is 53:3–4. Lk 22:44. Jn 11:33; 12:27.
Being buffeted. Mt 26:67. Lk 22:64.
Being nailed to the cross. Ps 22:16, with Lk 23:33.
Being scourged. Mt 27:26. Jn 19:1.
Being subject to weariness. Jn 4:6.
Birth. Mt 1:16, 25; 2:2. Lk 2:7, 11.

Burial. Mt 27:59–60. Mk 15:46.
Circumcision. Lk 2:21.
Conception in the virgin's womb. Mt 1:18. Lk 1:31.
Death. Jn 19:30.
Enduring indignities. Lk 23:11.
Having a human soul. Mt 26:38. Lk 23:46. Ac 2:31.
Hungering. Mt 4:2; 21:18.
Increase in wisdom and stature. Lk 2:52.
Partaking of flesh and blood. Jn 1:14. He 2:14.
Resurrection. Ac 3:15. 2 Tm 2:8.
Side being pierced. Jn 19:34.
Sleeping. Mt 8:24. Mk 4:38.
Thirsting. Jn 4:7; 19:28.
Weeping. Lk 19:41. Jn 11:35.
Submitted to the evidence of the senses. Lk 24:39. Jn 20:27. 1 Jn 1:1–2.
WAS OF THE SEED OF
Abraham. Gn 22:18, with Gl 3:16. He 2:16.
David. 2 S 7:12, 16. Ps 89:35–36. Jr 23:5. Mt 22:42. Mk 10:47. Ac 2:30; 13:23. Ro 1:3.
The woman. Gn 3:15. Is 7:4. Jr 31:22. Lk 1:31. Gl 4:4.
Without sin. He 7:26, 28. 1 Jn 3:5. 1 P 2:22. He 4:15. Jn 18:38; 8:46.

HUMILITY
Afflictions intended to produce. Lv 26:41. Dt 8:3. Lm 3:20.
Before honor. Pr 15:33.
Blessedness of. Mt 5:3.
A characteristic of saints. Ps 34:2.
Christ an example of. Mt 11:29. Jn 13:14–15. Php 2:5–8.
Excellency of. Pr 16:19.
Leads to riches, honor, and life. Pr 22:4.
Necessary to the service of God. Mi 6:8.
SAINTS SHOULD
Be clothed with. 1 P 5:5.
Beware of false. Cl 2:18, 23.
Put on. Cl 3:12.
Walk with. Ep 4:1–2.
Temporal judgments averted by. 2 Ch 7:14; 12:6–7.
THEY WHO HAVE
Delivered by God. Jb 22:29.
Enjoy the presence of God. Is 57:15.
Exalted by God. Lk 14:11; 18:14.
Greatest in Christ's kingdom. Mt 18:4; 20:26–28.

Heard by God.   Pss 9:12; 10:17.
Lifted up by God.   Ja 4:10.
Receive more grace.   Pr 3:34. Ja 4:6.
Regarded by God.   Ps 138:6. Is 66:2.
Upheld by honor.   Pr 18:12; 29:23.
Want of, condemned.   2 Ch 33:23; 36:12. Jr
44:10. Dn 5:22.

HUMILITY OF CHRIST
Declared by himself.   Mt 11:29.
EXHIBITED IN HIS
Associating with the despised.   Mt
9:10–11. Lk 15:1–2.
Becoming a servant.   Mt 20:28. Lk 22:27.
Php 2:7.
Birth.   Lk 2:4–7.
Death.   Jn 10:15, 17–18. Php 2:8. He
12:2.
Entry into Jerusalem.   Zc 9:9, with Mt
21:5, 7.
Exposing himself to reproach and con-
tempt.   Pss 22:6; 69:9, with Ro 15:3. Is
53:3.
Obedience.   Jn 6:38. He 10:9.
Partaking of our infirmities.   He 4:15; 5:7.
Poverty.   Lk 9:58. 2 Co 8:9.
Refusing honors.   Jn 5:41; 6:15.
Subjection to his parents.   Lk 2:51.
Submitting to sufferings.   Is 50:6; 53:7,
with Ac 8:32. Mt 26:37–39.
Station in life.   Mt 13:55. Jn 9:29.
Submitting to ordinances.   Mt 3:13–15.
Taking our nature.   Php 2:7. He 2:16.
Washing his disciples' feet.   Jn 13:5.
His exaltation, the result of.   Php 2:9.
On account of, he was despised.   Mk 6:3. Jn
9:29.
Saints should imitate.   Php 2:5–8.

HUSBANDS
DUTY OF, TO WIVES
Be faithful to them.   Pr 5:19. Ml 2:14–15.
Comfort them.   1 S 1:8.
Consult with them.   Gn 31:4–7.
Dwell with them for life.   Gn 2:24. Mt
19:3–9.
Love them.   Ep 5:25, etc. Cl 3:19.
Not to leave them, though unbelieving.   1
Co 7:11–12, 14, 16.
Regard them as themselves.   Gn 2:23,
with Mt 19:5.

Respect them.   1 P 3:7.
Have authority over their wives.   Gn 3:16. 1
Co 11:3. Ep 5:23.
Not to interfere with their duties to Christ.
Lk 14:26, with Mt 19:29.
Should have but one wife.   Gn 2:24. Mk
10:6–8. 1 Co 7:2–4.

HYPOCRITES
The apostasy to abound with.   1 Tm 4:2.
Beware of the principles of.   Lk 12:1.
Christ knew and detected.   Mt 22:18.
DESCRIBED AS
Apparently zealous in the things of God.
Is 58:2.
Censorious.   Mt 7:3–5. Lk 13:14–15.
Covetous.   Ezk 33:31. 2 P 2:3.
Devouring widows' houses.   Mt 23:14.
Exact in minor, but neglecting important
duties.   Mt 23:23–14.
Glorying in appearance only.   2 Co 5:12.
Having but a form of godliness.   2 Tm 3:5.
Loving preeminence.   Mt 23:6–7.
Ostentatious.   Mt 6:2, 5, 16; 23:5.
Professing but not practicing.   Ezk
33:31–32. Mt 23:3. Ro 2:17–23.
Regarding tradition more than the word of
God.   Mt 15:1–3.
Seeking only outward purity.   Lk 11:39.
Self-righteous.   Is 65:5. Lk 18:11.
Trusting in privileges.   Jr 7:4. Mt 3:9.
Using but lip worship.   Is 29:13, with Mt.
15:8.
Vile.   Is 32:6.
Willfully blind.   Mt 23:17, 19, 26.
Zealous in making proselytes.   Mt 23:15.
Destroy others by slander.   Pr 11:9.
Fearfulness shall surprise.   Is 33:14.
God has no pleasure in.   Is 9:17.
God knows and detects.   Is 29:15–16.
Heap up wrath.   Jb 36:13.
Hope of, perishes.   Jb 8:13; 27:8–9.
In power, are a snare.   Jb 34:30.
Joy of, but for a moment.   Jb 20:5.
Punishment of.   Jb 15:34. Is 10:6. Jr 42:20,
22. Mt 24:51.
Shall not come before God.   Jb 13:16.
Spirit of, hinders growth in grace.   1 P 2:1.
Woe to.   Is 29:15. Mt 23:13.
Worship of, not acceptable to God.   Is
1:11–15; 58:3–5. Mt 15:9.

I

IDLENESS AND SLOTH

Accompanied by conceit. Pr 26:16.
Akin to extravagance. Pr 18:9.
Effects of, afford instruction to others. Pr 24:30–32.
False excuses for. Pr 20:4; 22:13.
Forbidden. Ro 12:11. He 6:12.
Illustrated. Pr 26:14. Mt 25:18, 26.

LEAD TO
Bondage. Pr 12:24.
Disappointment. Pr 13:4; 21:25.
Hunger. Pr 19:15; 24:34.
Poverty. Pr 10:4; 20:13.
Ruin. Pr 24:30–31. Ec 10:18.
Tattling and meddling. 1 Tm 5:13.
Want. Pr 20:4; 24:34.
Produce apathy. Pr 12:27; 26:15.
Remonstrance against. Pr 6:6, 9.

IDOLATRY

Accompanied by feasts. 2 K 10:20. 1 Co 10:27–28.
Adopted by Solomon. 1 K 11:5–8.
Adopted by the wicked kings. 1 K 21:26. 2 K 21:21. 2 Ch 28:2–4; 33:3, 7.
All forms of, forbidden by the law of Moses. Ex 20:4–5.
All heathen nations given up to. Ps 96:5. Ro 1:23, 25. 1 Co 12:2.
Altars raised for. 1 K 18:26. Ho 8:11.
Angels refuse to receive the worship of. Rv 22:8–9.
Captivity of Israel on account of. 2 K 17:6–18.
Captivity of Judah on account of. 2 K 17:19–23.
Changing the glory of God into an image. Ro 1:23, with Ac 17:29.
Changing the truth of God into a lie. Ro 1:25, with Is 44:20.

CONSISTS IN
Bowing down to images. Ex 20:5. Dt 5:9.
Covetousness. Ep 5:5. Cl 3:5.
Fearing other gods. 2 K 17:35.
Looking to other gods. Ho 3:1.
Sacrificing to images. Ps 106:38. Ac 7:41.
Sacrificing to other gods. Ex 22:20.
Sensuality. Php 3:19.
Setting up idols in the heart. Ezk 14:3–4.
Serving other gods. Dt 7:4. Jr 5:19.
Speaking in the name of other gods. Dt 18:20.
Swearing by other gods. Ex 23:13. Jsh 23:7.
Walking after other gods. Dt 8:19.
Worshiping angels. Cl 2:18.
Worshiping dead men. Ps 106:28.
Worshiping devils. Mt 4:9–10. Rv 9:20.
Worshiping images. Is 44:17 Dn 3:5, 10, 15.
Worshiping other gods. Dt 30:17. Ps 81:9.
Worshiping the host of heaven. Dt 4:19; 17:3.
Worshiping the true God by an image, etc. Ex 32:4–6, with Ps 106:19–20.
Curse denounced against. Dt 27:15.

DESCRIBED AS
Abominable. 1 P 4:3.
An abomination to God. Dt 7:25.
Bloody. Ezk 23:39.
Defiling. Ezk 20:7; 36:18.
Hateful to God. Dt 16:22. Jr 44:4.
Irrational. Ac 17:29. Ro 1:21–23.
Unprofitable. Jg 10:14. Is 46:7.
Vain and foolish. Ps 115:4–8. Is 44:19. Jr 10:3.
Destruction of, promised. Ezk 36:25. Zc 13:2.
Divination connected with. 2 Ch 33:6.
Early notice of, among God's professing people. Gn 31:19, 30; 35:1–4. Jsh 24:2.
Everything connected with, should be destroyed. Ezk 34:13. Dt 7:5. 2 S 5:21. 2 K 23:14.
Example of the kings encouraged Israel in. 1 K 12:30. 2 K 21:11. 2 Ch 33:9.
Exhortations to turn from. Ezk 14:6; 20:7. Ac 14:15.
Forbidden. Ex 20:2–3. Dt 5:7.
Good kings of Judah endeavored to destroy. 2 Ch 15:16; 34:7.

Great prevalence of, in Israel. Is 2:8. Jr 2:28. Ezk 8:10.

IDOLS, ETC., MENTIONED IN SCRIPTURE

Adrammelech. 2 K 17:31.
Anammelech. 2 K 17:31.
Ashima. 2 K 17:30.
Ashtoreth. Jg 2:13. 1 K 11:33.
Baal. Jg 2:11–13; 6:25.
Baal-berith. Jg 8:33; 9:4, 46.
Baal-peor. Nu 25:1–3.
Baal-zebub. 2 K 1:2, 16.
Baal-zephon. Ex 14:2.
Bel. Jr 50:2; 51:44.
Chemosh. Nu 21:29. 1 K 11:33.
Chinn. Am 5:26.
Dagon. Jg 16:23. 1 S 5:1–3.
Diana. Ac 19:24, 27.
Huzzab. Na 2:7.
Jupiter. Ac 14:12.
Mercury. Ac 14:12.
Merodach. Jr 50:2.
Molech or Milcom. Lv 18:21. 1 K 11:5, 33.
Nebo. Is 46:1.
Nergal. 2 K 17:30.
Nibhaz and Tartak. 2 K 17:31.
Nisroch. 2 K 19:37.
Queen of heaven. Jr 44:17, 25.
Remphan. Ac 7:43.
Rimmon. 2 K 5:18.
Succoth-benoth. 2 K 17:30.
Tammuz. Ezk 8:14.

Incompatible with the service of God. Gn 35:2–3. Jsh 24:23.

THE JEWS

Brought, out of Egypt with them. Ezk 23:8, with Ac 7:39–41.
Followed the Assyrians in. Ezk 16:28–30; 23:5–7.
Followed the Canaanites in. Jg 2:11–13. 1 Ch 5:25.
Followed the Moabites in. Nu 25:1–3.
Followed the Syrians in. Jg 10:6.
Forbidden to practice. Ex 20:1–5; 23:24.
Often mixed up, with God's worship. Ex 32:1–5. 1 K 12:27–28.
Practiced, in Egypt. Jsh 24:14. Ezk 23:3, 19.

Making idols for the purpose of, described and ridiculed. Is 44:10–20.

Led the heathen to consider their gods to have but a local influence. 1 K 20:23. 2 K 17:26.

Led the heathen to think their gods visited the earth in bodily shapes. Ac 14:11.

Led to abominable sins. Ro 1:26, 27–32. Ac 15:20.

OBJECTS OF

Angels. Cl 2:18.
Departed spirits. 1 S 28:14–15.
Earthly creatures. Ro 1:23.
Heavenly bodies. 2 K 23:5. Ac 7:42.
Images. Dt 29:17. Ps 115:4. Is 44:17.

Objects of, carried in procession. Is 46:7. Am 5:26. Ac 7:43.

OBJECTS OF, DESCRIBED AS

Abominations. Is 44:19. Jr 32:34.
Dumb idols. Hk 2:18. 1 Co 12:2.
Dumb stones. Hk 2:19.
Gods that cannot save. Is 45:20.
Gods that have not made the heavens. Jr 10:11.
Graven images. Is 45:20. Ho 11:2.
Helpless. Jr 10:5.
Idols of abomination. Ezk 16:36.
Images of abomination. Ezk 7:20.
Molten gods. Ex 34:17. Lv 19:4.
Molten images. Dt 27:15. Hk 2:18.
New gods. Dt 32:17. Jg 5:8.
No gods. Jr 5:7. Gl 4:8.
Nothing. Is 41:24. 1 Co 8:4.
Numerous. 1 Co 8:5.
Other gods. Jg 2:12, 17. 1 K 14:9.
Senseless idols. Dt 4:28. Ps 115:5, 7.
Stocks. Jr 3:9. Ho 4:12.
Strange gods. Gn 35:2, 4. Jsh 24:20.
Stumbling blocks. Ezk 14:3.
Teachers of lies. Hk 2:18.
Vanities of the Gentiles. Jr 14:22.
Vanity. Jr 18:15.
Wind and confusion. Is 41:29.

OBJECTS OF, WORSHIPED

By bowing to them. 1 K 19:18. 2 K 5:18.
By burning children. Dt 12:31. 2 Ch 33:6. Jr 19:4, 5. Ezk 16:21.
By cutting the flesh. 1 K 18:28.
By kissing the hand to them. Jb 31:26–27.
By kissing them. 1 K 19:18. Ho 13:2.
In groves. Ex 34:13.
In private houses. Jg 17:4–5.
In secret places. Is 57:8.
In temples. 2 K 5:18.
On high places. Nu 22:41. Jr 2:20.
On the tops of houses. 2 K 23:12. Zp 1:5.
Under trees. Is 56:5. Jr 2:20.
With incense. Jr 48:35.
With libations. Is 57:6. Jr 19:13.

With prayer. 1 K 18:26. Is 44:17.
With sacrifices. Nu 22:40. 2 K 10:24.
With singing and dancing. Ex 32:18–19.
1 Co 10:7.
Obstinate sinners judicially given up to. Dt
4:28; 28:64. Ho 4:17.

PUNISHMENT OF
Banishment. Jr 8:3. Ho 8:5–8. Am
5:26–27.
Dreadful judgments ending in death. Jr
8:2; 16:1–11.
Eternal torments. Rv 14:9–11; 21:8.
Exclusion from heaven. 1 Co 6:9–10. Ep
5:5.
Judicial death. Dt 17:2–5.
Renounced on conversion. 1 Th 1:9.
Rites of, obscene and impure. Ex 32:25.
Nu 25:1–3. 2 K 17:9. Is 57:6, 8–9. 1 P 4:3.
Saints preserved by God from. 1 K 19:18,
with Ro 11:4.
Saints refuse to receive the worship of. Ac
10:25–26.; 14:11–15.

SAINTS SHOULD
Flee from. 1 Co 10:14.
Keep from. Jsh 23:7. 1 Jn 5:21.
Not covenant with those who practice. Ex
34:12, 15. Dt 7:2.
Not have anything connected with, in their
houses. Dt 7:26.
Not have religious intercourse with those
who practice. Jsh 23:7. 1 Co 5:11.
Not intermarry with those who practice.
Ex 34:16. Dt 7:3.
Not partake of anything connected with.
1 Co 10:19–20.
Refuse to engage in, though threatened
with death. Dn 3:18.
Testify against. Ac 14:15; 19:26.
Temples built for. Ho 8:14.

THEY WHO PRACTICE.
Are estranged from God. Ezk 14:5.
Are ignorant and foolish. Ro 1:21–22.
Are mad upon it. Jr 50:38.
Are vain in their imaginations. Ro 1:21.
Ask counsel of their idols. Ho 4:12.
Boast of it. Ps 97:7.
Carried away by it. 1 Co 12:2.
Defile the sanctuary of God. Ezk 5:11.
Forget God. Dt 8:19. Jr 18:15.
Forsake God. 2 K 22:17. Jr 16:11.
Go after it in heart. Ezk 20:16.
Go astray from God. Ezk 44:10.
Hate God. 2 Ch 19:2–3.
Have fellowship with devils. 1 Co 10:20.
Hold fast their deceit. Jr 8:5.

Inflame themselves. Is 56:5.
Look to idols for deliverance. Is 44:17;
45:20.
Pollute the name of God. Ezk 20:39.
Provoke God. Dt 31:20. Is 65:3. Jr 25:6.
Swear by their idols. Am 8:14.
Victims sacrificed for, often adorned with gar-
lands. Ac 14:13.
A virtual forsaking of God. Jr 2:9–13.
Warnings against. Dt 4:15–19.
Woe denounced against. Hk 2:19.
A work of the flesh. Gl 5:19–20.

IGNORANCE
Associated with unrighteousness. Pr 1:22. Jr
4:22. Ac 17:30. Ro 10:3.
Offerings for. Lv 5:15–16. Nu 15:22, 24, 28.
Results of. Ro 10:3. 2 P 3:5. Is 5:13.

IGNORANCE OF GOD
EVIDENCED BY
Living in sin. Ti 1:16. 1 Jn 3:6.
Not keeping his commandments. 1 Jn 2:4.
Want of love. 1 Jn 4:8.
Ignorance of Christ is. Jn 8:19.
Is no excuse for sin. Lv 4:2. Lk 12:48.

LEADS TO
Alienation from God. Ep 4:18.
Error. Mt 22:29.
Idolatry. Is 44:19. Ac 17:29, 30.
Persecuting saints. Jn 15:21; 16:3.
Sinful lusts. 1 Th 4:5. 1 P 1:14.

MINISTERS SHOULD
Aid those in. He 5:2. 2 Tm 2:24–25.
Labor to remove. Ac 17:23.
Punishment of. Ps 79:6. 2 Th 1:8.
The wicked choose. Jb 21:14. Ro 1:28.
The wicked in a state of. Jr 9:3. Jn 15:21;
17:25. Ac 17:30.

IMITATION
Of Christ. 1 P 2:23.
Of God. Ep 5:1.
Of men of faith, value of. He 6:12.
Of prophets, need of. Ja 5:10.
Of the apostles. 1 Th 1:6.
Of the good, protection in. 1 P 3:13. 3 Jn
1:11.
Of the wicked, evil of. 2 K 17:15.

IMPOSSIBILITY
Does not apply to faith. Mt 17:20.
Means nothing to God. Mt 19:26. Lk 1:37;
18:27.
Of escaping God. Ps 139:7–12.

Of God to fail.   Ti 1:2.
Of loving God without loving people.   1 Jn
4:20.
Of pleasing God without faith.   He 11:6.

INCENSE
An article of extensive commerce.   Rv 18:13.
Brought from Sheba.   Jr 6:20.
Called frankincense.   S S 4:6, 14.
Common, not to be offered to God.   Ex 30:9.
Designed for atonement.   Nu 16:46–47.
For God's service mixed with sweet spices.
Ex 25:6; 37:29.
ILLUSTRATIVE OF
The merits of Christ.   Rv 8:3–4.
Prayer.   Ps 141:2. Ml 1:11. Rv 5:8.
THE JEWS
Not accepted in offering, on account of sin.
Is 1:13; 66:3.
Offered to idols on altars of brick.   Is 65:3.
Prayed when offering.   Lk 1:10.
Punished for offering to idols.   2 Ch 34:25.
Korah and his company punished for offering.
Nu 16:16–35.
Levites had charge of.   1 Ch 9:29.
Nadab and Abihu destroyed for offering, with
strange fire.   Lv 10:1–2.
None but priests to offer.   Nu 16:40. Dt
33:10.
OFFERED
By the high priest in the most holy place on
the day of atonement.   Lv 16:12–13.
In censers.   Lv 10:1. Nu 16:17, 46.
Morning and evening.   Ex 30:7–8.
On the altar of gold.   Ex 30:1, 6; 40:5.
Perpetually.   Ex 30:8.
With fire from off the altar of burnt-offer-
ing.   Lv 16:12. Nu 16:46.
Offering of, allotted to the priests.   Lk 1:9.
Presented to Christ by the wise men.   Mt
2:11.
Put on meat offerings.   Lv 2:1–2, 15–16, 6:15.
Recipe for mixing.   Ex 30:34–36.
Used in idolatrous worship.   Jr 48:35.
Uzziah punished for offering.   2 Ch
26:16–21.

INDIVIDUAL, VALUE OF
God and one sparrow.   Lk 12:6–7.
Joy over one recovered child.   Lk 15:4, 7.
One-by-one love.   Is 27:12.

INDUSTRY
Characteristic of godly women.   Pr 31:13,
etc.

Commanded.   Ep 4:28. 1 Th 4:11.
Early rising necessary to.   Pr 31:15.
Illustrated.   Pr 6:6–8.
LEADS TO
Affection of relatives.   Pr 31:28.
General commendation.   Pr 31:31.
Increase of substance.   Pr 13:11.
Required of man after the fall.   Gn 3:23.
Required of man in a state of innocence.   Gn
2:15.
REQUISITE TO SUPPLY
Our own wants.   Ac 20:34. 1 Th 2:9.
Wants of others.   Ac 20:35. Ep 4:28.
The slothful devoid of.   Pr 24:30–31.
To be suspended on the sabbath.   Ex 20:10.

INDWELLING OF THE HOLY SPIRIT
In his church, as his temple.   1 Co 3:16.
In the body of saints, as his temple.   1 Co
6:19. 2 Co 6:16.
Is abiding.   1 Jn 2:27.
IS THE MEANS OF
Fructifying.   Gl 5:22.
Guiding.   Jn 16:13. Gl 5:18.
Quickening.   Ro 8:11.
Opposed by the carnal nature.   Gl 5:17.
Promised to saints.   Ezk 36:27.
A proof of adoption.   Ro 8:15. Gl 4:5.
A proof of being Christ's.   Ro 8:9. 1 Jn 4:13.
Saints enjoy.   Is 63:11. 2 Tm 1:14.
Saints full of.   Ac 6:5. Ep 5:18.
THOSE WHO HAVE NOT
Are sensual.   Jde 1:19.
Are without Christ.   Ro 8:9.

INGRATITUDE
A characteristic of the wicked.   Ps 38:20. 2
Tm 3:2.
OFTEN EXHIBITED
By relations.   Jb 19:14.
By servants.   Jb 19:15–16.
To benefactors.   Ps 109:5. Ec 9:15.
To friends in distress.   Ps 38:11.
Punishment of.   Pr 17:13. Jr 18:20–21.
Saints avoid the guilt of.   Ps 7:4–5.
SHOULD BE MET WITH
Faithfulness.   Gn 31:38–42.
Persevering love.   2 Co 12:15.
Prayer.   Pss 35:12–13; 109:4.

INGRATITUDE TO GOD
A characteristic of the wicked.   Ro 1:21.
Exceeding folly of.   Dt 32:6.
Guilt of.   Ps 106:7, 21. Jr 2:11–13.
Illustrated.   Is 5:1–7. Ezk 16:1–15.

Inexcusable. Is 1:2–3. Ro 1:21.
Prosperity likely to produce. Dt 31:20; 32:15. Jr 5:7–11.
Punishment of. Ne 9:20–27. Ho 2:8–9.
Unreasonable. Jr 5:5–6, 31. Mi 6:2–3.
Warnings against. Dt 8:11–14. 1 S 12:24–25.

INJUSTICE
A bad example leads to. Ex 23:2.
Brings a curse. Dt 27:17, 19.
Covetousness leads to. Jr 6:13. Ezk 22:12. Mi 2:2.
Forbidden. Lv 19:15, 35. Dt 16:19.
God
    Abominates. Pr 17:15; 20:10.
    Approves not of. Lm 3:35–36.
    Hears the cry of those who suffer. Ja 5:4.
    Provoked to avenge. Ps 12:5.
    Regards. Ec 5:8.
Intemperance leads to. Pr 31:5.
Of the least kind, condemned. Lk 16:10.
Punishment of. Pr 11:7; 28:8. Am 5:11–12. Am 8:5, 8. 1 Th 4:6.
Saints Should
    Bear patiently. 1 Co 6:7.
    Hate. Pr 29:27.
    Take no vengeance for. Mt 5:39.
    Testify against. Ps 58:1–2. Mi 3:8–9.
Specially to Be Avoided Toward
    The poor. Ex 23:6. Pr 22:16, 22–23.
    Servants. Jb 31:13–14. Dt 24:14. Jr 22:13.
    The stranger and fatherless. Ex 22:21–22. Dt 24:17. Jr 22:3.
The Wicked
    Deal with. Is 26:10.
    Judge with. Ps 82:2. Ec 3:16. Hk 1:4.
    Practice without shame. Jr 6:13, 15. Zp 3:5.

INSECTS
Created by God. Gn 1:24–25.
Divided into
    Clean and fit for food. Lv 11:21–22.
    Unclean and abominable. Lv 11:23–24.
Fed by God. Pss 104:25, 27; 145:9, 15.
Mentioned in Scripture
    Ant. Pr 6:6; 30:25.
    Bald locust. Lv 11:22.
    Bee. Jg 14:8. Ps 118:12. Is 7:18.
    Beetle. Lv 11:22.
    Cankerworm. Jl 1:4. Na 3:15–16.
    Caterpillar. Ps 78:46. Is 33:4.

Earthworm. Jb 25:6. Mi 7:17.
Flea. 1 S 24:14.
Fly. Ex 8:22. Ec 10:1. Is 7:18.
Gnat. Mt 23:24.
Grasshopper. Lv 11:22. Jg 6:5. Jb 39:20.
Hornet. Dt 7:20.
Locust. Ex 10:12–13.
Lice. Ex 8:16. Ps 105:31.
Maggot. Ex 16:20.
Moth. Jb 4:19; 27:18. Is 50:9.
Palmer worm. Jl 1:4. Am 4:9.
Spider. Jb 8:14. Pr 30:28.

INSPIRATION OF THE BIBLE
Apostles appealed to. Ac 8:32; 28:23.
Continually affirmed. Dt 6:6. 1 K 16:1. Jr 13:1. 1 Co 2:13. 2 P 1:21.
Inspired by God. 2 Tm 3:16. He 1:1.
Inspired by the Holy Spirit. 2 P 1:21. Ac 1:16.
Presents Christ. Jn 5:39. Ac 18:28.
Will judge those not accepting it. Jn 12:48. He 10:28.

INSPIRATION OF THE HOLY SPIRIT
All scripture given by. 2 S 23:2. 2 Tm 3:16.
Design of
    To control ministers. Ac 16:6.
    To direct ministers. Ezk 3:24–27. Ac 11:12; 13:2.
    To give power to ministers. Mi 3:8. Ac 1:8.
    To reveal future events. Ac 1:16; 28:25. 1 P 1:11.
    To reveal the mysteries of God. Am 3:7. 1 Co 2:10.
    To testify against sin. 2 K 17:13. Ne 9:30. Mi 3:8. Jn 16:8–9.
Despisers of, punished. 2 Ch 36:15–16. Zc 7:12.
Foretold. Jl 2:28, with Ac 2:16–18.
Irresistible. Am 3:8.
Modes of
    By a voice. Is 6:8. Ac 8:29. Rv 1:10.
    By dreams. Nu 12:6. Dn 7:1.
    By secret impulse. Jg 13:25. 2 P 1:21.
    By visions. Nu 12:6. Ezk 11:24.
    Various. He 1:1.
Necessary to prophesying. Nu 11:25–27. 2 Ch 20:14–17.

INTEGRITY
And bribes. Ac 8:18–23.
And honesty. 2 Co 7:2.

Characterizes righteous men.   Nu 16:15. Jb 27:5. Ps 26:11. Pr 11:3.
Protects the righteous.   Pr 11:3. Ps 25:21.
Required of mankind.   Dt 6:5.

INTERCESSION
Brings special blessings.   1 S 7:5–9. Nu 6:23–26. Ja 5:14–16.
DIVINE EXAMPLES
Christ.   Jn 17:1–26. He 7:25. Ro 8:34. 1 Jn 2:1.
Holy Spirit.   Ro 8:26.
HUMAN EXAMPLES.
Job.   Jb 42:8–10.
Moses.   Nu 14:19.
Stephen.   Ac 7:60.
Should be made for everyone.   1 Tm 2:1. Ep 6:18.
Should be made for specific individuals.   Ro 15:30. He 13:18.

INTEREST OR USURY
Curse attending the giving or receiving of unlawful, alluded to.   Jr 15:10.
Illustrative of the improvement of talents received from God.   Mt 25:27. Lk 19:23.
THE JEWS
Allowed to take, from strangers.   Dt 23:20.
Forbidden to take, from brethren.   Dt 23:19.
Forbidden to take, from brethren specially when poor.   Ex 22:25. Lv 25:35–37.
Often guilty of taking.   Ne 5:6–7. Ezk 22:12.
Required to restore.   Ne 5:9–13.
Judgments denounced against those who exacted unlawful.   Is 24:1–2. Ezk 18:13.
Lending of money or other property for increase.   Lv 25:37.
Those enriched by unlawful, not allowed to enjoy their gain.   Ps 28:8.
True and faithful Israelites never took, from their brethren.   Ps 15:5. Ezk 18:8–9.

INTOXICATION
Brings woe.   Pr 23:29–30.
Causes shame.   Jl 1:5. Ps 69:12.
Inconsistent with Christianity.   Ro 13:13. Ep 5:18.

IRON
Admits of a high polish.   Ezk 27:19.
An article of commerce.   Ezk 27:12, 19. Rv

18:12.
Canaan abounded with.   Dt 8:9; 33:25.
DESCRIBED AS
Fusible.   Ezk 22:20.
Malleable.   Is 2:4.
Strong and durable.   Jb 40:18. Dn 2:40.
Dug out of the earth.   Jb 28:2.
From the north hardest and best.   Jr 15:12.
Great quantity of, provided for the temple.   1 Ch 22:3, 14, 16; 29:2.
Hardened into steel.   2 S 22:35. Jb 20:24.
ILLUSTRATIVE OF
A hard barren soil.   Dt 28:23.
Insensibility of conscience, when seared with.   1 Tm 4:2.
Severe affliction.   Dt 4:20. Ps 107:10.
Severe exercise of power.   Ps 2:9. Rv 2:27.
Strength.   Dn 2:33, 40.
Stubbornness.   Is 48:4.
MADE INTO
Armor.   2 S 23:7. Rv 9:9.
Bars.   Ps 107:16. Is 45:2.
Bedsteads.   Dt 3:11.
Chariots.   Jg 4:3.
Fetters.   Pss 105:18; 149:8.
Gates.   Ac 12:10.
Graving tools.   Jb 19:24. Jr 17:1.
Idols.   Dn 5:4, 23.
Implements for husbandry.   1 S 13:20–21. 2 S 12:31.
Nails and hinges.   1 Ch 22:3.
Pillars.   Jr 1:18.
Rods.   Ps 2:9. Rv 2:27.
Tools for artificers.   Jsh 8:31. 1 K 6:7.
Weapons of war.   1 S 13:19; 17:7.
Yokes.   Dt 28:48. Jr 28:13–14.
Miraculously made to swim.   2 K 6:6.
Mode of purifying, taken in war.   Nu 31:21–23.
Of greater gravity than water.   2 K 6:5.
Of small comparative value.   Is 60:17.
Sharpens things made of it.   Pr 27:17.
Taken in war often dedicated to God.   Jsh 6:19, 24.
Used from the earliest age.   Gn 4:22.
Working in, a trade.   1 S 13:19. 2 Ch 2:7, 14.

ISRAEL
See Holy Land; Jews; Judea.

ISRAELITES
See Jews.

JK ❧

JERUSALEM

Allotted to the tribe of Benjamin. Jsh 18:28.

Ancient Jebusi or Jebus. Jsh 15:8; 18:28. Jg 19:10.

Ancient Salem. Gn 14:18. Ps 76:2.

CALAMITIES OF, MENTIONED

Besieged but not taken by Rezin and Pekah. Is 7:1. 2 K 16:5.

Besieged but not taken by Sennacherib. 2 K 18:17; 19.

Besieged by Nebuchadnezzar. 2 K 24:10–11.

Taken and burned by Nebuchadnezzar. 2 K 25. Jr 39:1–8.

Taken and made tributary by Pharaoh-Necho. 2 K 23:33–35.

Taken and plundered by Jehoash king of Israel. 2 K 14:13–14.

Taken and plundered by Shishak. 1 K 14:25–26. 2 Ch 12:1–4.

Threatened by Sanballat. Ne 4:7–8.

CALLED

A city not forsaken. Is 62:12.

City of God. Pss 46:4; 48:1.

City of Judah. 2 Ch 25:28.

City of righteousness. Is 1:26.

City of solemnities. Is 33:20.

City of the great king. Ps 48:2. Mt 5:5,

City of the Lord. Is 60:14.

City of truth. Zc 8:3.

Faithful city. Is 1:21, 26.

Holy city. Ne 11:1. Is 48:2. Mt 4:5.

Throne of the Lord. Jr 3:17.

Zion. Ps 48:12. Is 33:20.

Zion of the holy one of Israel. Is 60:14.

CHRIST

Did many miracles in. Jn 4:45.

Lamented over. Mt 23:37. Lk 19:41.

Preached in. Lk 21:37–38. Jn 18:20.

Publicly entered, as king. Mt 21:9–10.

Was put to death at. Lk 9:31. Ac 13:27, 29.

DESCRIBED AS

Beautiful for situation. Ps 48:2.

Comely. S S 6:4.

Compact. Ps 122:3.

Full of business and tumult. Is 22:3,

Great. Jr 22:8.

Joy of the whole earth. Ps 48:2. Lm 2:15,

The perfection of beauty. Lm 2:15.

Populous. Lm 1:1.

Princess among the provinces. Lm 1:1.

Wealth, etc., in the time of Solomon. 1 K 10:26–27.

Enlarged by David. 2 S 5:9.

Entered by gates. Ps 122:2. Jr 17:19–21.

First Christian council held at. Ac 15:4, 6.

Gospel first preached at. Lk 24:47. Ac 2:14.

Hezekiah made an aqueduct for. 2 K 20:20.

Idolatry of. 2 Ch 28:24. Ezk 8:7–10.

ILLUSTRATIVE OF

The church. Gl 4:25–26. He 12:22.

The church glorified. Rv 3:12; 21:2, 10.

Saints under God's protection (by its strong position). Ps 125:2.

Instances of God's care and protection of. 2 S 24:16. 2 K 19:32–34. 2 Ch 12:7.

THE JEBUSITES

Finally dispossessed of, by David. 2 S 5:6–8.

Formerly dwelt in. Jg 19:10–11.

Held possession of, with Judah and Benjamin. Jsh 15:63. Jg 1:21.

THE JEWS

Lamented the affliction of. Ne 1:2–4.

Loved. Ps 137:5–6.

Prayed for prosperity of. Pss 51:18; 122:6.

Prayed toward. Dn 6:10, with 1 K 8:44.

Went up to, at the feasts. Lk 2:42, with Ps 122:4.

The king of, defeated and slain by Joshua. Jsh 10:5–23.

Made the royal city. 2 S 5:9; 20:3.

Miraculous gift of the Holy Ghost first given at. Ac 1:4; 2:1–5.

Partly taken and burned by Judah. Jg 1:8.

Persecution of the Christian church commenced at. Ac 4:1; 8:1.

PROPHECIES RESPECTING

Christ to enter, as king. Zc 9:9.

The gospel to go forth from. Is 2:3; 40:9.

Its capture accompanied by severe calamities. Mt 24:21, 29. Lk 21:23–24.

Signs preceding its destruction Mt 24:6–15. Lk 21:7–11, 25, 28.

To be a quiet habitation. Is 33:20.

To be a terror to her enemies. Zc 12:2–3.

To be a wilderness. Is 64:10.

To be destroyed by the Romans. Lk 19:42–44.

To be made a heap of ruins. Jr 9:11; 26:18.

To be rebuilt by Cyrus. Is 44:26–28.

To be taken by king of Babylon. Jr 20:5.

Protected by forts and bulwarks. Ps 48:12–13.

Protected by God. Is 31:5.

Rebuilt after the captivity by order of Cyrus. Is 44:26–28.

Roman government transferred from, to Caesarea. Ac 23:23–24; 25:1–13.

Seat of government under the Romans. Mt 27:2, 19.

Specially chosen by God. 2 Ch 6:6. Ps 135:21.

Spoils of war placed in. 1 S 17:54. 2 S 8:7.

Surrounded by a wall. 1 K 3:1.

Surrounded by mountains. Ps 125:2.

The temple built in. 2 Ch 3:1. Ps 68:29.

Was the tomb of the prophets. Lk 13:33–34.

Wickedness of. Is 1:1–4. Jr 5:1–5. Mi 3:10.

Wickedness of, the cause of its calamities. 2 K 21:12–15. 2 Ch 24:18. Lm 1:8. Ezk 5:5–8.

JEWELS AND PRECIOUS STONES

FORMS

Agate, possibly used in windows. Ex 28:9. Is 54:12.

Alabaster, used in bottles to hold perfume or myrrh. Mk 16:3. Lk 7:37.

Amethyst, a purple quartz stone. Ex 39:12. Rv 21:20.

Beryl, a green or red stone. Ex 28:20. Rv 21:20.

Carbuncle, a green or red stone. Ex 28:17. Is 54:12.

Carnelian, a red quartz. Ex 28:17. Ezk 28:13. Rv 4:3. Rv 21:20.

Chalcedony, a green stone. Rv 21:19.

Chrysolite, yellow topaz or quartz. Rv 21:20.

Chrysoprasus, a light green chalcedony. Rv 21:20.

Coral, a red or black marine growth. Jb 28:18. Ezk 27:16.

Crystal, a form of quartz, glass, or ice. Jb 28:17. Rv 4:6; 21:11.

Diamond, a hard opaque stone probably quite different from the modern diamond. Ex 28:18. Ezk 28:13.

Emerald, a green or red stone. Ex 28:18. Rv 4:3.

Hyacinth: See Jacinth.

Jacinth, a blue or blue-green stone. Rv 9:17; 21:20.

Jasper, green jade or green or translucent quartz. Ex 29:20. Ezk 28:13. Rv 4:3, 21:11, 18–19.

Lapis lazuli: See Sapphire.

Ligure, a yellow stone. Ex 39:12.

Onyx, a green or black and white stone. Gn 2:12. Ex 25:7. Jb 28:16.

Pearl, a stone produced by an oyster. Mt 13:45–46. Rv 17:4.

Ruby, a bright red stone. Jb 28:18. Pr 8:11.

Sapphire, a deep blue stone. Ex 24:10. Is 54:11.

Sardius, a brown or red form of quartz. Ex 28:17. Ezk 28:13. Rv 21:20.

Sardonyx, a multicolored stone. Rv 21:20.

Topaz, a yellow stone. Ex 28:17. Jb 28:19. Rv 21:20.

ILLUSTRATIVE OF

Love and affection. Gn 24:22. Ml 3:17.

Selfish ornamentation. 1 Tm 2:9. Rv 17:4.

USED AS

Adornment. Is 3:18ff.

Investment and merchandise. Pr 3:15. Ja 2:2. Rv 18:12.

Offerings. Ex 32:1; 35:22.

JEWS

An agricultural people. Gn 46:32.

ALL OTHER NATIONS

Envied. Ne 4:1. Is 26:11. Ezk 35:11.

Hated. Ps 44:10. Ezk 35:5.

Oppressed. Ex 3:9. Jg 2:18; 4:3.

Persecuted. Lm 1:3; 5:5.

Rejoiced at calamities of. Pss 44:13–14; 80:5–6. Ezk 36:4.

Beloved for their fathers' sake. Dt 4:37; 10:15, with Ro 11:28.

BLESSEDNESS OF

Blessing. Gn 27:29.

Favoring. Gn 12:3. Ps 122:6.

CALLED

Children of Israel. Gn 50:25. Is 27:12.

Children of Jacob. 1 Ch 16:13.
Hebrews. Gn 14:13; 40:15. 2 Co 11:22.
Israelites. Ex 9:7. Jsh 3:17.
Jeshurun. Dt 32:15.
Seed of Abraham. Ps 105:6. Is 41:8.
Seed of Israel. 1 Ch 16:13.
Seed of Jacob. Jr 33:36.
Cast off for unbelief. Ro 11:17, 20.
Chosen and loved by God. Dt 7:6–7.
CHRIST
Descended from. Jn 4:22. Ro 9:5.
Expected by. Ps 14:7. Mt 11:3. Lk 2:25,
38. Jn 8:56.
Murdered by. Ac 7:52. 1 Th 2:15.
Promised to. Gn 49:10. Dn 9:25.
Regarded as the restorer of national great-
ness. Mt 20:21. Lk 24:21. Ac 1:6.
Rejected by. Is 53:3. Mk 6:3. Jn 1:11.
Sent to. Mt 15:24; 21:37. Ac 3:20, 22, 26.
Sprang from. Ro 9:5. He 7:14.
Circumcised in token of their covenant rela-
tion. Gn 17:10–11. Ac 7:8.
A commercial people. Ezk 27:17.
Compassion of Christ for. Mt 23:37. Lk
19:41.
Condemned for associating with other nations.
Jg 2:1–3. Jr 2:18.
Covenant established with. Ex 6:4; 24:6–8;
34:27.
Degenerated as they increased in national
greatness. Am 6:4.
DENUNCIATIONS AGAINST THOSE WHO
Aggravated the afflictions of. Zc 1:14–15.
Contended with. Is 41:11; 49:25.
Cursed. Gn 27:29. Nu 24:9.
Hated. Ps 129:5. Ezk 35:5–6.
Oppressed. Is 49:26; 51:21–23.
Slaughtered. Ps 79:1–7. Ezk 35:5–6.
Deprived of civil and religious privileges. Ho
3:4.
Descended from Abraham. Ps 105:6. Is
51:2. Jn 8:33, 39. Ro 9:7.
DESCRIBED AS
A holy nation. Ex 19:6.
A holy people. Dt 7:6; 14:21.
A kingdom of priests. Ex 19:6.
A peculiar people. Dt 14:2.
A peculiar treasure. Ex 19:5. Ps 135:4.
A special people. Dt 7:6.
The Lord's portion. Dt 32:9.
Desired and obtained kings. 1 S 8:5, 22.
Despised all strangers. 1 S 17:36. Mt
16:26–27. Ep 2:11.
Despised by the nations. Ezk 36:3.

Distinction of castes among, noticed. Is
65:5. Lk 7:39; 15:2. Ac 26:5.
Divided into twelve tribes. Gn 35:22; 49:28.
Divided into two kingdoms after Solomon. 1
K 11:31–32; 12:19–20.
Enemies of, obliged to acknowledge them as
divinely protected. Jsh 2:9–11. Es 6:13.
Gentiles made one with, under the gospel.
Ac 10:15, 28; 15:8–9. Gl 3:28. Ep
2:14–16.
God mindful of. Ps 98:3. Is 49:15–16.
Gospel preached first to. Mt 10:6. Lk 24:47.
Ac 1:8.
Had an ecclesiastical establishment. Ex 28:1.
Nu 18:6. Ml 2:4–7.
Had courts of justice. Dt 16:18.
Had a series of prophets to promote national
reformation. Jr 7:25; 26:4–5; 35:15; 44:4.
Ezk 38:17.
Held no intercourse with strangers. Jn 4:9.
Ac 11:2–3.
Imprecated the blood of Christ upon them-
selves and their children. Mt 27:25.
In the desert forty years. Nu 14:33. Jsh 5:6.
Many of, believed the gospel. Ac 21:20.
MODERN, DIVIDED INTO
Hebrews or pure Jews. Ac 6:1. Php 3:5.
Hellenists or Grecians. Ac 6:1; 9:29.
Many sects and parties. Mt 16:6. Mk
8:15.
NATIONAL CHARACTER OF
Attached to customs of the law. Ac 6:14;
21:21; 22:3.
Attached to Moses. Jn 9:28–29. Ac 6:11.
Backsliding. Jr 2:11–13; 8:5.
Covetous. Jr 6:13. Ezk 33:31. Mi 2:2.
Cowardly. Ex 14:10. Nu 14:3. Is 51:12.
Distrustful of God. Nu 14:11. Ps 78:22.
Fond of their brethren. Ex 2:11–12. Ro
9:1–3.
Fond of traditional customs. Jr 44:17.
Ezk 20:18, 30, with 21. Mk 7:3–4.
Formal in religion. Is 29:13. Ezk 33:31.
Mt 15:7–9.
Idolatrous. Is 2:8; 57:5.
Ignorant of the true sense of scripture. Ac
13:27. 2 Co 3:13–15.
Love their country. Ps 137:6.
Proud of descent, etc. Jr 13:9. Jn 8:33,
41.
Rebellious. Dt 9:7, 24. Is 1:2.
Self-righteous. Is 65:5. Ro 10:3.
Stubborn and stiff-necked. Ex 32:9. Ac
7:51.

Unfaithful to covenant engagements. Jr 3:6–8; 31:32. Ezk 16:59.

Ungrateful to God. Dt 32:15. Is 1:2.

None hated or oppressed, with impunity. Ps 137:8–9. Ezk 25:15–16; 35:6. Ob 1:10–16.

OBJECTS OF GOD'S

Choice. Dt 7:6.

Love. Dt 7:8; 23:5. Jr 31:3.

Protection. Ps 105:15. Zc 2:8.

Obliged to unite against enemies. Nu 32:20–22. Jg 19:29; 20. 1 S 11:7–8.

Often displeased God by their sins. Nu 25:3. Dt 32:16. 1 K 16:2. Is 1:4; 5:24–25.

Often distinguished in war. Jg 7:19–23. 1 S 14:6–13; 17:32–33. Ne 4:16–22.

Often subdued and made tributary. Jg 2:13–14; 4:2; 6:2, 6. 2 K 23:33.

The only people who had knowledge of God. Ps 76:1, with 1 Th 4:5. Ps 48:3, with Ro 1:28.

The only people who worshiped God. Ex 5:17, with Ps 96:5. Ps 115:3–4. Jn 4:22.

People of God. Dt 32:9. 2 S 7:24. Is 51:16.

Pray importunately for. Ps 122:6. Is 62:1, 6–7. Jr 31:7. Ro 10:1.

Privileges of. Ps 76:1–2. Ro 3:1–2; 9:4–5.

PROHIBITED FROM

Associating with others. Ac 10:28.

Covenanting with others. Ex 23:32. Dt 7:2.

Following practices of others. Dt 12:29–31; 18:9–14.

Marrying others. Dt 7:3. Jsh 23:12.

PROMISES RESPECTING

Blessing to the Gentiles by conversion. Is 2:1–5; 60:5; 66:19. Ro 11:12, 15.

Future glory. Is 60:19; 62:3–4. Zp 3:19–20. Zc 2:5.

Future prosperity. Is 60:6–7, 9, 17; 61:4–6. Ho 14:5–6.

Gentiles assisting in their restoration. Is 49:22–23; 60:10, 14; 61:4–6.

Joy occasioned by conversion of. Is 44:23; 49:13; 52:8–9; 66:10.

Pardon of sin. Is 44:22. Ro 11:27.

The pouring out of the Spirit upon them. Ezk 39:29. Zc 12:10.

The removal of their blindness. Ro 11:25. 2 Co 3:14–16.

Restoration to their own land. Is 11:15–16; 14:1–3; 27:12–13. Jr 16:14–15. Ezk 36:24; 37:21, 25; 39:25, 28. Lk 21:24.

Reunion of. Jr 3:18. Ezk 37:16–17, 20–22. Ho 1:11. Mi 2:12.

Salvation. Is 59:20, with Ro 11:26.

Sanctification. Jr 33:8. Ezk 36:25. Zc 12:1, 9.

Subjection of Gentiles to. Is 60:11–12, 14.

That Christ shall dwell among. Ezk 43:7, 9. Zc 14:4.

Their humiliation for the rejection of Christ. Zc 12:10.

Their return and seeking to God. Ho 3:5.

PROMISES RESPECTING, MADE TO

Abraham. Gn 12:1–3; 13:14–17; 15:18; 17:7–8.

Isaac. Gn 26:2–5, 24.

Jacob. Gn 28:12–15; 35:9–12.

Themselves. Ex 6:7–8; 19:5–6. Dt 26:18–19.

PUNISHED FOR

Breaking the covenant. Is 23:5. Jr 11:10.

Changing the ordinances. Is 24:5.

Idolatry. Ps 78:58–64. Is 65:3–7.

Imprecating upon themselves the blood of Christ. Mt 27:25.

Killing the prophets. Mt 23:37–38.

Transgressing the law. Is 1:4, 7; 24:5–6.

Unbelief. Ro 11:20.

Punishment for rejecting and killing Christ illustrated. Mt 21:37–43.

Received proselytes from other nations. Ac 2:10, with Ex 12:44, 48.

RELIGION OF

According to rites prescribed by God. Lv 18:4. Dt 12:8–11. He 9:1.

Typical. He 9:8–11; 10:1.

Restored to their own land by Cyrus. Ezr 1:1–4.

Saints remember. Ps 102:14; 137:5. Jr 51:50.

Scattered among the nations. Dt 28:64. Ezk 6:8; 36:19.

Scattered and peeled. Is 18:2, 7. Ja 1:1.

Separated from all other nations. Ex 33:16. Lv 20:24. 1 K 8:53.

Separated to God. Ex 33:16. Nu 23:9. Dt 4:34.

Settled in Canaan. Nu 32:32. Jsh 14:1–5.

Shall finally be saved. Ro 11:26–27.

Sojourned in Egypt. Ex 12:40–41.

Spiritual seed of true believers always among. 1 K 19:18. Is 6:13. Ro 9:6–7; 11:1, 5.

Strengthened by God in war. Lv 26:7–8. Jsh 5:13–14; 8:1–2.

Taken captive to Assyria and Babylon. 2 K
17:23; 18:11; 24:16; 25:11.

Taken out of Egypt by God. Ex 12:42, Dt
5:15; 6:12.

Their country trodden under foot by the Gentiles. Dt 28:49–52. Lk 21:24.

Their house desolate. Mt 24:38.

Their national greatness. Gn 12:2. Dt
33:29.

Their national privileges. Ro 3:2; 9:4–5.

Their vast numbers. Gn 22:17. Nu 10:36,

Trusted to their privileges for salvation. Jr
7:4. Mt 3:9.

Unbelieving, persecuted the Christians. Ac
17:5, 13. 1 Th 2:14–16.

Under God's special protection. Dt
32:10–11; 33:27–29. Pss 105:13–15;
121:3–5.

Under the theocracy until the time of Samuel.
Ex 19:4–6, with 1 S 8–7.

JORDAN RIVER

Despised by foreigners. 2 K 5:12.

Eastern boundary of Canaan. Nu 34:12.

Empties into the Dead Sea. Nu 34:12.

Ferry boats often used on. 2 S 19:18.

Fordable in some places. Jsh 2:7. Jg 12:5–6.

The Jews had great pride in. Zc 11:3.

Moses not allowed to cross. Dt 3:27; 31:2.

Often overflowed. Jsh 3:15. 1 Ch 12:15.

Overflowing of, called the swelling of Jordan.
Jr 12:5; 49:19.

PASSAGE OF ISRAEL OVER

Accomplished. Jsh 3:17, 4:1, 10–11.

Alluded to. Pss 74:15; 114:3, 5.

Commemorated by a pillar of stones in Gilgal. Jsh 4:2–8, 20–24.

Commemorated by a pillar of stones raised
in it. Jsh 4:9.

In an appointed order. Jsh 3:1–8.

A pledge that God would drive the Canaanites, etc., out of their land. Jsh
3:10.

Preceded by priests with the ark. Jsh 3:6,
11, 14.

Promised. Dt 4:22; 9:1; 11:31.

PLAINS OF

Afforded clay for molding brass, etc. 1 K
7:46. 2 Ch 4:17.

Chosen by Lot for a residence. Gn 13:11,

Exceeding fertile. Gn 13:10.

Infested with lions. Jr 49:19; 50:44.

Thickly wooded. 2 K 6:2.

REMARKABLE EVENTS CONNECTED WITH

Baptism of multitudes by John the Baptist.
Mt 3:6. Mk 1:5. Jn 1:28.

Baptism of our Lord. Mt 3:13, 15. Mk
. 1:9.

Division of its waters by Elijah. 2 K 2:8.

Division of its waters by Elisha. 2 K 2:14.

Division of its waters to let Israel pass over.
Jsh 3:12–16; 5:1.

Healing of Naaman the leper. 2 K 5:10,
14.

Return of its waters to their place. Jsh
4:18.

Slaughter of Moabites. Jg 3:28–29.

Slaughter of the Ephraimites. Jg 12:4–6.

JOY

Afflictions of saints succeeded by. Pss 30:5;
126:5. Is 35:10. Jn 16:20.

Christ appointed to give. Is 61:3.

The coming of Christ will afford exceeding, to
saints. 1 P 4:14.

Enjoined to saints. Ps 32:11. Php 3:1.

EXPERIENCED BY

Believers. Lk 24:52. Ac 16:34.

The just. Pr 21:15.

Parents of good children. Pr 23:24.

Peacemakers. Pr 12:20.

The wise and discreet. Pr 15:23.

A fruit of the Spirit. Gl 5:22.

Fullness of, in God's presence. Ps 16:11.

God gives. Ec 2:26. Ps 4:7.

God's word affords. Ne 8:12. Jr 15:6.

Gospel good tidings of. Lk 2:10–11.

Gospel to be received with. 1 Th 1:6.

Holy, illustrated. Is 9:3. Mt 13:44.

Increased to the meek. Is 29:19.

Liberality in God's service should cause. 1
Ch 29:9, 17.

MINISTERS SHOULD

Come to their people with. Ro 15:32.

Desire to render an account with. Php
2:16. He 13:17.

Esteem their people as their. Php 4:1. 1
Th 2:20.

Finish their course with. Ac 20:24.

Have, in the faith and holiness of their people. 2 Co 7:4. 1 Th 3:9. 3 Jn 1:4.

Pray for, for their people. Ro 15:13.

Promote, in their people. 2 Co 1:24. Php
1:25.

OF SAINTS IS

For deliverance from bondage. Ps 105:43.
Jr 31:10–13.

For divine protection. Pss 5:11; 16:8–9.
For divine support. Pss 28:7; 63:7.
For election. Lk 10:20.
For manifestation of goodness. 2 Ch 7:10.
For salvation. Ps 21:1. Is 61:10.
For supplies of grace. Is 12:3.
For temporal blessings. Jl 2:23–24.
For the hope of glory. Ro 5:2.
For the success of the gospel. Ac 15:3.
For the victory of Christ. Jn 16:33.
In Christ. Lk 1:47. Php 3:3.
In God. Pss 89:16; 149:2. Hk 3:18. Ro 5:11.
In the Holy Ghost. Ro 14:17.
OF SAINTS MADE FULL BY
Abiding in Christ. Jn 15:10–11.
Answers to prayer. Jn 16:24.
Communion. 2 Tm 1:4. 1 Jn 1:3–4. 2 Jn 1:12.
Faith in Christ. Ro 15:13.
The favor of God. Ac 2:28.
The word of Christ. Jn 17:13.
OF SAINTS SHOULD BE
Abundant. 2 Co 8:2.
Animated. Ps 32:11. Lk 6:23.
Constant. 2 Co 6:10. Php 4:4.
Exceeding. Pss 21:6; 68:3.
Expressed in hymns. Ep 5:19. Ja 5:13.
For evermore. 1 Th 5:16.
Full of glory. 1 P 1:8.
Great. Zc 9:9. Ac 8:8.
In hope. Ro 12:12.
In sorrow. 2 Co 6:10.
Under calamities. Hk 3:17–18.
Under persecutions. Mt 5:11–12. Lk 6:22–23. He 10:34.
Under trials. Ja 1:2. 1 P 1:6.
Unspeakable. 1 P 1:8.
With awe. Ps 2:11.
OF THE WICKED
Is delusive. Pr 14:13.
Is derived from earthly pleasures. Ec 2:10; 11:9.
Is derived from folly. Pr 15:21.
Is short-lived. Jb 20:5. Ec 7:6.
Shall be taken away. Is 16:10.
Should be turned into mourning. Ja 4:9.
Pray for restoration of. Pss 51:8, 12; 85:6.
Prepared for saints. Ps 97:11.
Promised to saints. Ps 132:16. Is 35:10; 55:12; 56:7.
Promote, in the afflicted. Jb 29:13.
The reward of saints at the judgment day. Mt 25:21.

Saints shall be presented to God with exceeding. 1 P 4:13, with Jde 1:24.
Saints should afford, to their ministers. Php 2:2. Phm 1:20.
Saints should have, in all their undertakings. Dt 12:18.
Serve God with. Ps 100:2.
Strengthening to saints. Ne 8:10.
Vanity of seeking, from earthly things. Ec 2:10–11; 11:8.

JOY OF GOD OVER HIS PEOPLE
Greatness of, described. Zp 3:17.
Illustrated. Is 62:5. Lk 15:23–24.
LEADS HIM TO
Comfort them. Is 65:19.
Deliver them. 2 S 22:20.
Do them good. Dt 28:63. Jr 32:41.
Give them the inheritance. Nu 14:8.
Prosper them. Dt 30:9.
ON ACCOUNT OF THEIR
Faith. He 11:5–6.
Fear of him. Ps 147:11.
Hope in his mercy. Ps 147–11.
Meekness. Ps 149:4.
Praying to him. Pr 15:8.
Repentance. Lk 15:7, 10.
Uprightness. 1 Ch 29:17. Pr 11:20.

JUBILEE, FEAST OF
Began upon the day of atonement. Lv 25:9.
CALLED THE
Acceptable year. Is 61:2.
Year of liberty. Ezk 46:17.
Year of the redeemed. Is 63:4.
ENACTMENTS RESPECTING
Cessation of all field labor. Lv 25:11.
Fruits of the earth to be common property. Lv 25:12.
Redemption of sold property. Lv 25:23–27.
Release of Hebrew servants. Lv 25:40–41, 54.
Restoration of all inheritances. Lv 25:10, 13, 28; 27:24.
Held every fiftieth year. Lv 25:8, 10.
Houses in walled cities not redeemed within a year, exempted from the benefit of. Lv 25:30.
Illustrative of the gospel. Is 61:1–2. Lk 4:18–19.
Proclaimed by trumpets. Lv 25:9. Ps 89:15.
Sale of property calculated from. Lv 25:15–16.

Value of devoted property calculated from.
Lv 27:14–23.
Was specially holy.   Lv 25:12.

JUDAH, TRIBE OF
Bounds of inheritance.   Jsh 15:1–12.
Descended from Jacob's fourth son.   Gn 29:35.
Encamped with its standard east of the tabernacle.   Nu 2:3.
Families of.   Nu 26:19–21.
First and most vigorous in driving out the Canaanites.   Jg 1:3–20.
First to submit to David.   2 S 2:10.
First went against Gibeah.   Jg 20:18.
Furnished kings to Israel.   1 S 13:14; 15:28; 16:6, 13. 2 S 2:4; 7:16–17.
Furnished to Israel the first judge.   Jg 3:9.
Helped Saul in his wars.   1 S 11:8; 15:4.
Last tribe carried into captivity.   2 K 17:18, 20; 25:21.
Led the first division of Israel in their journeys.   Nu 10:14.
Offering of, at dedication.   Nu 7:12–17.
Officer placed over by David.   1 Ch 27:18.
On Gerizim said amen to the blessings.   Dt 27:12.
Other tribes jealous of, on account of David.   2 S 19:41–43; 20:1–2.
Our Lord sprang from.   Mt 1:3–16. Lk 3:23–33. He 7:14.
Persons Selected from to
   Divide the land.   Nu 34:19.
   Number the people.   Nu 1:7.
   Spy out the land.   Nu 13:6.
Predictions respecting.   Gn 49:8–12. Dt 33:7.
Reigned over alone by David seven years and a half.   2 S 2:11; 5:5.
Remarkable Persons of
   Absalom.   2 S 15:1.
   Achan.   Jsh 7:18.
   Adonijah.   1 K 1:5–6.
   Bezaleel.   Ex 31:2.
   Boaz.   Ru 2:1.
   Caleb.   Nu 14:24.
   David.   1 S 16:1, 13.
   Elhanan.   2 S 21:19.
   Elihu.   1 Ch 27:18.
   Elimelech.   Ru 1:1–2.
   Jesse.   Ru 4:22.
   Jonathan.   2 S 21:21.
   Kings of Judah.   1 and 2 K.
   Nashon.   Nu 7:12.
   Obed.   Ru 4:21.
   Pethahiah.   Ne 11:24.
   Solomon.   1 K 1:32–39.
Reproved for tardiness in bringing back David after Absalom's rebellion.   2 S 19:11–15.
Strength of, on leaving Egypt.   Nu 1:26–27; 2:4.
With Benjamin, alone adhered to the house of David.   1 K 12:21.

JUDEA
Called
   Jewry.   Dn 5:13, with Jn 7:1.
   The land of Judah.   Mt 2:6.
Comprised the whole of the ancient kingdom of Judah.   1 K 12:21–24.
Jerusalem the capital of.   Mt 4:23.
John the Baptist preached in.   Mt 3:1.
A mountainous district.   Lk 1:39, 65.
One of the divisions of the Holy Land under the Romans.   Lk 3:1.
Our Lord
   Born in.   Mt 2:1, 5–6.
   Frequently visited.   Jn 11:7.
   Often left, to escape persecution.   Jn 4:1–3.
   Tempted in the wilderness of.   Mt 4:1.
Parts of, desert.   Mt 3:1. Ac 8:26.
Several Christian churches in.   Ac 9:31. 1 Th 2:14.
Towns of
   Arimathea.   Mt 27:57. Jn 19:38.
   Azotus or Ashdod.   Ac 8:40.
   Bethany.   Jn 11:1, 18.
   Bethlehem.   Mt 2:1, 6, 16.
   Bethphage.   Mt 21:1.
   Emmaus.   Lk 24:13.
   Ephraim.   Jn 11:54.
   Gaza.   Ac 8:26.
   Jericho.   Lk 10:30; 19:1.
   Joppa.   Ac 9:36; 10:5, 8.
   Lydda.   Ac 9:32, 35, 38.

JUDGES, EXTRAORDINARY
During four hundred and fifty years.   Ac. 13:20.
Israel not permanently or spiritually benefited by.   Jg 2:17–19.
Names of
   Abdon.   Jg 12:13.
   Abimelech.   Jg 9:6.
   Deborah.   Jg 4:4.
   Ehud.   Jg 3:15.
   Eli.   1 S 4:18.

Elon. Jg 12:11.
Gideon. Jg 6:11.
Ibzan. Jg 12:8.
Jair. Jg 10:3.
Jephthah. Jg 11:1.
Othniel. Jg 3:9–10.
Samson. Jg 13:24–25; 16:31.
Samuel. 1 S 7:6, 15–17.
Shamgar. Jg 3:31.
Tola. Jg 10:1.
Not without intermission. Jg 17:6; 18:1; 19:1; 21:25.
The office of, not always for life, or hereditary. Jg 8:23, 29.
Raised up to deliver Israel. Jg 2:16.
Remarkable for their faith. He 11:32.
Upheld and strengthened by God. Jg 2:18.

JUDGMENT
The books shall be opened at. Dn 7:10.
CALLED THE
Day of destruction. Jb 21:30.
Day of judgment and perdition of ungodly men. 2 P 3:7.
Day of wrath. Ro 2:5. Rv 6:17.
Judgment of the great day. Jde 1:6.
Revelation of the righteous judgment of God. Ro 2:5.
CERTAINTY OF, A MOTIVE TO
Faith. Is 28:16–17.
Holiness. 2 Co 5:9–10. 2 P 3:11, 14.
Prayer and watchfulness. Mk 13:33.
Repentance. Ac 17:30–31.
Christ will acknowledge saints at. Mt 25:34–40. Rv 3:5.
A day appointed for. Ac 17:31. Ro 2:16.
Devils shall be condemned at. 2 P 2:4. Jde 1:6.
Final punishment of the wicked will succeed. Mt 13:40–42; 25:46.
A first principle of the gospel. He 6:2.
Neglected advantages increase condemnation at. Mt 11:20–24. Lk 11:31–32.
None, by nature, can stand in. Pss 130:3; 143:2. Ro 3:19.
Of Christians, by the gospel. Ja 2:12.
Of heathens, by the law of conscience. Ro 2:12, 14–15.
Of Jews by the law of Moses. Ro 2:12.
Perfect love will give boldness in. 1 Jn 4:17.
Predicted in the Old Testament. 1 Ch 16:33. Pss 9:7; 96:13. Ec 3:17.
Saints shall be enabled to stand in. Ro 8:33–34.

Saints shall be rewarded at. 2 Tm 4:8. Rv 11:18.
Saints shall sit with Christ in. 1 Co 6:2. Rv 20:4.
Shall be administered by Christ. Jn 5:22, 27. Ac 10:42. Ro 14:10. 2 Co 5:10.
SHALL BE HELD UPON
All men. He 9:27; 12:23.
All nations. Mt 25:32.
Quick and dead. 2 Tm 4:1; 1 P 4:5.
The righteous and wicked. Ec 3:17.
Small and great. Rv 20:12.
Shall be in righteousness. Ps 98:9. Ac 17:31.
SHALL BE OF ALL
Actions. Ec 11:9; 12:14. Rv 20:13.
Thoughts. Ec 12:14. 1 Co 4:5.
Words. Mt 12:36–37. Jde 1:15.
Shall take place at the coming of Christ. Mt 25:31. 2 Tm 4:1.
Time of, unknown to us. Mk 13:32.
Warn the wicked of. Ac 24:25. 2 Co 5:11.
The wicked dread. Ac 24:25. He 10:27.
The wicked shall be condemned in. Mt 7:22–23; 25:41.
The word of Christ shall be a witness against the wicked in. Jn 12:48.

JUDGMENTS
Are frequently tempered with mercy. Jr 4:27; 5:10, 15–18. Am 9:8.
Are from God. Dt 32:39. Jb 12:23. Am 3:6. Mi 6:9.
Are in all the earth. 1 Ch 16:14.
ARE SENT AS PUNISHMENT FOR
Despising the warnings of God. 2 Ch 36:16. Pr 1:24–31. Jr 44:4–6.
Disobedience to God. Lv 26:14–16. 2 Co 7:19–20.
Idolatry. 2 K 22:17. Jr 16:18.
Iniquity. Is 26:21. Ezk 24:13–14.
Murmuring against God. Nu 14:29.
Persecuting saints. Dt 32:43.
Sins of rulers. 1 Ch 21:2, 12.
DIFFERENT KINDS OF
Abandonment by God. Ho 4:17.
Blotting out the name. Dt 29:20.
Captivity. Dt 28:41. Ezk 39:23.
Continued sorrows. Pss 32:10; 78:32–33. Ezk 24:23.
Cursing men's blessings. Ml 2:2.
Desolation. Ezk 33:29. Jl 3:19.
Destruction. Jb 31:3. Ps 34:16. Pr 2:22.
Enemies. 2 S 24:13.
Famine. Dt 28:38–40. Am 4:7–9.

Famine of hearing the word. Am 8:11.
Pestilence. Dt 28:21–22. Am 4:10.
The sword. Ex 22:24. Jr 19:7.
INFLICTED UPON
All enemies of saints. Jr 30:16.
False gods. Ex 12:12. Nu 33:4.
Individuals. Dt 29:20. Jr 23:34.
Nations. Gn 15:14. Jr 51:20–21.
Posterity of sinners. Ex 20:5. Ps 37:28.
Lm 5:7.
Manifest the righteous character of God. Ex
9:14–16. Ezk 39:21. Dn 9:14.
MAY BE AVERTED BY
Forsaking iniquity. Jr 18:7–8.
Humiliation. Ex 33:3–4, 14. 2 Ch 7:14.
Prayer. Jg 3:9–11. 2 Ch 7:13–14.
Turning to God. Dt 30:1–3.
SAINTS
Acknowledge the justice of. 2 S 24:17.
Ezr 9:13. Ne 9:33. Jr 14:7.
Pray for those under. Ex 32:11–13. Nu
11–2. Dn 9:3.
Preserved during. Jb 5:19–20. Ps 91:7. Is
26:20. Ezk 9:6. Rv 7:3.
Provided for, during. Gn 47:12. Pss
35:19; 37:19.
Sympathize with those under. Jr 9:1;
13:17. Lm 3:48.
Sent for correction. Jb 37:13. Jr 30:11.
Sent for the deliverance of saints. Ex 6:6.
Should be a warning to others. Lk 13:3, 5.
SHOULD LEAD TO
Contrition. Ne 1:4. Es 4:3. Is 22:12.
Humiliation. Jsh 7:6. 2 Ch 12:6. Lm
3:1–20. Jl 1:13. Jnh 3:5–6.
Learning righteousness. Is 26:9.
Prayer. 2 Ch 20:9.

JUSTICE
Brings its own reward. Jr 22:15.
Christ an example of. Ps 98:9. Is 11:4. Jr.
23:5.
Commanded. Dt 16:20. Is 56:1.
Gifts impede. Ex 23:8.
GOD
Delights in. Pr 11:1.
Displeased with the want of. Ec 5:8.
Gives wisdom to execute. 1 K 3:11–12.
Pr 2:6, 9.
Requires. Mi 6:8.
Sets the highest value on. Pr 21:3.
Promises to. Is 33:15–16. Jr 7:5, 7.
SAINTS SHOULD
Always do. Ps 119:121. Ezk 18:8–9.

Pray for wisdom to execute. 1 K 3:9.
Receive instruction in. Pr 1:3.
Study the principles of. Php 4:8.
Take pleasure in doing. Pr 21:15.
Teach others to do. Gn 18:19.
Specially required in rulers. 2 S 23:3. Ezk
45:9.
TO BE DONE
In buying and selling. Lv 19:36. Dt
25:15.
In executing judgment. Dt 16:18. Jr
21:12.
To servants. Cl 4:1.
To the fatherless and widows. Is 1:17.
To the poor. Pr 29:14; 31:9.
THE WICKED
Abhor. Mi 3:9.
Afflict those who act with. Jb 12:4. Am
5:12.
Banish. Is 59:14.
Call not for. Is 59:4.
Pass over. Lk 11:42.
Scorn. Pr 19:28.

JUSTICE OF GOD
Acknowledge. Ps 51:4, with Ro 3:4.
DECLARED TO BE
The habitation of his throne. Ps 89:14.
Impartial. 2 Ch 19:7. Jr 32:19.
Incomparable. Jb 4:1.
Incorruptible. Dt 10:17. 2 Ch 19:7.
Plenteous. Jb 37:23.
Undeviating. Jb 8:3; 34:12.
Unfailing. Zp 3:5.
Without respect of persons. Ro 2:11. Cl
3:25. 1 P 1:17.
Denied by the ungodly. Ezk 33:17, 20.
EXHIBITED IN
All his ways. Ezk 18:25, 29.
The final judgment. Ac 17:31.
Forgiving sins. 1 Jn 1:9.
His government. Ps 9:4. Jr 9:24.
His judgments. Gn 18:25. Rv 19:2.
Redemption. Ro 3:26.
Magnify. Pss 98:9; 99:3–4.
Not to be sinned against. Jr 50:7.
A part of his character. Dt 32:4. Is 45:21.

JUSTIFICATION BEFORE GOD
The act of God. Is 50:8. Ro 8:33.
BY FAITH
Does not make void the law. Ro 3:30–31.
1 Co 9:21.

Excludes boasting. Ro 3:27; 4:2. 1 Co 1:29, 31.

Revealed under the old dispensation. Hk 2:4, with Ro 1:17.

Promised to Christ. Is 45:25; 53:11.

UNDER THE GOSPEL

Blessedness of. Ps 32:1–2, with Ro 4:6–8.

By imputation of Christ's righteousness. Is 61:10. Jr 23:6. Ro 3:22; 5:18. 1 Co 1:30. 2 Co 5:21.

By the blood of Christ. Ro 5:9.

By the resurrection of Christ. Ro 4:25. 1 Co 15:17.

Ensures glorification. Ro 8:30.

Entitles to an inheritance. Ti 3:7.

Frees from condemnation. Is 50:8–9; 54:17, with Ro 8:33–34.

In the name of Christ. 1 Co 6:11.

Is by faith alone. Jn 5:24. Ac 13:39. Ro 3:30; 5:1. Gl 2:16.

Is not of faith and works united. Ac 15:1–29. Ro 3:28; 11:6. Gl 2:14–21; 5:4.

Is not of works. Ac 13:39. Ro 8:3. Gl 2:16; 3:11.

Is of grace. Ro 3:24; 4:16; 5:17–21.

UNDER THE LAW

Man cannot attain to. Jb 9:2–3, 20; 25:4. Pss 130:3; 143:2, with Ro 3:20. Ro 9:31–32.

Requires perfect obedience. Lv 18:5, with Ro 10:5; 2:13. Ja 2:10.

The wicked shall not attain to. Ex 23:7.

KINDNESS

An attribute of God. Is 54:8. Ep 2:7. Ti 3:4–7.

A characteristic of decent people. Jb 29:15. Pr 31:26. 1 Co 13:4.

A Christian necessity. 2 P 1:7. Cl 3:12.

A fundamental requirement. Mi 6:8. Mt 25:40.

KINGDOM OF GOD

Announced. Mt 3:2; 4:23.

Compared to growing things. Mk 4:1–11, 26–32.

A future certainty. Mt 6:10. Lk 22:16. 1 Co 6:9.

A present reality. Lk 17:21. Cl 1:13.

Promised. Dn 2:44.

L 🌺

LABOR

Divinely ordained.   Gn 2:5, 15; 3:19. 2 Th 3:10, 12.

Required in the Christian life.   He 4:11. 1 Co 3:9. Cl 4:12.

To be done well.   Ec 9:10.

Worthwhile in the Lord.   1 Co 15:58.

LAMB

Considered a great delicacy.   Am 6:4.

Covenants confirmed by gift of.   Gn 21:28–30.

DESCRIBED AS
Patient.   Is 53:7.
Playful.   Ps 114:4, 6.

Exposed to danger from wild beasts.   1 S 17:34.

An extensive commerce in.   Ezr 7:17. Ezk 27:21.

The first-born of an ass to be redeemed with.   Ex 13:13; 34:20.

ILLUSTRATIVE OF
Anything dear or cherished.   2 S 12:3, 9.
Christ as a sacrifice.   Jn 1:29. Rv 5:6.
Complete destruction of the wicked (when consumed in sacrifice).   Ps 37:20.
Israel deprived of God's protection (when deserted and exposed).   Ho 4:16.
The Lord's people.   Is 5:17; 11:6.
Ministers among the ungodly (when among wolves).   Lk 10:3.
Patience of Christ.   Is 53:7. Ac 8:32.
Purity of Christ.   1 P 1:19.
Weak believers.   Is 40:11. Jn 21:15.
The wicked under judgments (when brought to slaughter).   Jr 51:40.

Numbers of, given by Josiah to the people for sacrifice.   2 Ch 35:7.

OFFERED IN SACRIFICE
At a year old.   Ex 12:5. Nu 6:14.
At the passover.   Ex 12:3, 6–7.
By the wicked not accepted.   Is 1:11; 66:3.
During the earliest times.   Gn 4:4; 22:7–8.
Every morning and evening.   Ex 29:38–39. Nu 28:3–4.
Females.   Nu 6:14.

Males.   Ex 12:5.
While sucking.   1 S 7:9.

Shepherds care for.   Is 40:11.

Tribute often paid in.   2 K 3:4. Is 16:1.

USED FOR
Clothing.   Pr 27:26.
Food.   Dt 32:14. 2 S 12:4.
Sacrifice.   1 Ch 29:21. 2 Ch 29:32.

The young of the flock.   Ex 12:5. Ezk 45:15.

LAMPS

DESCRIBED AS
Burning.   Gn 15:17.
Shining.   Jn 5:35.

Design of.   2 P 1:19.

Illumination of the tents of Arab chiefs by, alluded to.   Jb 29:3–4.

ILLUSTRATIVE OF
Complete destruction of those who curse parents (when totally quenched).   Pr 20:20.
Destruction of the wicked (when put out).   Jb 18:5–6; 21:17.   Pr 13:9.
Glory of the cherubim.   Ezk 1:13.
God's guidance.   2 S 22:29. Ps 18:28.
Graces of the Holy Ghost.   Rv 4:5.
Ministers.   Jn 5:35.
Omniscience of Christ.   Dn 10:6. Rv 1:14.
Salvation of God.   Gn 15:17. Is 62:1.
Severe judgments.   Rv 8:10.
Spirit of man.   Pr 20:27.
A succession of heirs.   1 K 11:36; 15:4.
Wise rulers.   2 S 21:17.
The word of God.   Ps 119:105. Pr 6:23.

Lighted with oil.   Mt 25:3, 8.

Often kept lighting all night.   Pr 31:18.

Oil for, carried in vessels.   Mt 25:4.

Placed on a stand to give light to all in the house.   Mt 5:15.

Probable origin of dark lantern.   Jg 7:16.

Required to be constantly trimmed.   Mt 25:7.

Sometimes supplied with oil from a bowl through pipes.   Zc 4:2.

USED FOR LIGHTING
Chariots of war by night. Na 2:3–4.
Marriage processions. Mt 25:1.
Persons going out at night. Jn 18:3.
Private apartments. Ac 20:8.
The tabernacle. Ex 25:37.

LANGUAGE
Ancient kingdoms often comprehended nations of different. Es 1:22. Dn 3:4; 6:25.
CALLED
Speech. Mk 14:70. Ac 14:11.
Tongue. Ac 1:19. Rv 5:9.
CONFUSION OF
Divided men into separate nations. Gn 10:5, 20, 31.
Originated the varieties in. Gn 11:7.
A punishment for presumption, etc. Gn 11:2–6.
Scattered men over the earth. Gn 11:8–9.
Great variety of, spoken by men. 1 Co 14:10.
INTERPRETATION OF
Antiquity of engaging persons for. Gn 42:23.
A gift of the Holy Ghost. 1 Co 12:10.
The Jews punished by being given up to people of a strange. Dt 28:49. Is 28:11. Jr 5:15.
Most important in the early church. 1 Co 14:5, 13, 27–28.
KINDS OF, MENTIONED
Arabic, etc. Ac 2:11.
Chaldee. Dn 1:4.
Egyptian. Pss 81:5; 114:1. Ac 2:10.
Greek. Ac 21:37.
Hebrew. 2 K 18:28. Ac 26:14.
Latin. Lk 23:38.
Lycaonian. Ac 14:11.
Syriac. 2 K 18:26. Ezr 4:7.
Of all mankind one at first. Gn 11:1, 6.
Of some nations difficult. Ezk 3:5–6.
POWER OF SPEAKING DIFFERENT
Conferred by laying on of the apostles' hands. Ac 8:17–18; 19:6.
A gift of the Holy Ghost. 1 Co 12:10.
Given on the day of Pentecost. Ac 2:3–4.
Followed receiving the gospel. Ac 10:44–46.
Necessary to spread of the gospel. Ac 2:7–11.
Promised. Mk 16:17.
A sign to unbelievers. 1 Co 14:22.
Sometimes abused. 1 Co 14:2–12, 23.

Term barbarian applied to those who spoke a strange. 1 Co 14:11.

LAST
CHRIST
Alpha and Omega. Rv 21:6.
Beginning and end. Rv 2:3.
GOD
At the end. 1 Co 15:24.
The first and the. Is 44:6.
With the ———. Is 41:4.
TIMES
Day. Jn 6:39.
Days. Ac 2:17. 2 Tm 3:1.
Of the apostles' ———. 1 Co 4:9.
These ——— days. He 1:1.
Time. Mt 21:37. 1 Jn 2:18.
Times. 1 P 1:20.

LAW OF GOD
Absolute and perpetual. Mt 5:18.
All men have transgressed. Ro 3:9, 19.
Blessedness of keeping. Ps 119:1. Mt 5:19. 1 Jn 3:22, 24. Rv 22:14.
CHRIST
Came to fulfill. Mt 5:17.
Explained. Mt 7:12; 22:37–40.
Magnified. Is 42:21.
Conscience testifies to. Ro 2:15.
DESCRIBED AS
Exceedingly broad. Ps 119:96.
Holy, just, and good. Ro 7:12.
Not grievous. 1 Jn 5:3.
Perfect. Ps 19:7. Ro 12:2.
Pure. Ps 19:8.
Spiritual. Ro 7:14.
Truth. Ps 119:142.
Designed to lead to Christ. Gl 3:24.
Established by faith. Ro 3:31.
GIVEN
Through Moses. Ex 31:18. Jn 7:19.
Through the ministration of angels. Ac 7:53. Gl 3:19. He 2:2.
To Adam. Gn 2:16–17, with Ro 5:12–14.
To Noah. Gn 9:6.
To the Israelites. Ex 20:2, etc. Ps 78:5.
Gives the knowledge of sin. Ro 3:20; 7:7.
Love of, produces peace. Ps 119:165.
Love the fulfilling of. Ro 13:8, 10. Gl 5:14. Ja 2:8.
Man by nature not in subjection to. Ro 7:5; 8:7.
Man cannot be justified by. Ac 13:39. Ro 3:20, 28. Gl 2:16; 3:11.

Man cannot render perfect obedience to. 1 K 8:46. Ec 7:20. Ro 3:10.

Man's duty to keep. Ec 12:13.

OBEDIENCE TO

A characteristic of saints. Rv 12:17.

Of prime importance. 1 Co 7:19.

A test of love. 1 Jn 5:3.

Punishment for disobeying. Ne 9:26–27. Is 65:11–13. Jr 9:13–16.

REQUIRES

Obedience of the heart. Ps 51:6. Mt 5:28; 22:37.

Perfect obedience. Dt 27:26. Gl 3:10. Ja 2:10.

The rule of life to saints. 1 Co 9:21. Gl 5:13–14.

The rule of the judgment. Ro 2:12.

SAINTS

Delight in. Ps 119:77. Ro 7:22.

Freed from the bondage of. Ro 6:14; 7:4, 6. Gl 3:13.

Freed from the curse of. Gl 3:13.

Have written on their hearts. Jr 31:33, with He 8:10.

Keep. Ps 119:55.

Lament over the violation of by others. Ps 119:136.

Love. Ps 119:97, 113.

Pledge themselves to walk in. Ne 10:29.

Pray for power to keep. Ps 119:34.

Pray to understand. Ps 119:18.

Prepare their hearts to seek. Ezr 7:10.

Should make the subject of their conversation. Ex 13:9.

Should remember. Ml 4:4.

Sin is a transgression of. 1 Jn 3:4.

To be used lawfully. 1 Tm 1:8.

THE WICKED

Cast away. Is 5:24.

Despise. Am 2:4.

Forget. Ho 4:6.

Forsake. 2 Ch 12:1. Jr 9:13.

Refuse to hear. Is 30:9. Jr 6:19.

Refuse to walk in. Ps 78:10.

Worketh wrath. Ro 4:15.

LAW OF MOSES

Additions made to, in the plains of Moab by Jordan. Nu 36:13.

ALL ISRAELITES REQUIRED

To know. Ex 18:16.

To lay up in their hearts. Dt 6:6; 11:18.

To observe. Dt 4:6; 6:2.

To remember. Ml 4:4.

To teach their children. Dt 6:7; 11:19.

Book of, laid up in the Sanctuary. Dt 31:26.

A burdensome yoke. Ac 15:10.

CALLED

Book of Moses. 2 Ch 25:4; 35:12.

Book of the law. Dt 30:10. Jsh 1:8.

A fiery law. Dt 33:2.

Ministration of condemnation. 2 Co 3:9.

Ministration of death. 2 Co 3:7.

Lively oracles. Ac 7:38.

Royal law. Ja 2:8.

Word spoken by angels. He 2:2.

CHRIST

Abrogated, as a covenant of works. Ro 7:4.

Attended all feasts of. Jn 2:23; 7:2, 10, 37.

Bore the curse of. Dt 21:23, with Gl 3:13.

Came not to destroy but to fulfill. Mt 5:17–18.

Circumcised according to. Lk 2:21. Ro 15:8.

Fulfilled all precepts of. Ps 40:7–8.

Fulfilled all types and shadows of. He 9:8, 11–14; 10:1, 11–14.

Made under. Gl 4:4.

Magnified and made honorable. Is 42:41.

Could not annul the covenant of grace made in Christ. Gl 3:17.

Could not give righteousness and life. Gl 3:21, with Ro 8:3–4. He 10:1.

A covenant of works to the Jews as a nation. Dt 28:1, 15, with Jr 31:32.

Darkness, etc., at giving of, illustrative of obscurity of Mosaic dispensation. He 12:18–24.

DIVIDED INTO

Ceremonial, relating to manner of worshiping God. Lv 7:37–38. He 9:1–7.

Civil, relating to administration of justice. Dt 17:9–11. Ac 23:3; 24:6.

Moral, embodied in the ten commandments. Dt 5:22; 10:4.

Entire, written in a book. Dt 31:9.

GIVEN

After the exodus. Dt 4:45. Ps 81:4–5.

At Horeb. Dt 4:10, 15; 5:2.

By disposition of angels. Ac 7:53.

From the Mount Sinai. Ex 19:11, 20.

In the desert. Ezk 20:10–11.

Through Moses as mediator. Dt 5:5, 27–28. Jn 1:17. Gl 3:19.

To no other nation. Dt 4:8. Ps 147:20.

To the Jews. Lv 26:46. Ps 78:5.

Good kings enforced. 2 K 23:24–25. 2 Ch 31:21.

THE JEWS

Accused Christians of speaking. Ac 6:11–14; 21:28.

Accused Christ of breaking. Jn 19:7.

Broke it themselves. Jn 7:19.

Dishonored God by breaking. Ro 2:23.

From regard to, rejected Christ. Ro 9:31–33.

Held those ignorant of, accursed. Jn 7:49.

Shall be judged by. Jn 5:45. Ro 2:12.

Zealous for. Jn 9:28–29. Ac 21:20.

Kings to write out and study. Dt 17:18–19.

The law of God. Lv 26:46.

A means of national reformation. 2 Ch 34:19–21. Ne 8:13–18.

None to approach the Mount while God gave. Ex 19:13, 21–24. He 12:20.

Not the manifestation of the grace of God. Jn 1:17. (See also Ro 8:3–4.)

Priests and Levites to teach. Dt 33:8–10. Ne 8:7. Ml 2:7.

Primitive Jewish converts would have all Christians observe. Ac 15:1.

Public instruction given to youth in. Lk 2:46. Ac 22:3.

PUBLICLY READ

At the feast of tabernacles in the sabbatical year. Dt 31:10–13.

By Ezra. Ne 8:2–3.

By Joshua. Jsh 8:34–35.

In the synagogues every sabbath. Ac 13:15; 15:21.

Rehearsed by Moses. Dt 1:1–3.

Remarkable phenomena connected with, at giving. Ex 19:16–19.

A schoolmaster to lead to Christ. Gl 3:24.

Scribes were learned in, and expounded. Ezr 7:6. Mt 23:2.

A shadow of good things to come. He 10:1.

Tables of, laid up in the ark. Dt 10:5.

TAUGHT THE JEWS

All punishments awarded according to. Jn 8:5; 19:7. He 10:28.

To love and fear God. Dt 6:5; 10:12–13. Mt 22:36, 38.

To love their neighbor. Lv 19:18. Mt 22:39.

Strict justice and impartiality. Lv 19:35–36.

Terror of Israel at receiving. Ex 19:16; 20:18–20. Dt 5:5, 23–25.

LEAVEN

Diffusive properties of. 1 Co 5:6.

First fruits of wheat offered with. Lv 23:17.

FORBIDDEN

During the feast of passover. Ex 12:15–20.

To be offered with blood. Ex 34:25.

To be offered, etc., with meat offerings which were burned. Lv 2:11; 10:12.

ILLUSTRATIVE OF

Doctrines of Pharisees, etc. Mt 16:6, 12.

False teachers. Gl 5:8–9.

Malice and wickedness. 1 Co 5:8.

The rapid spread of the gospel. Mt 13:33. Lk 13:21.

Ungodly professors. 1 Co 5:6–7.

Used in making bread. Ho 7:4.

Used with thank offerings. Lv 7:13. Am 4:5.

LEPROSY

Ceremonies at cleansing of. Lv 14:3–32.

Christ gave power to heal. Mt 10:8.

A common disease among the Jews. Lk 4:27.

GARMENTS

Incurably infected with, burned. Lv 13:51–52.

Infected with, to have the piece first torn out. Lv 13:56.

Suspected of but not infected, washed and pronounced clean. Lv 13:53–54, 58–59.

Suspected of, shown to priest. Lv 13:49.

Suspected of, shut up seven days. Lv 13:50.

HOUSES

Ceremonies at cleansing of. Lv 14:49–53.

Incurably infected with, pulled down and removed. Lv 14:43–45.

Infected with, communicated uncleanness to every one who entered them. Lv 14:46–47.

Suspected of but not infected, pronounced clean. Lv 14:48.

Suspected of, emptied. Lv 14:36.

Suspected of, inspected by priest. Lv 14:37.

Suspected of, reported to priest. Lv 14:35.

Suspected of, shut up seven days. Lv 14:38.

To have the part infected with, first removed, and the rest scraped, etc. Lv 14:39, 42.

An incurable disease. 2 K 5:7.

INFECTED
Garments. Lv 13:47.
Houses. Lv 14:34.
Men. Lk 17:12.
Women. Nu 12:10.
Less inveterate when it covered the whole body. Lv 13:13.
Often began with a bright red spot. Lv 13:2, 24.
Often hereditary. 2 S 3:29. 2 K 5:27.
Often sent as a punishment for sin. Nu 12:9–10. 2 Ch 26:19.
PARTS AFFECTED BY
The beard. Lv 13:20.
The forehead. 2 Ch 26:19.
The hand. Ex 4:6.
The head. Lv. 13:44.
The whole body. Lk 5:12.
Power of Christ manifested in curing. Mt 8:3. Lk 5:13; 17:13–14.
Power of God manifested in curing. Nu 12:13–14. 2 K 5:8–14.
THE PRIESTS
Examined all persons healed of. Lv 14:2. Mt 8:4. Lk 17:14.
Examined persons suspected of. Lv 13:2, 9.
Had rules for distinguishing. Lv 13:5–44.
Judged and directed in cases of. Dt 24:8.
Shut up for seven days persons suspected of. Lv 13:4.
THOSE AFFLICTED WITH
Associated together. 2 K 7:3. Lk 17:12.
Ceremonially unclean. Lv 13:8, 11, 22, 44.
Cut off from God's house. 2 Ch 26:21.
Dwelt in a separate house. 2 K 15:5.
Excluded from priest's office. Lv 22:2–4.
Had their heads bare, clothes rent, and lip covered. Lv 13:45.
Separated from intercourse with others. Nu 5:2; 12:14–15.
To cry unclean when approached. Lv 13:45.
Turned the hair white or yellow. Lv 13:3, 10, 30.
Turned the skin white. Ex 4:6. 2 K 5:27.

LEVITES
CEREMONIES AT CONSECRATION OF
Cleansing and purifying. Nu 8:7.
Elders of Israel laying their hands on them. Nu 8:9–10.
Making a sin offering for. Nu 8:8, 12.

Presenting them to God as an offering for the people. Nu 8:11, 15.
Setting before the priests and presenting them as their offering to God. Nu 8:13.
Chosen by God for service of the sanctuary. 1 Ch 15:2, with Nu 3:6.
DAVID
By his last words had them numbered from twenty years old. 1 Ch 23:24, 27.
Divided them into four classes. 1 Ch 23:4–6.
Made them attend in courses. 2 Ch 8:14; 31:17.
Made them serve from twenty on account of the lightness of their duties. 1 Ch 23:26, 28–32.
Numbered them first from thirty years old. 1 Ch 23:2–3.
Subdivided them into twenty-four courses. 1 Ch 23:6, with 25:8–31.
Descended from Jacob's third son. Gn 29:34. He 7:9–10.
Encamped around the tabernacle. Nu 1:50, 52–53; 3:23, 29, 35.
Entered on their service at age twenty-five. Nu 8:24.
FAMILIES, AS NUMBERED
Of Gershon. Nu 3:18, 21–22.
Of Kohath. Nu 3:19, 27–28.
Of Merari. Nu 3:20, 33–34.
Forty-eight cities appointed for. Nu 35:2–8.
Given to Aaron and sons. Nu 3:9; 8:19.
Had a part of the offerings. Dt 18:1–2.
Had chiefs or officers over them. Nu 3:24, 30, 35. 1 Ch 15:4–10. 2 Ch 35:9. Ezr 8:29.
Had no inheritance in Israel. Dt 10:9. Jsh 13:33; 14:3.
The Jews to be kind and benevolent to. Dt 12:12, 18–19; 14:29; 16:11, 14.
Marched in the center of Israel. Nu 2:17.
Not numbered with Israel. Nu 1:47–49.
Numbered as ministers at age thirty. Nu 4:3, 23, etc.
Numbered separately after the people from a month old. Nu 3:14–16, 39.
Originally consisted of three families or divisions. Nu 3:17. 1 Ch 6:16–48.
Priests to get a tenth of their tithes. Nu 18:26–32.
Prophecies respecting. Gn 49:5, 7. Dt 33:8–11.
Punished with death for encroaching on the priestly office. Nu 18:3.

Punishment of Korah and others, for offering incense. Nu 16:1–35.

Served in courses after captivity. Ezr 6:18.

SERVICES OF

Blessing the people. Dt 10:8.

Conducting the sacred music. 1 Ch 23:5–30. 2 Ch 5:12–13. Ne 12:24, 27–43.

Doing the service of tabernacle. Nu 8:19, 22.

Guarding king's person and house in time of danger. 2 K 11:5–9. 2 Ch 23:5, 7.

Judging and deciding in controversies. Dt 17:9. 1 Ch 23:4. 2 Ch 19:8.

Keeping sacred instruments and vessels. Nu 3:8. 1 Ch 9:28–29.

Keeping sacred oil, flour, etc. 1 Ch 9:29–30.

Keeping sacred treasures. 1 Ch 26:20.

Keeping the charge of the sanctuary. Nu 18:3. 1 Ch 23:32.

Keeping the gates of the temple. 1 Ch 9:17–26.

Ministering to priests. Nu 3:6–7; 18:2.

Ministering to the Lord. Dt 10:8.

Ministering to the people. 2 Ch 35:3.

Preparing the sacrifices for the priests. 1 Ch 23:31. 2 Ch 35:11.

Preparing the showbread. 1 Ch 9:31–32; 23:29.

Purifying the holy things. 1 Ch 23:28.

Regulating weights and measures. 1 Ch 23:29.

Singing praises before the army. 2 Ch 20:21–22.

Taking charge of the tithes, offerings, etc. 2 Ch 31:11–19. Ne 12:44.

Taking down, putting up, and carrying the tabernacle, etc. Nu 1:50–51; 4:5–33.

Teaching the people. 2 Ch 17:8–9; 30:22; 35:3. Ne 8:7.

Superannuated at age fifty. Nu 8:25.

Taken instead of the first-born of Israel. Nu 3:12–13, 40–45. Nu 8:16–18.

Tithes given to, for their support. Nu 18:21, 24. 2 Ch 31:4–5. Ne 12:44–45. (*See also* He 7:5.)

Were all under control of the high priest's deputy. Nu 3:32. 1 Ch 9:20.

Were consecrated. Nu 8:6, 14.

When superannuated, required to perform less arduous duties. Nu 8:26.

While in attendance, lodged around the temple. 1 Ch 9:27.

Zeal against idolatry a cause of their appointment. Ex 32:26–28, with Dt 33:9–10.

LIBERALITY

Blessings connected with. Ps 41:1. Pr 22:9. Ac 20:35.

Characteristic of saints. Ps 112:9. Is 32:8.

Christ set an example of. 2 Co 8:9.

Exercise of, provokes others to. 2 Co 9:2.

Exhortations to. Lk 3:11; 11:41. Ac 20:35. 1 Co 16:1. 1 Tm 6:17–18.

God never forgets. He 6:10.

Labor to be enabled to exercise. Ac 20:35. Ep 4:28.

Pleasing to God. 2 Co 9:7. He 13:16.

Promises to. Ps 112:9. Pr 11:25; 28:27. Ec 11:1–2. Is 58:10.

SHOULD BE EXERCISED

Abundantly. 2 Co 8:7; 9:11–13.

According to ability. Dt 16:10, 17. 1 Co 16:2.

In forwarding missions. Php 4:14–16.

In giving alms. Lk 12:33.

In lending to those in want. Mt 5:42.

In relieving the destitute. Is 58:7.

In rendering personal services. Php 2:30.

In the service of God. Ex 35:21–29.

Toward all men. Gl 6:10.

Toward enemies. Pr 25:21.

Toward saints. Ro 12:13. Gl 6:10.

Toward servants. Dt 15:12–14.

Toward strangers. Lv 25:35.

Toward the poor. Dt 15:11. Is 58:7.

Willingly. Ex 25:2. 2 Co 8:12.

Without ostentation. Mt 6:1–3.

With simplicity. Ro 12:8.

Unprofitable, without love. 1 Co 13:3.

WANT OF

Brings many a curse. Pr 28:27.

A proof of not having faith. Ja 2:14–16.

A proof of not loving God. 1 Jn 3:17.

LIBERTY, CHRISTIAN

Called the glorious liberty of the children of God. Ro 8:21.

CONFERRED

By Christ. Gl 4:3–5; 5:1.

By God. Cl 1:13.

By the Holy Ghost. Ro 8:15. 2 Co 3:17.

Through the gospel. Jn 8:32.

Confirmed by Christ. Jn 8:36.

FALSE TEACHERS

Abuse. Jde 1:4.

Promise to others. 2 P 2:19.

Try to destroy. Gl 2:4.
Foretold. Is 42:7; 61:1.
The gospel is the law of. Ja 1:25, 2:12.
Is FREEDOM FROM
Bondage of man. 1 Co 9:19.
Corruption. Ro 8:21.
Curse of the law. Gl 3:13.
Fear of death. He 2:15.
Jewish ordinances. Gl 4:3. Cl 2:20.
Law. Ro 7:6; 8:2.
Sin. Ro 6:7, 18.
Proclaimed by Christ. Is 61:1. Lk 4:18.
Saints are called to. Gl 5:13.
SAINTS SHOULD
Assert. 1 Co 10:29.
Not abuse. Gl 5:13.. 1 P 2:16.
Not offend others by. 1 Co 8:9; 10:29, 32.
Praise God for. Ps 116:16–17.
Stand fast in. Gl 2:5; 5:1.
Walk in. Ps 119:45.
The service of Christ is. 1 Co 7:22.
Types. Lv 25:10–17. Gl 4:22–26, 31.
The wicked, devoid of. Jn 8:34, with Ro 6:20.

LIFE, ETERNAL
Cannot be inherited by works. Ro 2:7, with 3:10–19.
Christ is. 1 Jn 1:2; 5:20.
Exhortation to seek. Jn 6:27.
GIVEN
By Christ. Jn 6:27; 10:28.
By God. Ps 113:3. Ro 6:23.
In answer to prayer. Ps 21:4.
In Christ. 1 Jn 5:11.
Through Christ. Ro 5:21; 6:23.
To all given to Christ. Jn 17:2.
To those who believe in Christ. Jn 3:15–16, 6:40, 47.
To those who believe in God. Jn 5:24.
To those who hate life for Christ. Jn 12:25.
RESULTS FROM
Drinking the water of life. Jn 4:14.
Eating of the tree of life. Rv 2:7.
Eating the bread of life. Jn 6:50–58.
Revealed by Christ. Jn 6:68. 2 Tm 1:10.
Revealed in the scriptures. Jn 5:39.
The self-righteous think to inherit, by works. Mk 10:17.
SAINTS
Are preserved unto. Jn 10:28–29.
Have hope of. Ti 1:2; 3:7.

Have promises of. 1 Tm 4:8. 2 Tm 1:1. Ti 1:2. 1 Jn 2:25.
Look for the mercy of God unto. Jde 1:21.
May have assurance of. 2 Co 5:1. 1 Jn 5:13.
Shall go into. Mt 25:46.
Shall inherit. Mt 19:29.
Shall reap, through the Spirit. Gl 6:8.
Shall reign in. Dn 7:18. Ro 5:17.
Shall rise unto. Dn 12:2. Jn 5:29.
Should lay hold of. 1 Tm 6:12, 19.
They who are ordained to, believe the gospel. Ac 13:48.
To know God and Christ is. Jn 17:3.
THE WICKED
Have not. 1 Jn 3:15.
Judge themselves unworthy of. Ac 13:46.

LIFE, NATURAL
Be not overanxious to provide for the wants of. Mt 6:25.
BE THANKFUL FOR
Its preservation. Ps 103:4. Jn 2:6.
The supply of its wants. Gn 48:15.
Cares and pleasures of, dangerous. Lk 8:14; 21:34. 2 Tm 2:4.
COMPARED TO
A dream. Ps 73:20.
An eagle hasting to the prey. Jb 9:26.
A flower. Jb 14:2.
Grass. 1 P 1:24.
A handbreadth. Ps 39:5.
A pilgrimage. Gn 47:9.
A shadow. Ec 6:12.
A shepherd's tent removed. Is 38:18.
A sleep. Ps 90:5.
A swift post. Jb 9:25.
A swift ship. Jb 9:26.
A tale told. Ps 90:9.
A thread cut by the weaver. Is 38:12.
A vapor. Ja 4:14.
Water spilt on the ground. 2 S 14:14.
A weaver's shuttle. Jb 7:6.
Wind. Jb 7:7.
DESCRIBED AS
Full of trouble. Jb 14:1.
Limited. Jb 7:1; 14:5.
Short. Jb 14:1. Ps 89:47.
Uncertain. Ja 4:13–15.
Vain. Ec 6:12.
The dissatisfied despise. Ec 2:17.
Enjoyment of consists not in abundance of possessions. Lk 12:15.
Forfeited by sin. Gn 2:17; 3:17–19.

God as the author of. Gn 2:7. Ac 17:28.
God preserves. Pss 36:6; 66:9.
God's loving-kindness better than. Ps 63:3.
In the hand of God. Jb 12:10. Dn 5:23.
Miraculously restored by Christ. Mt 9:18, 25. Lk 7:15, 22. Jn 11:43.
Obedience to God tends to prolong. Dt 30:20.
Obedience to parents tends to prolong. Ex 20:12. Pr 4:10.
Of others, not to be taken away. Ex 20:13.
Of saints, specially protected by God. Jb 2:6. Ac 18:10. 1 P 3:13.
Of the wicked, not specially protected by God. Jb 36:6. Ps 78:50.
Preserved by discretion. Pr 13:3.
Saints have true enjoyment of. Ps 128:2. 1 Tm 4:8.
Shortness of, should lead to spiritual improvement. Dt 32:29. Ps 90:12.
Should be laid down, if necessary, for Christ. Mt 10:39. Lk 14:26. Ac 20:24.
Should be laid down, if necessary, for the brethren. Ro 16:4. 1 Jn 3:16.
SHOULD BE SPENT IN
  Doing good. Ec 3:12.
  Fear of God. 1 P 1:17.
  Living unto God. Ro 14:8. Php 1:21.
  Peace. Ro 12:18. 1 Tm 2:2.
  Service of God. Lk 1:75.
Should be taken all due care of. Mt 10:23. Ac 27:34.
Sometimes judicially shortened. 1 S 2:32–33. Jb 36:14.
Sometimes prolonged, in answer to prayer. Is 38:2–5. Ja 5:15.
Value of. Jb 2:4. Mt 6:25.
We know not what is good for us in. Ec 6:12.
The wicked have their portion of good during. Ps 17:14. Lk 6:24; 16:25.

LIFE, SPIRITUAL

All saints have. Ep 2:1, 5. Cl 2:13.
Christ the author of. Jn 5:21, 25; 6:33, 51–53; 14:6. 1 Jn 4:9.
DESCRIBED AS
  A life unto God. Ro 6:11. Gl 2:19.
  Living in the Spirit. Gl 5:25.
  Newness of life. Ro 6:4.
Evidenced by love to the brethren. 1 Jn 3:14.
Fear of God is. Pr 14:27; 19:23.
God the author of. Ps 36:9. Cl 2:13.
Has its infancy. Lk 10:21. 1 Co 3:1–2. 1 Jn 2:12.

Has its maturity. Ep 4:13. 1 Jn 2:13–14.
Has its origin in the new birth. Jn 3:3–8.
Has its youth. 1 Jn 2:13–14.
Hidden with Christ. Cl 3:3.
The Holy Ghost the author of. Ezk 37:14, with Ro 8:9–13.
Hypocrites destitute of. Jde 1:12. Rv 3:1.
Illustrated. Ezk 37:9–10. Lk 15:24.
Lovers of pleasure destitute of. 1 Tm 5:6.
MAINTAINED BY
  Christ. Jn 6:57. 1 Co 10:3–4.
  Faith. Gl 2:20.
  Prayer. Ps 69:32.
  The word of God. Dt 8:3, with Mt 4:4.
Pray for the increase of. Pss 119:25; 143:11.
Revived by God. Ps 85:6. Ho 6:2.
Saints praise God for. Ps 119:175.
Seek to grow in. Ep 4:15. 1 P 2:2.
Should animate the services of saints. Ro 12:1. 1 Co 14:15.
Spiritual-mindedness is. Ro 8:6.
The wicked alienated from. Ep 4:18.
The word of God is the instrument of. Is 55:3. 2 Co 3:6. 1 P 4:6.

LIGHT

Communicated to the body through the eye. Pr 15:30. Mt 6:22.
Created by God. Gn 1:3. Is 45:7.
DESCRIBED AS
  Agreeable. Ec 11:7.
  Bright. Jb 37:21.
  Diffusive. Jb 25:3, with 36:30.
  Manifesting objects. Jn 3:20–21. Ep 5:13.
  Shining. 2 S 23:4. Jb 41:18.
  Useful and precious. Ec 2:13.
DIVIDED INTO
  Artificial. Jr 25:10. Ac 16:29.
  Extraordinary or miraculous. Ex 14:20. Ps 78:14. Ac 9:3; 12:7.
  Natural. Jb 24:14. Is 5:30.
God the only source of. Ja 1:17.
ILLUSTRATIVE OF
  Christ the source of all wisdom. Lk 2:32. Jn 1:4, 9; 8:12; 12:46.
  Favor of God. Ps 4:6. Is 2:5.
  Future glory of saints. Ps 97:11. Cl 1:12.
  Glory of Christ. Ac 9:3, 5; 26:13.
  Glory of God. Ps 104:2, with 1 Tm 6:16.
  Glory of the church. Is 60:1–3.
  Gospel. 2 Co 4:4. 1 P 2:9.
  Guidance of God. Pss 27:1; 36:9.
  Ministers. Mt 5:14. Jn 5:35.

Path of the just. Pr 4:18.
Purity of Christ. Mt 17:2.
Purity of God. 1 Jn 1:5.
Saints. Lk 16:8. Ep 5:8. Php 2:15.
The soul of man. Jb 18:5–6.
Whatever makes manifest. Jn 3:21. Ep 5:13.
Wisdom of God. Dn 2:22.
Wise rulers. 2 S 21:17; 23:4.
Word of God. Ps 119:105, 130. 2 P 1:19.
Separated from darkness. Gn 1:4.
Sun, moon, and stars appointed to communicate to the earth. Gn 1:14–17. Jr 31:35.
Theory of, beyond man's comprehension. Jb 38:19–20, 24.

LION

Attacks and destroys men. 1 K 13:24; 20:36.
Attacks the sheepfolds. 1 S 17:34. Am 3:12. Mi 5:8.
Canaan infested by. 2 K 17:25–26.
Conceals itself by day. Ps 104:22.
Criminals often thrown to. Dn 6:7, 16, 24.
DESCRIBED AS
    Active. Dt 33:22.
    Courageous. 2 S 17:10.
    Fearless even of man. Is 31:4. Na 2:11.
    Fierce. Jb 10:16; 28:8.
    Majestic in movement. Pr 30:29–30.
    Superior in strength. Jg 14:18. Pr 30:30.
    Voracious. Ps 17:12.
Disobedient prophet slain by. 1 K 13:24, 26.
God provides for. Jb 38:39. Ps 104:21, 28.
God's power exhibited in restraining. 1 K 13:28. Dn 6:22, 27.
Greatness of its teeth alluded to. Ps 58:6. Jl 1:6.
Hunting of, alluded to. Jb 10:16.
ILLUSTRATIVE OF
    Boldness of saints. Pr 28:1.
    Brave men. 2 S 1:23; 23:20.
    Christ. Rv 5:5.
    Cruel and powerful enemies. Is 5:29. Jr 49:19, 51:38.
    The devil. 1 P 5:8.
    God in executing judgments. Is 38:13. Lm 3:10. Ho 5:14; 13:8.
    God in protecting his church. Is 31:4.
    Imaginary fears of the slothful. Pr 22:13; 26:13.
    Israel. Nu 24:9.
    A king's wrath (when roaring). Pr 19:12; 20:2.
    Natural man subdued by grace (when tamed). Is 11:7; 65:25.
    Persecutors. Ps 22:13. 2 Tm 4:17.
    Tribe of Gad. Dt 33:20.
    Tribe of Judah. Gn 49:9.
INHABITS
    Deserts. Is 30:6.
    Forests. Jr 5:6.
    Mountains. S S 4:8.
    Thickets. Jr 4:7.
Lurks for its prey. Ps 10:9.
Often carries its prey to its den. Na 2:12.
Often perishes for lack of food. Jb 4:11.
Rends its prey. Dt 33:20. Ps 7:2.
Roars when seeking prey. Ps 104:21. Is 31:4.
SLAIN BY
    Benaiah. 2 S 23:20.
    David. 1 S 17:35–36.
    Samson. Jg 14:5–6.
Swarm of bees found in the carcass of, by Samson. Jg 14:8.

LIPS

Blessings and. 1 S 1:13. Pss 45:2; 66:13–14. Jb 33:3. He 13:15.
Evil and. Pss 22:7; 140:9. Pr 24:2, 28. Is 59:3.
May glorify God. Ps 51:15. Ro 10:9.
Reveal the heart. Mt 12:34.
Require Christian control. Pss 19:14; 141:3. Mt 5:37. Cl 4:6.
Source of good or evil. Pr 18:21. Ja 3:9–10.

LISTENING

Emphasized in the way of faith. Is 55:3. Mt 11:15. Rv 2:7.
Neglected by the unrighteous. Ne 9:16.
Required by God. Ps 34:11.

LOCUST

Carried every way by the wind. Ex 10:13, 19.
Clean and fit for food. Lv 11:21–22.
DESCRIBED AS
    Like horses prepared for battle. Jl 2:4, with Rv 9:7.
    Rapid in movement. Is 33:4.
    Voracious. Ex 10:15.
    Wise. Pr 30:24, 27.
Flies in bands and with order. Pr 30:27.
ILLUSTRATIVE OF
    Destruction of God's enemies (by its destruction). Na 3:15.
    Destructive enemies. Jl 1:6–7; 2:2–9.
    False teachers of the apostasy. Rv 9:3.

Ungodly rulers. Ne 3:17.

Immensely numerous. Ps 105:34. Na 3:15.

THE JEWS

Deprecated the plague of. 1 K 8:37–38.

Often plagued by. Jl 1:4; 2:25.

Promised deliverance from the plague of, on humiliation, etc. 2 Ch 7:13–14.

Threatened with, as a punishment for sin. Dt 28:38, 42.

Used, as food. Mt 3:4.

One of the plagues of Egypt. Ex 10:4–15.

A small insect. Pr 30:24, 27.

LONELINESS

MAY BE AN OCCASION FOR

Communion. Ex 24:2.

Meditation. Jn 6:15.

Prayer. Lk 9:18.

Thanksgiving. Dn 6:10.

Not good for man. Gn 2:18. Ps 68:6.

Sometimes necessary. Ps 38:11. 2 Tm 4:16.

LONG-SUFFERING OF GOD

An encouragement to repent. Jl 2:13.

EXERCISED TOWARD

His people. Is 30:18. Ezk 20:17.

The wicked. Ro 9:22. 1 P 3:20.

Exhibited in forgiving sins. Ro 3:25.

Illustrated. Lk 13:6, 9.

Limits set to. Gn 6:3. Jr 44:22.

Part of his character. Ex 34:6. Nu 14:18. Ps 86:15.

Plead in prayer. Jr 15:15.

Salvation the object of. 2 P 3:15.

Should lead to repentance. Ro 2:4. 2 P 3:9.

Through Christ's intercession. Lk 13:8.

THE WICKED

Abuse. Ec 8:11. Mt 24:48–49.

Despise. Ro 2:4.

Punished for despising. Ne 9:30. Mt 24:48–51. Ro 2:5.

LORD'S SUPPER

See Communion of the Lord's Supper.

LOVE

Covers sin. Pr 10:12.

Fulfills the law. Ro 13:8.

God is. 1 Jn 4:8, 16.

The greatest thing in the world. 1 Co 13.

The highest principle. Mt 22:37–38.

Is of God. 1 Jn 4:7.

Marks the child of God. Jn 13:35. 1 Jn 4:7.

See also Brotherly Love.

LOVE OF CHRIST

The banner over his saints. S S 2:4.

The ground of his saints' love to him. Lk 7:47.

Illustrated. Mt 18:11–13.

MANIFESTED IN HIS

Coming to seek the lost. Lk 19:10.

Dying for us. Jn 15:13. 1 Jn 3:16.

Giving himself for us. Gl 2:20.

Interceding for us. He 7:25; 9:24.

Praying for his enemies. Lk 23:34.

Rebukes and chastisements. Rv 3:19.

Sending the Spirit. Ps 68:18. Jn 16:7.

Washing away our sins. Rv 1:5.

Obedient saints abide in. Jn 15:10.

Passeth knowledge. Ep 3:19.

To his church. S S 4:8–9; 5:1. Jn 15:9. Ep 5:25.

To be imitated. Jn 13:34; 15:12. Ep 5:2. 1 Jn 3:16.

Saints obtain victory through. Ro 8:37.

TO SAINTS IS

Constraining. 2 Co 5:14.

Indissoluble. Ro 8:35.

Unchangeable. Jn 13:1.

Unquenchable. S S 8:7.

To saints, shall be acknowledged even by enemies. Rv 3:9.

To the Father. Ps 91:14. Jn 14:31.

To those who love him. Pr 8:17. Jn 14:21.

LOVE OF GOD

Christ abides in. Jn 15:10.

Christ the special object of. Jn 15:9; 17:26.

DESCRIBED AS

Abiding. Zp 3:17.

Constraining. Ho 11:4.

Everlasting. Jr 31:3.

Great. Ep 2:4.

Sovereign. Dt 7:8; 10:15.

Unalienable. Ro 8:39.

Unfailing. Is 49:15–16.

EXHIBITED IN

Adoption. 1 Jn 3:1.

Chastisements. He 12:6.

Christ's dying for us while sinners. Ro 5:8. 1 Jn 4:10.

Defeating evil counsels. Dt 23:5.

Drawing us to himself. Ho 11:4.

Election. Ml 1:2–3. Ro 9:11–13.

Forgiving sin. Is 38:17.

Freeness of salvation. Ti 3:4–7.

The giving of Christ. Jn 3:16.

Quickening souls. Ep 2:4–5.

Redemption. Is 43:3–4; 63:9.
The sending of Christ. 1 Jn 4:9.
Temporal blessings. Dt 7:13.
Irrespective of merit. Dt 7:7. Jb 7:17.
MANIFESTED TOWARD
The cheerful giver. 2 Co 9:7.
The destitute. Dt 10:18.
His saints. Jn 16:27; 17:23. 2 Th 2:16. 1 Jn 4:16.
Perishing sinners. Jn 3:16. Ti 3:4.
A part of his character. 2 Co 13:11. 1 Jn 4:8.
PERFECTED IN SAINTS
By brotherly love. 1 Jn 4:12.
By obedience. 1 Jn 2:5.
Saints know and believe. 1 Jn 4:16.
Saints should abide in. Jde 1:21.
Shed abroad in the heart by the Holy Ghost. Ro 5:5.
The source of our love to him. 1 Jn 4:19.
To be sought in prayer. 2 Co 13:14.

LOVE TO CHRIST

A characteristic of saints. S S 1:4.
Decrease of, rebuked. Rv 2:4.
An evidence of adoption. Jn 8:42.
Exhibited by God. Mt 17:5. Jn 5:20.
Exhibited by saints. 1 P 1:8.
His love to us a motive to. 2 Co 5:14.
His personal excellence is deserving of. S S 5:9–16.
Increase of, to be prayed for. Php 1:9.
MANIFESTED IN
Ministering to him. Mt 27:55, with 25:40.
Obeying him. Jn 14:15, 21, 23.
Preferring him to all others. Mt 10:37.
Seeking him. S S 3:2.
Taking up the cross for him. Mt 10:38.
Pray for grace to those who have. Ep 6:24.
Promises to. 2 Tm 4:8. Ja 1:12.
SHOULD BE
Ardent. S S 2:5; 8:6.
Even unto death. Ac 21:13. Rv 12:11.
In proportion to our mercies. Lk 7:47.
Sincere. Ep 6:24.
Supreme. Mt 10:37.
Unquenchable. S S 8:7.
With the soul. S S 1:7.
THEY WHO HAVE
Are loved by Christ. Pr 8:17. Jn 14:21.
Are loved by the Father. Jn 14:21, 23; 16:27.
Enjoy communion with God and Christ. Jn 14:23.

Want of, denounced. 1 Co 16:22.
The wicked, destitute of. Ps 35:19, with Jn 15:18, 25.

LOVE TO GOD

Better than all sacrifices. Mk 12:33.
A characteristic of saints. Ps 5:11.
Commanded. Dt 11:1. Jsh 22:5.
Exhibited by Christ. Jn 14:31.
Exhort one another to. Ps 31:23.
The first great commandment. Mt 22:38.
God faithful to those who have. Dt 7:9.
God tries the sincerity of. Dt 13:3.
Hypocrites, without. Lk 11:42. Jn 5:42.
Love of the world a proof of not having. 1 Jn 2:15.
Perfected, gives boldness. 1 Jn 4:17–18.
Perfected in obedience. 1 Jn 2:5.
Persevere in. Jde 1:21.
Pray for. 2 Th 3:5.
PRODUCED BY
Answers to prayer. Ps 116:1.
The Holy Ghost. Gl 5:22. 2 Th 3:5.
The love of God to us. 1 Jn 4:19.
Promises connected with. Dt 11:13–15. Ps 69:36. Is 56:6–7. Ja 1:12.
SHOULD PRODUCE
Hatred of sin. Ps 97:10.
Joy. Ps 5:11.
Love to saints. 1 Jn 5:1.
Obedience to God. Dt 30:20. 1 Jn 5:3.
THEY WHO HAVE
Are delivered by him. Ps 91:14.
Are known of him. 1 Co 8:3.
Are preserved by him. Ps 145:20.
Have all things working for their good. Ro 8:28.
Partake of his mercy. Ex 20:6. Dt 7:9.
They who love not others, without. 1 Jn 4:20.
The uncharitable, without. 1 Jn 3:17.
With all the heart. Dt 6:5, with Mt 22:37.

LOVE TO MAN

An abiding principle. 1 Co 13:8, 13.
An active principle. 1 Th 1:3. He 6:10.
After the example of Christ. Jn 13:34; 15:12. Ep 5:2.
All things should be done with. 1 Co 16:14.
The bond of perfectness. Cl 3:14.
A bond of union. Cl 2:2.
Commanded by Christ. Jn 13:34; 15:12. 1 Jn 3:23.
Commanded by God. 1 Jn 4:21

The end of the commandment. 1 Tm 1:5.

Especially enjoined upon ministers. 1 Tm 4:12. 2 Tm 2:22.

AN EVIDENCE OF

Being in the light. 1 Jn 2:10.

Discipleship with Christ. Jn 13:35.

Spiritual life. 1 Jn 3:14.

Explained. 1 Co 13:4–7.

Faith works by. Gl 5:6.

A fruit of the Spirit. Gl 5:22. Cl 1:8.

The fulfilling of the law. Ro 13:8–10. Gl 5:14. Ja 2:8.

Good and pleasant. Ps 133:1–2.

Greatest sacrifices are nothing without. 1 Co 13:3.

Hypocrites devoid of. 1 Jn 3:10.

Love of God is a motive to. Jn 13:34. 1 Jn 4:11.

Love to self is the measure of. Mk 12:33.

Necessary to true happiness. Pr 15:17.

Of God. 1 Jn 4:7.

Purity of heart leads to. 1 P 1:22.

SAINTS SHOULD

Abound in. Php 1:9. 1 Th 3:12.

Be disinterested in. 1 Co 10:24; 13:5. Php 2:4.

Be fervent in. 1 P 1:22; 4:8.

Be sincere in. Ro 12:9. 2 Co 6:6; 8:8. 1 Jn 3:18.

Continue in. 1 Tm 2:15. He 13:1.

Follow after. 1 Co 14:1.

Provoke each other to. 2 Co 8:7; 9:2. He 10:24.

Put on. Cl 3:14.

The second great commandment. Mt 22:37–39.

Should be connected with brotherly kindness. Ro 12:10. 2 P 1:7.

SHOULD BE EXHIBITED IN

Clothing the naked. Is 58:7. Mt 25:36.

Covering the faults of others. Pr 10:12, with 1 P 4:8.

Forbearing. Ep 4:2.

Forgiving injuries. Ep 4:32. Cl 3:13.

Loving each other. Gl 5:13.

Ministering to the wants of others. Mt 25:35. He 6:10.

Rebuking. Lv 19:17. Mt 18:15.

Relieving strangers. Lv 25:35. Mt 25:35.

Supporting the weak. Gl 6:2. 1 Th 5:14.

Sympathizing. Ro 12:15. 1 Co 12:26.

Visiting the sick, etc. Jb 31:16–22. Ja 1:27.

SHOULD BE EXHIBITED TOWARD

All men. Gl 6:10.

Enemies. Ex 23:4–5. 2 K 6:22. Mt 5:44. Ro 12:14, 20. 1 P 3:9.

Families. Ep 5:25. Ti 2:4.

Fellow countrymen. Ex 32:32. Ro 9:2–3; 10:1.

Ministers. 1 Th 5:13.

Saints. 1 P 2:17. 1 Jn 5:1.

Strangers. Lv 19:34. Dt 10:19.

Supernatural gifts are nothing without. 1 Co 13:1–2.

Taught by God. 1 Th 4:9.

LOVING-KINDNESS OF GOD

Consideration of the dealings of God gives a knowledge of. Ps 107:43.

DESCRIBED AS

Better than life. Ps 63:3.

Everlasting. Is 54:8.

Excellent. Ps 36:7.

Good. Ps 69:16.

Great. Ne 9:17.

Marvelous. Pss 17:7; 31:21.

Merciful. Ps 117:2.

Multitudinous. Is 63:7.

Former manifestations of, to be pleaded in prayer. Pss 25:6; 89:49.

Never utterly taken from saints. Ps 89:33. Is 54:10.

Praise God for. Pss 92:2; 138:2.

PRAY FOR ITS

Continuance. Ps 36:10.

Exhibition. Pss 17:7; 143:8.

Extension. Gn 24:12. 2 S 2:6.

Proclaim to others. Ps 40:10.

SAINTS

Are ever mindful of. Pss 26:3; 48:9.

Are heard according to. Ps 119:149.

Betrothed in. Ho 2:19.

Comforted by. Ps 119:76.

Crowned with. Ps 103:4.

Drawn by. Jr 31:3.

Look for mercy through. Ps 51:1.

Preserved by. Ps 40:11.

Quickened after. Ps 119:88.

Receive mercy through. Is 54:8.

Should expect, in affliction. Ps 42:7–8.

Through Christ. Ep 2:7. Ti 3:4–6.

See also Pity.

LOWLINESS

Accompanies the presence of God. Is 57:15. Mt 5:3.

Brings wisdom. Pr 11:2. Mt 11:25.
Exhorted. Ro 12:16. Php 2:3.
Marks the person God helps. Mt 8:8. Lk 18:9–14.

LOYALTY
Extolled. Ps 31:23.
Must be wholehearted. Mt 6:24. Ja 1:8.
To friends. Ru 1:14. Pr 27:6; 17:17.
To God. Mt 6:24. Lk 9:62. 1 Co 10:21.

LUKEWARMNESS
Indicates spiritual instability. Ho 7:8. Ja 1:6, 8.
Offensive to God. Rv 3:16. 1 K 18:21. Lk 16:13.

LUST
Marks false spiritual leaders. Jde 1:16, 18.
May bring spiritual death. Ja 1:15.
Must be controlled by God. Gl 5:17. Ro 13:14.

LYING
An abomination to God. Pr 12:22.
Antinomians guilty of. 1 Jn 1:6; 2:4.
A characteristic of the apostasy. 2 Th 2:9. 1 Tm 4:2.
The devil excites men to. 1 K 22:22. Ac 5:3.
The devil the father of. Jn 8:44.
The evil of rulers hearkening to. Pr 29:12.
Excludes from heaven. Rv 21:27; 22:15.
False prophets addicted to. Jr 23:14. Ezk 22:28.
False witnesses addicted to. Pr 14:5, 25.

Folly of concealing hatred by. Pr 10:18.
Forbidden. Lv 19:11. Cl 3:9.
Hateful to God. Pr 6:16–19.
A hindrance to prayer. Is 59:2–3.
Hypocrites addicted to. Ho 11:12.
Hypocrites a seed of. Is 57:4.
LEADS TO
　Hatred. Pr 26:28.
　Love of impure conversation. Pr 17:4.
Often accompanied by gross crimes. Ho 4:1–2.
Poverty preferable to. Pr 19:22.
Punishment for. Pss 5:6; 120:3–4. Pr 19:5. Jr 50:36.
SAINTS
　Avoid. Is 63:8. Zp 3:13.
　Hate. Ps 119:163. Pr 13:5.
　Pray to be preserved from. Ps 119:29. Pr 30:8.
　Reject those who practice. Ps 101:7.
　Respect not those who practice. Ps 40:4.
Shall be detected. Pr 12:19.
They who are guilty of, shall be cast into hell. Rv 21:8.
Unbecoming in rulers. Pr 17:7.
Vanity of getting riches by. Pr 21:6.
THE WICKED
　Are addicted to, from their infancy. Ps 58:3.
　Bring forth. Ps 7:14.
　Delight in. Ps 62:4.
　Give heed to. Pr 17:4.
　Love. Ps 52:3.
　Prepare their tongues for. Jr 9:3, 5.
　Seek after. Ps 4:2.

M

MAGIC
Forbidden. Dt 13:1–18; 18:9–14.
Of Sceva and his sons. Ac 19:11–20.
Of Simon of Samaria. Ac 8:9–24.
Of the Egyptian sorcerers. Ex 7:1–12.

MAGISTRATES
Appointed by God. Ro 13:1
Ministers of God. Ro 13:4, 6.
Not a terror to the good, but to the evil. Ro 13:3.
Purpose of their appointment. Ro 13:4. 1 P 2:14.

SHOULD
Be diligent in ruling. Ro 12:8.
Be faithful to the Sovereign. Dn 6:4.
Be impartial. Ex 23:6. Dt 1:17.
Defend the poor, etc. Jb 29:12, 16.
Enforce the laws. Ezr 7:26.
Hate covetousness. Ex 18:21.
Judge for God, not for man. 2 Ch 19:6.
Judge righteously. Dt 1:16; 16:18; 25:1.
Judge wisely. 1 K 3:16–28.
Know the law of God. Ezr 7:25.
Not take bribes. Ex 23:8. Dt 16:19.
Rule in the fear of God. 2 S 23:3. 2 Ch 19:7.
Seek wisdom from God. 1 K 3:9.
Subjection to their authority enjoined. Mt 23:2–3. Ro 13:1. 1 P 2:13–14.
Their office to be respected. Ac 23:5.
To be prayed for. 1 Tm 2:1–2.
To be wisely selected and appointed. Ex 18:21. Ezr 7:25.
Wicked, illustrated. Pr 28:15.

MALICE
Brings its own punishment. Ps 7:15–16.
Christian liberty not to be made a cloak for. 1 P 2:16.
Forbidden. 1 Co 14:20. Cl 3:8. Ep 4:26–27.
God requites. Ps 10:14. Ezk 36:5.
A hindrance to growth in grace. 1 P 2:1–2.
Incompatible with the worship of God. 1 Co 5:7–8.
Pray for those who injure you through. Mt 5:44.
Punishment of. Am 1:11–12. Ob 1:10–15.
Saints avoid. Jb 31:29–30. Ps 35:12–14.
Springs from an evil heart. Mt 15:19–20. Gl 5:19.

THE WICKED
Are filled with. Ro 1:29.
Conceive. Ps 7:14.
Live in. Ti 3:3.
Speak with. 2 Jn 1:10.
Visit saints with. Ps 83:3. Mt 22:6.

MAN
Able to sustain bodily affliction. Pr 18:14.
Allowed to eat flesh after the flood. Gn 9:3.
All the ways of, clean in his own eyes. Pr 16:2.
Approved of by God. Gn 1:31.
Banished from paradise. Gn 3:23–24.
Blessed by God. Gn 1:28; 5:2.
Born in sin. Ps 51:5.
Born to trouble. Jb 5:7.

CALLED
Flesh. Gn 6:12. Jl 2:28.
The potsherd of the earth. Is 45:9.
Vain man. Jb 11:12. Ja 2:20.
A worm. Jb 25:6.
Cannot be just with God. Jb 9:2; 25:4. Ps 143:2. Ro 3:20.
Cannot cleanse himself. Jb 15:14. Jr 2:22.
Cannot direct his ways. Jr 10:23. Pr 20:24.
Cannot profit God. Jb 22:2. Ps 16:2.
Cannot retain his spirit from death. Ec 8:8.

CHRIST
Approved of God as. Ac 2:22.
As such, the cause of the resurrection. 1 Co 15:21–22.
Called the second, as covenant head of the church. 1 Co 15:47.
Head of every. 1 Co 11:3.
Knew what was in. Jn 2:25.
Made in the likeness of. Php 2:7.
A refuge, to sinners. Is 32:2.

Took on him nature of. Jn 1:14. He 2:14, 16.

Was found in fashion as. Php 2:8.

Clothed by God with skins. Gn 3:21.

COMPARED TO

Clay in the potter's hands. Is 64:8. Jr 18:2, 6.

Grass. Is 40:6–8. 1 P 1:24.

A sleep. Ps 90:5.

Vanity. Ps 144:4.

A wild ass's colt. Jb 11:12.

Covered himself with fig leaves. Gn 3:7.

CREATED

After consultation, by the Trinity. Gn 1:26.

By Christ. Jn 1:3. Cl 1:16.

By God. Gn 1:27. Is 45:12.

By the Holy Ghost. Jb 33:4.

From the dust. Gn 2:7. Jb 33:6.

In knowledge (inferred). Cl 3:10.

In the image of God. Gn 1:26. Ja 3:9.

In uprightness. Ec 7:29.

A living soul. Gn 2:7. 1 Co 15:45.

Male and female. Gn 1:27; 5:2.

On the sixth day. Gn 1:31.

A type of Christ. Ro 5:14.

Under obligations to obedience. Gn 2:16–17.

Upon the earth. Dt 4:32. Jb 20:4.

Days of, as the days of a hireling. Jb 7:1.

Days of, compared to a shadow. 1 Ch 29:15.

Disobeyed God by eating part of the forbidden fruit. Gn 3:1–12.

Every herb and tree given to, for food. Gn 1:29.

Fearfully and wonderfully made. Ps 139:14.

Filled with shame after the fall. Gn 3:10.

Gave names to other creatures. Gn 2:19–20.

GOD

Destroys the hopes of. Jb 14:19.

Enables to speak. Pr 16:1.

Instructs. Ps 94:10.

Makes his beauty consume away. Ps 39:11.

Makes the wrath of, to praise him. Ps 76:10.

Orders the goings of. Pr 5:21; 20:24.

Prepares the heart of. Pr 16:1.

Preserves. Jb 7:20. Ps 36:6.

Provides for. Ps 145:15–16.

Turns, to destruction. Ps 90:3.

God's purpose in creation completed by making. Gn 2:5, 7.

Has an appointed time on the earth. Jb 7:1.

Has but few days. Jb 14:1.

Has sought out many inventions. Ec 7:29.

Help of, vain. Ps 60:11.

Ignorant of what is good for him. Ec 6:12.

Ignorant of what is to come after him. Ec 10:14.

Inferior to angels. Ps 8:5, with He 2:7.

Intellect of, matured by age. 1 Co 13:11.

Involved posterity in his ruin. Ro 5:12–19.

Made by God in his successive generations. Jb 10:8–11; 31:15.

Made for God. Pr 16:4, with Rv 4:11.

Made wise by the inspiration of the Almighty. Jb 32:8–9.

More valuable than other creatures. Jb 35:11.

Nature and constitution different from other creatures. 1 Co 15:39.

Not good for, to be alone. Gn 2:18.

No trust to be placed in. Ps 118:8. Is 2:22.

Of every nation, made of one blood. Ac 17:26.

Of the earth earthy. 1 Co 15:47.

Ordinary limit of his life. Ps 90:10.

Originally naked and not ashamed. Gn 2:25.

Placed in the garden of Eden. Gn 2:15.

POSSESSED OF

Affections. 1 Ch 29:3. Cl 3:2.

Body. Mt 6:25.

Conscience. Ro 2:15. 1 Tm 4:2.

Memory. Gn 41:9. 1 Co 15:2.

Soul. Lk 12:20. Ac 14:22. 1 P 4:19.

Spirit. Pr 18:14; 20:17. 1 Co 2:11.

Understanding. Ep 1:18; 4:18.

Will. 1 Co 9:17. 2 P 1:21.

Punished for disobedience. Gn 3:16–19.

Quickened by the breath of God. Gn 2:7; 7:22. Jb 33:4.

Received dominion over other creatures. Gn 1:28. Ps 8:6–8.

Shall be recompensed according to his works. Ps 62:12. Ro 2:6.

Sinks under trouble of mind. Pr 18:14.

Unprofited by all his labor and travail. Ec 2:22; 6:12.

Unworthy of God's favor. Jb 7:17. Ps 8:4.

Walks in a vain show. Ps 39:6.

Whole duty of. Ec 12:13.

Wiser than other creatures. Jb 35:11.

Woman formed to be a help for. Gn 21:2–25.

Would give all his possessions for the preservation of life. Jb 2:4.

MANIFESTATION
Of Christ and his glory. Mt 17. Jn 1:14;
2:11. 1 Jn 3:5. 1 Tm 3:16.
Of everyone's work. 1 Co 3:13.
Of iniquity and evil. Jn 3:21. 2 Tm 3:9.
Of the being and love of God. Ro 1:19. 1 Jn
4:9. Ti 3:4.
Of the Holy Spirit. 1 Co 12:7.
Of the judgments of God. Rv 15:4.
Of the righteousness of God. Ro 3:21.
Of the sons of God. Ro 8:19. 1 Jn 3:10.

MANNA
CALLED
Angel's food. Ps 78:25.
Bread from heaven. Ex 16:4. Jn 6:31.
Bread of heaven. Ps 105:40.
Corn of heaven. Ps 78:24.
God's manna. Ne 9:20.
Spiritual meat. 1 Co 10:3.
Ceased when Israel entered Canaan. Ex
16:35. Jsh 5:12.
DESCRIBED AS
Like coriander seed. Ex 16:31. Nu 11:7.
Like hoar frost. Ex 16:14.
Like in color to bedellium. Nu 11:7.
Like in taste to oil. Nu 11:8.
Like in taste to wafers made with honey.
Ex 16:31.
White. Ex 16:31.
Fell after the evening dew. Nu 11:9.
Fell not on the sabbath. Ex 16:26–27.
Gathered every morning. Ex 16:21.
GIVEN
As a sign of Moses's divine mission. Jn
6:30–31.
As a test of obedience. Ex 16:4.
For forty years. Ne 9:21.
In answer to prayer. Ps 105:40.
Through Moses. Jn 6:31–32.
To exhibit God's glory. Ex 16:7.
To humble and prove Israel. Dt 8:16.
To teach that man does not live by bread
only. Dt 8:3, with Mt 4:4.
When Israel murmured for bread. Ex
16:2–3.
A golden pot of, laid up in the holiest for a
memorial. Ex 16:32–34. He 9:4.
He that gathered much or little had sufficient
and nothing over. Ex 16:18.
ILLUSTRATIVE OF
Blessedness given to saints. Rv 2:17.
Christ. Jn 6:32–35.

THE ISRAELITES
At first covetous of. Ex 16:17.
Counted inferior to food of Egypt. Nu
11:4–6.
Ground, made into cakes and baked in pans.
Nu 11:8.
Loathed. Nu 21:5.
Punished for despising. Nu 11:10–20.
Punished for loathing. Nu 21:6.
Kept longer than a day (except on the sabbath)
became corrupt. Ex 16:19–20.
Melted away by the sun. Ex 16:21.
Miraculously given to Israel for food in the
wilderness. Ex 16:4, 15. Ne 9:15.
An omer of, gathered for each person. Ex
16:16.
Previously unknown. Dt 8:3, 16.
Two portions of, gathered the sixth day on
account of the sabbath. Ex 16:5, 22–26.

MARRIAGE
THE BRIDE
Adorned with jewels for. Is 49:18; 61:10.
Attended by bridesmaids. Ps 15:9.
Called to forget her father's house. Ps
45:10.
Given a handmaid at. Gn 24:59; 29:24,
29.
Gorgeously appareled. Ps 45:13–14.
Received presents before. Gn 24:53.
Stood on the right of bridegroom. Ps 45:9.
THE BRIDEGROOM
Adorned with ornaments. Is 61:10.
Attended by many friends. Jg 14:11. Jn
3:29.
Crowned with garlands. S S 3:11.
Presented with gifts. Ps 45:12.
Rejoiced over the bride. Is 62:5.
Returned with the bride to his house at
night. Mt 25:1–6.
CELEBRATED
For seven days. Jg 14:12.
With feasting. Gn 29:22. Jg 14:10. Mt
22:2–3. Jn 2:1–10.
With great rejoicing. Jr 33:11. Jn 3:29.
Contracted at the gate and before witnesses.
Ru 4:1, 10–11.
Contracted in patriarchal age with near rela-
tions. Gn 20:12; 24:24; 28:2.
Consent of the parties necessary to. Gn
24:57–58. 1 S 18:20; 25:41.
A covenant relationship. Ml 2:4.
DESIGNED FOR
Happiness of man. Gn 2:18.

Increasing the species.   Gn 1:28; 9:1.
Preventing fornication.   1 Co 7:2.
Raising up a godly seed.   Ml 2:15.
Divinely instituted.   Gn 2:24.
Dowry given to the woman's parents before.
Gn 29:18; 34:12.   1 S 18:27–28.   Ho 3:2.
Early introduction of polygamy.   Gn 4:19.
Elder daughters usually given in, before the
younger.   Gn 29:26.
EXPRESSED BY
Giving daughters to sons and sons to daugh-
ters.   Dt 7:3.   Ezr 9:12.
Joining together.   Mt 19:6.
Making affinity.   1 K 3:1.
Taking to wife.   Ex 2:1.
Followed by a benediction.   Gn 24:60.   Ru
4:11–12.
Garments provided for guests at.   Mt 22:12.
High priest not to contract with a widow or a
divorced or profane person.   Lv 21:14.
Honorable for all.   He 13:4.
ILLUSTRATIVE OF
Christ's union with his church.   Ep
5:23–24, 32.
God's union with the Jewish nation.   Is
54:5.   Jr 3:14.   Ho 2:19–20.
Indissoluble during the joint lives of the par-
ties.   Mt 19:6.   Ro 7:2–3.   1 Co 7:39.
Infidelity of those contracted in, punished as if
married.   Dt 22:23–24.   Mt 1:19.
THE JEWS
Betrothed themselves some time before.
Dt 20:7.   Jg 14:5, 7–8.   Mt 1:18.
Careful in contracting for their children.
Gn 24:2–3; 28:1–2.
Considered being debarred from a re-
proach.   Is 4:1.
Contracted when young.   Pr 2:17.   Jl 1:8.
Exempted from going to war immediately
, after.   Dt 20:7.
Forbidden to contract, with idolaters.   Dt
7:3–4.   Jsh 23:12.   Ezr 9:11–12.
Forbidden to contract with their near rela-
tions.   Lv 18:6.
Obliged to contract with a brother's wife
who died without seed.   Dt 25:5.   Mt
22:24.
Often contracted in their own tribe.   Ex
2:1.   Nu 36:6–13.   Lk 1:5, 27.
Often contracted with foreigners.   1 K
11:1.   Ne 13:23.
Often punished by being debarred from.
Jr 7:34; 16:9; 25:10.

Sometimes guilty of polygamy.   1 K 11:1,
3.
Were allowed divorce from, because of
hardness of their hearts.   Dt 24:1, with
Mt 19:7–8.
Lawful in all.   1 Co 7:2, 28.   1 Tm 5:14.
Modes of demanding women in.   Gn 24:3–4;
34:6, 8.   1 S 25:39–40.
Often contracted by parents for children.
Gn 24:49–51; 34:6, 8.
Parents might refuse to give their children in.
Ex 22:17.   Dt 7:3.
Priest not to contract with divorced or im-
proper persons.   Lv 21:7.
Should be only in the Lord.   1 Co 7:39.
Should be with the consent of parents.   Gn
28:8.   Jg 14:2–3.

MARRIAGE, CHRISTIAN
Christians not under Jewish ceremonial laws.
Ac 15:1–29.   Gl 3:1—5:6.   Ro 7:4–6.
PURPOSES OF
Fellowship and well-being.   Gn 2:18.
Glory of God.   1 Co 6:15, 20.
Godly seed.   Ml 2:14–15.   1 Co 7:14.
Prevention of sin.   1 Co 7:2, 9.
RESTRICTIONS OF
In the Lord.   1 Co 6:16–20; 7:39.   2 Co
6:4.
Permanent.   Mt 19:6.   Ro 7:2–3.   1 Co
7:39.

MARRIAGE, INTERRACIAL
BACKGROUND
All nations of one blood.   Ac 17:26.
All races descended from Adam.   Gn 1:27;
2:20; 5.   Ro 5:12–21.
All races descended from Noah.   Gn 7:23;
9:18–19.
David and Jesus descended from interracial
marriage.   Ru 4:22.   Mt 1:1, 5–6.
God's interest in marriage not racial but
spiritual.   Ml 2:14–15.   Mt 19:4–6.
Jews often married outside race.   1 K 11:1.
Punishment of Aaron and Miriam for speaking
against Moses' Ethiopian wife.   Nu
12:1–10.
RESTRICTIONS ON JEWISH MARRIAGE
Daughters of Zelophehad not to marry out-
side own tribe.   Nu 27:1–11.
High priest not to marry a widow.   Lv
21:14.
Jews not to marry heathen.   Ex 34:12–16.

MARTYRDOM

The apostasy guilty of inflicting. Rv 17:6; 18:24.

Death endured for the word of God and testimony of Christ. Rv 6:9; 20:4.

Inflicted at the instigation of the devil. Rv 2:10, 13.

Of saints, shall be avenged. Lk 11:50–51. Rv 18:20–24.

Reward of. Rv 2:10; 6:11.

SAINTS

Forewarned of. Mt 10:21; 24:9. Jn 16:2.

Should be prepared for. Mt 16:24–25. Ac 21:13.

Should not fear. Mt 10:28. Rv 2:10.

Should resist sin unto. He 12:4.

MASSACRE

ATTEMPED UNSUCCESSFULLY AGAINST

Abimelech's rivals. Jg 9:1–6.

Athaliah's rivals. 2 K 11:2.

Innocent and faith-filled individuals. Ac 9:1. Rv 12:11; 20:4.

Jesus. Mt 2:16.

The Jews. Ex 1:16–18.

The work of the devil and his servants. Jn 8:44. Mt 19:18. Ex 20:13 Gn 9:6. 1 P 4:15. Mt 15:19; 26:52.

MASTERS

Authority of, established. Cl 3:22. 1 P 2:18.

Benevolent, blessed. Dt 15:18.

DUTY OF, TOWARD SERVANTS

Not to defraud them. Gn 31:7.

Not to keep back their wages. Lv 19:13. Dt 24:15.

Not to rule over them with rigor. Lv 25:43. Dt 24:14.

To act justly. Jb 31:13, 15. Cl 4:1.

To deal with them in the fear of God. Ep 6:9. Cl 4:1.

To esteem them highly, if saints. Phm 1:16.

To forbear threatening them. Ep 6:9.

To take care of them in sickness. Lk 7:3.

Should receive faithful advice from servants. 2 K 5:13–14.

Should select faithful servants. Gn 24:2. Ps 101:6–7.

SHOULD WITH THEIR HOUSEHOLDS

Fear God. Ac 10:2.

Observe the sabbath. Ex 20:10. Dt 5:12–14.

Put away idols. Gn 35:2.

Serve God. Jsh 24:15.

Worship God. Gn 35:3.

Unjust, denounced. Jr 22:13. Ja 5:4.

MASTERY

Of Christ. He 2:8. 1 P 3:22. Php 3:21. 1 Co 15:28.

Of God. Ps 98:1. 1 Ch 29:12. Dn 4:17. Rv 19:6.

Over one's own spirit. Pr 16:32; 25:28.

Over the body. 1 Co 9:27.

Over the realm of evil. Lk 10:19.

MEAT OFFERINGS

Always seasoned with salt. Lv 2:13.

CONSISTED OF

Barley meal. Nu 5:15.

Fine flour. Lv 2:1.

Fine flour baked in a frying pan. Lv 2:7.

Fine flour baked in a pan. Lv 2:5.

Green ears of corn parched. Lv 2:14.

Unleavened cakes baked in the oven. Lv 2:4.

High priest's deputy had care of. Nu 4:16.

THE JEWS

Condemned for offering to idols. Is 57:6.

Often not accepted in. Am 5:22.

Often prevented from offering, by judgments. Jl 1:9, 13.

Laid up in a chamber of the temple. Ne 10:39; 13:5. Ezk 42:13.

Materials for public, often provided by the princes. Nu 7:13, 19, 25. Ezk 45:17.

No leaven used with. Lv 2:11; 6:17.

Not to be offered on altar of incense. Ex 30:9.

OFFERED

By the high priest every day, half in the morning and half in the evening. Lv 6:20–22.

By the poor for a trespass offering. Lv 5:11.

On the altar of burnt offering. Ex 40:29.

With all burnt sacrifices. Nu 15:3–12.

With the daily sacrifices. Ex 29:40–42.

Of jealousy, without oil or incense. Nu 5:15.

Oil and incense used with. Lv 2:1, 4, 15.

The priest's portion. Lv 2:3; 6:17.

A small part consumed on the altar for a memorial. Lv 2:2, 9, 16; 6:15.

To be eaten by the males of the house of Aaron alone. Lv 6:18.

To be eaten in the holy place. Lv 6:16.

Were most holy. Lv 6:17.

When offered for a priest, entirely consumed by fire. Lv 6:23.

MEDITATION
Brings vision and help. Ps 63:1–8.
Characterizes the godly person. Ps 1:1–2.
A Christian duty. 1 Tm 4:15.
SHOULD BE CENTERED ON
  The good and true. Php 4:8.
  The Lord. Ps 63:6.
  The message of God. Ps 119:67.
  The promises of God. Ps 119:148.
  The works of God. Ps 143:5.

MEEKNESS
A characteristic of wisdom. Ja 3:17.
Blessedness of. Mt 5:5.
CHRIST
  Set an example of. Ps 45:4. Is 53:7. Mt 11:29; 21:5. 2 Co 10:1. 1 P 2:21–23.
  Taught. Mt 5:38–45.
A fruit of the Spirit. Gl 5:22–23.
The gospel to be preached to those who possess. Is 61:1.
MINISTERS SHOULD
  Follow after. 1 Tm 6:11.
  Instruct opposers with. 2 Tm 2:24–25.
  Urge, on their people. Ti 3:1–2.
Necessary to a Christian walk. Ep 4:1–2. 1 Co 6:7.
Precious in the sight of God. 1 P 3:4.
SAINTS SHOULD
  Answer for their hope with. 1 P 3:15.
  Exhibit. Ja 3:13.
  Put on. Cl 3:12–13.
  Receive the word of God with. Ja 1:21.
  Restore the erring with. Gl 6:1.
  Seek. Zp 2:3.
  Show, to all men. Ti 3:2.
THEY WHO ARE GIFTED WITH
  Are beautified with salvation. Ps 149:4.
  Are exalted. Ps 147:6. Mt 23:12.
  Are guided and taught. Ps 25:9.
  Are preserved. Ps 76:9.
  Are richly provided for. Ps 22:26.
  Increase their joy. Is 29:19.
  Shall inherit the earth. Ps 37:11.

MEMORY, MEMORIALS
Blessed, of the just. Pr 10:7.
DIVINE
  God's name and revelation. Ex 3:15. Ps 135:13.
  The Lord's Supper. Lk 22:19.

Passover. Ex 12:14.
THINGS TO REMEMBER
  The apostolic testimony. Jde 1:17.
  The heritage of the past. Dt 32:7.
  The Lord's day. Ex 20:8.
  The Lord's deliverance. Dt 16:3.
  The Lord's leadings. Dt 8:2.
  The Lord's resurrection. 2 Tm 2:8.
  The words of Jesus. Ac 20:35.
Value of. 2 P 1:15–21. Ezr 9:5–15.

MERCY
After the example of God. Lk 6:36.
Beneficial to those who exercise. Pr 11:17.
Blessedness of showing. Pr 14:21. Mt 5:7.
A characteristic of saints. Ps 37:26. Is 57:1.
Denunciations against those devoid of. Ho 4:1, 3. Mt 18:23–35. Ja 2:13.
Enjoined. 2 K 6:21–23. Ho 12:6. Ro 12:20–21. Cl 3:12.
Hypocrites devoid of. Mt 23:23.
SHOULD BE SHOWN
  To animals. Pr 12:10.
  To backsliders. Lk 15:18–20. 2 Co 2:6–8.
  To our brethren. Zc 7:9.
  To the poor. Pr 14:31. Dn 4:27.
  To those that are in distress. Lk 10:37.
  With cheerfulness. Ro 12:8.
To be engraved on the heart. Pr 3:3.
Upholds the throne of kings. Pr 20:28.

MERCY OF GOD
DESCRIBED AS
  Abundant. 1 P 1:3.
  Everlasting. 1 Ch 16:34. Pss 89:28; 106:1; 107:1; 136.
  Filling the earth. Ps 119:64.
  Great. Nu 14:18. Is 54:7.
  High as heaven. Pss 36:5; 103:11.
  Manifold. Ne 9:27. Lm 3:32.
  New every morning. Lm 3:23.
  Over all his works. Ps 145:9.
  Plenteous. Pss 86:5, 15; 103:8.
  Rich. Ep 2:4.
  Sure. Is 55:3. Mi 7:20.
  Tender. Pss 25:6; 103:4. Lk 1:78.
God's delight. Mi 7:18.
A ground of hope. Pss 130:7; 147:11.
A ground of trust. Ps 52:8.
MANIFESTED
  In long-suffering. Lm 3:22. Dn 9:9.
  In salvation. Ti 3:5.
  In the sending of Christ. Lk 1:78.
  To his people. Dt 32:43. 1 K 8:23.

To repentant sinners. Ps 32:5. Pr 28:13.
Is 55:7. Lk 15:18–20.
To returning backsliders. Jr 3:12. Ho
14:4. Jl 2:13.
To the afflicted. Is 49:13; 54:7.
To the fatherless. Ho 14:3.
To them that fear him. Ps 103:17. Lk
1:50.
To whom he will. Ho 2:23, with Ro 9:15,
18.
With everlasting kindness. Is 54:8.
Part of his character. Ex 34:6–7. Ps 62:12.
Ne 9:17. Jnh 4:2, 10–11. 2 Co 1:3.
SHOULD BE
Magnified. 1 Ch 16:34. Pss 115:1;
118:1–4, 29. Jr 33:11.
Pleaded in prayer. Pss 6:4; 25:6; 51:1.
Rejoiced in. Ps 31:7.
Sought for others. Gl 6:16. 1 Tm 1:2. 2
Tm 1:18.
Sought for ourselves. Ps 6:2.
Typified by. Ex 25:17.

MERCY SEAT
Bezaleel given wisdom to make. Ex 31:2–3,
7.
Blood of sacrifices on the day of atonement
sprinkled upon and before. Lv 16:14–15.
Cherubim formed out of, and at each end of it.
Ex 25:18–20. He 9:5.
Covered with a cloud of incense on the day of
atonement. Lv 16:13.
GOD
Appeared over in the cloud. Lv 16:2.
Dwelt over. Ps 80:1.
Spoke from above. Ex 25:22. Nu 7:89.
ILLUSTRATIVE OF
Christ. Ro 3:25, with He 9:3.
The throne of grace. He 4:16.
Made of pure gold. Ex 25:17; 37:6.
Moses commanded to make. Ex 25:17.
Placed upon the ark of testimony. Ex 25:21;
26:34; 40:20.

MESSENGERS OF GOD
Sent for the world's salvation. Jn 3:17. He
1:1–2.
Sent to assure of God's presence. Hg 1:13.
Sent to minister. He 1:14.
Sent to prepare for the Messiah. Ml 3:1. Lk
1:76.
Sent to prepare the way. Gn 24:7.
Sent to reveal God's word. Mt 23:34.

MESSIAH
BRINGING ABOUT
An end to divisions and enmities. Ep
2:1–22.
Everlasting righteousness. Dn 9:24. 2 Co
5:21.
A new covenant. Jr 31:31–34. Mt
26:26–30.
Redemption from sin. 1 P 1:18–20.
PROMISED
At the fall. Gn 3:15.
For Bethlehem. Mi 5:2, 5.
Through Balaam. Nu 22—24:17.
Through David's ancestry. Is 11:1–10.
To Abraham. Gn 12:1–3.
REVEALED
At his birth. Mt 1:16, 23.
Through the apostles. Ac 17:3; 18:28.
To his followers. Jn 1:41; 6:41, 69.

MILK
Canaan abounded with. Ex 3:8, 17. Jsh 5:6.
DIFFERENT KINDS MENTIONED
Of camels Gn 32:15.
Of cows. Dt 32:14. 1 S 6:7.
Of goats. Pr 27:27.
Of sea monsters. Lm 4:3.
Of sheep. Dt 32:14.
Flocks and herds fed for supply of. Pr 27:23,
27. Is 7:21–22. 1 Co 9:7.
ILLUSTRATIVE OF
Blessings of the gospel. Is 55:1. Jl 3:18.
Doctrines of the gospel. S S 5:1.
First principles of God's word. 1 Co 3:2.
He 5:12. 1 P 2:2.
Godly and edifying discourses. S S 4:11.
Temporal blessings. Gn 49:12.
Wealth of the Gentiles. Is 60:16.
Kept by the Jews in bottles. Jg 4:19.
MADE INTO
Butter. Pr 30:33.
Cheese. Jb 10:10.
Used as food by the Jews. Gn 18:8. Jg 5:25.
Young animals not to be boiled in that of the
mother. Ex 23:19.

MILLS
Antiquity of. Ex 11:5.
Female servants usually employed at. Ex
11:5. Mt 24:41.
ILLUSTRATIVE OF
Degradation, etc., when grinding. Is
47:1–2.

Desolation, when ceasing. Jr 25:10. Rv 18:22.

Male captives often employed at. Jg 16:21. Lm 5:13.

STONES USED IN

Hard. Jb 41:24.

Heavy. Mt 18:6.

Large. Rv 18:21.

Not to be taken in pledge. Dt 24:6.

Often thrown down on enemies during sieges. Jg 9:53. 2 S 11:21.

USED FOR GRINDING

Corn. Is 47:2.

Manna in the wilderness. Nu 11:8.

MIND

Blinded. Lk 24:16. 2 Co 3:14.

Discouraged. He 12:3.

Hardened. Is 5:13. Dn 5:20.

Opened. Lk 24:31. Ep 1:18.

Power of. Pr 23:7; 4:23. Ro 8:6. 1 P 1:13.

Protection of. Php 4:7.

Renewed. Ro 12:1–2. Ep 4:23.

MINISTERS

ARE BOUND TO

Build up the church. 2 Co 12:19. Ep 4:12.

Comfort. 2 Co 1:4–6.

Convince gainsayers. Ti 1:9.

Endure hardness. 2 Tm 2:3.

Exhort. Ti 1:9; 2:15.

Feed the church. Jr 3:15. Jn 21:15–17. Ac 20:28. 1 P 5:2.

Pray for their people. Jl 2:17. Cl 1:9.

Preach the gospel to all. Mk 16:15. 1 Co 1:17.

Rebuke. Ti 1:13; 2:15.

Strengthen the faith of their people. Lk 22:32. Ac 14:22.

Teach. 2 Tm 2:2.

Wage a good warfare. 1 Tm 1:18. 2 Tm 4:7.

Warn affectionately. Ac 20:31.

Watch for souls. He 13:17.

Authority of, is for edification. 2 Co 10:8; 13:10.

Called by God. Ex 28:1, with He 5:4.

Commissioned by Christ. Mt 28:19.

Compared to earthen vessels. 2 Co 4:7.

DESCRIBED AS

Ambassadors for Christ. 2 Co 5:20.

Defenders of the faith. Php 1:7.

Ministers of Christ. 1 Co 4:1.

Servants of Christ's people. 2 Co 4:5.

Stewards of the mysteries of God. 1 Co 4:1.

Entrusted with the gospel. 1 Th 2:4.

Excellency of. Ro 10:15.

Have authority from God. 2 Co 10:8; 13:10.

Labors of, vain, without God's blessing. 1 Co 3:7; 15:10.

Necessity for. Mt 9:37–38. Ro 10:14.

Pray for the increase of. Mt 9:38.

Qualified by God. Is 6:5–7. 2 Co 3:5–6.

Sent by the Holy Ghost. Ac 13:2, 4.

Should avoid giving unnecessary offense. 1 Co 10:32–33. 2 Co 6:3.

SHOULD BE

Affectionate to their people. Php 1:7. 1 Th 2:8, 11.

Apt to teach. 1 Tm 3:2. 2 Tm 2:24.

Blameless. 1 Tm 3:2. Ti 1:7.

Devoted. Ac 20:24. Php 1:20–21.

Disinterested. 2 Co 12:14. 1 Th 2:6.

Examples to the flock. Php 3:17. 2 Th 3:9. 1 Tm 4:12. 1 P 5:3.

Gentle. 1 Th 2:7. 2 Tm 2:24.

Holy. Ex 28:36. Lv 21:6. Ti 1:8.

Hospitable. 1 Tm 3:2. Ti 1:8.

Humble. Ac 20:19.

Impartial. 1 Tm 5:21.

Patient. 2 Co 6:4. 2 Tm 2:24.

Prayerful. Ep 3:14. Php 1:4.

Pure. Is 52:11. 1 Tm 3:9.

Self-denying. 1 Co 9:27.

Sober, just, and temperate. Lv 10:9. Ti 1:8.

Strict in ruling their own families. 1 Tm 3:4, 12.

Strong in grace. 2 Tm 2:1.

Studious and meditative. 1 Tm 4:13, 15.

Watchful. 2 Tm 4:5.

Willing. Is 6:8. 1 P 5:2.

Should make full proof of their ministry. 2 Tm 4:5.

SHOULD NOT BE

Contentious. 1 Tm 3:3. Ti 1:7.

Crafty. 2 Co 4:2.

Easily dispirited. 2 Co 4:8–9; 6:10.

Entangled by cares. Lk 9:60. 2 Tm 2:4.

Given to wine. 1 Tm 3:3. Ti 1:7.

Greedy of filthy lucre. Ac 20:33. 1 Tm 3:3, 8. 1 P 5:2.

Lords over God's heritage. 1 P 5:3.

Men pleasers. Gl 1:10. 1 Th 2:4.

SHOULD PREACH

According to the oracles of God. 1 P 4:11.

Christ crucified.   Ac 8:5, 35. 1 Co 2:2.

Everywhere.   Mk 16:20. Ac 8:4.

Fully, and without reserve.   Ac 5:20; 20:20, 27. Ro 15:19.

Not setting forth themselves.   2 Co 4:5.

Not with enticing words of man's wisdom. 1 Co 1:17; 2:1, 4.

Repentance and faith.   Ac 20:21.

With boldness.   Is 58:1. Ezk 2:6. Mt 10:27–28.

With consistency.   2 Co 1:18–19.

With constancy.   Ac 6:4. 2 Tm 4:2.

With faithfulness.   Ezk 3:17–18.

With good will and love.   Php 1:15–17.

With heedfulness.   1 Tm 4:16.

Without charge, if possible.   1 Co 9:18. 1 Th 2:9.

Without deceitfulness.   2 Co 2:17; 4:2. 1 Th 2:3, 5.

With plainness of speech.   2 Co 3:12.

With zeal.   1 Th 2:8.

Should seek the salvation of their flock.   1 Co 10:33.

Specially protected by God.   2 Co 1:10.

THEIR PEOPLE ARE BOUND TO

Attend to their instructions.   Ml 2:7. Mt 23:3.

Follow their holy example.   1 Co 11:1. Php 3:17.

Give them joy.   2 Co 1:14; 2:3.

Help them.   Ro 16:9. Php 4:3.

Hold them in reputation.   Php 2:29. 1 Th 5:13. 1 Tm 5:17.

Imitate their faith.   He 13:7.

Love them.   2 Co 8:7. 1 Th 3:6.

Not to despise them.   Lk 10:16. 1 Tm 4:12.

Obey them.   1 Co 16:16. He 13:17.

Pray for them.   Ro 15:30. 2 Co 1:11. Ep 6:19. He 13:18.

Regard them as God's messengers.   1 Co 4:1. Gl 4:14.

Support them.   2 Ch 31:4. 1 Co 9:7–11. Gl 6:6.

WHEN FAITHFUL

Approve themselves as the ministers of God.   2 Co 6:4.

Are rewarded.   Mt 24:47. 1 Co 3:14; 9:17, 18. 1 P 5:4.

Commend themselves to the consciences of men.   2 Co 4:2.

Glory in their people.   2 Co 7:4.

Rejoice in the faith and holiness of their people.   1 Th 2:19, 20; 3:6–9.

Thank God for his gifts to their people.   1 Co 1:4. Php 1:3. 1 Th 3:9.

WHEN UNFAITHFUL

Deal treacherously with their people.   Jn 10:12.

Delude men.   Jr 6:14. Mt 15:14.

Described.   Is 56:10–12. Ti 1:10–11.

Seek gain.   Mi 3:11. 2 P 2:3.

Shall be punished.   Ezk 33:6–8. Mt 24:48–51.

Woe to those who do not preach the gospel. 1 Co 9:16.

MIRACLES

DESCRIBED AS

Marvelous things.   Ps 78:12.

Marvelous works.   Is 29:14. Ps 105:5.

Signs and wonders.   Jr 32:21. Jn 4:48. 2 Co 12:12.

Evidences of a divine commission.   Ex 4:1–5. Mk 16:20.

FAITH REQUIRED IN

Those for whom they were performed. Mt 9:28; 13:58. Mk 9:22–24. Ac 14:9.

Those who performed.   Mt 17:20; 21:21. Jn 14:12. Ac 3:16; 6:8.

First preaching of the gospel confirmed by. Mk 16:20. He 2:4.

A gift of the Holy Ghost.   1 Co 12:10.

Guilt of rejecting the evidence afforded by. Mt 11:20–24. Jn 15:24.

Instrumental to the early propagation of the gospel.   Ac 8:6. Ro 15:18–19.

Insufficient of themselves to produce conversion   Lk 16:31.

Jesus followed on account of.   Mt 4:23–25; 14:35–36. Jn 6:2, 26; 12:18.

Jesus proved to be the Messiah by.   Mt 11:4–6. Lk 7:20–22. Jn 5:36. Ac 2:22.

MANIFEST

The glory of Christ.   Jn 2:11; 11:4.

The glory of God.   Jn 11:4.

The works of God.   Jn 9:3.

Messiah expected to perform.   Mt 11:2–3. Jn 7:31.

Power of God necessary to.   Jn 3:2.

Should be remembered.   1 Ch 16:12. Ps 105:5.

Should be told to future generations.   Ex 10:2. Jg 6:13.

Should produce faith.   Jn 2:23; 20:30–31.

Should produce obedience.   Dt 11:1–3; 29:2–3, 9.

They who wrought, disclaimed all power of their own. Ac 3:12.

WERE PERFORMED

By the power of Christ. Mt 10:1.
By the power of God. Ex 8:19. Ac 14:3; 15:12; 19:11.
By the power of the Holy Ghost. Mt 12:28. Ro 15:19.
In the name of Christ. Mk 16:17. Ac 3:16; 4:30.

THE WICKED

Desire to see. Mt 27:42. Lk 11:29; 23:8.
Do not consider. Mk 6:52.
Do not understand. Ps 106:7.
Forget. Ne 9:17. Ps 78:1, 11.
Often acknowledge. Jn 11:47. Ac 4:16.
Proof against. Nu 14:22. Jn 12:37.

MIRACLES OF CHRIST

Blind restored to sight. Mt 9:27–30. Mk 8:22–25. Jn 9:1–7.
Centurion's servant healed. Mt 8:5–13.
Cures performed before the messengers of John. Lk 7:21–22.
Dead raised to life. Mt 9:18–19, 23–25. Lk 7:12–15. Jn 11:11–44.
Deaf and dumb cured. Mk 7:32–35.
Devils cast out. Mt 8:28–32; 9:32–33; 15:22–28; 17:14–18. Mk 1:23–27.
Dropsy cured. Lk 14:2–4.
Fig tree blighted. Mt 21:19.
His appearance to his disciples, the doors being shut. Jn 20:19.
His ascension. Ac 1:9.
His resurrection. Lk 24:6, with Jn 10:18.
His transfiguration. Mt 17:1–8.
His walking on the sea. Mt 14:25–27.
Impotent man healed. Jn 5:5–9.
Issue of blood stopped. Mt 9:20–22.
Lepers cleansed. Mt 8:3. Lk 17:14.
Malchus healed. Lk 22:50–51.
Many diseases healed. Mt 4:23–24; 14:14; 15:30. Mk 1:34. Lk 6:17–19.
The multitude fed. Mt 14:15–21; 15:32–38.
Nets full of fish. Lk 5:4–6. Jn 21:6.
Nobleman's son healed. Jn 4:46–53.
Paralytic healed. Mk 2:3–12.
Peter's wife's mother healed. Mt 8:14–15.
Peter walking on the sea. Mt 14:29.
Sudden arrival of the ship. Jn 6:21.
Tempest stilled. Mt 8:23–26; 14:32.
Tribute money from fish. Mt 17:27.
Water turned into wine. Jn 2:6–10.

Withered hand restored. Mt 12:10–13.
Woman healed of infirmity. Lk 13:11–13.

MIRACLES THROUGH EVIL AGENTS

Deceive the ungodly. 2 Th 2:10–12. Rv 13:14; 19:20.
A mark of the apostasy. 2 Th 2:3, 9. Rv 13:13.
Not to be regarded. Dt 13:3.
Performed through the power of the devil. 2 Th 2:9. Rv 16:14.

WROUGHT

By false christs. Mt 24:24.
By false prophets. Mt 24:24. Rv 19:20.
In support of false religions. Dt 13:1–2.

MIRACLES WROUGHT THROUGH SERVANTS OF GOD

THE APOSTLES

Wonders and signs done. Ac 2:43; 5:12.

ELIJAH

Child restored to life. 1 K 17:22–23.
Drought caused. 1 K 17:1. Ja 5:17.
Meal and oil multiplied. 1 K 17:14–16.
Men destroyed by fire. 2 K 1:10–12.
Rain brought. 1 K 18:41–45. Ja 5:18.
Sacrifice consumed by fire. 1 K 18:36, 38.
Taken to heaven. 2 K 2:11.
Waters of Jordan divided. 2 K 2:8.

ELISHA

Children torn by bears. 2 K 2:24.
Child restored to life. 2 K 4:32–35.
Gehazi struck with leprosy. 2 K 5:27.
Iron caused to float. 2 K 6:6.
Man restored to life. 2 K 13:21.
Naaman healed. 2 K 5:10, 14.
Oil multiplied. 2 K 4:1–7.
Syrians restored to sight. 2 K 6:20.
Syrians smitten with blindness. 2 K 6:18.
Waters healed. 2 K 2:21–22.
Waters of Jordan divided. 2 K 2:14.

ISAIAH

Hezekiah healed. 2 K 20:7.
Shadow put back on the dial. 2 K 20:11.

JOSHUA

Jericho taken. Jsh 6:6–20.
Jordan restored to its course. Jsh 4:18.
Midianites destroyed. Jg 7:16–22.
Sun and moon stayed. Jsh 10:12–14.
Waters of Jordan divided. Jsh 3:10–17.

MOSES AND AARON

Amalek vanquished. Ex 17:11–13.
Boils and blains brought. Ex 9:10–11.

Darkness brought. Ex 10:22.
Egyptians overwhelmed. Ex 14:26–28.
First-born destroyed. Ex 12:29.
Flies brought. Ex 8:21–24.
Flies removed. Ex 8:31.
Frogs brought. Ex 8:6.
Frogs removed. Ex 8:13.
Hail brought. Ex 9:23.
Hail removed. Ex 9:33.
Hand healed. Ex 4:7.
Hand made leprous. Ex 4:6.
Healing by bronze serpent. Nu 21:8–9.
Korah destroyed. Nu 16:28–32.
Lice brought. Ex 8:17.
Locusts brought. Ex 10:13.
Locusts removed. Ex 10:19.
Murrain of beasts. Ex 9:3–6.
Red Sea divided. Ex 14:21–22.
River turned into blood. Ex 7:20.
Rod changed into a serpent. Ex 4:3; 7:10.
Rod restored. Ex 4:4.
Water brought from rock in Horeb. Ex 17:6.
Water brought from rock in Kadesh. Nu 20:11.
Water sweetened. Ex 15:25.
Water turned into blood. Ex 4:9, 30.

PAUL
Elymas smitten with blindness. Ac 13:11.
Eutychus restored to life. Ac 20:10–12.
Father of Publius healed. Ac 28:8.
Lame man cured. Ac 14:10.
Special miracles. Ac 19:11–12.
Unclean spirit cast out. Ac 16:18.
Viper's bite made harmless. Ac 28:5.

PAUL AND BARNABAS
Empowered to work signs and wonders. Ac 14:3.

PETER
Death of Ananias. Ac 5:5.
Death of Sapphira. Ac 5:10.
Dorcas restored to life. Ac 9:40.
Eneas made whole. Ac 9:34.
Lame man cured. Ac 3:7.
The sick healed. Ac 5:15–16.

PHILIP
Unclean spirits cast out, palsied and lame healed. Ac 8:6–7.
Miracles and signs. Ac 8:13.

THE PROPHET OF JUDAH
Altar rent. 1 K 13:5.
Jeroboam's hand withered. 1 K 13:4.
Withered hand restored. 1 K 13:6.

SAMSON
Dagon's house pulled down. Jg 16:30.
The gates of Gaza carried away. Jg 16:3.
A lion killed. Jg 14:6.
Philistines killed. Jg 14:19; 15:15.

SAMUEL
Thunder and rain in harvest. 1 S 12:18.

THE SEVENTY DISCIPLES
Sent to heal sick. Lk 10:9.
Empowered to subject devils. Lk 10–17.

STEPHEN
Wonders and miracles done. Ac 6:8.

MIRACULOUS GIFTS OF THE HOLY SPIRIT

Christ endowed with. Mt 12:28.

COMMUNICATED
By the laying on of the apostles' hands. Ac 8:17–18; 19:6.
For the confirmation of the gospel. Mk 16:20. Ac 14:3. Ro 15:19. He 2:4.
For the edification of the church. 1 Co 12:7; 14:12–13.
Upon the preaching of the gospel. Ac 10:44–46.
Counterfeited by antichrist. Mt 24:24. 2 Th 2:9. Rv 13:13–14.
Dispensed, according to his sovereign will. 1 Co 12:11.
Enumerated. 1 Co 12:8–10, 28; 14:1.
Foretold. Is 35:4–6. Jl 2:28–29.
Might be possessed without saving grace. Mt 7:22–23. 1 Co 13:1–2.
Of different kinds. 1 Co 12:4–6.
Poured out on the day of Pentecost. Ac 2:1–4.
Temporary nature of. 1 Co 13:8.
To be sought after. 1 Co 12:31; 14:1.

MISCEGENATION

See Marriage, Interracial.

MISSIONARIES

ALL CHRISTIANS SHOULD BE AS
In admonishing others. 1 Th 5:14. 2 Th 3:15.
In aiding ministers in their labors. Ro 16:3, 9. 2 Co 11:9. Php 4:14–16. 3 Jn 1:6.
In declaring what God has done for them. Pss 66:16; 116:16–19.
In dedicating themselves to the service of God. Jsh 24:15. Ps 27:4.
In devoting all property to God. 1 Ch

29:2–3, 14, 16. Ec 11:1. Mt 6:19–20.
Mk 12:44. Lk 12:33; 18:22, 28. Ac 2:45;
4:32–34.
In encouraging the weak. Is 35:3–4. Ro
14:1; 15:1. 1 Th 5:14.
In the family. Dt 6:7. Ps 78:5–8. Is
38:19. 1 Co 7:16.
In first giving their own selves to the Lord.
2 Co 8:5.
In following Christ. Lk 14:27; 18:22.
In forsaking all for Christ. Lk 5:11.
In giving a reason for their faith. Ex
12:26–27.
In hating life for Christ. Lk 14:26.
In holy boldness. Ps 119:46.
In holy conduct. 1 P 2:12.
In holy conversation. Ps 37:30, with Pr
10:31. Pr 15:7. Ep 4:29. Cl 4:6.
In holy example. Mt 5:16. Php 2:15. 1
Th 1:7.
In interceding for others. Cl 4:3. He
13:18. Ja 5:16.
In inviting others to embrace the gospel.
Ps 34:8. Is 2:3. Jn 1:46; 4:29.
In joyfully suffering for Christ. He 10:34.
In old age. Dt 32:7. Ps 71:18.
In openly confessing Christ. Mt 10:32.
In preferring Christ above all relations. Lk
14:26. 1 Co 2:2.
In reproving others. Lv 19:17. Ep 5:11.
In seeking the edification of others. Ro
14:19; 15:2. 1 Th 5:11.
In showing forth God's praises. Is 43:21.
In talking of God and his works. Pss
71:24; 77:12; 119:27; 145:11–12.
In teaching and exhorting. Pss 34:11;
51:13. Cl 3:16. He 3:13; 10:25.
In their intercourse with the world. Mt
5:16. Php 2:15–16. 1 P 2:12.
In visiting and relieving the poor and the
sick. Lv 25:35. Ps 112:9, with 2 Co
9:9. Mt 25:36. Ac 20:35. Ja 1:27.
In youth. Pss 71:17; 148:12–13.
With a superabundant liberality. Ex
36:5–7. 2 Co 8:3.
With a willing heart. Ex 35:29. 1 Ch
29:9, 14.
Blessedness of. Dn 12:3.
Encouragement to. Pr 11:25, 30. 1 Co 1:27.
Ja 5:19–20.
Faithful stewards. 1 P 4:10–11.
Follow the example of Christ. Ac 10:38.
However weak. 1 Co 1:27.
Illustrated. Mt 25:14. Lk 19:13, etc.
An imperative duty. Jn 5:23. Lk 19:40.

Principle of. 2 Co 5:14–15.
Their calling as saints. Ex 19:6. 1 P 2:9.
Women and children as well as men. Ps 8:2.
Pr 31:26. Mt 21:15–16. Php 4:3. 1 Tm
5:10. Ti 2:3–5. 1 P 3:1.
Zeal of idolaters should provoke. Jr 7:18.

MISSIONARY WORK BY MINISTERS
According to the purpose of God. Lk
24:46–47. Gl 1:15–16. Cl 1:25–27.
Aid those engaged in. Ro 16:1–2. 2 Co 11:9.
3 Jn 1:5–8.
Be ready to engage in. Is 6:8.
Christ engaged in. Mt 4:17, 23; 11:1. Mk
1:38, 39. Lk 8:1.
Christ sent his disciples to labor in. Mk 3:14;
6:7. Lk 10:1–11.
Commanded. Mt 28:19. Mk 16:15.
Directed by the Holy Ghost. Ac 13:2.
Excellency of. Is 52:7, with Ro 10:15.
God qualifies for. Ex 3:11, 18; 4:11–12, 15.
Is 6:5–9.
God strengthens for. Jr 1:7–9.
Guilt and danger of shrinking from. Jnh
1:3–4.
Harmony should subsist among those engaged
in. Gl 2:9.
Holy Ghost calls to. Ac 13:2.
No limits to the sphere of. Is 11:9. Mk
16:15. Rv 14:6.
Obligations to engage in. Ac 4:19–20. Ro
1:13–15. 1 Co 9:16.
Opportunities for, not to be neglected. 1 Co
16:9.
Required. Lk 10:2. Ro 10:14–15.
Requires wisdom and meekness. Mt 10:16.
SUCCESS OF
A cause of joy. Ac 15:3.
A cause of praise. Ac 11:18; 21:19–20.
To be prayed for. Ep 6:18–19. Cl 4:3.
Warranted by predictions concerning the hea-
then, etc. Is 42:10–12; 66:19.
Worldly concerns should not delay. Lk
9:59–62.

MOMENT
Afflictions last but a. 2 Co 4:17.
Divine anger endures but a. Ps 30:5.
We are kept every. Is 27:3.
We shall be changed in a. 1 Co 15:52.

MONEY
Brass introduced as, by the Romans. Mt
10:9.
Changing of, a trade. Mt 21:12. Jn 2:15.

Custom of presenting a piece of.   Jb 42:11.
Gold and silver used as.   Gn 13:2. Nu 22:18.
Jews forbidden to take usury for.   Lv 25:37.
Love of, the root of all evil.   1 Tm 6:10.
Of the Jews regulated by the standard of the
sanctuary.   Lv 5:15. Nu 3:47.
Of the Romans, stamped with the image of
Caesar.   Mt 22:20–21.
PIECES OF, MENTIONED
Farthing.   Mt 5:26. Lk 12:6.
Fourth of a shekel.   1 S 9:8.
Gerah, the twentieth of a shekel.   Nu 3:47.
Half shekel or bekah.   Ex 30:15.
Mite.   Mk 12:42. Lk 21:2.
Penny.   Mt 20:2. Mk 6:37.
Pound.   Lk 19:13.
Shekel of silver.   Jg 17:10. 2 K 15:20.
Talent of gold.   1 K 9:14. 2 K 23:33.
Talent of silver.   1 K 16:24. 2 K 5:22–23.
Third of a shekel.   Ne 10:32.
Power and usefulness of.   Ec 7:12; 10:19.
Usually taken by weight.   Gn 23:16. Jr
32:10.
Was current with the merchants.   Gn 23:16.
WAS GIVEN
As alms.   1 S 2:36. Ac 3:3, 6.
As offerings.   2 K 12:7–9. Ne 10:32.
As wages.   Ezr 3:7. Mt 20:2. Ja 5:4.
For lands.   Gn 23:9. Ac 4:37.
For merchandise.   Gn 43:12. Dt 2:6.
For slaves.   Gn 37:28. Ex 21:21.
For tribute.   2 K 23:33. Mt 22:19.

MONOTHEISM
Christ and his Father are one.   Jn 10:30.
The Holy Spirit is sent by Father and Son.   Jn
14:16; 15:26.
The Holy Spirit is the Spirit of God and of
Christ.   Ro 8:9, 14. 1 Co 3:16.
There is only one God.   Dt 4:39; 6:4. 1 Co
8:4, 6. Ep 4:5–6.

MONTHS
Commenced with first appearance of new
moon.   Nu 10:10, with Ps 81:3.
Idolaters prognosticated by.   Is 47:13.
The Jews computed time by.   Jg 11:37. 1 S
6:1. 1 K 4:7.
NAMES OF THE TWELVE
First, Nisan or Abib.   Ex 13:4. Ne 2:1.
Second, Zif.   1 K 6:1, 37.
Third, Sivan.   Es 8:9.
Fourth, Thammuz.   Zc 8:19.
Fifth, Ab.   Zc 7:3.
Sixth, Ehul.   Ne 6:15.

Seventh, Ethanim.   1 K 8:2.
Eighth, Bul.   1 K 6:38.
Ninth, Chisleu.   Zc 7:1.
Tenth, Tebeth.   Es 2:16.
Eleventh, Sebat.   Zc 1:7.
Twelfth, Adar.   Ezr 6:15. Es 3:7.
Observance of, condemned.   Gl 4:10.
Originally had no names.   Gn 7:11; 8:4.
Patriarchs computed time by.   Gn 29:14.
Sun and moon designed to mark out.   Gn
1:14.
Year composed of twelve.   1 Ch 27:2–15. Es
2:12. Rv 22:2.

THE MOON
APPOINTED
By an ordinance forever.   Pss 72:5, 7;
89:37. Jr 31:36.
For the benefit of all.   Dt 4:19.
For a light in the firmament.   Gn 1:15.
For signs and seasons.   Gn 1:14. Ps
104:19.
To divide day from night.   Gn 1:14.
To light the earth by night.   Jr 31:35.
To rule the night.   Gn 1:16. Ps 136:9.
Called the lesser light.   Gn 1:16.
Created by God.   Gn 1:14. Ps 8:3.
DESCRIBED AS
Bright.   Jb 31:26.
Fair.   S S 6:10.
First appearance of, a time of festivity.   1 S
20:5–6. Ps 81:3.
Has a glory of its own.   1 Co 15:41.
ILLUSTRATIVE OF
Changeableness of the world.   Rv 12:1.
Deep calamities (when withdrawing her
light).   Is 13:10. Jl 2:10; 3:15. Mt
24:29.
Fairness of the church.   S S 6:10.
Glory of Christ in the church.   Is 60:20.
Judgments (when becoming as blood).   Rv
6:12.
Influences vegetation.   Dt 33:14.
Lunacy attributed to the influence of.   Ps
121:6, with Mt 4:24.
Made to glorify God.   Ps 148:3.
MIRACLES CONNECTED WITH
Signs in, before the destruction of Jerusa-
lem.   Lk 21:25.
Standing still in Ajalon.   Jsh 10:12–13.
Worshiped as the queen of heaven.   Jr 7:18;
41:17–19, 25.
WORSHIPING OF
Condemned as atheism.   Jb 31:26, 28.
Forbidden to the Jews.   Dt 4:19.

Jews often guilty of. 2 K 23:5. Jr 8:2.
Jews punished for. Jr 8:1–3.
To be punished with death. Dt 17:3–6.

MORALITY
Characterizes the kingdom of God, and the new heavens and new earth. Ro 14:17. 2 P 3:13.
Enlightens the darkness. Is 58:10.
Exalts a nation. Pr 14:34. Is 26:2.
The heart of religion. Mi 6:6–8.
Indispensable for Christians. Mt 5:47. 1 Jn 2:29.
Prescribed by God. Pr 3:1, 2. Ti 2:7. He 13:20–21.
Religious ceremony useless without. Am 5:21, 24.

MORNING
Began with first dawn. Jsh 6:15. Ps 119:147.
Continued until noon. 1 K 18:26. Ne 8:3.
First dawning of, called the eyelids of. Jb 3:9; 41:18.
First part of the natural day. Mk 16:2.
ILLUSTRATIVE OF
   Glory of Christ (star of). Rv 22:16.
   Glory of the church (when breaking forth). S S 6:10. Is 58:8.
   Heavy calamities (spread upon the mountains). Jl 2:2.
   Rapid movements (wings of). Ps 139:9.
   Resurrection day. Ps 49:14.
   Reward of saints (star of). Rv 2:28.
   Short-lived profession of hypocrites (clouds in). Ho 6:4.
THE JEWS
   Ate but little in. Ec 10:16.
   Began their journeys in. Gn 22:3.
   Contracted covenants in. Gn 26:31.
   Devoted a part of, to prayer and praise. Pss 5:3; 59:16; 88:13.
   Gathered the manna in. Ex 16:21.
   Generally rose early in. Gn 28:18. Jg 6:28.
   Held courts of justice in. Jr 21:12. Mt 27:1.
   Offered a part of the daily sacrifice in. Ex 29:38–39. Nu 28:4–7.
   Transacted business in. Ec 11:6. Mt 20:1.
   Went to the temple in. Lk 21:38. Jn 8:2.
Ordained by God. Jb 38:12.
Outgoings of, made to rejoice. Ps 65:8.

A red sky in, a sign of bad weather. Mt 16:3.
Second part of the day at the creation. Gn 1:5, 8, 13, 19, 23, 31.
Ushered in by the morning star. Jb 38:7.
Was frequently cloudless. 2 S 23:4.

MOTHER
Blessings of. Ps 113:9. Is 40:11.
Comfort of. Is 66:12–13.
Duties of. Ti 2:4. Pr 31:26–27, 30.
Gift of God. Ps 113:9.
Praised by her family. Pr 31:28.
To be honored and cared for. Ep 6:2. Pr 23:22. Gn 32:11. Jn 19:27.
Tribute to. Pr 31:1–31.

MOUNTAINS
ABOUNDED WITH
   Deer. 1 Ch 12:8. S S 2:8.
   Forests. 2 K 19:23. 2 Ch 2:2, 8–10.
   Game. 1 S 26:20.
   Herbs. Pr 27:25.
   Minerals. Dt 8:9.
   Precious things. Dt 33:15.
   Spices. S S 4:6; 8:14.
   Stone for building. 1 K 5:14, 17. Dn 2:45.
   Vineyards. 2 Ch 26:10. Jr 31:5.
   Wild beasts. S S 4:8. Hk 2:17.
AFFORDED
   Pasturage. Ex 3:1. 1 S 25:7. 1 K 22:17. Ps 147:8. Am 4:1.
   Refuge in time of danger. Gn 14:10. Jg 6:2. Mt. 24:16. He 11:38.
Beacons or ensigns often raised upon. Is 13:2; 30:17.
CALLED
   Ancient mountains. Dt 33:15.
   Everlasting hills. Gn 49:26.
   Everlasting mountains. Hk 3:6.
   God's mountains. Is 49:11.
   Perpetual hills. Hk 3:6.
   Pillars of heaven. Jb 26:11.
Canaan abounded in. Dt 11:11.
Collect the vapors which ascend from the earth. Ps 104:6, 8.
Defenses. Ps 125:2.
Elevated parts of the earth. Gn 7:19–20.
GOD
   Causes to melt. Jg 5:5. Ps 97:5. Is 64:1, 3.
   Causes to skip. Ps 114:4, 6.
   Causes to smoke. Pss 104:32; 144:5.

Causes to tremble. Na 1:5. Hk 3:10.
Formed. Am 4:13.
Gives strength to. Ps 95:4.
Makes waste. Is 42:15.
Overturns. Jb 9:5; 28:9.
Parches with drought. Hg 1:11.
Removes. Jb 9:5.
Scatters. Hk 3:6.
Set fast. Ps 65:6.
Sets the foundations of, on fire. Dt 32:22.
Waters, from his chambers. Ps 104:13.
Weighs, in a balance. Is 40:12.

ILLUSTRATIVE OF
Abundance (when dripping wine). Am 9:13.
The church of God. Is 2:2. Dn 2:35, 44–45.
Desolation (when made waste). Is 42:15. Ml 1:3.
Destructive enemies (when burning). Jr 51:25. Rv 8:8.
Difficulties. Is 40:4. Zc 4:7. Mt 17:20.
Exceeding joy (when breaking forth into song). Is 44:23; 55:12.
God's righteousness. Ps 36:6.
Heavy judgments (threshing of). Is 41:15.
Persons in authority. Ps 72:3. Is 44:23.
Proud and haughty persons. Is 2:14.
Made to glorify God. Ps 148:9.
Many very high. Ps 104:18. Is 2:14.

MENTIONED IN SCRIPTURE
Abarim. Nu 33:47–48.
Amalek. Jg 12:15.
Ararat. Gn 8:4.
Bashan. Ps 68:15.
Bethel. 1 S 13:2.
Carmel. Jsh 15:55; 19:26. 2 K 19:23.
Ebal. Dt 11:29; 27:13.
Ephraim. Jsh 17:15. Jg 2:9.
Gerizim. Dt 11:29. Jg 9:7.
Gilboa. 1 S 31:1. 2 S 1:6, 21.
Gilead. Gn 31:21, 25. S S 4:1.
Hachilah. 1 S 23:19.
Hermon. Jsh 13:11.
Hor. Nu 20:22; 34:7–8.
Horeb. Ex 3:1.
Lebanon. Dt 3:25.
Mizar. Ps 42:6.
Moreh. Jg 7:1.
Moriah. Gn 22:2. 2 Ch 3:1.
Nebo (part of Abarim). Nu 32:3. Dt 34:1.
Olives, or mount of corruption. 1 K 11:7, with 2 K 23:13. Lk 21:37.

Pisgah (part of Abarim). Nu 21:20. Dt 34:1.
Seir. Gn 14:6; 36:8.
Sinai. Ex 19:2, 18, 20, 23; 31:18.
Sion. 2 S 5:7.
Tabor. Jg 4:6, 12, 14.
Often inhabited. Gn 36:8. Jsh 11:21.
Often selected as places for idolatrous worship. Dt 12:2. 2 Ch 21:11.
Proclamations often made from. Is 40:9.
Sometimes selected as places for divine worship. Gn 22:2, 5. Ex 3:12. Is 2:2.
Sources of springs and rivers. Dt 8:7. Ps 104:8–10.
Volcanic fires of, alluded to. Is 64:1–2. Jr 51:25. Na 1:5–6.

MOUTH
See Lips.

MURDER
A characteristic of the devil. Jn 8:44.
Comes from the heart. Mt 15:19.
Connected with idolatry. Ezk 22:3–4. 2 K 3:27.
Cries for vengeance. Gn 4:10.

DEFILES THE
Hands. Is 59:3.
Land. Nu 35:33. Ps 106:38.
Person and garments. Lm 4:13–14.

DESCRIBED AS KILLING
By the blow of a stone. Nu 35:17.
By a hand weapon of wood. Nu 35:18.
By an instrument of iron. Nu 35:16.
By lying in wait. Nu 35:20. Dt 19:11.
From hatred. Nu 35:20–21. Dt 19:11.
With premeditation. Ex 21:14.
Early introduction of. Gn 4:8.
Excludes from heaven. Gl 5:21. Rv 22:15.
Explained by Christ. Mt 5:21–22.
Forbidden. Gn 9:6. Ex 20:13. Dt 5:17, with Ro 13:9.
Forbidden by Mosaic law. Ex 20:13. Dt 5:17.

GOD
Abominates. Pr 6:16–17.
Curses those guilty of. Gn 4:11.
Rejects the prayers of those guilty of. Is 1:15; 59:2–3.
Requires blood for. Gn 9:5. Nu 35:33. 1 K 2:32.
Will avenge. Dt 32:43. 1 K 21:19. Ps 9:12. Ho 1:4.
Hatred is. 1 Jn 3:15.

Imputed to the nearest city if murderer unknown. Dt 21:1–3.

The Jews often guilty of. Is 1:21.

Killing a thief in the day, counted as. Ex 22:3.

The law made to restrain. 1 Tm 1:9.

Mode of clearing those suspected of. Dt 21:3–9. (*See* Mt 27:24.)

Not concealed from God. Is 26:21. Jr 2:34.

Of saints, specially avenged. Dt 32:43. Mt 23:35. Rv 18:20, 24.

Often committed by night. Ne 6:10. Jb 24:14.

PERSONS GUILTY OF

Fearful and cowardly. Gn 4:14.

Flee from God's presence. Gn 4:16.

Had no protection from altars. Ex 21:14.

Not protected in refuge cities. Dt 19:11–12.

Not to be pitied or spared. Dt 19:13.

Wanderers and vagabonds. Gn 4:14.

PUNISHMENT FOR

Curse of God. Gn 4:11.

Death. Gn 9:5–6. Ex 21:12. Nu 35:16, 30.

Inflicted by the nearest of kin. Nu 35:19, 21.

Not to be commuted. Nu 35:32.

Punishment of, not commuted under the law. Nu 35:31.

Represented as a sin crying unto heaven. Gn 4:10, with He 12:24. Rv 6:10.

SAINTS

Deprecate the guilt of. Ps 51:14.

Should warn others against. Gn 37:22. Jr 26:15.

Specially warned against. 1 P 4:15.

To be proved by at least two witnesses. Nu 35:30. Dt 19:11, 15.

Why forbidden by God. Gn 9:6.

THE WICKED

Devise. Gn 27:41; 37:18.

Encourage others to commit. 1 K 21:8–10. Pr 1:11.

Filled with. Ro 1:29.

Have hands full of. Is 1:15.

Intent on. Jr 22:17.

Lie in wait to commit. Ps 10:8–10.

Perpetrate. Jb 24:14. Ezk 22:3.

Swift to commit. Pr 1:16. Ro 3:15.

A work of the flesh. Gl 5:21.

MURMURING

AGAINST

Christ. Lk 5:30; 15:2; 19:7. Jn 6:41–43, 52.

Disciples of Christ. Mk 7:2. Lk 5:30; 6:2.

God. Pr 19:3.

Ministers of God. Ex 17:3. Nu 16:41.

The service of God. Ml 3:14.

The sovereignty of God. Ro 9:19–20.

A characteristic of the wicked. Jde 1:10.

Forbidden. 1 Co 10:10. Php 2:14.

Guilt of encouraging others in. Nu 13:31–33, with 14:36–37.

Illustrated. Mt 20:11. Lk 15:29–30.

Provokes God. Nu 14:2, 11. Dt 9:8, 22.

Punishment of. Nu 11:1; 14:27–29; 16:45–46. Ps 106:25–26.

Saints cease from. Is 29:23–24.

Tempts God. Ex 17:2.

Unreasonableness of. Lm 3:39.

MUSIC

Appointed to be used in the temple. 1 Ch 16:4–6; 23:5–6; 25:1. 2 Ch 29:25.

Considered efficacious in mental disorders. 1 S 16:14–17, 23.

Custom of sending away friends with. Gn 31:27.

Designed to promote joy. Ec 2:8, 10.

DIVIDED INTO

Instrumental. Dn 6:18.

Vocal. 2 S 19:35. Ac 16:25.

Early invention of. Gn 4:21.

Effects produced on the prophets of old by. 1 S 10:5–6.

Generally put aside in times of affliction. Ps 137:2–4. Dn 6:18.

ILLUSTRATIVE OF

Calamities (when ceasing). Is 24:8–9. Rv 18:22.

Heavenly felicity. Rv 5:8–9.

Joy and gladness. Zp 3:17. Ep 5:19.

INSTRUMENTS

Great diversity of. Ec 2:8.

Invented by David. 1 Ch 23:5. 2 Ch 7:6.

The Jews celebrated for inventing. Am 6:5.

Made of almug wood. 1 K 10:12.

Made of brass. 1 Co 13:1.

Made of fir wood. 2 S 6:5.

Made of horns of animals. Jsh 6:8.

Made of silver. Nu 10:2.

Many with strings. Pss 33:2; 150:4.

Often expensively ornamented. Ezk 28:13.

INSTRUMENTS NAMED

Cymbals. 1 Ch 16:5. Ps 150:5.
Cornet. Ps 98:6. Ho 5:8.
Dulcimer. Dn 3:5.
Flute. Dn 3:5.
Harp. Ps 137:2. Ezk 26:13.
Organ. Gn 4:21. Jb 21:12. Ps 150:4.
Pipe. 1 K 1:40. Is 5:12. Jr 48:36.
Psaltery. Pss 33:2; 71:22.
Sackbut. Dn 3:5.
Tabret. 1 S 10:5. Is 24:8.
Timbrel. Ex 15:20. Ps 68:25.
Trumpet. 2 K 11:14. 2 Ch 29:27.
Viol. Is 14:11. Am 5:23.

Movements of armies regulated by. Jsh 6:8. 1 Co 14:8.

USED BY THE JEWS

At consecration of temple. 2 Ch 5:11–13
At coronation of kings. 2 Ch 23:11, 13.
At dedication of city walls. Ne 12:27–28.
At laying foundation of temple. Ezr 3:9–10.
In commemorating great men. 1 Ch 35:25.
In dances. Mt 11:17. Lk 15:25.
In funeral ceremonies. Mt 9:23.
In private entertainments. Is 5:12. Am 6:5.

In religious feasts. 2 Ch 30:21.
In sacred processions. 2 S 6:4–5, 15. 1 Ch 13:6–8; 15:27–28.
To celebrate victories. Ex 15:20. 1 S 18:6–7.
Used in idol worship. Dn 3:5.
Vanity of all unsanctified. Ec 2:8, 11.

MUTABILITY

God has not. Pss 89:34; 102:25. Ml 3:6. Ja 1:17.
Heavens have. Is 34:4. Ps 102:25–26. He 1:12.
Times and seasons have. Dn 2:20–21.
Universe has. 2 P 3:10. Rv 21:1.
Visible things have. 2 Co 4:18.
World has. 1 Co 7:31.

MYRRH

Given at Christ's birth. Mt 2:11.
Offered at Christ's death. Mk 15:23.
Used in Christ's tomb. Jn 19:39–40.

MYSTERY

Of the faith. 1 Tm 3:9.
Of God. Dt 21:29. Ro 11:33.
Of godliness. 1 Tm 3:16.
Of heaven. 1 Co 2:9.
Of iniquity. 2 Th 2:7.
Of our coming transformation. 1 Co 15:51.

N

NAME
Importance of good. Pr 22:1. Ec 7:1.
OF BELIEVERS
Everlasting. Is 56:5.
In the book of life. Php 4:3.
Written in heaven. Lk 10:20.
OF GOD
Blessed. Ps 72:19.
Eternal. Ps 135:13.
Excellent. Ps 148:13.
Glorious. Is 63:14. Dt 28:58.
Great. Ml 1:11.
Holy. Ps 99:3.
Not to be taken in vain. Ex 20:7.
OF JESUS CHRIST
Above every name. Php 2:9–10. He 1:4.
Ep 3:15.
We are baptized in. Ac 2:38; 8:16.
We are saved by. Ac 4:12.
We have life in. Jn 20:31.
We may pray in. Jn 14:13.
We should gather in. Mt 18:20.
Wonderful. Is 9:6.

NATIONS
All one blood. Ac 17:26.
All will serve God. Ps 72:11.
Divided after building the tower of Babel.
Gn 11:8.
Glory to be brought into the New Jerusalem.
Rv 21:24.
Insignificant compared to God. Is 40:15.
Israel separated from other. Lv 20:24.
Redeemed are from every nation. Rv 5:9.

NATURE, HUMAN
Assumed by Christ. Jn 1:14. Php 2:7.
Born to trouble. Jb 5:7.
Created by God. Gn 1:26.
Crowned with honor. Pss 8:5; 21:5.
Lower than angels. Ps 8:5.

NATURE OF CHRISTIANS
NEW
Created by Christ. 2 Co 5:17.

Promised by the prophets. Jr 31:33. Ezk
36:26.
Voluntarily put on. Ep 4:24. Cl 3:10.
OLD
Corrupt. Ep 4:22.
Crucified with Christ. Ro 6:6
Voluntarily put off. Ep 4:22. Cl 3:9.

NAZARITES
DIFFERENT KINDS OF
By a particular vow. Nu 6:2.
From the womb. Jg 13:5. Lk 1:15.
Esteemed pure. Lm 4:7.
IF DEFILED DURING VOW, TO
Bring two turtledoves for a burnt offering.
Nu 6:10–11.
Recommence their vow with a trespass
offering. Nu 6:12.
Shave the head the seventh day. Nu 6:9.
ILLUSTRATIVE OF
Christ. He 7:26.
Saints. 2 Co 6:17. Ja 1:27.
ON COMPLETION OF VOW, TO
Be brought to tabernacle door. Nu
6:13.
Have the left shoulder of the ram of the
peace offering waved upon their hands by
the priest. Nu 6:19–20, with Lv 7:32.
Offer sacrifices. Nu 6:14–17.
Shave their heads. Nu 6:18. Ac 18:18;
21:24.
Persons separated to the service of God. Nu
6:2.
PROHIBITED FROM
Cutting or shaving the head. Nu 6:5. Jg
13:5; 16:17.
Defiling themselves by the dead. Nu
6:6–7.
Grapes or anything made from the vine.
Nu 6:3–4. Jg 13:14.
Wine or strong drink. Nu 6:3. Lk
1:15.
Raised up for the good of the nation. Am
2:11.
Required to be holy. Nu 6:8.
Ungodly Jews tried to corrupt. Am 2:12.

THE NEEDY

The early church cared for. Ac 4:35. Ro 12:13.

Jesus helped. Mt 9:12.

The Lord regards. Pss 40:17; 102:17.

We are to aid. Dt 15:11; 24:14. Mt 25:34–40.

The wicked trample. Am 8:6. Is 10:2. Jb 24:4.

NEW BIRTH

All saints partake of. Ro 8:16–17. 1 P 2:2. 1 Jn 5:1.

Connected with adoption. Is 43:6–7. Jn 1:12–13.

Corruption of human nature requires. Jn 3:6. Ro 8:7–8.

DESCRIBED AS

Circumcision of the heart. Dt 30:6, with Ro 2:29. Cl 2:11.

The inward man. Ro 7:22. 2 Co 4:16.

A new creation. 2 Co 5:17. Gl 6:15. Ep 2:10.

A new heart. Ezk 36:26.

A new spirit. Ezk 11:19. Ro 6:6.

Newness of life. Ro 6:4.

Partaking of the divine nature. 2 P 1:4.

Putting on the new man. Ep 4:24.

A spiritual resurrection. Ro 6:4–6. Ep 2:1, 5. Cl 2:12; 3:1.

The washing of regeneration. Ti 3:5.

EFFECTED BY

Christ. 1 Jn 2:29.

God. Jn 1:13. 1 P 1:3.

The Holy Ghost. Jn 3:6. Ti 3:5.

EVIDENCED BY

Brotherly love. 1 Jn 4:7.

Faith in Christ. 1 Jn 5:1.

Righteousness. 1 Jn 2:29.

For the glory of God. Is 43:7.

The ignorant cavil at. Jn 3:4.

Manner of effecting illustrated. Jn 3:8.

None can enter heaven without. Jn 3:3.

Of the mercy of God. Ti 3:5.

Of the will of God. Ja 1:18.

Preserves from Satan's devices. 1 Jn 5:18.

PRODUCES

Delight in God's law. Ro 7:22.

Hatred of sin. 1 Jn 3:9; 5:18.

Knowledge of God. Jr 24:7. Cl 3:10.

Likeness to Christ. Ro 8:29. 2 Co 3:18. 1 Jn 3:2.

Likeness to God. Ep 4:24. Cl 3:10.

Victory over the world. 1 Jn 5:4.

THROUGH THE INSTRUMENTALITY OF

The ministry of the gospel. 1 Co 4:15.

The resurrection of Christ. 1 P 1:3.

The word of God. Ja 1:18. 1 P 1:23.

NEW MOON, FEAST OF

Celebrated with blowing of trumpets. Nu 10:10. Ps 8:3–4.

Disliked by the ungodly. Am 8:5.

Held first day of the month. Nu 10:10.

The Jews deprived of, for sin. Ho 2:11.

Mere outward observance of, hateful to God. Is 1:13–14.

Observance of, by Christians, condemned. Cl 2:16, with Gl 4:10.

Observed with great solemnity. 1 Ch 23:31. 2 Ch 2:4; 8:13; 31:3.

Restored after captivity. Ezr 3:5. Ne 10:33.

Sacrifices at. Nu 28:11–15.

A SEASON FOR

Entertainments. 1 S 20:5, 18.

Inquiring of God's messengers. 2 K 4:23.

Worship in God's house. Is 66:23. Ezk 46:1.

NEW NATURE

See Nature (New) of Christians.

NIGHT

Belongs to God. Ps 74:16.

Caused by God. Ps 104:20.

Commenced at sunset. Gn 28:11.

Continued until sunrise. Ps 104:22. Mt 28:1, with Mk 16:2.

The darkness first called. Gn 1:5.

Designed for rest. Ps 104:23.

Divided into four watches by the Romans. Lk 12:38, with Mt 14:25. Mk 13:35.

Eastern fishermen continued their employment during. Lk 5:5. Jn 21:3.

Eastern shepherds watched over their flocks during. Gn 31:40. Lk 2:8.

Favorable to the purposes of the wicked. Gn 31:39. Jb 24:14–15. Ob 1:5. 1 Th 5:2.

FREQUENTLY

Accompanied by heavy dews. Nu 11:9. Jg 6:38, 40. Jb 29:19. S S 5:2.

Cold and frosty. Gn 31:40. Jr 36:30.

Very dark. Pr 7:9.

GOD FREQUENTLY

Executed his judgments in. Ex 12:12. 2 K 19:35. Jb 27:20. Dn 5:30.

Revealed his will in. Gn 31:24; 46:2. Nu 22:20. Dn 7:2.

Visited his people in. 1 K 3:5. Ps 17:3.

Heavenly bodies designed to separate day from. Gn 1:14.

ILLUSTRATIVE OF
Death. Jn 9:4.
Seasons of severe calamities. Is 21:12. Am 5:8.
Seasons of spiritual desertion. S S 3:1.
Spiritual darkness. Ro 13:12.

THE JEWS
Forbidden to allow malefactors to hang during. Dt 21:23.
Forbidden to keep the wages of servants during. Lv 19:13.
In affliction, spent in prayer. Ps 22:2.
In affliction, spent in sorrow and humiliation. Pss 6:6; 30:5. Jl 1:13.
Often kept lamps burning during. Pr 31:18.

Moon and stars designed to rule and give light by. Gn 1:16–18. Jr 31:35.

Originally divided into three watches. Lm 2:19, with Jg 7:19. Ex 14:24.

REGULAR SUCCESSION OF
Established by covenant. Gn 8:22. Jr 33:20.
Ordained for the glory of God. Ps 19:2.
Unsuitable for labor. Jn 9:4.
Unsuitable for traveling. Jn 11:10
Wearisome to the afflicted. Jb 7:3–4.

Wild beasts go forth in search of prey during. 2 S 21:10. Ps 104:21–22.

NILE RIVER

ABOUNDED IN
Crocodiles. Ezk 29:3.
Fish. Ex 7:21. Ezk 29:4.
Reeds and flags. Is 19:6–7.

Annual overflow of its banks alluded to. Jr 46:8. Am 8:8; 9:5.

CALLED
The Egyptian sea. Is 11:15.
The river. Gn 41:1, 3.
Sihor. Jsh 13:3. Jr 2:18.
The stream of Egypt. Is 27:12.

Empties itself into the Mediterranean Sea by seven streams. Is 11:15.

THE EGYPTIANS
Bathed in. Ex 2:5.
Carried on extensive commerce by. Is 23:3.

Drank of. Ex 7:21, 24.

Took great pride in. Ezk 29:9.

Were punished by destruction of its fish. Is 19:8.

Were punished by failure of its waters. Is 19:5–6.

REMARKABLE EVENTS CONNECTED WITH
Male children drowned in. Ex 1:22.
Miraculous generation of frogs. Ex 8:3.
Moses exposed on its banks. Ex 2:3.
Its waters turned into blood. Ex 7:15, 20.

NINEVEH

Ancient capital of Assyria. 2 K 19:36. Is 37:37.

Called the bloody city. Na 3:1.

DESCRIBED AS
Commercial. Na 3:16.
Extensive. Jnh 3:3.
Full of joy and carelessness. Zp 2:15.
Full of lies and robbery. Na 3:1.
Full of witchcraft, etc. Na 3:4.
Great. Jnh 1:2; 3:2.
Idolatrous. Na 1:14.
Populous. Jnh 4:11.
Rich. Na 2:9.
Strong. Na 3:12.
Vile. Na 1:14.
Wicked. Jnh 1:2.

Destruction of, averted. Jnh 3:10; 4:11.

Inhabitants of, repented at Jonah's preaching. Jnh 3:5–9. Mt 12:41. Lk 11:32.

Jonah sent to proclaim the destruction of. Jnh 1:2; 3:1–2, 4.

Origin and antiquity of. Gn 10:11.

PREDICTIONS RESPECTING
Being taken while the people were drunk. Na 1:10; 3:11.
Captivity of its people. Na 3:10.
Coming up of the Babylonish armies against. Na 2:1–4; 3:2.
Complete desolation. Zp 2:13–15.
Degradation and contempt put on. Na 3:5–7. Zp 2:15.
Destruction of its idols. Na 1:14; 2:7.
Destruction of its people. Na 1:12; 3:3.
Feebleness of its people. Na 3:13.
Spoiling of its treasures. Na 2:9.
Utter destruction. Na 1:8–9.

Situated on the river Tigris. Na 2:6, 8.

O

OAK TREE
Absalom in his flight, intercepted by and suspended from. 2 S 18:9–10, 14.

THE ANCIENTS OFTEN
Buried their dead under. Gn 35:8. 1 Ch 10:12.
Erected monuments under. Jsh 24:26.
Performed idolatrous rites under. Is 1:29; 57:5. Ezk 6:13. Ho 4:13.
Rested under. Jg 6:11, 19. 1 K 13:14.
Bashan celebrated for. Is 2:13.

DESCRIBED AS
Casting its leaves in winter. Is 6:13.
Strong. Am 2:9.
Thick-spreading. 2 S 18:9. Ezk 6:13.
Idolaters often made idols of. Is 44:14.

ILLUSTRATIVE OF
The church. Is 6:13.
Strong and powerful men. Am 2:9.
Wicked rulers. Is 2:13. Zc 11:2.
The wicked under judgments (when fading). Is 1:30.
Jacob buried his family idols under. Gn 35:4.
The Tyrians made oars of. Ezk 27:6.

OATHS
Antiquity of. Gn 14:22; 24:3, 8.
Custom of swearing by the life of the king. Gn 42:15–16.

EXPRESSIONS USED AS
As the Lord liveth. Jg 8:19. Ru 3:13.
As my soul liveth. 1 S 1:26; 25:26.
Before God I lie not. Gl 1:20.
By the fear of Isaac. Gn 31:53.
By the Lord. 2 S 19:7. 1 K 2:42.
God so do to thee, and more also. 1 S 3:17.
God is witness. 1 Th 2:5.
I call God for a record. 2 Co 1:23.
I charge you by the Lord. 1 Th 5:27.
The Lord do so to me, and more also. Ru 1:17.
God used, to show the immutability of his counsel. Gn 22:16. Nu 14:28. He 6:17.

INSTANCES OF RASH, ETC.
Herod. Mt 14:7–9.
Jephthah. Jg 11:30–36.
The Jews who sought to kill Paul. Ac 23:21.
Joshua. Jsh 9:15–16.
Saul. 1 S 14:27, 44.

THE JEWS
Condemned for false. Zc 5:4. Ml 3:5.
Condemned for profane. Jr 23:10. Ho 4:2.
Fell into many errors respecting. Mt 23:16–22.
Forbidden to take false. Lv 6:3. Zc 8:17.
Forbidden to take in the name of any created thing. Mt 5:34–36. Ja 5:12.
Forbidden to take in the name of idols. Jsh 23:7.
Forbidden to take rash, or unholy. Lv 5:4.
Generally respected the obligation of. Jsh 9:19–20. 2 S 21:7. Ps 15:4. Mt 14:9.
Often guilty of falsely taking. Lv 6:3. Jr 5:2; 7:9.
Often guilty of rashly taking. Jg 21:7. Mt 14:7; 26:72.
To take in truth, judgment, etc. Jr 4:2.
To use God's name alone in. Dt 6:13; 10:20. Is 65:16.
Judicial form of administering. 1 K 22:16. Mt 26:63.
Lawful purpose of, explained. He 6:16.
Often accompanied by placing the hand under the thigh of the person sworn to. Gn 24:2, 9; 47:29.
Often accompanied by raising up the hand. Gn 14:22. Dn 12:7. Rv 10:5–6.
To be taken in fear and reverence. Ec 9:2.

USED FOR
Binding to performance of any particular act. Gn 24:3–4; 50:25. Jsh 2:12.
Binding to performance of sacred duties. Nu 30:2. 2 Ch 15:14–15. Ne 10:29. Ps 132:2.
Confirming covenants. Gn 26:28; 31:44, 53. 1 S 20:16–17.

OBEDIENCE TO GOD
Angels engaged in. Ps 103:20.
Better than sacrifice. 1 S 15:22.
Blessedness of. Dt 11:27; 28:1–13. Lk 11:28. Ja 1:25.
A characteristic of saints. 1 P 1:14.
Christ an example of. Mt 3:15. Jn 15:10. Php 2:5–8. He 5:8.
Commanded. Dt 13:4.
Confess your failure in. Dn 9:10.
Exhortations to. Jr 26:13; 38:20.
Impossible without faith. He 11:6.
INCLUDES
  Keeping his commandments. Ec 12:13.
  Obeying Christ. Ex 23:21. 2 Co 10:5.
  Obeying his law. Dt 11:27. Is 42:24.
  Obeying his voice. Ex 19:5. Jr 7:23.
  Obeying the gospel. Ro 1:5; 6:17; 10:16–17.
  Submission to higher powers. Ro 13:1.
Justification obtained by that of Christ. Ro 5:19.
Obligations to. Ac 4:19–20; 5:29.
Pray to be taught. Pss 119:35; 143:10.
Prepare the heart for. 1 S 7:3. Ezr 7:10.
Promises to. Ex 23:22. 1 S 12:14. Is 1:19. Jr 7:23.
Punishment of refusing. Dt 11:28.
Resolve upon. Ex 24:7. Jsh 24:24.
Saints elected to. 1 P 1:2.
SHOULD BE
  Constant. Php 2:12.
  From the heart. Dt 11:13. Ro 6:17.
  Undeviating. Dt 28:14.
  Unreserved. Jsh 22:2–3.
  With willingness. Ps 18:44. Is 1:19.
To be universal in the latter days. Dn 7:27.
The wicked refuse. Ex 5:2. Ne 9:17.

OBSTACLES
Christ can overcome. Ro 8:35–37.
Faith can take away. Mt 21:21.
God may set up. Jr 6:21. Ho 2:6.
God removes. Is 40:4; 45:2. Mk 16:4.
Religious leaders sometimes cause. Is 57:14.
Riches can be. Mk 10:24.
We must avoid creating. Ro 14:13. 1 Co 8:9.

OFFENSES
All things that cause, shall be gathered out of Christ's kingdom. Mt 13:41.
Blessedness of not taking, at Christ. Mt 11:6.

Denunciation against those who cause. Mt 18:7. Mk 9:42.
MINISTERS SHOULD
  Be cautious of giving. 2 Co 6:3.
  Remove that which causes. Is 57:14.
Occasions of, forbidden. 1 Co 10:32. 2 Co 6:3.
Occasions of, must arrive. Mt 18:7.
Persecution, a cause of, to mere professors. Mt 13:21; 24:10; 26:31.
Punishment for occasioning. Ezk 44:12. Ml 2:8–9. Mt 18:6–7.
SAINTS SHOULD
  Avoid those who cause. Ro 16:17.
  Be cautious of giving. Ps 73:15. Ro 14:13. 1 Co 8:9.
  Be without. Php 1:10.
  Cut off what causes, to themselves. Mt 5:29–30. Mk 9:43–47.
  Have a conscience void of. Ac 24:16.
  Not let their liberty occasion, to others. 1 Co 8:9.
  Not take. Jn 16:1.
  Reprove those who cause. Ex 32:21. 1 S 2:24.
  Use self-denial rather than occasion. Ro 14:21. 1 Co 8:13.
THE WICKED TAKE, AT
  Christ as the bread of life. Jn 6:58–61.
  Christ as the cornerstone. Is 8:14, with Ro 9:33. 1 P 2:8.
  Christ crucified. 1 Co 1:23. Gl 5:11.
  The low station of Christ. Is 53:1–3. Mt 13:54–57.
  The necessity of inward purity. Mt 15:11–12.
  The righteousness of faith. Ro 9:32.

OFFENSES AGAINST THE HOLY SPIRIT
Blasphemy against him, unpardonable. Mt 12:31–32. 1 Jn 5:16.
EXHIBITED IN
  Danger of trifling with the Holy Ghost. He 6:4–6.
  Disregarding his testimony. Ne 9:30.
  Doing despite unto him. He 10:29.
  Grieving him. Ep 4:30.
  Lying to him. Ac 5:3–4.
  Quenching him. 1 Th 5:19.
  Resisting him. Ac 7:51.
  Tempting him. Ac 5:9.
  Undervaluing his gifts. Ac 8:19–20.

Vexing him. Is 63:10.
Exhortations against. Ep 4:30. 1 Th 5:19.

OFFERINGS
Antiquity of. Gn 4:3–4.
Could not make the offerer prefect. He 9:9.
Declared to be most holy. Nu 18:9.
DIFFERENT KINDS OF
Burnt. Lv 1:3–17. Ps 66:15.
Drink. Gn 35:14. Ex 29:40. Nu 15:5.
First fruits. Ex 22:29. Dt 18:4.
Free-will. Lv 23:38. Dt 16:10; 23:23.
Gifts. Ex 35:22. Nu 7:2–88.
Heave. Ex 29:27–28. Lv 7:14. Nu 15:19.
Incense. Ex 30:8. Ml 1:11. Lk 1:9.
Jealousy. Nu 5:15.
Meat. Lv 2. Nu 15:4.
Peace. Lv 3:1–17; 7:11.
Personal, for redemption. Ex 30:13, 15.
Sin. Lv 4:3–35; 6:25; 10:17.
Thank. Lv 7:12; 22:29. Ps 50:14.
Tithe. Lv 27:30. Nu 18:21. Dt 14:22.
Trespass. Lv 5:6–19; 6:6; 7:1.
Wave. Ex 29:26. Lv 7:30.
Hezekiah prepared chambers for. 2 Ch 31:11.
ILLUSTRATIVE OF
Christ's offering of himself. Ep 5:2.
The conversion of the Gentiles. Ro 15:16.
The conversion of the Jews. Is 66:20.
THE JEWS OFTEN
Abhorred, on account of the sins of the priests. 1 S 2:17.
Defrauded God of. Ml 3:8.
Gave the worst they had as. Ml 1:8, 13.
Presented to idols. Ezk 20:28.
Rejected in, because of sin. Is 1:13. Ml 1:10.
Slow in presenting. Ne 13:10–12.
Laid up in the temple. 2 Ch 31:12. Ne 10:37.
Made by strangers, to be the same as by the Jews. Nu 15:14–16.
Many offenses under the law, beyond the efficacy of. 1 S 3:14. Ps 51:16.
REQUIRED TO BE
Best of their kind. Ml 1:14.
Brought in a clean vessel. Is 66:20.
Brought to the place appointed of God. Dt 12:6. Ps 27:6. He 9:9.
Brought without delay. Ex 22:29–30.
Laid before the altar. Mt 5:23–24.
Offered in love and charity. Mt 5:23–24.
Offered in righteousness. Ml 3:3.

Offered willingly. Lv 22:19.
Perfect. Lv 22:21.
Presented by the priest. He 5:1.
THINGS FORBIDDEN AS
The price of a dog. Dt 23:18.
The price of fornication. Dt 23:18.
Whatever was blemished. Lv 22:20.
Whatever was imperfect. Lv 22:24.
Whatever was unclean. Lv 27:11, 27.
To be made to God alone. Ex 22:20. Jg 13:16.
Unacceptable without gratitude. Ps 50:8, 14.

OIL
Canaan abounded in. Dt 8:8.
Comes from the earth. Ps 104:14–15. Ho 2:22.
Dealing in, a trade. 2 K 4:7.
DESCRIBED AS
Healing. Is 1:6, with Lk 10:34.
Penetrating. Ps 109:18.
Smooth. Pr 5:3.
Soft. Ps 55:21.
Exported. 1 K 5:11. Ezk 27:17. Ho 12:1.
Extracted by presses. Hg 2:16, with Mi 6:15.
Failure of, a severe calamity. Hg 1:11.
First fruits of, given to God. Dt 18:4. 2 Ch 31:5. Ne 10:37.
Given by God. Ps 104:14–15. Jr 31:12. Jl 2:19, 24.
ILLUSTRATIVE OF
The consolation of the gospel. Is 61:3.
Kind reproof. Ps 141:5.
The unction of the Holy Spirit. Pss 45:7; 89:20. Zc 4:12.
Jews often extravagant in the use of. Pr 21:17.
KEPT IN
Boxes. 2 K 9:1.
Cellars. 1 Ch 27:28.
Cruises. 1 K 17:12.
Horns. 1 K 1:39.
Pots. 2 K 4:2.
Storehouses. 2 Ch 32:28.
KINDS OF, MENTIONED
Myrrh. Es 2:12.
Olive. Ex 30:24. Lv 24:2.
Miraculous increase of. 2 K 4:2–6.
Ointments of the Jews made of perfumes mixed with. Ex 30:23–25. Jn 12:3.
The poor employed in extracting. Jb 24:11.
Sold by measure. 1 K 5:11. Lk 16:6.
Stores of, laid up in fortified cities. 2 Ch 11:11.

USED

For anointing the person. Pss 23:5;
104:15. Lk 7:46.

For anointing the sick. Mk 6:13. Ja 5:14.

For anointing to offices of trust. Ex 29:7.
1 S 10:1. 1 K 19:16.

For food. 1 K 17:12. Ezk 16:13.

For lamps. Ex 25:6; 27:20. Mt 25:3.

In God's worship. Lv 7:10. Nu 15:4–10.

In idolatrous worship. Lv 7:10. Nu
15:4–10.

Was titheable by the law. Dt 12:17.

When fresh, especially esteemed. Ps 92:10.

OLD

Christ's new covenant replaces the old. He
8:6–13.

The new is implicit in the old commandment.
1 Jn 2:7.

———— and new both to be treasured. Mt
13:52.

———— has given way to new. 2 Co 5:17.

———— landmarks not to be removed. Pr
22:28.

———— men and women counseled. Ti
2:2–4.

———— men will dream dreams. Ac 2:17.

———— things may not go with new. Mt
9:16–17. Lk 5:36–39.

———— wine is better than new. Lk 5:39.

OLD AGE

May be a time of danger or decline. 1 K 11:4.
Ps 71:9.

Should be a time of special blessing. Pr 22:6.
Is 65:20. Ac 2:17.

A time of ripeness and fruition. Ps 92:14.

To be honored. Lv 19:32. Pr 16:31.

OLD NATURE

See Nature (Old) of Christians.

OLIVE TREE

Assyria abounded in. 2 K 18:32.

Beaten to remove the fruit. Dt 24:20.

Canaan abounded in. Dt 6:11; 8:8.

CULTIVATED

Among rocks. Dt 32:13.

In olive yards. 1 S 8:14. Ne 5:11.

On the sides of mountains. Mt 21:1.

DESCRIBED AS

Bearing goodly fruit. Jr 11:16, with Ja
3:12.

Fair and beautiful. Jr 11:16, with Ho 14:6.

Fat and unctuous. Jg 9:9. Ro 11:17.

Green. Jr 11:16.

Failure of, a great calamity. Hk 3:17–18.

Fruit of, during sabbatical year left for the
poor, etc. Ex 23:11.

Fruit of, trodden in presses to extract the oil.
Mi 6:15, with Hg 2:16.

Gleaning of, left for the poor. Dt 24:20.

Good for the service of God and man. Jg
9:9.

Grafting of, alluded to. Ro 11:24.

ILLUSTRATIVE OF

Children of pious parents. Ps 128:3.

Christ. Ro 11:17, 24. Zc 4:3, 12.

Gentiles (when wild). Ro 11:17, 24.

The Jewish church. Jr 11:16.

The remnant of grace (gleaning of). Is
17:6; 24:13.

The righteous. Ps 52:8. Ho 14:6.

The two witnesses. Rv 11:3–4.

Kings of Israel largely cultivated. 1 Ch
27:28.

Often cast its flowers. Jb 15:33.

Often cast its fruit. Dt 28:40.

Often grew wild. Ro 11:17.

Often suffered from caterpillars. Am 4:9.

Oil procured from. Ex 27:20. Dt 8:8.

Probable origin of its being the emblem of
peace. Gn 8:11.

Pruning of, alluded to. Ro 11:18–19.

Shaken when fully ripe. Is 17:6.

USED FOR MAKING

Booths at feast of tabernacles. Ne 8:15.

Cherubim in the temple. 1 K 6:23.

Doors and posts of the temple. 1 K
6:31–33.

ONE

God is one. Dt 6:4.

———— in Christ. Gl 3:28.

———— Lord, one faith, one baptism. Ep
4:5.

———— thing have I desired. Ps 27:4.

———— thing I do. Php 3:13.

———— thing I know. Jn 9:25.

———— thing lacking. Lk 18:22.

———— thing needful. Lk 10:42.

ONENESS

Of the church. 1 Co 1:13; 12:4–31.

Of the first believers. Ac 2:44–47; 4:32.

Of all nations. Ac 17:24–26.

Of husband and wife. Gn 2:24. 1 Co 6:16.

Of Jesus and his Father. Jn 10:30.

OPPORTUNITY
Easily lost. 1 K 20:40. Jn 9:4. Jr 8:20.
For good deeds. Gl 6:10.
For salvation. 2 Co 6:2.
For satisfaction. Rv 22:17.
Present and immediate. Es 4:14. Jn 4:35.
Ro 13:11.

OPPOSITION
Depth of spiritual. Ep 6:12.
Power over. Lk 10:19.
Technique for meeting. Ep 6:11–19.
To Christ. He 12:3. Mt 26:3–4.
To the doer of righteousness. Jn 15:20.
To God. 2 Th 2:3–4. 2 Tm 6:20.
To the Holy Spirit. Ac 7:51.
To the speaker of truth. Is 30:10. Jr 11:21.

OPPRESSION
Divinely prohibited. Lv 25:14. Ja 5:4.
Relieved by God. Dt 26:7. Ps 9:9.
To be opposed by the godly. Is 1:17. Ac
7:24. Ja 2:5–8. Gl 6:2.

ORPHANS
Afflict not. Ex 23:22.
Blessedness of taking care of. Dt 14:29. Jb
29:12–13. Jr 7:6–7.
A curse on those who oppress. Dt 27:19.
Defend. Ps 82:3. Is 1:17.
Defraud not. Pr 23:10.
Do no violence to. Jr 22:3.
Find mercy in God. Ho 14:3.
GOD WILL
Be a father of. Ps 68:5.
Be a helper of. Ps 10:14.
Execute the judgment of. Dt 10:18. Ps
10:18.
Hear the cry of. Ex 22:23.
Punish those who judge not. Jr 5:28–29.
Punish those who oppress. Ex 22:24. Is
10:1–3. Ml 3:5.
Let them share in our blessings. Dt 14:29.
Oppress not. Zc 7:10.
Promises with respect to. Jr 49:11.
A type of Zion in affliction. Lm 5:3.
Visit in affliction. Ja 1:27.
THE WICKED
Judge not for. Ps 1:23. Jr 5:28.
Murder. Ps 94:6.
Oppress. Jb 24:3.
Overwhelm. Jb 6:27.
Rob. Is 10:2.

Vex. Ezk 22:7.
Wrong not, in judgment. Dt 24:17.

OVERCOMING
Faith overcomes the world. 1 Jn 5:4.
In practice we are to overcome evil with good.
Ro 12:21.
In principle we have overcome evil. 1 Jn
2:13–14.
OVERCOMERS WILL
Be clothed in the white of purity and hear
Christ confess his name. Rv 3:5.
Become a pillar in the temple of God and be
given three great names. Rv 3:12.
Be granted power over the nations. Rv
2:26.
Enjoy the tree of life. Rv 2:7.
Not be subject to spiritual death. Rv 2:11.
Sit with Christ on his throne. Rv 3:21.

OX
Clean and fit for food. Dt 14:4.
Custom of sending the pieces of, to collect the
people to war. 1 S 11:7.
DESCRIBED AS
Beautiful. Jr 46:20. Ho 10:11.
Not without sagacity. Is 1:3.
Strong. Ps 144:14. Pr 14:4.
FED
In stalls. Hk 3:17.
In the valleys. 1 Ch 27:29. Is 65:10.
On the hills. Is 7:25.
With corn. Is 30:24.
With grass. Jb 40:15. Ps 106:20. Dn
4:25.
FORMED A PART OF THE
Patriarchal wealth. Gn 13:2, 5; 26:14. Jb
1:3.
Wealth of Israel in Egypt. Gn 50:8. Ex
10:9; 12:32.
Wealth of the Jews. Nu 32:4. Ps 144:14.
Goes to the slaughter unconscious. Pr 7:22.
Herdmen appointed over. Gn 13:7. 1 S
21:7.
Horns and hoofs of, alluded to. Ps 69:31.
ILLUSTRATIVE OF
Backsliding Israel (a heifer sliding back).
Ho 4:16.
Beauty and wealth of Egypt (a fair heifer)
Jr 46:20.
A beloved wife (a heifer). Jg 14:18.
Fierce enemies (bulls). Pss 22:12; 68:30.
The glory of Joseph (a firstling bull). Dt
33:17.

Greedy mercenaries (fatted calves). Jr 46:21.

The impatient under judgment (in a net). Is 51:20.

Intractable sinners (when unaccustomed to the yoke). Jr 31:18.

Israel's fondness for ease, not obedience (a heifer taught). Ho 10:11.

Luxurious Chaldees (a heifer at grass). Jr 50:11.

Ministers (when engaged in husbandry). Is 30:24; 32:20.

Ministers' right to support (when not muzzled in treading corn). 1 Co 9:9–10.

Moab in affliction (a heifer three years old). Is 15:5. Jr 48:34.

Proud and wealthy rulers (kine). Am 4:1.

The provision of the gospel (when prepared for a feast). Pr 9:2. Mt 22:4.

A rash youth (when led to slaughter). Pr 7:22.

Saints under persecution (when led to slaughter). Jr 11:19.

Years of plenty (when well favored). Gn 41:2, 26, 29.

Years of scarcity (when lean). Gn 41:3, 27, 30.

INCLUDES THE

Bull. Gn 32:15. Jb 21:10.

Bullock. Ps 50:9. Jr 46:21.

Cow. Nu 18:17. Jb 21:10.

Heifer. Gn 15:9. Nu 19:2.

Increase of, promised. Dt 7:13; 28:4.

LAWS RESPECTING

Fallen under its burden, to be raised up again. Dt 22:4.

Fat of, not to be eaten. Lv 7:23.

If stolen to be restored double. Ex 22:4.

Killing a man, to be stoned. Ex 21:28–32.

Mode of reparation for one, killing another. Ex 21:35–36.

Not to be muzzled when treading out the corn. Dt 25:4. 1 Co 9:9.

Not to be yoked with an ass in the same plow. Dt 22:10.

Of others, if lost or hurt through neglect, to be made good. Ex 22:9–13.

Of others, not to be coveted. Ex 20:17. Dt 5:21.

Straying to be brought back to its owner. Ex 23:4. Dt 22:1–2.

To rest on the sabbath. Ex 23:12. Dt 5:14.

Lowing of, alluded to. 1 S 15:14. Jb 6:5.

Male firstlings of, belonged to God. Ex 34:19.

Often found wild. Dt 14:5.

Often given as a present. Gn 12:16; 20:14.

Often stall-fed for slaughter. Pr 15:17.

Publicly sold. 2 S 24:24. Lk 14:19.

Rapid manner of collecting its food alluded to. Nu 22:4.

Required great care and attention. Pr 27:23.

Sea of brass rested on figures of. 1 K 7:25.

Tithe of, given to the priests. 2 Ch 31:6.

Urged on by the goad. Jg 3:31.

USED FOR

Carrying burdens. 1 Ch 12:40.

Drawing wagons, etc. Nu 7:3. 1 S 6:7.

Food. 1 K 1:9; 19:21. 2 Ch 18:2.

Plowing. 1 K 19:19. Jb 1:14. Am 6:12.

Sacrifice. Ex 20:24. 2 S 24:22.

Tilling (earing) the ground. Is 30:24; 32:20.

Treading out the corn. Ho 10:11.

The wicked often took, in pledge from the poor. Jb 24:3.

Young of, considered a great delicacy. Gn 18:7. Am 6:4.

PQ

PALACES
DESCRIBED AS
High. Ps 78:69.
Pleasant. Is 13:22.
Polished. Ps 144:12.
ILLUSTRATIVE OF
The godly children of saints. Ps 144:12.
The place of Satan's dominion. Lk 11:21.
The splendor of the church. S S 8:9.
Jerusalem celebrated for. Ps 48:3, 13.
OF KINGS
Afforded support to all the king's retainers.
Ezr 4:14. Dn 1:5.
Called the house of the kingdom. 2 Ch
2:1, 12.
Called the king's house. 2 K 25:9. 2 Ch
7:11.
Called the king's palace. Es 1:5.
Called the royal house. Es 1:9.
Contained treasures of the king. 1 K
15:18. 2 Ch 12:9; 25:24.
Gorgeous apparel suited to, alone. Lk
7:25.
Often attended by eunuchs as servants. 2
K 20:18. Dn 1:3–4.
Royal decrees issued from. Es 3:15; 8:14.
Royal decrees laid up in. Ezr 6:2.
Splendidly furnished. Es 1:6.
Surrounded with gardens. Es 1:5.
Surrounded with terraces. 2 Ch 9:11.
Under governors. 1 K 4:6. Ne 7:2.
Were strictly guarded. 2 K 11:5.
OFTEN AS A PUNISHMENT
Burned with fire. 2 Ch 36:19. Jr 17:27.
Desolate. Ezk 19:7.
Forsaken. Is 32:14.
The habitation of dragons, etc. Is 13:22.
Overgrown with thorns, etc. Is 34:13.
Scenes of bloodshed. Jr 9:21.
Spoiled. Am 3:11.
Often the storehouses of rapine. Am 3:10.
The spider makes its way even into. Pr 30:28.
TERM APPLIED TO
House of the high priest. Mt 26:58.
Houses of great men. Am 3:9. Mi 5:5.
Residences of kings. Dn 4:4; 6:18.

Temple of God. 1 Ch 29:1, 19.
Were entered by gates. Ne 2:8.

PALM TREE
Blasted as a punishment, Jl 1:12.
BRANCHES WERE
Carried at feast of tabernacles. Lv 23:40.
The emblem of victory. Rv 7:9.
Spread before Christ. Jn 12:13.
Used for constructing booths. Ne 8:15.
DESCRIBED AS
Flourishing. Ps 92:12.
Fruitful to a great age. Ps 92:14.
Tall. S S 7:7.
Upright. Jr 10:5.
First mention of, in scripture. Ex 15:27.
ILLUSTRATIVE OF
The church. S S 7:7–8.
The righteous. Ps 92:12.
The upright appearance of idols. Jr 10:5.
Jericho celebrated for. Dt 34:3. Jg 1:16.
Represented in carved work on the walls and
doors of the temple of Solomon. 1 K 6:29,
32, 35. 2 Ch 3:5.
Requires a moist and fertile soil. Ex 15:27.
Tents often pitched under the shade of. Jg
4:5.

PARABLES
OF CHRIST
Barren fig tree. Lk 13:6–9.
Beam and mote. Lk 6:41–42.
Blind leading the blind. Lk 6:39.
Builder of a tower. Lk 14:28–30, 33.
Children of the bride chamber. Mt 9:15.
Cloud and wind. Lk 12:54–57.
Creditor and debtors. Lk 7:41–47.
Faithful and evil servants. Mt 24:45–51.
Fig tree leafing. Mt 24:32–34.
Good Samaritan. Lk 10:30–37.
Good shepherd. Jn 10:1–6.
House divided against itself. Mk 3:25.
Importunate friend. Lk 11:5–9.
Importunate widow. Lk 18:1–8.
Kingdom divided against itself. Mk 3:24.
King going to war. Lk 14:31–33.

Laborers hired. Mt 20:1–16.
Leaven. Mt 13:33.
Lighted candle. Mk 4:21. Lk 11:33–36.
Lost piece of silver. Lk 15:8–10.
Lost sheep. Lk 15:3–7.
Man of the house watching. Mt 24:43.
Man taking a far journey. Mk 13:34–37.
Marriage feast. Mt 22:2–14.
Meats defiling not. Mt 15:10–15.
Men bidden to a feast. Lk 14:7–11.
Mustard seed. Mt 13:31–32. Lk 13:19.
Net cast into the sea. Mt 13:47–50.
New cloth on an old garment. Mt 9:16.
New wine and old bottles. Mt 9:17.
Pearl of great price. Mt 13:45–46.
Pharisee and publican. Lk 18:9–14.
Pounds. Lk 19:12–27.
Prodigal son. Lk 15:11–32.
Rich fool. Lk 12:16–21.
Rich man and Lazarus. Lk 16:19–31.
Savor of salt. Lk 14:34–35.
Seed growing secretly. Mk 4:26–29.
Sower. Mt 13:3, 18. Lk 8:5, 11.
Strong man armed. Mk 3:27. Lk 11:21.
Talents. Mt 25:14–30.
Tares. Mt 13:24–30, 36–43.
Ten virgins. Mt 25:1–13.
Treasure hid in a field. Mt 13:44.
Tree and its fruit. Lk 6:43–45.
Two sons. Mt 21:28–32.
Unclean spirit. Mt 12:43.
Unjust steward. Lk 16:1–8.
Unmerciful servant. Mt 18:23–35.
Vine and branches. Jn 15:1–5.
Wicked husbandmen. Mt 21:33–45.
Wise and foolish builders. Mt 7:24–27.
Of the Old Testament. Jg 9:8–15. 2 S 12:1–4; 14:5–7.

PARDON

All saints enjoy. Cl 2:13. 1 Jn 2:12.
Blessedness of. Ps 32:1, with Ro 4:7.
Blood of Christ alone is efficacious for. Zc 13:1, with 1 Jn 1:7.
Encouragement to pray for. 2 Ch 7:14.
EXHIBITS GOD'S
  Compassion. Mi 7:18–19.
  Faithfulness. 1 Jn 1:9.
  Forbearance. Ro 3:25.
  Goodness. 2 Ch 30:18. Ps 86:5.
  Grace. Ro 5:15–16.
  Justice. 1 Jn 1:9.
  Loving-kindness. Ps 51:1.
  Mercy. Ex 34:7. Ps 51:1

EXPRESSED BY
  Blotting out sin. Ac 3:19.
  Blotting out transgression. Is 44:22.
  Casting sins into the sea. Mi 7:19.
  Covering sin. Ps 32:1.
  Forgiving transgression. Ps 32:1.
  Not imputing sin. Ro 4:8.
  Not mentioning transgression. Ezk 18:22.
  Remembering sins no more. He 10:17.
  Removing transgression. Ps 103:12.
GRANTED
  Abundantly. Is 55:7. Ro 5:20.
  According to the riches of grace. Ep 1:7.
  By Christ. Mk 2:5. Lk 7:48.
  By God alone. Dn 9:9. Mk 2:7.
  For the name's sake of Christ. 1 Jn 2:12.
  Freely. Is 43:25.
  On the exaltation of Christ. Ac 5:31.
  Readily. Ne 9:17. Ps 86:5.
  Through the blood of Christ. Mt 26:28. Ro 3:25. Cl 1:14.
  Through Christ. Lk 1:69, 77. Ac 5:31; 13:38.
  To those who believe. Ac 10:43.
  To those who confess their sins. 2 S 12:13. Ps 32:5. 1 Jn 1:9.
  To those who repent. Ac 2:38.
Legal sacrifices ineffectual for. He 10:4.
Ministers are appointed to proclaim. Is 40:1–2. 2 Co 5:19.
None without shedding of blood. Lv 17:11, with He 9:22.
Outward purifications ineffectual for. Jb 9:30–31. Jr 2:22.
PRAY FOR
  Others. Ja 5:15. 1 Jn 5:16.
  Yourselves. Pss 25:11, 18; 51:1. Mt 6:12. Lk 11:4.
Promised. Is 1:18. Jr 31:34, with He 8:12. Jr 50:20.
Should be preached in the name of Christ. Lk 24:47.
SHOULD LEAD TO
  Fearing God. Ps 130:4.
  Loving God. Lk 7:47.
  Praising God. Ps 103:2–3.
  Returning to God. Is 44:22.
WITHHELD FROM
  Apostates. He 10:26–27. 1 Jn 5:16.
  Blasphemers against the Holy Ghost. Mt 12:32. Mk 3:28–29.
  The impenitent. Lk 13:2–5.
  The unbelieving. Jn 8:21, 24.
  The unforgiving. Mk 11:26. Lk 6:37.

PARENTS

Children received from God. Gn 33:5. 1 S
1:27. Ps 127:3.

DUTY OF, TO CHILDREN

Bless them. Gn 48:15. He 11:20.

Bring them to Christ. Mt 19:13–14.

Command them to obey God. Dt 32:46.
1 Ch 28:9.

Correct them. Pr 13:24; 19:18; 23:13;
29:17. He 12:7.

Instruct them in God's world. Dt 4:9;
11:19. Is 38:19.

Love them. Ti 2:4.

Not make unholy connections for them.
Gn 24:1–4; 28:1–2.

Not provoke them. Ep 6:4. Cl 3:21.

Pity them. Ps 103:13.

Provide for them. Jb 42:15. 2 Co 12:14.
1 Tm 5:8.

Rule them. 1 Tm 3:4, 12.

Tell them of God's judgments. Jl 1:3.

Tell them of the miraculous works of God.
Ex 10:2. Ps 78:4.

Train them up for God. Pr 22:6. Ep
6:4.

Negligence of, sorely punished. 1 S 3:13.

SHOULD PRAY FOR THEIR CHILDREN

For their spiritual welfare. Gn 17:18. 1
Ch 29:19.

When in sickness. 2 S 12:16. Mk 5:23.
Jn 4:46, 49.

When in temptation. Jb 1:5.

Sins of, visited on their children. Ex 20:5. Is
14:20. Lm 5:7.

WHEN FAITHFUL

Are blessed by their children. Pr 31:28.

Leave a blessing to their children. Ps
112:2. Pr 11:21. Is 65:23.

WHEN WICKED

Instruct their children in evil. Jr 9:14. 1 P
1:18.

Set a bad example to their children. Ezk
20:18. Am 2:4.

Wicked children, a cause of grief to. Pr 10:1;
17:25.

PARTAKERS

SHOULD NOT TAKE PART IN

Adultery. Ps 50:18.

Other men's sins. 1 Tm 5:22.

The table of devils. 1 Co 10:21.

SHOULD TAKE PART IN

The bread of communion. 1 Co 10:17.

Grace. Php 1:7.

The heavenly calling. He 3:1.

The holiness of God. He 12:10.

The Holy Spirit. He 6:4.

The inheritance of the saints. Cl 1:12.

The nature of God. 2 P 1:4.

The promise of salvation. Ep 3:6.

Spiritual blessings. Ro 11:17.

The sufferings of Christ. 1 P 4:13.

PARTIALITY

There is none with God. Ac 10:34. Ro
10:12. Mt 5:45.

There must be none with us. Dt 1:17. 1 Tm
5:21. Jb 13:10. Ja 2:4.

There should be none in the realm of justice.
Lv 19:15. Cl 4:1.

PASCHAL LAMB, TYPICAL NATURE OF

Blood of, not sprinkled on threshold. Ex
12:7. He 10:29.

Blood of, sprinkled on lintel and door posts.
Ex 12:22. He 9:13–14; 10:22. 1 P 1:2.

Blood of, to be shed. Ex 12:7. Lk 22:20.

Chosen beforehand. Ex 12:3. 1 P 2:4.

Eaten in haste. Ex 12:11. He 6:18.

Eaten with bitter herbs. Ex 12:8. Zc 12:10.

Eaten with the loins girt. Ex 12:11. Lk
12:35. Ep 6:14. 1 P 1:13.

Eaten with shoes on. Ex 12:11. Ep 6:15.

Eaten with staff in hand. Ex 12:11. Ps
23:4.

Eaten with unleavened bread. Ex 12:39. 1
Co 5:7–8. (See also 2 Co 1:12.)

Killed at the place where the Lord put his
name. Dt 16:2, 5–7. 2 Ch 35:1. Lk
13:33.

Killed by the people. Ex 12:6. Ac 2:23.

Killed in the evening. Ex 12:6. Mk 15:34,
37.

A male of the first year. Ex 12:5. Is 9:6.

Not a bone of, broken. Ex 12:46. Jn 19:36.

Not eaten raw. Ex 12:9. 1 Co 11:28–29.

Not taken out of the house. Ex 12:46. Ep
3:17.

Roasted with fire. Ex 12:8. Ps 22:14–15.

Shut up four days that it might be closely examined. Ex 12:6. Jn 8:46; 18:38

Taken out of the flock. Ex 12:5. He 2:14,
17.

A type of Christ. Ex 12:3. 1 Co 5:7.

What remained of it till morning to be burned.
Ex 12:10. Mt 7:6. Lk 11:3.

Without blemish. Ex 12:5. 1 P 1:19.

PASSOVER, FEAST OF

All males to appear at. Ex 23:17. Dt 16:16.

CALLED THE

Days of unleavened bread. Ac 12:3; 20:6.

Feast of unleavened bread. Mk 14:1. Lk 22:1.

Jew's Passover. Jn 2:13; 11:55.

Lord's Passover. Ex 12:11, 27.

Passover. Nu 9:5. Jn 2:23.

Children to be taught the nature and design of. Ez 12:26–27; 13:8.

Christ always observed. Mt 26:17–20. Lk 22:15. Jn 2:13, 23.

COMMEMORATES THE

Deliverance of Israel from bondage of Egypt. Ex 12:17, 42; 13:9. Dt 16:3.

Passing over the first-born. Ex 12:12–13.

Commenced the fourteenth of the first month at even. Ex 12:2, 6, 18. Lv 23:5. Nu 9:3.

Custom of releasing a prisoner at. Mt 27:15. Lk 23:16–17.

Day before the sabbath in, called the preparation. Jn 19:14, 31.

First and last days of, holy convocations. Ex 12:16. Nu 28:18, 25.

First sheaf of barley harvest offered the day after the sabbath in. Lv 23:10–14.

Illustrative of redemption through Christ. 1 Co 5:7–8.

Improper keeping of, punished. 2 Ch 30:18, 20.

Lasted seven days. Ex 12:15. Lv 23:6.

LEAVEN

Nothing with, to be eaten. Ex 12:20.

Not to be in any of their quarters. Ex 13:7. Dt 16:4.

Not to be in their houses during. Ex 12:19.

Punishment for eating. Ex 12:15, 19.

The Lord's Supper instituted at. Mt 26:26–28.

Might be kept in second month by those who were unclean at the appointed time. Nu 9:6–11. 2 Ch 30:2–3, 15.

Moses kept through faith. He 11:28.

Neglect of, punished with death. Nu 9:13.

No uncircumcised person to keep. Ex 12:43, 45.

Ordained by God. Ex 12:1–2.

Paschal lamb eaten first day of. Ex 12:6, 8.

People of Jerusalem lent their rooms to strangers for. Lk 22:11–12.

Purification necessary to the due observance of. 2 Ch 30:15–19. Jn 11:55.

REMARKABLE CELEBRATIONS OF

After the captivity. Ezr 6:19–20.

Before the death of Christ. Lk 22:15.

In Hezekiah's reign. 2 Ch 30:1.

In Josiah's reign. 2 K 23:22–23. 2 Ch 35:1, 18.

In the wilderness of Sinai. Nu 9:3–5.

On entering the land of promise. Jsh 5:10–11.

On leaving Egypt. Ex 12:28, 50.

The sabbath in, a high day. Jn 19:31.

Sacrifices during. Lv 23:8. Nu 28:19–24.

Strangers and servants when circumcised might keep. Ex 12:44, 48.

To be perpetually observed during the Mosaic dispensation. Ex 12:14; 13:10.

Unleavened bread eaten at. Ex 12:15. Dt 16:3.

PASTORS

GOOD

Are examples to the flock. 1 P 5:3.

Are faithful. 1 S 2:35.

Are ministers for good. Ro 13:4.

Commend themselves by purity, knowledge, patience, kindness, the Holy Spirit, and love unfeigned. 2 Co 6:6.

Do not lord it over the flock. 1 P 5:3.

Do not strive. 2 Tm 2:24.

Do not work for mere money nor by constraint. 1 P 5:2.

Do the work of evangelists. 2 Tm 4:5.

Feed the sheep. Jr 23:4. 1 P 5:2.

Give themselves to prayer and the ministry of the word. Ac 6:4.

Serve God. Rv 22:3.

Take heed to themselves and to their flock. Ac 20:28

Work willingly and eagerly. 1 P 5:2.

POOR

Are brutish. Jr 10:21

Cannot understand. Is 56:11.

Do not care for the sheep. Jn 10:13.

Lead the sheep astray. Jr 50:6.

Scatter the sheep. Jr 23:1.

See also Ministers; Shepherds.

PATIENCE

Christ an example of. Is 53:7, with Ac 8:32. Mt 27:14.

Commended. Ec 7:8. Rv 2:2–3.

Enjoined. Ti 2:2. 2 P 1:6.

Exercise, toward all. 1 Th 5:14.

God the God of. Ro 15:5.

Illustrated. Ja 5:7.
Ministers approved by. 2 Co 6:4.
Ministers should follow after. 1 Tm 6:11.
Necessary to the inheritance of the promises.
He 6:12; 10:36.
PRODUCES
Experience. Ro 5:4.
Hope. Ro 15:4.
Saints strengthened unto all. Cl 1:11.
SHOULD BE ACCOMPANIED BY
Faith. 2 Th 1:4. He 6:12. Rv 13:10.
Godliness. 2 P 1:6.
Joyfulness. Cl 1:11.
Long-suffering. Cl 1:11.
Temperance. 2 P 1:6.
SHOULD BE EXERCISED IN
Bearing the yoke. Lm 3:27.
Bringing forth fruits. Lk 8:15.
Running the race set before us. He 12:1.
Tribulation. Lk 21:19. Ro 12:12.
Waiting for Christ. 1 Co 1:7. 2 Th 3:5.
Waiting for God. Pss 37:7; 40:1.
Waiting for God's salvation. Lm 3:26.
Waiting for the hope of the gospel. Ro
8:25. Gl 5:5.
Well-doing. Ro 2:7. Gl 6:9.
Should have its perfect work. Ja 1:4.
Suffering with, for well-doing, is acceptable
with God. 1 P 2:20.
They who are in authority should exercise.
Mt 18:26. Ac 26:3.
Trials of saints lead to. Ro 5:3. Ja 1:3.

PAYMENT
FOR OUR DEEDS
Bountiful sowing brings bountiful harvest.
2 Co 9:6.
Laborer is worthy of reward. 1 Tm 5:18.
Wage of sin is death. Ro 6:23.
Will be made in kind. Lk 6:38.
TO GOD
Should be made regularly. 1 Co 16:2.
Should be proportionate to what we have.
Lv 27:32.
Should honor him. Pr 3:9.
TO MEN
Should be made when due. Pr 12:14.
Should not be made in kind but in grace.
1 P 3:9. Lk 6:35.

PEACE
Advantages of. Pr 17:1. Ec 4:6.
Blessedness of. Ps 133:1.
Blessedness of promoting. Mt 5:9.

A bond of union. Ep 4:3.
The church shall enjoy. Pss 125:5; 128:6. Is
2:4. Ho 2:18.
Exhort others to. Gn 45:24.
Fruit of righteousness should be sown in. Ja
3:18.
God the author of. Ps 147:14. Is 45:7. 1 Co
14:33.
GOD BESTOWS UPON THOSE WHO
Endure his chastisements. Jb 5:17, 23–24.
Obey him. Lv 26:6.
Please him. Pr 16:7.
Ministers should exhort to. 2 Th 3:12.
Necessary to the enjoyment of life. Ps 34:12,
14, with 1 P 3:10–11.
Pray for that of the church. Ps 122:6–8.
RESULTS FROM
Government of Christ. Is 2:4.
Heavenly wisdom. Ja 3:17.
Praying for rulers. 1 Tm 2:2.
Seeking the peace of those with whom we
dwell. Jr 29:7.
SAINTS SHOULD
Cultivate. Ps 120:7.
Endeavor to have with all men. Ro 12:18.
He 12:14.
Follow. 2 Tm 2:22.
Follow the things which make for. Ro
14:19.
Have with each other. Mk 9:50. 1 Th
5:13.
Live in. 2 Co 13:11.
Love. Zc 8:19.
Seek. Ps 34:14, with 1 P 3:11.
Speak. Es 10:3.
Shall abound in the latter days. Is 2:4; 11:13;
32:18.
THE WICKED
Enjoy not. Is 48:22. Ezk 7:25.
Hate. Ps 120:6.
Hypocritically speak. Ps 28:3.
Opposed to. Ps 120:7.
Speak not. Ps 35:20.

PEACE, SPIRITUAL
ACCOMPANIES
Acquaintance with God. Jb 22:21.
Faith. Ro 15:13.
Love of God's law. Ps 119:165.
Righteousness. Is 32:17.
Spiritual-mindedness. Ro 8:6.
Announced by angels. Lk 2:14.
Benediction of ministers should be. Nu 6:26.
Lk 10:5.

Bequeathed by Christ. Jn 14:27.
Christ gives. 2 Th 3:16.
Christ guides into the way of. Lk 1:79.
Christ our. Ep 2:14.
Christ the Lord of. 2 Th 3:16.
Christ the prince of. Is 9:6.
Divine wisdom is the way of. Pr 3:17.
Established by covenant. Is 54:10. Ezk 34:25. Ml 2:5.
Follows upon justification. Ro 5:1.
A fruit of the Spirit. Ro 14:17. Gl 5:22.
God ordains. Is 26:12.
God speaks, to his saints. Ps 85:8.
God the God of. Ro 15:33. 2 Co 13:11. 1 Th 5:23. He 13:20.
The gospel is good tidings of. Ro 10:15.

OF SAINTS
Abundant. Ps 72:7. Jr 33:6.
Consummated after death. Is 57:2.
Great. Ps 119:165. Is 54:13.
Passeth all understanding. Php 4:7.
Secure. Jb 34:29.

PREACHED
By Christ. Ep 2:17.
By ministers. Is 52:7, with Ro 10:15.
Through Christ. Ac 10:36.

PROMISED TO
The church. Is 66:12.
The Gentiles. Zc 9:10.
The meek. Ps 37:11.
Returning backsliders. Is 57:18–19.
Saints. Ps 72:3, 7. Is 55:12.
Those who confide in God. Is 26:3.

SAINTS
Blessed with. Ps 29:11.
Die in. Ps 37:37. Lk 2:29.
Enjoy. Ps 119:165.
Have in Christ. Jn 16:33.
Have with God. Is 27:5. Ro 5:1.
Kept by. Php 4:7.
Kept in perfect. Is 26:3.
Repose in. Ps 4:8.
Ruled by. Cl 3:15.
Wish, to each other. Gl 6:16. Php 1:2. Cl 1:2. 1 Th 1:1.
Supports under trials. Jn 14:27; 16:33.
Through the atonement of Christ. Is 53:5. Ep 2:14, 15. Cl 1:20.
We should love. Zc 8:19.

THE WICKED
Are promised, by false teachers. Jr 6:14.
Know not the things of. Lk 19:42.
Know not the way of. Is 59:8. Ro 3:17.

Promise, to themselves. Dt 29:19.
There is none for. Is 48:22; 57:21.

PEARLS
And excessive adorning are not appropriate for children of God. 1 Tm 2:9. Rv 17:4.
Are not to be cast before swine. Mt 7:6.
Are the gates of the heavenly city. Rv 21:21.
The kingdom is like a merchant seeking. Mt 13:45.
Wisdom is worth more than. Jb 28:18.

PENITENCE
See Repentance.

PENTECOST, FEAST OF
All males to attend. Ex 23:16–17. Dt 16:16.

CALLED THE
Day of the first fruits. Nu 28:26.
Day of Pentecost. Ac 2:1.
Feast of harvest. Ex 23:16.
Feast of weeks. Ex 34:22. Dt 16:10.
First fruits of bread presented at. Lv 23:17. Dt 16:10.
Held fiftieth day after offering first sheaf of barley harvest. Lv 23:15–16. Dt 16:9.
A holy convocation. Lv 23:21. Nu 28:26.
Holy Spirit given to apostles at. Ac 2:1–3.
Law given from Mount Sinai upon. Ex 19:1, 11, with Ex 12:6, 12.
Observed by the early church. Ac 20:16. 1 Co 16:8.
Sacrifices at. Lv 23:18–19. Nu 28:27–31.
A time of holy rejoicing. Dt 16:11–12.
To be perpetually observed. Lv 23:21.

PERFECTION
All saints have, in Christ. 1 Co 2:6. Php 3:15. Cl 2:10.
Blessedness of. Ps 37:37. Pr 2:21.
Charity the bond of. Cl 3:14.
The church shall attain to. Jn 17:23. Ep 4:13.
Exhortation to. 2 Co 7:1; 13:11.
God's perfection the standard of. Mt 5:48.

IMPLIES
Entire devotedness. Mt 19:21.
Purity and holiness in speech. Ja 3:2.
Impossibility of attaining to. 2 Ch 6:36. Ps 119:96.
Ministers appointed to lead saints to. Ep 4:12. Cl 1:28.
Of God. Pss 18:32; 138:8.
Patience leads to. Ja 1:4.

Pray for. He 13:20–21. 1 P 5:10.
Saints claim not. Jb 9:20. Php 3:12.
Saints commanded to aim at. Gn 17:1. Dt 18:13.
Saints follow after. Pr 4:18. Php 3:12.
THE WORD OF GOD
Designed to lead us to. 2 Tm 3:16–17.
The rule of. Ja 1:25.

PERSECUTION

All that live godly in Christ shall suffer. 2 Tm 3:12.
Blessedness of enduring, for Christ's sake. Mt 5:10. Lk 6:22.
Cannot separate from Christ. Ro 8:35.
Christ patient under. Is 53:7.
Christ suffered. Ps 69:26. Jn 5:16.
Christ voluntarily submitted to. Is 50:6.
False teachers shrink from. Gl 6:12.
God delivers out of. Dn 3:25, 28. 2 Co 1:10. 2 Tm 3:11.
God forsakes not his saints under. 2 Co 4:9.
Hope of future blessedness supports under. 1 Co 15:19, 32. He 10:34–35.
Hypocrites cannot endure. Mk 4:17.
Illustrated. Mt 21:33–39.
Inconsistent with the spirit of the gospel. Mt 26:52.
Lawful means may be used to escape. Mt 2:13; 10:23; 12:14–15.
Men by nature addicted to. Gl 4:29.
Of saints, a persecution of Christ. Zc 2:8, with Ac 9:4–5.
ORIGINATES IN
Hatred to God and Christ. Jn 15:20, 24.
Hatred to the gospel. Mt 13:21.
Ignorance of God and Christ. Jn 16:3.
Mistaken zeal. Ac 13:50; 26:9–11.
Pride. Ps 10:2.
Pray for those suffering. 2 Th 3:2.
Preachers of the gospel subject to. Gl 5:11.
Punishment for. Ps 7:13. 2 Th 1:6.
Saints may expect. Mk 10:30. Lk 21:12. Jn 15:20.
Saints suffer, for the sake of God. Jr 15:15.
SAINTS SUFFERING, SHOULD
Commit themselves to God. 1 P 4:19.
Exhibit patience. 1 Co 4:12.
Glorify God. 1 P 4:16.
Pray for deliverance. Pss 7:1; 119:86.
Pray for those who inflict. Mt 5:44.
Rejoice. Mt 5:12. 1 P 4:13.
Return blessing for. Ro 12:14.
Sometimes unto death. Ac 22:4.

THE WICKED
Active in. Ps 143:3. Lm 4:19.
Addicted to. Pss 10:2; 69:26.
Encourage each other in. Ps 71:11.
Rejoice in its success. Ps 13:4. Rv 11:10.

PERSEVERANCE

Blessedness of. Ja 1:25.
A characteristic of saints. Pr 4:18.
Encouragement to. He 12:2–3.
An evidence of belonging to Christ. Jn 8:31. He 3:6, 14.
An evidence of reconciliation with God. Cl 1:21–23.
IN WELL-DOING
Is not in vain. 1 Co 15:58. Gl 6:9.
Leads to assurance of hope. He 6:10–11.
Leads to increase of knowledge. Jn 8:31–32.
MAINTAINED THROUGH
Faith. 1 P 1:5.
The fear of God. Jr 32:40.
The intercession of Christ. Lk 22:31–32. Jn 17:11.
The power of Christ. Jn 10:28.
The power of God. Ps 37:24. Php 1:6.
Ministers should exhort to. Ac 13:43; 14:22.
Promised to saints. Jb 17:9.
Promises to. Mt 10:22; 24:13. Rv 2:26–28.
TO BE MANIFESTED IN
Continuing in the faith. Ac 14:22. Cl 1:23. 2 Tm 4:7.
Holding fast hope. He 3:6.
Prayer. Ro 12:12. Ep 6:18.
Seeking God. 1 Ch 16:11.
Waiting upon God. Ho 12:6.
Well-doing. Ro 2:7. 2 Th 3:13.
WANT OF
Excludes from the benefits of the gospel. He 6:4–6.
Illustrated. Mk 4:5, 17.
Punished. Jn 15:6. Ro 11:22.

PERSISTENCE

IN PRAYER
The early Christians' example. Ac 2:42.
Paul's example. 2 Co 12:7–8. Ac 20:18–35.
The psalmist's example. Ps 55:17.
OF GOD
Christ persisted with Peter. Mt 26:32–33. Lk 22:61. Jn 21:1–17.
God loves and calls with everlasting love. Jr 31:3.

The Lord called Samuel three times. 1 S 3:8.

The Lord revealed himself repeatedly in spite of men's indifference. He 1:1. Lk 20:9–15. 2 P 3:9.

Where sin abounds, grace abounds much more. Ro 5:20.

OF THE RIGHTEOUS

In good things. 1 Th 5:21. Gl 6:9. 2 Th 3:13.

The just man's resilience. Pr 24:16.

Peter's continued knocking. Ac 12:16.

PERSUASION

Our assurance. Ro 8:38–39. 2 Tm 1:12. He 11:13.

Our duty. Ac 26:28. 2 Co 5:11. 1 P 3:15.

Our security. Ro 15:14.

PHARISEES

As a body, rejected John's baptism. Lk 7:30.

Believed in the resurrection, etc. Ac 23:8.

By descent especially esteemed. Ac 23:6.

CHARACTER OF

Active in proselytizing. Mt 23:15.

Ambitious of precedence. Mt 23:6.

Avaricious. Mt 23:14. Lk 16:14.

Cruel in persecuting. Ac 9:1–2.

Fond of distinguished titles. Mt 23:7–10.

Fond of public salutations. Mt 23:7.

Outwardly moral. Lk 18:11. Php 3:5–6.

Oppressive. Mt. 23:4.

Particular in paying all dues. Mt 23:23.

Rigid in fasting. Lk 5:33; 18:12.

Self-righteous. Lk 16:15; 18:9.

Zealous of the law. Ac 15:5. Php 3:5.

Zealous of tradition. Mk 7:3, 5–8. Gl 1:14.

CHRIST

Asked for signs by. Mt 12:38; 16:1.

Called an evil and adulterous generation. Mt 12:39.

Called fools and blind guides. Mt 23:17, 24.

Called serpents and generation of vipers. Mt 23:33.

Compared to graves that appear not. Lk 11:44.

Compared to whited sepulchres. Mt 23:27.

Condemned by, for associating with sinners. Mt 9:11. Lk 7:39; 15:1–2.

Declared the doctrines of, to be hypocrisy. Mt 16:6, 11–12. Lk 12:1.

Declared the imaginary righteousness of, to be insufficent for salvation. Mt 5:20.

Denounced woes against. Mt 23:13, etc.

Left Judea for a time on account of. Jn 4:1–3.

Offended by his doctrine. Mt 15:12; 21:45. Lk 16:14.

Often invited by. Lk 7:36; 11:37.

Tempted by, with questions about the law. Mt 19:3; 22:15–16, 35.

Watched by, for evil. Lk 6:7.

Had disciples. Lk 5:33. Ac 22:3.

Imputed Christ's miracles to Satan's power. Mt 9:34; 12:24.

Made broad their phylacteries, etc. Mt 23:5.

Many priests and Levites. Jn 1:19, 24.

Many rulers, lawyers, and scribes. Jn 3:1. Ac 5:34; 23:9.

Often sought to destroy Christ. Mt 12:14; 21:46. Jn 11:47, 53, 57.

A sect of the Jews. Ac 15:5.

Sent officers to apprehend Christ. Jn 7:32, 45.

Some came to John for baptism. Mt 3:7.

Strictest observers of the Mosaic ritual. Ac 26:5.

Their opinions a standard to others. Jn 7:48.

PHILISTINES

Always confederated with the enemies of Israel. Ps 83:7. Is 9:11–12.

CALLED

Caphtorims. Dt 2:23.

Cherethites. 1 S 30:14. Zp 2:5.

CHARACTER OF

Idolatrous. Jg 16:23. 1 S 5:2.

Proud. Zc 9:6.

Superstitious. Is 2:6.

Warlike. 1 S 17:1; 28:1.

Conquered the Avims and took west coast of Canaan. Dt 2:23.

COUNTRY OF

Called Philistia. Pss 87:4; 108:9.

Divided into five states or lordships. Jsh 13:3. Jg 3:3. 1 S 6:16.

Given by God to the Israelites. Jsh 13:2–3; 15:45, 47.

Had many flourishing cities. 1 S 6:17.

DAVID

Distrusted by. 1 S 29:2–7.

Fled to, for safety. 1 S 27:1–7.

Gained the confidence of Achish king of. 1 S 28:2; 29:9.

Had a guard composed of. 2 S 8:18, with Ezk 25:16. Zp 2:5.

Often defeated during Saul's reign. 1 S 19:8; 23:1–5.

Often defeated in the course of his reign. 2 S 5:17–23; 8:1; 21:15–22; 23:8–12.

Procured Saul's daughter for a hundred foreskins of. 1 S 18:25–27.

Slew Goliath the champion of. 1 S 17:40–50.

Defeated by Hezekiah. 2 K 18:8.

Defeated by Israel at Ephes-dammin and pursued to Ekron. 1 S 17:1, 52.

Defeated by Uzziah. 2 Ch 26:6–7.

Defeated Israel and slew Saul. 1 S 31:1–10.

Defeated Israel at Ebenezer. 1 S 4:1–2.

Defied Israel by their champion. 1 S 17:4–10.

Descended from Casluhim. Gn 10:13–14.

Distressed Judah under Ahaz. 2 Ch 28:18–19.

First dwelt in the land of Caphtor. Jr 47:4. Am 9:7.

Gathered all their armies to Aphek against Israel. 1 S 28:1; 29:1.

Governed by kings in the patriarchal age. Gn 21:22, 34; 26:8.

Invaded the land of Israel with a great army. 1 S 13:5, 17–23.

Israel condemned for imitating. Jg 10:6. Am 6:2; 9:7.

Jonathan and his armor bearer smote a garrison of, at the passages. 1 S 14:1–14.

Jonathan smote a garrison of, at Geba. 1 S 13:3–4.

Men of great strength and stature among. 1 S 17:4–7. 2 S 21:16, 18–20.

Miraculously discomfited. 1 S 14:15–23.

Miraculously routed at Mizpeh. 1 S 7:7–14.

Nadab besieged in Gibbethon. 1 K 15:27.

Oppressed Israel after the death of Jair for eighteen years. Jg 10:7–8.

Oppressed Israel for forty years after the death of Abdon. Jg 13:1.

Plagued for retaining the ark. 1 S 5:6–12.

PROPHECIES RESPECTING

Base men to be their rulers. Zc 9:6.

Destruction and desolation of their cities. Jr 47:5. Zp 2:4.

Dismay at ruin of Tyre. Zc 9:3, 5.

Hatred and revenge against Israel to be fully recompensed. Ezk 25:15–17. Am 1:6–8.

Punishment with other nations. Jr 25:20.

Their country to be a future possession to Israel. Ob 1:19. Zp 2:7.

To help in Israel's restoration. Is 11:14.

Union with Syria against Israel. Is 9:11–12.

Utter destruction by Pharaoh king of Egypt. Jr 47:1–4. Zp 2:5–6.

Put the ark into Dagon's house. 1 S 5:1–4.

SAMSON

Blinded and imprisoned by. Jg 16:21

Burned vineyards, etc., of. Jg 15:3–5.

Intermarried with. Jg 14:1, 10.

Promised as a deliverer from. Jg 13:5.

Pulled down the house of Dagon and destroyed immense numbers of. Jg 16:29–30.

Slew a thousand with the jawbone of an ass. Jg 15:15–16.

Slew many for burning his wife. Jg 15:7–8.

Slew thirty, near Askelon. Jg 14:19.

Saul constantly at war with. 1 S 14:52.

Sent back the ark and were healed. 1 S 6:1–18.

Sent by God against Jehoram. 2 Ch 21:16–17.

Shamgar slew six hundred and delivered Israel. Jg 3:31.

Some left to prove Israel. Jg 3:1–3.

Took the ark. 1 S 4:3–11.

Ziklag, a town of, taken and plundered by the Amalekites. 1 S 30:1–2, 16.

PILGRIMS AND STRANGERS

All saints are. Ps 39:12. 1 P 1:1.

AS SAINTS THEY

Are actuated by faith. He 11:9.

Are exposed to persecution Ps 120:5–7. Jn 17:14.

Are not at home in this world. He 11:9.

Are not mindful of this world. He 11:15.

Are strengthened by God. Dt 33:25. Ps 81:6–7.

Die in faith. He 11:13.

Forsake all for Christ. Mt 19:27.

Hate worldly fellowship. Ps 120:5–6.

Have a heavenly conversation. Php 3:20.

Have the example of Christ. Lk 9:58.

Have their faces toward Zion. Jr 50:5.

Invite others to go with them. Nu 10:29.

Keep the promises in view. He 11:13.

Long for their pilgrimage to end. Ps 55:6. 2 Co 5:1–8.

Look for a heavenly city. He 11:10.

Look for a heavenly country. He 11:16.
Pass their sojourning in fear. 1 P 1:17.
Pray for direction. Ps 43:3. Jr 50:5.
Rejoice in the statutes of God. Ps 119:54.
Shine as lights in the world. Php 2:15.
Should abstain from fleshly lusts. 1 P 2:11.
Should have their treasure in heaven. Mt
6:19. Lk 12:33. Cl 3:1–2.
Should not be over anxious about worldly
things. Mt 6:25.
The world is not worthy of. He 11:38.
Described. Jn 17:16.
God is not ashamed to be called their God.
He 11:16.
Saints are called to be. Gn 12:1, with Ac 7:3.
Lk 14:26–27, 33.
Saints confess themselves. 1 Ch 29:15. Pss
39:12; 119:19. He 11:13.

PILLARS
Divine glory appeared to Israel in the form of.
Ex 13:21–22. Nu 12:5.
ILLUSTRATIVE OF
The church. 1 Tm 3:15.
Ministers. Jr 1:18. Gl 2:9.
Saints who overcome in Christ. Rv 3:12.
Stability of Christ. S S 5:15. Rv 10:1.
Stability of the earth. 1 S 2:8. Ps 75:3.
Stability of the heavens. Jb 26:11.
Lot's wife became, of salt. Gn 19:26.
MADE OF
Brass. 1 K 7:15.
Iron. Jr 1:18.
Marble. Es 1:6.
Silver. S S 3:10.
Wood. 1 K 10:12.
OF MEMORIAL
In honor of idols. Lv 26:1. Dt 7:5.
Often anointed. Gn 28:18; 31:13.
Often had inscriptions. Jb 19:24.
To commemorate remarkable events. Ex
24:4. Jsh 4:20, 24.
To mark the graves of the dead. Gn 35:20.
To perpetuate names. 2 S 18:18.
To witness covenants. Gn 31:52.
To witness vows. Gn 28:18; 31:13.
Sometimes of a heap of stones. Jsh 4:8–9,
20.
Sometimes of a single stone. Gn 28:18.
The supports of a building. Jg 16:29.
Two placed in the temple porch. 1 K
7:15–21.
Veil and hangings of the tabernacle supported
by. Ex 26:32, 37; 36:36, 38.

PITY
GOD'S IS
Toward all. Jn 3:16. Ps 145:9. Mt
5:45.
Toward his people. Jl 2:18.
Toward little ones. Mt 10:42.
Toward the poor. Pr 19:17.
Toward the weak and needy. Ps 72:13.
Toward those who trust him Ps 103:13.
OURS SHOULD BE
At the heart of our life. Cl 3:12.
Characteristic. Mt 5:7; 5:46–48.
Continual. 1 P 3:8.
Fundamental to our faith. Ho 6:6.
See also Loving-kindness of God.

PLAGUE OR PESTILENCE
Attributed to a destroying angel. Ex 12:23,
with 2 S 24:16.
Desolating effects of. Ps 91:7. Jr 16:6–7.
Am 6:9–10.
Described as noisome. Ps 91:3.
Egypt often afflicted with. Jr. 42:17, with
Am 4:10.
Equally fatal day and night. Ps 91:5–6.
ILLUSTRATIVE OF
The diseased state of man's heart. 1 K
8:38.
God's judgments upon the apostasy. Rv
18:4, 8.
Inflicted by God. Ps 78:50. Jr 21:6. Ezk
14:19. Hk 3:5.
Israel threatened with, as a punishment for
disobedience. Lv 26:24–25. Dt 28:21.
The Jews sought deliverance from, by prayer.
1 K 8:37, 38. 2 Ch 20:9.
Often broke out suddenly. Ps 106:29.
Often followed war and famine. Jr 27:13;
28:8; 29:17–18.
One of God's four sore judgments. Ezk
14:21.
Predicted to happen before destruction of
Jerusalem. Mt 24:7. Lk 21:11.
SENT UPON
David's subjects for his numbering the peo-
ple. 2 S 24:15.
The Egyptians. Ex 12:29–30.
Israel for despising manna. Nu 11:33.
Israel for making a golden calf. Ex 32:35.
Israel for murmuring at destruction of
Korah. Nu 16:46–50.
Israel for worshiping Baal-peor. Nu 25:18.
Specially fatal in cities. Lv 26:25. Jr 21:6,
9.

PLANS
Folly of forgetting God in. Ps 52:7.
Importance of. Lk 14:28, 31.
Urgency of including God in. Pr 3:6.

PLEASURE
Dangers in. Ti 3:3 He 11:25.
Emptiness of worldly. Ec 2.
From God. Ps 16:6, 11. Pr 3:17. Ac 2:26.
Influence of. Lk 8:14. 2 P 2:13.
Of God. Php 2:13. Ps 149:4.

PLOWING
Breaking up or tilling the earth. Jr 4:3. Ho 10:12.
Difficulty of, on rocky ground. Am 6:12.
Followed by harrowing and sowing. Is 28:24–25.
ILLUSTRATIVE OF
   Continued devotedness (by the attention and constancy required in). Lk 9:62.
   A course of sin. Jb 4:8. Ho 10:13.
   The labor of ministers. 1 Co 9:10.
   Peace and prosperity. Is 2:4. Mi 4:3.
   Repentance and reformation. Jr 4:3.
   A severe course of affliction. Ho 10:11.
Noah the supposed inventor of. Gn 5:29.
PERFORMED
   By a plow. Lk 9:62.
   During the cold winter season. Pr 20:4.
   Generally by servants. Is 61:5. Lk 17:7.
   In long and straight furrows. Ps 129:3.
   Sometimes by the owner of the land himself. 1 K 19:19.
   With oxen. 1 S 14:14. Jb 1:14.
With an ox and an ass yoked together, forbidden to the Jews. Dt 22:10.

POLLUTION
Of the altar of God. Ex 20:25. Dn 8:11.
Of the Lord's Day. Is 56:2.
Of sin removed. 1 Jn 1:7.
Of the sinful nature. Ep 4:22.
Of the ungodly. Lv 19:31. Ac 15:20.

POMEGRANATE TREE
Blasting of, a great calamity. Jl 1:12.
Canaan abounded with. Nu 13:23. Dt 8:8.
Egypt abounded with. Nu 20:5.
God's favor exhibited, in making fruitful. Hg 2:19.
ILLUSTRATIVE OF
   The church (as an orchard). S S 4:13.

The graces of the church (in its fruit). S S 4:3; 6:7.
   Saints. S S 6:11; 7:12.
THE JEWS
   Cultivated, in orchards. S S 4:13.
   Drank the juice of. S S 8:2.
   Often dwelt under shade of. 1 S 14:2.
REPRESENTATIONS OF ITS FRUIT
   On the high priest's robe. Ex 39:24–26.
   On the pillars of the temple. 1 K 7:18.

POOLS AND PONDS
ARTIFICIAL, DESIGNED FOR
   Preserving fish. Is 19:10.
   Supplying cities with water. 2 K 20:20.
   Supplying gardens, etc., with water. Ec 2:6.
Egypt abounded in. Ex 7:19.
Filled by the rain. Ps 84:6.
ILLUSTRATIVE OF
   The gifts of the Spirit (in the wilderness). Is 35:7; 41:18.
   Great desolation (turning cities into). Is 14:23.
   Nineveh. Na 2:8.
Made by God. Is 35:7.
Made by man. Is 19:10.
MENTIONED IN SCRIPTURE
   Bethesda. Jn 5:2.
   Gibeon. 2 S 2:13.
   Hebron. 2 S 4:12.
   The king's pool. Ne 2:14.
   The lower pool. Is 22:9.
   The old pool. Is 22:11.
   Samaria. 1 K 22:38.
   Siloam. Jn 9:7.
   The upper pool. 2 K 18:17. Is 7:3.
Water of, brought into the city by a ditch or conduit. Is 22:11, with 2 K 20:20.

THE POOR
CARE FOR
   A characteristic of saints. Ps 112:9, with 2 Co 9:9. Pr 29:7.
   A fruit of repentance. Lk 3:11.
   Illustrated. Lk 10:33–35.
   Should by urged. 2 Co 8:7–8. Gl 2:10.
Christ delivers. Ps 72:12.
Christ lived as one of. Mt 8:20.
Christ preached to. Lk 4:18.
CONDITION OF, OFTEN RESULTS FROM
   Bad company. Pr 28:19.
   Drunkenness and gluttony. Pr 23:21.
   Sloth. Pr 20:18.

Defend. Ps 82:3–4.
Despise not. Pr 14:21. Ja 2:2–4.
Do justice to. Ps 82:3. Jr 22:3, 16.
GIVE TO
  Cheerfully. 2 Co 8:12; 9:7.
  Liberally. Dt 14:29; 15:8, 11.
  Not grudgingly. Dt 15:10. 2 Co 9:7.
  Specially if saints. Ro 12:13. Gl 6:10.
  Without ostentation. Mt 6:1.
GOD
  Delivers. Jb 36:15. Ps 35:10.
  Despises not the prayer of. Ps 102:17.
  Exalts. 1 S 2:8. Ps 107:41.
  Forgets not. Ps 9:18.
  Hears. Ps 69:33. Is 41:17.
  Is reproached by mocking. Pr 17:5.
  Is reproached by oppressing. Pr 14:31.
  Is the refuge of. Ps 14:6.
  Maintains the right of. Ps 140:12.
  Protects. Pss 12:5; 109:31.
  Provides for. Pss 68:10; 146:7.
  Regards equally with the rich. Jb 34:19.
Guilt of defrauding. Ja 5:4.
Harden not the heart against. Dt 15:7.
Made by God. Jb 34:19. Pr 22:2.
MAY BE
  Liberal. Mk 12:42. 2 Co 8:2.
  Rich in faith. Ja 2:5.
  Upright. Pr 19:1.
  Wise. Pr 28:11.
NEGLECT TOWARD, IS
  Inconsistent with love to God. 1 Jn 3:17.
  A neglect of Christ. Mt 25:42–45.
  A proof of unbelief. Ja 2:15–17.
Offerings of, acceptable to God. Jk
  12:42–44. 2 Co 8:2, 12.
Oppression of, illustrated. 2 S 12:1–6.
Oppress not. Dt 24:14. Zc 7:10.
Pray for. Ps 74:19, 21.
Provided for under the law. Ex 23:11. Lv
  19:9–10.
PUNISHMENT FOR
  Acting unjustly toward. Jb 20:19, 29;
    22:6, 10. Is 10:1–3. Am 5:11–12.
  Oppressing. Pr 22:16. Ezk 22:29, 31.
  Refusing to assist. Jb 22:7, 10. Pr 21:13.
  Spoiling. Is 3:13–15. Ezk 18:13.
Relieve. Lv 25:35. Mt 19:21.
Rob not. Pr 22:22.
Rule not, with rigor. Lv 25:39, 43.
Shall never cease out of the land. Dt 15:11.
  Zp 3:12. Mt 26:11.
SHOULD
  Commit themselves to God. Ps 10:14.

Hope in God. Jb 5:16.
Rejoice in God. Is 29:19.
When converted, rejoice in their exaltation.
  Ja 1:9.
Shut not the hand against. Dt 15:7.
Such by God's appointment. 1 S 2:7. Jb
  1:21.
Take no usury from. Lv 25:36.
THEY WHO IN FAITH BELIEVE
  Are blessed. Dt 15:10. Ps 41:1. Pr 22:9.
    Ac 20:35.
  Are happy. Pr 14:21.
  Have promises. Pr 28:27. Lk 14:13–14.
  Have the favor of God. He 13:16.
THE WICKED
  Care not for. Jn 12:6.
  Crush. Am 4:1.
  Defraud. Am 8:5–6.
  Despise the counsel of. Ps 14:6.
  Devour. Hk 3:14.
  Grind the faces of. Is 3:15.
  Oppress. Jb 24:4–10. Ezk 18:12.
  Persecute. Ps 10:2.
  Regard not the cause of. Pr 29:7.
  Sell. Am 2:6.
  Tread down. Am 5:11.
  Vex. Ezk 22:20.
Wrong not in judgment. Ex 23:6.

POSSIBILITY
By faith. Mt 17:20; 19:26. Mk 9:23.
In anything. Ro 8:37–38. Ep 3:20.
In weakness. 2 Co 12:10. He 11:34.
Of strength. 2 Ch 32:7. Ps 27:1; 55:22.
Through Christ. Php 4:13. Ro 8:37.
With God. Jg 6:12. Mk 14:36.

POVERTY
See The Poor.

POWER OF CHRIST
Able to subdue all things. Php 3:21.
As man, from the Father. Ac 10:38.
As Son of God, the power of God. Jn
  5:17–19; 10:28–30.
DESCRIBED AS
  Everlasting. 1 Tm 6:16.
  Glorious. 2 Th 1:9.
  Over all flesh. Jn 17:2.
  Over all things. Jn 3:35. Ep 1:22.
  Supreme. Ep 1:20–21. 1 P 3:22.
  Unlimited. Mt 28:18.
EXHIBITED IN
  Creation. Jn 1:3, 10. Cl 1:16.

Destroying the works of Satan. 1 Jn 3:8.
Enabling others to work miracles. Mt 10:1. Mk 16:17–18. Lk 10:17.
Forgiving sins. Mt 9:6. Ac 5:31.
Giving eternal life. Jn 17:2.
Giving spiritual life. Jn 5:21, 25–26.
His teaching. Mt 7:28–29. Lk 4:32.
Overcoming Satan. Cl 2:15. He 2:14.
Overcoming the world. Jn 16:33.
Raising himself from the dead. Jn 2:19–21; 10:18.
Raising the dead. Jn 5:28–29.
Salvation. Is 63:1. He 7:25.
Upholding all things. Cl 1:17. He 1:3.
Working miracles. Mt 8:27. Lk 5:17.
Ministers should make known. 2 P 1:16.
Present in the assembly of saints. 1 Co 5:4.
Rests upon saints. 2 Co 12:9.
SAINTS
Bodies of, shall be changed by. Php 3:21.
Made willing by. Ps 110:3.
Preserved by. 2 Tm 1:12; 4:18.
Strengthened by. Php 4:13. Tm 4:17.
Succored by. He 2:18.
Shall be specially manifested at his second coming. Mk 13:26. 2 P 1:16.
Shall subdue all power. 1 Co 15:24.
The wicked shall be destroyed by. Ps 2:9. Is 11:4; 63:3. 2 Th 1:9.

POWER OF GOD
All things possible to. Mt 19:26.
Can save by many or by few. 1 S 14:6.
DESCRIBED AS
Effectual. Is 43:13. Ep 3:7.
Everlasting. Is 26:4. Ro 1:20.
Glorious. Ex 15:6. Is 63:12.
Great. Ps 79:11. Na 1:3.
Incomparable. Ex 15:11–12. Dt 3:24. Jb 40:9. Ps 89:8.
Incomprehensible. Jb 26:14. Ec 3:11.
Irresistible. Dt 32:39. Dn 4:35.
Mighty. Jb 9:4. Ps 89:13.
Sovereign. Ro 9:21.
Strong. Pss 89:13; 136:12.
Unsearchable. Jb 5:9; 9:10.
Efficiency of ministers is through. 1 Co 3:6–8. Gl 2:8. Ep 3:7.
Exerted in behalf of saints. 2 Ch 16:9.
EXHIBITED IN
Creation. Ps 102:25. Jr 10:12.
Delivering his people. Ps 106:8.
Destruction of the wicked. Ex 9:16. Ro 9:22.

Establishing and governing all things. Pss 65:6; 66:7.
Making the gospel effectual. Ro 1:16. 1 Co 1:18, 24.
Miracles of Christ. Lk 11:20.
Resurrection of Christ. 2 Co 13:4. Cl 2:12.
Resurrection of saints. 1 Co 6:14.
EXPRESSED BY THE
Arm of God. Jb 40:9. Is 52:10.
Finger of God. Ex 8:19. Ps 8:3.
Hand of God. Ex 9:3, 15. Is 48:13.
Thunder of his power, etc. Jb 26:14.
Voice of God. Pss 29:3, 5; 68:33.
The faith of saints stands in. 1 Co 2:5.
A ground of trust. Is 26:4. Ro 4:21.
The heavenly host magnify. Rv 4:11; 5:13; 11:17.
Nothing too hard for. Gn 18:14. Jr 32:27.
One of his attributes. Ps 62:11.
SAINTS
Delivered by. Ne 1:10. Dn 3:17.
Exalted by. Jb 36:22.
Have confidence in. Jr 20:11.
Kept by, unto salvation. 1 P 1:5.
Long for exhibitions of. Ps 63:1–2.
Receive increase of grace by. 2 Co 9:8.
Strengthened by. Ep 6:10. Cl 1:11.
Supported in affliction by. 2 Co 6:7. 2 Tm 1:8.
Upheld by. Ps 37:17. Is 41:10.
SHOULD BE
Acknowledged. 1 Ch 29:11. Is 33:13.
Feared. Jr 5:22. Mt 10:28.
Magnified. Ps 21:13. Jde 1:25.
Pleaded in prayer. Ps 79:11. Mt 6:13.
The source of all strength. 1 Ch 29:12. Ps 68:35.
THE WICKED
Have against them. Ezr 8:22.
Know not. Mt 22:29.
Shall be destroyed by. Lk 12:5.
Works in and for saints. 2 Co 13:4. Ep 1:19; 3:20.

POWER OF THE HOLY SPIRIT
Christ commenced his ministry in. Lk 4:14.
Christ wrought his miracles by. Mt 12:28.
EXHIBITED IN
The conception of Christ. Lk 1:35.
Creation. Gn 1:2. Jb 26:13. Ps 104:30.
Giving spiritual life. Ezk 37:11–14, with Ro 8:11.

Making the gospel efficacious. 1 Co 2:4. 1 Th 1:5.

Overcoming all difficulties. Zc 4:6–7.

Raising Christ from the dead. 1 P 3:18.

Working miracles. Ro 15:19.

God's word the instrument of. Ep 6:17.

The power of God. Mt 12:28, with Lk 11:20.

Promised by Christ. Ac 1:8.

Promised by the Father. Lk 24:49.

Qualifies ministers. Lk 24:49. Ac 1:8.

SAINTS

Abound in hope by. Ro 15:13.

Enabled to speak the truth boldly by. Mi 3:8. Ac 6:5, 10. 2 Tm 1:7–8.

Helped in prayer by. Ro 8:26.

Strengthened by. Ep 3:16.

Upheld by. Ps 51:12.

PRAISE

Acceptable through Christ. He 13:15.

Accompanied with musical instruments. 1 Ch 16:41–42. Ps 150:3, 5.

CALLED THE

Calves of the lips. Ho 14:2.

Fruit of the lips. He 13:15.

Garment of praise. Is 61:3.

Sacrifice of praise. He 13:15.

Sacrifices of joy. Ps 27:6.

Voice of melody. Is 51:3.

Voice of praise. Ps 66:8.

Voice of a psalm. Ps 98:5.

Voice of triumph. Ps 47:1.

Christ worthy of. Rv 5:12.

DUE TO GOD ON ACCOUNT OF

All spiritual blessings. Ps 103:2. Ep 1:3.

All temporal blessings. Pss 104:1, 14; 136:25.

Answering prayer. Pss 28:6; 118:21.

Constant preservation. Ps 71:6–8.

The continuance of blessings. Ps 68:19.

Deliverance. Pss 40:1–3; 124:6.

Fulfilling of his promises. 1 K 8:56.

His consolation. Ps 42:5. Is 12:1.

His counsel. Ps 16:7. Jr 32:19.

His excellency. Ex 15:7. Ps 148:13.

His faithfulness and truth. Is 25:1.

His glory. Ps 138:5. Ezk 3:12.

His goodness. Pss 107:8; 118:1; 136:1. Jr 33:11.

His greatness. 1 Ch 16:25. Ps 145:3.

His holiness. Ex 15:11. Is 6:3.

His judgment. Ps 101:1.

His loving-kindness and truth. Ps 138:2.

His majesty. Ps 96:1, 6. Is 24:14.

His mercy. 2 Ch 20:21. Pss 89:1; 118:1–4; 136.

His power. Ps 21:13.

His salvation. Ps 18:46. Is 35:10; 61:10. Lk 1:68–69.

His wisdom. Dn 2:20. Jde 1:25.

His wonderful works. Pss 89:5; 150:2. Is 25:1.

The hope of glory. 1 P 1:3–4.

Pardon of sin. Ps 103:1–3. Ho 14:2.

Protection. Pss 28:7; 59:17.

Spiritual health. Ps 103:3.

God glorified by. Pss 22:23; 50:23.

God worthy of. 2 S 22:4.

Good and comely. Pss 33:1; 147:1.

The heavenly host engage in. Is 6:3. Lk 2:13. Rv 4:9–11; 5:12.

OBLIGATORY UPON

All creation. Pss 148:1–10; 150:6.

All men. Pss 107:8; 145:21.

Angels. Pss 103:20; 148:2.

Children. Ps 8:2, with Mt 21:16.

Gentiles. Ps 117:1, with Ro 15:11.

High and low. Ps 148:1, 11.

Saints. Pss 30:4; 149:5.

Small and great. Rv 19:5.

Young and old. Ps 148:1, 12.

Offered to Christ. Jn 12:13.

A part of public worship. Pss 9:14; 100:4; 118:19–20. He 2:12.

Posture suited to. 1 Ch 23:30. Ne 9:5.

SAINTS SHOULD

Be endowed with the spirit of. Is 61:3.

Declare. Is 42:12.

Express their joy by. Ja 5:13.

Glory in. 1 Ch 16:35.

Invite others to. Pss 34:3; 95:1.

Pray for ability to offer. Pss 51:15; 119:175.

Render, under affliction. Ac 16:25.

Show forth. Is 43:21. 1 P 2:9.

Triumph in. Ps 106:47.

SHOULD BE OFFERED

Continually. Pss 35:28; 71:6.

Day and night. Rv 4:8.

Day by day. 2 Ch 30:21.

During life. Ps 104:33.

Forever and ever. Ps 145:1–2.

In psalms and hymns, etc. Ps 105:2. Ep 5:19. Cl 3:16.

More and more. Ps 71:14.

Throughout the world. Ps 113:3.

With gladness. 2 Ch 29:30. Jr 33:11.

With joy. Pss 63:5; 98:4.

With the lips.   Pss 63:3; 119:171.
With the mouth.   Pss 51:15; 63:5.
With the soul.   Pss 103:1; 104:1, 35.
With thankfulness.   1 Ch 16:4. Ne 12:24.
Ps 147:7.
With the understanding.   Ps 47:7, with 1
Co 14:15.
With the whole heart.   Pss 9:1; 111:1;
138:1.
With uprightness of heart.   Ps 119:7.

PRAYER

Acceptable through Christ.   Jn 14:13–14;
15:16; 16:23–24.
ACCOMPANIED WITH
Confession.   Ne 1:4, 7. Dn 9:4–11.
Fasting.   Ne 1:4. Dn 9:3. Ac 13:3.
Praise.   Ps 66:17.
Repentance.   1 K 8:33. Jr 36:7.
Self-abasement.   Gn 18:27.
Thanksgiving.   Php 4:6. Cl 4:2.
Watchfulness.   Lk 21:36. 1 P 4:7.
Weeping.   Jr 31:9. Ho 12:4.
Ascends to heaven.   2 Ch 30:27. Rv 5:8.
Avoid hindrances in.   1 P 3:7.
Commanded.   Is 55:6. Mt 7:7. Php 4:6.
DESCRIBED AS
Beseeching the Lord.   Ex 32:11.
Bowing the knees.   Ep 3:14.
Calling upon the name of the Lord.   Gn
12:8. Ps 116:4. Ac 22:16.
Crying to heaven.   2 Ch 32:20.
Crying unto God.   Pss 27:7; 34:6.
Drawing near to God.   Ps 73:28. He
10:22.
Lifting up the heart.   Lm 3:41.
Lifting up the soul.   Ps 25:1.
Looking up.   Ps 5:3.
Making supplication.   Jb 8:5. Jr 36:7.
Pouring out the heart.   Ps 62:8.
Pouring out the soul.   1 S 1:15.
Seeking the face of the Lord.   Ps 27:8.
Seeking unto God.   Jb 8:5.
An evidence of conversion.   Ac 9:11.
Experience of past mercies an incentive to.
Pss 4:1; 116:2.
Faint not in.   Lk 18:1.
For mercy and grace to help in time of need.
He 4:16.
For spiritual blessings.   Mt 6:33.
For temporal blessings.   Gn 28:20. Pr 30:8.
Mt 6:11.
God hears.   Pss 10:17; 65:2.
God responds.   Ps 99:6. Is 58:9.

THE HOLY SPIRIT
As the spirit of adoption, leads to.   Ro
8:15. Gl 4:6.
Helps our infirmities in.   Ro 8:26.
Promised as a spirit of.   Zc 12:10.
Model for.   Mt 6:9–13.
Of the righteous, avails much.   Ja 5:16.
Of the upright, a delight to God.   Pr 15:8.
Ostentation in, forbidden.   Mt 6:5.
PLEAD IN THE
Covenant of God.   Jr 14:21.
Faithfulness of God.   Ps 143:1.
Mercy of God.   Ps 51:1. Dn 9:18.
Promises of God.   Gn 32:9–12. Ex 32:13.
1 K 8:26. Ps 119:49.
Righteousness of God.   Dn 9:16.
POSTURES IN
Bowing down.   Ps 95:6.
Falling on the face.   Nu 16:22. Jsh 5:14.
1 Ch 21:16. Mt 26:39.
Kneeling.   2 Ch 6:13. Ps 95:6. Lk 22:41.
Ac 20:36.
Lifting up the hands.   Ps 28:2. Lm 2:19. 1
Tm 2:8.
Spreading forth the hands.   Is 1:15.
Standing.   1 K 8:22. Mk 11:25.
SHOULD BE OFFERED UP
Everywhere.   1 Tm 2:8.
In everything.   Php 4:6.
In faith.   Mt 21:22. Ja 1:6.
In a forgiving spirit.   Mt 6:12.
In full assurance of faith.   He 10:22.
In the Holy Ghost.   Ep 6:18. Jde 1:20.
Night and day.   1 Tm 5:5.
With boldness.   He 4:16.
With confidence in God.   Pss 56:9; 86:7.
1 Jn 5:14.
With deliberation.   Ec 5:2.
With desire to be answered.   Pss 27:7;
102:2; 108:6; 143:1.
With desire to be heard.   Ne 1:6. Pss
17:1; 55:1–2; 61:1.
With earnestness.   1 Th 3:10. Ja 5:17.
With the heart.   Jr 29:13. Lm 3:41.
With holiness.   1 Tm 2:8.
With humility.   2 Ch 7:14; 33:12.
With importunity.   Gn 32:26. Lk 11:8–9;
18:1–7.
With preparation of heart.   Jb 11:13.
With the soul.   Ps 42:4.
With the spirit and understanding.   Jn 4
22–24. 1 Co 14:15.
With submission to God.   Lk 22:42.
With a true heart.   He 10:22.

With truth. Ps 145:18. Jn 4:24.
With unfeigned lips. Ps 17:1.
With the whole heart. Ps 119:58, 145,
Without ceasing. 1 Th 5:17.
Promises of Christ encourage to. Lk 11:9–10. Jn 14:13–14.
Promises of God encourage to. Is 65:24. Am 5:4. Zc 13:9.
Quickening grace necessary to. Ps 80:18.
Rise early for. Pss 5:3; 119:147.
Seek divine teaching for. Lk 11:1.
Shortness of time a motive to. 1 P 4:7.
To BE OFFERED
    Through Christ. Ep 2:18. He 10:19.
    To Christ. Lk 23:42. Ac 7:59.
    To God. Ps 5:2. Mt 4:10.
    To the Holy Ghost. 2 Th 3:5.
Vain repetitions in, forbidden. Mt 6:5.

PRAYER, ANSWERS TO
Christ gives. Jn 4:10, 14; 14:14.
Christ received. Jn 11:42. He 5:7.
DENIED THOSE WHO
    Are blood-shedders. Is 1:15; 59:3.
    Are deaf to the cry of the poor. Pr 21:13.
    Are the enemies of saints. Ps 18:40–41.
    Are hypocrites. Jb 27:8–9.
    Are idolaters. Jr 11:11–14. Ezk 8:15–18.
    Are proud. Jb 35:12–13.
    Are self-righteous. Lk 18:11–12, 14.
    Are wavering. Ja 1:6–7.
    Ask amiss. Ja 4:3.
    Cruelly oppress saints. Mi 3:2–4.
    Forsake God. Jr 14:10, 12.
    Hear not the law. Pr 28:9. Zc 7:11–13.
    Live in sin. Is 59:2. Jn 9:31.
    Offer unworthy service to God. Ml 1:7–9,
    Regard iniquity in the heart. Ps 66:18.
    Reject the call of God. Pr 1:24–25, 28.
God gives. Pss 99:6; 118:5; 138:3.
GRANTED
    Beyond expectation. Jr 33:3. Ep 3:20.
    Sometimes after delay. Lk 18:7.
    Sometimes differently from our desire. 2 Co 12:8–9.
    Sometimes immediately. Is 65:24. Dn 9:21, 23; 10:12.
    Through the grace of God. Is 30:19.
A motive for continued prayer. Ps 116:2.
Promised. Is 58:9. Jr 29:12. Mt 7:7.
Promised especially in times of trouble. Pss 50:15; 91:15.
RECEIVED BY THOSE WHO
    Abide in Christ. Jn 15:7.

    Are poor and needy. Is 41:17.
    Are righteous. Ps 34:15. Ja 5:16.
    Ask according to God's will. 1 Jn 5:14.
    Ask in faith. Mt 21:22. Ja 5:15.
    Ask in the name of Christ. Jn 14:13.
    Call upon God in truth. Ps 145:18.
    Call upon God under affliction. Pss 18:6; 106:44. Is 30:19–20.
    Call upon God under oppression. Is 19:20.
    Fear God. Ps 145:19.
    Humble themselves. 2 Ch 7:14. Ps 9:12.
    Keep God's commandments. 1 Jn 3:22.
    Return to God. 2 Ch 7:14. Jb 22:23, 27.
    Seek God. Ps 34:4.
    Seek God with all the heart. Jr 29:12–13.
    Set their love upon God. Ps 91:14–15.
    Wait upon God. Ps 40:1.
SAINTS
    Are assured of. 1 Jn 5:15.
    Bless God for. Ps 66:20.
    Love God for. Ps 116:1.
    Praise God for. Pss 116:17; 118:21.

PRAYER, INTERCESSORY
Beneficial to the offerer. Jb 42:10.
By ministers for their people. Ep 1:16; 3:14–19. Php 1:4.
Christ set an example of. Lk 22:32; 23:34. Jn 17:9–24.
Commanded. 1 Tm 2:1. Ja 5:14, 16.
Encouragement to. Ja 5:16. 1 Jn 5:16.
Seek an interest in. 1 S 12:19. He 13:18.
SHOULD BE OFFERED UP FOR
    All in authority. 1 Tm 2:2.
    All men. 1 Tm 2:1.
    All saints. Ep 6:18.
    Children. Gn 17:18. Mt 15:22.
    The church. Ps 122:6. Is 62:6–7.
    Enemies among whom we dwell. Jr 29:7.
    Fellow countrymen. Ro 10:1.
    Friends. Jb 42:8.
    Kings. 1 Tm 2:2.
    Masters. Gn 24:12–14.
    Ministers. 2 Co 1:11. Php 1:19.
    Persecutors. Mt 5:44.
    Servants. Lk 7:2–3.
    The sick. Ja 5:14.
    Those who envy us. Nu 12:13.
    Those who forsake us. 2 Tm 4:16.
    Those who murmur against God. Nu 11:1–2; 14:13, 19.
Sin of neglecting. 1 S 12:23.

Unavailing for the obstinately impenitent.   Jr
7:13–16; 14:10–11.

PRAYER, PRIVATE
Christ was constant in.   Mt 14:23; 26:36, 39.
Mk 1:35. Lk 9:18, 29.
Commanded.   Mt 6:6.
An evidence of conversion.   Ac 9:11.
Nothing should hinder.   Dn 6:10.
Rewarded openly.   Mt 6:6.
Shall be heard.   Jb 22:27.
SHOULD BE OFFERED
Day and night.   Ps 88:1.
Evening, morning, and noon.   Ps 55:17.
Without ceasing.   1 Th 5:17.

PRAYER, PUBLIC
Acceptable to God.   Is 56:7.
CHRIST
Attended. Mt 12:9.   Lk 4:16.
Promises answers to.   Mt 18:19.
Sanctifies by his presence.   Mt 18:20.
Exhortation to.   He 10:25.
God promises to bless in.   Ex 20:24.
God promises to hear.   2 Ch 7:14, 16.
Instituted form of.   Lk 11:2.
Saints delight in.   Pss 42:4; 122:1.
Should not be made in an unknown tongue.
1 Co 14:14–16.
Urge others to join in.   Ps 95:6. Zc 8:21.

PRAYER, SOCIAL AND FAMILY
Christ promises to be present at.   Mt 18:20.
Promise of answers to.   Mt 18:19.
Punishment for neglecting.   Jr 10:25.

PREACHING
PURPOSE OF
Convince, reprove, exhort, teach.   2 Tm
4:2.
Encourage, comfort, do people good.   1
Co 14:3.
RESULTS OF
Believers are built up through.   1 Co 14:3.
Ep 4:12.
Some consider foolishness.   1 Co 1:18–21.
Some find life through.   Lk 11:32; 8:15. 1
Co 3:6–23.
Some postpone a decision.   Ac 17:32;
26:28.
Some reject outright.   2 P 2:4–5.
SUBJECT OF
Christ's cross.   1 Co 1:18, 23.
Christ's resurrection.   Ac 17:18.

Forgiveness.   Ac 13:38.
God's kingdom.   Lk 9:2, 60.
Good news or gospel.   Lk 4:18, 43. Ro
1:15. 1 Co 1:17. Ep 1:3.
Jesus Christ.   1 Co 1:23. 2 Co 4:5.
Peace.   Ac 10:36.
Repentance.   Mk 1:15.
Righteousness of life.   2 P 2:5. Ac 24:25.
1 Tm 4:11—6:5.
The unsearchable riches of Christ.   Ep
3:8.
The word of faith.   Ro 10:8.
The word of God.   2 Tm 4:2. He 4:2.

PRECIOUSNESS OF CHRIST
As the cornerstone of the church.   Is 28:16,
with 1 P 2:6.
As the source of all grace.   Jn 1:14. Cl 1:19.
Illustrated.   S S 2:3; 5:10–16. Mt 13:44–46.
ON ACCOUNT OF HIS
Atonement.   1 P 1:19, with He 12:24.
Care and tenderness.   Is 40:11.
Excellence and grace.   Ps 45:2.
Goodness and beauty.   Zc 9:17.
Name.   S S 1:3. He 1:4.
Promises.   2 P 1:4.
Words.   Jn 6:68.
To God.   Mt 3:17. 1 P 2:4.
To saints.   S S 5:10. Php 3:8. 1 P 2:7.
Unsearchable.   Ep 3:8.

PREJUDICE
Christ condemned for not having.   Mt 9:11.
Christ rejected through.   Lk 4:24. Jn 1:46;
7:52.
Condemned.   Pr 28:21. Ja 2:3–4, 9.
God's lack of.   Jb 13:10. Ac 10:34. Ep 6:9.

PREPARATION
IN GOD'S PLAN
For deliverance of the Israelites from Egypt.
Gn 2:1—4:31.
For our future.   Jn 14:2. 1 Co 2:9–10.
For the ministry of Christ.   Lk 4:1–15.
For the work of Christ.   Ml 3:1. Lk 1:76;
3:1–17.
IN OUR LIVES
For the Lord's coming.   Lk 12:35–36.
To do good works.   Ti 3:1.
To seek the Lord.   Ho 10:12.

PRESENCE
OF CHRIST
In all things.   Ro 8:35–38.

In our hearts. Ep 3:17.
In our suffering. 2 Co 1:5. Php 3:10.
When two or three worship. Mt 18:20.
With his disciples. Mt 28:20.

OF GOD
Demands thanksgiving. Ps 95:2.
Forever. He 13:5.
In Eden. Gn 3:8.
In our trials. Is 43:2.
Source of help. Ps 46:5.
Source of joy. Ps 16:11.
With his people. Ex 33:14. Jsh 3:10.

PRESENTS
Antiquity of. Gn 32:13; 43:15.
Considered essential on all visits of business.
1 S 9:7.
Generally presented in person. Gn 43:15, 26.
Jg 3:17. 1 S 25:27.
Generally procured a favorable reception. Pr
18:16; 19:6.

GIVEN
As tribute. Jg 3:15. 2 S 8:2. 2 Ch 17:5.
At marriages. Gn 24:53. Ps 45:12.
By kings to each other in token of inferi-
ority. 1 K 10:25. 2 Ch 9:23–24. Ps
72:10.
In token of friendship. 1 S 18:3–4.
On all occasions of public rejoicing. Ne
8:12. Es 9:19.
On occasions of visits. 2 K 8:8.
On recovering from sickness. 2 K 20:12.
On restoration to prosperity. Jb 42:10–11.
On sending away friends. Gn 45:22. Jr
40:5.
To appease the angry feelings of others.
Gn 32:20. 1 S 25:27–28, 35.
To confirm covenants. Gn 21:28–30.
To judges to secure a favorable hearing. Pr
17:23. Am 2:6.
To kings to engage their aid. 1 K 15:18.
To reward service. 2 S 18:12. Dn 2:6, 48.
To show respect. Jg 6:18.
Laid out and presented with great ceremony.
Gn 43:25. Jg 3:18. Mt 2:11.
Not bringing, considered a mark of disrespect
and disaffection. 1 S 10:27. 2 K 17:4.
Of persons of rank, of great value and variety.
2 K 5:5. 2 Ch 9:1.
Often borne by servants. Jg 3:18.
Often conveyed on camels, etc. 1 S 25:18. 2
K 8:9. 2 Ch 9:1.
Receiving of, a token of good will. Gn
33:10–11.

Sometimes sent before the giver. Gn 32:21.
THINGS GIVEN AS
Cattle. Gn 32:14–15, 18.
Eatables. Gn 43:11. 1 S 25:18. 1 K 14:3.
Garments. Gn 45:22. 1 S 18:4.
Gold and silver vessels. 1 K 10:25.
Horses and mules. 1 K 10:25.
Money. Gn 45:22. 1 S 9:8. Jb 42:11.
Ornaments. Gn 24:22, 47. Jb 42:11.
Precious stones. 1 K 10:2.
Servants. Gn 20:14; 29:24, 29.
Weapons of war. 1 S 18:4.
When small or defective, refused. Ml 1:8.

PRESUMPTION
A characteristic of antichrist. 2 Th 2:4.
A characteristic of the wicked. 2 P 2:10.
EXHIBITED IN
Esteeming our own ways right. Pr 12:15.
Opposing God. Jb 15:25–26.
Planning for futurity. Lk 12:18. Ja 4:13.
Pretending to prophecy. Dt 18:22.
Seeking precedence. Lk 14:7–11.
Self-righteousness. Ho 12:8. Rv 3:17.
Spiritual pride. Is 65:5. Lk 18:11.
Willful commission of sin. Ro 1:32.
Pray to be kept from sins of. Ps 19:13.
Punishment for. Nu 15:30. Rv 18:7–8.
Saints avoid. Ps 131:1.

PRIDE
A CHARACTERISTIC OF
The devil. 1 Tm 3:6.
False teachers. 1 Tm 6:3–4.
The wicked. Hk 2:4–5. Ro 1:30.
The world. 1 Jn 2:16.
Comes from the heart. Mk 7:21–23.
Defiles a man. Mk 7:20, 22.
Exhortation against. Jr 13:15.
FOLLOWED BY
Debasement. Pr 29:23. Is 28:3.
Destruction. Pr 16:18; 18:12.
Shame. Pr 11:2.
Forbidden. 1 S 2:3. Ro 12:3, 16.
Hardens the mind. Dn 5:20.
Hateful to Christ. Pr 8:12–13.
Hateful to God. Pr 6:16–17; 15:5.
A hindrance to improvement. Pr 26:12.
A hindrance to seeking God. Ps 10:4. Ho
7:10.
LEADS MEN TO
Contempt and rejection of God's word and
ministers. Jr 43:2.
Contention. Pr 13:10; 28:25.

A persecuting spirit. Ps 10:2.
Self-deception. Jr 49:16. Ob 1:3.
Wrath. Pr 21:24.

OFTEN ORIGINATES IN
Inexperience. 1 Tm 3:6.
Possession of power. Lv 26:19. Ezk 30:6.
Possession of wealth. 2 K 20:13.
Religious privileges. Zp 3:11.
Self-righteousness. Lk 18:11–12.
Unsanctified knowledge. 1 Co 8:1.

SAINTS
Give not way to. Ps 131:1.
Hate, in others. Ps 101:5.
Mourn over, in others. Jr 13:17.
Respect not, in others. Ps 40:4.
Shall abound in the last days. 2 Tm 3:2.
A sin. Pr 21:4.

THEY WHO ARE GUILTY OF, SHALL BE
Abased. Dn 4:37, with Mt 23:12.
Brought into contempt. Is 23:9.
Brought low. Ps 18:27. Is 2:12.
Marred. Jr 13:9.
Punished. Zp 2:10–11. Ml 4:1.
Recompensed. Ps 31:23.
Resisted. Ja 4:6.
Scattered. Lk 1:51.
Subdued. Ex 18:11. Is 13:11.
The wicked encompassed with. Ps 73:6.
Woe to. Is 23:1, 3.

PRIESTS

After the exodus, young men (first-born)
deputed to act as. Ex 24:5, with 19:22.
All except seed of Aaron excluded from being.
Nu 3:10; 16:40; 18:7.

CEREMONIES AT CONSECRATION OF
Anointing with oil. Ex 30:30; 40:13.
Clothing with the holy garments. Ex
29:8–9; 40:14. Lv 8:13.
Lasted seven days. Ex 29:35–37. Lv 8:33.
Offering sacrifices. Ex 29:10–19. Lv
8:14–23.
Partaking of the sacrifices of consecration.
Ex 29:31–33. Lv 8:31–32.
Placing in their hands the wave-offering.
Ex 29:22–24. Lv 8:25–26.
Purification by blood of the consecration
ram. Ex 29:20–21. Lv 8:23–24.
Washing in water. Ex 29:4. Lv 8:6.
Divided by David into twenty-four courses. 1
Ch 24:1–19. 2 Ch 8:14; 35:4–5.
During patriarchal age heads of families acted
as. Gn 8:20; 12:8; 35:7.

Each course of, had its president or chief. 1
Ch 24:6, 31. 2 Ch 36:14.
First notice of persons acting as. Gn 4:3–4.
The four courses which returned from Babylon
subdivided into twenty-four. Ezr 2:36–39,
with Lk 1:5.

GARMENTS OF
Bonnet. Ex 28:40; 39:28.
Coat or tunic. Ex 28:40; 39:27.
Girdle. Ex 28:40.
Laid up in holy chambers. Ezk 44:19.
Linen breeches. Ex 28:42; 39:28.
Often provided by the people. Ezr
2:68–69. Ne 7:70, 72.
Purified by sprinkling of blood. Ex 29:21.
Worn always while engaged in the service of
the tabernacle. Ex 28:43; 39:41.
Worn at consecration. Ex 29:9; 40:15.
Worn by the high priest on the day of
atonement. Lv 16:4.
Generally participated in punishment of the
people. Jr 14:18. Lm 2:20.

ILLUSTRATIVE OF
Christ. He 10:11–12.
Saints. Ex 19:6. 1 P 2:9.
Made of the lowest of the people by Jeroboam
and others. 1 K 12:31. 2 K 17:32.
Might purchase and hold other lands in posses-
sion. 1 K 2:26. Jr 32:8–9.
No blemished or defective persons could be
consecrated. Lv 21:17–23.
On special occasions, persons not of Aaron's
family acted as. Jg 6:24–27. 1 S 7:9. 1 K
18:33.
Publicly consecrated. Ex 28:3. Nu 3:3.
Punishment for invading the office of. Nu
16:1–35; 18:7. 2 Ch 36:14.

REQUIRED TO
Prove their genealogy before they exercised
the office. Ezr 2:62. Ne 7:64.
Remain in the tabernacle seven days after
consecration. Lv 8:33–36.
Wash in the bronze laver before they performed their services. Ex 30:18–21.

REVENUES OF
All devoted things. Nu 18:14.
All restitutions when the owner could not
be found. Nu 5:8.
First-born of animals or their substitutes.
Nu 18:17–18, with Ex 13:12–13.
First fruits. Nu 18:8, 12–13. Dt 18:4.
First of the wool of sheep. Dt 18:4.
A fixed portion of the spoil taken in war.
Nu 31:29, 41.

Part of all sacrifices. Lv 6:6–10, 31–34. Nu 6:19–20; 18:8–11. Dt 18:3.

Redemption money of the first-born. Nu 3:48, 51; 18:15–16.

Showbread after its removal. Lv 24:9. 1 S 21:4–6. Mt 12:4.

Tenth of the tithes paid to the Levites. Nu 18:26, 28. Ne 10:37–38. He 7:5.

Sanctified by God for the office. Ex 29:44.

SERVICES OF

Blessing the people. Nu 6:23–27.

Blowing the trumpets on various occasions. Nu 10:1–10. Jsh 6:3–4.

Burning incense. Ex 30:7–8. Lk 1:9.

Carrying the ark. Jsh 3:6, 17; 6:12.

Covering the sacred things of the sanctuary before removal. Nu 4:5–15.

Deciding in cases of jealousy. Nu 5:14–15.

Deciding in cases of leprosy. Lv 13:2–59; 14:34–45.

Divided by lot. Lk 1:9.

Encouraging the people when they went to war. Dt 20:1–4.

Ineffectual for removing sin. He 7:11; 10:11.

Judging in cases of controversy. Dt 17:8–13; 21:5.

Keeping the charge of the tabernacle, etc. Nu 18:1, 5, 7.

Keeping the sacred fire always burning on the altar. Lv 6:12–13.

Lighting and trimming the lamps of the sanctuary. Ex 27:20–21. Lv 24:3–4.

Offering first fruits. Lv 23:10–11. Dt 26:3–4.

Offering sacrifices. Lv 1—6. 2 Ch 29:34; 35:11.

Placing and removing showbread. Lv 24:5–9.

Purifying the unclean. Lv 15:30–31.

Teaching the law. Dt 33:8, 10. Ml 2:7.

Valuing things devoted. Lv 27:8.

Sons of Aaron appointed as, by perpetual statute. Ex 29:9; 40:15.

SPECIAL LAWS RESPECTING

All bought and home-born servants to eat of their portion. Lv 22:11.

Children of, married to strangers, not to eat of their portion. Lv 22:12.

No sojourner or hired servant to eat of their portion. Lv 22:10.

Not to defile themselves by eating what died or was torn. Lv 22:8.

Not to defile themselves for the dead except the nearest of kin. Lv 21:1–6.

Not to drink wine, etc., while attending in the tabernacle. Lv 10:9. Ezk 44:21.

Not to marry divorced or improper persons. Lv 21:7.

Restitution to be made to, by persons ignorantly eating of their holy things. Lv 22:14–16.

While unclean could not eat of the holy things. Lv 22:3–7.

While unclean could not perform any service. Lv 22:1, 2, with Nu 19:6–7.

Thirteen of the Levitical cities given to, for residence. 1 Ch 6:57–60, with Nu 35:1–8.

WERE SOMETIMES

Corrupters of the law. Is 28:7, with Ml 2:8.

Drunken. Is 28:7.

Greedy. 1 S 2:13–17.

Profane and wicked. 1 S 2:22–24.

Slow to sanctify themselves for God's service. 2 Ch 29:34.

Unjust. Jr 6:13.

Were to live by the altar, as they had no inheritance. Dt 18:1–2. 1 Co 9:13.

PRISONS

Antiquity of. Gn 39:20.

Confinement in, often awarded as a punishment. Ezr 7:26.

Confinement in, considered a severe punishment. Lk 22:33.

Dungeons attached to. Jr 38:6. Zc 9:11.

ILLUSTRATIVE OF

Bondage to sin and Satan. Is 42:7; 49:9; 61:1.

Deep afflictions. Ps 142:7.

Hell. Rv 20:7.

KEEPERS OF

Often used severity. Jr 37:16, 20. Ac 16:24.

Put to death if prisoners escaped. Ac 12:19.

Responsible for the prisoners. Ac 16:23, 27.

Sometimes acted kindly. Gn 39:21. Ac 16:33–34.

Sometimes entrusted the care of the prison to well-conducted prisoners. Gn 39:22–23.

Strictly guarded the doors. Ac 12:6.

KINDS OF, MENTIONED

Common. Ac 5:18.

State. Jr 37:21, with Gn 39:20.

The king had power to commit to. 1 K 22:27.

The king had power to release from. Gn 40:21.

Magistrates had power to commit to. Mt 5:25.

Magistrates had power to release from. Ac 16:35–36.

PERSONS CONFINED IN

Clothed in prison dress. 2 K 25:29.

Fed on bread and water. 1 K 22:27.

Might have their condition ameliorated by the king. Jr 37:20–21.

Often bound with fetters. Gn 42:19. Ezk 19:9. Mk 6:17.

Often chained to two soldiers. Ac 12:6.

Often executed in. Gn 40:22. Mt 14:10.

Often fastened in stocks. Jr 29:26. Ac 16:24.

Often kept to hard labor. Jg 16:21.

Often placed in dungeons. Jr 38:6. Ac 16:24.

Often subjected to extreme suffering. Pss 79:11; 102:20; 105:18.

Said to be in hold. Ac 4:3.

Said to be in ward. Lv 24:12.

Sometimes allowed to be visited by their friends. Mt 11:2; 25:36. Ac 24:23.

PLACES USED AS

Court of the king's house. Jr 32:2.

House of the captain of the guard. Gn 40:3.

House of the king's scribe. Jr 37:15.

Prisoner's own house, where he was kept bound to a soldier. Ac 28:16, 30, with 2 Tm 1:16–18.

Under the care of a keeper. Gn 39:21.

USED FOR CONFINING

Condemned criminals till executed. Lv 24:12. Ac 12:4–5.

Debtors till they paid. Mt 5:26; 18:30.

Enemies taken captive. Jg 16:21. 2 K 17:4. Jr 52:11.

Persons accused of crimes. Lk 23:19.

Persons accused of heresy. Ac 4:3; 5:18; 8:3.

Persons under the king's displeasure. 1 K 22:27. 2 Ch 16:10. Mk 6:17.

Suspected persons. Gn 42:19.

PRIVILEGES OF SAINTS

Abiding in Christ. Jn 15:4–5.

Access to God by Christ. Ep 3:12.

All things working together for their good. Ro 8:28. 2 Co 4:15–17.

Being of the household of God. Ep 2:19.

Calling upon God in trouble. Ps 50:15.

Committing themselves to God. Ps 31:5. Ac 7:59. 2 Tm 1:12.

HAVING

Christ for their intercessor. Ro 8:34. He 7:25. 1 Jn 2:1.

Christ for their shepherd. Is 40:11, with Jn 10:14, 16.

The promises of God. 2 Co 7:1. 2 P 1:4.

HAVING GOD FOR THEIR

Deliverer. 2 S 22:2. Ps 18:2.

Father. Dt 32:6. Is 63:16; 64:8.

Friend. 2 Ch 20:7, with Ja 2:23.

Glory. Ps 3:3. Is 60:19.

Guide. Ps 48:14. Is 58:11.

Habitation. Pss 90:1; 91:9.

Helper. Ps 33:20. He 13:6.

Keeper. Ps 121:4–5.

King. Pss 5:2; 41:4. Is 44:6.

Lawgiver. Ne 9:13–14. Is 33:22.

Light. Ps 27:1. Is 60:19. Mi 7:8.

Portion. Ps 73:26. Lm 3:24.

Redeemer. Ps 19:14. Is 43:14.

Refuge. Ps 46:1, 11. Is 25:4.

Salvation. Pss 18:2; 27:1. Is 12:2.

Shield. Gn 15:1. Ps 84:11.

Strength. Pss 18:2; 27:1; 46:1.

Tower. 2 S 22:3. Ps 61:3.

Interceding for others. Gn 18:23–33. Ja 5:16.

Membership with the church of the first-born. He 12:23.

Partaking of the divine nature. 2 P 1:4.

Possession of all things. 1 Co 3:21–22.

Profiting by chastisement. Ps 119:67. He 12:10–11.

Secure during public calamities. Jb 5:20, 23. Pss 27:1–5; 91:5–10.

Suffering for Christ. Ac 5:41. Php 1:29.

Their names written in the book of life. Rv 13:8; 20:15.

Union in God and Christ. Jn 17:21.

PROCRASTINATION

Condemned by Christ. Lk 9:59–62.

Danger of, illustrated. Mt 5:25. Lk 13:25.

MOTIVES FOR AVOIDING

The present the accepted time. 2 Co 6:2.

The present the best time. Ec 12:1.

The uncertainty of life. Pr 27:1.

Saints avoid. Pss 27:8; 119:60.

To Be Avoided in
Glorifying God. Jr 13:16.
Hearkening to God. Ps 95:7–8, with He 3:7–8.
Keeping God's commandments. Ps 119:60.
Making offerings to God. Ex 22:29.
Performance of vows. Dt 23:21. Ec 5:4.
Seeking God. Is 55:6

PROFITABLE THINGS
God's chastening. He 12:10.
Doing God's will. Ti 3:8
Godliness. 1 Tm 4:8; 6:6.
Labor. Pr 14:23.
Scripture. 2 Tm 3:16.
Wisdom. Jb 22:2.

PROMISES OF GOD
Are
Confirmed by an oath. Ps 89:3–4. He 6:17.
Confirmed in Christ. Ro 15:8.
Contained in the scriptures. Ro 1:2.
Exceeding great and precious. 2 P 1:4.
Fulfilled in Christ. 2 S 7, 12, with Ac 13:23. Lk 1:69–73
Given to those who believe. Gl 3:22.
Good. 1 K 8:56.
Holy. Ps 105:42.
Inherited through faith and patience. He 6:12, 15; 10:36.
Made in Christ. Ep 3:6. 2 Tm 1:1.
Obtained through faith. He 11:33.
Performed in due season. Jr 33:14. Ac 7:17. Gl 4:4.
Through the righteousness of faith. Ro 4:13, 16.
Yea and amen in Christ. 2 Co 1:20.
The covenant established upon. He 8:6.
Fear, lest ye come short of. He 4:1.
Gentiles shall be partakers of. Ep 3:6.
God faithful to. Ti 1:2. He 10:23.
God remembers. Ps 105:42. Lk 1:54–55.
Inheritance of the saints is. Ro 4:13. Gl 3:18.
The law could not annul. Gl 3:17.
The law not against. Gl 3:21.
Made to
Abraham. Gn 12:3, 7, with Gl 3:16.
All who are called of God. Ac 2:39.
Christ. Gl 3:16, 19.
David. 2 S 7:12. Ps 89:3–4, 35–36.
The fathers. Ac 13:32. Ac 26:6–7.

Isaac. Gn 26:3–4.
The Israelites. Ro 9:4.
Jacob. Gn 28:14.
Those who love him. Ja 1:12; 2:5.
Man, by nature, has no interest in. Ep 2:12.
Not one shall fail. Jsh 23:14. 1 K 8:56.
Saints
Children of. Ro 9:8. Gl 4:28.
Expect the performance of. Lk 1:38, 45. 2 P 3:13.
Have implicit confidence in. He 11:11.
Heirs of. Gl 3:29. He 6:17; 11:9.
Plead, in prayer. Gn 32:9, 12. 1 Ch 17:23, 26. Is 43:26.
Sometimes, through infirmity, tempted to doubt. Ps 77:8, 10.
Stagger not at. Ro 4:20.
Scoffers despise. 2 P 3:3–4.
Should lead to perfecting holiness. 2 Co 7:1.
Should wait for the performance of. Ac 1:4.
Subjects of
Adoption. 2 Co 6:18, with 7:1.
Blessing. Dt 1:11.
Christ. 2 S 7:12–13, with Ac 13:22–23.
A crown of life. Ja 1:12.
Entering into rest. Jsh 22:4, with He 4:1.
Eternal life. Ti 1:2. 1 Jn 2:25.
Forgiveness of sins. Is 1:18. He 8:12.
The gospel. Ro 1:1–2.
The Holy Spirit. Ac 2:33. Ep 1:13.
Life in Christ. 2 Tm 1:1.
The life that now is. 1 Tm 4:8.
New heavens and earth. 2 P 3:13.
Preservation in affliction. Is 43:2.
Putting the law into the heart. Jr 31:33, with He 8:10.
Second coming of Christ. 2 P 3:4.

PROPHECIES CONCERNING CHRIST
Anointed with the Spirit. Ps 45:7. Is 11:2; 61:1. Fulfilled: Mt 3:16. Jn 3:34. Ac 10:38.
Ascension. Ps 68:18. Fulfilled: Lk 24:51. Ac 1:9.
Bearing reproach. Pss 22:6; 69:7, 9, 20. Fulfilled: Jn 1:11; 7:3.
Betrayed by a friend. Pss 41:9; 55:12–14. Fulfilled: Jn 13:18, 21.
Born in Bethlehem of Judea. Mi 5:2. Fulfilled: Mt 2:1. Lk 2:4–6.
Born of a virgin. Is 7:14. Fulfilled: Mt 1:18. Lk 2:7.
Buried with the rich. Is 53:9. Fulfilled: Mt 27:57–60.

Called Immanuel. Is 7:14. *Fulfilled:* Mt 1:22–23.

Called out of Egypt. Ho 11:1. *Fulfilled:* Mt 2:15.

Chief cornerstone of the church. Is 28:16. *Fulfilled:* 1 P 2:6–7.

Coming at a set time. Gn 49:10. Dn 9:24–25. *Fulfilled:* Lk 2:1.

Coming into the temple. Hg 2:7, 9. Ml 3:1. *Fulfilled:* Mt 21:12. Lk 2:27–32. Jn 2:13–16.

Conversion of the Gentiles to him. Is 11:10; 42:1. *Fullfilled:* Mt 1:17, 21. Jn 10:16. Ac 10:45, 47.

Death. Is 53:12. *Fulfilled:* Mt 27:50.

Disciples forsaking him. Zc 13:7. *Fulfilled:* Mt 26:31, 56.

Entering on his public ministry. Is 61:1–2. *Fulfilled:* Lk 4: 16–21, 43.

Entering publicly into Jerusalem. Zc 9:9. *Fulfilled:* Mt 21:1–5.

Exercising the priestly office in heaven. Zc 6:13. *Fulfilled:* Ro 8:34.

Flesh not seeing corruption. Ps 16:10. *Fulfilled:* Ac 2:31.

Forsaken by God. Ps 22:1. *Fulfilled:* Mt 27:46.

Gall and vinegar given him to drink. Ps 69:21. *Fulfilled:* Mt 27:34.

Garments parted, and lots cast for his vesture. Ps 22:18. *Fulfilled:* Mt 27:35.

Great persons coming to adore him. Ps 72:10. *Fulfilled:* Mt 2:1–11.

Hands and feet nailed to the cross. Ps 22:16. *Fulfilled:* Jn 19:18; 20:25.

Hated by the Jews. Ps 69:4. Is 49:7. *Fulfilled:* Jn 15:24–25.

Intensity of his sufferings. Ps 22:14–15. *Fulfilled:* Lk 22:42, 44.

Intercession for his murderers. Is 53:12. *Fulfilled:* Lk 23:34.

Jews and Gentiles combining against him. Ps 2:1–2. *Fulfilled:* Lk 23:12. Ac 4:27.

King in Zion. Ps 2:6. *Fulfilled:* Lk 1:32. Jn 18:33–37.

Meekness and want of ostentation. Is 42:2. *Fulfilled:* Mt 12:15–16, 19.

Ministry commencing in Galilee. Is. 9:1–2. *Fulfilled:* Mt 4:12–16, 23.

Mocked. Ps 22:7–8. *Fulfilled:* Mt 27:39–44.

Numbered with the transgressors. Is 53:12. *Fulfilled:* Mk 15:28.

Patience and silence under sufferings. Is 53:7. *Fulfilled:* Mt 26:63; 27:12–14.

Perpetuity of his kingdom. Is 9:7. Dn 7:14. *Fulfilled:* Lk 1:32–33.

Pierced. Zc 12:10. *Fulfilled:* Jn 19:34, 37.

Preaching by parables. Ps 78:2. *Fulfilled:* Mt 13:34–35.

Preceded by John the Baptist. Is 40:3. Ml 3:1. *Fulfilled:* Mt 3:1, 3. Lk 1:17.

Price given for the potter's field. Zc 11:13. *Fulfilled:* Mt 27:7.

A priest after the order of Melchizedek. Ps 110:4. *Fulfilled:* He 5:5–6.

A prophet like unto Moses. Dt 18:15–18. *Fulfilled:* Ac 3:20–22.

Poverty. Is 53:2. *Fulfilled:* Mk 6:3. Lk 9:58.

Rejected by his brethren. Ps 69:8. Is 63:3. *Fulfilled:* Jn 1:11; 7:3.

Rejected by the Jewish rulers. Ps 118:22. *Fulfilled:* Mt 21:42. Jn 7:48.

Resurrection. Ps 16:10. Is 26:19. *Fulfilled:* Lk 24:6, 31, 34.

Righteous government. Ps 45:6–7. *Fulfilled:* Jn 5:30. Rv 19:11.

Seed of Abraham. Gn 17:7; 22:18. *Fulfilled:* Gl 3:16.

Seed of David. Ps 132:11. Jr 23:5. *Fulfilled:* Ac 13:23. Ro 1:3.

Seed of Isaac. Gn 21:12. *Fulfilled:* He 11:17–19.

Seed of the woman. Gn 3:15. *Fulfilled:* Gl 4:4.

Sitting on the right hand of God. Ps 110:1. *Fulfilled:* He 1:3.

Slaying of the children of Bethlehem. Jr 31:15. *Fulfilled:* Mt 2:16–18.

Smitten on the cheek. Mi 5:1. *Fulfilled:* Mt 27:30.

Sold for thirty pieces of silver. Zc 11:12. *Fulfilled:* Mt 26:15.

Son of God. Ps 2:7. *Fulfilled:* Lk 1:32, 35.

Spit on and scourged. Is 50:6. *Fulfilled:* Mk 14:65. Jn 19:1.

A stone of stumbling to the Jews. Is 8:4. *Fulfilled:* Ro 9:32. 1 P 2:8.

Suffering for others. Is 53:4–6, 12. Dn 9:26. *Fulfilled:* Mt 20:28.

Tenderness and compassion. Is 40:11; 42:3. *Fulfilled:* Mt 12:15, 20. He 4:15.

That a bone of him should not be broken. Ex 12:46. Ps 34:20. *Fulfilled:* Jn 19:33, 36.

Universal dominion. Ps 72:8. Dn 7:14. *Fulfilled:* Php 2:9, 11.

Visage marred. Is 52:14; 53:3. *Fulfilled:* Jn 19:5.

Without guile. Is 53:9. *Fulfilled:* 1 P 2:22.

Working miracles. Is 35:5–6. *Fulfilled:* Mt 11:4–6. Jn 11:47.

Zeal. Ps 69:9. *Fulfilled:* Jn 2:17.

PROPHECY

Blessedness of reading, hearing, and keeping. Rv 1:3; 22:7.

Came not by the will of man. 2 P 1:21.

Christ the great subject of. Ac 3:22–24; 10:43. 1 P 1:10–11.

Despise not. 1 Th 5:20.

Foretelling future events. Gn 49:1. Nu 24:14.

For the benefit of after ages. 1 P 1:12.

Fulfilled respecting Christ. Lk 24:44.

A gift of Christ. Ep 4:11. Rv 11:3.

A gift of the Holy Ghost. 1 Co 12:10.

Gift of, promised. Jl 2:28, with Ac 2:16–17.

Gift of, sometimes possessed by unconverted men. Nu 24:2–9. 1 S 19:20, 23. Mt 7:22. Jn 11:49–51. 1 Co 13:2.

Give heed to. 2 P 1:19.

Given from the beginning. Lk 1:70.

God accomplishes. Is 44:26. Ac 3:18.

God gives, through Christ. Rv 1:1.

God the author of. Is 44:7; 45:21.

Guilt of pretending to the gift of. Jr 14:14; 23:13–14. Ezk 13:2–3.

How tested. Dt 13:1–3; 18:22.

A light in a dark place. 2 P 1:19.

Not of private interpretation. 2 P 1:20.

PUNISHMENT FOR

Adding to, or taking from. Rv 22:18–19.

Not giving ear to. Ne 9:30.

Pretending to the gift of. Dt 18:20. Jr 14:15; 23:15.

Receive in faith. 2 Ch 20:20. Lk 24:25.

A sure word. 2 P 1:19.

THEY WHO UTTERED

Filled with the Holy Ghost. Lk 1:67.

Moved by the Holy Ghost. 2 P 1:21.

Ordained by God. 1 S 3:20. Jr 1:5.

Raised up by God. Am 2:11.

Sent by Christ. Mt 23:34.

Sent by God. 2 Ch 36:15. Jr 7:25.

Spoke by the Holy Ghost. Ac 1:16; 11:28; 28:25.

Spoke in the name of the Lord. 2 Ch 33:18. Ja 5:10.

Spoke with authority. 1 K 17:1.

PROPHETS

Assisted the Jews in their great national undertakings. Ezr 5:2.

Christ exercised the office of. Mt 24. Mk 10:32–34.

Christ predicted to exercise the office of. Dt 18:15, with Ac 3:22.

Consulted in all difficulties. 1 S 9:6; 28:15. 1 K 14:2–4; 22:7.

EXTRAORDINARY

Often endowed with miraculous power. Ex 4:1–4. 1 K 17:23. 2 K 5:3–8.

Specially raised up on occasions of emergency. 1 S 3:19–21. Is 6:8–9. Jr 1:5.

Felt deeply on account of the calamities they predicted. Is 16:9–11. Jr 9:1–7.

God avenged all injuries done to. 2 K 9:7. 1 Ch 16:21–22. Mt 23:35–38. Lk 11:50.

GOD COMMUNICATED TO

At sundry times and in divers ways. He 1:1.

By angels. Dn 8:15–26. Rv 22:8–9.

By an audible voice. Nu 12:8. 1 S 3:4–14.

By dreams and visions. Nu 12:6. Jl 2:28.

His secret things. Am 3:7.

God spoke of old by. Ho 12:10. He 1:1.

Great patience of, under suffering. Ja 5:10.

Historiographers of the Jewish nation. 1 Ch 29:29. 2 Ch 9:29.

Interpreters of dreams, etc. Dn 1:17.

THE JEWS

Often imprisoned them. 1 K 22:27. Jr 32:2; 37:15–16.

Often left without, on account of sin. 1 S 3:1. Ps 74:9. Am 8:11–12.

Often put them to death. 1 K 18:13; 19:10. Mt 23:34–37.

Often tried to make them speak smooth things. 1 K 22:13. Is 30:10. Am 2:12.

Persecuted them. 2 Ch 36:16. Mt 5:12.

Required to hear and believe. Dt 18:15, with 2 Ch 20:20.

MENTIONED IN SCRIPTURE

Aaron. Ex 7:1.

Agabus. Ac 11:28; 21:10.

Ahijah. 1 K 11:29; 12:15. 2 Ch 9:29.

Amos. Am 1:1; 7:14–15.

Anna. Lk 2:36.

Azariah the son of Oded. 2 Ch 15:2, 8.

Daniel. Dn 12:11, with Mt 24:15.

Daughters of Philip. Ac 21:9.

David. Ps 16:8–11, with Ac 2:25, 30.

Deborah. Jg 4:4.

Elijah. 1 K 17:1.

Elisha. 1 K 19:16.
Enoch. Gn 5:21–24, with Jde 1:14.
Ezekiel. Ezk 1:3.
Gad. 2 S 24:11. 1 Ch 29:29.
Habakkuk. Hk 1:1.
Haggai. Ezr 5:1; 6:14. Hg 1:1.
Hanani. 2 Ch 16:7.
Hosea. Ho 1:1.
Huldah. 2 K 22:14.
Iddo. 2 Ch 9:29; 12:15.
Isaiah. 2 K 19:2. 2 Ch 26:22. Is 1:1.
Jacob. Gn 49:1.
Jeduthun. 2 Ch 35:15.
Jehu the son of Hanani. 1 K 16:1, 7, 12.
Jeremiah. 2 Ch 36:12, 21. Jr 1:1–2.
Joel. Jl 1:1. Ac 2:16.
John. Rv 1:1.
Jonah. 2 K 14:25. Jnh 1:1. Mt 12:39.
Malachi. Ml 1:1.
Micah. Mi 1:1.
Micaiah the son of Imlah. 1 K 22:7–8.
Miriam. Ex 15:20.
Moses. Dt 18:18.
Nahum. Na 1:1.
Nathan. 2 S 7:2; 12:1. 1 K 1:10.
Noah. Gn 9:25–27.
Obadiah. Ob 1:1.
Oded. 2 Ch 28:9.
Paul. 1 Tm 4:1.
Peter. 2 P 2:1–2.
Prophet of Judah. 1 K 13:1.
Prophet sent to Eli. 1 S 2:27.
Prophet sent to Israel. Jg 6:8.
Samuel. 1 S 3:20.
Shemaiah. 1 K 12:22. 2 Ch 12:7, 15.
Zacharias the father of John. Lk 1:67.
Zadok. 2 S 15:27.
Zechariah son of Iddo. Ezr 5:1. Zc 1:1.
Zephaniah. Zp 1:1.
Messengers of God. 2 Ch 36:15. Is 44:26.
Often accompanied by music while predicting. 1 S 10:5. 2 K 3:15.
Often committed their predictions to writing. 2 Ch 21:12. Jr 36:2.
Often in their actions, etc., signs were made to the people. Is 20:2–4. Jr 19:1, 10–11; 27:2–3; 43:9; 51:63. Ezk 4:1–13; 5:1–4; 7:23; 12:3–7; 21:6–7; 24:1–24. Ho 1:2–9
Often led a wandering and unsettled life. 1 K 18:10–12; 19:3, 8, 15. 2 K 4:10.
Often left without divine communications on account of sins of the people. 1 S 28:6. Lm 2:9. Ezk 7:26.

Often spoke in parables and riddles. 2 S 12:1–6. Is 5:1–7. Ezk 17:2–10.
One generally attached to the king's household. 2 S 24:11. 2 Ch 29:25; 35:15.
ORDINARY
Numerous in Israel. 1 S 10:5. 1 K 18:4.
Sacred bards of the Jews. Ex 15:20–21. 1 S 10:5, 10. 1 Ch 25:1.
Trained up and instructed in schools. 2 K 2:3, 5, with 1 S 19–20.
PREDICTIONS OF
Frequently proclaimed at the gate of the Lord's house. Jr 7:2.
Proclaimed in the cities and streets. Jr 11:6.
Were all fulfilled. 2 K 10:10. Is 44:26. Ac 3:18. Rv 10:7.
Written on rolls and read to the people. Is 8:1. Jr 36:2.
Written on tables and fixed up in some public place. Hk 2:2.
Presented with gifts by those who consulted them. 1 S 9:7–8. 1 K 14:3.
Servants of God. Jr 35:15.
Simple in their manner of life. Mt 3:4.
Sometimes received divine communications and uttered predictions under great bodily and mental excitement. Jr 23:9. Ezk 3:14–15. Dn 7:28; 10:8. Hk 3:2, 16.
Sometimes thought it right to reject presents. 2 K 5:15–16.
Sometimes uttered their predictions in verse. Dt 32:44. Is 5:1.
Spoke in the name of the Lord. 2 Ch 33:18. Ezk 3:11. Ja 5:10.
Watchmen of Israel. Ezk 3:17.
WERE CALLED
Holy men of God. 2 P 1:21.
Holy prophets. Lk 1:70. Rv 18:20; 22:6.
Men of God. 1 S 9:6.
Prophets of God. Ezr 5:2.
Seers. 1 S 9:9.
Were esteemed as holy men. 2 K 4:9.
Were mighty through faith. He 11:32–40.
Were often married men. 2 K 4:1. Ezk 24:18.
WERE REQUIRED
Not to speak anything but what they received from God. Dt 18:20.
To be bold and undaunted. Ezk 2:6; 3:8–9.
To be vigilant and faithful. Ezk 3:17–21.
To declare everything that the Lord commanded. Jr 26:2.

To receive with attention all God's communications. Ezk 3:10.

WERE SENT TO

Denounce the wickedness of kings. 1 S 15:10, 16–19. 2 S 12:7–12. 1 K 18:18; 21:17–22.

Exhort to faithfulness and constancy in God's service. 2 Ch 15:1–2, 7.

Predict the coming, etc., of Christ. Lk 24:44. Jn 1:45. Ac 3:24; 10:43.

Predict the downfall of nations. Is 15:1; 17:1, etc. Jr 47—51.

Reprove the wicked and exhort to repentance. 2 K 17:13. 2 Ch 24:19. Jr 25:4–5.

Were under the influence of the Holy Ghost while prophesying. Lk 1:67. 2 P 1:21.

Women sometimes endowed as. Jl 2:28.

Wore a coarse dress of haircloth. 2 K 1:8. Zc 13:4. Mt 3:4. Rv 11:3.

Writings of, read in the synagogues every sabbath. Lk 4:17. Ac 13:15.

PROPHETS, FALSE

Called foolish prophets. Ezk 13:3.

Compared to foxes in the desert. Ezk 13:4.

Compared to wind. Jr 5:13.

DESCRIBED AS

Covetous. Mi 3:11.

Crafty. Mt 7:15.

Drunken. Is 28:7.

Immoral and profane. Jr 23:11, 14.

Light and treacherous. Zp 3:4.

Influenced by evil spirits. 1 K 22:21–22.

Involved the people in their own ruin. Is 9:15–16. Jr 20:6. Ezk 14:10.

Judgments denounced against. Jr 8:1–2; 14:15; 28:16–17; 29:32.

Made use of by God to prove Israel. Dt 13:3.

Mode of trying and detecting. Dt 13:1–2; 18:21–22. 1 Jn 4:1–3.

Not sent or commissioned by God. Jr 14:14; 23:21; 29:31.

Often deceived by God as a judgment. Ezk 14:9.

Often practiced divination and witchcraft. Jr 14:14. Ezk 22:28. Ac 13:6.

Often presented to dreams, etc. Jr 23:28, 32.

THE PEOPLE

Deprived of God's word by. Jr 23:30.

Encouraged and praised. Jr 5:31. Lk 6:26.

Led into error by. Jr 23:13. Mi 3:5.

Made to forget God's name by. Jr 23:27.

Oppressed and defrauded by. Ezk 22:25.

Taught profaneness and sin by. Jr 23:14–15.

Warned not to listen to. Dt 13:3. Jr 23:16; 27:9, 15–16.

PREDICTED TO ARISE

Before destruction of Jerusalem. Mt 24:11, 24.

In the latter times. 2 P 2:1.

Pretended to be sent by God. Jr 23:17–18, 31.

PROPHESIED

Falsely. Jr 5:31.

In the name of false gods. Jr 2:8.

Lies in the name of the Lord. Jr 14:14.

Out of their own heart. Jr 23:16, 26. Ezk 13:2.

Peace, when there was no peace. Jr 6:14; 23:17. Ezk 13:10. Mi 3:5.

Women sometimes' acted as. Ne 6:14. Rv 2:20.

PROSELYTES

Described. Es 8:17. Is 56:3.

Entitled to all privileges. Ex 12:48. Is 56:3–7.

From the Ammonites and Moabites, restricted forever from holding office in the congregation. Dt 23:3.

From the Egyptians and Edomites, restricted to the third generation from holding office in the congregation. Dt 23:7–8.

Latterly called devout Greeks. Jn 12:20, with Ac 17:4.

Many embraced the gospel. Ac 6:5; 13:43.

Pharisees, etc., zealous in making. Mt 23:15.

REQUIRED

To be circumcised. Gn 17:13, with Ex 12:48.

To enter into covenant to serve the Lord. Dt 29:10–13, with Ne 10:28–29.

To give up all heathen associates. Ru 1:16; 2:11. Ps 45:10. Lk 14:26.

To give up all heathen practices. Ezr 6:21.

To observe the law of Moses as Jews. Ex 12:49.

Unfaithfulness in, punished. Ezk 14:7.

Went up to the feasts. Ac 2:10; 8:27.

PROSPERITY

MATERIAL

Dangers of. Ps 73:12. Pr 28:20. Mk 10:24. Lk 18:25.

From the Lord. 1 S 2:7. 2 K 18:7.

Limitations of. Ps 49:10. 1 Tm 6:7. Ja
1:11.

SPIRITUAL

Of the Christian. 3 Jn 1:2.
Of liberal souls. Pr 11:25.
Of those who love God. Ps 122:6.
Of those who trust God. Ps 23:1.

PROTECTION

AFFORDED TO

The church. Ps 48:3. Zc 2:4–5.
The perfect in heart. 2 Ch 16:9.
The oppressed. Ps 9:9.
The poor. Pss 14:6; 72:12–14.
Returning sinners. Jb 22:23, 25.
Those who hearken to God. Pr 1:33.
God able to afford. 1 P 1:5. Jde 1:24.
God faithful to afford. 1 Th 5:23–24. 2 Th
3:3.
Illustrated. Dt 32:11. Ps 125:1–2. Pr 18:10.
Is 25:4; 31:5. Lk 13:34.

NOT TO BE FOUND IN

Horses. Ps 33:17. Pr 21:31.
Hosts. Jsh 11:4–8, with Ps 33:16.
Idols. Dt 32:37–39. Is 46:7.
Man. Ps 146:3. Is 30:7.
Riches. Pr 11:4, 28. Zp 1:18.

OF GOD IS

Effectual. Jn 10:28–30. 2 Co 12:9.
Encouraging. Is 41:10; 50:7.
Indispensable. Ps 127:1.
Often afforded through means inadequate
in themselves. Jg 7:7. 1 S 17:45, 50. 2
Ch 14:11.
Perpetual. Ps 121:8.
Seasonable. Ps 46:1.
Unfailing. Dt 31:6. Jsh 1:5.
Uninterrupted. Ps 121:3.

SAINTS

Acknowledge God as their. Pss 18:2; 62:2;
89:18.
Praise God for. Ps 5:11.
Pray for. Ps 17:5, 8. Is 51:9.

VOUCHSAFED TO SAINTS, IN

All dangers. Ps 91:3–7.
All places. Gn 28:15. 2 Ch 16:9.
Calamities. Pss 57:1; 59:16.
Death. Ps 23:4.
Defeating the counsels of enemies. Is
8:10.
Defending them against their enemies.
Dt 20:1–4; 33:27. Is 59:19.
Keeping their feet. 1 S 2:9. Pr 3:26.
Keeping them from evil. 2 Th 3:3.

Keeping them from falling. Jde 1:24.
Keeping them from temptation. Rv 3:10.
Keeping them in the way. Ex 23:20.
Persecution. Lk 21:18.
Preserving them. Ps 145:20.
Providing a refuge for them. Pr 14:26. Is
4:6; 32:2.
Sleep. Pss 3:5; 4:8. Pr 3:24.
Strengthening them. 2 Tm 4:17.
Temptation. 1 Co 10:13. 2 P 2:9.
Upholding them. Pss 37:17, 24; 63:8.

WITHDRAWN FROM THE

Backsliding. Jsh 23:12–13. Jg 10:13.
Disobedient. Lv 26:14–17.
Obstinately impenitent. Mt 23:38.
Presumptuous. Nu 14:40–45.
Unbelieving. Is 7:9.

PROVIDENCE OF GOD

All pervading. Ps 139:1–5.

ALL THINGS ORDERED BY

For good to saints. Ro 8:28.
For his glory. Is 63:14.
Cannot be defeated. 1 K 22:30, 34. Pr
21:30.
Care over his works. Ps 145:9.
Connected with the use of means. 1 K 21:19,
with 22:37–38. Mi 5:2, with Lk 2:1–4. Ac
27:22, 31–32.
Danger of denying. Is 10:13–17. Ezk
28:2–10. Dn 4:29–31. Ho 2:8–9.
Ever watchful. Ps 121:4. Is 27:3.

EXERCISED IN

Bringing his words to pass. Nu 26:65. Jsh
21:45. Lk 21:32–33.
Defeating wicked designs. Ex 15:9–19. 2
S 17:14, 15. Ps 33:10.
Delivering saints. Ps 91:3. Is 31:5.
Determining the period of human life.
Pss 31:15; 39:5. Ac 17:26.
Directing all events. Jsh 7:14. 1 S 6:7–10,
12. Pr 16:33. Is 44:7. Ac 1:26.
Leading saints. Dt 8:2, 15. Is 63:12.
Ordaining the conditions and circum-
stances of men. 1 S 2:7–8. Ps 75:6–7.
Ordering the minutest matters. Mt
10:29–30. Lk 21:18.
Ordering the ways of men. Pr 16:9; 19:21;
20:24.
Overruling wicked designs for good. Gn
45:5–7; 50:20. Php 1:12.
Preserving his creatures. Ne 9:6. Ps 36:6.
Mt 10:29.

Preserving the course of nature. Gn 8:22.
Jb 26:10. Ps 104:5–9.
Prospering saints. Gn 24:48, 56.
Protecting saints. Pss 91:4; 140:7.
Providing for his creatures. Pss
104:27–28; 136:25; 147:9. Mt 6:26.
Ruling the elements. Jb 37:9–13. Is 50:2.
Jn 1:4, 15. Na 1:4.
Special preservation of saints. Pss 37:28;
91:11. Mt 10:30.
Man's efforts are vain without. Ps 127:1–2.
Pr 21:31.
Result of depending upon. Lk 22:35.
Righteous. Ps 145:17. Dn 4:37
SAINTS SHOULD
Commit their works unto. Pr 16:3.
Encourage themselves in. 1 S 30:6.
Have full confidence in. Pss 16:8; 139:10.
Pray in dependence upon. Ac 12:5.
Pray to be guided by. Gn 24:12–14;
28:20–21. Ac 1:24.
Trust in. Mt 6:33–34; Mt 10:9, 29–31.
SHOULD BE ACKNOWLEDGED
In adversity. Jb 1:21. Ps 119:75.
In all things. Pr 3:6.
In our daily support. Gn 48:15.
In prosperity. Dt 8:18. 1 Ch 29:12.
In public calamities. Am 3:6.
Sometimes dark and mysterious. Pss 36:6;
73:16; 77:19. Ro 11:33.
The wicked made to promote the designs of.
Is 10:5–12. Ac 3:17–18.

PRUDENCE
Exemplified by Christ. Is 52:13. Mt
21:24–27; 22:15–21.
Exhibited in the manifestation of God's grace.
Ep 1:8.
Intimately connected with wisdom. Pr 8:12.
Necessity for, illustrated. Mt 25:3, 9. Lk
14:28–32.
OF THE WICKED
Defeated by God. Is 29:14. 1 Co 1:19.
Denounced by God. Is 5:21; 29:15.
Fails in the times of perplexity. Jr 49:7.
Keeps them from the knowledge of the gospel. Mt 11:25.
Saints act with. Ps 112:5.
Saints should specially exercise, in their intercourse with unbelievers. Mt 10:16. Ep
5:15. Cl 4:5.
THEY WHO HAVE
Are preserved by it. Pr 2:11.
Crowned with knowledge. Pr 14:18.

Deal with knowledge. Pr 13:16.
Foresee and avoid evil. Pr 22:3.
Get knowledge. Pr 18:15.
Keep silence in the evil time. Am 5:12.
Look well to their goings. Pr 14:15.
Not ostentatious of knowledge. Pr 12:23.
Regard reproof. Pr 15:5.
Suppress angry feelings, etc. Pr 12:16;
19:11.
Understand their own ways. Pr 14:8.
Understand the ways of God. Ho 14:9.
Virtuous wives act with. Pr 31:16, 26.
The wise celebrated for. Pr 16:21.
The young should cultivate. Pr 3:21.

PUBLICANS
Chiefs of, very rich. Lk 19:2.
Collectors of the public taxes. Lk 5:27.
THE JEWS
Classed with the most infamous characters.
Mt 11:19; 21:32.
Despised. Lk 18:11.
Despised our Lord for associating with.
Mt 9:11; 11:19.
MANY OF
Attended the preaching of Christ. Mk
2:15. Lk 15:1.
Believed the preaching of John. Mt 21:32.
Embraced the gospel. Mt 21:31.
Received John's baptism. Lk 3:12; 7:29.
Matthew the apostle was of. Mt 10:3.
Often guilty of extortion. Lk 19:8.
Often hospitable. Lk 5:29; 19:6.
Often kind to their friends. Mt 5:46–47.
Suspected of extortion. Lk 3:13.

PUNISHMENT OF THE WICKED
BECAUSE OF
Covetousness. Is 57:17. Jr 51:13.
Disobeying God. Ne 9:26-27. Ep 5:6.
Disobeying the gospel. 2 Th 1:8.
Evil ways and doings. Jr 21:14. Ho 4:9;
12:2.
Idolatry. Lv 26:30. Is 10:10–11.
Ignorance of God. 2 Th 1:8.
Iniquity. Jr 36:31. Ezk 3:17–18; 18:4, 13,
20. Am 3:2.
Oppressing. Is 49:26. Jr 30:16, 20.
Persecuting. Jr 11:21–22. Mt 23:34–36.
Pride. Is 10:12; 24:21. Lk 14:11.
Rejection of the law of God. 1 S 15:23.
Ho 4:6–9.
Sin. Lm 3:39.

Unbelief. Mk 16:16. Ro 11:20. He 3:18–19; 4:2.

Comes from God. Lv 26:18. Is 13:11.

Commences frequently in this life. Pr 11:31.

Consummated at the day of judgment. Mt 25:31, 46. Ro 2:5, 16. 2 P 2:9.

Deferred, emboldens them in sin. Ec 8:11.

The fruit of sin. Jb 4:8. Pr 22:8. Ro 6:21. Gl 6:8.

Future, awarded by Christ. Mt 16:27; 25:31, 41.

FUTURE, DESCRIBED AS

Blackness of darkness. 2 P 2:17. Jde 1:13.

Damnation of hell. Mt 23:33.

Darkness. Mt 8:12. 2 P 2:17.

Death. Ro 5:12–17; 6:23.

Eternal damnation. Mk 3:29.

Everlasting burnings. Is 33:14.

Everlasting destruction. Pss 52:5; 92:7. 2 Th 1:9.

Everlasting fire. Mt 25:41. Jde 1:7.

Hell. Ps 9:17. Mt 5:29. Lk 12:5; 16:23.

Often sudden and unexpected. Pss 35:8; 64:7. Pr 29:1. Lk 12:20. 1 Th 5:3.

Resurrection of damnation. Jn 5:29.

The righteousness of God requires. 2 Th 1:6.

Rising to shame and everlasting contempt. Dn 12:2.

Second death. Rv 2:11; 21:8.

Torment forever and ever. Rv 14:11.

Torment with fire. Rv 14:10.

Wine of the wrath of God. Rv 14:10.

The wrath of God. Jn 3:36.

IN THIS LIFE BY

Bringing down their pride. Is 13:11.

Cutting off. Ps 94:23.

Deliverance unto enemies. Ne 9:27.

Famine. Lv 26:19–20, 26, 29. Ps 107:34.

Fear. Lv 26:36–37. Jb 18:11.

Noisome beasts. Lv 26:22.

Put in slippery places. Ps 73:3–19.

Reprobate mind. Ro 1:28.

Sickness. Lv 26:16. Ps 78:50.

Trouble and distress. Is 8:22. Zp 1:15.

War. Lv 26:25, 32-33. Jr 6:4.

No combination avails against. Pr 11:21.

Often brought about by evil designs. Es 7:10. Pss 37:15; 57:6.

The reward of sin. Jb 4:8. Pr 22:8. Ro 6:21. Gl 6:8.

SHALL BE

Accompanied by remorse. Is 66:24, with Mk 9:44.

According to their deeds. Mt 16:27. Ro 2:6, 9. 2 Co 5:10.

According to the knowledge possessed by them. Lk 12:47–48.

Increased by neglect of privileges. Mt 11:21–24. Lk 10:13–15.

Without mitigation. Lk 16:23–26.

Should be a warning to others. Nu 26:10. 1 Co 10:6–11. Jde 1:7.

PUNISHMENTS

Antiquity of. Gn 4:13–14.

CAPITAL, KINDS OF

Beheading. Gn 40:19. Mk 6:16, 27.

Bruising in mortars. Pr 27:22.

Burning. Gn 38:24. Lv 20:14. Dn 3:6.

Casting headlong from a rock. 2 Ch 25:12.

Casting into the sea. Mt 18:6.

Crucifying. Mt 20:19; 27:35.

Cutting in pieces. Dn 2:5. Mt 24:51.

Exposing to wild beasts. Dn 6:16, 24. (See also 1 Co 15:32.)

Hanging. Nu 25:4. Dt 21:22–23. Jsh 8:29. 2 S 21:12. Es 7:9–10.

Not permitted to the Jews by the Romans. Jn 18:31.

Sawing asunder. He 11:37.

Slaying with the sword. 1 S 15:33. Ac 12:2.

Stoning. Lv 24:14. Dt 13:10. Ac 7:59.

SECONDARY, KINDS OF

Banishment. Ezr 7:26. Rv 1:9.

Binding with chains and fetters. Ps 105:18.

Confinement in a dungeon. Jr 38:6. Zc 9:11.

Confinement in stocks. Jr 20:2. Ac 16:24.

Confiscating the property. Ezr 7:26.

Cutting off hands and feet. 2 S 4:12.

Cutting off nose and ears. Ezk 23:25.

Fine, or giving of money. Ex 21:22. Dt 22:19.

Imprisonment. Ezr 7:26. Mt 5:25.

Mutilating the hands and feet. Jg 1:5–7.

Plucking out the hair. Ne 13:25. Is 50:6.

Putting out the eyes. Jg 16:21. 1 S 11:2.

Restitution. Ex 21:36; 22:1–4. Lv 6:4–5; 24:18.

Retaliation or injuring according to the injury done. Ex 21:24. Dt 19:21.

Scourging. Dt 25:2–3. Mt 27:26. Ac 22:25. 2 Co 11:24.

Selling the criminal, etc. Mt 18:25.

Torturing.   Mt 18:34. He 11:37.

Sometimes deferred for a considerable time.
1 K 2:5–6, 8–9.

Sometimes deferred until God was consulted.
Nu 15:34.

Strangers not exempted from.   Lv 20:2.

A warning to others.   Dt 13:11; 17:13; 19:20.

WERE INFLICTED

By order of kings.   2 S 1:13–16. 1 K
2:23–46.

By order of magistrates.   Jb 31:11. Ac
16:22. Ro 13:4.

By the people.   Nu 15:35–36. Dt 13:9.

By soldiers.   2 S 1:15. Mt 27:27–35.

By the witnesses.   Dt 13:9, with 17:7. Jn
8:7. Ac 7:58–59.

Immediately after sentence was passed.
Dt 25:2. Jsh 7:25.

On murderers without commutation.   Nu
35:31–32.

On the guilty.   Dt 24:16. Pr 17:26.

Without partiality.   Dt 13:6–8.

Without pity.   Dt 19:13, 21.

Were sometimes commuted.   Ex 21:29–30.

PURIFICATION

Availed to sanctifying the flesh.   He 9:13.

Consequence of neglecting those prescribed
by law.   Lv 17:16. Nu 19:13, 20.

ILLUSTRATIVE OF

Purification by the blood of Christ.   He
9:9–12.

Regeneration.   Ep 5:26. 1 Jn 1:7.

Insufficient for spiritual purification.   Jb
9:30–31. Jr 2:22.

The Jews laid great stress on.   Jn 3:25.

MEANS USED FOR

Running water.   Lv 15:13.

Water mixed with blood.   Ex 24:5–8, with
He 9:19.

Water of separation.   Nu 19:9.

Multiplied by traditions.   Mt 15:2. Mk
7:3–4.

Of the healed leper.   Lv 14:8–9.

Of high priest on day of atonement.   Lv 16:4,
24.

Of individuals who were ceremonially unclean.
Lv 15:2–13. Lv 17:15; 22:4–7. Nu
19:7–12, 21.

Of Israel at the exodus.   Ex 14:32. 1 Co 10:2.

Of Israel before receiving the law.   Ex 19:10.

Of Levites before consecration.   Nu 8:6–7.

Of Nazarites after vow expired.   Ac 21:24,
26.

Of priests before consecration.   Ex 29:4.

Of priests performed in the bronze laver.   Ex
30:18. 2 Ch 4:6.

Of things for burnt offerings.   2 Ch 4:6.

Used by the devout before entering God's
house.   Ps 26:6. He 10:22.

Vessels in the houses of the Jews for.   Jn 2:6.

WAS BY

Sprinkling.   Nu 19:13, 18. He 9:19.

Washing parts of the body.   Ex 30:19.

Washing the whole body.   Lv 8:6; 14:9.

PURIM, FEAST OF

Began fourteenth of twelfth month.   Es 9:17.

Confirmed by royal authority.   Es 9:29–32.

Instituted by Mordecai.   Es 9:20.

The Jews bound themselves to keep.   Es
9:27–28.

Lasted two days.   Es 9:21.

Mode of celebrating.   Es 9:17–19, 22.

To commemorate the defeat of Haman's
wicked design.   Es 3:7–15, with 9:24–26.

PURITY

Of heart, blessing of.   Mt 5:8.

Of life, necessity of.   Is 52:11. 1 P 1:22.

Of mind, value of.   Ti 1:15.

Of religion, essence of.   Ja 1:27.

Of spirit, witness of.   Php 2:15.

Of thought, desirability of.   Php 4:8.

PURPOSE

OF CHRIST

To bring good news and deliverance.   Lk
4:18.

To bring life.   Jn 10:10.

To witness to the truth.   Jn 18:37.

OF CHRISTIANS

To achieve the heavenly goal.   Php
3:13–14.

To cleave to the Lord.   Ac 11:22, 23.

To have the best gifts.   1 Co 9:25.

To seek the things above.   Cl 3:1–2.

OF GOD

Our purity.   1 Th 3:13.

Our salvation.   Ep 3:11. 2 Tm 1:9.

QUIET

Achievement of.   Is 32:17.

Power of.   Is 30:15.

Value of.   Ec 4:6.

R

RACE

CHOICE OF JEWISH
To bless all races. Gn 12:1–3.
To special responsibility. Am 3:2.

CHURCH AND
Paul's proclamation of racial equality in Christ. Ep 2:11–22. Gl 3:23–29. Cl 3:1–17.
Peter's overcoming of racial prejudice. Ac 10:1–48; 11:1–18.
Philip's Ethiopian convert. Ac 8:26–40.
Reconciling early racial divisions. Ac 6:1–7.

GOD AND
Loves the world. Jn 3:16.
Will gather all nations together. Is 66:18.
Will heal all nations. Rv 22:2.

JESUS AND
Denounced as a Samaritan. Jn 8:48.
Healing a Gentile. Mt 8:5–13.
Healing a Syrophoenician girl. Mk 7:24–30.
Praising hated Samaritans. Lk 10:25–37; 17:16.
Talking with a Samaritan woman. Jn 4.
Transcending racial differences. Jn 4:19–24. Cl 3:11.
Uniting races. Ep 2:11–22.
Worldwide unity of. Gn 1:27; 7:23; 9:18, 19. Ac 17:26.

RAIN
Appearance of a cloud from the west indicated. 1 K 18:44. Lk 12:54.
Canaan abundantly supplied with. Dt 11:11.
Caused by condensing of the clouds. Jb 36:27–28. Ps 77:17. Ec 11:3.

DESIGNED FOR
Making the earth fruitful. He 6:7.
Refreshing the earth. Pss 68:9; 72:6.
Replenishing the springs and fountains of the earth. Ps 104:8.

DIVIDED INTO
Great. Ezr 10:9.
Overflowing. Ezk 38:22.
Plentiful. Ps 68:9.

Small. Jb 37:6.
Sweeping. Pr 28:3.
The former, after harvest, to prepare for sowing. Dt 11:14. Jr 5:24.
Frequently withheld on account of iniquity. Dt 11:17. Jr 3:3; 5:25. Am 4:7.

GOD
Causes to come down. Jl 2:23.
Exhibits goodness in giving. Ac 14:17.
Exhibits greatness in giving. Jb 36:26–27.
Gives. Jb 5:10.
Made a decree for. Jb 28:26.
Prepares. Ps 147:8.
Sends upon the evil and good. Mt 5:45.
Should be feared on account of. Jr 5:24.
Should be praised for. Ps 147:7–8.

ILLUSTRATIVE OF
Christ in the communication of his graces. Ps 72:6. Ho 6:3.
The doctrine of faithful ministers. Dt 32:2.
God's judgments (when destructive). Jb 20:23. Ps 11:6. Ezk 38:22.
A poor man oppressing the poor (when destructive). Pr 28:3.
Righteousness. Ho 10:12.
Spiritual blessings. Pss 68:9; 84:6. Ezk 34:26.
The word of God. Is 55:10–11.
Impotence of idols exhibited in not being able to give. Jr 14:22.

INSTANCES OF EXTRAORDINARY
After long drought in Ahab's reign. 1 K 18:45.
After the captivity. Ezr 10:9, 13.
During wheat harvest in the days of Samuel. 1 S 12:17–18.
Plague of, upon Egypt. Ex 9:18, with 23.
Time of the flood. Gn 7:4, 12.
The latter, before harvest. Jl 2:23. Zc 10:1.
The north wind drives away. Pr 25:23.
Not sent upon the earth immediately after creation. Gn 2:5.
Often destroyed houses, etc. Ezk 13:13–15. Mt 7:27.

Often impeded traveling in the east. 1 K 18:44, with Is 4:6.

Often succeeded by heat and sunshine. 2 S 23:4. Is 18:4.

Promised in due season to the obedient. Lv 26:4. Dt 11:14. Ezk 34:26–27.

Rainbows often appear during. Gn 9:14, with Ezk 1:28.

Rarely falls in Egypt. Dt 11:10. Zc 14:18.

Storm and tempest often with. Mt 7:25, 27.

Thunder and lightning often with. Ps 135:7.

Unusual in harvest time. Pr 26:1.

WANT OF
Causes the earth to open. Jb 29:23. Jr 14:4.
Dries up springs and fountains. 1 K 17:7.
Occasions famine. 1 K 18:1–2.
Removed by prayer. 1 K 8:35–36. Ja 5:18.

Withheld for three years and six months in the days of Elijah. 1 K 17:1. Ja 5:17.

RAVEN

Called the raven of the valley. Pr 30:17.

DESCRIBED AS
Black. S S 5:11.
Carnivorous. Pr 30:17.
Improvident. Lk 12:24.
Solitary in disposition. Is 34:11.

Elijah fed by. 1 K 17:4–6.

God provides food for. Jb 38:41. Ps 147:9. Lk 12:24.

Plumage of, illustrative of the glory of Christ. S S 5:11.

Sent by Noah from the ark. Gn 8:7.

Unclean and not to be eaten. Lv 11:15. Dt 14:14.

REAPING

Both men and women engaged in. Ru 2:8–9.

Corn after, bound up into sheaves. Gn 37:7. Ps 129:7.

Cutting of the corn in harvest. Jb 24:6, with Lv 23:10.

ILLUSTRATIVE OF
The final judgment. Mt 13:30, 39–43.
Gathering in souls to God. Jn 4:38.
The judgments of God on the antichristian world. Rv 14:14–16.
Ministers receiving temporal provision for spiritual labors. 1 Co 9:11.
Receiving the reward of righteousness. Ho 10:12. Gl 6:8–9.
Receiving the reward of wickedness. Jb 4:8. Pr 22:8. Ho 8:7. Gl 6:8.

THE JEWS NOT TO REAP
The corners of their fields. Lv 19:9, with 23:22.
During the sabbatical year. Lv 25:5.
During the year of jubilee. Lv 25:11.
The fields of others. Dt 23:25.

The Jews often hindered from, on account of their sins. Mi 6:15.

Mode of gathering the corn for, alluded to. Ps 129:7. Is 17:5.

Often unprofitable on account of sin. Jr 12:13.

PERSONS ENGAGED IN
Fed by the master who himself presided at their meals. Ru 2:14.
Received wages. Jn 4:36. Ja 5:4.
Under the guidance of a steward. Ru 2:5–6.
Visited by the master. Ru 2:4. 2 K 4:18.

Sickle used for. Dt 16:9. Mk 4:29.

A time of great rejoicing. Ps 126:5–6.

REBELLION AGAINST GOD

CONNECTED WITH
Contempt of God. Ps 107:11.
Injustice and corruption. Is 1:23.
Stubbornness. Dt 31:27.

EXHIBITED IN
Departing from him. Is 59:13.
Departing from his instituted worship. Ex 32:8–9. Jsh 22:16–19.
Departing from his precepts. Dn 9:5.
Despising his counsels. Ps 107:11.
Despising his law. Ne 9:26.
Distrusting his power. Ezk 17:15.
Murmuring against him. Nu 20:3, 10.
Rebelling against governors appointed by him. Jsh 1:18.
Refusing to hearken to him. Dt 9:23. Ezk 20:8. Zc 7:11.
Rejecting his government. 1 S 8:7; 15:23.
Revolting from him. Is 1:5; 31:6.
Sinning against light. Jb 24:13. Jn 15:22. Ac 13:41.
Unbelief. Dt 9:23. Ps 106:24–25.
Walking after our own thoughts. Is 65:2.

Forbidden. Nu 14:9. Jsh 22:19.

Forgiven upon repentance. Ne 9:26–27.

God alone can forgive. Dn 9:9.

God ready to forgive. Ne 9:17.

GUILT OF
Aggravated by God's fatherly care. Is 1:2.
Aggravated by God's unceasing invitations to return to him. Is 65:2.

To be confessed.   Lm 1:18, 20.   Dn 9:5.
To be deprecated.   Jsh 22:29.
The heart is the seat of.   Jr 5:23.   Mt 15:18–19.   He 3:12.
Heinousness of.   1 S 15:23.
Ingratitude of, illustrated.   Is 1:2–3.
Man is prone to.   Dt 31:27.   Ro 7:14–18.

MINISTERS
Cautioned against.   Ezk 2:8.
Sent to those guilty of.   Ezk 2:3–7; 3:4–9.   Mk 12:4–8.
Should remind their people of past.   Dt 9:7; 31:27.
Should testify against.   Is 30:8–9.   Ezk 17:12; 44:6.
Should warn against.   Nu 14:9.

Promises to those who avoid.   Dt 28:1–13, 1 S 12:14.
Provokes Christ.   Ex 23:20–21, with 1 Co 10:9.
Provokes God.   Nu 16:30.   Ne 9:26.
Punished.   Lv 26:14–39.   1 S 12:15.   Is 1:20.   Jr 4:16–18.   Ezk 20:8, 38.
Punishment for teaching.   Jr 28:16.
Religious instruction designed to prevent.   Ps 78:5, 8.

THEY WHO ARE GUILTY OF
Agrravate their sin by.   Jb 34:37.
Brought low for.   Ps 107:11–12.
Cast out in their sins for.   Ps 5:10.
Cast out of the church for.   Ezk 20:38.
Delivered into the hands of enemies on account of.   Ne 9:26–27.
Denounced.   Is 30:1.
Have God as their enemy.   Is 63:10.
Have God's hand against them.   1 S 12:15, with Ps 106:26–27.
Impoverished for.   Ps 68:6.
Increase in, though chastised.   Is 1:5.
Persevere in.   Dt 9:7, 24.
Practice hypocrisy to hide.   Ho 7:14.
Restored through Christ alone.   Ps 68:18.
Warned not to exalt themselves.   Ps 66:7.
Vexes the Holy Spirit.   Is 63:10.

RECONCILIATION WITH BRETHREN

Messiah to unite the generations.   Ml 4:6.
Prodigal son welcomed by his father but not by his self-righteous brother.   Lk 15:25–32.
Racially divided Christians reconciled by appointment of deacons.   Ac 6:1–7.
Worshiper first reconciled with an offended brother.   Mt 5:23, 24.

RECONCILIATION WITH GOD

Blotting out the handwriting of ordinances is necessary to.   Ep 2:16.   Cl 2:14.

EFFECTED FOR MEN
By the blood of Christ.   Ep 2:13.   Cl 1:20.
By Christ as High Priest.   He 2:17.
By the death of Christ.   Ro 5:10.   Ep 2:16.   Cl 1:21–22.
By God in Christ.   2 Co 5:19.
While alienated from God.   Cl 1:21.
While enemies to God.   Ro 5:10.
Without strength.   Ro 5:6.
Yet sinners.   Ro 5:8.

EFFECTS OF
Access to God.   Ro 5:2.   Ep 2:18.
Peace of God.   Ro 5:1.   Ep 2:16–17.
Union of Jews and Gentiles.   Ep 2:14.
Union of things in heaven and earth.   Cl 1:20, with Ep 1:10.

Ministers, in Christ's stead, should beseech men to seek.   2 Co 5:20.
The ministry of, committed to ministers.   2 Co 5:18–19.
Necessity for, illustrated.   Mt 5:24–26.
A pledge of final salvation.   Ro 5:10.
Predicted.   Dn 9:24, with Is 53:5.
Proclaimed by angels at the birth of Christ.   Lk 2:14.
Types.   Lv 8:15; 16:20.

REDEMPTION

Christ is made, unto us.   1 Co 1:30.
Christ sent to effect.   Cl 4:4–5.
Corruptible things cannot purchase.   1 P 1:18.
Defined.   1 Co 6:20; 7:23.

DESCRIBED AS
Eternal.   He 9:12.
Plenteous.   Ps 130:7.
Precious.   Ps 49:8.

Is by the blood of Christ.   Ac 20:28.   He 9:12.   1 P 1:19.   Rv 5:9.
Is by Christ.   Mt 20:28.   Gl 3:13.

IS FROM
All evil.   Gn 48:16.
All iniquity.   Ps 130:8.   Ti 2:14.
All troubles.   Ps 25:22.
The bondage of the law.   Gl 4:5.
The curse of the law.   Gl 3:13.
Death.   Ho 13:14.
Destruction.   Ps 103:4.
Enemies.   Ps 106:10–11.   Jr 15:21.
The power of sin.   Ro 6:18, 22.
The power of the grave.   Ps 49:15.

This present evil world.   Gl 1:14.
Vain conversation.   1 P 1:18.
Is of God.   Is 43:1, with Lk 1:68.   Is
44:21–23.
Man cannot effect.   Ps 49:7.
MANIFESTS THE
Grace of God.   Is 52:3.
Love and pity of God.   Is 63:9. Jn 3:16.
Ro 6:8. 1 Jn 4:10.
Power of God.   Is 50:2.
Old Testament saints partakers of.   He 9:15.
Present life the only season for.   Jb 36:18–19.
PROCURES FOR US
Adoption.   Gl 4:4–5.
Forgiveness of sin.   Ep 1:7. Cl 1:14.
Justification.   Ro 3:24.
Purification.   Ti 2:14.
A subject for praise.   Is 44:22–23; 51:11.
SUBJECTS OF
The body.   Ro 8:23.
The inheritance.   Ep 1:14.
The life.   Ps 103:4. Lm 3:58.
The soul.   Ps 49:15.
THEY WHO PARTAKE OF
Alone can learn the songs of heaven.   Rv
14:3–4.
Are a peculiar people.   2 S 7:23. Ti 2:14,
with 1 P 2:9.
Are assured of.   Jb 19:25. Ps 31:5.
Are first fruits unto God.   Rv 14:4.
Are the property of God.   Is 43:1. 1 Co
6:20.
Are sealed unto the day of.   Ep 4:30.
Are zealous of good works.   Ep 2:10. Ti
2:14. 1 P 2:9.
Commit themselves to God.   Ps 31:5.
Have an earnest of the completion of.   Ep
1:14, with 2 Co 1:22.
Praise God for.   Pss 71:23, 103:4. Rv 5:9.
Pray for the completion of.   Pss 26:11; 44:26.
Shall return to Zion with joy.   Is 35:10.
Should be without fear.   Is 43:1.
Should glorify God for.   1 Co 6:20.
Wait for the completion of.   Ro 8:23. Php
3:20–21. Ti 2:11–13.
Walk safely in holiness.   Is 35:8–9.

RED HEIFER
Ashes of, collected and mixed with water for
purification.   Nu 19:9, 11–22.
Blood of, sprinkled seven times before the
tabernacle.   Nu 19:4.
Cedar, hyssop, etc., burned with.   Nu 19:6.

COMMUNICATED UNCLEANNESS TO
The man that burned her.   Nu 19:8.
The man who gathered the ashes.   Nu
19:10.
The priest that offered her.   Nu 19:7.
Could only purify the flesh.   He 9:13.
Entire, to be burned.   Nu 19:5.
To be given to Eleazar the priest to offer.   Nu
19:3.
To be slain without the camp.   Nu 19:3.
To be without spot or blemish.   Nu 19:2.
A type of Christ.   He 9:12–14.

REGENERATION
See New Birth; Redemption; Remission of
Sin; Salvation.

RELIGION
At its best.   Ja 1:27. Mi 6:8. Mk 12:33. Ro
13:10.
At its worst.   Ho 6:6. Is 1:10–14. Mi 6:6–7.
Ja 1:26.
Of the Athenians.   Ac 17:22.
Of the Christian.   He 10:23.
Of the heart.   1 Co 13.
Of Paul before his conversion.   Ac 26:5.
Of the scribes and Pharisees.   Mt 23.

REMEMBRANCE
God's people are in his.   Is 49:16. Ml 3:16.
Lord's supper is his.   1 Co 11:24.
Prayer should include.   2 Tm 1:3.
Righteous to be in everlasting.   Ps 112:6.
We need a stirring of.   2 P 1:12.
Woman's generosity to be a.   Mt 26:13.

REMISSION OF SIN
Baptism to accompany.   Ac 2:38.
Blessing accompanies.   Ps 32:1.
Christian fellowship may grant.   Jn 20:22–23.
Confession necessary for.   1 Jn 1:9.
Faith receives.   Ac 10:43.
Lack of a forgiving spirit negates.   Mt 6:15.
Repentance is required for.   Mk 1:4. Ac
2:38.
Secured through Christ's blood.   Mt 26:28.
1 Co 15:3.

RENEWAL
Of mind, a means of transformation of life.
Ro 12:1–2.
Of mind, our duty.   Ep 4:23.
Of spirit, from God.   Pss 51:10; 23:3. Is
57:15.

Of strength, from waiting on the Lord. Is 40:31.

Of the inner nature, daily. 2 Co 4:16.

Of the Lord's work, prayed for. Hk 3:2.

Of those completely apostate, impossible. He 6:6.

REPARATIONS
See Restitution.

REPENTANCE
By the operation of the Holy Ghost. Zc 12:10

Called repentance unto life. Ac 11:18.

Called repentance unto salvation. 2 Co 7:10.

Christ came to call sinners to. Mt 9:13.

Christ exalted to give. Ac 5:31.

Commanded by Christ. Rv 2:5, 16; 3:3.

Commanded to all by God. Ezk 18:30–32. Ac 17:30.

Conviction of sin necessary to. 1 K 8:38. Pr 28:13. Ac 2:37–38; 19:18.

Danger of neglecting. Mt 11:20–24. Lk 13:3, 5. Rv 2:22.

Denied to apostates. He 6:4–6.

Exhortations to. Ezk 14:6; 18:30. Ac 2:38; 3:19.

Given by God. Ac 11:18. 2 Tm 2:25.

Godly sorrow works. 2 Co 7:10.

Joy in heaven over one sinner brought to. Lk 15:7, 10.

Ministers should rejoice over their people on their. 2 Co 7:9.

Necessary to the pardon of sin. Ac 2:38; 3:19; 8:22.

Neglect of, followed by swift judgment. Rv 2:5, 16.

Not to be repented of. 2 Co 7:10.

PREACHED
By the apostles. Mk 6:12. Ac 20:21.

By Christ. Mt 4:17. Mk 1:15.

By John the Baptist. Mt 3:2.

In the name of Christ. Lk 24:47.

Present time the season for. Ps 95:7–8, with He 3:7–8. Pr 27:1. Is 55:6. 2 Co 6:2. He 4:7.

SHOULD BE ACCOMPANIED BY
Confession. Lv 26:40. Jb 33:27.

Conversion. Ac 3:19; 26:20.

Faith. Mt 21:32. Mk 1:15. Ac 20:21.

Greater zeal in the path of duty. 2 Co 7:11.

Humility. 2 Ch 7:14. Ja 4:9–10.

Prayer. 1 K 8:33. Ac 8:22.

Self-abhorrence. Jb 42:6.

Shame and confusion. Ezr 9:6–15. Jr 31:19. Ezk 16:61, 63. Dn 9:7–8.

Turning from idolatry. Ezk 14:6. 1 Th 1:9.

Turning from sin. 2 Ch 6:26.

Should be evidenced by fruits. Is 1:16–17. Dn 4:27. Mt 3:8. Ac 26:20.

WE SHOULD BE LED TO, BY
The chastisements of God. 1 K 8:47. Rv 3:19.

The goodness of God. Ro 2:4.

The long-suffering of God. Gn 6:3, with 1 P 3:20. 2 P 3:9.

What it is. Is 45:22. Mt 6:19–21. Ac 14:15. 2 Co 5:17. Cl 3:2. 1 Th 1:9. He 12:1–2.

THE WICKED
Averse to. Jr 8:6. Mt 21:32.

Condemned for neglecting. Mt 11:20.

Neglect the time given for. Rv 2:21.

Not led to, by the judgments of God. Rv 9:20–21; 16:9.

Not led to, by miraculous interference. Lk 16:30–31.

REPROOF
Attention to, a proof of prudence. Pr 15:5.

Christ gives, in love. Rv 3:19.

Christ sent to give. Is 2:4; 11:3.

Contempt of, leads to remorse. Pr 5:12.

DECLARED TO BE
Better than secret love. Pr 27:5.

Better than the praise of fools. Ec 7:5.

An excellent oil. Ps 141:5.

More profitable to saints than stripes to a fool. Pr 17:10.

Eventually brings more respect than flattery. Pr 28:23.

God gives, to his own children. 2 S 7:14. Jb 5:17. Pss 94:12; 119:67, 71, 75. He 12:6–7.

God gives, to the wicked. Ps 50:21. Is 51:20.

Hatred of, leads to destruction. Pr 15:10; 29:1.

Hatred of, a proof of brutishness. Pr 12:1.

The Holy Spirit gives. Jn 16:7–8.

Hypocrites not qualified to give. Mt 7:5.

LEADS TO
Happiness. Pr 6:23.

Honor. Pr 13:18.

Knowlege Pr 19:25.

Understanding. Pr 15:32

Wisdom. Pr 15:31; 29:15.

Ministers empowered to give. Mi 3:8.

Ministers sent to give. Jr 44:4. Ezk 3:17.

REPROOF

MINISTERS SHOULD GIVE
Fearlessly. Ezk 2:3–7.
Openly. 1 Tm 5:20.
Sharply, if necessary. Ti 1:13.
Unreservedly. Is 58:1.
With all authority. Ti 2:15.
With Christian love. 2 Th 3:15.
With long-suffering, etc. 2 Tm 4:2.
Of those who offend, a warning to others. Lv
19:17. Ac 5:3–4, 9. 1 Tm 5:20. Ti 1:10,
13.
ON ACCOUNT OF
Fearfulness. Mk 4:40. Lk 24:37–38.
Hardness of heart. Mk 8:17; 16:14.
Hypocrisy. Mt 15:7; 23:13, etc.
Impenitence. Mt 11:20–24.
Not understanding. Mt 16:9, 11. Mk
7:18. Lk 24:25. Jn 8:43; 13:7–8.
Oppressing our brethren. Ne 5:7.
Reviling Christ. Lk 23:40.
Sinful practices. Mt 21:13. Lk 3:19. Jn
2:16.
Unbelief. Mt 17:17, 20. Mk 16:14.
Unruly conduct. 1 Th 5:14.
Vain boasting. Lk 22:34.
A proof of faithful friendship. Pr 27:6.
Rejection of, leads to error. Pr 10:17.
SAINTS SHOULD
Delight in those who give. Pr 24:25.
Give. Lv 19:17. Ep 5:11.
Give no occasion for. Php 2:15.
Love those who give. Pr 9:8.
Receive kindly. Ps 141:5.
The scriptures are profitable for. Ps 19:7–11.
2 Tm 3:16.
Should be accompanied by exhortation to re-
pentance. 1 S 12:20–25.
They who give, hated by scorners. Pr 9:8;
15:12.
WHEN FROM GOD
Is despised by the wicked. Pr 1:30.
Is for correction. Ps 39:11.
Pray that it be not in anger. Ps 6:1.
Should not discourage saints. He 12:5.

REPTILES

Created by God. Gn 1:24–25.
Jews condemned for worshiping. Ezk
8:10.
Made for praise and glory of God. Ps
148:10.
MENTIONED IN SCRIPTURE
Adder or asp. Pss 58:4; 91:13. Pr 23:32.
Chameleon. Lv 11:30.

Cockatrice or basilisk. Is 11:8; 59:5.
Dragon. Dt 32:33. Jb 30:29. Jr 9:11.
Flying fiery serpent. Dt 8:15. Is 30:6.
Frog. Ex 8:2. Rv 16:13.
Horse leech. Pr 30:15.
Lizard. Lv 11:30.
Scorpion. Dt 8:15.
Serpent. Jb 26:13. Mt 7:10.
Snail. Lv 11:30. Ps 58:8.
Tortoise. Lv 11:29.
Viper. Ac 28:3.
No image or similitude of, to be made for
worshiping. Dt 4:16, 18.
Placed under the dominion of man. Gn
1:26.
Solomon wrote a history of. 1 K 4:33.
Unclean and not eaten. Lv 11:31, 40–43. Ac
10:11–14.
Worshiped by the Gentiles. Ro 1:23.

REQUIREMENTS

Of the entrance into the kingdom: conversion.
Mt 18:3.
Of the law: love. Ro 13:10.
Of the Lord: justice, mercy, and humble fel-
lowship with God. Mi 6:8.
Of salvation: belief in Christ. Jn 8:24.
Of worship: sincerity and true devotion of
spirit. Jn 4:24.

RESIGNATION

Christ set an example of. Mt 26:39–44. Jn
12:27; 18:11.
Commanded. Pss 37:7; 46:10.
Exhortation to. Ps 37:1–11.
MOTIVES TO
God's faithfulness. 1 P 4:19.
God's greatness. Ps 46:10.
God's justice. Ne 9:33.
God's love. He 12:6.
God's wisdom. Ro 11:32–33.
Our own sinfulness. Lm 3:39. Mi 7:9.
SHOULD BE EXHIBITED IN
Bodily suffering. Jb 2:8–10.
Chastisements. He 12:9.
Loss of children. Jb 1:18–19, 21.
Loss of goods. Jb 1:15–16, 21.
The prospect of death. Ac 21:13. 2 Co
4:16—5:1.
Submission to the sovereignty of God in his
purposes. Ro 9:20–21.
Submission to the will of God. 2 S 15:26.
Ps 42:5, 11. Mt 6:10.
The wicked are devoid of. Pr 19:3.

RESPONSIBILITY
Corporate. Jsh 22:16. 1 Co 5:1–2.
For the earth. Gn 1:28. Ps 115:16.
For one another. Ro 14:13; 15:1. 1 Co 8:11.
1 Jn 4:11.
For sexual partnerships. 1 Co 6:12–20.
For what we hear. Mk 4:24.
For what we see. Mk 9:47.
For whatever we do. 1 Co 10:31.
Individual. Dt 24:16. Jr 31:30. Ro 14:12.
Marital. 1 Co 7:3–5.
National. Am 1:3—3:2. Pr 14:34.
Parental. 1 S 3:13. Ep 6:4.

REST
Christ's call to. Mt 11:28.
Eternal. Ps 104:23. Rv 14:13.
God's day for. Ex 23:12.
The Lord's provision for. Pss 23:2; 37:7. He
4:9.

RESTITUTION
DIVINE PROVISIONS FOR, IN THE CASE OF
Accidentally destroying property. Ex
22:5–6.
Disappearing, injured, or destroyed property. Ex 22:7–15.
Ill-gotten gains. Nu 5:6–10.
Seduction of a virgin. Ex 22:16–17.
Stealing an animal. Ex 22:1, 4.
Example approved by Christ. Lk 19:8–9.

RESURRECTION
Assumed and proved by our Lord. Mt
22:29–32. Lk 14:14. Jn 5:28–29.
Blessedness of those who have part in the first.
Rv 20:6.
Called in question by some in the primitive
church. 1 Co 15:12.
Certainty of, proved by the resurrection of
Christ. 1 Co 15:12–20.
Credibility of, shown by the resurrection of
individuals. Mt 9:25; 27:53. Lk 7:14. Jn
11:44. He 11:35.
Denied by the Sadducees. Mt 22:23. Lk
20:27. Ac 23:8.
Doctrine of the Old Testament. Jb 19:26.
Pss 16:10; 49:15. Is 26:19. Dn 12:2. Ho
13:14.
EFFECTED BY THE POWER OF
Christ. Jn 5:28–29; 6:39–40, 44.
God. Mt 22:29.
The Holy Spirit. Ro 8:11.
Expected by the Jews. Jn 11:24. He 11:35.

Explained away by false teachers. 2 Tm 2:18.
First principle of the gospel. 1 Co 15:13–14.
He 6:1–2.
Illustrated. Ezk 37:1–10. 1 Co 15:36–37.
Illustrative of the new birth. Jn 5:25.
Not contrary to reason. Jn 12:24. 1 Co
15:35–49.
Not incredible. Mk 12:24. Ac 26:8.
Of saints, shall be followed by the change of
those then alive. 1 Co 15:51, with 1 Th
4:17.
OF THE WICKED, SHALL BE TO
Damnation. Jn 5:29.
Shame and everlasting contempt. Dn
12:2.
Preached by the apostles. Ac 4:2; 17:18;
24:15.
PREACHING OF, CAUSED
Mocking. Ac 17:32.
Persecution. Ac 23:6; 24:11–15.
SAINTS IN, SHALL
Be as the angels. Mt 22:30
Be glorified with Christ. Cl 3:4.
Be recompensed. Lk 14:14.
Have bodies like Christ's. Php 3:21. 1 Jn
3:2.
Have glorious bodies. 1 Co 15:43.
Have incorruptible bodies. 1 Co 15:42.
Have powerful bodies. 1 Co 15:43.
Have spiritual bodies. 1 Co 15:44.
Rise first. 1 Co 15:23. 1 Th 4:16.
Rise through Christ. Jn 11:25. Ac 4:2. 1
Co 15:21–22.
Rise to eternal life. Dn 12:2. Jn 5:29.
Saints should look forward to. Dn 12:13.
Php 3:11. 2 Co 5:1.
Shall be of all the dead. Jn 5:28. Ac 24:15.
Rv 20:13.

RESURRECTION OF CHRIST
THE APOSTLES
At first did not understand the predictions
respecting. Mk 9:10. Jn 20:9.
Reproved for their unbelief of. Mk 16:14.
Very slow to believe. Mk 16:13. Lk 24:9,
11, 37–38.
Asserted and preached by the apostles. Ac
25:19; 26:23.
An assurance of the judgment. Ac 17:31.
ATTESTED BY
Angels. Mt 28:5–7. Lk 24:4–7, 23.
Apostles. Ac 1:22; 2:32; 3:15; 4:33.
His enemies. Mt 28:11–15.

EFFECTED BY

His own power. Jn 2:19; 10:18.

The power of God. Ac 2:24; 3:15. Ro 8:11. Ep 1:20. Cl 2:12.

The power of the Holy Ghost. 1 P 3:18.

An emblem of the new birth. Ro 6:4. Cl 2:12.

First fruits of our resurrection. Ac 26:23. 1 Co 15:20, 23.

Followed by his exaltation. Ac 4:10–11. Ro 8:34. Ep 1:20. Php 2:9–10. Rv 1:18.

Foretold by himself. Mt 20:9. Mk 9:9; 14:28. Jn 2:19–22.

Foretold by the prophets. Ps 16:10, with Ac 13:34–35. Is 26:19.

Fraud impossible in. Mt 27:63–66.

HE APPREARED AFTER, TO

All the apostles. Lk 24:51. Ac 1:9. 1 Co 15:7.

Above five hundred brethren. 1 Co 15:6.

Apostles, except Thomas. Jn 20:19, 24.

Apostles, Thomas being present. Jn 20:26.

Apostles at the sea of Tiberias. Jn 21:1.

Apostles in Galilee. Mt 28:16–17.

James. 1 Co 15:7.

Mary Magdalene. Mk 16:9. Jn 20:18.

Paul. 1 Co 15:8.

Simon Peter. Lk 24:34.

Two disciples. Lk 24:13–31.

The women. Mt 28:9.

He gave many infallible proofs of. Lk 24:35, 39, 43. Jn 20:20, 27. Ac 1:3.

NECESSARY TO

The efficacy of faith. 1 Co 15:14, 17.

The efficacy of preaching. 1 Co 15:14.

Forgiveness of sins. 1 Co 15:17.

The fulfillment of scripture. Lk 24:45–46.

Hope. 1 Co 15:19.

Justification. Ro 4:25; 8;34.

On the first day of the week. Mk 16:9.

On the third day after his death. Lk 24:26. Ac 10:40. 1 Co 15:4.

A proof of his being the Son of God. Ps 2:7, with Ac 13:33. Ro 1:4.

SAINTS

Begotten to a lively hope by. 1 P 1:3, 21.

Desire to know the power of. Php 3:10.

Shall rise in the likeness of. Ro 6:5. 1 Co 15:49, with Php 3:21.

Should keep, in remembrance. 2 Tm 2:8.

Truth of the gospel involved in. 1 Co 15:14–15.

RETALIATION OR REVENGE

Be thankful for being kept from taking. 1 S 25:32–33.

Christ an example of forbearing. Is 53:7. 1 P 2:23.

Forbidden by our Lord. Lv 19:18. Pr 24:17, 29. Mt 5:39–41. Ro 12:17, 19. 1 Th 5:15. 1 P 3:9.

Inconsistent with Christian spirit. Lk 9:55.

INSTEAD OF TAKING, WE SHOULD

Bless. Ro 12:14.

Exercise forbearance. Mt 5:38–41.

Exhibit love. Lv 19:18. Lk 6:35.

Give place unto wrath. Ro 12:19.

Overcome others by kindness. Pr 25:21–22, with Ro 12:20.

Trust in God. Pr 20:22. Ro 12:16.

Keep others from taking. 1 S 24:10; 25:24–31; 26:9.

Proceeds from a spiteful heart. Ezk 25:15.

Punishment for. Ezk 25:15–17. Am 1:11–12.

Rebuked by Christ. Lk 9:54–55.

The wicked are earnest after. Jr 20:10.

REVERENCE

For Christ. Mt 8:2; 14:33; 28:16, 17. He 1:6. Php 2:10.

For God. 1 Ch 16:25. Hk 2:20.

For the Lord's day. Es 20:8. Rv 1:10.

For the Lord's house. Lv 19:30. Jn 2:16.

For the Lord's name. Ex 20:7.

For parents. Ex 20:12. Ep 6:1–3.

For spiritual leaders. He 13:7, 17.

REVILING AND REPROACHING

Blessedness of enduring, for Christ's sake. Mt 5:11. Lk 6:22.

Conduct of Christ under. 1 P 2:23.

Excludes from heaven. 1 Co 6:10.

Forbidden. 1 P 3:9.

Happiness of enduring, for Christ's sake. 1 P 4:14.

Ministers should not fear. Ezk 2:6.

Of Christ, predicted. Ps 69:9, with Ro 15:3. Ps 89:51.

Of rulers specially forbidden. Ex 22:28, with Ac 23:4–5.

Punishment for. Zp 2:8–9. Mt 5:22.

SAINTS

Endure. 1 Tm 4:10. He 10:33.

Endure for Christ's sake. Lk 6:22.

Endure for God's sake. Pr 69:7.

May take pleasure in. 2 Co 12:10.
Pray under. 2 K 19:4, 16. Ps 89:50.
Return blessings for. 1 Co 4:12. 1 P 3:9.
Should expect. Mt 10:25.
Should not fear. Is 51:7.
Sometimes depressed by. Pss 42:10–11;
   44:16; 69:20.
Supported under. 2 Co 12:10.
Trust in God under. Pss 57:3; 119:42.
THE WICKED UTTER, AGAINST
   Christ. Mt 27:39. Lk 7:34.
   God. Pss 74:22; 79:12.
   God, by oppressing the poor. Pr 14:31.
   Rulers. 2 P 2:10–11. Jde 1:8–9.
   Saints. Ps 102:8. Zp 2:8.

REWARD OF SAINTS
As servants of Christ. Cl 3:24.
Be careful not to lose. 2 Jn 1:8.
DESCRIBED AS
   Beholding the face of God. Ps 17:15. Mt
      5:8. Rv 22:4.
   Beholding the glory of Christ. Jn 17:24.
   Being glorified with Christ. Ro 8:17–18.
      Cl 3:4. Php 3:21. 1 Jn 3:2.
   Being with Christ. Jn 12:26; 14:3. Php
      1:23. 1 Th 4:17.
   A city which had foundation. He 11:10.
   A crown of glory. 1 P 5:4.
   A crown of life. Ja 1:12. Rv 2:10.
   A crown of righteousness. 2 Tm 4:8.
   An enduring substance. He 10:34.
   Entering into the joy of the Lord. Mt
      25:21, with He 12:2.
   An eternal weight of glory. 2 Cl 4:17.
   Everlasting life. Lk 18:30. Jn 6:40;
      17:2–3. Ro 2:7; 6:23. 1 Jn 5:11.
   Everlasting light. Is 60:19.
   Fullness of Joy. Ps 16:11.
   A house, eternal in the heavens. 2 Co
      5:1.
   An incorruptible crown. 1 Co 9:25.
   Inheritance eternal. He 9:15.
   Inheritance incorruptible, etc. 1 P 1:4.
   Inheritance of all things. Rv 21:7.
   Inheritance with saints in light. Ac 20:32;
      26:18. Cl 1:12.
   Joint heirship with Christ. Ro 8:17.
   A kingdom. Mt 25:34. Lk 22:29.
   A kingdom immovable. He 12:28.
   The prize of the high calling of God in
      Christ. Php 3:14.
   Reigning forever and ever. Rv 22:5.

   Reigning with Christ. 2 Tm 2:12. Rv
      3:21; 5:10; 20:4.
   Rest. He 4:9. Rv 14:13.
   Shining as the stars. Dn 12:3.
   Sitting in judgment with Christ. Dn 7:22.
      Mt 19:28. Lk 22:30, with 1 Co 6:2.
   Treasure in heaven. Mt 19:21. Lk 12:33.
Hope of, a cause of rejoicing. Ro 5:2.
Is
   From God. Ro 2:7. Cl 3:24. He 11:6.
   Full. 2 Jn 1:8.
   Great. Mt 5:12. Lk 6:35. He 10:35.
   Inestimable. Is 64:4, with 1 Co 2:9.
   Of God's good pleasure. Mt 20:14–15.
      Lk 12:32.
   Of grace through faith alone. Ro 4:4–5,
      16; 11:6.
   Satisfying. Ps 17:15.
   Sure. Pr 11:18.
Not on account of their merits. Ro 4:4–5.
Prepared by Christ. Jn 14:2
Prepared by God. He 11:16.
Present afflictions not to be compared with.
   Ro 8:18. 2 Co 5:17.
PROSPECT OF, SHOULD LEAD TO
   Diligence. 2 Jn 8.
   Enduring suffering for Christ. 2 Co
      4:16–18. He 11:26.
   Faithfulness unto death. Rv 2:10.
   Pressing forward. Php 3:14.
Saints may feel confident of. Ps 73:24. Is
   25:8–9. 2 Co 5:1. 2 Tm 4:8.
Shall be given at the second coming of Christ.
   Mt 16:17. Rv 22:12.

RICHES
Be not overanxious for. Pr 30:8.
The blessing of the Lord brings. Pr 10:22.
CANNOT
   Deliver in the day of God's wrath. Zp
      1:18. Rv 6:15–17.
   Redeem the soul. Ps 49:6–9.
   Secure prosperity. Ja 1:11.
Danger   of   misusing,   illustrated. Lk
   16:19–25.
Deceitfulness of, chokes the word. Mt 13:22.
DENUNCIATIONS AGAINST THOSE WHO
   Abuse. Ja 5:1, 5.
   Get by vanity. Pr 13:11; 21:6.
   Get unlawfully. Jr 17:11.
   Hoard up. Ec 5:13–14. Ja 5:3.
   Increase by oppression. Pr 22:16. Hk
      2:6–8. Mi 2:2–3.
   Receive their consolation from. Lk 6:24.

Spend upon their appetite. Jb 20:15–17.
Trust in. Pr 11:28.

DESCRIBED AS
Corruptible. Ja 5:2. 1 P 1:18.
Deceitful. Mt 13:22.
Fleeting. Pr 23:5. Rv 18:16–27.
Liable to be stolen. Mt 6:19.
Perishable. Jr 48:36.
Temporary. Pr 27:24.
Thick clay. Hk 2:6.
Uncertain. 1 Tm 6:17.
Unsatisfying. Ec 4:8; 5:10.
Folly and danger of trusting to, illustrated.
Lk 12:16–21.
Give worldly power. Pr 22:7.
God gives. 1 S 2:7. Ec 5:19.
God gives power to obtain. Dt 8:18.
Guilt of rejoicing in. Jb 31:25, 28.
Guilt of trusting in. Jb 31:24, 28. Ezk
28:4–5, 8.
Heavenly treasure superior to. Mt 6:19–20.
Labor not for. Pr 23:4.
Life consists not in abundance of. Lk 12:15.
Love of, the root of all evil. 1 Tm 6:10.
Of the wicked, laid up for the just. Pr 13:22.
Often an obstruction to the reception of the
gospel. Mk 10:23–25.

OFTEN LEAD TO
Anxiety. Ec 5:12.
Denying God. Pr 30:8–9.
Forgetting God. Dt 8:13–14.
Forsaking God. Dt 32:15.
Fraud. Ja 5:4.
Oppression. Ja 2:6.
An overbearing spirit. Pr 18:23.
Pride. Ezk 28:5. Ho 12:8.
Rebelling against God. Ne 9:25–26.
Rejecting Christ. Mt 19:22; Mk 10:22.
Self-sufficiency. Pr 28:11.
Sensual indulgence. Lk 16:19. Ja 5:5.
Violence. Mi 6:12.
Profit not in the day of wrath. Pr 11:4.

THEY WHO COVET
Bring trouble on their families. Pr 15:27.
Bring trouble on themselves. 1 Tm 6:10.
Err from the faith. 1 Tm 6:10.
Fall into hurtful lusts. 1 Tm 6:9.
Fall into temptation and a snare. 1 Tm
6:9.
Use unlawful means to acquire. Pr 28:20.

THEY WHO POSSESS, SHOULD
Ascribe them to God. 1 Ch 29:12.
Be liberal in all things. 1 Tm 6:18.

Devote them to God's service. 1 Ch 29:3.
Mk 12:42–44.
Esteem it a privilege to be allowed to give.
1 Ch 29:14.
Give of them to the poor. Mt 19:21. 1 Jn
3:17.
Not boast of obtaining them. Dt 8:17.
Not glory in them. Jr 9:23.
Not hoard them up. Mt 6:19.
Not set the heart on them. Ps 62:10.
Not be high-minded. 1 Tm 6:17.
Not trust in them. Jb 31:24. 1 Tm 6:17.
Use them in promoting the salvation of oth-
ers. Lk 16:9.
When converted, rejoice in being humbled.
Ja 1:9–10.
This world's, belong to God. Hg 2:8.
True, described. Ep 3:8 1 Co 1:30. Cl 2:3.
1 P 2:7.
Vanity of heaping up. Ps 39:6. Ec 5:10–11.

THE WICKED
Boast themselves in. Pss 49:6; 52:7.
Have trouble with. Pr 15:6. 1 Tm 6:9–10.
Heap up. Jb 27:16. Ps 39:6. Ec 2:26.
Keep, to their hurt. Ec 5:13.
Must leave, to others. Ps 49:10.
Often increase in. Ps 73:12.
Often spend their days in. Jb 21:13.
Profit not by. Pr 11:4; 13:7. Ec 5:11.
Swallow down. Jb 20:15.
Trust in the abundance of. Ps 52:7.

RIGHTEOUSNESS

BLESSEDNESS OF
Being persecuted for. Mt 5:10.
Doing. Ps 106:3.
Having imputed, without works. Ro 4:6.
Hungering and thirsting after. Mt 5:6.
Suffering for. 1 P 3:14.
Turning others to. Dn 12:3.
Blessing of God not attributed to our works of.
Dt 9:5.
Brings its own reward. Pr 11:18. Is 3:10.
Cannot come by the law. Gl 2:21; 3:21.
Chastisements yield the fruit of. He 12:11.

CHRIST
Fulfilled all. Mt 3:15.
Has brought in everlasting. Dn 9:24.
Is the end of the law for. Ro 10:4.
Is made unto his people. 1 Co 1:30.
Is the Son of. Ml 4:2.
Loves. Ps 45:7, with He 1:9.
Preached. Ps 40:9.
Put on, as a breastplate. Is 59:17.

Shall execute.   Ps 99:4. Jr 23:6.
Shall judge with.   Ps 72:2. Is 11:4. Ac 17:31. Rv 19:11.
Shall reign in.   Ps 45:6. Is 32:1, He 1:8.
Was girt with.   Is 11:5.
Was sustained by.   Is 59:16.
A crown of glory to the aged.   Pr 16:31.
Effect of, quietness and assurance forever.   Is 32:17.
An evidence of the new birth.   1 Jn 2:29.
The fruit of the Spirit is in all.   Ep 5:9.
God looks for.   Is 5:7.
God loves.   Ps 11:7.
Has no fellowship with unrighteousness.   2 Co 6:14.
Judgment should be executed in.   Lv 19:15.
Judgments designed to lead to.   Is 26:9.
Keeps saints in the right way.   Pr 11:5; 13:6.
The kingdom of God is.   Ro 14:17.
MINISTERS SHOULD
  Be armed with.   2 Co 6:7.
  Be clothed with.   Ps 132:9.
  Be preachers of.   2 P 2:5.
  Follow after.   1 Tm 6:11. 2 Tm 2:22.
  Pray for fruit of, in their people.   2 Co 9:10. Php 1:11.
  Reason of.   Ac 24:25.
Nations exalted by.   Pr 14:34.
No justification by works of.   Ro 3:20; 9:31–32. Gl 2:16.
None by nature have.   Jb 15:14. Ps 14:3, with Ro 3:10.
Obedience to God's law.   Dt 6:25, with Ro 10:5. Lk 1:6, with Ps 1:2.
Of saints endures forever.   Ps 112:3, 9, with 2 Co 9:9.
Promised to the church.   Is 32:16; 45:8; 61:11; 62:1.
Promised to saints.   Is 60:21; 61:3.
SAINTS
  Are covered with the robe of.   Is 61:10.
  Are led in the paths of.   Ps 23:3.
  Are renewed in.   Ep 4:24.
  Are servants of.   Ro 6:16, 18.
  Characterized by.   Gn 18:25. Ps 1:5–6.
  Count their own, as filthy rags.   Is 64:6.
  Do.   1 Jn 2:29; 3:7.
  Follow after.   Is 51:1.
  Have, imputed.   Ro 4:11, 22.
  Have, in Christ.   Is 45:24; 54:17. 2 Co 5:21.
  Hunger and thirst after.   Mt 5:6
  Know.   Is 51:7.
  Offer the sacrifice of.   Ps 4:5; 51:19.

  Pray for the spirit of.   Ps 51:10.
  Put no trust in their own.   Php 3:6–8.
  Put on.   Jb 29:14.
  Receive, from God.   Ps 24:5.
  Shall receive a crown of.   2 Tm 4:8,
  Shall see God's face in.   Ps 17:15.
  Should have on the breastplate of.   Ep 6:14.
  Should live in.   Ti 2:12. 1 P 2:24.
  Should seek.   Zp 2:3.
  Should serve God in.   Lk 1:75.
  Should yield their members as instruments of.   Ro 6:13.
  Should yield their members servants to.   Ro 6:19.
  Wait for the hope of.   Gl 5:5.
  Walk before God in.   1 K 3:6.
  Work, by faith.   He 11:33.
The scriptures instruct in.   2 Tm 3:16.
Shall be glad in the Lord.   Ps 64:10.
Tends to life.   Pr 11:19; 12:28.
THEY WHO WALK IN AND FOLLOW
  Are abundantly provided for.   Pr 13:25. Mt 6:25–33.
  Are accepted with God.   Ac 10:35.
  Are blessed by God.   Ps 5:12.
  Are bold as a lion.   Pr 28:1.
  Are delivered out of all troubles.   Ps 34:19. Pr 11:8.
  Are enriched.   Ps 112:3. Pr 15:6.
  Are exalted by God.   Jb 36:7.
  Are the excellent of the earth.   Ps 16:3, with Pr 12:26.
  Are heard by God.   Lk 18:7. Ja 5:16.
  Are loved by God.   Ps 146:8. Pr 15:9.
  Are never forsaken by God.   Ps 37:25.
  Are objects of God's watchful care.   Jb 36:7. Ps 34:15. Pr 10:3. 1 P 3:12.
  Are righteous.   1 Jn 3:7.
  Are tried by God.   Ps 11:5.
  Dwell in security.   Is 33:15–16.
  Find it with life and honor.   Pr 21:21.
  Have their desires granted.   Pr 10:24.
  Have their prayers heard.   Ps 34:17. Pr 15:29. 1 P 3:12.
  Know the secret of the Lord.   Ps 25:14. Pr 3:32.
  Shall be ever remembered.   Ps 112:6.
  Shall flourish as a branch.   Pr 11:28.
  Shall hold on their way.   Jb 17:9.
  Shall never be moved.   Pss 15:2, 5; 55:22, Pr 10:30; 12:3.
  Think and desire good.   Pr 11:23; 12:5.

The throne of kings established by. Pr 16:12; 25:5.

Unregenerate man seeks justification by works of. Lk 18:9. Ro 10:3.

THE WICKED

Are enemies of. Ac 13:10.

Are far from. Ps 119:150. Is 46:12.

Are free from. Ro 6:20.

Do not. 1 Jn 3:10.

Do not obey. Ro 2:8, with 2 Th 2:12.

Follow not after. Ro 9:30.

Hate those who follow. Ps 34:21.

Leave off. Am 5:7, with Ps 36:3.

Love lying rather than. Ps 52:3.

Make mention of God, not in. Is 48:1.

Should awake to. 1 Co 15:34.

Should break off their sins by. Dn 4:27.

Should sow to themselves in. Ho 10:12.

Slay those who follow. Ps 37:32. 1 Jn 3:12, with Mt 23:35.

Speak contemptuously against those who follow. Ps 31:18. Mt 27:39–44.

Though favored, will not learn. Is 26:10, with Ps 106:43.

Vainly wish to die as those who follow. Nu 23:10.

Work of, shall be peace. Is 32:17.

RIGHTEOUSNESS IMPUTED

Blessedness of those who have. Ro 4:6.

Christ brings in an everlasting righteousness. Dn 9:24.

Christ called the Lord our righteousness. Jr 23:6.

Christ the end of the law for. Ro 10:4.

DESCRIBED AS

Christ being made righteousness unto us. 1 Co 1:30.

Our being made the righteousness of God, in Christ. 2 Co 5:21.

The righteousness of faith. Ro 4:13; 9:30; 10:6.

The righteousness of God by faith in Christ. Ro 3:22.

The righteousness of God, without the law. Ro 3:21.

Exhortation to seek righteousness. Mt 6:33.

A free gift. Ro 5:17.

The Gentiles attained to. Ro 9:30.

God's righteousness never to be abolished. Is 51:6.

THE JEWS

Ignorant of. Ro 10:3.

Stumble at righteousness by faith. Ro 9:32.

Submit not to. Ro 10:3.

Of the Lord. Is 54:17.

Predicted. Is 56:1. Ezk 16:14.

Promises made through. Ro 4:13.

Revealed in the gospel. Ro 1:17.

SAINTS

Clothed with the robe of righteousness. Is 61:10.

Desire to be found in. Php 3:9.

Exalted in righteousness. Ps 89:16.

Glory in having. Is 45:24–25.

Have, on believing. Ro 4:5, 11, 24.

RIGHTEOUSNESS OF GOD

Angels acknowledge. Rv 16:5.

Christ acknowledged. Jn 17:25.

Christ committed his cause to. 1 P 2:23.

DESCRIBED AS

Abundant. Ps 48:10.

Beyond computation. Ps 71:15.

Enduring forever. Ps 111:3.

Everlasting. Ps 119:142.

The habitation of his throne. Ps 97:2.

Very high. Ps 71:19.

EXHIBITED IN

His acts. Jg 5:11 1 S 12:7.

His commandments. Dt 4:8. Ps 119:172.

His government. Pss 96:13; 98:9.

His judgments. Pss 19:9; 119:7, 62.

His testimonies. Ps 119:138, 144.

His ways. Ps 145:17.

His word. Ps 119:123.

The final judgment. Ac 17:31.

The gospel. Ps 85:10, with Ro 3:25–26.

The punishment of the wicked. Ro 2:5. 2 Th 1:6. Rv 16:7; 19:2.

God delights in the exercise of. Jr 9:24.

Heavens shall declare. Pss 50:6; 97:6.

His care and defense of his people designed to teach. Mi 6:4–5.

Illustrated. Ps 36:6.

Leads him to love righteousness. Ps 11:7.

Part of his character. Pss 7:9; 116:5; 119:137.

SAINTS

Acknowledge in his dealings. Ezr 9:15.

Acknowledge, though the wicked prosper. Jr 12:1, with Ps 73:12–17.

Ascribe to him. Jb 36:3. Dn 9:7.

Confident of beholding. Mi 7:9.

Declare to others. Ps 22:31.

Do not conceal. Ps 40:10.

Magnify. Pss 7:17; 51:14; 145:7.

Mention, only. Ps 71:16.
Plead, in prayer. Ps 143:11. Dn 9:16.
Recognize in the fulfillment of his promises.
Ne 9:8.
Talk of. Pss 35:28; 71:15, 24.
Upheld by. Is 41:10.
Shown openly before the heathen. Ps 98:2.
Shown to the posterity of saints. Ps 103:17.

WE SHOULD PRAY
For its continued manifestation. Ps 36:10.
To be answered in. Ps 143:1.
To be delivered in. Pss 31:1; 71:2.
To be judged according to. Ps 35:24.
To be led in. Ps 5:8.
To be quickened in. Ps 119:40.
The wicked have no interest in. Ps 69:27.

RINGS
Antiquity of. Gn 24:22; 38:18.

ILLUSTRATIVE OF
Favor (when put on the hands). Lk 15:22.
The glory of Christ. S S 5:14.
Made of gold and set with precious stones.
Nu 31:50–51. S S 5:14.
Numbers of, taken from Midianites. Nu
31:50.

OF KINGS
Given to favorites as a mark of honor. Gn
41:42. Es 3:10; 8:2.
Used for sealing decrees. Es 3:12; 8:8, 10.
Rich men distinguished by. Ja 2:2.
Women of rank adorned with. Is 3:16, 21.

WORN
In the ears. Jb 42:11. Ho 2:11. Ezk
16:12.
In the nose. Is 3:21.
On the arms. 2 S 1:10.
On the hands. Gn 41:42.

RIVERS
BANKS OF
Covered with flags. Ex 2:3, 5.
Frequented by doves. S S 5:12.
Frequented by wild beasts. Jr 49:19.
Frequently overflowed. Jsh 3:15. 1 Ch
12:15.
Peculiarly fruitful. Ps 1:3. Is 32:20.
Places of common resort. Ps 137:1.
Planted with trees. Ezk 47:7.
Baptism often performed in. Mt 3:6.
Cities often built beside. Pss 46:6; 137:1.
Enclosed within banks. Dn 12:5.
Flow through valleys. Ps 104:8, 10.
Gardens often made beside. Nu 24:6.

God's power over, unlimited. Is 50:2. Na
1:4.

ILLUSTRATIVE OF
Abundance. Jb 20:17; 29:6.
The abundance of grace in Christ. Is 32:2,
with Jn 1:16.
The gifts and graces of the Holy Spirit. Ps
46:4. Is 41:18; 43:19–20. Jn 7:38–39.
God's judgments (when drying up). Is
19:1–8. Jr 51:36. Na 1:4. Zc 10:11.
God's judgments (when overflowing). Is
8:7–8; 28:3, 18. Jr 47:2.
Heavy afflictions. Ps 69:2. Is 43:2.
Peace of saints (in their steady course). Is
66:12.
People flying from judgments. Is 23:10.
The permanent prosperity of saints (fruit-
fulness of trees planted by). Ps 1:3. Jr
17:8.
Many, fordable in some places. Gn 32:22.
Jsh 2:7. Is 16:2.

MENTIONED IN SCRIPTURE
Abana. 2 K 5:12.
Arnon. Dt 2:36. Jsh 12:1.
Chebar. Ezk 1:1, 3; 10:15, 20.
Euphrates. Gn 2:14.
Gihon. Gn 2:13.
Gozan. 2 K 17:6. 1 Ch 5:26.
Hiddekel. Gn 2:14.
Jabbok. Dt 2:37. Jsh 12:2.
Jordan. Jsh 3:8. 2 K 5:10.
Kanah. Jsh 16:8.
Kishon. Jg 5:21.
Of Ahava. Ezr 8:15.
Of Babylon. Ps 137:1.
Of Damascus. 2 K 5:12.
Of Eden. Gn 2:10.
Of Egypt. Gn 15:18.
Of Ethiopia. Is 18:1.
Of Jotbath. Dt 10:7.
Of Judah. Jl 3:18.
Of Philippi. Ac 16:13.
Pharpar. 2 K 5:12.
Pison. Gn 2:11.
Ulai. Dn 8:16.
Of Canaan, abounded with fish. Lv 11:9–10.
Often the boundaries of kingdoms, etc. Jsh
22:25. 1 K 4:24.
Run into the sea. Ec 1:7. Ezk 47:8.

SOME ARE
Broad. Is 33:21.
Deep. Ezk 47:5. Zc 10:11.
Great and mighty. Gn 15:18. Ps 74:15.

Parted into many streams. Gn 2:10. Ps
11:15.
Rapid. Jg 5:21.
Source of. Jb 28:10. Ps 104:8, 10.

USEFUL FOR
Bathing. Ex 2:5.
Commerce. Is 23:3.
Promoting vegetation. Gn 2:10.
Supplying drink to the people. Jr 2:18.

ROCKS
Bees often made their honey among. Dt
32:13. Ps 81:16.
Casting down from, a punishment. 2 Ch
25:12.
A defense to a country. Is 33:16.

DESCRIBED AS
Barren. Ezk 26:4, 14. Am 6:12. Lk 8:6.
Durable. Jb 19:24.
Hard. Jr 5:3.
Dreaded by mariners. Ac 27:29.
God's power exhibited in removing, etc. Jb
14:18. Na 1:6.
Hammers used for breaking. Jr 23:29.
Houses often built on. Mt 7:24–25.

ILLUSTRATIVE OF
The ancestor of a nation. Is 51:1.
Christ as a stumbling stone to the wicked.
Is 8:14. Ro 9:33. 1 P 2:8.
Christ as foundation of his church. Mt
16:18, with 1 P 2:6.
Christ as refuge of his people. Is 32:2.
Christ as source of spiritual gifts. 1 Co
10:4.
God as creator of his people. Dt 32:18.
God as defense of his people. Ps 31:2–3.
God as refuge of his people. Ps 94:22.
God as salvation of his people. Dt 32:15.
Pss 89:26; 95:1.
God as the strength of his people. Pss
18:1–2; 62:7. Is 17:10.
A place of safety. Pss 27:5; 40:2.
Whatever we trust in. Dt 32:31, 37.
Important events often engraved upon. Jb
19:24.

INHABITED BY
Conies. Ps 104:18.
Doves. S S 2:14. Jr 48:28.
Eagles. Jb 39:28. Jr 49:16.
Wild goats. Jb 39:1.
Man's industry in cutting through. Jb
28:9–10.

MENTIONED IN SCRIPTURE
Adullam. 1 Ch 11:15.

Bozez. 1 S 14:4.
Engedi. 1 S 24:1–2.
Etam. Jg 15:8.
Horeb in Rephidim. Ex 17:1–6.
Meribah in Kadesh. Nu 20:1–11.
Oreb. Jg 7:25. Is 10:26.
Rimmon. Jg 20:45.
Sela-hammahlekoth in the wilderness of
Maon. 1 S 23:25, 28.
Selah in the Valley of Salt. 2 K 14:7. 2 Ch
25:11–12.
Seneh. 1 S 14:4.

MIRACLES CONNECTED WITH
Broken in pieces by the wind. 1 K 19:11.
Fire ascended out of. Jg 6:21.
Rent at the death of Christ. Mt 27:51.
Water brought from. Ex 17:6. Nu 20:11.
Often composed of flint. Dt 8:15; 32:13.
Often had boles and clefts. Ex 33:22
Often sharp-pointed and craggy. 1 S 14:4.
The olive tree flourished among. Dt 32:13.
Jb 29:6.
Shadow of, welcome to travelers during the
heat of the day. Is 32:2.
Tombs often hewn from. Is 22:16. Mt
27:60.

USED AS
Altars. Jg 6:20–21, 26; 13:19.
Places for idolatrous worship. Is 57:5.
Places for shelter by the poor in their dis-
tress. Jb 24:8; 30:3, 6.
Places of observation. Ex 33:21. Nu 23:9.
Places of safety in danger. 1 S 13:6. Is
2:19. Jr 16:16. Rv 6:15.

ROMAN EMPIRE
Called the world (from its extent). Lk 2:1.

CITIZENSHIP OF
Exempted from the degradation of scourg-
ing. Ac 16:37–38; 22:25.
Obtained by birth. Ac 22:28.
Obtained by purchase. Ac 22:28.

EMPERORS OF, MENTIONED
Augustus. Lk 2:1.
Claudius. Ac 11:28.
Nero. Php 4:22. 2 Tm 4:17.
Tiberius. Lk 3:1.

GRECIAN GAMES ADOPTED BY
Crowning of conquerors. 1 Co 9:25. Php
3:14. 2 Tm 4:8.
Foot races. 1 Co 9:24. Php 2:16; 3:11–14;
He 12:1–2.
Gladiatorial fights. 1 Co 4:9; 15:32.
Rules observed in conducting. 2 Tm 2:5.

Training of combatants. 1 Co 9:25, 27.
Wrestling. Ep 6:12.

Judea a province of, under a procurator or a governor. Lk 3:2. Ac 23:24, 26; 25:1.

JUDICIAL AFFAIRS OF

Accusation in writing placed over the head of those executed. Jn 19:19.

Accused persons protected from popular violence. Ac 23:20, 24–27.

Accusers and accused confronted together. Ac 23:35; 25:16–19.

All appeals made to the emperor. Ac 25:11–12.

Criminals delivered over to the soldiers for execution. Mt 27:26–27.

Garments of those executed given to the soldiers. Mt 27:35. Jn 19:23.

Persons accused, examined by scourging. Ac 22:24, 29.

Power of life and death vested in its authorities. Jn 18:31, 39–40; 19:10.

Prisoners chained to soldiers for safety. Ac 21:33, with 12:6. 2 Tm 1:16, with Ac 28:16.

Those who appealed to Caesar, to be brought before him. Ac 26:32.

MILITARY AFFAIRS OF

Crowning of soldiers who distinguished themselves. 2 Tm 4:7–8.

Danger of sentinels' sleeping. Mt 28:13–14.

Different military officers, etc. Ac 21:31; 23:23–24.

Expunging from the muster roll names of soldiers guilty of crimes. Rv 3:5.

Hardship endured by soldiers. 2 Tm 2:3.

Italian and Augustus' band. Ac 10:1; 27:1.

Soldiers not allowed to entangle themselves with earthly cares. 2 Tm 2:4.

The soldier's special comrade who shared his toils and dangers. Php 2:25.

Strict obedience to superiors. Mt 8:8–9.

Triumph of victorious generals. 2 Co 2:14–16. Cl 2:15.

Use of the panoply or defensive armor. Ro 13:12. 2 Co 6:7. Ep 6:11–17.

PREDICTIONS RESPECTING

Its division into ten parts. Dn 2:41–43; 7:20, 24.

Its universal dominion. Dn 7:23.

Origin of papal power in. Dn 7:8, 20–25.

REPRESENTED BY

Legs of iron in Nebuchadnezzar's vision. Dn 2:33, 40.

Terrible beast in Daniel's vision. Dn 7:7, 19.

Rome the capital of. Ac 18:2; 19:21.

S

THE SABBATH
Blessedness of honoring. Is 58:13–14.
Blessedness of keeping. Is 56:2, 6.
CALLED
  God's holy day. Is 58:13.
  The Lord's day. Rv 1:10.
  The rest of the holy sabbath. Ex 16:23.
  The sabbath of rest. Ex 31:15.
  The sabbath of the Lord. Ex 20:10. Lv
    23:3. Dt 5:14.
CHRIST
  Is Lord of. Mk 2:27.
  Taught on. Lk 4:31; 6:6.
  Was accustomed to observe. Lk 4:16.
Denunciations against those who profane.
  Ex 31:14–15. Nu 15:32–36.
Divine worship to be celebrated on. Ezk
  46:3. Ac 16:13.
First day of the week kept as, by primitive
  church. Jn 20:26. Ac 20:7. 1 Co 16:2.
GOD
  Blessed. Gn 2:3. Ex 20:11.
  Commanded to be kept. Lv 19:3, 30.
  Commanded to be sanctified. Ex 20:8.
  Hallowed. Ex 20:11.
  Sanctified. Gn 2:3. Ex 31:15.
  Shows considerate kindness in appointing.
    Ex 23:12.
  Shows favor in appointing. Ne 9:14.
  Will have his goodness commemorated in
    the observance of. Dt 5:15.
Grounds of its institution. Gn 2:2–3. Ex
  20:11.
Instituted by God. Gn 2:3.
Made for man. Mk 2:27.
Necessary wants may be supplied on. Mt
  12:1. Lk 13:15; 14:1.
No burdens to be carried on. Ne 13:19. Jr
  17:21.
No manner of work to be done on. Ex 20:10.
  Lv 23:3
No purchases to be made on. Ne 10:31;
  13:15–17.
Observance of, to be perpetual. Ex
  31:16–17, with Mt 5:17–18.

Punishment of those who profane. Ex
  31:14–15. Nu 15:32–36.
SAINTS
  Honor God in observing. Is 58:13.
  Observe. Ne 13:22.
  Rejoice in. Ps 118:24. Is 58:13.
  Testify against those who desecrate. Ne
    13:15, 20–21.
The scriptures to be read on. Ac 13:27;
  15:21.
Servants and cattle should be allowed to rest
  upon. Ex 20:10. Dt 5:14.
Seventh day observed as. Ex 20:9, 11.
A sign of the covenant. Ex 31:13, 17.
A type of the heavenly rest. He 4:4, 9.
THE WICKED
  Bear burdens on. Ne 13:15.
  Do their own pleasure on. Is 58:13.
  Hide their eyes from. Ezk 22:26.
  May be judicially deprived of. Lm 2:6.
    Ho 2:11.
  Mock at. Lm 1:7.
  Pollute. Is 56:2. Ezk 20:13, 16.
  Profane. Ne 13:17. Ezk 22:8.
  Sometimes pretend to be zealous for. Lk
    13:14. Jn 9:16.
  Traffic on. Ne 10:31; 13:15–16.
  Wearied by. Am 8:5.
  Work on. Ne 13:15.
The word of God to be preached on. Ac
  13:14–15, 44; 17:2; 18:4.
Works connected with religious service lawful
  on. Nu 28:9. Mt 12:5. Jn 7:23.
Works of mercy lawful on. Mt 12:12. Lk
  13:16. Jn 9:14.

SABBATICAL YEAR, FEAST OF
ENACTMENTS RESPECTING
  Cessation of all field labor. Lv 25:4–5.
  The fruits of the earth to be common prop-
    erty. Ex 23:11. Lv 25:6–7.
  No release to strangers during. Dt 15:3.
  Public reading of the law at feast of taberna-
    cles. Dt 31:10–13.
  Release of all Hebrew servants. Ex 21:2.
    Dt 15:12.

Remission of debts. Dt 15:1–3. Ne 10:31.

Jews threatened for neglecting. Lv 26:34–35, 43. Jr 34:13–18.

Kept every seventh year. Ex 23:11. Lv 25:4.

Release of, not to hinder the exercise of benevolence. Dt 15:9–11.

Restored after the captivity. Ne 10:31.

A sabbath for the land. Lv 25:2.

The seventy years' captivity a punishment for neglecting. 2 Ch 36:20–21.

Surplus of sixth year to provide for. Lv 25:20–22.

SACKCLOTH

ILLUSTRATIVE OF

Heavy afflictions (when girding with). Is 3:24; 22:12; 32:11.

Joy and gladness (when putting off). Ps 30:11.

Severe judgments (when covering the heavens with). Is 50:3.

Severe judgments (when heavens became black as). Rv 6:12.

The Jews lay in, when in deep affliction. 2 S 21:10. 1 K 21:27. Jl 1:13.

Made of coarse hair. Mt 3:4, with Rv 6:12.

No one clothed in, allowed into the palaces of kings. Es 4:2.

Of a black color. Rv 6:12.

Rough aand unsightly. Zc 13:4.

WORN

At funerals. 2 S 3:31.

By God's prophets. 2 K 1:8. Is 20:2. Mt 3:4. Rv 11:3.

By persons in affliction. Ne 9:1. Ps 69:11. Jnh 3:5.

Frequently next the skin in deep affliction. 1 K 21:27. 2 K 6:30. Jb 16:15.

Girt about the loins. Gn 37:34. 1 K 20:31.

In the streets. Is 15:3.

Often over the whole person. 2 K 19:1–2.

Often with ropes on the head. 1 K 20:31.

With ashes on the head. Es 4:1.

SACRIFICES

Always offered upon altars. Ex 20:24.

CONSISTED OF

Clean animals or bloody sacrifices. Gn 8:20.

Fruits of the earth or unbloody sacrifices. Gn 4:4. Lv 2:1.

Could not take away sin. Ps 40:6. He 9:9; 10:1–11.

Covenants of God confirmed by. Gn 15:9–17. Ex 24:5–8, with He 9:19–20. Ps 50:5.

DIFFERENT KINDS OF

Burnt offering wholly consumed by fire. Lv 1. 1 K 18:38.

Peace offering. Lv 3.

Sin offering for sins of ignorance. Lv 4.

Trespass offering for intentional sins. Lv 6:1–7; 7:1–7.

Divine institution of. Gn 3:21, with 1:29 and 9:3; 4:4–5, with He 11:4.

Fat of, not to remain until morning. Ex 23:8.

For public use, often provided by the state. 2 Ch 31:3.

Generally the best of their kind. Gn 4:4. 1 S 15:22. Ps 66:15. Is 1:11.

ILLUSTRATIVE OF

Benevolence. Php 4:18. He 13:16.

A broken spirit. Ps 51:17.

Devotedness. Ro 12:1. Php 2:17.

Martyrdom. Php 2:7. 2 Tm 4:6.

Prayer. Ps 141:2.

Righteousness. Pss 4:5; 51:19.

Thanksgiving. Pss 27:6; 107:22; 116:17. He 13:15.

Imparted a legal purification. He 9:13, 22.

THE JEWS

Condemned for bringing defective and blemished. Ml 1:13–14.

Condemned for not offering. Is 43:23–24.

Condemned for not treating with respect. 1 S 2:29. Ml 1:12.

Condemned for offering, to idols. 2 Ch 34:25. Is 65:3, 7. Ezk 20:28, 31.

Unaccepted in, on account of sin. Is 1:11, 15; 66:3. Ho 8:13.

No leaven offered with, except for thanksgiving. Ex 23:18, with Lv 7:13.

OFFERED

After the departure of Israel from Egypt. Ex 5:3, 17; 18:12; 24:5.

At all the feasts. Nu 10:10.

By the patriarchs. Gn 22:2, 13; 31:54; 46:1. Jb 1:5.

Daily. Ex 29:38–39. Nu 28:3–4.

For individuals. Lv 1:2; 17:8.

For the whole nation. Lv 16:15–30. 1 Ch 29:21.

From the earliest age. Gn 4:3–4.

In faith of a coming Savior. He 11:4, 17, 28.

Monthly. Nu 28:11.

Under the Mosaic dispensation. Lv 1—7. He 10:1–3.

Weekly. Nu 28:9–10.

Yearly. Lv 16:3. 1 S 1:3, 21; 20:6.

Offered to false gods, are offered to devils. Lv 17:7. Dt 32:17. Ps 106:37. 1 Co 10:20.

Offering of, an acknowledgment of sin. He 10:3.

Often consumed by fire from heaven. Lv 9:24. 1 K 18:38. 2 Ch 7:1.

On great occasions, very numerous. 2 Ch 5:6; 7:5.

PRIESTS

Appointed to offer. 1 S 2:28. Ezk 44:11, 15. He 5:1, 8:3.

Had a portion of and lived by. Ex 29:27–28. Dt 18:3. Jsh 13:11. 1 Co 9:13.

Required to be perfect and without blemish. Lv 22:19. Dt 15:21; 17:1. Ml 1:8, 14.

To be brought to the place appointed by God. Dt 12:6. 2 Ch 7:12.

To be offered to God alone. Ex 22:20. Jg 13:16. 2 K 17:36.

Were accepted when offered in sincerity and faith. Gn 4:4, with He 11:4. Gn 8:21.

Were bound to the horns of the altar. Ps 118:27.

Were salted with salt. Lv 2:13. Mk 9:49.

Were typical of Christ's sacrifice. 1 Co 5:7. Ep 5:2. He 10:1, 11–12.

When bloody, accompanied with meat and drink offering. Nu 15:3–12.

When offered to God, an acknowledgment of his being the supreme God. 2 K 5:17. Jnh 1:16.

Without obedience, worthless. 1 S 15:22. Pr 21:3. Mk 12:33.

SADDUCEES

CHRIST

Cautioned his disciples against their principles. Mt 16:6, 11–12.

Silenced. Mt 22:34.

Tempted by. Mt 16:1.

Vindicated the resurrection against. Mt 22:24–32. Mk 12:19–27.

Denied the resurrection and a future state. Mt 22:23. Lk 20:27.

Persecuted the early Christians. Ac 4:1; 5:17–18, 40.

Refused baptism by John. Mt 3:7.

The resurrection a cause of dispute between them and the Pharisees. Ac 23:6–9.

A sect of the Jews. Ac 5:17.

SAINTS (Those Who Belong to God)

Are perfected through the church's ministry. Ep 4:12.

Christ will appear with and be glorified in. 1 Th 3:13. 2 Th 1:10. Jde 1:14.

COMPARED TO

Babes. Mt 11:25. 1 P 2:2.

Branches of a vine. Jn 15:2, 4–5.

Calves of the stall. Ml 4:2.

Cedars in Lebanon. Ps 92:12.

Corn. Ho 14:7.

Dew and showers. Mi 5:7.

Doves. Ps 68:13. Is 60:8.

Eagles. Ps 103:5. Is 40:31.

Fruitful trees. Ps 1:3. Jr 17:8.

Gold. Jb 23:10. Lm 4:2.

Good figs. Jr 24:2–7.

Good fishes. Mt 13:48.

Good servants. Mt 25:21.

Green olive trees. Ps 52:8. Ho 14:6.

Jewels. Ml 3:17.

Lambs. Is 40:11. Jn 21:15.

Lebanon. Ho 14:5–7.

Lights. Mt 5:14. Php 2:15.

Lilies. S S 2:2. Ho 14:5.

Lions. Pr 28:1. Mi 5:8.

Little children. Mt 18:3. 1 Co 14:20.

Lively stones. 1 P 2:5.

Members of the body. 1 Co 12:20, 27.

Mount Zion. Ps 125:1–2.

Obedient children. 1 P 1:14.

Palm trees. Ps 92:12.

Pomegranates. S S 4:13.

Runners in a race. 1 Co 9:24. He 12:1.

Salt. Mt 5:13.

Sheep. Ps 78:52. Mt 25:33. Jn 10:4.

Soldiers. 2 Tm 2:3–4.

Stars. Dn 12:3.

Stones of a crown. Zc 9:16.

Strangers and pilgrims. 1 P 2:11.

Sun. Jg 5:31. Mt 13:43.

Thirsting deer. Ps 42:1.

Treasure. Ex 19:5. Ps 135:4.

Trees planted by rivers. Ps 1:3.

Unfailing springs. Is 58:11.

Vessels of gold and silver. 2 Tm 2:20.

Vines. S S 6:11. Ho 14:7.

Watered gardens. Is 58:11.

Wheat. Mt 3:12; 13:29–30.

Willows by streams. Is 44:4.

Wrestlers. 2 Tm 2:5.
Divine intercession for. Ro 8:27.
God will not forsake. Ps 37:28. 1 S 2:9.
Paul considered himself the least. Ep 3:8.
Paul ministered to. Ro 15:25.
We are the saints. Pss 31:23; 34:9. Ro 1:7.
Will judge the world. 1 Co 6:2.

SAINTS, CHARACTER OF
Attentive to Christ's voice. Jn 10:3-4.
Blameless and harmless. Php 2:15.
Bold. Pr 28:1. Ro 13:3.
Contrite. Is 57:15; 66:2.
Devout. Ac 8:2; 22:12.
Faithful. Rv 17:14.
Fearing God. Mt 3:16. Ac 10:2.
Following Christ. Jn 10:4, 27.
Godly. Ps 4:3. 2 P 2:9.
Guileless. Jn 1:47.
Holy. Dt 7:6; 14:2. Cl 3:12.
Humble. Ps 34:2. 1 P 5:5.
Hungering after righteousness. Mt 5:6.
Just. Gn 6:9. Hk 2:4. Lk 2:25.
Led by the Spirit. Ro 8:14.
Liberal. Is 32:8. 2 Co 9:13.
Loving. Cl 1:4. 1 Th 4:9.
Lowly. Pr 16:19.
Meek. Is 29:19. Mt 5:5.
Merciful. Ps 37:26. Mt 5:7.
New creatures. 2 Co 5:17. Ep 2:10.
Obedient. Ro 16:19. 1 P 1:14.
Poor in spirit. Ps 51:17. Mt 5:3.
Prudent. Pr 16:21.
Pure in heart. Mt 5:8. 1 Jn 3:3.
Righteous. Is 60:21. Lk 1:6.
Sincere. 2 Co 1:12; 2:17.
Steadfast. Ac 2:42. Cl 2:5.
Taught of God. Is 54:13. 1 Jn 2:27.
True. 2 Co 6:8.
Undefiled. Ps 119:1.
Upright. 1 K 3:6. Ps 15:2.
Watchful. Lk 12:37.
Zealous of good works. Ti 2:14; 3:8.

SALT
Characterized as good and useful. Mk 9:50.
ILLUSTRATIVE OF
Desolation (pits of). Zp 2:9.
Grace in the heart. Mk 9:50.
Graceless professors (without savor). Mt 5:13. Mk 9:50.
Preparation of the wicked for destruction (salted with fire). Mk 9:49.
Saints. Mt 5:13.

Wisdom in speech. Cl 4:6.
Liberally afforded to the Jews after the captivity. Ezr 6:9; 7:22.
Lost its savor when exposed to the air. Mt 5:13. Mk 9:50.
MIRACLES CONNECTED WITH
Elisha healed the bad water with. 1 K 2:21.
Lot's wife turned into a pillar of. Gn 19:26.
OFTEN FOUND
In pits. Zp 2:9.
In springs. Ja 3:12.
Near the Dead Sea. Nu 34:12. Dt 3:17.
Partaking of another's, a bond of friendship. Ezr 4:14.
Places sown with, to denote perpetual desolation. Jg 9:45.
Places where it abounded barren and unfruitful. Jr 17:6. Ezk 47:11.
USED FOR
Ratifying covenants. Nu 18:19. 2 Ch 13:5.
Seasoning food. Jb 6:6.
Seasoning sacrifices. Lv 2:13. Ezk 43:24.
Strengthening newborn infants. Ezk 16:4.
Valley of, celebrated for victories. 2 S 8:13. 2 K 14:7. 1 Ch 18:12.

SALUTATIONS
Antiquity of. Gn 18:2; 19:1.
Denied to persons of bad character. 2 Jn 1:10.
EXPRESSIONS USED AS
All hail. Mt 28:9.
Art thou in health? 2 S 20:9.
Blessed be thou of the Lord. 1 S 15:13.
The blessing of the Lord be upon you, we bless you in the name of the Lord. Ps 129:8.
God be gracious unto thee. Gn 43:29.
Hail. Mt 26:49. Lk 1:28.
The Lord be with you. Ru 2:4.
The Lord bless thee. Ru 2:4.
Peace be to this house. Lk 10:5.
Peace be with thee. Jg 19:20.
Peace to thee, and peace to thine house, and peace unto all that thou hast. 1 S 25:6.
GIVEN
By all passers-by. 1 S 10:3-4. Ps 129:8.
By brethren to each other. 1 S 17:22.
By inferiors to their superiors. Gn 47:7.
By superiors to inferiors. 1 S 30:21.
On entering a house. Jg 18:15. Mt 10:12. Lk 1:40-41, 44.

Given to Christ in derision. Mt 27:39, with Mk 15:18.

Jews condemned for giving only to their own countrymen. Mt 5:47.

OFTEN ACCOMPANIED BY

Bowing frequently to the ground. Gn 33:3.

Embracing and kissing the feet. Mt 28:9. Lk 7:38, 45.

Falling on the neck and kissing. Gn 33:4; 45:14–15. Lk 15:20.

Falling prostrate on the ground. Es 8:3. Mt 2:11. Lk 8:41.

Kissing the dust. Ps 72:9. Is 49:23.

Laying hold of the beard with the right hand. 2 S 20:9.

Often perfidious. 2 S 20:9. Mt 26:49.

Often sent by letter. Ro 16:21–23. 1 Co 16:21. Cl 4:18. 2 Th 3:17.

Often sent through messengers. 1 S 25:5, 14. 2 S 8:10.

Persons in haste excused from giving or receiving. 2 K 4:29. Lk 10:24.

Pharisees condemned for seeking in public. Mt 23:7. Mk 12:38.

SALVATION

All the earth shall see. Is 52:10. Lk 3:6.

Announced after the fall. Gn 3:15.

Came to the Gentiles through the fall of the Jews. Ro 11:11.

CHRIST

Appointed for. Is 49:6.

The Author of. He 5:9.

Brings, with him. Is 62:11. Lk 19:9.

Came to effect. Mt 18:11. 1 Tm 1:15.

The Captain of. He 2:10.

Died to effect. Jn 3:14–15. Gl 1:4.

Exalted to give. Ac 5:31.

Has. Zc 9:9.

Mighty to effect. Is 63:1. He 7:25.

Raised up for. Lk 1:69.

Confession of Christ necessary to. Ro 10:10.

DELIVERANCE FROM

The devil. Cl 2:15. He 2:14–15.

Enemies. Lk 1:71, 74.

Eternal death. Jn 3:16–17.

Sin. Mt 1:21, with 1 Jn 3:5.

This present evil world. Gl 1:4.

Uncleanness. Ezk 36:29.

Wrath. Ro 5:9. 1 Th 1:10.

DESCRIBED AS

Common. Jde 1:3.

Eternal. Is 45:17; 51:6. He 5:9.

From generation to generation. Is 51:8.

Glorious. 2 Tm 2:10.

Great. He 2:3.

To the uttermost. He 7:25.

Final perseverance necessary to. Mt 10:22.

From sin, to be worked out with fear and trembling. Php 2:12.

God is willing to give. Tm 2:4.

Godly sorrow produces repentance unto. 2 Co 7:10.

The gospel is the power of God unto. Ro 1:16. Co 1:18.

The heavenly host ascribe to God. Rv 7:10; 19:1.

ILLUSTRATED BY

Chariots. Hk 3:8.

Clothing. 2 Ch 6:41. Pss 132:16; 149:4. Is 61:10.

A cup. Ps 116:13.

A helmet. Is 59:17.

A horn. Ps 18:2. Lk 1:69.

A lamp. Is 62:1.

A rock. Dt 32:15. 2 S 22:47. Ps 95:1.

A shield. 2 S 22:36.

A tower. 2 S 22:51.

A victory. 1 Co 15:57.

Walls and bulwarks. Is 26:1; 60:18.

Wells. Is 12:3.

Is

By Christ. Is 63:9. Ep 5:23.

By Christ alone. Is 45:21–22; 59:16. Ac 4:12.

Far off from the wicked. Ps 119:155. Is 59:11.

Not by works. Ro 11:6. Ep 2:9. 2 Tm 1:9. Ti 3:5.

Of the appointment of God. 1 Th 5:9.

Of God. Pss 3:8; 37:39. Jr 3:23.

Of grace. Ep 2:5, 8. 2 Tm 1:9. Ti 2:11.

Of the long-suffering of God. 2 P 3:15.

Of love. Ro 5:8. 1 Jn 4:9–10.

Of mercy. Ps 6:4. Ti 3:5.

Of the purpose of God. 2 Tm 1:9.

Through faith in Christ. Mk 16:16. Ac 16:31. Ro 10:9. Ep 2:8. 1 P 1:5.

MINISTERS

Are a sweet savor of Christ, unto God, in those who obtain. 2 Co 2:15.

Give the knowledge of. Lk 1:77.

Should be clothed with. 2 Ch 6:41. Ps 132:16.

Should endure suffering that the elect may obtain. 2 Tm 2:10.

Should exhort to. Ezk 3:18–19. Ac 2:40.

Should labor to lead others to. Ro 11:14.
Should use self-denial to lead others to. 1 Co 9:22.
Show the way of   Ac 16:17.
No escape for those who neglect.   He 2:3.
Now is the day of.   Is 49:8. 2 Co 6:2.
Of the Gentiles, predicted.   Is 45:22; 49:6; 52:10.
Of Israel, predicted.   Is 35:4; 45:17. Zc 9:16. Ro 11:26.
Preaching the word is the appointed means of. 1 Co 1:21.
Reconciliation to God, a pledge of.   Ro 5:10.
Regeneration necessary to.   Jn 3:3.
Revealed in the gospel.   Ep 1:13. 2 Tm 1:10.

SAINTS

Appointed to obtain.   1 Th 5:9.
Are heirs of.   He 1:14.
Ascribe, to God.   Ps 25:5. Is 12:2.
Beautified with.   Ps 149:4.
Chosen to.   2 Th 2:13. 2 Tm 1:9.
Clothed with.   Is 61:10.
Commemorate, with thanks.   Ps 116:13.
Daily approach nearer to.   Ro 13:11.
Declare.   Pss 40:10; 71:15.
Earnestly look for.   Ps 119:123.
Evidence, by works.   He 6:9–10.
Glory in.   1 Co 1:31. Gl 6:14.
Have a token of, in their patient suffering for Christ.   Php 1:28–29.
Have, through grace.   Ac 15:11.
Hope for.   Lm 3:26. Ro 8:24.
Kept by the power of God unto.   1 P 1:5.
Long for.   Ps 119:81, 174.
Love.   Ps 40:16.
Praise God for.   1 Ch 16:23. Ps 96:2.
Pray for assurance of.   Ps 35:3.
Pray for a joyful sense of.   Ps 51:12.
Pray to be visited with.   Pss 85:7; 106:4; 119:41.
Rejoice in.   Pss 9:14; 21:1. Is 25:9
Receive, as the end of their faith.   1 P 1:9.
Satisfied by.   Lk 2:30.
Wait for.   Gn 49:18. Lm 3:26.
Welcome the tidings of.   Is 52:7, with Ro 10:15.

The scriptures are able to make wise unto.   2 Tm 3:15. Ja 1:21.
Searched into and exhibited by the prophets. 1 P 1:10.

SOUGHT IN VAIN FROM

Earthly power.   Jr 3:23.
Idols.   Is 45:20. Jr 2:28.
Types.   Nu 21:4–9, with Jn 3:14–15.

SAMARIA, ANCIENT

Had many cities.   1 K 13:32.
Inhabitants of, carried captive to Assyria.   2 K 17:6, 23; 18:11.
A mountainous country.   Jr 31:5. Am 3:9.

PEOPLE OF, CHARACTERIZED AS

Corrupt and wicked.   Ezk 16:46–47. Ho 7:1. Am 3:9–10.
Idolatrous.   Ezk 23:5. Am 8:14. Mi 1:7.
Proud and arrogant.   Is 9:9.
Predictions respecting its destruction.   Is 8:4; 9:11–12. Ho 13:16. Am 3:11–12. Mi 1:6.
Repeopled from Assyria.   2 K 17:24–25.

SAMARIA THE CAPITAL OF

Besieged and taken by Shalmaneser.   2 K 17:5–6; 18:9–10.
Besieged by Benhadad.   1 K 20:1–12.
Besieged second time by Benhadad.   2 K 6:24.
Built by Omri king of Israel.   1 K 16:23–24.
Burial place of the kings of Israel.   1 K 16:28; 22:37. 2 K 13:13.
Called after Shemer, the owner of the hill on which it was built.   1 K 16:24.
Called the head of Ephraim.   Is 7:9.
Called the mountain of Samaria.   Am 4:1; 6:1.
Deliverance of, effected.   1 K 20:15–21.
Deliverance of, predicted.   1 K 20:13–14.
Delivered by miraculous means.   2 K 7:6–7.
Elisha predicted plenty in.   2 K 7:1–2.
A fenced city, well provided with arms.   2 K 10:2.
Kings of Israel sometimes took their titles from.   1 K 21:1. 2 K 1:3.
Pool of Samaria near to.   1 K 22:38.
Prophet Elisha dwelt in.   2 K 2:25; 5:3; 6:32.
Remarkable plenty in, as foretold by Elisha. 2 K 7:16–20.
The residence of the kings of Israel.   1 K 16:29. 2 K 1:2; 3:1, 6.
Suffered severely from famine.   2 K 6:25–29.
Territory of Ephraim and Manasseh properly so-called.   Jsh 17:17–18. Is 28:1.
Whole kingdom of Israel sometimes called. Ezk 16:46, 51. Ho 8:5–6.

SAMARIA, MODERN

Christ after his resurrection commanded the gospel to be preached in.   Ac 1:8.

Christ at first forbade his disciples to visit. Mt 10:5.

Christ preached in. Jn 4:39–42.

CITIES OF, MENTIONED

Antipatris. Ac 23:31.

Samaria. Ac 8:5.

Sychar. Jn 4:5.

The gospel first preached in, by Philip. Ac 8:5.

Had many cities, etc. Mt 10:5. Lk 9:52.

INHABITANTS OF

Abhorred by the Jews. Jn 8:48.

Boasted descent from Jacob. Jn 4:12.

Expected the Messiah. Jn 4:25, 29.

Had no dealings with the Jews. Lk 9:52–53. Jn 4:9.

More humane and grateful than the Jews. Lk 10:33–36; 17:16–18.

Opposed the Jews after their return from captivity. Ne 4:1–18.

Professed to worship God. Ezr 4:2.

Ready to hear and embrace the gospel. Jn 4:39–42. Ac 8:6–8.

Their religion mixed with idolatry. 2 K 17:41, with Jn 4:22.

Their true descent. 2 K 17:24, Ezr 4:9–10.

Were superstitious. Ac 8:9–11.

Worshiped on Mount Gerizim. Jn 4:20.

Many Christian churches in. Ac 9:31.

Persecuted Christians fled to. Ac 8:1.

Situated between Judea and Galilee. Lk 17:11. Jn 4:3–4.

SANCTIFICATION

All saints are in a state of. Ac 20:32; 26:18. 1 Co 6:11.

Christ made, of God, unto us. 1 Co 1:30.

The church made glorious by. Ep 5:26–27.

Described as separation to the service of God. Ps 4:3. 2 Co 6:17.

EFFECTED BY

Christ. He 2:11; 13:12.

God. Ezk 37:28. 1 Th 5:23. Jde 1:1.

The Holy Ghost. Ro 15:16. 1 Co 6:11.

God wills all saints to have. 1 Th 4:3.

In Christ. 1 Co 1:2.

MINISTERS

Set apart to God's service by. Jr 1:5.

Should exhort their people to walk in. 1 Th 4:1, 3.

Should pray that their people may enjoy complete. 1 Th 5:23.

None can inherit the kingdom of God without. 1 Co 6:9–11.

Offering up of saints acceptable through. Ro 15:16.

Saints elected to salvation through. 2 Th 2:13. 1 P 1:2.

Saints fitted for the service of God by. 2 Tm 2:21.

SHOULD LEAD TO

Holiness. Ro 6:22. Ep 5:7–9.

Mortification of sin. 1 Th 4:3–4.

Through the atonement of Christ. He 10:10; 13:12.

Through the word of God. Jn 17:17, 19. Ep 5:26.

Types. Gn 2:3. Ex 13:2; 19:14; 40:9–15. Lv 27:14–16.

SANCTUARY

Brings understanding. Ps 73:17.

A house of prayer for all peoples. Is 56:7. Mt 21:13.

Isaiah beheld the Lord in. Is 6.

The Lord is in. Ps 11:4.

Not to be desecrated. Jn 2:16.

The righteous love. Ps 26:8.

Strength and beauty are in. Ps 96:6.

To be reverenced. Lv 19:30.

SATAN

See The Devil.

SATISFACTION

For the hungry. Lk 6:21.

From drinking divine waters. Is 55:1. Jn 4:14.

From good news. Pr 25:25.

From the Lord's likeness. Ps 17:15.

Of the humble, the mourning, the meek. Mt 5:3–12.

Of the redeemed in heaven. Rv 7:16.

With good things. Ps 103:2, 5.

With long life. Ps 91:16.

SAVIOR

See Christ, the Savior ; Redemption; Salvation.

SCAPEGOAT

Chosen by lot. Lv 16:8.

COMMUNICATED UNCLEANNESS TO

The high priest. Lv 16:24.

The man who led him away. Lv 16:26.

High priest transferred the sins of Israel to, by

confessing them with both hands upon its head. Lv 16:21.

Part of the sin offering on the day of atonement. Lv 16:5, 7.

Sent into the wilderness by the hands of a fit person. Lv 16:21–22.

A type of Christ. Is 53:6, 11–12.

SCIENCES
Architecture. Dt 8:12. 1 Ch 29:19.
Arithmetic. Gn 15:5. Lv 26:8. Jb 29:18.
Astrology. Is 47:13.
Astronomy. Jb 38:31–32. Is 13:10.
Botany. 1 K 4:33.
Geography. Gn 10:1–30. Is 11:11.
History and chronology. 1 K 22:39. 2 K 1:18. 1 Ch 9:1; 29:29.
Mechanics. Gn 6:14–16; 11:4. Ex 14:6–7.
Medicine. Jr 8:22. Mk 5:26.
Music. 1 Ch 16:4–7; 25:6.
Navigation. 1 K 9:27. Ps 107:23.
Surveying. Jsh 18:4–9. Ne 2:12–16. Ezk 40:5–6. Zc 2:2.
Zoology. 1 K 4:33.

SCORNING AND MOCKING
Characteristic of the latter days. 2 P 3:3. Jde 1:18.
Christ endured. Mt 9:24; 27:29.
Drunkards addicted to. Ps 69:12. Ho 7:5.
Idolaters addicted to. Is 57:3–6.
Punishment for. 2 Ch 36:17. Pr 19:29. Is 29:20. Lm 3:64–66.
SAINTS ENDURE, ON ACCOUNT OF THEIR
Being children of God. Gn 21:9, with Gl 4:29.
Faith. He 11:36.
Faithfulness in declaring the word of God. Jr 20:7–8.
Uprightness. Jb 12:4.
Zeal for God's house. Ne 2:19.
Sufferings of Christ by, predicted. Ps 22:6–8. Is 53:3. Lk 18:32.
THEY WHO ARE ADDICTED TO
Are avoided by saints. Ps 1:1. Jr 15:17.
Are contentious. Pr 22:10.
Are hated by men. Pr 24:9.
Are proud and haughty. Pr 21:24.
Are scorned by God. Pr 3:34.
Bring others into danger. Pr 29:8.
Delight in. Pr 1:22.
Go not to the wise. Pr 15:12.
Hate those who reprove. Pr 9:8.
Hear not rebuke. Pr 13:1.

Love not those who reprove. Pr 15:12.
Shall themselves endure. Ezk 23:32.
Walk after their own lusts. 2 P 3:3.
THE WICKED INDULGE IN, AGAINST
All solemn admonitions. 2 Ch 30:6–10.
The gifts of the Spirit. Ac 2:13.
God's ministers. 2 Ch 36:16.
God's ordinances. Lm 1:7.
God's threatenings. Is 5:19. Jr 17:15.
The resurrection of the dead. Ac 17:32.
Saints. Ps 123:4. Lm 3:14, 63.
The second coming of Christ. 2 P 3:3–4.
Woe denounced against. Is 5:18–19.

SCRIBES
ACTED AS
Keepers of the muster rolls of the host. 2 K 25:19. 2 Ch 26:11. Jr 52:25.
Notaries in courts of justice. Jr 32:11–12.
Religious teachers. Ne 8:2–6.
Secretaries to kings. 2 S 8:17; 20:25. 2 K 12:10. Es 3:12.
Secretaries to prophets. Jr 36:4, 26.
Writers of public documents. 1 Ch 24:6.
Antiquity of. Jg 5:14.
FAMILIES CELEBRATED FOR FURNISHING
Kenites. 1 Ch 2:55.
Levi. 1 Ch 24:6. 2 Ch 34:13.
Zebulun. Jg 5:14.
Generally men of great wisdom. 1 Ch 27:32.
Illustrative of well-instructed ministers of the gospel. Mt 13:52.
MODERN
Active in procuring our Lord's death. Mt 26:3. Lk 23:10.
Condemned by Christ for hypocrisy. Mt 23:15.
Esteemed wise and learned. 1 Co 1:20.
Often offended at our Lord's conduct and teaching. Mt 21:15. Mk 2:6–7, 16; 3:22.
Persecuted the early Christians. Ac 4:5, 18, 21; 6:12.
Regarded as interpreters of scripture. Mt 2:4; 17:10. Mk 12:35.
Sat in Moses' seat. Mt 23:2.
Tempted our Lord. Jn 8:3.
Their manner of teaching contrasted with that of Christ. Mt 7:29. Mk 1:22.
Were doctors of the law. Mk 12:28, with Mt 22:35.
Were frequently Pharisees. Ac 23:9.
Wore long robes and loved pre-eminence. Mk 12:38–39.

Often learned in the law. Ezr 7:6.
Were ready writers. Ps 45:1.
Wore an inkhorn at their girdles. Ezk 9:2–3.

THE SCRIPTURES

Advantage of possessing. Ro 3:2.
All should desire to hear. Ne 8:1.

ARE

Able to make wise unto salvation through faith in Christ. 2 Tm 3:15.
Full and sufficient. Lk 16:29, 31.
Profitable both for doctrine and practice. 2 Tm 3:16–17.
An unerring guide. Pr 6:23. 2 P 1:19.
Blessedness of hearing and obeying. Lk 11:28. Ja 1:25.

CALLED THE

Book. Ps 40:7. Rv 22:19.
Book of the law. Ne 8:3. Gl 3:10.
Book of the Lord. Is 34:16.
Holy Scriptures. Ro 1:2. 2 Tm 3:15.
Law of the Lord. Ps 1:2. Is 30:9.
Oracles of God. Ro 3:2. 1 P 4:11.
Scripture of truth. Dn 10:21.
Sword of the Spirit. Ep 6:17.
Word. Ja 1:21–23. 1 P 2:2.
Word of Christ. Cl 3:16.
Word of God. Lk 11:28. He 4:12.
Word of truth. Ja 1:18.

Christ enables us to understand. Lk 24:45.
Christ sanctioned, by appealing to them. Mt 4:4. Mk 12:10. Jn 7:42.
Christ taught out of. Lk 24:27.
Contain the promises of the gospel. Ro 1:2.
Denunciations against those who add to or take from. Rv 22:18–19.

DESCRIBED AS

Perfect. Ps 19:7.
Precious. Ps 19:10.
Pure. Pss 12:6; 119:140. Pr 30:5.
Quick and powerful. He 4:12.
True. Ps 119:160. Jn 17:17.

DESIGNED FOR

Admonishing. Ps 19:11. 1 Co 10:11.
Building up in the faith. Ac 20:32.
Cleansing the heart. Jn 15:3. Ep 5:26.
Cleansing the ways. Ps 119:9.
Comforting. Ps 119:82. Ro 15:4.
Converting the soul. Ps 19:7.
Illuminating. Ps 119:130.
Keeping from destructive paths. Ps 17:4.
Making wise the simple. Ps 19:7.
Producing faith. Jn 20:31.
Producing hope. Ps 119:49. Ro 15:4.

Producing obedience. Dt 17:19–20.
Promoting growth in grace. 1 P 2:2.
Quickening. Ps 119:50, 93.
Regenerating. Ja 1:18. 1 P 1:23.
Rejoicing the heart. Pss 19:8; 119:111.
Sanctifying. Jn 17:17. Ep 5:26.
Supporting life. Dt 8:3, with Mt 4:4.
Destruction of, punished. Jr 36:29–31.
Everything should be tried by. Is 9:20. Ac 17:11.
Given by inspiration of God. 2 Tm 3:16.
Given by inspiration of the Holy Ghost. Ac 1:16. He 3:7. 2 P 1:21.
The Holy Ghost enables us to understand. Jn 16:13. 1 Co 2:10–14.
Ignorance of, a source of error. Mt 22:29. Ac 13:27.
Intended for the use of all men. Ro 16:26.
The letter of, without the spirit, killeth. Jn 6:63, with 2 Co 3:6.
Let them dwell richly in you. Cl 3:16.
Mere hearers of, deceive themselves. Ja 1:22.
No prophecy of, is of any private interpretation. 2 P 1:20.
Nothing to be taken from or added to. Dt 4:2; 12:32.
One portion of, to be compared with another. 1 Co 2:13.
Record divine prophecies. 2 P 1:19–21.
Reveal the laws, statutes, and judgments of God. Dt 4:5, 14, with Ex 24:3–4.

SAINTS

Delight in. Ps 1:2.
Esteem above all things. Jb 23:12.
Esteem as a light. Ps 119:105.
Grieve when men disobey. Ps 119:158.
Hide in their hearts. Ps 119:11.
Hope in. Ps 119:74, 81, 147.
Keep in remembrance. Ps 119:16.
Long after. Ps 119:82.
Love exceedingly. Ps 119:86, 113, 159, 167.
Meditate in. Pss 1:2; 119:99, 148.
Obey. Ps 119:67. Lk 8:21. Jn 17:6.
Plead the promises of, in prayer. Ps 119:25, 28, 41, 76, 169.
Pray to be conformed to. Ps 119:133.
Pray to be taught. Ps 119:12–13, 33, 66.
Regard as sweet. Ps 119:103.
Rejoice in. Ps 119:162. Jr 15:16.
Speak of. Ps 119:172.
Stand in awe of. Ps 119:161. Is 66:2.
Trust in. Ps 119:42.

SHOULD BE

Appealed to.   1 Co 1:31. 1 P 1:16.

Believed.   Jn 2:22.

Known.   2 Tm 3:15.

Laid up in the heart.   Dt 6:6; 11:18.

Not handled deceitfully.   2 Co 4:2.

Not only heard, but obeyed.   Mt 7:24, with Lk 11:28. Ja 1:22.

Read.   Dt 17:19. Is 34:16.

Read publicly to all.   Dt 31:11–13. Ne 8:3. Jr 36:6. Ac 13:15.

Received, not as the word of men, but as the word of God.   1 Th 2:13.

Received with meekness.   Ja 1:21.

Searched.   Jn 5:39; 7:52.

Searched daily.   Ac 17:11.

The standard of teaching.   1 P 4:11.

Talked of continually.   Dt 6:7.

Taught to all.   2 Ch 17:7–9. Ne 8:7–8.

Taught to children.   Dt 6:7; 11:19. 2 Tm 3:15.

Used against our spiritual enemies.   Mt 4:4, 7, 10, with Ep 6:11, 17.

Testify of Christ.   Jn 5:39. Ac 10:43; 18:28. 1 Co 15:3.

They who search, are truly noble.   Ac 17:11.

THE WICKED

Corrupt.   2 Co 2:17.

Frequently wrest, to their own destruction. 2 P 3:16.

Make, of none effect through their traditions.   Mk 7:9–13.

Obey not.   Ps 119:158.

Reject.   Jr 8:9.

Stumble at.   1 P 2:8.

Work effectually in them that believe.   1 Th 2:13.

Written for our instruction.   Ro 15:4.

THE SEA

CALLED THE

Deep.   Jb 41:31. Ps 107:24. 2 Co 11:25.

Great and wide sea.   Ps 104:25.

Great waters.   Ps 77:19.

Caused to foam by Leviathan.   Jb 41:31–32.

Clouds the garment of.   Jb 38:9.

COMMERCIAL NATIONS

Derived great wealth from.   Dt 33:19.

Often built cities on the borders of.   Gn 49:13. Ezk 27:3. Na 3:8.

Darkness the swaddling band of.   Jb 38:9.

Gathering together of waters originally called. Gn 1:10.

GOD

Created.   Ex 20:11. Ps 95:5. Ac 14:15.

Does what he pleases in.   Ps 135:6.

Dries up, by his rebuke.   Is 50:2. Na 1:4.

Founded the earth upon.   Ps 24:2.

Made the birds and fishes out of.   Gn 1:20–22.

Measures the waters of.   Is 40:12.

Set bounds to, by a perpetual decree.   Jb 26:10; 38:8, 10–11. Pr 8:27, 29.

Shakes, by his word.   Hg 2:6.

Stills, by his power.   Pss 65:7; 89:9; 107:29.

Great rivers often called.   Is 11:15. Jr 51:36.

ILLUSTRATIVE OF

Devastating armies (its waves).   Ezk 26:3–4.

Diffusion of spiritual knowledge over the earth in the latter days (covered with waters).   Is 11:9. Hk 2:14.

Heavy afflictions.   Is 43:2. Lm 2:13.

Hostile armies (when roaring).   Is 5:30. Jr 6:23.

The peace of heaven (when smooth as glass).   Rv 4:6; 15:2.

Righteousness (its waves).   Is 48:18.

The unsteady (its waves).   Ja 1:6.

The wicked (when troubled).   Is 57:20.

Inhabited by innumerable creatures great and small.   Ps 104:25–26.

Lakes often called.   Dt 3:17. Mt 8:24, 27, 32.

Made to glorify God.   Pss 69:34; 148:7.

NAMES MENTIONED

Adriatic or Sea of Adria.   Ac 27:27.

Mediterranean or Great Sea.   Nu 34:6. Dt 11:24; 34:2. Zc 14:8.

Red Sea.   Ex 10:19; 13:18; 23:31.

Salt or Dead Sea.   Gn 14:3. Nu 34:12.

Sea of Galilee.   Mt 4:18; 8:32. Jn 6:1.

Sea of Jazer.   Jr 48:32.

Sea of Joppa or Sea of the Philistines.   Ezr 3:7, with Ex 23:31.

Numerous islands in.   Ezk 26:18.

Of great depth.   Ps 69:22.

Of immense extent.   Jb 11:9. Ps 104:25.

Passed over in ships.   Pss 104:26; 107:23.

Raised by the wind.   Ps 107:25–26. Jnh 1:4.

Replenished by rivers.   Ec 1:7. Ezk 47:8.

The renewed earth shall be without.   Rv 21:1.

Rivers supplied by exhalations from.   Ec 1:7.

Sailing on, dangerous.   Ac 27:9, 20. 2 Co 11:26.

Sand the barrier of.   Jr 5:22.

Shall give up its dead at the last day.   Rv 20:13.

Shore of, covered with sand. Gn 22:17. 1 K
4:29. Jb 6:3. Ps 78:27.

WAVES OF
Mighty. Ps 93:4. Ac 27:41.
Multitudinous. Jr 51:42.
Raised upon high. Pss 93:3; 107:25
Tossed to and fro. Jr 5:22.
Tumultuous. Lk 21:25. Jde 1:13.
Wonders of God seen in. Ps 107:24.

SEALING OF THE HOLY SPIRIT
Christ received. Jn 6:27.
Is unto the day of redemption. Ep 4:30.
Judgment suspended until all saints receive.
Rv 7:3.
Saints receive. 2 Co 1:22. Ep 1:13.
Type. Ro 4:11.
The wicked do not receive. Rv 9:4.

SEALS
Called signets. Gn 38:18, 25.
Generally worn as rings or bracelets. Jr
22:24.
ILLUSTRATIVE OF
Appropriation of saints to God by the
Spirit. 2 Co 1:22. Ep 1:13; 4:30.
Circumcision. Ro 4:11.
Converts. 1 Co 9:2.
Full approval. Jn 3:33.
Restraint. Jb 9:7; 37:7. Rv 20:3.
Secrecy. Dn 12:4. Rv 5:1; 10:4.
Security. S S 4:12. 2 Tm 2:19. Rv 7:2–8;
20:3.
What is dear or valued. S S 8:6. Jr 22:24.
Hg 2:23.
IMPRESSIONS OF
Attached to all royal decrees. 1 K 21:8. Es
3:12; 8:8.
Attached to covenants. Ne 9:38; 10:1.
Attached to leases and transfers of property.
Jr 32:9–12, 44.
Attached to the victims approved for sac-
rifice, alluded to. Jn 6:27.
Frequently taken in clay. Jb 38:14.
Set upon treasures. Dt 32:34.
Used for security. Dn 6:17. Mt 27:66.
Were given by kings as a badge of authority.
Gn 41:41–42.
Inscriptions upon, alluded to. 2 Tm 2:19.
Precious stones set in gold used as. Ex 28:11.

SECOND COMING OF CHRIST
Blessedness of being prepared for. Mt 24:6.
Lk 12:37–38.

CALLED THE
Appearing of Jesus Christ. 1 P 1:7.
Day of our Lord Jesus Christ. 1 Co 1:8.
Coming of the day of God. 2 P 3:12.
Glorious appearing of the great God and
our Savior. Ti 2:13.
Last time. 1 P 1:5.
Revelation of Jesus Christ. 1 P 1:13.
Times of refreshing from the presence of
the Lord. Ac 3:19.
Times of restitution of all things. Ac 3:21,
with Ro 8:21.
Every eye shall see him at. Rv 1:7.
FORETOLD BY
Angels. Ac 1:10–11.
Apostles. Ac 3:20. 1 Tm 6:14.
Himself. Mt 25:31. Jn 14:3.
Prophets. Dn 7:13. Jde 1:14.
Heavens and earth shall be dissolved, etc., at.
2 P 3:10, 12.
Illustrated. Mt 25:6. Lk 12:36, 39; 19:12,
15.
MANNER OF
Accompanied by angels. Mt 16:27; 25:31.
Mk 8:38. 2 Th 1:7.
As he ascended. Ac 1:9, 11.
As the lightning. Mt 24:27.
As a thief in the night. 1 Th 5:2. 2 P 3:10.
Rv 16:15.
In clouds. Mt 24:30; 26:64. Rv 1:7.
In flaming fire. 2 Th 1:8.
In the glory of his Father. Ml 16:27.
In his own glory. Mt 25:31.
Suddenly. Mk 13:36.
Unexpectedly. Mt 24:44. Lk 12:40.
With his saints. 1 Th 3:13. Jde 1:14.
With a shout and the voice of the Archan-
gel, etc. 1 Th 4:16.
With power and great glory. Mt 24:30.
The man of sin to be destroyed at. 2 Th 2:8.
Not to make atonement. He 9:28, with Ro
6:9–10 and He 10:14.
PURPOSES OF, TO
Be admired in them that believe. 2 Th
1:10.
Be glorified in his saints. 2 Th 1:10.
Bring to light the hidden things of darkness,
etc. 1 Co 4:5.
Completete the salvation of saints. He
9:28. 1 P 1:5.
Destroy death. 1 Co 15:25–26.
Judge. Ps 50:3–4, with Jn 5:22. 2 Tm 4:1.
Jde 1:15. Rv 20:11–13.
Reign. Is 24:23. Dn 7:14. Rv 11:15.

SAINTS

Assured of. Jb 19:25–26.

Faith of, shall be found unto praise at. 1 P 1:7.

Haste unto. 2 P 3:12.

Look for. Php 3:20. Ti 2:13.

Love. 2 Tm 4:8.

Pray for. Rv 22:20.

Shall appear with him in glory at. Cl 3:4.

Shall be blameless at. 1 Co 1:8. 1 Th 3:13; 5:23. Jde 1:24.

Shall be like him at. Php 3:21. 1 Jn 3:2.

Shall be preserved unto. Php 1:6.

Shall not be ashamed at. 1 Jn 2:28; 4:17.

Shall receive a crown of glory at. 2 Tm 4:8. 1 P 5:4.

Shall reign with him at. Dn 7:27. 2 Tm 2:12. Rv 5:10; 20:6; 22:5.

Shall see him as he is, at. 1 Jn 3:2.

Should be patient unto. 2 Th 3:5. Ja 5:7–8.

Should be ready for. Mt 24:44. Lk 12:40.

Should watch for. Mt 24:42. Mk 13:35–37. Lk 21:36.

Wait for. 1 Co 1:7. 1 Th 1:10.

Saints alive at, shall be caught up to meet him. 1 Th 4:17.

Should be always considered as at hand. Ro 13:12. Php 4:5. 1 P 4:7

Signs preceding. Mt 24:3, etc.

They who shall have died in Christ shall rise first at. 1 Th 4:16.

Time of, unknown. Mt 24:36. Mk 13:32.

THE WICKED

Presume upon the delay of. Mt 24:28.

Scoff at. 2 P 3:3–4.

Shall be punished at. 2 Th 1:8–9.

Shall be surprised by. Mt 24:37–39. 1 Th 5:3.

SECURITY

IN GOD

Our caretaker. 1 P 5:7.

Our champion. 2 S 5:24. 2 Ch 32:8.

Our defense. Ps 62:2.

Our dwelling place. Ps 90:1.

Our guardian. Ps 125:2. Is 31:5; 52:12.

Our help. Ps 94:17.

Our keeper. Ps 121:5.

Our rock. Dt 32:31.

Our safety. Pr 21:31.

Our stronghold in trouble. Na 1:7.

Our sustainer. Ps 55:22.

OF BELIEVERS

Chosen before the foundation of the world. Ep 1:4.

None can take them from Christ's hand, nor from God's. Jn 10:28, 29.

Predestined, called, justified, glorified. Ro 8:30.

Shall never perish. Jn 10:28.

SEED

Difference between, and the plant which grows from it, noticed. 1 Co 15:37–38.

Each kind of, has its own body. 1 Co 15:38.

Every herb, tree and grass yields its own. Gn 1:11–12, 29.

Ground carefully plowed and prepared for. Is 28:24–25.

ILLUSTRATIVE OF

Spiritual life. 1 Jn 3:9.

The word of God. Lk 8:11. 1 P 1:23.

In Egypt required to be artificially watered. Dt 11:19.

THE JEWS PUNISHED BY

Its being choked by thorns. Jr 12:13, with Mt 13:7.

Its increase being consumed by enemies. Lv 26:16. Dt 28:33, 51.

Its increase being consumed by locusts, etc. Dt 28:38. Jl 1:4.

Its rotting in the ground. Jl 1:17. Ml 2:3.

Its yielding but little increase. Is 5:10. Hg 1:6.

MOSAIC LAWS RESPECTING

Different kinds of, not to be sown in the same field. Lv 19:19. Dt 22:9.

If dry, exempted from uncleanness though touched by an unclean thing. Lv 11:37.

If wet, rendered unclean by contact with an unclean thing. Lv 11:38.

Not to be sown during the sabbatical year. Lv 25:4, 20.

Not to be sown in year of jubilee. Lv 25:11.

The tithe of, to be given to God. Lv 27:30.

Often sown beside rivers. Ec 11:1. Is 32:20.

Often trodden into the ground, by the feet of oxen, etc. Is 32:20.

Required to be watered by the rain. Is 55:10.

SOWING

Necessary to its productiveness. Jn 12:24. 1 Co 15:36.

Often attended with danger. Ps 126:5–6.

Often attended with great waste. Mt 13:4–5, 7.

Required constant diligence. Ec 11:4, 6.

Time for, called seedtime. Gn 8:22.

SOWING, ILLUSTRATIVE OF

The burial of the body. 1 Co 15:26–38.

Christian liberality. Ec 11:6. 2 Co 9:6.

The death of Christ and its effects. Jn 12:24.

Men's works producing a corresponding recompense. Jb 4:8. Ho 10:12. Gl 6:7–8.

Preaching the gospel. Mt 13:3, 32. 1 Co 9:11.

Scattering or dispersing a people. Zc 10:9.

Yearly return of time of sowing, secured by covenant. Gn 8:21–22.

Yielded an abundant increase in Canaan. Gn 26:12. (See also Mt 13:23.)

SEEKING GOD

Afflictions designed to lead to. Ps 78:33–34. Ho 5:15.

Blessedness of. Ps 119:2.

By prayer. Jb 8:5. Dn 9:3.

Commanded. Is 55:6. Mt 7:7.

Ends in praise. Ps 22:26.

ENSURES

Being heard of him. Ps 34:4.

Gifts of righteousness. Ho 10:12.

His being found. Dt 4:29. 1 Ch 28:9. Pr 8:17. Jr 29:13.

His favor. Lm 3:25.

His not forsaking us. Ps 9:10.

His protection. Ezr 8:22.

Life. Ps 69:32. Am 5:4, 6.

Prosperity. Jb 8:5–6. Ps 34:10.

Understanding all things. Pr 28:5.

Imperative upon all. Is 8:19.

INCLUDES SEEKING

Christ. Ml 3:1. Lk 2:15–16.

The city which God has prepared. He 11:10, 16; 13–14.

His commandments. 1 Ch 28:8. Ml 2:7.

His face. Pss 27:8; 105:4.

His kingdom. Mt 6:33. Lk 12:31.

His name. Ps 83:16.

His precepts. Ps 119:45, 94.

His righteousness. Mt 6:33.

His strength. 1 Ch 16:11. Ps 105:4.

His word. Is 34:16.

Honor which comes from him. Jn 5:44.

Justification by Christ. Gl 2:16–17.

In his house. Dt 12:5. Ps 27:4.

Is never in vain. Is 45:19.

Leads to joy. Pss 70:4; 105:3.

None, by nature, are found to be engaged in. Ps 14:2, with Ro 3:11. Lk 12:23, 30.

Promise connected with. Ps 69:32.

Punishment of those who neglect. Zp 1:4–6.

SAINTS

Characterized by. Ps 24:6.

Desirous of. Jb 5:8.

Early in. Jb 8:5. Ps 63:1. Is 26:9.

Earnest in. S S 3:2, 4.

Engage in, with the whole heart. 2 Ch 15:2. Ps 119:10.

Prepare their hearts for. 2 Ch 30:19.

Purpose, in heart. Ps 27:8.

Set their hearts to. 2 Ch 11:16.

Specially exhorted to. Zp 2:3.

Shall be rewarded. He 11:6.

SHOULD BE

Evermore. Ps 105:4.

Immediate. Ho 10:12.

In the day of trouble. Ps 77:2.

While he may be found. Is 55:6.

With diligence. He 11:6.

With the heart. Dt 4:29. 1 Ch 22:19.

They who neglect denounced. Is 31:1.

THE WICKED

Are gone out of the way of. Ps 14:2–3, with Ro 3:11–12.

Not led to, by affliction. Is 9:13.

Prepare not their hearts for. 2 Ch 12:14.

Refuse, through pride. Ps 10:4.

Rejected, when too late in. Pr 1:28.

Sometimes pretend to. Ezr 4:2. Is 58:2.

SELF-CONTROL

For a clear conscience. Ac 24:16.

The fruit of the Holy Spirit. Gl 5:22, 23.

Over our bodies. Ro 6:12.

Over our lips. Ps 141:3. Ja 1:26.

Over our spirits. Pr 16:32; 25:28.

Reward of. Rv 21:7.

Through divine help. Jr 10:23.

Value of. Pr 16:32; 25:28.

SELF-DELUSION

A characteristic of the wicked. Ps 49:18.

EXHIBITED IN THINKING THAT

Christ shall not come to judge. 2 P 3:4.

Gifts entitle us to heaven. Mt 7:21–22.

God will not punish our sins. Ps 10:11 Jr 5:12.

Our lives shall be prolonged. Is 56:12 Lk 12:19. Ja 4:13.

Our own ways are right.   Pr 14:12.

Privileges entitle us to heaven.   Mt 3:9. Lk 13:25–26.

We are above adversity.   Ps 10:6.

We are better than others.   Lk 18:11.

We are pure.   Pr 30:12.

We are rich in spiritual things.   Rv 3:17.

We may have peace while in sin.   Dt 29:19.

We should adhere to established wicked practices.   Jr 44:17.

Fatal consequences of.   Mt 7:23; 24:48–51. Lk 12:20. 1 Th 5:3.

Frequently persevered in, to the last.   Mt 7:22; 25:11–12. Lk 13:24–25.

Obstinate sinners often given up to.   Ps 81:11–12. Ho 4:17. 2 Th 2:10–11.

Prosperity frequently leads to.   Ps 30:6. Ho 12:8. Lk 12:17–19.

SELF-DENIAL

Becomes strangers and pilgrims.   He 11:13–15. 1 P 2:11.

Christ set an example of.   Mt 4:8–10; 8:20. Jn 6:38. Ro 15:3. Php 2:6–8.

Danger of neglecting.   Mt 16:25–26. 1 Co 9:27.

Happy result of.   2 P 1:4.

Ministers especially called to exercise.   2 Co 6:4–5.

NECESSARY

In following Christ.   Lk 14:27–33.

In the warfare of saints.   2 Tm 2:4.

To the triumph of saints.   1 Co 9:25–27.

Reward of.   Mt 19:28–29. Ro 8:13.

SHOULD BE EXERCISED IN

Abstaining from fleshly lusts,   1 P 2:11.

Assisting others.   Lk 3:11.

Being crucified unto the world.   Gl 6:14.

Being crucified with Christ.   Ro 6:6.

Controlling the appetite.   Pr 23:2.

Crucifying the flesh.   Gl 5:24.

Denying ungodliness and worldly lusts.   Ro 6:12. Ti 2:12.

Even lawful things.   1 Co 10:23.

Forsaking all.   Lk 14:33.

Mortifying deeds of the body.   Ro 8:13.

Mortifying sinful lusts.   Mk 9:43. Cl 3:5.

No longer living to lusts of men.   1 P 4:2.

Not pleasing ourselves.   Ro 15:1–3.

Not seeking our own profit.   1 Co 10:24, 33; 13:5. Php 2:4.

Preferring Christ to all earthly relations.   Mt 8:21–22. Lk 14:26.

Preferring the profit of others.   Ro 14:20–21. 1 Co 10:24, 33.

Putting off the old man which is corrupt.   Ep 4:22. Cl 3:9.

Taking up the cross and following Christ.   Mt 10:38; 16:24.

A test of devotedness to Christ.   Mt 10:37–38. Lk 9:23–24.

SELF-EXAMINATION

Advantages of.   1 Co 11:31. Gl 6:4. 1 Jn 3:20–22.

Cause of difficulty in.   Jr 17:9.

Enjoined.   2 Co 13:5.

Necessary before the communion.   1 Co 11:28.

SHOULD BE ENGAGED IN

With diligent search.   Ps 77:6. Lm 3:40.

With holy awe.   Ps 4:4.

With prayer for divine searching.   Pss 26:2; 139:23–24.

With purpose of amendment.   Ps 119:59. Lm 3:40.

SELFISHNESS

All men addicted to.   Ep 2:3. Php 2:21.

Characteristic of the last days.   2 Tm 3:1–2.

Contrary to the law of God.   Lv 19:18. Mt 22:39. Ja 2:8.

Especially forbidden to saints.   1 Co 10:24. Php 2:4.

Example of Christ condemns.   Jn 4:34. Ro 15:3. 2 Co 8:9.

EXHIBITED IN

Being lovers of ourselves.   2 Tm 3:2.

Living to ourselves.   2 Co 5:15.

Neglect of the poor.   1 Jn 3:17.

Performing duty for reward.   Mi 3:11.

Pleasing ourselves.   Ro 15:1.

Seeking after gain.   Is 56:11.

Seeking our own.   1 Co 10:33. Php 2:21.

Seeking undue precedence.   Mt 20:21.

Serving God for reward.   Ml 1:10.

God hates.   Ml 1:10.

Inconsistent with Christian love.   1 Co 13:5.

Inconsistent with the communion of saints.   Ro 12:4–5, with 1 Co 12:12–27.

Love of Christ should constrain us to avoid.   2 Co 5:14–15.

Ministers should be devoid of.   1 Co 9:19–23; 10:33.

Saints falsely accused of.   Jb 1:9–11.

SELF-RIGHTEOUSNESS
Denunciation against. Mt 23:27–28.
Folly of. Jb 9:20.
Hateful to God. Lk 16:15.
Illustrated. Lk 18:10–12.
Is boastful. Mt 23:30.
IS VAIN BECAUSE OUR RIGHTEOUSNESS Is
But external. Mt 23:25–28. Lk 11:39–44.
But partial. Mt 23:25. Lk 11:42.
Ineffectual for salvation. Jb 9:30–31. Mt 5:20, with Ro 3:20.
No better than filthy rags. Is 64:6.
Unprofitable. Is 57:12.
Man is prone to. Pr 20:6; 30:12.
Saints renounce. Php 3:7–10.
THEY WHO ARE GIVEN TO
Are abominable before God. Is 65:5.
Are pure in their own eyes. Pr 30:12.
Audaciously approach God. Lk 18:11.
Condemn others. Mt 9:11–13. Lk 7:39.
Consider their own way right. Pr 21:2.
Despise others. Is 65:5. Lk 18:9.
Proclaim their own goodness. Pr 20:6.
Reject the righteousness of God. Ro 10:3.
Seek to justify themselves. Lk 10:29.
Seek to justify themselves before men. Lk 16:15.
Warning against. Dt 9:4.

SELF-WILL AND STUBBORNNESS
Characteristic of the wicked. Pr 7:11. 2 P 2:10.
EXHIBITED IN
Going backward and not forward. Jr 7:24.
Hardening the heart. 2 Ch 36:13.
Hardening the neck. Ne 9:16.
Rebelling against God. Dt 31:27. Ps 78:8.
Refusing to hearken to God. Pr 1:24.
Refusing to hearken to the messengers of God. 1 S 8:19. Jr 44:16. Zc 7:11.
Refusing to hearken to parents. Dt 21:18–19.
Refusing to receive correction. Dt 21:18. Jr 5:3; 7:28.
Refusing to walk in the ways of God. Ne 9:17. Ps 78:10. Is 42:24. Jr 6:16.
Resisting the Holy Ghost. Ac 7:51.
Walking in the counsels of an evil heart. Jr 7:24, with 23:17.
Forbidden. 2 Ch 30:8. Pss 75:5; 95:8.
God knows. Is 48:4.
Heinousness of. 1 S 15:23.

Illustrated. Ps 32:9. Jr 31:18.
MINISTERS SHOULD
Be without. Ti 1:7.
Pray that their people may be forgiven for. Ex 34:9. Dt 9:27.
Warn their people against. He 3:7–12.
PROCEED FROM
An evil heart. Jr 7:24.
Pride. Ne 9:16, 29.
Unbelief. 2 K 17:14.
Punishment for. Dt 21:21. Pr 29:1.
The wicked cease not from. Jg 2:19.

SERPENTS
All kinds of, can be tamed. Ja 3:7.
Called crooked. Jb 26:13. Is 27:1.
Characterized as subtle. Gn 3:1. Mt 10:16.
Created by God. Jb 26:13.
Cursed above all creatures. Gn 3:14.
Dangerous to travelers. Gn 49:17.
Doomed to creep on their bellies. Gn 3:14.
Doomed to eat their food mingled with dust. Gn 3:14. Is 65:25. Mi 7:17.
ILLUSTRATIVE OF
Baneful effects of wine (by their poisonous bite). Pr 23:31–32.
The devil. Gn 3:1, with 2 Co 11:3. Rv 12:9; 20:2.
Enemies who harass and destroy. Is 14:29. Jr 8:17.
Hypocrites. Mt 23:33.
Malice of the wicked (by their sharp tongues). Ps 140:3.
The tribe of Dan. Gn 49:17.
INFEST
Deserts. Dt 8:15.
Hedges. Ec 10:8.
Holes in walls. Am 5:19.
Man's aversion and hatred to. Gn 3:15.
Many kinds of, poisonous. Dt 32:24. Ps 58:4.
MIRACLES CONNECTED WITH
Israelites cured by looking at one of brass. Nu 21:8–9. Jn 3:14–15.
Moses' rod turned into. Ex 4:3; 7:9, 15.
Power over, given to the disciples. Mk 16:18. Lk 10:19.
Often sent as a punishment. Nu 21:6. Dt 32:24. 1 Co 10:9.
Produced from eggs. Is 59:5.
Unclean and unfit for food. Mt 7:10.
Were often enchanted or fascinated. Ec 10:11.

SERVANTS

Are inferior to their masters. Lk 22:27.

CHARACTERISTICS OF GOOD

Adorn the doctrine of God their Savior in all things. Ti 2:10.
Blessed by God. Mt 24:46.
Brethren beloved in the Lord. Phm 1:16.
Bring God's blessing upon their masters. Gn 30:27, 30; 39:3.
Deserve the confidence of their masters. Gn 24:2, 4, 10; 39:4.
Guided by God. Gn 24:7, 27.
Have God with them. Gn 31:42; 39:21. Ac 7:9–10.
The Lord's freemen. 1 Co 7:22.
Often advanced by masters. Gn 39:4–5.
Often exalted. Gn 41:40. Pr 17:2.
Partakers of gospel privileges. 1 Co 12:13. Gl 3:28. Ep 6:8. Cl 3:11.
Prospered by God. Gn 39:3.
Protected by God. Gn 31:7.
Servants of Christ. Cl 3:24.
Shall be rewarded. Ep 6:8. Cl 3:24.
To be honored. Gn 24:31. Pr 27:18.

CHARACTERISTICS OF WICKED

Covetousness. 2 K 5:20.
Deceit. 2 S 19:26. Ps 101:6–7.
Do not bear to be exalted. Pr 30:21–22, with Is 3:5.
Eyeservice. Ep 6:6. Cl 3:22.
Gluttony. Mt 24:49.
Lying. 2 K 5:22, 25.
Quarrelsomeness. Gn 13:7; 26:20.
Shall be punished. Mt 24:50.
Stealing. Ti 2:10.
Unmerciful to their fellows. Mt 18:30.
Will not submit to correction. Pr 29:19.

Christ condescended to the office of. Mt 20:28. Lk 22:27. Jn 13:5. Php 2:7.

DIVIDED INTO

Female. Gn 16:6; 32:5.
Male. Gn 24:34; 32:5.
Hired. Mk 1:20. Lk 15:17.
Slave or bond. Gn 43:18. Lv 25:46.

DUTIES OF, TO MASTERS

Not to answer them rudely. Ti 2:9.
Not to defraud them. Ti 2:10.
Not to serve them with eyeservice, as men-pleasers. Ep 6:6. Cl 1:22.
To attend to their call. Ps 123:2.
To be anxious for their welfare. 1 S 25:14–17. 2 K 5:2–3.
To be earnest in transacting their business. Gn 24:54–56.

To be faithful to them. Lk 16:10–12. 1 Co 4:2. Ti 2:10.
To be industrious in laboring for them. Ne 4:16, 23.
To be kind and attentive to their guests. Gn 43:23–24.
To be profitable to them. Lk 19:15–16, 18. Phm 1:11.
To be prudent in the management of their affairs. Gn 24:31–49.
To be subject to them. 1 P 2:18.
To be submissive even to the forward. Gn 16:6, 9. 1 P 2:18.
To bless God for mercies shown to them. Gn 24:27, 48.
To honor them. Ml 1:6. 1 Tm 6:1.
To obey them. Ep 6:5. Ti 2:9.
To please them well in all things. Ti 2:9.
To pray for them. Gn 24:12.
To prefer their business to their own necessary food. Gn 24:33.
To revere them the more, when they are believers. 1 Tm 6:2.
To sympathize with them. 2 S 12:18.

Early mention of. Gn 9:25–26.

HIRED

Anxiety of, for the end of their daily toil, alluded to. Jb 7:2.
Called hirelings. Jb 7:1. Jn 10:12–13.
Engaged by the day. Mt 20:2.
Engaged by the year. Lv 25:53. Is 16:14.
Hebrew slaves serving strangers to be treated as. Lv 25:39–40.
Hebrew slaves serving their brethren to be treated as. Lv 25:39–40.
If foreigners not allowed to partake of the Passover or holy things. Ex 12:45. Lv 22:10.
Not to be oppressed. Dt 24:14.
Often oppressed and their wages kept back. Ml 3:5. Ja 5:4.
Often stood in the market place waiting for employment. Mt 20:1–3.
Often well fed and taken care of. Lk 15:17.
To be esteemed worthy of their hire. Lk 10:7.
To be paid without delay at the expiration of their service. Lv 19:13. Dt 24:15.
To partake of the produce of the land in the sabbatical year. Lv 25:6.

ILLUSTRATIONS OF BOND

Christ. Ps 40:6, with He 10:5. Php 2:7–8.
Saints. 1 Co 6:20; 7:23.

The wicked.   2 P 2:19, with Ro 6:16, 19.

Persons devoted to God so called.   Ps 119:49. Is 56:6. Ro 1:1.

Persons of low condition so called.   Ec 10:7.

Persons devoted to the service of another so called.   Ex 24:13. 1 K 19:21.

The property of masters increased by faithful. Gn 30:29–30.

Should be compassionate to their fellows. Mt 18:33.

Should be contented in their situation.   1 Co 7:20–21.

Should follow Christ's example.   1 P 2:21.

SHOULD SERVE

As doing the will of God from the heart. Ep 6:6.

As the servants of Christ.   Ep 6:5–6.

For conscience toward God.   1 P 2:19.

Heartily, as to the Lord, and not unto men. Ep 6:7. Cl 3:23.

In the fear of God.   Ep 6:5. Cl 3:22.

In singleness of heart.   Ep 6:5. Cl 3:22.

With good will.   Ep 6:7.

SLAVE OR BOND

All Israelites sold as, to be free at the jubilee. Lv 25:10, 40–41, 54.

By birth.   Gn 14:14. Ps 116:16. Jr 2:14.

By purchase.   Gn 17:27; 37:36.

Called bondmen.   Gn 43:18; 44:9.

Captives taken in war often kept as.   Dt 20:14. 2 K 5:2.

Could not, when set free, demand wives or children procured during servitude.   Ex 21:3–4.

Custom of branding alluded to.   Gl 6:17.

Engaged in the most menial offices.   1 S 25:41. Jn 13:4–5.

Israelites sold as, refusing their liberty, to have their ears bored to the door.   Ex 21:5–6. Dt 15:16–17.

Israelites sold to strangers as, might be redeemed by their nearest of kin.   Lv 25:47–55.

Laws respecting marriage with female.   Ex 21:7–11.

Laws respecting, often violated.   Jr 34:8–16.

Laws respecting the killing of.   Ex 21:20–21.

Maimed or injured by masters, to have their freedom.   Ex 21:26–27.

Masters to be recompensed for injury done to.   Ex 21:32.

More valuable than hired servants.   Dt 15:18.

Of others, not to be coveted or enticed away.   Ex 20:17. Dt 5:21.

Persons belonging to other nations might be purchased as.   Lv 25:44.

Persons of distinction had many.   Gn 14:14. Ec 2:7.

Persons unable to pay their debts liable to be sold as.   2 K 4:1. Ne 5:4–5. Mt 18:25.

Seeking protection, not to be delivered up to masters.   Dt 23:15.

Seizing and stealing of men for, condemned and punished by the law.   Ex 21:16. Dt 24:7. 1 Tm 1:10.

Sometimes intermarried with their master's family.   1 Ch 2:34–35.

Sometimes rose to rank and station.   Ec 10:7.

Strangers sojourning in Israel might be purchased as.   Lv 25:45.

Thieves unable to make restitution sold as. Ex 22:3.

To be allowed to rest on the sabbath.   Ex 20:10.

To be furnished liberally, when their servitude expired.   Dt 15:13–14.

To participate in all national rejoicings. Dt 12:18; 16:11, 14.

When foreigners, to be circumcised.   Gn 17:13, 27. Ex 12:44.

When Israelites, not to be treated with rigor.   Lv 25:39–40, 46.

When Israelites, to have their liberty after six years' service.   Ex 21:2. Dt 15:12.

Subjects of a prince or king so called.   Ex 9:20; 11:8.

The term often used to express humility.   Gn 18:3; 33:5. 1 S 20:7. 1 K 20:32.

When patient under injury, acceptable to God.   1 P 2:19–20.

SERVICE

Aiding Christ's brethren.   Mt 25:40.

Caring for one another.   Gl 5:13.

Dedication for.   Is 6:8. Ro 12:1–2.

Doing good.   Is 6:8.

Feeding the hungry.   Ja 2:15, 16.

Helping the weak.   Ro 15:1. Ac 20:35.

Of God.   Lk 1:74. Ro 12:11.

Of the Lord.   Ep 6:7.

Through prayer.   He 12:12.

SEX
See Lust; Marriage.

SHEEP
Bleating of, alluded to.   Jg 5:16. 1 S 15:14.
Clean and used as food.   Dt 14:4.
Constituted a great part of patriarchal wealth.
Gn 13:5; 25:35; 26:14.

DESCRIBED AS
Agile.   Ps 114:4, 6.
Covered with a fleece.   Jb 31:20.
Innocent.   2 S 24:17.
Remarkably prolific.   Pss 107:41; 144:13.
S S 4:2. Ezk 36:37.
Sagacious.   Jn 10:4–5.

False prophets assume the simple appearance
of.   Mt 7:15.
Females of, called ewes.   Ps 78:71.

FIRSTLINGS OF
Not to be dedicated as a free-will offering.
Lv 27:26.
Not to be redeemed.   Nu 18:17.
Not to be shorn.   Dt 15:19.

First wool of, given to the priests.   Dt 18:4.
Flesh of, used extensively as food.   1 S 25:18.
1 K 1:19; 4:23. Ne 5:18. Is 22:13.

FLOCKS OF
Attended by members of the family.   Gn
29:6. Ex 2:16. 1 S 16:11.
Attended by servants.   1 S 17:20. Is 61:5.
Conducted to the richest pastures.   Ps
23:2.
Fed in the valleys.   Is 65:10.
Fed on the mountains.   Ex 3:1. Ezk 34:6,
13.
Fled from strangers.   Jn 10:5.
Followed the shepherd.   Jn 10:4, 27.
Frequently covered the pastures.   Ps
65:13.
Guarded by dogs.   Jb 30:1.
Kept in folds or cotes.   1 S 24:3. 2 S 7:8.
Jn 10:1.
Made to rest at noon.   Ps 23:2, with S S
1:7.
Watered every day.   Gn 29:8–10. Ex
2:16–17.

FREQUENTLY
Cut off by disease.   Ex 9:3.
Destroyed by wild beasts.   Jr 50:17. Mi
5:8. Jn 10:12.
Given as presents.   2 S 17:29. 1 Ch 12:40.
Given as tribute.   2 K 3:4. 2 Ch 17:11.
Taken in great numbers in war.   Jg 6:4. 1
S 14:32. 1 Ch 5:21. 2 Ch 14:15.

ILLUSTRATIVE OF
The Jews.   Pss 74:1; 78:52; 79:13.
The patience, etc., of Christ (in their pa-
tience and simplicity).   Is 53:7.
The people of Christ.   Jn 10:7–26;
21:16–17. He 13:20. 1 P 5:2.
Restored sinners (when found).   Lk 15:5,
7.
Separation of saints from the wicked (when
separated from goats).   Mt 25:32–33.
Those under God's judgment.   Ps 44:11.
Those who depart from God (in their
proneness to wander).   Ps 119:176. Is
53:6. Ezk 34:16.
The unregenerate (when lost).   Mt 10:6.
The wicked (in their death).   Ps 49:14.

Males of, called rams.   1 S 15:23. Jr 51:40.
Milk of, used as food.   Dt 32:14. Is 7:21–22.
1 Co 9:7.
Offered in sacrifice from the earliest age.   Gn
4:4; 8:20; 15:9–10.
Offered in sacrifice under the law.   Ex 20:24.
Lv 1:10. 1 K 8:5, 63.

PLACES CELEBRATED FOR
Bashan.   Dt 32:14.
Bozra.   Mi 2:12.
Kedar.   Ezk 27:21.
Nebaioth.   Is 60:7.

Skins of, made into a covering for the taberna-
cle.   Ex 25:5; 36:19; 39:34.
Skins of, worn as clothing by the poor.   He
11:37.
Time of shearing, a time of rejoicing.   1 S
25:2, 11, 36. 2 S 13:23.
Tithe of, given to the Levites.   2 Ch 31:4–6.
Under man's care from the earliest age.   Gn
4:4.
Washed and shorn every year.   S S 4:2.
Wool of, made into clothing.   Jb 31:20. Pr
31:13. Ezk 34:3.
Young of, called lambs.   Ex 12:3. Is 11:6.

SHEPHERDS
An abomination to the Egyptians.   Gn 46:34.

CARE OF SHEEP BY, EXHIBITED IN
Attending them when sick.   Ezk 34:16.
Defending them when attacked by wild
beasts.   1 S 17:34–36. Am 3:12.
Going before and leading them.   Pss
77:20; 78:52; 80:1.
Knowing them.   Jn 10:14.
Numbering them when they return from
pasture.   Jr 33:13.

Searching them out when lost and straying. Ezk 34:12. Lk 15:4–5.

Seeking out good pasture for them. 1 Ch 4:39–41. Ps 23:2.

Tenderness to the ewes in lamb, and to the young. Gn 33:13–14. Ps 78:71.

Watching over them by night. Lk 2:8.

Carried a staff or rod. Lv 27:32. Ps 23:4.

Dwelt in tents while tending their flocks. S S 1:8. Is 38:12.

Early mention of. Gn 4:2.

Had hired keepers under them. 1 S 17:20.

ILLUSTRATIVE OF

Bad ministers (when ignorant and foolish). Is 56:11. Jr 50:6. Ezk 34:2, 10. Zc 11:7–8, 15–17.

Christ as the good shepherd. Ezk 34:23. Zc 13:7. Jn 10:14. He 13:20.

Christ seeking the lost (when searching out straying sheep). Ezk 34:12. Lk 15:2–7.

God as leader of Israel. Pss 77:20; 80:1.

Kings as the leaders of the people. Is 44:28. Jr 6:3; 49:19.

Ministers of the gospel. Jr 23:4.

Tenderness of Christ (by their care and tenderness). Is 40:11. Ezk 34:13–16.

Members of the family, both male and female, acted as. Gn 29:6. 1 S 16:11; 17:15.

Unfaithfulness of hireling, alluded to. Jn 10:12.

Usually carried a scrip or bag. 1 S 17:40.

SHIELDS

BEFORE WAR

Anointed. 2 S 1:21, with Is 21:5.

Gathered together. Jr 51:11.

Often made red. Na 2:3.

Repaired. Jr 46:3.

Uncovered. Is 22:6.

A disgrace to lose or throw away. 2 S 1:21.

FREQUENTLY MADE OF OR COVERED WITH

Brass. 1 K 14:27.

Gold. 2 S 8:7. 1 K 10:17.

ILLUSTRATIVE OF

Faith. Ep 6:16.

Favor of God. Ps 5:12.

Protection of God. Gn 15:1. Ps 33:20.

Salvation of God. 2 S 22:36. Ps 18:35.

Truth of God. Ps 91:4.

In times of peace, hung up in towers of armories. Ezk 27:10, with S S 4:4.

KINDS OF

Buckler or target. 2 Ch 9:15, with 1 Ch 5:18. Ezk 26:8.

Small shield. 2 Co 9:16.

Many of the Israelites used, with expertness. 1 Ch 12:8, 24, 34. 2 Ch 14:8; 25:5.

Often borne by an armor bearer. 1 S 17:7.

Of the vanquished, often burned. Ezk 39:9.

Part of defensive armor. Ps 115:9, with 140:7.

Provided by the kings of Israel in great abundance. 2 Ch 11:12; 26:14; 32:5.

Said to belong to God. Ps 47:9.

Scarce in Israel in the days of Deborah and Barak. Jg 5:8.

SHIPS

Antiquity of, among the Jews. Gn 49:13. Jg 5:17.

Commanded by a master. Jnh 1:6. Ac 27:11.

Course of, frequently directed by the heavenly bodies. Ac 27:20.

Course of, through the midst of the sea, wonderful. Pr 30:18–19.

DESCRIBED AS

Gallant. Is 33:21.

Large. Ja 3:4.

Strong. Is 23:14.

Swift. Jb 9:26.

EMPLOYED IN

Carrying passengers. Jnh 1:3. Ac 27:2, 6; 28:11.

Fishing. Mt 4:21. Lk 5:4–9. Jn 21:3–8.

Trading. 1 K 22:48. 2 Ch 8:18; 9:21.

War. Nu 24:24. Dn 11:30, 40.

ENDANGERED BY

Quicksands. Ac 27:17.

Rocks. Ac 27:29.

Storms. Jnh 1:4. Mk 4:37–38.

Generally impelled by sails. Ac 27:2–7.

Generally made of the fir tree. Ezk 27:5.

Governed and directed by the helm. Ja 3:4.

Guided in their course by pilots. Ezk 27:8, 27–29.

ILLUSTRATIVE OF

Departure from the faith (when wrecked). 1 Tm 1:19.

Industrious women. Pr 31:14.

MENTIONED IN SCRIPTURE

Adramyttium. Ac 27:2.

Alexandria. Ac 27:6.

Chaldea. Is 43:14.

Chittim. Nu 24:24. Dn 11:30.

Tarshish. Is 23:1; 60:9.

Tyre. 2 Ch 8:18.

NAVIGATED

Lakes. Lk 5:1–2.

The ocean. Pss 104:26; 106:23.
Rivers. Is 33:21.
Often impelled by oars. Jnh 1:13. Jn 6:19.
Often the property of individuals. Ac 27:11.
Often wrecked. 1 K 22:48. Ps 48:7. Ac 27:41–44. 2 Co 11:25.
PARTS OF, MENTIONED
Anchors. Ac 27:29, 40.
Boats. Ac 27:30, 32.
Forepart or foreship. Ac 27:30, 41.
Hind part or stern. Ac 27:29, 41.
Hold or between the sides. Jnh 1:5.
Mast. Is 33:23. Ezk 27:5.
Oars. Is 33:21. Ezk 27:6.
Rudder bands. Ac 27:40.
Rudder or helm. Ja 3:4.
Sails. Is 33:23. Ezk 27:7.
Tackling. Is 33:23. Ac 27:19.
Probably originated from the ark made by Noah. Gn 7:17–18.
Seams of, calked. Ezk 27:9, 27.
Solomon built a navy of. 1 K 9:26.
Sometimes made of bulrushes. Is 18:2.
Soundings usually taken for, in dangerous places. Ac 27:28.
Stern of, occupied by passengers. Mk 4:38.
Usually distinguished by signs or figure heads. Ac 28:11.
When damaged, sometimes undergirded with cables. Ac 27:17.
Worked by mariners or sailors. Ezk 27:9, 27. Jnh 1:5. Ac 27:30.

SHOES
The apostles prohibited from taking for their journey more than the pair they had on. Mt 10:10. Mk 6:9. Lk 10:4.
Bound around the feet with latchets or strings. Jn 1:27. Ac 12:8.
Called sandals. Mk 6:9. Ac 12:8.
Carrying for another, a degrading office, only performed by slaves. Mt 3:11.
CUSTOMS CONNECTED WITH
A man who refused to marry a deceased brother's wife disgraced by her pulling off his shoes. Dt 25:9–10.
The right of redemption resigned by a man's giving one of his shoes to the next of kin. Ru 4:7–8.
Early use of. Gn 14:23.
ILLUSTRATIVE OF
The beauty conferred on saints. S S 7:1, with Lk 15:22.
Being engaged in war and slaughter (when bloody). 1 K 2:5.

An ignominious and servile condition (when taken off). Is 47:2. Jr 2:25.
The preparation of the gospel. Ep 6:15.
Subjection (when thrown over a place). Pss 60:8; 108:9.
THE JEWS
Never wore in mourning. 2 S 15:30. Is 20:2–3. Ezk 24:17, 23.
Put off when they entered sacred places. Ex 3:5. Jsh 5:15.
Put on before beginning a journey. Ex 12:11.
Loosing of, for another, a degrading office. Mk 1:7. Jn 1:27.
Of Israel, preserved for forty years, while journeying in the wilderness. Dt 29:5.
OF LADIES OF DISTINCTION
Often highly ornamental. S S 7:1.
Often made of badgers' skins. Ezk 16:10.
Probably often adorned with tinkling ornaments. Is 3:18.
Often given as bribes. Am 2:6; 8:6.
Soles of, sometimes plated with brass or iron. Dt 33:25.
Worn out by a long journey. Jsh 9:5, 13.

SHOWBREAD
Cakes of fine flour (twelve). Lv 24:5.
Called hallowed bread. 1 S 21:4.
Changed every sabbath day. Lv 24:8.
Frankincense placed on. Lv 24:7.
ILLUSTRATIVE OF
Christ as the bread of life. Jn 6:48.
The church. 1 Co 5:7; 10:17.
Materials for, provided by the people. Lv 24:8. Ne 10:32, 33.
Not lawful for any but priests to eat, except in extreme cases. 1 S 21:4–6, with Mt 12:4.
Once removed from the table, given to the priests. Lv 24:9.
Placed in two rows on the table by the priests. Ex 25:30; 40:23. Lv 24:6.
Prepared by Levites. 1 Ch 9:32; 23:29.
TABLE OF
Covered with gold. Ex 25:24.
Dimensions, etc., of. Ex 25:23.
Directions for removing. Nu 4:7.
Had an ornamental border. Ex 25:25.
Had dishes, spoons, covers, and bowls of gold. Ex 25:29.
Had rings of gold in the corners for the staves. Ex 25:26–27.

Had staves of shittim wood covered with gold. Ex 25:28.

Placed in the north side of the tabernacle. Ex 40:22. He 9:2.

SICKNESS

The apostles endowed with power to heal. Mt 10:1.

Christ compassionated those in. Is 53:4, with Mt 8:16–17.

CHRIST HEALED, BY

Being present. Mk 1:31. Mt 4:23.

Imposition of hands. Mk 6:5. Lk 13:13.

Not being present. Mt 8:13.

A touch. Mt 8:3.

The touch of his garment. Mt 14:35–36. Mk 5:27–34.

A word. Mt 8:8, 13.

Faith required in those healed of, by Christ. Mt 9:28–29. Mk 5:34; 10:52.

GOD

Abandons the wicked to. Jr 34:17.

Comforts saints in. Ps 41:3.

Exhibits his love in healing. Is 38:17.

Exhibits his mercy in healing. Php 2:27.

Exhibits his power in healing. Lk 5:17.

Heals. Dt 32:39. Ps 103:3. Is 38:5, 9.

Hears the prayers of those in. Pss 30:2; 107:18–20.

Often manifests saving grace to sinners during. Jb 33:19–24. Ps 107:17–21.

Permits saints to be tried by. Jb 2:5–6.

Persecutes the wicked by. Jr 29:18.

Preserves saints in time of. Ps 91:3–7.

Promises to heal. Ex 23:25. 2 K 20:5.

Strengthens saints in. Ps 41:3.

God's aid should be sought in. 2 Ch 16:12.

Healing of, lawful on the sabbath. Lk 13:14–16.

Illustrates sin. Lv 13:45–46. Is 1:5. Jr 8:22. Mt 9:12.

Not visiting those in, an evidence of not belonging to Christ. Mt 25:43, 45.

Often brought on by intemperance. Ho 7:5.

Often incurable by human means. Dt 28:27. 2 Ch 21:18.

Often sent as a punishment of sin. Lv 26:14–16. 2 Ch 21:12–15. 1 Co 11:30.

One of God's four sore judgments on a guilty land. Ezk 14:19–21.

The power of healing, one of the miraculous gifts bestowed on the early church. 1 Co 12:9, 30. Ja 5:14–15.

Pray for those afflicted with. Ac 28:8. Ja 5:14–15.

SAINTS

Acknowledge that it comes from God. Ps 31:1–8. Is 38:12, 15.

Are resigned under. Jb 2:10.

Ascribe recovery from to God. Is 38:20.

Feel for others in. Ps 35:13.

Mourn under, with prayer. Is 38:14.

Praise God for recovery from. Ps 103:1–3. Is 38:19. Lk 17:15.

Pray for recovery from. Is 38:2–3.

Thank God publicly for recovery from. Is 38:20. Ac 3:8.

Visit those in. Mt 25:36.

SENT BY

The devil. Jb 2:6–7. Lk 9:39; 13:16.

God. Dt 28:59–61; 32:39. 2 S 12:15. Ac 12:23.

Visiting those in, an evidence of belonging to Christ. Mt 25:34, 36, 40.

THE WICKED

Forsake those in. 1 S 30:13.

Have much sorrow, etc., with. Ec 5:17.

Visit not those in. Mt 25:43.

SILVER

CALLED, WHEN PURIFIED

Choice silver. Pr 8:19.

Refined silver. 1 Ch 29:4.

Comparative value of. Is 60:17.

DESCRIBED AS

Fusible. Ezk 22:20, 22.

Malleable. Jr 10:9.

White and shining. Ps 68:13–14.

Found in the earth in veins. Jb 28:1.

Generally found in an impure state. Pr 25:4.

Given by David and his subjects for making the temple. 1 Ch 28:14; 29:2, 6–9.

Given by the Israelites for making the tabernacle. Ex 25:3; 35:24.

ILLUSTRATIVE OF

Diligence required for attaining knowledge (in the labor of seeking it). Pr 2:4.

Good rulers. Is 1:22–23.

Medo-Persian kingdom. Dn 2:32, 39.

Saints purified by affliction. Ps 66:10. Zc 13:9.

The tongue of the just. Pr 10:20.

The wicked (by its dross). Is 1:22 Ezk 22:18.

The wicked (when reprobate). Jr 6:30.

The words of the Lord. Ps 12:6.

MADE INTO

Beds or couches. Es 1:6.

Bowls. Nu 7:13, 84.

Candlesticks. 1 Ch 28:15.

Chains. Is 40:19.
Cups. Gn 44:2.
Dishes. Nu 7:13, 84, 85.
Idols. Ps 115:4. Is 2:20; 30:22.
Ornaments and hooks for the pillars of the tabernacle. Ex 27:17; 38:19.
Ornaments for the person. Ex 3:22.
Sockets for the boards of the tabernacle. Ex 26:19, 25, 32; 36:24, 26, 30, 36.
Tables. 1 Ch 28:16.
Thin plates. Jr 10:9.
Vessels. 2 S 8:10. Ezr 6:5.
Wires (alluded to). Ec 12:6.
Often given as presents. 1 K 10:25. 2 K 5:5, 23.
Patriarchs rich in. Gn 13:2; 24:35.
Purified by fire. Pr 17:3. Zc 13:9.
Taken in war, often consecrated to God. Jsh 6:19. 2 S 8:11. 1 K 15:15.
Taken in war, purified by fire. Nu 31:22–23.
Tarshish carried on extensive commerce in. Jr 10:9. Ezk 27:12.
Tribute often paid in. 2 Ch 17:11. Ne 5:15.
Used as money from the earliest age. Gn 23:15–16; 37:28. 1 K 16:24.
Very abundant in the reign of Solomon. 1 K 10:21–22, 27. 2 Ch 9:20–21, 27.
Wisdom to be esteemed more than. Jb 28:15. Pr 3:14; 8:10, 19; 16:16.
Working in, a trade. Ac 19:24.

SIMPLICITY

Beware of being corrupted from that which is in Christ. 2 Co 11:3.
Exhortation to. Ro 16:19. 1 P 2:2.
Illustrated. Mt 6:22.
Necessity for. Mt 18:2–3.
Opposed to fleshly wisdom. 2 Co 1:12.
SHOULD BE EXHIBITED
    Concerning evil. Ro 16:19.
    Concerning malice. 1 Co 14:20.
    Concerning our own wisdom. 1 Co 3:18.
    In acts of benevolence. Ro 12:8.
    In all our conduct. 2 Co 1:12.
    In preaching the gospel. 1 Th 2:3–7.
THEY WHO HAVE THE GRACE OF
    Are made wise by God. Mt 11:25.
    Are made wise by the word of God. Pss 19:7; 119:130.
    Are preserved by God. Ps 116:6.
    Made circumspect by instruction. Pr 1:4.
    Profit by the correction of others. Pr 19:25; 21:11.

SIN

Aggravated by neglected advantages. Lk 12:47. Jn 15:22.
All men are shapen in. Ps 51:5.
All men conceived and born in. Gn 5:3. Jb 15:14; 25:4. Ps 51:5.
All the imaginations of the unrenewed heart are. Gn 6:5; 8:21.
All unrighteousness is. 1 Jn 5:17.
Blessings withheld on account of. Jr 5:25.
Christ alone was without. 2 Co 5:21. He 4:15; 7:26. 1 Jn 3:5.
Christ's blood cleanses from. 1 Jn 1:7.
Christ's blood redeems from. Ep 1:7.
Christ was manifested to take away. Jn 1:29. 1 Jn 3:5.
Confusion of face belongs to those guilty of. Dn 9:7–8.
Death the punishment of. Gn 2:17. Ezk 18:4.
Death the wages of. Ro 6:23.
DESCRIBED AS
    The abominable thing that God hates. Pr 15:9. Jr 44:4, 11.
    Besetting. He 12:1.
    Coming from the heart. Mt 15:19.
    Dead works. He 6:1; 9:14.
    Deceitful. He 3:13.
    Defiling. Pr 30:12. Is 59:3.
    Disgraceful. Pr 14:34.
    The fruit of lust. Ja 1:15.
    Like scarlet and crimson. Is 1:18.
    Often manifold. Am 5:12.
    Often mighty. Am 5:12.
    Often presumptuous. Ps 19:13.
    Often very great. Ex 32:30. 1 S 2:17.
    Reaching unto heaven. Rv 18:5.
    Rebellion against God Dt 9:7. Jsh 1:18.
    Reproaching the Lord. Nu 15:30. Ps 74:18.
    Sometimes open and manifest. 1 Tm 5:24.
    Sometimes secret. Ps 90:8. 1 Tm 5:24.
    The sting of death. 1 Co 15:56.
    Works of darkness. Ep 5:11.
Entered into the world by Adam. Gn 3:6–7, with Ro 5:12.
Excludes from heaven. 1 Co 6:9–10. Gl 5:19–21. Ep 5:5. Rv 21:27.
Fear of God restrains. Ex 20:20. Ps 4:4. Pr 16:6.
GOD
    Abominates. Dt 25:16. Pr 6:16–19.

Alone can forgive. Ex 34:7. Dn 9:9. Mi 7:18. Mk 2:7.

Has opened a fountain for. Zc 13:1.

Is provoked to anger by. 1 K 16:2.

Is provoked to jealousy by. 1 K 14:22.

Marks. Jb 10:14.

Punishes. Is 13:11. Am 3:2.

Recompenses. Jr 16:18. Rv 18:6.

Remembers. Rv 18:5.

God's word keeps us from. Pss 17:4; 119:11.

Ground cursed on account of. Gn 3:17–18.

Guilt of concealing. Jb 31:33. Pr 28:13.

The Holy Ghost convinces of. Jn 16:8–9.

If we say that we have no, we deceive ourselves, and the truth is not in us. 1 Jn 1:8.

If we say that we have no, we make God a liar. 1 Jn 1:10.

THE LAW

By its strictness stirs up. Ro 7:5, 8, 11.

Curses those guilty of. Gl 3:10.

Gives knowledge of. Ro 3:20; 7:7.

Is the strength of. 1 Co 15:56.

Is transgressed by every. Ja 2:10–11, with 1 Jn 3:4.

Made to restrain. 1 Tm 1:9–10.

Shows exceeding sinfulness of. Ro 7:13.

LEADS TO

Disease. Jb 20:11.

Disquiet. Ps 38:3.

Shame. Ro 6:21.

Ministers should warn the wicked to forsake. Ezk 33:9. Dn 4:27.

No man can atone for. Mi 6:7.

No man can cleanse himself from. Jb 9:30–31. Pr 20:9. Jr 2:22.

No man is without. 1 K 8:46. Ec 7:20.

Of the devil. 1 Jn 3:8, with Jn 8:44.

Omission of what we know to be good is. Ja 4:17.

Prayer hindered by. Ps 66:18. Is 59:2.

SAINTS

Abhor themselves on account of. Jb 42:6. Ezk 20:43.

Ashamed of having committed. Ro 6:21.

Cannot live in. 1 Jn 3:9; 5:18.

Dead to. Ro 6:2, 11. 1 P 2:24.

Have yet the remains of, in them. Ro 7:17, 23, with Gl 5:17.

Made free from. Ro 6:18.

Profess to have ceased from. 1 P 4:1.

Resolve against. Jb 34:32.

Scripture concludes all under. Gl 3:22.

Shall find out the wicked. Nu 32:23.

SHOULD BE

Abhorred. Ro 12:9.

Avoided even in appearance. 1 Th 5:22.

Confessed. Jb 33:27. Pr 28:13.

Departed from. Ps 34:14. 2 Tm 2:19.

Guarded against. Pss 4:4; 39:1.

Hated. Ps 97:10. Pr 8:13. Am 5:15.

Mortified. Ro 8:13. Cl 3:5.

Mourned over. Ps 38:18. Jr 3:21.

Put away. Jb 11:14.

Striven against. He 12:4.

Wholly destroyed. Ro 6:6.

Specially strive against besetting. He 12:1.

The thought of foolishness is. Pr 24:9.

Toil and sorrow originated in. Gn 3:16–17, 19, with Jb 14:1.

Transgression of the law. 1 Jn 3:4.

WE SHOULD PRAY TO GOD

To cleanse us from. Ps 51:2.

To deliver us from. Mt 6:13.

To forgive our. Ex 34:9. Lk 11:4.

To keep us from. Ps 19:13.

To make us know our. Jb 13:23.

To search for, in our hearts. Ps 139:23–24.

Whatever is not of faith is. Ro 14:23.

When finished brings forth death. Ja 1:15.

THE WICKED

Boast of. Is 3:9.

Cannot cease from. 2 P 2:14.

Dead in. Ep 2:1.

Defy God in committing. Is 5:18–19.

Delight in those who commit. Ps 10:3. Ho 7:3. Ro 1:32.

Encourage themselves in. Ps 64:5.

Encouraged in by prosperity. Jb 21:7–15. Pr 10:16.

Excuse. Gn 3:12–13. 1 S 15:13–15.

Expect impunity in. Pss 10:11; 50:21; 94:7.

Guilty of, in everything they do. Pr 21:4. Ezk 21:24.

Heap up. Ps 78:17. Is 30:1.

Led by despair to continue in. Jr 2:25; 18:12.

Make a mock at. Pr 14:9.

Plead necessity for. 1 S 13:11–12.

Servants to. Jn 8:34. Ro 6:16.

Shall bear the shame of. Ezk 16:52.

Tempt others to. Gn 3:6. 1 K 16:2; 21:25. Pr 1:10–14.

Throw the blame of, on God. Gn 3:12. Jr 7:10.

Throw the blame of, on others. Gn 3:12–13. Ex 32:22–24.

Try to conceal, from God. Gn 3:8, 10; with Jb 31:33.

SINCERITY
Blessedness of. Ps 32:2.
A characteristic of the doctrines of the gospel, 1 P 2:2.
Christ an example of. 1 P 2:22.
Exhortations to. Ps 34:13. 1 Co 5:8. 1 P 2:1.
The gospel sometimes preached without. Php 1:16.
Ministers should exemplify. Ti 2:7.
Opposed to fleshly wisdom. 2 Co 1:12.
Pray for, on behalf of others. Php 1:10.
SHOULD CHARACTERIZE
Our faith. 1 Tm 1:5.
Our love to Christ. Ep 6:24.
Our love to God. 2 Co 8:8, 24.
Our love to one another. Ro 12:9, 1 P 1:22. 1 Jn 3:18.
Our service to God. Jsh 24:14. Jn 4:23–24.
Our whole conduct. 2 Co 1:12.
The preaching of the gospel. 2 Co 2:17, 1 Th 2:3–5.
The wicked devoid of. Pss 5:9; 55:21.

SIN OFFERING
Aaron, etc., rebuked for burning and not eating that of the congregation, its blood not having been brought into the tabernacle. Lv 10:16–18, with Lv 9:9, 15.
BLOOD OF
For a priest or for the congregation, brought by the priest into the tabernacle. Lv 4:5, 16.
For a priest or for the congregation, put upon the horns of the altar of incense. Lv 4:7, 18.
For a priest or for the congregation, sprinkled seven times before the Lord, outside the veil, by the priest with his finger. Lv 4:6, 17.
For a ruler or for a private person, put upon the horns of the altar of burnt offering by the priest with his finger. Lv 4:25, 30.
In every case, poured at the foot of the altar of burnt offering. Lv 4:7, 18, 25, 30; 9:9.
CONSISTED OF
A female kid or female lamb for a private person. Lv 4:28, 32.
A male kid for a ruler. Lv 4:23.

A young bullock for priests. Lv 4:3; 9:2, 8; 16:3, 6.
A young bullock or he-goat for the congregation. Lv 4:14; 16:9. 2 Ch 29:23.
Eaten by the priests in a holy place, when its blood had not been brought into the tabernacle. Lv 6:26, 29–30.
Fat of the inside, kidneys, etc., burned on the altar of burnt offering. Lv 4:8–10, 19, 26, 31; 9:10.
For a priest or the congregation, the skin, carcass, etc., burned outside the camp. Lv 4:11–12, 21; 6:30; 9:11.
Killed in the same place as the burnt offering. Lv 4:24; 6:25.
Laws respecting the vessels used for boiling the flesh of. Lv 6:28.
OFFERED
At the consecration of Levites. Nu 8:8.
At the consecration of priests. Ex 29:10, 14. Lv 8:14.
At the expiration of a Nazarite's vow. Nu 6:14.
For sins of ignorance. Lv 4:2, 13, 22, 27.
On the day of atonement. Lv 16:3, 9.
Probable origin of. Gn 4:4, 7.
Sins of the offerer transferred to, by imposition of hands. Lv 4:4, 15, 24, 29. 2 Ch 29:23.
A type of Christ's sacrifice. 2 Co 5:21. He 13:11–13.
Whatever touched the flesh of, was rendered holy. Lv 6:27.

SINS, NATIONAL
Aggravated by privileges. Is 5:4–7. Ezk 20:11–13. Am 2:4; 3:1–2. Mt 11:21–24.
Bring down national judgments. Mt 23:35–36; 27:25.
Cause the withdrawal of privileges. Lm 2:9, Am 8:11. Mt 23:37–39.
DEFILE
The land. Lv 18:25. Nu 35:33–34. Ps 106:38. Is 24:5. Mi 2:10.
National worship. Is 1:10–15, Am 5:21–22. Hg 2:14.
The people. Lv 18:21. Ezk 14:11.
Denunciations against. Is 1:24; 30:1. Jr 5:9; 6:27–30.
Lead the heathen to blaspheme. Ezk 36:20, 23. Ro 2:24.
MINISTERS SHOULD
Mourn over. Ezr 10:6. Jr 13:17. Ezk 6:11. Jl 2:17.

Pray for forgiveness of. Ex 32:31–32. Jl 2:17.

Testify against. Is 30:8, 9; 58:1. Ezk 2:3–5; 22:2. Jnh 1:2.

Try to turn the people from. Jr 23:22.

National prayer rejected on account of. Is 1:15; 59:2.

National worship rejected on account of. Is 1:10–14. Jr 6:19–20; 7:9–14.

Often caused and encouraged by rulers. 1 K 12:26–33; 14:16. 2 Ch 21:11–13. Pr 29:12.

Often caused by prosperity. Dt 32:15. Ne 9:28. Jr 48:11. Ezk 16:49; 28:5.

Pervade all ranks. Is 1:5. Jr 5:1–5; 6:13.

Punishment for. Is 3:8. Jr 12:17; 25:12. Ezk 28:7–10.

Punishment for, averted on repentance. Jg 10:15–16. 2 Ch 12:6–7. Ps 106:43–46. Jnh 3:10.

A reproach to a people. Pr 14:34.

Saints especially mourn over. Ps 119:136. Ezk 9:4.

SHOULD BE
Confessed. Lv 26:40. Dt 30:2. Jg 10:10. 1 K 8:47–48.
Mourned over. Jl 2:12.
Repented of. Jr 18:8. Jnh 3:5.
Turned from. Is 1:16. Ho 14:1–2. Jnh 3:10.

SLANDER

An abomination unto God. Pr 6:16, 19.

A characteristic of the devil. Rv 12:10.

Christ exposed to. Ps 35:11. Mt 26:60.

Comes from the evil heart. Mt 15:19. Lk 6:45.

A deceitful work. Ps 52:2.

Destructive. Pr 11:9.

EFFECTS OF
Deadly wounds. Pr 18:8; 26:22.
Discord among brethren. Pr 6:19.
Murder. Ps 31:13. Ezk 22:9.
Separating friends. Pr 16:28; 17:9.
Strife. Pr 26:20.

End of, is mischievous madness. Ec 10:13.

Forbidden. Ex 23:1. Ep 4:31. Ja 4:11.

Hypocrites addicted to. Pr 11:9.

Idleness leads to. 1 Tm 5:13.

Illustrated. Pr 12:18; 25:18.

INCLUDES
Babbling. Ec 10:11.
Backbiting. Ro 1:30. 2 Co 12:20.
Bearing false witness. Ex 20:16. Dt 5:20. Lk 3:14

Defaming. Jr. 20:10. 1 Co 4:13.

Evil speaking. Pss 41:5; 109:20.

Evil surmising. 1 Tm 6:4.

Judging uncharitably. Ja 4:11–12.

Raising false reports. Ex 23:1.

Repeating matters. Pr 17:9.

Tale-bearing. Lv 19:16.

Tattling. 1 Tm 5:13.

Whispering. Ro 1:29. 2 Co 12:20.

Men shall give account for. Mt 12:36. Ja 1:26.

Ministers exposed to. Ro 3:8. 1 Co 6:8.

Ministers' wives should avoid. 1 Tm 3:11.

Nearest relations exposed to. Ps 50:20.

Often arises from hatred. Pss 41:7; 109:3.

Punishment for. Dt 19:16–21. Ps 101:5.

Rulers exposed to. 2 P 2:10. Jde 1:8.

SAINTS
Blessed in enduring. Mt 5:11.
Characterized as avoiding. Ps 15:1, 3.
Exposed to. Pss 38:12; 109:2. 1 P 4:4.
Should be warned against. Ti 3:1–2.
Should give no occasion for. 1 P 2:12; 3:16.
Should keep their tongue from. Ps 34:13, with 1 P 3:10.
Should lay aside. Ep 4:31. 1 P 2:1.
Should return good for. 1 Co 4:13.

Should be discountenanced with anger. Pr 25:23.

Should not be listened to. 1 S 24:9.

They who indulge in are fools. Pr 10:18.

They who indulge in, not to be trusted. Jr 9:4.

Tongue of, is a scourge. Jb 5:21.

Venomous. Ps 140:3. Ec 10:11.

The wicked addicted to. Ps 50:20. Jr 6:28; 9:4.

The wicked love. Ps 52:4.

Women warned against. Ti 2:3.

SOBRIETY

Commanded. 1 P 1:13; 5:8.

The gospel designed to teach. Ti 2:11–12.

Motives to. 1 P 4:7; 5:8.

REQUIRED IN
Aged men. Ti 2:2.
All saints. 1 Th 5:6, 8.
Ministers. 1 Tm 3:2–3. Ti 1:8.
Wives of ministers. 1 Tm 3:11.
Young men. Ti 2:6.
Young women. Ti 2:4.

We should estimate our character and talents with. Ro 12:3.

We should live in. Ti 2:12.
With prayer. 1 P 4:7.
With watchfulness. 1 Th 5:6.
Women should exhibit, in dress. 1 Tm 2:9.

SONG
Gift of a new. Ps 33:3; 40:3. Is 42:10.
God gives. Ps 77:6.
In glad worship. Ps 100:2.
The Lord is our. Ex 15:2. Jb 30:9.
Of salvation. Ps 32:7. Is 35:6; 65:14.
Spiritual. Ep 5:19. Cl 3:16.

SORROW
Comforted. Is 40; 61:1–3. Ja 4:9.
KINDS OF
    Godly. 2 Co 7:10.
    Natural. Lk 22:45. Ro 9:2.
    Resulting from sin. Ps 51.

SPEAR
Called the glittering spear. Jb 39:23. Hk 3:11.
DIFFERENT KINDS OF
    Darts. 2 S 18:14. Jb 41:26, 29.
    Javelins. Nu 25:7. 1 S 18:10.
    Lances. Jr 50:42.
First mention of, in scripture. Jsh 8:18.
Frequently thrown from the hand. 1 S 18:11; 19:10.
Frequently used by horse soldiers. Na 3:3.
Furbished before war. Jr 46:4.
Illustrative of the bitterness of the wicked. Ps 57:4.
THE ISRAELITES
    Acquainted with the making of. 1 S 13:19.
    Frequently used. Ne 4:13, 16.
    Ill provided with, in the times of Deborah and Saul. Jg 5:8. 1 S 13:22.
Made into pruning hooks in peace. Is 2:4. Mi 4:3.
An offensive weapon. 2 S 23:8, 18.
Often retained in the hand of the person using. Nu 25:7. 2 S 2:23.
PARTS OF, MENTIONED
    Head of iron or brass. 1 S 17:7, with 2 S 21:16.
    Staff of wood. 1 S 17:7.
Probably pointed at both ends. 2 S 2:23.
Provided by the kings of Israel in great abundance. 2 Ch 11:12; 32:5.
Pruning hooks made into, before war. Jl 3:10.

Stuck in the ground beside the bolster during sleep. 1 S 26:7–11.
Those who used, called spearmen. Ps 68:30. Ac 23:23.

STARS
Appear after sunset. Ne 4:21, with Jb 3:9.
Appear of different magnitudes. 1 Co 15:41.
Astrology and stargazing practiced by the Babylonians, etc. Is 47:13.
CALLED
    The host of heaven. Dt 17:3. Jr 33:22.
    Stars of heaven. Is 13:10.
    Stars of light. Ps 148:3.
Exhibit the greatness of God's power. Ps 8:3, with Is 40:26.
False gods frequently worshiped under the representation of. Am 5:26. Ac 7:43.
GOD
    Appointed to give light by night. Gn 1:16, with Gn 14. Ps 136:9. Jr 31:35.
    Created. Gn 1:16. Ps 8:3; 148:5.
    Established forever. Ps 148:3, 6. Jr 31:36.
    Numbers and names. Ps 147:4.
    Obscures. Jb 9:7.
    Set, in the firmament of heaven. Gn 1:17.
Idolaters worshiped. Jr 8:2; 19:13.
ILLUSTRATIVE OF
    Angels. Jb 38:7.
    Christ. Nu 24:17.
    Christ (bright and morning star). Rv 22:16.
    False teachers (wandering). Jde 1:13.
    Glory to be given to faithful saints (morning star). Rv 2:28.
    Ministers. Rv 1:16, 20; 2:1.
    Pride and carnal security (setting the host among). Ob 1:4.
    Princes and subordinate governors. Dn 8:10. Rv 8:12.
    The reward of faithful ministers (by shining). Dn 12:3.
    Severe judgments (when withdrawing their light). Is 13:10. Ezk 32:7. Jl 2:10; 3:15.
Impure in the sight of God. Jb 25:5.
Infinite in number. Gn 15:5. Jr 33:22.
The Israelites forbidden to worship. Dt 4:19; 17:2–4.
Made to praise God. Ps 148:3.
MENTIONED IN SCRIPTURE
    Arcturus. Jb 9:9; 38:32.
    Mazzaroth. Jb 38:32.
    Morning star. Rv 2:28.

Orion. Jb 9:9; 38:31. Am 5:8.

Pleiades. Jb 9:9; 38:31. Am 5:8.

One of extraordinary brightness (a meteor) appeared at Christ's birth. Mt 2:2, 9.

Punishment for worshiping. Dt 17:5-7.

Revolve in fixed orbits. Jg 5:20.

Shine in the firmament of heaven. Dn 12:3.

Use of, in navigation alluded to. Ac 27:20.

When grouped together, called constellations. 2 K 23:5. Is 13:10.

STEADFASTNESS

A characteristic of saints. Jb 17:9. Jn 8:31.

Commanded. Php 4:1. 2 Th 2:15. Ja 1:6-8.

Exhibited by God in all his purposes and ways. Nu 23:19. Dn 6:26. Ja 1:17.

Godliness necessary to. Jb 11:13-15.

MINISTERS

Encouraged by, in their people. 1 Th 3:8.

Exhorted to. 2 Tm 1:13-14. Ti 1:9.

Rejoiced by, in their people. Cl 2:5.

Should exhort to. Ac 13:43; 14:22.

Should pray for, in their people. 1 Th 3:13. 2 Th 2:17.

Principle of, illustrated. Mt 7:24-25. Jn 15:4. Cl 2:7.

Saints praise God for. Ps 116:8.

Saints pray for. Ps 17:5.

SECURED BY

The intercession of Christ. Lk 22:31-32.

The power of God. Pss 55:22; 62:2. 1 P 1:5. Jde 1:24.

The presence of God. Ps 16:8.

Trust in God. Ps 26:1.

SHOULD BE MANIFESTED

Even under affliction. Ps 44:17-19. Ro 8:35-37. 1 Th 3:3.

In cleaving to God. Dt 10:20. Ac 11:23.

In continuing in the apostles' doctrine and fellowship. Ac 2:42.

In holding fast our profession. He 4:14; 10:23.

In holding fast the confidence and rejoicing of the hope. He 3:6, 14.

In holding fast what is good. 1 Th 5:21.

In keeping the faith. Cl 2:5. 1 P 5:9.

In maintaining Christian liberty. Gl 5:1.

In standing fast in the faith. 1 Co 16:13.

In striving for the faith of the gospel. Php 1:27, with Jde 1:3.

In the work of the Lord. 1 Co 15:58.

Want of, illustrated. Lk 8:6, 13. Jn 15:6. 2 P 2:17. Jde 1:12.

The wicked devoid of. Ps 78:8, 37.

STONES, PRECIOUS

Art of engraving upon, early known to the Jews. Ex 28:9, 11, 21.

Art of setting, known to the Jews. Ex 28:20.

Brilliant and glittering. 1 Ch 29:2. Rv 21:11.

Brought from Ophir. 1 K 10:11. 2 Ch 9:10.

Brought from Sheba. 1 K 10:1, 2. Ezk 27:22.

CALLED

Jewels. Is 61:10. Ezk 16:12.

Precious jewels. 2 Ch 20:25. Pr 20:15.

Stones of fire. Ezk 28:14, 16.

Stones to be set. 1 Ch 29:2.

Dug out of the earth. Jb 28:5-6.

Extensive commerce in. Ezk 27:22. Rv 18:12.

Given by chief men for the temple. 1 Ch 29:8.

Given by the Jews for the tabernacle. Ex 25:7.

Highly prized by the ancients. Pr 17:8.

ILLUSTRATIVE OF

Beauty and stability of the church. Is 54:11-12.

Glory of heavenly Jerusalem. Rv 21:11.

Preciousness of Christ. Is 28:16. 1 P 2:6.

Saints. Ml 3:17. 1 Co 3:12.

Seductive splendor and false glory of the apostasy. Rv 17:4; 18:16.

Stability of heavenly Jerusalem. Rv 21:19.

Worldly glory of nations. Ezk 28:13-16.

MENTIONED IN SCRIPTURE

Agate. Ex 28:19. Is 54:12.

Amethyst. Ex 28:19. Rv 21:20.

Beryl. Dn 10:6. Rv 21:20.

Carbuncle. Ex 28:17. Is 54:12.

Chalcedony. Rv 21:19.

Chrysolyte. Rv 21:20.

Chrysoprasus. Rv 21:20.

Coral. Jb 28:18.

Diamond. Ex 28:18. Jr 17:1. Ezk 28:13.

Emerald. Ezk 27:16. Rv 4:3.

Jacinth. Rv 9:17; 21:20.

Jasper. Rv 4:3; 21:11, 19.

Onyx. Ex 28:20. Jb 28:16.

Pearl. Jb 28:18. Mt 13:45-46. Rv 21:21.

Ruby. Jb 28:18. Lm 4:7.

Sapphire. Ex 24:10. Ezk 1:26.

Sardine or sardius. Ex 28:17. Rv 4:3.

Sardonyx. Rv 21:20.

Topaz. Jb 28:19. Rv 21:20.

Of divers colors. 1 Ch 29:2.

Of great variety. 1 Ch 29:2.

Often given as presents. 1 K 10:2, 10.

A part of the treasure of kings. 2 Ch 32:27.

Prepared by David for the temple. 1 Ch 29:2.

USED FOR

Adorning the breastplate of judgment. Ex 28:17–20; 39:10–14.

Adorning the high priest's ephod. Ex 28:12.

Adorning the temple. 2 Ch 3:6.

Decorating the person. Ezk 28:13.

Honoring idols. Dn 11:38.

Ornamenting royal crowns. 2 S 12:30.

Setting in seals and rings. S S 5:12.

STRANGERS IN ISRAEL

All foreigners sojourning in Israel counted as, Ex 12:49.

CHIEFLY CONSISTED OF

Captives taken in war. Dt 21:10.

Foreign servants. Lv 25:44–45.

Persons who came into Israel for the sake of religious privileges. 1 K 8:41.

Persons who sought employment among the Jews. 1 K 7:13; 9:27.

The remnant of the mixed multitude who came out of Egypt. Ex 12:38.

The remnant of the nations of the land. 1 K 9:20. 2 Ch 8:7.

Could worship in the outer court of the temple. 1 K 8:41–43, with Rv 11:2. (*See also* Ep 2:14.)

The Jews condemned for oppressing. Ps 94:6. Ezk 22:7, 29.

LAWS RESPECTING

Allowed to eat what died of itself. Dt 14:21.

The Jews might purchase and have them as slaves. Lv 25:44–45.

The Jews might take usury from. Dt 23:20.

Might offer their burnt offerings on the altar of God. Lv 17:8; 22:18. Nu 15:14.

Might purchase Hebrew servants subject to release. Lv 25:47–48.

Not to be chosen as kings in Israel. Dt 17:15.

Not to be vexed or oppressed. Ex 22:21; 23:9. Lv 19:33.

Not to blaspheme God. Lv 24:16.

Not to eat blood. Lv 17:10–12.

Not to eat of the Passover while uncircumcised. Ex 12:43–44.

Not to practice idolatrous rites. Lv 20:2.

Not to work on the sabbath. Ex 20:10; 23:12. Dt 5:14.

Subject to the civil law. Lv 24:22.

To be loved. Lv 19:34. Dt 10:19.

To be relieved in distress. Lv 25:35.

To enjoy the benefit of the cities of refuge. Nu 35:15.

To have justice done to them in all disputes. Dt 1:16; 24:17.

To have the gleaning of the harvest. Lv 19:10; 23:22. Dt 24:19–22.

To have the law read to them. Dt 31:12. Jsh 8:32–35.

To participate in the rejoicing of the people. Dt 14:29; 16:11, 14; 26:11.

Motives urged on the Jews for being kind to. Ex 22:21; 23:9.

Under the care and protection of God. Dt 10:18. Ps 146:9.

Very numerous in Solomon's reign. 2 Ch 2:17.

Were frequently employed in public works. 1 Ch 22:2. 2 Ch 2:18.

STRENGTH

God is our. Ps 73:26; 27:1. Is 40:29.

In weakness. 2 Co 12:10. He 11:34.

Love with. Mk 12:30.

Must be demonstrated. 2 Ch 32:7, 1 Co 16:13.

Quietness is. Is 30:7.

Through Christ. Php 4:13.

Through the Spirit. Ep 3:16. Cl 1:11.

STRIFE

Appeased by slowness to anger. Pr 15:18.

Christ an example of avoiding. Is 42:2, with Mt 12:15–19. Lk 9:52–56. 1 P 2:23.

Danger of joining in, illustrated. Pr 26:17.

Difficulty of stopping, a reason for avoiding it. Pr 17:14.

Evidence of a carnal spirit. 1 Co 3:3.

Evidences a love of transgression. Pr 17:19.

EXCITED BY

A contentious disposition. Pr 26:21.

Curious questions. 1 Tm 6:4. 2 Tm 2:23.

Drunkenness. Pr 23:29–30.

Frowardness. Pr 16:28.

Hatred. Pr 10:12.

Lusts. Ja 4:1.

Pride. Pr 13:10; 28:25.

Scorning. Pr 22:10.

Talebearing. Pr 26:20.

Wrath. Pr 15:18; 30:33.

Excludes from heaven. Gl 5:20–21.
Existed in primitive church. 1 Co 1:11.
Fools engage in. Pr 18:6.
Forbidden. Pr 3:30; 25:8.
Honorable to cease from. Pr 20:3.
Hyprocrites make religion a pretense for. Is 58:4.

LEADS TO
Blasphemy. Lv 24:10–11.
Confusion and every evil work. Ja 3:16.
Injustice. Hk 1:3–4.
Mutual destruction. Gl 5:15.
Violence. Ex 21:18, 22.

MINISTERS SHOULD
Avoid. 1 Tm 3:3. 2 Tm 2:24.
Avoid questions that lead to. 2 Tm 2:23. Ti 3:9.
Not preach through. Php 1:15–16.
Reprove. 1 Co 1:11–12; 3:3; 11:17–18.
Warn against. 1 Co 1:10. 2 Tm 2:14.
Promoters of, should be expelled. Pr 22:10.
Punishment for. Ps 55:9.
Saints kept from tongues of. Ps 31:20.

SAINTS SHOULD
Avoid. Gn 13:8. Ep 4:3.
Avoid questions that lead to. 2 Tm 2:14.
Do all things without. Php 2:14.
Not act from. Php 2:3.
Not walk in. Ro 13:13.
Praise God for protection from. 2 S 22:44. Ps 18:43.
Seek God's protection from. Ps 35:1. Jr 18:19.
Submit to wrong rather than engage in. Pr 20:22. Mt 5:39–40. 1 Co 6:7.
Shameful in saints. 2 Co 12:20. Ja 3:14.
Strength and violence of, illustrated. Pr 17:14; 18:19.
Temporal blessings embittered by. Pr 17:1.
A work of the flesh. Gl 5:20.

SUMMER

The ancients had houses or apartments suited to. Jg 3:20, 24. Am 3:15.
Ants provide their winter food during. Pr 6:8; 30:25.
Approach of, indicated by shooting out of leaves on trees. Mt 24:32.

CHARACTERIZED BY
Excessive drought. Ps 32:4.
Excessive heat. Jr 17:8.
Illustrative of seasons of grace. Jr 8:20.
Made by God. Ps 74:17.

Many kinds of fruit ripened and used during. 2 S 16:1. Jr 40:10; 48:32.
The wise are diligent during. Pr 10:5.
Yearly return of, secured by covenant. Gn 8:22.

THE SUN

Called the greater light. Gn 1:16.
Clearness of its light alluded to. S S 6:10.

COMPARED TO
A bridegroom coming forth from his chamber. Ps 19:5.
A strong man rejoicing to run a race. Ps 19:5.

GOD
Appointed to divide seasons, etc. Gn 1:14.
Appointed to rule the day. Gn 1:16. Ps 136:8. Jr 31:35.
Causes to know its time of setting. Ps 104:19.
Causes to rise both on evil and good. Mt 5:45.
Created. Gn 1:14, 16. Ps 74:16.
Exercises sovereign power over. Jb 9:7.
Placed in the firmament. Gn 1:17.

ILLUSTRATIVE OF
Christ's coming. Ml 4:2.
The future glory of saints (in its brightness). Dn 12:3, with Mt 13:43.
The glory of Christ. Mt 17:2. Rv 1:16; 10:1.
God's favor. Ps 84:11.
Public ignominy (when before or in sight of). 2 S 12:11, 12. Jr 8:3.
The purity of the church (in its clearness). S S 6:10.
Perpetual blessedness (no more going down). Is 60:20.
Premature destruction (going down at noon). Jr 15:9. Am 8:9.
Severe calamities (darkened). Ezk 32:7. Jl 2:10, 31, with Mt 24:29. Rv 9:2.
Supreme rulers. Gn 37:9. Is 13:10.
The triumph of saints (in its power). Jg 5:31.
Indicates the hours of the day by the shadow on the dial. 2 K 20:9.

THE JEWS
Commenced their day with the rising of. Gn 19:23–24, with 27–28. Jg 9:33.
Commenced their evening with the setting of. Gn 28:11. Dt 24:13. Mk 1:32.
Consecrated chariots and horses, as symbols of. 2 K 23:11.

Expressed the east by rising of. Nu 21:11.
Dt 4:41, 47. Jsh 12:1.
Expressed the west by setting of. Ja 1:4.
Expressed the whole earth by, from rising of, to setting of. Pss 50:1; 113:3. Is 45:6.
Forbidden to worship. Dt 4:19; 17:3.
Worshiped. 2 K 23:5. Jr 8:2.
Made to praise and glorify God. Ps 148:3.
MIRACLES CONNECTED WITH
Darkened at the crucifixion. Lk 23:44–45.
Shadow put back on the dial. 2 K 20:11.
Standing still for a whole day in the valley of Ajalon. Jsh 10:12–13.
The power and brilliancy of its rising alluded to. Jg 5:31. 2 S 23:4.
RAYS OF
Change the color of the skin. S S 1:6.
Frequently destructive to human life. 2 K 4:18–20. Ps 121:6. Is 49:10.
Pleasant to man. Jb 30:28, with Ec 11:7.
Produce and ripen fruit. Dt 33:14.
Soften and melt some substances. Ex 16:21.
Wither and burn up the herbs of the field. Mk 4:6. Ja 1:11.
Worshipers of, turned their faces toward the east. Ezk 8:16.

SWEARING FALSELY

Blessedness of abstaining from. Ps 24:4–5.
False witnesses guilty of. Dt 19:16, 18.
Forbidden. Lv 19:12. Nu 30:2. Mt 5:33.
Fraud often leads to. Lv 6:2–3.
Hateful to God. Zc 8:17.
Saints abstain from. Jsh 9:20. Ps 15:4.
We should not love. Zc 8:17.
THE WICKED
Addicted to. Jr 5:2. Ho 10:4.
Plead excuses for. Jr 7:9–10.
Shall be cut off for. Zc 5:3.
Shall be judged on account of. Ml 3:5.
Shall have a curse upon their houses for. Zc 5:4.

SWEARING, PROFANE

All kinds forbidden as desecration of God's name. Ex 20:7. Mt 5:34–36; 23:21–22. Ja 5:12.
Guilt of. Ex 20:7. Dt 5:11.
Nations visited for. Jr 23:10. Ho 4:1–3.
Punishment for. Lv 24:16, 23. Pss 59:12; 109:17–18.

THE WICKED
Addicted to. Ps 10:7. Ro 3:14.
Clothe themselves with. Ps 109:18.
Love. Ps 109:17.
Woe denounced against. Mt 23:16.

SWINE

DESCRIBED AS
Destructive to agriculture. Ps 80:13.
Fierce and ungenerous. Mt 7:6.
Filthy in its habits. 2 P 2:22.
Fed upon husks. Lk 15:16.
The Gergesenes punished for having. Mt 8:31–32. Mk 5:11, 14.
Herding of, considered as the greatest degradation to a Jew. Lk 15:15.
ILLUSTRATIVE OF
Hypocrites. 2 P 2:22.
The wicked. Mt 7:6.
Kept in large herds. Mt 8:30.
Sacrificing of, an abomination. Is 66:3.
Unclean and not to be eaten. Lv 11:7–8.
Ungodly Jews condemned for eating. Is 65:4; 66:17.
When wild, inhabited the woods. Ps 80:13.

SWORD

Brandished over the head. Ezk 32:10.
Carried in a sheath or scabbard. 1 Ch 21:27. Jr 47:6. Ezk 21:3–5.
DESCRIBED AS
Bright. Na 3:3.
Glittering. Dt 32:41. Jb 20:25.
Hurtful. Ps 144:10.
Oppressive. Jr 46:16.
Sharp. Ps 57:4.
Frequently had two edges. Ps 149:6.
Hebrews early acquainted with making of. 1 S 13:19.
ILLUSTRATIVE OF
Deep mental affliction. Lk 2:35.
The end of the wicked. Pr 5:4.
False witnesses. Pr 25:18.
Judicial authority. Ro 13:4.
The justice of God. Dt 32:41. Zc 13:7.
Peace and friendship (when sheathed). Jr 47:6.
Perpetual calamity (not departing from one's house). 2 S 12:10.
Persecuting spirit of the wicked. Ps 37:14.
The protection of God. Dt 33:29.
Rapine (when living by). Gn 27:40.
Severe and heavy calamities. Ezk 5:2, 17; 14:17; 21:9.

The tongue of the wicked. Pss 57:4; 64:3, Pr 12:18.

War and contention. Mt 10:34.

War and destruction (when drawn). Lv 26:33. Ezk 21:3–5.

The wicked. Ps 17:13.

The word of Christ. Is 49:2, with Rv 1:16.

The word of God. Ep 6:17, with He 4:12.

In time of peace made into plowshares. Is 2:4. Mi 4:3.

In time of war plowshares made into. Jl 3:10.

Often sent as a punishment. Ezr 9:7. Ps 78:62.

Often threatened as a punishment. Lv 26:25, 33. Dt 32:25.

One of God's four sore judgments. Ezk 14:21.

Pointed. Ezk 21:15.

Probable origin of. Gn 3:24.

Sharpened and furbished before going to war. Ps 7:12. Ezk 21:9.

Suspended from the girdle. 1 S 17:39. 2 S 20:8. Ne 4:18. Ps 45:3.

Those slain by, communicated ceremonial uncleanness. Nu 19:16.

Thrust through enemies. Ezk 16:40.

USED

By heathen nations. Jg 7:22. 1 S 15:33.

By the Jews. Jg 20:2. 2 S 24:9.

By the patriarchs. Gn 34:25; 48:22.

For destruction of enemies. Nu 21:24. Jsh 6:21.

For punishing criminals. 1 S 15:33. Ac 12:2.

For self-defense. Lk 22:36.

Sometimes for self-destruction. 1 S 31:4–5. Ac 16:27.

SYNAGOGUES

The apostles frequently taught and preached in. Ac 9:20; 13:5; 17:1, 17.

The building of, considered a noble and meritorious work. Lk 7:5.

Chief seats in, reserved for elders. Mt 23:6.

CHRIST OFTEN

Attended. Lk 4:16.

Performed miracles in. Mt 12:9–10. Mk 1:23. Lk 13:11.

Preached and taught in. Mt 4:23. Mk 1:39. Lk 13:10.

Each sect had its own. Ac 6:9.

Early notice of their existence. Ps 74:8.

GOVERNED BY

Ordinary rulers. Mk 5:22. Ac 13:15.

A president or chief ruler. Ac 18:8, 17.

Had seats for the congregation. Ac 13:14.

OFFENDERS WERE OFTEN

Expelled from. Jn 9:22, 34; 12:42; 16:2.

Given up to, for trial. Lk 12:11; 21:12.

Punished in. Mt 10:17; 23:34. Ac 22:19.

Often used as courts of justice. Ac 9:2.

Places in which the Jews assembled for worship. Ac 13:5, 14.

Portion of scripture for the day sometimes read by one of the congregation. Lk 4:16.

Probably originated in the schools of the prophets. 1 S 19:18–24. 2 K 4:23.

Provided with a chazan or minister, who had charge of the sacred books. Lk 4:17, 20.

Revival of, after the captivity. Ne 8:1–8.

Service in, on the sabbath day. Lk 4:16. Ac 13:14.

SERVICE OF, CONSISTED OF

Expounding the word of God. Ne 8:8. Lk 4:21.

Praise and thanksgiving. Ne 9:5.

Prayer. Mt 6:5.

Reading the word of God. Ne 8:18; 9:3; 13:1. Ac 15:21.

Sometimes several, in the same city. Ac 6:9; 9:2.

Strangers invited to address the congregation in. Ac 13:15.

SYRIA

Abana and Pharpar rivers of. 2 K 5:12.

Army of, miraculously routed. 2 K 7:5–6.

Asa sought aid of, against Israel. 1 K 15:18–20.

Benhadad king of, besieged Samaria. 1 K 20:1–12.

Besieged Samaria again. 2 K 6:24–29.

Damascus the capital of. Is 7:8.

DAVID

Dedicated the spoils of. 2 S 8:11–12.

Destroyed an army of, which assisted Hadadezer. 2 S 8:5.

Destroyed a second army of. 2 S 10:15–19.

Garrisoned and made tributary. 2 S 8:6.

Obtained renown by his victory over. 2 S 8:13.

Sent Joab against the armies of, hired by the Ammonites. 2 S 10:6–14.

Death of the king of, and the cruelty of his successor, foretold by Elisha. 2 K 8:7, 15.

Elijah anointed Hazael king over, by divine direction. 1 K 19:15.

Elisha predicted to Joash his three victories over. 2 K 13:14–19.

God smote with blindness those sent against Elisha by the king of. 2 K 6:14, 18–20.

The gospel preached and many churches founded in. Ac 15:23, 41.

Governed by kings. 1 K 22:31. 2 K 5:1.

INHABITANTS OF
Called Syrians. 2 S 10:11. 2 K 5:20.
Called Syrians of Damascus. 2 S 8:5.
A commercial people. Ezk 27:18.
An idolatrous people. Jg 10:6. 2 K 5:18.
Spoke the Syriac language. 2 K 18:26. Ezr 4:7. Dn 2:4.
A warlike people. 1 K 20:23, 25.

Israel delivered into the hands of, for the sins of Jehoahaz. 2 K 13:3, 7, 22.

Israel followed the idolatry of. Jg 10:6.

THE ISRAELITES
At peace with, for three years. 1 K 22:1.
Craftily drawn into a league with. 1 K 20:31–43.
Defeated by, and Ahab slain. 1 K 22:30–36.
Encouraged and assisted by God, overcame a second time. 1 K 20:28–30.
Forewarned of invasion by, at the return of the year. 1 K 20:22–25.
Harassed by frequent incursions of. 2 K 5:2; 6:23.
Heard the secrets of, from Elisha. 2 K 6:8–12.
Insignificant before. 1 K 20:26–27.
Under Ahab, encouraged and assisted by

God, overcame. 1 K 20:13–20.

Under Ahab, sought to recover Ramoth-gilead from. 1 K 22:3–29.

Joined with Israel against Ahaz and besieged Jerusalem. 2 K 16:5. Is 7:12.

Joram king of Israel, in seeking to recover Ramoth-gilead from, severely wounded. 2 K 8:28–29; 9:15.

More properly, the country around Damascus. 2 S 8:6.

Originally included Mesopotamia. Gn 25:20; 28:5. Dt 26:5, with Ac 7:2.

PROPHECIES RESPECTING
Burning of Damascus. Jr 49:27. Am 1:4.
Ceasing to be a kingdom. Is 17:1–3.
Destruction of its inhabitants. Jr 49:26.
Destruction of Rezin, king of. Is 7:8, 16.
Its calamities, the punishments of its sins. Am 1:3.
Its history in connection with the Macedonian empire. Dn 11:6, etc.
Its inhabitants to be captives. Am 1:5.
Spoliation of Damascus. Is 8:4.
Terror and dismay in, occasioned by its invasion. Jr 49:23–24.

Retook Elath and drove out the Jews. 2 K 16:6.

A savior raised up for Israel against. 2 K 13:5, 23–25.

Subdued and governed by the Romans. Lk 2:2.

Subdued and its inhabitants taken captive by Assyria. 2 K 16:9.

T

THE TABERNACLE

All offerings to be made at. Lv 17:4. Dt 12:5–6, 11, 13–14.

Anointed and consecrated with oil. Ex 40:9. Lv 8:10. Nu 7:1.

Ark and mercy seat put in the most holy place. Ex 26:33–34; 40:20–21. He 9:4.

BOARDS OF
> Had each two tenons fitted into sockets of silver. Ex 26:17, 19; 36:22–24.
>
> Made of shittim wood. Ex 26:15; 36:20.
>
> Six, and two corner boards for west side. Ex 26:22–25; 36:27–30.
>
> Supported by bars of shittim wood resting in rings of gold. Ex 26:26–29; 36:31–33.
>
> Ten cubits high by one and a half broad. Ex 26:16; 36:21.
>
> Twenty on north side. Ex 26:20; 36:25.
>
> Twenty on south side. Ex 26:18; 36:23.
>
> With the bars, covered with gold. Ex 26:29; 36:34.

CALLED THE
> House of the Lord. Jsh 6:24. 1 S 1:7, 24.
>
> Tabernacle of Joseph. Ps 78:67.
>
> Tabernacle of Shiloh. Ps 78:60.
>
> Tabernacle of testimony or witness. Ex 38:21. Nu 1:50; 17:7–8. 2 Ch 24:6. Ac 7:44.
>
> Tabernacle of the congregation. Ex 27:21; 33:7; 40:26.
>
> Tabernacle of the Lord. Jsh 22:19. 1 K 2:28. 1 Ch 16:39.
>
> Temple of the Lord. 1 S 1:9; 3:3.

The cloud of glory rested on, by night and day, during its abode in the wilderness. Ex 40:38. Nu 9:15–16.

COURT OF
> All the pillars of, filletted wth silver, etc. Ex 27:17; 38:17.
>
> All the vessels of, made of brass. Ex 27:19.
>
> Contained the bronze altar and laver of brass. Ex 40:29–30.
>
> The gate of, a hanging of blue, purple, etc., twenty cubits wide, suspended from four pillars, etc. Ex 27:16; 38:18.

One hundred cubits long and fifty cubits wide. Ex 27:18.

Surrounded by curtains of fine linen suspended from pillars in sockets of brass. Ex 27:9–15; 38:9–16.

COVERINGS OF
> First or inner, ten curtains of blue, purple, etc., joined with loops and golden taches. Ex 26:1–6; 36:8–13.
>
> Fourth or outward, badgers' skins. Ex 26:14; 36:19.
>
> Second, eleven curtains of goats' hair, etc. Ex 26:7–13; 36:14–18.
>
> Third, rams' skins dyed red. Ex 26:14; 36:19.

Designed for manifestation of God's presence and for his worship. Ex 25:8; 29:42–43.

Divided by a veil of blue, purple, etc., suspended from four pillars of shittim wood by gold hooks. Ex 26:31–33; 36:35–36; 40:21.

DIVIDED INTO
> The holy place. Ex 26:33. He 9:2–6.
>
> The most holy place. Ex 26:34. He 9:3, 7.

Divine wisdom given to Bezaleel, etc., to make. Ex 31:2–7; 35:30–35; 36:1.

Door of, a curtain of blue and purple suspended by gold rings from five pillars of shittim wood, etc. Ex 26:36–37; 36:37–38.

First reared on the first day of the second year after the exodus. Ex 40:2, 17.

Free-will offerings made at the dedication of the altar of. Nu 7:10–87.

Free-will offerings made at the first rearing of. Nu 7:1–9.

Had a court round about. Ex 40:8.

ILLUSTRATIVE OF
> The body. 2 Co 5:1. 2 P 1:13.
>
> Christ. Is 4:6. Jn 1:14. (Greek) He 9:8–9, 11.
>
> Christ's body (the veil). He 10:20.
>
> The church. Ps 15:1. Is 16:5; 54:2. He 8:2. Rv 21:2–3.
>
> Heaven (the holy of holies). He 6:19–20; 9:12, 24; 10:19.

The obscurity of the Mosaic dispensation (the veil). He 9:8, 10, with Ro 16:25–26. Rv 11:19.

Journeys of Israel regulated by the cloud on. Ex 40:36–37.

THE LEVITES

Appointed over and had charge of. Nu 1:50; 8:24; 18:2–4.

Carried. Nu 4:15, 25, 31.

Did the inferior service of. Nu 3:6–8.

Pitched their tents around. Nu 1:53; 3:23, 29, 35.

Took down and put up. Nu 1:51.

The Lord appeared in, over the mercy seat. Ex 25:22. Lv 16:2. Nu 7:89.

Made of the free-will offerings of the people. Ex 25:1–8; 35:4–5, 21–29.

Moses commanded to make, after a divine pattern. Ex 25:9; 26:30. He 8:5.

A movable tent suited to the unsettled condition of Israel. 2 S 7:6–7.

A permanent house substitued for, when the kingdom was established. 2 S 7:5–13.

THE PRIESTS

Alone could enter. Nu 18:3, 5.

Performed all services in. Nu 3:10; 18:1–2. He 9:6.

Were the ministers of. He 8:2.

Punishment for defiling. Lv 15:31. Nu 19:13.

Sanctified by the glory of the Lord. Ex 29:43; 40:34. Nu 9:15.

SET UP

At Gilgal. Jsh 5:10–11.

By Moses at Mount Sinai. Ex 40:18–19, with Nu 10:11–12.

In Nob. 1 S 21:1–6.

In Shiloh. Jsh 18:1; 19:51.

Lastly at Gibeon. 1 Ch 16:39; 21:29.

Sprinkled and purified with blood. He 9:21.

The table of showbread, the golden candlestick, and the altar of incense placed in the holy place. Ex 36:35; 40:22, 24, 26. He 9:2.

TABERNACLES, FEAST OF

All males obliged to appear at. Ex 23:16–17.

Began fifteenth of seventh month. Lv 23:34, 39.

Called the feast of ingathering. Ex 34:22.

Commemorated the sojourn of Israel in the desert. Lv 23:43.

CUSTOMS OBSERVED AT

Bearing branches of palms. Lv 23:40. Rv 7:9.

Drawing water from the pool of Siloam. Is 12:3. Jn 7:2, 37–39.

Singing hosannas. Ps 118:24–29. Mt 21:8–9.

First and last days of, holy convocations. Lv 23:35, 39. Nu 29:12, 35.

Held after harvest and vintage. Dt 16:13.

Lasted seven days. Lv 23:34, 41. Dt 16:13, 15.

The law publicly read every seventh year at. Dt 31:10–12. Ne 8:18.

OBSERVED

Perpetually. Lv 23:41.

With rejoicing. Dt 16:14–15.

The people dwelt in booths during. Lv 23:42. Ne 8:15–16.

REMARKABLE CELEBRATIONS OF

After the captivity. Ezr 3:4. Ne 8:17.

At the dedication of Solomon's temple. 1 K 8:2, 65.

Sacrifices during. Lv 23:36–37. Nu 29:13–39.

TALENT

Differs in different individuals. Mt 25:15.

Given by God. 1 Co 12:4.

To be used. 1 Tm 4:14. Ro 12:6.

TEACHING

Commanded. Pr 19:20. Cl 1:28.

FALSE

Described. Is 56:11.

Motive in. Ti 1:10, 11.

Warned against. Jr 12:6. He 13:9.

From God, promised. 1 S 12:23. Ex 4:15. Lk 12:12.

From God, requested. Ps 25:4; 86:11.

From nature. Jb 12:7, 8. 1 Co 11:14.

In the church. Ac 5:42. Ro 12:7. Cl 1:28. 1 Tm 4:11. Ti 1:11. He 5:12.

Parents' duty. Dt 4:10; 11:19.

Teachers worthy of honor. 1 Co 9:9. 1 Tm 5:17.

TEMPLE, FIRST

All dedicated things placed in. 2 Ch 5:1.

Appointed as a house of prayer. Is 56:7, with Mt 21:13.

Appointed as a house of sacrifice. 2 Ch 7:12.

Ark of God brought into, with great solemnity. 1 K 8:1–9. 2 Ch 5:2–10.

Built on Mount Moriah on the threshing floor of Ornan or Araunah. 1 Ch 21:28–30, with 22:1. 2 Ch 3:1.

CALLED

House of the God of Jacob. Is 2:3.
The house of the Lord. 2 Ch 23:5, 12.
The mountain of the Lord's house. Is 2:2.
Mount Zion. Ps 74:2.
Zion. Ps 84:1–7.

Cedar of, carved with flowers, etc. 1 K 6:18.
Ceiled with fir wood and gilt. 2 Ch 3:5.
Complete destruction of, predicted. Jr 26:18, with Mi 3:12.

DAVID

Anxious to build. 2 S 7:2. 1 Ch 22:7; 29:3. Ps 132:2–5.
Being a man of war, not permitted to build. 2 S 7:5–9, with 1 K 5:3. 1 Ch 22:8.
Charged his princes to assist in building. 1 Ch 22:17–19.
Charged Solomon to build. 1 Ch 22:6–7, 11.
Free-will offerings of the people for building. 1 Ch 29:6–9.
Made preparations for building. 1 Ch 22:2–5, 14–16; 29:2–5.
Prayed that Solomon might have wisdom to build. 1 Ch 29:19.
Told by the prophet that Solomon should build. 2 S 17:12–13. 1 Ch 17:12.

Dedicated to God by Solomon. 1 K 8:12–66. 2 Ch 6.

DIVIDED INTO

Oracle or most holy place. 1 K 6:19.
Porch. 2 Ch 3:4.
Sanctuary or greater house. 2 Ch 3:5.

Filled with the cloud of glory. 1 K 8:10–11. 2 Ch 5:13; 7:2.
Floor and walls of, covered with cedar and fir wood. 1 K 6:15.
Garnished with precious stones. 2 Ch 3:6.
God promised to dwell in. 1 K 6:12–13.

HISTORICAL NOTICES OF

Defiled and its treasures given by Ahaz to the king of Assyria. 2 K 16:14, 18. 2 Ch 28:20–21.
Its treasures, etc., given by Hezekiah to the Assyrians, to procure a treaty. 2 K 18:13–16.
Pillaged and burned by the Babylonians. 2 K 25:8, 13–17. 2 Ch 36:18–19.
Pillaged by Shishak king of Egypt. 1 K 14:25–26. 2 Ch 12:9.
Polluted by the idolatrous worship of

Manasseh. 2 K 21:4–7. 2 Ch 33:4–5, 7.
Purified and divine worship restored under Hezekiah. 2 Ch 29:3–35.
Purified by Josiah. 2 K 23:4–7, 11–12.
Repaired by Jehoash at the instigation of Jehoiada. 2 K 12:4–14. 2 Ch 24:4–13.
Repaired by Josiah in the eighteenth year of his reign. 2 K 22:3–7. 2 Ch 34:8–13.
Treasures of given by Jehoash to propitiate the Syrians. 2 K 12:17–18.

ILLUSTRATIVE OF

The bodies of saints. 1 Co 6:19.
Christ. Jn 2:19, 21.
The spiritual church. 1 Co 3:16. 2 Co 6:16. Ep 2:20–22.

Inside and out covered with gold. 1 K 6:21–22. 2 Ch 3:7.
Its magnificence. 2 Ch 2:5, 9.

ORACLE OR MOST HOLY PLACE

Doors and posts of, of olivewood carved and gilded. 1 K 6:31–32.
A partition of chains of gold between it and outer house. 1 K 6:21.
Separated from the outer house by a veil. 2 Ch 3:14.
Twenty cubits every way. 1 K 6:16, 20.
Two cherubim of gilded olivewood made within. 1 K 6:23–28. 2 Ch 3:11–13.

PORCH

One hundred and twenty cubits high. 2 Ch 3:4.
Pillars with their chapiters described. 1 K 7:15–22. 2 Ch 3:15–17.
Twenty cubits long and ten broad. 1 K 6:3.

Sacred fire sent down from heaven at its dedication. 2 Ch 7:3.

SANCTUARY OR GREATER HOUSE

Door posts of olivewood carved and gilded. 1 K 6:33. 2 Ch 3:7.
Folding doors of fir wood carved and gilded. 1 K 6:34–35.
Forty cubits long. 2 K 6:17.

SOLOMON

Applied to Hiram for a skilful workman to superintend, etc., the building of. 2 Ch 2:7, 13–14.
Built without the noise of hammers, ax, or any tool. 1 K 6:7.
Commenced second day of second month of fourth year of Solomon. 1 K 6:1, 37. 2 Ch 3:2.

Contracted with Hiram for wood, stone, and labor. 1 K 5:6–12. 2 Ch 2:8–10.

Determined to build. 2 Ch 2:1.

Employed all the strangers in preparing for. 2 Ch 2:2, 17–18, with 1 K 5:15.

Employed thirty thousand Israelites in the work. 1 K 5:13–14.

Specially instructed for. 2 Ch 3:3.

Surrounded with three stories of chambers communicating with the interior on the right side. 1 K 6:5–6, 8, 10.

Was but a temple built with hands. Ac 7:47–48.

Was finished in the eighth month of the eleventh year of Solomon. 1 K 6:38.

Was lighted by narrow windows. 1 K 6:4.

Was roofed with cedar. 1 K 6:9.

Was seven years in building. 1 K 6:38.

Was three score cubits long, twenty broad, and thirty high. 1 K 6:2. 2 Ch 3:3.

TEMPLE, SECOND

Beautiful gate of, mentioned. Ac 3:2.

Built on the site of the first temple. Ezr 2:6, etc.

CHRIST

Frequently taught in. Mk 14:49.

Miraculously transported to a pinnacle of, Mt 4:5. Lk 4:9.

Predicted its destruction. Mt 24:2. Mk 13:2. Lk 21:6.

Presented in. Lk 2:22, 27.

Purified, at the close of his ministry. Mt 21:12–13.

Purified, at the commencement of his ministry. Jn 2:15–17.

To appear in. Hg 2:7, with Ml 3:1.

Completed the third of the twelfth month in the sixth year of Darius. Ezr 6:15.

CYRUS

Decree for building, predicted. Is 44:28.

Furnished means for building. Ezr 6:4.

Gave a decree for building, in the first year of his reign. Ezr 1:1–2; 6:3.

Gave permission to the Jews to go to Jerusalem to build. Ezr 1:3.

Gave the vessels of the first temple for. Ezr 1:7–11; 6:5.

Ordered those who remained in Babylon to contribute to the building of. Ezr 1:4.

Dedication of, celebrated with joy and thankfulness. Ezr 6:16–18.

Decree of Cyrus found and confirmed by Darius. Ezr 6:1–2, 6–12.

Desecrated by the Romans. Dn 9:27, with Mt 24:15.

Desecration of, foretold. Dn 9:27; 11:31.

Dimensions. Ezr 6:3–4.

Divine worship commenced before foundation was laid. Ezr 3:1–6.

Foundation of, laid the second month of the second year after the captivity. Ezr 3:8.

Future glory of, predicted. Hg 2:7–9.

Grief of those who had seen the first temple. Ezr 3:12. Hg 2:3.

Its completion by Zerubbabel foretold, to encourage the Jews. Zc 4:4–10.

THE JEWS

Considered it blasphemy to speak against. Mt 26:61. Ac 6:13; 21:28.

Desecrated by the selling of oxen, etc. Jn 2:14.

Encouraged to proceed in building. Hg 1:8; 2:19. Zc 8:9.

Prayed outside while the priest offered incense within. Lk 1:10. (See also Lk 18:10.)

Punished for not persevering in building. He 1:6, 9–11; 2:15, 17. Zc 8:10.

Reproved for not building. Hg 1:1–5.

Joy of those who had not seen the first temple. Ezr 3:13.

Magnificence of its building and ornaments. Jn 2:20. Mk 13:1. Lk 21:5.

Materials for building, procured from Tyre and Sidon. Ezr 3:7.

No Gentile allowed to enter the inner courts of. Ac 21:27–30.

Rededicated and cleansed by Judas Maccabaeus after its desecration by Antiochus. Jn 10:22.

Repaired and beautified by Herod, which occupied forty-six years. Jn 2:20.

Resumed by Zerubbabel and Jeshua. Ezr 5:2.

THE SAMARITANS, ETC.

Procured its interruption for fifteen years. Ezr 4:24.

Proposed to assist in building. Ezr 4:1–2.

Their help refused by the Jews. Ezr 4:3.

Weakened the hands of the Jews in building. Ezr 4:4–5.

Wrote to Artazerxes Smerdis to interrupt the building. Ezr 4:6–16.

Separation between the outer or Gentile court and that of the Jews alluded to. Ep 2:13–14.

Solemnities connected with laying the foundation of. Ezr 3:9–11.

Solomon's porch connected with.   Jn 10:23. Ac 3:11.

Tatnai the governor wrote to Darius to know if the building had his sanction.   Ezr 5:3–17.

Veil of, rent at our Lord's death.   Mt 27:51.

TEMPTATION

Always conformable to the nature of man.   1 Co 10:13.

Blessedness of those who meet and overcome. Ja 1:2–4, 12.

CHRIST

Endured from the devil.   Mk 1:13.

Endured from the wicked.   Mt 16:1; 22:18. Lk 10:25.

Intercedes for his people under.   Lk 22:31–32. Jn 17:15.

Is able to succor those under.   He 2:18.

Keeps faithful saints from the hour of.   Rv 3:10.

Overcame.   Mt 4:11.

Resisted by the word of God.   Mt 4:4, 7, 10.

Sympathizes with those under.   He 4:15.

COMES FROM

Covetousness.   Pr 28:20. 1 Tm 6:9–10.

Lusts.   Ja 1:14.

The devil is the author of.   1 Ch 21:1. Mt 4:1. Jn 13:2. 1 Th 3:5.

The devil will renew.   Lk 4:13.

Does not come from God.   Ja 1:13.

Evil associates, the instruments of.   Pr 1:10; 7:6; 16:29.

GOD

Cannot be the subject of.   Ja 1:13.

Enables the saints to bear.   1 Co 10:13.

Knows how to deliver saints out of.   2 P 2:9.

Will make a way for saints to escape out of. 1 Co 10:13.

Will not suffer saints to be exposed to, beyond their powers to bear.   1 Co 10:13.

Has strength through the weakness of the flesh.   Mt 26:41.

Mere professors fall away in time of.   Lk 8:13.

OFTEN ARISES THROUGH

Poverty.   Pr 30:9. Mt 4:2–3.

Prosperity.   Pr 30:9. Mt 4:8.

Worldly glory.   Nu 22:17. Dn 4:30; 5:2. Mt 4:8.

Often ends in sin and perdition.   1 Tm 6:9. Ja 1:15.

Often strengthened by the perversion of God's

word.   Mt 4:6.

PERMITTED AS A TRIAL OF

Disinterestedness.   Jb 1:9–12.

Faith.   1 P 1:7. Ja 1:2–3.

Saints may be in heaviness through.   1 P 1:6.

SAINTS SHOULD

Avoid the way of.   Pr 4:14–15.

Not occasion to others.   Ro 14:13.

Pray to be kept from.   Mt 6:13; 26:41.

Resist in faith.   Ep 6:16. 1 P 5:9.

Restore those overcome by.   Gl 6:1.

Watch against.   Mt 26:41. 1 P 5:8.

To distrust of God's providence.   Mt 4:3.

To presumption.   Mt 4:6.

To worshiping the god of this world.   Mt 4:9.

TENTS

Antiquity of.   Gn 4:20.

CALLED

Curtains.   Is 54:2. He 3:7.

Tabernacles.   Nu 24:5. Jb 12:6. He 11:9.

Custom of sitting and standing at the door of. Gn 18:1. Jg 4:20.

Ease and rapidity of their removal alluded to. Is 38:12.

Fastened by cords to stakes or nails.   Is 54:2. Jr 10:20, with Jg 4:21.

ILLUSTRATIVE OF

The great extension of the church (when enlarging).   Is 54:2.

The heavens (when spread out).   Is 40:22.

PITCHED

In the neighborhood of wells, etc.   Gn 13:10, 12; 26:17–18. 1 S 29:1.

On the tops of houses.   2 S 16:22.

Under trees.   Gn 18:1, 4. Jg 4:5.

With order and regularity.   Nu 1:52.

Sending persons to seek a convenient place for, alluded to.   Dt 1:33.

Separate, for females of the family.   Gn 24:67.

Separate, for servants.   Gn 31:33.

Spread out.   Is 40:22.

Those of the Jews contrasted with those of the Arabs.   Nu 24:5, with S S 1:5.

USED BY

All eastern nations.   Jg 6:5. 1 S 17:4. 2 K 7:7. 1 Ch 5:10.

The Arabs.   Is 13:20.

Israel in the desert.   Ex 33:8. Nu 24:2.

Patriarchs.   Gn 13:5; 25:27. He 11:9.

The people of Israel in all their wars.   1 S 4:3, 10; 29:1. 1 K 16:16.

The Rechabites.   Jr 35:7, 10.

Shepherds while tending their flocks.   S S
1:8. Is 38:12.

THANKSGIVING

Christ set an example of.   Mt 11:25; 26:27.
Jn 6:11; 11:41.
Commanded.   Ps 50:14. Php 4:6.
Expressed in psalms.   1 Ch 16:7.
A good thing.   Ps 92:1.
The heavenly host engaged in.   Rv 4:9,
7:11–12; 11:16–17.
Ministers appointed to offer in public.   1 Ch
16:4, 7; 23:30. 2 Ch 31:2.
Of hypocrites, full of boasting.   Lk 18:11.
SAINTS
   Abound in the faith with.   Cl 2:7.
   Come before God with.   Ps 95:2.
   Exhorted to.   Ps 105:1. Cl 3:15.
   Habitually offer.   Dn 6:10.
   Magnify God by.   Ps 69:30.
   Offer sacrifices of.   Ps 116:17.
   Resolved to offer.   Pss 18:49; 30:12.
   Should enter God's gate with.   Ps 100:4.
Should always accompany praise.   Ps 92:1.
He 13:15.
Should always accompany prayer.   Ne 11:17.
Php 4:6. Cl 4:2.
Should be accompanied by intercession for
others.   1 Tm 2:1. 2 Tm 1:3. Phm 1:4.
SHOULD BE OFFERED
   Always.   Ep 1:16; 5:20. 1 Th 1:2.
   At the remembrance of God's holiness.
   Pss 30:4; 97:12.
   Before taking food.   Jn 6:11. Ac 27:35.
   For all men.   1 Tm 2:1.
   For all things.   2 Co 9:11. Ep 5:20.
   For appointment to the ministry.   1 Tm
   1:12.
   For Christ's power and reign.   Rv 11:17.
   For deliverance through Christ from in-
   dwelling sin.   Ro 7:23–25.
   For faith exhibited by others.   Ro 1:8. 2
   Th 1:3.
   For love exhibited by others.   2 Th 1:3.
   For the conversion of others.   Ro 6:17.
   For the gift of Christ.   2 Co 9:15.
   For the goodness and mercy of God.   Pss
   106:1; 107:1; 136:1–3.
   For the grace bestowed on others.   1 Co
   1:4. Php 1:3–5. Cl 1:3–6.
   For the nearness of God's presence.   Ps
   75:1.
   For the reception and effectual working of

   the word of God in others.   1 Th 2:13.
   For the supply of our bodily wants.   Ro
   14:6–7. 1 Tm 4:3–4.
   For the triumph of the gospel.   2 Co 2:14.
   For the zeal exhibited by others.   2 Co
   8:16.
   For victory over death and the grave.   1 Co
   15:57.
   For willingness to offer our property for
   God's service.   1 Ch 29:6–14.
   For wisdom and might.   Dn 2:23.
   In behalf of ministers.   2 Co 1:11.
   In everything.   1 Th 5:18.
   In the name of Christ.   Ep 5:20.
   In private worship.   Dn 6:10.
   In public worship.   Ps 35:18.
   Through Christ.   Ro 1:8. Cl 3:17. He
   13:15.
   To Christ.   1 Tm 1:12.
   To God.   Ps 50:14.
   Upon the completion of great undertakings.
   Ne 12:31, 40.
The wicked averse to.   Ro 1:21.

THEFT

An abomination.   Jr 7:9–10.
All earthly treasure exposed to.   Mt 6:19.
Brings a curse on those who commit it.   Ho
4:2–3. Zc 5:3–4. Ml 3:5.
Brings the wrath of God upon those who com-
mit it.   Ezk 22:29, 31.
Connected with murder.   Jr 7:9. Ho 4:2.
Defiles a man.   Mt 15:20.
Excludes from heaven.   1 Co 6:10.
Forbidden.   Ex 20:15, with Mk 10:19. Ro
13:9.
From the poor, specially forbidden.   Pr 22:22.
Heavenly treasure secure from.   Mt 6:20. Lk
12:33.
Illustrates the guilt of false teachers.   Jr
23:30. Jn 10:1, 8, 10.
Includes fraud concerning wages.   Lv 19:13.
Ml 3:5. Ja 5:4.
Includes fraud in general.   Lv 19:13.
Mosaic law respecting.   Ex 22:1–8.
Proceeds from the heart.   Mt 15:19.
Saints warned against.   Ep 4:28. 1 P 4:15
Shame follows the detection of.   Jr 2:26.
THEY WHO CONNIVE AT
   Hate their own souls.   Pr 29:24.
   Shall be reproved of God.   Ps 50:18, 21
THE WICKED
   Addicted to.   Ps 119:61.
   Associate with those who commit.   Is 1:23.

Commit, under shelter of the night. Jb 24:14. Ob 1:5.
Consent to those who commit. Ps 50:18.
Destroy themselves by. Pr 21:7.
Lie in wait to commit. Ho 6:9.
May, for a season, prosper in. Jb 12:6.
Plead excuses for. Jr 7:9–10.
Repent not of. Rv 9:21.
Store up the fruits of. Am 3:10.
Woe denounced against. Is 10:2. Na 3:1.

THRESHING
Cattle employed in, not to be muzzled. Dt 25:4. 1 Co 9:9. 1 Tm 5:18.
Continued until the vintage in years of abundance. Lv 26:5.
Followed by a winnowing with a shovel or fan. Is 30:24; 41:16. Mt 3:12.
ILLUSTRATIVE OF
The church in her conquests. Is 41:15–16. Mi 4:13.
The church overcoming opposition (an instrument for, with teeth). Is 41:15.
Complete destruction (dust made by). 2 K 13:7.
The judgments of God. Is 21:10. Jr 51:33. Hk 3:12.
The labors of ministers. 1 Co 9:9–10.
Preparing the enemies of the church for judgments (gathering the sheaves). Mi 4:12.
PERFORMED
By cart wheels. Is 27:27–28.
By instruments with teeth. Is 41:15. Am 1:3.
By rod or staff. Is 28:27.
By the feet of horses and oxen. Is 28:28. Ho 10:11. (See also 2 S 24:22.)
PLACE FOR
Called the barn floor. 2 K 6:27.
Called the corn floor. Ho 9:1.
Called the floor. Jg 6:37. Is 21:10.
Called the threshing floor. Nu 18:27. 2 S 24:18.
Fullness of, promised as a blessing. Jl 2:24.
Generally on high ground. 1 Ch 21:18, with 2 Ch 3:1.
The Jews slept on, during the time of. Ru 3:7.
Often robbed. 1 S 23:1.
Scarcity in, a punishment. Ho 9:2.
Sometimes beside the wine press for concealment. Jg 6:11.
Used also for winnowing the corn. Ru 3:2.

Was large and roomy. Gn 50:10.
Removing or separating corn, etc., from the straw. 1 Ch 21:20.

TIME
All events of, predetermined by God. Ac 17:26.
All God's purposes fulfilled in due time. Mk 1:15. Gl 4:4.
An appointed season. Ne 2:6. Ec 3:1, 17.
COMPUTED BY
Days. Gn 8:3. Jb 1:4. Lk 11:3.
Hours, after the captivity. Dn 5:5. Jn 11:9.
Moments. Ex 33:5. Lk 4:5. 1 Co 15:52.
Months. Nu 10:10. 1 Ch 27:1. Jb 3:6.
Weeks. Dn 10:2. Lk 18:12.
Years. Gn 15:13. 2 S 21:1. Dn 9:2.
Duration of the world. Jb 22:16. Rv 10:6.
ERAS FROM WHICH COMPUTED
Accession of kings. 1 K 6:1; 15:1. Is 36:1. Jr 1:2. Lk 3:1.
Building of the temple. 1 K 9:10. 2 Ch 8:1.
The captivity. Ezk 1:1; 33:21; 40:1.
The exodus from Egypt. Ex 19:1; 40:17. Nu 9:1; 33:38. 1 K 6:1.
The jubilee. Lv 25:15.
Nativity of the patriarchs during the patriarchal age. Gn 7:11; 8:13; 17:1.
Heavenly bodies appointed as a means for computing. Gn 1:14.
In prophetic language, a prophetic year, or 365 natural years. Dn 12:7. Rv 12:14.
Measure of the continuance of anything. Jg 18:31.
PARTICULAR PERIODS OF, MENTIONED
Accepted time. Is 49:8. 2 Co 6:2.
Ancient time. Is 45:21.
Evil time. Ps 37:19. Ex 9:12.
Time of healing. Jr 14:19.
Time of need. Ne 4:16.
Time of reformation. He 9:10.
Time of refreshing. Ac 3:19.
Time of restitution of all things. Ac 3:21.
Time of tempatation. Lk 8:13.
Time of trouble. Ps 27:5. Jr 14:8.
Time of visitation. Jr 46:21; 50:27.
Part of a period of, usually counted as the whole. 1 S 13:1. Es 4:16, with 5:1.
Shortness of man's portion of. Ps 89:47.
Should be redeemed. Ep 5:16. Cl 4:5.
Should be spent in the fear of God. 1 P 1:17.
Sundial early invented for pointing out. 2 K 20:9–11.

TITHE

Antiquity of the custom of giving to God's ministers. Gn 14:20. He 7:6.

Considered a just return to God for his blessings. Gn 28:22.

CONSISTED OF A TENTH

Of all cattle. Lv 27:32.

Of all the produce of the land. Lv 27:30.

Of holy things dedicated. 2 Ch 31:6.

Given by God to the Levites for their services. Nu 18:21, 24. Ne 10:37.

The Jews reproved for withholding. Ml 3:8.

The Jews slow in giving. Ne 13:10.

The Pharisees scrupulous in paying. Lk 11:42; 18:12.

Pious governors of Israel caused the payment of. 2 Ch 31:5. Ne 13:11–12.

Punishment for changing. Lv 27:33.

Reasonableness of appointing, for the Levites. Nu 18:20, 23–24. Jsh 13:33.

Rulers appointed over, for distributing. 2 Ch 31:12. Ne 13:13.

A SECOND

Or its value yearly brought to the tabernacle and eaten before the Lord. Dt 12:6–7, 17–19; 14:22–27.

To be consumed at home every third year to promote hospitality and charity. Dt 14:28–29; 26:12–15.

The tenth of anything. 1 S 8:15, 17.

The tenth of, given by the Levites to the priests as their portion. Nu 18:26, 28. Ne 10:38.

The tenth of, offered by the Levites as an heave offering to God. Nu 18:26–27.

Under the law, belonged to God. Lv 27:30.

When redeemed, to have a fifth part of the value added. Lv 27:31.

TITLES AND NAMES OF CHRIST

Adam, second. 1 Co 15:45.

Advocate. 1 Jn 2:1.

Almighty. Rv 1:8.

Alpha and Omega. Rv 1:8; 22:13.

Amen. Rv 3:14.

Angel. Gn 48:16. Ex 23:20–21.

Angel of God's presence. Is 63:9.

Angel of the Lord. Ex 3:2. Jg 13:15–18.

Apostle. He 3:1.

Arm of the Lord. Is 51:9; 53:1.

Author and Finisher of our faith. He 12:2.

Beginning of the creation of God. Rv 3:14.

Blessed and only Potentate. 1 Tm 6:15.

Branch. Jr 23:5. Zc 3:8; 6:12.

Bread of life. Jn 6:35, 48.

Captain of the Lord's hosts. Jsh 5:14–15.

Captain of salvation. He 2:10.

Chief Cornerstone. Ep 2:20. 1 P 2:6.

Chief Shepherd. 1 P 5:4.

Christ of God. Lk 9:20.

Commander. Is 55:4.

Consolation of Israel. Lk 2:25.

Counselor. Is 9:6.

David. Jr 30:9. Ezk 34:23.

Day-spring. Lk 1:78.

Deliverer. Ro 11:26.

Desire of all nations. Hg 2:7.

Door. Jn 10:7.

Elect of God. Is 42:1.

Emmanuel. Is 7:14, with Mt 1:23.

Eternal life. 1 Jn 1:2; 5:20.

Everlasting Father. Is 9:6.

Faithful witness. Rv 1:5; 3:14.

First and Last. Rv 1:17; 2:8.

First begotten of the dead. Rv 1:5.

First-born of every creature. Cl 1:15.

Forerunner. He 6:20.

Glory of the Lord. Is 40:5.

God. Is 40:9. Jn 20:28.

God blessed forever. Ro 9:5.

God's fellow. Zc 13:7.

Good Shepherd. Jn 10:14.

Governor. Mt 2:6.

Great High Priest. He 4:14.

Head of the church. Ep 5:23. Cl 1:18.

Heir of all things. He 1:2.

Holy One. Ps 16:10, with Ac 2:27, 31.

Holy One of God. Mk 1:24.

Holy One of Israel. Is 41:14.

Horn of salvation. Lk 1:69.

I am. Ex 3:14, with Jn 8:58.

Jehovah. Is 26:4.

Jesus. Mt 1:21. 1 Th 1:10.

Judge of Israel. Mi 5:1.

Just One. Ac 7:52.

King. Zc 9:9, with Mt 21:5.

King of Israel. Jn 1:49.

King of Kings. 1 Tm 6:15. Rv 17:14.

King of the Jews. Mt 2:2.

King of saints. Rv 15:3.

Lamb. Rv 5:6, 12; 13:8; 21:22; 22:3.

Lamb of God. Jn 1:29, 36.

Lawgiver. Is 33:22.

Leader. Is 55:4.

Life. Jn 14:6. Cl 3:4. 1 Jn 1:2.

Light of the world.   Jn 8:12
Lion of the tribe of Judah.   Rv 5:5.
Lord God Almighty.   Rv 15:3.
Lord God of the holy prophets.   Rv 22:6.
Lord of all.   Ac 10:36.
Lord of Glory.   1 Co 2:8.
Lord our righteousness.   Jr 23:6.
Mediator.   1 Tm 2:5.
Messenger of the covenant.   Ml 3:1.
Messiah.   Dn 9:25. Jn 1:41.
Mighty God.   Is 9:6.
Mighty One of Jacob.   Is 60:16.
Morning star.   Rv 22:16.
Nazarene.   Mt 2:23.
Offspring of David.   Rv 22:16.
Only begotten.   Jn 1:14.
Our Passover.   1 Co 5:7.
Plant of renown.   Ezk 34:29.
Prince of the kings of the earth.   Rv 1:5.
Prince of life.   Ac 3:15.
Prince of peace.   Is 9:6.
Prophet.   Lk 24:19. Jn 7:40.
Ransom.   1 Tm 2:6.
Redeemer.   Jb 19:25. Is 59:20; 60:16.
Resurrection and life.   Jn 11:25.
Rock.   1 Co 10:4.
Root of David.   Rv 22:16.
Root of Jesse.   Is 11:10.
Ruler of Israel.   Mi 5:2.
Savior.   2 P 2:20; 3:18.
Servant.   Is 42:1; 52:13.
Shepherd and Bishop of souls.   1 P 2:25.
Shiloh.   Gn 49:10.
Son of the blessed.   Mk 14:61.
Son of David.   Mt 9:27.
Son of God.   Lk 1:35. Jn 1:49.
Son of the highest.   Lk 1:32.
Son of man.   Jn 5:27; 6:37.
Son of the blessed.   Mk 14:61.
Son of the highest.   Lk 1:32.
Star.   Nu 24:17.
Sun of righteousness.   Ml 4:2.
Surety.   He 7:22.
True God.   1 Jn 5:20
True light.   Jn 1:9.
True vine.   Jn 15:1.
Truth.   Jn 14:6.
Way.   Jn 14:6.
Wisdom.   Pr 8:12.
Witness.   Is 55:4.
Wonderful.   Is 9:6.
Word.   Jn 1:1. 1 Jn 5:7.
Word of God.   Rv 19:13.
Word of life.   1 Jn 1:1.

TITLES AND NAMES OF THE CHURCH

Assembly of the saints.   Ps 89:7.
Assembly of the upright.   Ps 111:1.
Body of Christ.   Ep 1:22–23. Cl 1:24.
Branch of God's planting.   Is 60:21.
Bride of Christ.   Rv 21:9.
Church of God.   Ac 20:28.
Church of the first-born.   He 12:23.
Church of the Living God.   1 Tm 3:15.
City of the Living God.   He 12:22.
Congregation of the Lord's poor.   Ps 74:19.
Congregation of saints.   Ps 149:1.
Dove.   S S 2:14; 5:2.
Family in heaven and earth.   Ep 3:15.
Flock of God.   Ezk 34:15. 1 P 5:2.
Fold of Christ.   Jn 10:16.
General assembly of the first-born.   He 12:23.
Golden candlestick.   Rv 1:20.
God's building.   1 Co 3:9.
God's heritage.   Jl 3:2. 1 P 5:3.
God's husbandry.   1 Co 3:9.
Habitation of God.   Ep 2:22.
Heavenly Jerusalem.   Gl 4:26. He 12:22.
Holy city.   Rv 21:2.
Holy hill.   Ps 15:1.
Holy mountain.   Zc 8:3.
House of Christ.   He 3:6.
House of God.   1 Tm 3:15. He 10:21.
House of the God of Jacob.   Is 2:3.
Household of God.   Ep 2:19.
Inheritance.   Ps 28:9. Is 19:25.
Israel of God.   Gl 6:16.
King's daughter.   Ps 45:13.
Lamb's wife.   Rv 19:7; 21.
Lot of God's inheritance.   Dt 32:9.
Mount Zion.   Ps 2:6. He 12:22.
Mountain of the Lord's house.   Is 2:2.
New Jerusalem.   Rv 21:2.
Pillar and ground of the truth.   1 Tm 3:15.
Sanctuary of God.   Ps 114:2.
Sought out, a city not forsaken.   Is 62:12.
Spiritual house.   1 P 2:5.
Spouse of Christ.   S S 4:12; 5:1.
Temple of God.   1 Co 3:16–17.
Temple of the Living God.   2 Co 6:16.
Vineyard.   Jr 12:10. Mt 21:41.

TITLES AND NAMES OF THE DEVIL

Abbadon.   Rv 9:11.
Accuser of our brethren.   Rv 12:10.
Adversary.   1 P 5:8.
Angel of the bottomless pit.   Rv 9:11.
Apollyon.   Rv 9:11.

Beelzebub.   Mt 12:24.
Belial.   2 Co 6:15.
Crooked serpent.   Is 27:1.
Dragon.   Is 27:1. Rv 20:2.
Enemy.   Mt 13:39.
Evil spirit.   1 S 16:14.
Father of lies.   Jn 8:44.
God of this world.   2 Co 4:4.
Great red dragon.   Rv 12:3.
Leviathan.   Is 27:1.
Liar.   Jn 8:44.
Lying spirit.   1 K 22:22.
Murderer.   Jn 8:44.
Old serpent.   Rv 12:9; 20:2.
Piercing serpent.   Is 27:1.
Power of darkness.   Cl 1:13.
Prince of the devils.   Mt 12:24.
Prince of the power of the air.   Ep 2:2.
Prince of this world.   Jn 14:30.
Ruler of the darkness of this world.   Ep 6:12.
Satan.   1 Ch 21:1. Jb 1:6.
Serpent.   Gn 3:4, 14. 2 Co 11:3.
Spirit that worketh in the children of disobedi-
     ence.   Ep 2:2.
Tempter.   Mt 4:3. 1 Th 3:5.
Unclean spirit.   Mt 12:43.
Wicked one.   Mt 13:19, 38.

TITLES AND NAMES OF THE HOLY SPIRIT
Breath of the Almighty.   Jb 33:4.
Comforter.   Jn 14:16, 26; 15:26.
Eternal Spirit.   He 9:14.
Free Spirit.   Ps 51:12.
God.   Ac 5:3, 4.
Good Spirit.   Ne 9:20. Ps 143:10.
Holy Spirit.   Ps 51:11. Lk 11:13. Ep 1:13;
     4:30.
Lord.   2 Th 3:5.
Power of the highest.   Lk 1:35.
Seven Spirits of God.   Rv 1:4.
Spirit.   Mt 4:1. Jn 3:6. 1 Tm 4:1.
Spirit of adoption.   Rv 19:10.
Spirit of burning.   Is 4:4.
Spirit of Christ.   Ro 8:9. 1 P 1:11.
Spirit of counsel.   Is 11:2.
Spirit of the Father.   Mt 10:20.
Spirit of the fear of the Lord.   Is 11:2.
Spirit of glory.   1 P 4:14.
Spirit of God.   Gn 1:2. 1 Co 2:11. Jb 33:4.
Spirit of grace.   Zc 12:10. He 10:29.
Spirit of holiness.   Ro 1:4.
Spirit of judgment.   Is 4:4; 28:6.
Spirit of knowledge.   Is 11:2.

Spirit of life.   Ro 8:2. Rv 11:11.
Spirit of the Lord.   Is 11:2. Ac 5:9.
Spirit of the Lord God.   Is 61:1.
Spirit of might.   Is 11:2.
Spirit of prophecy.   Rv 19:10.
Spirit of revelation.   Ep 1:17.
Spirit of the Son.   Gl 4:6.
Spirit of truth.   Jn 14:17; 15:26.
Spirit of understanding.   Is 11:2.
Spirit of wisdom.   Is 11:2. Ep 1:17.

TITLES AND NAMES OF MINISTERS
Ambassadors for Christ.   2 Co 5:20.
Angels of the church.   Rv 1:20; 2:1.
Apostles.   Lk 6:13. Ep 4:11. Rv 18:20.
Apostles of Jesus Christ.   Ti 1:1.
Bishops.   Php 1:1. 1 Tm 3:1. Ti 1:7.
Deacons.   Ac 6:1. 1 Tm 3:8. Php 1:1.
Elders.   1 Tm 5:17. 1 P 5:1.
Evangelists.   Ep 4:11. 2 Tm 4:5.
Fishers of men.   Mt 4:19. Mk 1:17.
Laborers.   Mt 9:38, with Phm 1:1. 1 Th 2:2
Messengers of the church.   2 Co 8:23.
Messengers of the Lord of hosts.   Ml 2:7.
Ministers of Christ.   Ro 15:16. 1 Co 4:1.
Ministers of the church.   Cl 1:24–25.
Ministers of God.   2 Co 6:4.
Ministers of the gospel.   Ep 3:7. Cl 1:23.
Ministers of the Lord.   Jl 2:17.
Ministers of the New Testament.   2 Co 3:6.
Ministers of righteousness.   2 Co 11:15.
Ministers of the sanctuary.   Ezk 45:4.
Ministers of the word.   Lk 1:2.
Overseers.   Ac 20:28.
Pastors.   Jr 3:15. Ep 4:11.
Preachers.   Ro 10:14. 1 Tm 2:7.
Servants of the church.   2 Co 4:5.
Servants of God.   Ti 1:1. Ja 1:1.
Servants of Jesus Christ.   Php 1:1. Jde 1:1
Servants of the Lord.   2 Tm 2:24.
Shepherds.   Jr 23:4.
Soldiers of Christ.   Php 2:25. 2 Tm 2:3.
Stars.   Rv 1:20; 2:1.
Stewards of God.   Ti 1:7.
Stewards of the grace of God.   1 P 4:10.
Stewards of the mysteries of God.   1 Co 4:1
Teachers.   Is 30:20. Ep 4:11.
Watchmen.   Is 62:6. Ezk 33:7.
Witnesses.   Ac 1:8; 5:32; 26:16.
Workers together with God.   2 Co 6:1.

TITLES AND NAMES OF SAINTS
Believers.   Ac 5:14. 1 Tm 4:12.
Beloved brethren.   1 Co 15:58. Ja 2:5

Beloved of God. Ro 1:7.
Blessed of the Father. Mt 25:34,
Blessed of the Lord. Gn 24:31; 26:29,
Brethren. Mt. 23:8. Ac 12:17.
Brethren of Christ. Lk 8:21. Jn 20:17,
Called of Jesus Christ. Ro 1:6.
Children of Abraham. Gl 3:7.
Children of the bride chamber. Mt 9:15,
Children of the day. 1 Th 5:5.
Children of the Father. Mt 5:45.
Children of the free woman. Gl 4:31.
Children of God. Jn 11:52. 1 Jn 3:10.
Children of the highest. Lk 6:35.
Children of Jacob. Ps 105:6.
Children of the kingdom. Mt 13:38.
Children of light. Lk 16:8. Ep 5:8. 1 Th 5:5.
Children of the Living God. Ro 9:26.
Children of the Lord. Dt 14:1.
Children of promise. Ro 9:8. Gl 4:28.
Children of the resurrection. Lk 20:36.
Children of Zion. Ps 149:2. Jl 2:23.
Chosen generation. 1 P 2:9,
Chosen ones. 1 Ch 16:13.
Chosen vessels. Ac 9:15.
Christians. Ac 11:26; 26:28.
Dear children. Ep 5:1.
Disciples of Christ. Jn 8:31; 15:8.
Elect of God. Cl 3:12. Ti 1:1.
Epistles of Christ. 2 Co 3:3.
Excellent. Ps 16:3.
Faithful. Ps 12:1.
Faithful brethren in Christ. Cl 1:2.
Faithful of the land. Ps 101:6.
Fellow citizens with the saints. Ep 2:19.
Fellow heirs. Ep 3:6.
Fellow servants. Rv 6:11.
Friends of Christ. Jn 15:15.
Friends of God. 2 Ch 20:7. Ja 2:23.
Godly. Ps 4:3. 2 P 2:9.
Heirs of God. Ro 8:17.
Heirs of the grace of life. 1 P 3:7.
Heirs of the kingdom. Ja 2:5.
Heirs of promise. He 6:17. Gl 3:29.
Heirs of salvation. He 1:14.
Holy brethren. 1 Th 5:27. He 3:1,
Holy nation. Ex 19:6. 1 P 2:9.
Holy people. Dt 26:19. Is 62:12.
Holy priesthood. 1 P 2:5.
Joint heirs with Christ. Ro 8:17.
Just. Hk 2:4.
Kingdom of priests. Ex 19:6.
Kings and priests unto God. Rv 1:6.
Lambs. Is 40:11. Jn 21:15.

Lights of the world. Mt 5:14.
Little children. Jn 13:33, 1 Jn 2:1.
Lively stones. 1 P 2:5.
Lord's freemen. 1 Co 7:22.
Members of Christ. 1 Co 6:15. Ep 5:30.
Men of God. Dt 33:1, 1 Tm 6:11, 2 Tm 3:17.
Obedient children. 1 P 1:14.
Peculiar people. Dt 14:2. Ti 2:14. 1 P 2:9.
Peculiar treasure. Ex 19:5. Ps 135:4.
People near unto God. Ps 148:14.
People of God. He 4:9. 1 P 2:10.
People saved by the Lord. Dt 33:29,
Pillars in the temple of God. Rv 3:12.
Ransomed of the Lord. Is 35:10.
Redeemed of the Lord. Is 51:11.
Royal priesthood. 1 P 2:9.
Salt of the earth. Mt 5:13.
Servants of Christ. 1 Co 7:22. Ep 6:6,
Servants of righteousness. Ro 6:18.
Sheep of Christ. Jn 10:1–16; 21:16.
Sojourners with God. Lv 25:23. Ps 39:12,
Sons of God. Jn 1:12. Php 2:15. 1 Jn 3:1–2.
Trees of righteousness. Is 61:3.
Vessels of mercy. Ro 9:23.
Vessels unto honor. 2 Tm 2:21.
Witnesses for God. Is 44:8.

TITLES AND NAMES OF THE WICKED

Adversaries of the Lord. 1 S 2:10.
Children in whom is no faith. Dt 32:20.
Children of base men. Jb 30:8.
Children of Belial. Dt 13:13. 2 Ch 13:7,
Children of the devil. Ac 13:10. 1 Jn 3:10.
Children of disobedience. Ep 2:2. Cl 3:6.
Children of the flesh. Ro 9:8.
Children of fools. Jb 30:8.
Children of hell. Mt 23:15.
Children of iniquity. Ho 10:9,
Children of pride. Jb 41:34.
Children of strangers. Is 2:6.
Children of the wicked one. Mt 13:38.
Children of this world. Lk 16:8.
Children of transgression. Is 57:4,
Children of wickedness. 2 S 7:10.
Children of wrath. Ep 2:3.
Children that are corrupters. Is 1:4.
Children that will not hear the law of the Lord. Is 30:9.
Cursed children. 2 P 2:14.
Enemies of all righteousness. Ac 13:10.
Enemies of the cross of Christ. Php 3:18.
Enemies of God. Ps 37:20. Ja 4:4.

Evil and adulterous generation. Mt 12:39.
Evil doers. Ps 37:1. 1 P 2:14.
Evil generation. Dt. 1:35.
Evil men. Pr 4:14. 2 Tm 3:13.
Fools. Pr 1:7. Ro 1:22.
Froward generation. Dt 32:20.
Generation of vipers. Mt 3:7; 12:34.
Grievous revolters. Jr 6:28.
Haters of God. Ps 81:15. Ro 1:30.
Impudent children. Ezk 2:4.
Inventors of evil things. Ro 1:30.
Lying children. Is 30:9.
Men of the world. Ps 17:14.
People laden with iniquity. Is 1:4.
Perverse and crooked generation. Dt 32:5.
   Mt 17:17. Php 2:15.
Rebellious children. Is 30:1.
Rebellious house. Ezk 2:5, 8; 12:2.
Rebellious people. Is 30:9; 65:2.
Reprobates. 2 Co 13:5–7.
Scornful. Ps 1:1.
Seed of evil doers. Is 1:4; 14:20.
Seed of falsehood. Is 57:4.
Seed of the wicked. Ps 37:28.
Serpents. Mt 23:33.
Servants of corruption. 2 P 2:19.
Servants of sin. Jn 8:34. Ro 6:20.
Sinful generation. Mk 8:28.
Sinners. Ps 26:9. Pr 1:10.
Sons of Belial. 1 S 2:12. 1 K 21:10.
Sottish children. Jr 4:22.
Strange children. Ps 144:7.
Stubborn and rebellious generation. Ps 78:8.
Transgressors. Pss 37:38; 51:13.
Ungodly. Ps 1:1.
Ungodly men. Jde 1:4.
Unprofitable servants. Mt 25:30.
Untoward generation. Ac 2:40.
Vessels of wrath. Ro 9:22.
Wicked doers. Ps 101:8. Pr 17:4.
Wicked generation. Mt 12:45; 16:4.
Wicked of the earth. Ps 75:8.
Wicked ones. Jr 2:33.
Wicked servants. Mt 25:26.
Wicked transgressors. Ps 59:5.
Workers of iniquity. Ps 28:3; 36:12.

TOWERS
Antiquity of. Gn 11:4.
BUILT
   In cities. Jg 9:51.
   In the deserts. 2 Ch 26:10.
   In the forests. 2 Ch 27:4.
   In vineyards. Is 5:2. Mt 21:33.

On the walls of cities. 2 Ch 14:7; 26:9.
Frequently left desolate. Is 32:14. Zp 3:6.
Frequently strong and well fortified. Jg 9:51,
   with 2 Ch 26:9.
Frequently thrown down in war. Jg 8:17;
   9:49. Ezk 26:4.
Frequently very high. Is 2:15.
ILLUSTRATIVE OF
   God as the protector of his people. 2 S
      22:3, 51. Pss 18:2; 61:3.
   The grace and dignity of the church. S S
      4:4; 7:4; 8:10.
   Ministers. Jr 6:27.
   Mount Zion. Mi 4:8.
   The name of the Lord. Pr 18:10.
   The proud and haughty. Is 2:15; 30:25.
MENTIONED IN SCRIPTURE
   Babel. Gn 11:9.
   David. S S 4:4.
   Edar. Gn 35:21.
   Hananeel. Jr 31:38. Zc 14:10.
   Jezreel. 2 K 9:17.
   Lebanon. S S 7:4.
   Meah. Ne 12:39.
   Of the furnaces. Ne 3:11.
   Penuel. Jg 8:17.
   Shechem. Jg 9:46.
   Siloam. Lk 13:4.
   Syene. Ezk 29:10; 30:6.
   Thebez. Jg 9:50, 51.
Of Jerusalem, remarkable for number,
   strength, and beauty. Ps 48:12.
Used as armories. S S 4:4.
Used as citadels in times of war. Jg 9:51.
   Ezk 27:11.
Watchmen posted on, in times of danger. 2
   K 9:17. Hk 2:1.

TRAVELERS
After a long journey, described. Jsh 9:4–5,
   13.
Called wayfaring men. Jg 19:17. Is 35:8.
CARRIED WITH THEM
   Presents for those who entertained them.
      Gn 43:15. 1 K 10:2. 2 K 5:5. Mt 2:11.
   Provender for their beasts of burden. Gn
      42:27. Jg 19:19.
   Provisions for the way. Jsh 9:11–12. Jg
      19:19.
   Skins filled with water, wine, etc. Gn
      21:14–15. Jsh 9:13.
Ceasing of, threatened as a calamity. Is 33:8.
Estimated the length of their journey by the

number of days it took. Gn 31:23. Dt 1:2.
2 K 3:9.

FRIENDS OF

Frequently commended them to protection
of God. Gn 43:13–14. Ac 21:5.

Frequently took leave of them with sorrow.
Ac 20:37; 21:16.

Often sent them away with music. Gn
31:27.

Often supplied them with provision. Gn
21:14; 44:1. Jr 40:5.

Sometimes accompanied them a short way.
2 S 19:31. Ac 20:38; 21:5.

Frequently asked whence they came and
whither they went. Jg 19:17.

Generally began their journey early in the
morning. Jg 19:5.

Generally halted at wells or streams. Gn
24:11; 32:21, 23. Ex 15:27. 1 S 30:21. Jn
4:6.

Generally rested at noon. Gn 18:1, 3. Jn 4:6.

Generally stopped at night. Gn 24:11.

Generally treated with great hospitality. Gn
18:3–8; 19:2; 24:25, 32–33. Ex 2:20. Jg
19:20–21. Jb 31:32. (See also He 13:2.)

The Jews prohibited from taking long journeys
on the sabbath. Ex 20:10, with Ac 1:12.

OF DISTINCTION

Before setting out gave employment, etc.,
to their servants. Mt 25:14.

Frequently extorted provisions by the way.
Jg 8:5, 8. 1 S 25:4–13.

Generally attended by running footmen.
1 S 25:27. 1 K 18:46. 2 K 4:24. Ec 10:7.

Generally performed their journey in great
state. 1 K 10:2. 2 K 5:5, 9, etc.

Often preceded by heralds, etc., to have the
roads prepared. Is 40:3–4, with Mk
1:2–3.

Rode in chariots. 2 K 5:9. Ac 8:27–28.

Rode on asses, camels, etc. Gn 22:3;
24:64. Nu 22:21.

Often collected together and formed caravans.
Gn 37:25. Is 21:13. Lk 2:44.

Often engaged persons acquainted with the
country as guides. Nu 10:31–32. Jb
29:15.

Often left the highways for security. Jg 5:6.

Often traveled on foot. Gn 28:10, with
32:10. Ex 12:37. Ac 20:13.

ON ERRANDS REQUIRING DESPATCH

Saluted no man by the way. 2 K 4:29. Lk
10:4.

Went with great speed. Es 8:10. Jb 9:25.

On foot, how attired. Ex 12:11.

Pledges of hospitality alluded to. Rv 2:17.

Preparations made by, alluded to. Ezk
12:3–4.

Protected by those who .entertained them
Gn 19:6–8. Jg 19:23.

Public inn for, noticed. Gn 42:27. Ex 4:24.
Lk 2:7; 10:34.

Strangers civil to. Gn 18:2; 24:18–19.

TREES

Afford an agreeable shade in eastern countries
during the heat of the day. Gn 18:4. Jb
40:21.

CUT DOWN

By besieging armies for erecting forts. Dt
20:20. Jr 6:6.

For building. 2 K 6:2. 2 Ch 2:8, 10.

For fuel. Is 44:14–16. Mt 3:10.

For making idols. Is 40:20; 44:14, 17.

With axes. Dt 19:5. Ps 74:5. Mt 3:10.

Designed to beautify the earth. Gn 2:9.

DIFFERENT KINDS OF, MENTIONED

Bearing fruit. Ne 9:25. Ec 2:5. Ezk
47:12.

Deciduous. Is 6:13.

Evergreen. Ps 37:35. Jr 17:2.

Of the forest. Is 10:19.

Of the wood. S S 2:3.

Each kind has its own seed for propogating its
species. Gn 1:11–12.

Each kind known by its fruit. Mt 12:33.

Early custom of planting in consecrated
grounds. Gn 21:33.

Given as food to the animals. Gn 1:29, 30.
Dt 20:19.

God increases and multiplies the fruit of, for
his people. Lv 26:4. Ezk 34:27. Jl 2:22.

God often renders barren as a punishment.
Lv 26:20.

ILLUSTRATIVE OF

Christ. Ro 11:24. Rv 2:7; 22:2, 14.

Continued prosperity of saints (in their duration). Is 65:22.

The elect remnant in the church (casting
their leaves yet retaining their substance). Is 6:13.

The innocence of Christ (when green).
Lk 23:31.

The life and conversation of the righteous.
Pr 11:30; 15:4.

Kings, etc. Is 10:34. Ezk 17:24; 31:7–10.
Dn 4:10–14.

Saints (when evergreen). Ps 1:1–3.

Saints (when good and fruitful). Nu 24:6. Ps 1:3. Is 61:3. Jr 17:8. Mt 7:17–18.

The terror of the wicked (shaking of their leaves). Is 7:2.

Useless persons (when dry). Is 56:3.

The wicked (when producing evil fruit). Mt 7:17–19.

The wicked ripe for judgment (when dry). Lk 23:31.

Wisdom. Pr 3:18.

THE JEWS

Considered trees on which criminals were executed abominable. Is 14:19.

Often buried under. Gn 35:8. 1 S 31:13.

Often executed criminals on. Dt 21:22–23. Jsh 10:26. Gl 3:13. (*See also* Gn 40:19.)

Often pitched their tents under. Gn 18:1, 4. Jg 4:5. 1 S 22:6.

Prohibited from cutting down fruit-bearing, for sieges. Dt 20:19.

Prohibited from planting in consecrated places. Dt 16:21.

Made for the glory of God. Ps 148:9.

MENTIONED IN SCRIPTURE

Almond. Gn 43:11. Ec 12:5. Jr 1:11.

Almug or algum. 1 K 10:11–12. 2 Ch 9:10–11.

Aloe. Nu 24:6.

Apple. SS 2:3; 8:5. Jl 1:12.

Ash. Is 44:14.

Bay. Ps 37:35.

Box. Is 41:19.

Cedar. 1 K 10:27. Is 41:19.

Chestnut. Ezk 31:8.

Cyprus. Is 44:14.

Gif. Dt 8:8.

Fir. 1 K 5:10. 2 K 19:23. Ps 104:17.

Juniper. 1 K 19:4–5.

Mulberry. 2 S 5:23–24.

Mustard. Mt 13:32.

Myrtle. Is 41:19; 55:13. Zc 1:8.

Oak. Is 1:30.

Oil tree. Is 41:19.

Olive. Dt 6:11.

Palm. Ex 15:27.

Pine. Is 41:19.

Pomegranate. Dt 8:8. Jl 1:12

Shittah or shittim. Ex 36:20. Is 41:19.

Sycamore. 1 K 10:27. Ps 78:47. Am 7:14. Lk 19:4.

Teil. Is 6:13.

Vine Nu 6:4. Ezk 15:2.

Willow. Is 44:4. Ezk 17:5.

NOURISHED

By the earth. Gn 1:12; 2:9.

By the rain from heaven. Is 44:14.

Through their own sap. Ps 104:16.

Often propagated by birds who carry the seeds along with them. Ezk 17:3, 5.

OFTEN SUFFERED FROM

Fire. Jl 1:19.

Hail and frost. Ex 9:25. Ps 78:47.

Locusts. Ex 10:5, 15. Dt 28:42.

Of various sizes. Ezk 17:24.

Originally created by God. Gn 1:11–12; 2:9.

PARTS OF, MENTIONED

Branches. Lv 23:40. Dn 4:14.

Fruit or seeds. Lv 27:30. Ezk 36:30.

Leaves. Is 6:13. Dn 4:12. Mt 21:19.

Roots. Jr 17:8.

Stem or trunk. Is 11:1; 44:19.

Planted by man. Lv 19:23.

Sold with the land on which they grew. Gn 23:17.

Specially flourished beside rivers and streams of water. Ezk 47:12.

When cut down, often sprouted from the roots again. Jb 14:7.

TRESPASS OFFERING

Accompanied by confession. Lv 5:5.

Atonement made by. Lv 5:6, 10, 13, 16, 18; 6:7; 19:22.

Being for minor offenses, was lessened for the poor. Lv 5, with 4.

CONSISTED OF

A meat offering by the very poor. Lv 5:11–13.

A ram without blemish. Lv 5:15; 6:6.

A she lamb or kid. Lv 5:6.

Two turtle doves by those unable to bring a lamb. Lv 5:7–10.

Esteemed as a sin offering, and frequently so called. Lv 5:6, 9.

Generally accompanied by restitution. Lv 5:16; 6:5.

Illustrative of Christ. Is 53:10. Ezk 46:20.

A most holy offering. Lv 14:13.

OFFERED

For any sin of ignorance. Lv 5:17.

For breach of trust, or fraud. Lv 6:2–5.

For concealing knowledge of a crime. Lv 5:1.

For involuntarily touching unclean things. Lv 5:2–3.

For rash swearing. Lv 5:4.

For sins of ignorance in holy things. Lv 5:15.

The perquisite of the priest. Lv 14:13. Ezk 44:29.

Sometimes waved alive before the Lord. Lv 14:12–13.

SPECIAL Occasions of OFFERING
Cleansing of a leper. Lv 14:2, 12–14, 21–22.
For connection with a betrothed bondmaid. Lv 19:20–22.
Purification of Nazarites who had broken their vow. Nu 6:12.
Purification of those with issues. Lv 15:14–15.
Purification of women. Lv 12:6–8.

To be slain where the sin offering and burnt offering were slain. Lv 14:13. Ezk 40:39.

TRIAL
Of faith. He 11:17. 1 P 4:12.
Of the heart. Ps 66:10. 1 Th 2:4.
Of Jesus. Mt 4:1.
Of the righteous. Jb 23:10.
Promised, with victory. Jn 16:33.
Rewarded. Ja 1:12. 1 P 1:7.

TRIBES OF ISRAEL
All inheritance to remain in the tribe and family to which allotted. Nu 36:3–9.
Canaan divided among nine and a half of, by lot. Jsh 14:1–5.
Canaan to be divided among according to their numbers. Nu 33:54.
Descended from Jacob's sons. Gn 35:22–26.
Divided into four divisions while in the wilderness. Nu 10:14–28.
Divided on mounts Ebal and Gerizim to hear the law. Dt 27:12–13.
Each family of, had a chief or head. Nu 36:1. 1 Ch 4:38.
EACH OF THEM
Divided into families. Nu 1:2; 26:5–50. Jsh 7:14.
Under a president or chief. Nu 1:4–16.
Usually furnished an equal number of men for war. Nu 31:4.
Encamped in their divisions and by their standards around the tabernacle. Nu 2:2–31.
Manasseh and Ephraim numbered among, instead of Joseph and Levi. Gn 48:5. Jsh 14:3–4.
Names of, engraven on the breastplate of the high priest. Ex 28:21; 39:14.

Predictions respecting each of. Gn 49:3–27. Dt 33:6–35.
Remained as one people until the reign of Rehoboam. 1 K 12:16–20.
REUBEN, GAD, AND HALF MANASSEH
Settled on east side of Jordan. Dt 3:12–17. Jsh 13:23–32.
Were required to assist in subduing Canaan. Nu 32:6–32. Dt 3:18–20.
Situation of and bounds of the inheritance of each. Jsh 15—17.
Total strength of, on entering the land of Canaan. Nu 26:51.
Total strength of, on leaving Egypt. Ex 12:37. Nu 1:44–46; 2:32.
Twelve in number. Gn 49:28. Ac 26:12. Ja 1:1.

TRIBUTE
All saints exhorted to pay. Ro 13:6–7.
Christ, to avoid offense, wrought a miracle to pay for himself and Peter. Mt 17:24–27.
Exacted from all conquered nations. Jsh 16:10. Jg 1:30, 33, 35. 2 K 23:33, 35.
The Jews required to pay half a shekel to God as. Ex 30:12–16.
KINGS OF ISRAEL
Forbidden to levy unnecessary or oppressive. Dt. 17:17.
Often oppressed the people with. 1 K 12:4, 11.
Set officers over. 2 S 20:24. 1 K 1:6–7.
OFTEN EXACTED IN
Gold and silver. 2 K 23:33, 35.
Labor. 1 K 5:13–14; 9:15, 21.
Produce of land, etc. 1 S 8:15. 1 K 4:7.
Priests and Levites exempted from Ezr 7:24.
ROMAN
Christ showed to the Pharisees and Herodians the propriety of paying. Mt 22:15–22. Mk 12:13–17.
Collected by the publicans. Lk 3:12–13; 5:27.
Decree of Augustus for. Lk 2:1.
First levied in Judea when Cyrenius was governor. Lk 2:2.
Our Lord falsely accused of forbidding to pay. Lk 23:2.
Paid in Roman coin. Mt 22:19–20.
Persons enrolled for, in the native place of their tribe and family. Lk 2:3–5.
Resisted by the Galileans under Judas of Galilee. Ac 5:37, with Lk 13:1.

Sometimes exacted by kings from their own subjects. 1 S 8:10–17.

When oppressive, frequently led to rebellion. 1 K 12:14–20.

TRINITY
Baptism administered in name of. Mt 28:19.

Benediction given in name of. 2 Co 13:14.

Divine titles applied to the three Persons in. Ex 20:2, with Jn 20:28, and Ac 5:3–4.

Doctrine of, proved fron scripture. Mt 3:16–17; 28:19. Ro 8:9. 1 Co 12:3–6. 2 Co 13:14. Ep 4:4–6. 1 P 1:2. Jde 1:20, 21. Rv 1:4–5.

EACH PERSON IN, DESCRIBED AS

Author of all spiritual operations. He 13:21, with Cl 1:29, and 1 Co 12:11.

Creator. Gn 1:1, with Cl 1:16, and Jb 33:4. Ps 148:5, with Jn 1:3, and Jb 26:13.

Eternal. Ro 16:26, with Rv 22:13, and He 9:14.

Holy. Rv 4:8; 15:4, with Ac 3:14, and 1 Jn 2:20.

Inspiring the prophets, etc. He 1:1, with 2 Co 13:3, and Mk 13:11.

Omnipotent. Gn 17:1, with Rv 1:8, and Ro 15:19. Jr 32:17, with He 1:3, and Lk 1:35.

Omnipresent. Jr 23:24, with Ep 1:23, and Ps 139:7.

Omniscient. Ac 15:18, with Jn 21:17, and 1 Co 2:10–11.

Raising Christ from the dead. 1 Co 6:14, with Jn 2:19, and 1 P 3:18.

Sanctifier. Jde 1:1, with He 2:11, and 1 P 1:2.

Source of eternal life. Ro 6:23, with Jn 10:28, and Gl 6:8.

Supplying ministers to the church, Jr 3:15, with Ep 4:11, and Ac 20:28. Jr 26:5, with Mt 10:5, and Ac 13:2.

Teacher. Is 54:13, with Lk 21:15, and Jn 14:26. Is 48:17, with Gl 1:12, and 1 Jn 2:20.

True. Jn 7:28, with Rv 3:7.

Salvation the work of. 2 Th 2:13–14. Ti 3:4–6. 1 P 1:2.

TRIUMPH
In Christ. 2 Co 2:14. Ro 8:37.

In the Lord's praise. Ps 106:47.

Over death. 1 Co 15:55. Is 25:8.

Over evil. Rv 2:17; 6:2.

Over troubles. Is 43:2.

Over the world. 1 Jn 5:4.

TROUBLE
See Trial.

TRUMPET
Called the trump. 2 Co 15:52.

Feast of trumpets celebrated by blowing of. Lv 23:24. Nu 29:1.

An instrument of music. 1 Ch 13:8.

Jubilee introduced by blowing of. Lv 25:9.

MADE OF

Rams' horns. Jsh 6:4.

Silver. Nu 10:2.

MIRACLES CONNECTED WITH

Confusion produced in the camp of the Midianites by sound of. Jg 7:16, 22.

Falling of the walls of Jericho. Jsh 6:20.

Heard at Mount Sinai at giving of the law. Ex 19:16; 20:18.

Moses commanded to make two, for the tabernacle. Nu 10:2.

Priests to blow the sacred. Nu 10:8. 2 Ch 5:12; 7:6.

Required to give an intelligible and understood sound. 1 Co 14:8.

Solomon made a great many, for the service of the temple. 2 Ch 5:12.

SOUNDING OF, ILLUSTRATED

The bold and faithful preaching of ministers. Is 58:1. Ho 8:1. Jl 2:1.

God's power to raise the dead. 1 Co 15:52. 1 Th 4:16.

The latter-day judgments. Rv 8:2, 13.

The proclamation of the gospel. Ps 89:15.

USED FOR

Assembling the people to war. Jg 3:27.

Blowing at all religious processions and ceremonies. 1 Ch 13:8; 15:24, 28. 2 Ch 5:13; 15:14.

Blowing over the sacrifices on feast day. Nu 10:10. Ps 81:3.

Calling assemblies. Nu 10:2–3, 7.

Giving alarm in cases of danger. Ezk 33:2–6.

Proclaiming kings. 2 K 9:13; 11:14.

Regulating the journeys of the children of Israel. Nu 10:2, 5–6.

Sounding for a memorial when the people went into battle. Nu 10:9; 31:6–7.

War horse acquainted with the sound of. Jb 39:24–25.

TRUMPETS, FEAST OF
Held the first day of seventh month. Lv 23:24. Nu 29:1.

A holy convocation and rest. Lv 23:24–25.

A memorial of blowing of trumpets. Lv 23:24.

Sacrifices at. Nu 29:2–6.

TRUST
Blessedness of placing in God. Pss 2:12; 34:8; 40:4. Jr 17:7.

ENCOURAGEMENTS TO

The care of God for us. 1 P 5:7.

The everlasting strength of God. Is 26:4.

Former deliverances. Ps 9:10. 2 Co 1:10.

The goodness of God. Na 1:7.

The loving-kindness of God. Ps 36:7.

The rich bounty of God. 1 Tm 6:17.

Exhortations to, Pss 4:5; 115:9–11.

Fear of God leads to. Pr 14:26.

God the true object of. Ps 65:5.

KEEPS FROM

Desolation. Ps 34:22.

Fear. Ps 56:11. Is 12:2. He 13:6.

Sliding. Ps 26:1.

LEADS TO

Being compassed with mercy. Ps 32:10.

Deliverance from enemies. Ps 37:40.

Enjoyment of all temporal and spiritual blessings. Is 57:13.

Enjoyment of happiness. Pr 16:20.

Enjoyment of perfect peace. Is 26:3.

Fulfillment of all holy desires. Ps 37:5.

Prosperity. Pr 28:25.

Rejoicing in God. Pss 5:11; 33:21.

Safety in times of danger. Pr 29:25.

Stability. Ps 125:1.

The Lord knows those who have. Na 1:7.

Of saints, illustrated. Ps 91:12. Pr 18:10.

OF SAINTS IS

Despised by the wicked. Is 36:4, 7.

Fixed. 2 S 22:3. Ps 112:7.

Forever. Pss 52:8; 62:8. Is 26:4.

Grounded on the covenant. 2 S 23:5.

In Christ. Ep 3:12.

In God. Pss 11:1; 31:14. 2 Co 1:9.

In the mercy of God. Pss 13:5; 52:8.

In the word of God. Ps 119:42.

Not in carnal weapons. 1 S 17:38–39, 45. Ps 44:6. 2 Co 10:4.

Not in the flesh. Php 3:3–4.

Not in themselves. 2 Co 1:9.

Strong in the prospect of death. Ps 23:4.

Through Christ. 2 Co 3:4

Unalterable. Jb 13:15.

OF THE WICKED

Is in earthly alliances. Is 30:2. Ezk 17:15.

Is in falsehood. Is 28:15. Jr 13:25.

Is in idols. Is 42:17. Hk 2:18.

Is in man. Jg 9:26. Ps 118:8–9.

Is in their own heart. Pr 28:26.

Is in their own righteousness. Lk 18:9, 12.

Is in vanity. Jb 15:31. Is 59:4.

Is in wealth. Pss 49:6; 52:7. Pr 11:28. Jr 48:7. Mk 10:24.

Is not in God. Ps 78:22. Zp 3:2.

Is vain and delusive. Is 30:7. Jr 2:37.

Shall be destroyed. Jb 18:14. Is 28:18.

Shall make them ashamed. Is 20:5; 30:3, 5. Jr 48:13.

Of the wicked, illustrated. 2 K 18:21. Jb 8:14.

Saints plead, in prayer. Pss 25:21; 31:1; 141:8.

Should be from youth up. Ps 71:5.

Should be with the whole heart. Pr 3:5.

To be accompanied by doing good. Ps 37:3.

Woe and curse of false. Is 30:1–2; 31:1–3. Jr 17:5.

TRUTH
Abides continually with saints. 2 Jn 1:2.

CHRIST

Bears witness to. Jn 18:37.

Is. Jn 14:6, with Jn 7:18.

Spoke. Jn 8:45.

Was full of. Jn 1:14.

The church the pillar and ground of. 1 Tm 3:15.

The devil devoid of. Jn 8:44.

The fruit of the Spirit is in. Ep 5:9.

GOD

Desires in the heart. Ps 51:6.

Is a God of. Dt 32:4. Ps 31:5.

Regards with favor. Jr 5:3.

The gospel as, came by Christ. Jn 1:17.

THE HOLY GHOST

Guides into all. Jn 16:13.

Is the Spirit of. Jn 14:17.

IS

According to godliness. Ti 1:1.

In Christ. Ro 9:1. 1 Tm 2:7.

Part of the Christian armor. Ep 6:14.

Purifying. 1 P 1:22.

Sanctifying. Jn 17:17, 19.

John bears witness to. Jn 5:33.

Judgments of God are according to. Ps 96:13. Ro 2:2.

Kings are preserved by. Pr 20:28.

Magistrates should be men of. Ex 18:21.

MINISTERS SHOULD

Approve themselves by. 2 Co 4:2; 6:7–8; 7:14.

Speak. 2 Co 12:6. Gl 4:16.

Teach in. 1 Tm 2:7.

Revealed abundantly to saints. Jr 33:6.

SAINTS SHOULD

Esteem as inestimable. Pr 23:23.

Keep religious feasts with. 1 Co 5:8.

Meditate upon. Php 4:8.

Rejoice in. 1 Co 13:6.

Serve God in. Jsh 24:14. 1 S 12:24.

Speak, to one another. Zc 8:16. Ep 4:25.

Walk before God in. 1 K 2:4. 2 K 20:3.

Worship God in. Jn 4:24, with Ps 145:18.

Write upon the tables of the heart. Pr 3:3.

SHOULD BE

Acknowledged. 2 Tm 2:25.

Believed. 2 Th 2:12–13. 1 Tm 4:3.

Loved. 2 Th 2:10.

Manifested. 2 Co 4:2.

Obeyed. Ro 2:8. Gl 3:1.

Rightly divided. 2 Tm 2:15.

THEY WHO SPEAK

Are the delight of God. Pr 12:22.

Shall be established. Pr 12:19.

Show forth righteousness. Pr 12:17.

THE WICKED

Are destitute of. Ho 4:1. 1 Tm 6:5.

Are not valiant for. Jr 9:3.

Plead not for. Is 59:4.

Punished for want of. Jr 9:5, 9. Ho 4:1.

Resist. 2 Tm 3:8.

Speak not. Jr 9:5.

Uphold not. Is 59:14–15.

Turn away from. 2 Tm 4:4.

The word of God is. Dn 10:21. Jn 17:17.

TRUTH OF GOD

Always goes before his face. Ps 89:14.

DENIED BY

The devil. Gn 3:4–5.

The self-righteous. 1 Jn 1:10.

Unbelievers. 1 Jn 5:10.

DESCRIBED AS

Abundant. Ex 34:6.

Enduring to all generations. Ps 100:5.

Great. Ps 57:10.

Inviolable. Nu 23:19. Ti 1:2.

Plenteous. Ps 86:15.

Reaching to the clouds. Ps 57:10.

EXHIBITED IN HIS

Administration of justice. Ps 96:13.

Counsels of old. Is 25:1.

Dealings with saints. Ps 25:10.

Deliverance of saints. Ps 57:3.

Fulfillment of his covenant. Mi 7:20.

Fulfillment of promises in Christ. 2 Co 1:20.

Judicial statutes. Ps 19:9.

Punishment of the wicked. Rv 16:7.

Ways. Rv 15:3.

Word. Ps 119:160. Jn 17:17.

Works. Pss 33:4; 111:7. Dn 4:37.

He keeps, forever. Ps 146:6.

One of his attributes. Dt 32:4. Is 65:16.

Remembered toward saints. Ps 98:3.

A shield and buckler to saints. Ps 91:4.

United with mercy in redemption. Ps 85:10.

WE SHOULD

Confide in. Ps 31:5. Ti 1:2.

Magnify. Pss 71:22; 138:2.

Make known to others. Is 38:19.

Plead, in prayer. Ps 89:49.

Pray for its exhibition to others. 2 S 2:6.

Pray for its manifestation to ourselves. 2 Ch 6:17.

TYPES OF CHRIST

Aaron. Ex 28:1, with He 5:4–5. Lv 16:15, with He 9:7, 24.

Abel. Gn 4:8, 10. He 12:24.

Abraham. Gn 17:5, with Ep 3:15.

Adam. Ro 5:14. 1 Co 15:45.

Ark. Gn 7:16, with 1 P 3:20–21.

Ark of the covenant. Ex 25:16, with Ps 40:8. Is 42:6.

Atonement, sacrifices offered on the day of. Lv 16:15–16, with He 9:12, 24.

Bronze altar. Ex 27:1–2, with He 13:10.

Bronze serpent. Nu 21:9, with Jn 3:14–15.

Burnt offering. Lv 1:2, 4, with He 10:10.

Cities of refuge. Nu 35:6, with He 6:18.

David. 2 S 8:15, with Ezk 37:24. Ps 89:19–20, with Php 2:9.

Eliakim. Is 22:20–22, with Rv 3:7.

First fruits. Ex 22:29, with 1 Co 15:20.

Golden altar. Ex 40:5, 26–27, with Rv 8:3, and He 13:15.

Golden candlestick. Ex 25:31, with Jn 8:12.

Isaac. Gn 22:1–2, with He 11:17–19.

Jacob. Gn 32:28, with Jn 11:42. He 7:25.

Jacob's ladder. Gn 28:12, with Jn 1:51.

Jonah. Jnh 1:17, with Mt 12:40.

Joseph. Gn 50:19–20, with He 7:52.

Joshua.   Jsh 1:5–6, with He 4:8–9. Jsh 11:23, with Ac 20:32.
Laver of brass.   Ex 30:18–20, with Zc 13:1. Ep 5:26–27.
Leper's offering.   Lv 14:4–7, with Ro 4:25.
Manna.   Ex 16:11–15, with Jn 6:32–35.
Melchizedek.   Gn 14:18–20, with He 7:1–17.
Mercy seat.   Ex 25:17–22, with Ro 3:25. He 4:16.
Morning and evening sacrifices.   Ex 29:38–41, with Jn 1:29, 36.
Moses.   Nu 12:7, with He 3:2. Dt 18:15, with Ac 3:20–22.
Noah.   Gn 5:29. 2 Co 1:5.
Paschal lamb.   Ex 12:3–6, 46, with Jn 19:36. 1 Co 5:7.
Peace offering.   Lv 3:1, with Ep 2:14, 16.
Red heifer.   Nu 19:2–6, with He 9:13–14.

Rock of Horeb.   Ex 17:6, with 1 Co 10:4.
Samson.   Jg 16:30, with Cl 2:14–15.
Scapegoat.   Lv 16:20–22, with Is 53:6, 12.
Sin offering.   Lv 4:2–3, 12, with He 13:11–12.
Solomon.   2 S 7:12–13, with Lk 1:32–33. 1 P 2:5.
Tabernacle.   Ex 40:2, 34, with He 9:11. Cl 2:9.
Table and showbread.   Ex 25:23–30, with Jn 1:16. Jn 6:48.
Temple.   1 K 6:1, 38, with Jn 2:19, 21.
Tree of life.   Gn 2:9, with Jn 1:4. Rv 22:2.
Trespass offering.   Lv 6:1–7, with Is 53:10.
Veil of the tabernacle and temple.   Ex 40:21. 2 Ch 3:14, with He 10:20.
Zerubbabel.   Zc 4:7–9, with He 12:2–3.

U

UNBELIEF

All, by nature, concluded in. Ro 11:32.

Believers should hold no communion with those in. 2 Co 6:14.

Defilement inseparable from. Ti 1:15.

EXHIBITED IN

Departing from God. He 3:12.

Not believing the works of God. Ps 78:32.

Questioning the power of God. 2 K 7:2. Ps 78:19–20.

Rejecting Christ. Jn 16:9.

Rejecting evidence of miracles. Jn 12:37.

Rejecting the gospel. Is 53:1. Jn 12:38.

Rejecting the word of God. Ps 106:24.

Staggering at the promise of God. Ro 4:20.

An impediment to the performance of miracles. Mt 17:20. Mk 6:5.

Impugns the veracity of God. 1 Jn 5:10.

Is sin. Jn 16:9.

The Jews rejected for. Ro 11:20.

Miracles designed to convince those in. Jn 10:37–38. 1 Co 14:22.

The portion of, awarded to all unfaithful servants. Lk 12:46.

Pray for help against. Mk 9:24.

PROCEEDS FROM

The devil blinding the mind. 2 Co 4:4.

The devil taking away the word out of the heart. Lk 8:12.

Disinclination to the truth. Jn 8:45–46.

An evil heart. He 3:12.

Hardness of heart. Mk 16:14. Ac 19:9.

Judicial blindness. Jn 12:39–40.

Not being Christ's sheep. Jn 10:26.

Seeking honor from men. Jn 5:44.

Slowness of heart. Lk 24:25.

Rebuked by Christ. Mt 17:17. Jn 20:27.

THEY WHO ARE GUILTY OF

Are condemned already. Jn 3:18.

Cannot please God. He 11:6.

Excite others against saints. Ac 14:2.

Harden their necks. 2 K 17:14.

Have not the word of God in them. Jn 5:38.

Have the wrath of God abiding upon. Jn 3:36.

Malign the gospel. Ac 19:9.

Persecute the ministers of God. Ro 15:31.

Persevere in it. Jn 12:37.

Shall be cast into the lake of fire. Rv 21:8.

Shall be condemned. Mk 16:16. 2 Th 2:12.

Shall be destroyed. Jde 1:5.

Shall die in their sins. Jn 8:24.

Shall not be established. Is 7:9.

Shall not enter the rest. He 3:19; 4:11.

Warnings against. He 3:12; 4:11.

UNDERSTANDING

BELONGS TO GOD

His is infinite. Ps 147:5.

His is unsearchable. Is 40:28.

NEEDED BY

Believers. Lk 24:45. Mk 12:33.

Pastors. Jr 3:15.

Those who pray. 1 Co 14:15.

Those who sing. Ps 47:4.

Those who would find good. Pr 19:8.

SOUGHT BY

The psalmist. Ps 119:34, 125.

Solomon. 1 K 3:9–11; 4:29.

VALUE OF HAVING

A wellspring of life. Pr 16:22.

Will keep the righteous. Pr 2:11.

UNION WITH CHRIST

As head of the church. Ep 1:22–23; 4:15–16. Cl 1:18.

BENEFICIAL, RESULTS OF

Abundant fruitfulness. Jn 15:5.

Answers to prayer. Jn 15:7.

Being created anew. 2 Co 5:17.

Confidence at his coming. 1 Jn 2:28.

Freedom from condemnation. Ro 8:1.

Freedom from dominion of sin. 1 Jn 3:6.

Righteousness imputed. 2 Co 5:21. Php 3:9.

The spirit alive to righteousness. Ro 8:10.

Christ prayed that all saints might have. Jn 17:21, 23.

DESCRIBED AS

Christ being in us. Ep 3:17. Cl 1:27.

Our being in Christ. 2 Co 12:2. 1 Jn 5:20.

False teachers have not. Cl 2:18–19.

The gift of the Holy Ghost an evidence of. 1 Jn 4:13.

The Holy Ghost witnesses. 1 Jn 3:24.

Includes union with the Father. Jn 17:21. 1 Jn 2:24.

Is

Indissoluble. Ro 8:35.

Of God. 1 Co 1:30.

MAINTAINED BY

Abiding in him. Jn 15:4, 7.

Faith. Gl 2:20. Ep 3:17.

Feeding on him. Jn 6:56.

His word abiding in us. Jn 15:7. 1 Jn 2:24. 2 Jn 1:9.

Obeying him. 1 Jn 3:24.

Necessary to fruitfulness. Jn 15:4–5.

Necessary to growth in grace. Ep 4:15–16. Cl 2:19.

Punishment of those who have not. Jn 15:6.

SAINTS

Are complete through. Cl 2:10.

Enjoy, in the Lord's supper. 1 Co 10:16–17.

Exhorted to maintain. Jn 15:4. Ac 11:23. Cl 2:7.

Have assurance of. Jn 14:20.

Have in his death. Ro 6:3–8. Gl 2:20.

Have in love. S S 2:16; 7:10.

Have in mind. 1 Co 2:16. Php 2:5.

Have in spirit. 1 Co 6:17.

Have in sufferings. Php 3:10. 2 Tm 2:12.

Identified with Christ by. Mt 25:40, 45. Ac 9:4, with 8:1.

They who have, ought to walk as he walked. 1 Jn 2:6.

UNITY

See Oneness.

UNITY OF GOD

All saints acknowledge, in worshiping him. 2 S 7:22. 2 K 19:15. 1 Ch 17:20.

All should know and acknowledge. Dt 4:35. Ps 83:18.

ASSERTED BY

The apostles. 1 Co 8:4, 6. Ep 4:6. 1 Tm 2:5.

Christ. Mk 12:29. Jn 17:3.

God himself. Is 44:6, 8; 45:18, 21.

Moses. Dt 4:39; 6:4.

Consistent with the deity of Christ and of the Holy Ghost. Jn 10:30, with 1 Jn 5:7. Jn 14:9–11.

EXHIBITED IN HIS

Being alone good. Mt 19:17.

Being alone possessed of foreknowledge. Is 46:9–11.

Being the only Savior. Is 45:21–22.

Being the only source of pardon. Mi 7:18, with Mk 2:7.

Being the sole object of worship in heaven and earth. Ne 9:6. Mt 4:10.

Exercise of uncontrolled sovereignty. Dt 32:39.

Greatness and wonderful works. 2 S 7:22. Ps 86:10.

Unparalleled election and care of his people. Dt 4:32–35.

Works of creation and providence. Is 44:24; 45:5–8.

A ground for loving him supremely. Dt 6:4–5, with Mk 12:29–30.

A ground for obeying him exclusively. Dt 4:39–40.

Knowledge of, necessary to eternal life. Jn 17:3.

May be acknowledged without saving faith. Ja 2:19–20.

UNSELFISHNESS

Commanded. Lv 19:18. Dt 10:19. Mt 19:21. Jn 15:12. Php 2:4.

Covers sin. 1 P 4:8.

Described. 1 Co 13.

Encouraged. Ro 15:1. 2 Co 9:7.

Measure of. Lk 6:31.

Purpose of God's commandment. 1 Tm 1:5.

Reward for. Mt 7:2; 10:42. Pr 11:25; 22:9. Is 58:10. 2 Co 9:6.

UPRIGHTNESS

Being kept from presumptuous sins necessary to. Ps 19:13.

A characteristic of saints. Ps 111:1. Is 26:7.

GOD

Created man in. Ec 7:29.

Has pleasure in. 1 Ch 29:17.

Is perfect in. Is 26:7.

Pray for those who walk in. Ps 125:4.

Reprove those who deviate from. Gl 2:14.

Saints should resolve to walk in. Ps 26:11

SHOULD BE IN

Heart. 2 Ch 29:34. Ps 125:4.

Judging. Pss 58:1; 75:2.

Ruling. Ps 78:72.
Speech. Is 33:15.
Walk. Pr 14:2.

THEY WHO WALK IN
Abominated by the wicked. Pr 29:21.
A blessing to others. Pr 11:11.
Countenanced by God. Ps 11:7.
Defended by God. Pr 2:7.
Delighted in by God. Pr 11:20.
Direct their way. Pr 21:29.
Fear God. Pr 14:2.
Find strength in God's way. Pr 10:29.
Guided by integrity. Pr 11:3.
Hated by the wicked. Pr 29:10. Am 5:10.
Kept by righteousness. Pr 13:6.
Love Christ. S S 1:4.
Obtain good from God's word. Mi 2:7.
Obtain light in darkness. Ps 112:4.
Persecuted by the wicked. Ps 37:14.
Praise is comely for. Ps 33:1.
Prospered by God. Jb 8:6. Pr 14:11.
Recompensed by God. Ps 18:23–24.
Scorned by the wicked. Jb 12:4.
Their prayer delighted in by God. Pr 15:8.
Upheld in it by God. Ps 41:12.
Walk surely. Pr 10:9.

THEY WHO WALK IN SHALL
Be blessed. Ps 112:2.
Be delivered by righteousness. Pr 11:6.
Be delivered by their wisdom. Pr 12:6.
Be saved. Pr 28:18.
Dwell in the land. Pr 2:21.

Dwell on high and be provided for. Is 33:16.
Dwell with God. Pss 15:2; 140:13.
Enter into peace. Ps 37:37. Is 57:2.
Have dominion over the wicked. Ps 49:14.
Have an inheritance forever. Ps 37:18.
Have nothing good withheld. Ps 84:11.
Possess good things. Pr 28:10.
The truly wise walk in. Pr 15:21.
The way of, to depart from evil. Pr 16:17.

THE WICKED
Do not act with. Mi 7:2, 4.
Have not in heart. Hk 2:4.
Leave the path of. Pr 2:13.
With poverty, better than folly. Pr 19:1.
With poverty, better than sin with riches. Pr 28:6.

URIM AND THUMMIM
God to be consulted by. Nu 27:21.
Illustrative of the light and perfection of Christ, the true high priest. Dt 33:8. (*See also* Jn 1:4, 9, 17. Cl 2:3.)
Instances of consulting God by. Jg 1:1; 20:18, 28. 1 S 23:9–11; 1 S 30:7–8.
Placed in the breastplate of the high priest. Ex 28:30. Lv 8:8.
Sometimes no answer by, in consequence of the sin of those consulting. 1 S 28:6.
Wanting in the second temple. Ezr 2:63. Ne 7:65.

V

VALLEYS

ABOUNDED WITH
Doves. Ezk 7:16.
Fountains and springs. Dt 8:7, Is 41:18.
Lily of the valley. S S 2:1.
Ravens. Pr 30:17.
Rocks and caves. Jb 30:6. Is 57:5.
Trees. 1 K 10:27.

CALLED
Dales. Gn 14:17. 2 S 18:18.
Fat, when fruitful. Is 28:1, 4.
Rough, when uncultivated and barren. Dt 21:4.
Vales. Dt 1:7. Jsh 10:40.
Canaan abounded in. Dt 11:11.
The Canaanites held possession of, against Judah. Jg 1:19.
Described as tracts of land between mountains. 1 S 17:3.
The heathen supposed that certain deities presided over. 1 K 20:23, 28.

ILLUSTRATIVE OF
Affliction and death (when dark). Ps 23:4.
The church of Christ. S S 6:11.
Removing all obstructions to the gospel (when being filled up). Is 40:4. Lk 3:5.
The tents of Israel (when fruitful and well watered). Nu 24:6.

MENTIONED IN SCRIPTURE
Achor. Jsh 7:24. Is 65:10. Ho 2:15.
Ajalon. Jsh 10:12.
Baca. Ps 84:6.
Berachah. 2 Ch 20:26.
Bochim. Jg 2:5.
Charashim. 1 Ch 4:14.
Elah. 1 S 17:2; 21:9.
Eshcol. Nu 32:9. Dt 1:24.
Gad. 2 S 24:5.
Gerar. Gn 26:17.
Gibeon. Is 28:21.
Hamon-gog. Ezk 39:11.
Hebron. Gn 37:14.
Hinnom. Jsh 15:8; 18:16. 2 K 23:10, 2 Ch 28:3. Jr 7:32.
Jehoshaphat or decision. Jl 3:2, 14.
Jericho. Dt 34:3.

Jezreel. Ho 1:5.
Jiphthah-el. Jsh 19:14, 27.
Keziz. Jsh 18:21.
Lebanon. Jsh 11:17.
Megiddo. 2 Ch 35:22. Zc 12:11.
Moab where Moses was buried. Dt 34:6.
Rephaim. Jsh 15:8; 18:16. 2 S 5:18. Is 17:5.
Salt. 2 S 8:13. 2 K 14:17.
Shaveh. Gn 14:17. 2 S 18:18.
Shittim. Jl 3:18.
Siddim. Gn 14:3, 8.
Sorek. Jg 16:4.
Succoth. Ps 60:6.
Zared. Nu 21:12.
Zeboim. 1 S 13:18.
Zephathah. 2 Ch 14:10.

MIRACLES CONNECTED WITH
Ditches in, filled with water. 2 K 3:16–17.
The moon made to stand still over Ajalon. Jsh 10:12.
Water in, made to appear to the Moabites like blood. 2 K 3:22–23.
Of Israel, well tilled and fruitful. 1 S 6:13. Ps 65:13.
Often the scenes of great contests. Jg 5:15; 7:8, 22. 1 S 17:19.
Often the scenes of idolatrous rites. Is 57:5.
To be filled with hostile chariots, threatened as a punishment. Is 22:7.

VANITY

All earthly things are. Ec 1:2.
Almsgiving without charity is. 1 Co 13:3.
Beauty of man is. Ps 39:11. Pr 31:30.
Childhood and youth are. Ec 11:10.
Conduct of the ungodly is. 1 P 1:18.
A consequence of the fall. Ro 8:20.
Days of man are. Jb 7:16. Ec 6:12.
Every man is. Ps 39:11.
Every state of man is. Ps 62:9.
Faith without works is. Ja 2:14.
False teaching is. Jr 23:32.
Following those given to, leads to poverty. Pr 28:19.

Foolish questions, etc., are. 1 Tm 1:6–7;
6:20. 2 Tm 2:14, 16. Ti 3:9.

Fools follow those given to. Pr 12:11.

Heaping up riches is. Ec 2:26; 4:8.

Help of man is. Ps 60:11. Lm 4:17.

Idolatry is. 2 K 17:15. Ps 31:6. Is 44:9–10.
Jr 10:8; 18:15.

Love of riches is. Ec 5:10.

Lying words are. Jr 7:8.

Man at his best estate is. Ps 39:5.

Man like to. Ps 144:4.

Man's own righteousness is. Is 57:12.

Mere external religion is. 1 Tm 4:8. He
13:9.

Riches gotten by falsehood are. Pr 21:6.

Religion of hypocrites is. Ja 1:26.

SAINTS

Avoid. Ps 24:4.

Avoid those given to. Ps 26:4.

Hate the thoughts of. Ps 119:113.

Pray to be kept from. Ps 119:37. Pr 30:8.

They who trust in, rewarded with. Jb 15:31.

Thoughts of man are. Ps 94:11.

Treasures of wickedness are. Pr 10:2.

Unblessed riches are. Ec 6:2.

Wealth gotten by, diminishes. Pr 13:11.

THE WICKED

Allure others by words of. 2 P 2:18.

Count God's service as. Jb 21:15. Ml
3:14.

Especially characterized by. Jb 11:11.

Imagine. Ps 2:1. Ac 4:25. Ro 1:21.

Inherit. Jr 16:19.

Judicially given up to. Ps 78:33. Is 57:13.

Love. Ps 4:2.

Reap. Pr 22:8. Jr 12:13.

Speak. Pss 10:7; 12:2; 41:6.

Though full of, affect to be wise. Jb 11:12.

Walk after. Jr 2:5.

Walk in. Ps 39:6. Ep 4:17.

Worldly anxiety is. Pss 39:6; 127:2.

Worldly enjoyment is. Ec 2:3, 10–11.

Worldly labor is. Ec 2:11; 4:4.

Worldly pleasure is. Ec 2:1.

Worldly possessions are. Ec 2:4–11.

Worldly wisdom is. Ec 2:15, 21. 1 Co 3:20.

Worship of the wicked is. Is 1:13. Mt 6:7.

VEIL

A covering for the head usually worn by
women. Gn 38:14.

ILLUSTRATIVE OF

The spiritual blindness of the Gentile nations. Is 25:7.

The spiritual blindness of the Jewish nation.
2 Co 3:14–16.

Moses put one on to conceal the glory of his
face. Ex 34:33, with 2 Co 3:13.

Removing of, considered rude and insolent.
S S 5:7.

Removing of, threatened as a punishment to
ungodly women. Is 3:23.

WORN

As a token of modesty. Gn 24:65.

As a token of subjection. 1 Co 11:3, 6–7,
10.

For concealment. Gn 38:14.

VEIL, SACRED

Designed to conceal the ark, mercy seat, and
the symbol of the divine presence. Ex
40:3.

THE HIGH PRIEST

Alone allowed to enter within. He 9:6–7.

Allowed to enter but once a year. Lv 16:2.
He 9:7.

Could not enter without blood. Lv 16:3,
with He 9:7.

Hung between the holy and most holy place.
Ex 26:33. He 9:3.

ILLUSTRATIVE OF

The death of Christ which opened heaven
to saints (when rent). He 10:19–20, with
9:24.

Flesh of Christ which concealed his
divinity. He 10:20. (See also Is 53:2.)

Obscurity of the Mosaic dispensation. He
9:8.

Made by Bezaleel for the tabernacle. Ex
36:35.

Made by Solomon for the temple. 2 Ch 3:14.

Moses commanded to make. Ex 26:31.

Rent at the death of our Lord. Mt 27:51.
Mk 15:38. Lk 23:45.

Suspended from four pillars of shittim wood
overlaid with gold. Ex 26:32.

VICTORY

See Overcoming; Triumph.

VINE

Canaan abounded in. Dt 6:11; 8:8.

CULTIVATED

By the walls of houses. Ps 128:3.

In the valleys. S S 6:11.

In vineyards from the time of Noah. Gn
9:20.

On the sides of hills. Jr 31:5.

Dwarf and spreading particularly esteemed.
Ezk 17:6.

Foxes destructive to.   S S 2:15.

Frequently injured by hail and frost.   Pss
78:47; 105:32–33.

Frequently made unfruitful as a punishment.
Jr 8:13. Ho 2:12. Jl 1:7, 12. Hg 2:19.

FRUIT OF
Called grapes.   Gn 40:10.
Eaten dried.   1 S 25:18; 30:12.
Eaten fresh from the tree.   Dt 23:24.
Peculiarly sour when unripe.   Jr 31:30.
Sold in the markets.   Ne 13:15.
Made into wine.   Dt 32:14. Mt 26:29.

God made fruitful for his people when obedient.   Jl 2:22. Zc 8:12.

ILLUSTRATIVE OF
By the worthlessness of its wood, the un-
profitableness of the wicked.   Ezk
15:6–7.
Christ.   Jn 15:1–2.
God's purifying his people by afflictions
(when pruned).   Jn 15:2.
The graces of the church (by its rich clus-
ters).   S S 7:8.
The growth of saints in grace (by its quick
growth).   Ho 14:7.
Israel.   Ps 80:8. Is 5:2, 7.
Mere professors (by its unfruitful branches).
Jn 15:2, 6.
Peace and prosperity (when sitting under
one's own).   1 K 4:25. Mi 4:4. Zc 3:10.
Saints (by its fruitful branches).   Jn 15:5.
The wicked (when unfruitful).   Ho 10:1.

Its flowers perfumed the air.   S S 2:13. Ho
14:7.

Nazarites prohibited from eating.   Nu 6:3–4.

Of Sodom, bad, and unfit for use.   Dt 32:32.

Often degenerated.   Is 5:2. Jr 2:21.

Often found wild.   2 K 4:39. Ho 9:10.

PLACES CELEBRATED FOR
Egypt.   Pss 78:47; 80:8.
Eshcol.   Nu 13:23–24.
Lebanon.   Ho 14:7.
Sibmah.   Is 16:8–9.

Probably produced two crops a year.   Nu
13:20.

Proverbial allusion to fathers eating the unripe
fruit of.   Jr 31:29–30. Ezk 18:2.

Required to be dressed and pruned to increase
its fruitfulness.   Lv 25:3. 2 Ch 26:10. Is
18:5.

Sometimes cast its fruit before it came to perfection.   Jb 15:33. Ml 3:11.

Wild boar destructive to.   Ps 80:13.

Wood of fit only for burning.   Ezk 15:2–5.

Young cattle fed on its leaves and tender
shoots.   Gn 49:11.

VINEYARDS
Antiquity of.   Gn 9:20.

Cottages built in, for the keepers.   Is 1:8.

Design of planting.   Ps 107:37. 1 Co 9:7.

Estimated profit arising from, to the cultiva-
tors.   S S 8:12.

Estimated rent of.   S S 8:11. Is 7:23.

Frequently let out to husbandmen.   S S 8:11.
Mt 21:33.

Frequently walled or fenced with hedges.   Nu
22:24. Pr 24:31. Is 5:2, 5.

ILLUSTRATIVE OF
The elect (when cleaning grapes of).   Is
24:13.
The Jewish church.   Is 5:7; 27:2. Jr 12:10.
Mt 21:23.
Severe calamities (when failing).   Is 32:10.

In unfavorable seasons, produced but little
wine.   Is 5:10. Hg 1:9, 11.

LAWS RESPECTING
Compensation in kind to be made for injury
done to.   Ex 22:5.
Fruit of new, not to be eaten for three years.
Lv 19:23.
Fruit of new, to be eaten by the owners
from the fifth year.   Lv 19:25.
Fruit of new, to be holy to the Lord in the
fourth year.   Lv 19:24.
Gleaning of, to be left for the poor.   Lv
19:10. Dt 24:21.
Not to be cultivated during the sabbatical
year.   Ex 23:11. Lv 25:4.
Not to be planted with different kinds of
seed.   Dt 22:9.
Planters of, not liable to military service till
they had eaten of the fruit.   Dt 20:6.
Spontaneous fruit of, not to be gathered
during the sabbatical or jubilee year.   Lv
25:5, 11.
Strangers entering, allowed to eat fruit but
not to take any away.   Dt 23:24.

Members of the family often worked in.   S S
1:6. Mt 21:28–30.

Mode of hiring and paying laborers for working in.   Mt 20:1–2.

Of red grapes, particularly esteemed.   Is 27:2.

Often mortgaged.   Ne 5:3–4.

Of the kings of Israel, superintended by officers of state.   1 Ch 27:27.

Of the slothful man, neglected and laid waste. Pr 24:30–31.

The poor engaged in culture of. 2 K 25:12. Is 61:5.

Produce of, frequently destroyed by enemies. Jr 48:32.

Produce of, often destroyed by insects, etc. Dt 28:39. Am 4:9.

Provided with the apparatus for making wine. Is 5:2. Mt 21:33.

The Rechabites forbidden to plant. Jr 35:7–9.

Rent of, frequently paid by part of the fruit. Mt 21:34.

Stones carefully gathered out of. Is 5:2.

VINTAGE OR INGATHERING OF
Failure in, occasioned great grief. Is 16:9–10.

Sometimes continued to the time of sowing seed. Lv 26:5.

A time of great rejoicing. Is 16:10.

The wicked judicially deprived of the enjoyment of. Am 5:11. Zp 1:13.

VISIONS
False prophets pretended to have seen. Jr 14:14; 23:16.

Frequently difficult and perplexing to those who received them. Dn 7:15; 8:15. Ac 10:17.

God especially made himself known to prophets by. Nu 12:6.

God often made known his will by. Ps 89:19.

MENTIONED AS OCCURRING TO
Abraham. Gn 15:1.
Amos. Am 7:1–9; 8:1–6; 9:1.
Ananias. Ac 9:10–11.
Cornelius. Ac 10:3.
Daniel. Dn 2:19; 7—8; 10.
Eliphaz. Jb 4:13–16.
Ezekiel. Ezk 1:4–14; 8:2–14; 10; 11:24–25; 37:1–10; 40—48.
Isaiah. Is 6:1–8.
Jacob. Gn 46:2.
John. Rv 1:12; 4—22.
Moses. Ex 3:2–3. Ac 7:30–32.
Nathan. 2 S 7:4, 17.
Nebuchadnezzar. Dn 2:28; 4:5.
Paul. Ac 9:3, 6, 12; 16:9; 18:9; 22:18; 27:23. 2 Ch 12:1–4.
Peter. Ac 10:9–17.
Samuel. 1 S 3:2–15.
Zechariah. Zc 1:8; 3:1; 4:2; 5:2; 6:1.

Multiplied for the benefit of the people. Ho 12:10.

OFTEN ACCOMPANIED BY
An appearance of angels. Lk 1:22, with Lk 1:11; 24:23. Ac 10:3.

An appearance of human beings. Ac 9:12; 16:9.

An audible voice from heaven. Gn 15:1. 1 S 3:4–5.

A representative of the divine person and glory. Is 6:1.

OFTEN COMMUNICATED
At night. Gn 46:2. Dn 2:19.

In a trance. Nu 24:16. Ac 11:5.

Prophets of God skilled in interpreting. 2 Ch 26:5. Dn 1:17.

Recorded for the benefit of the people. Hk 2:2.

Sometimes withheld for a long season. 1 S 3:1.

Withholding of, a great calamity. Pr 29:18. Lm 2:9.

VOWS
As solemn promises to God. Ps 76:11.

Clean beasts the subjects of, not to be redeemed. Lv 27:9–10.

Danger of inconsiderately making. Pr 20:25.

Hire of a prostitute or price of a dog could not be the subject of. Dt 23:18.

MADE IN REFERENCE TO
Afflicting the soul. Nu 30:13.
Dedicating children to God. 1 S 1:11.
Devoting property to God. Gn 28:22.
Devoting the person to God. Nu 6:2.
Offering sacrifices. Lv 7:16; 22:18, 22. Nu 15:3.

Of children, void without consent of parents. Nu 30:3–5.

Of married women, void without consent of husbands. Nu 30:6–8, 10–13.

Of things corrupt or blemished an insult to God. Lv 22:23. Ml 1:14.

Of widows and women divorced from their husbands, binding. Nu 30:9.

Of wives, could only be objected to at the time of making. Nu 30:14–15.

RECORDED IN SCRIPTURE OF
Certain Jews with Paul. Ac 21:23–24, 26.
David. Ps 132:2–5.
Elkanah. 1 S 1:21.
Hannah. 1 S 1:11.
Israelites. Nu 21:2.
Jacob. Gn 28:20–22; 31:13.

Jephthah. Jg 11:30–31.
Jonah. Jnh 2:9.
Lemuel's mother. Pr 31:1–2.
Mariners who cast out Jonah. Jnh 1:16.
Paul. Ac 18:18.
Redeemed by paying a suitable compensation.
Lv 27:1–8, 11–23.

SHOULD BE
Performed faithfully. Nu 30:2.
Performed without delay. Dt 23:21, 23.
Voluntary. Dt 23:21–22.
Things dedicated by, to be brought to the
tabernacle. Dt 12:6, 11, 17–18, 26.

W

WAITING UPON GOD.
As THE
Giver of all temporal blessings. Pss 104:27–28; 145:15–16.
God of providence. Jr 14:22.
God of salvation. Ps 25:5.
Exhortations and encouragements to. Pss 27:14; 37:7. Ho 12:6.
For
Coming of Christ. 1 Co 1:7. 1 Th 1:10.
The consolation of Israel. Lk 2:25.
The fulfillment of his promises. Ac 1:4.
The fulfillment of his word. Hk 2:3.
Guidance and teaching. Ps 25:5.
Hope of righteousness by faith. Gl 5:5.
Mercy. Ps 123:2.
Pardon. Ps 39:7–8.
Protection. Pss 33:20; 59:9–10.
Salvation. Gn 49:18. Ps 62:1–2.
God calls us to. Zp 3:8.
Illustrated. Ps 123:2. Lk 12:36. Ja 5:7.
Is good. Ps 52:9.
The patience of saints often tried in. Ps 69:3.
Predicted of the Gentiles. Is 42:4; 60:9.
Saints
Have expectation from. Ps 62:5.
Plead, in prayer. Ps 25:21. Is 33:2.
Resolve on. Pss 52:9; 59:9.
Should Be
All the day. Ps 25:5.
Continually. Ho 12:6.
In the way of his judgments. Is 26:8.
Specially in adversity. Ps 59:1–9. Is 8:17.
With earnest desire. Ps 130:6.
With full confidence. Mi 7:7.
With hope in his word. Ps 130:5.
With patience. Pss 37:7; 40:1.
With resignation. Lm 3:26.
With the soul. Ps 62:1, 5.
They Who Engage in
Are blessed. Is 30:18. Dn 12:12.
Are heard. Ps 40:1.
Experience his goodness. Lm 3:25.
Shall be saved. Pr 20:22. Is 25:9.
Shall inherit the earth. Ps 37:9.
Shall not be ashamed. Ps 25:3. Is 49:23.
Shall receive the glorious things prepared by God for them. Is 64:4.
Shall rejoice in salvation. Is 25:9.
Shall renew their strength, etc. Is 40:31.
Wait upon him only. Ps 62:5.

WALKING WITH GOD
We Are Not to Walk
According to the flesh. Ro 8:4.
By sight but by faith. 2 Co 5:7.
Craftily. 2 Co 4:2.
In darkness. Jn 8:12. 1 Jn 1:6.
In disorder. 2 Th 3:6.
In our own ways. Ac 14:16.
In the way of Cain. Jde 1:11.
We Are to Walk
As children of light. Ep 5:8.
As Christ walked. 1 Jn 2:6.
By faith, not sight. 2 Co 5:7.
Circumspectly. Ep 5:15.
In love. Ep 5:2.
In the light. 1 Jn 1:7.
In newness of life. Ro 6:4.
In the Spirit. Gl 5:16, 25.

WALLS
Designed for defense. 1 S 25:16.
Designed for separation. Ezk 43:8. Ep 2:14.
Frequently made of stone and wood together. Ezr 5:8. Hk 2:11.
Hyssop frequently grew on. 1 K 4:33.
Illustrative of
The church as a protection to the nation. S S 8:9–10.
Hypocrites (whited). Ac 23:3.
Ordinances as a protection to the church. S S 2:9. Is 5:5.
Prophets in their testimony against the wicked (brazen). Jr 22:20.
Protection of God. Zc 2:5.
Salvation. Is 26:1; 60:18.
Separation of Jews and Gentiles (as partitions). Ep 2:14.
The teaching of false prophets (daubed with untempered mortar). Ezk 13:10–15.

Those who afford protection. 1 S 25:16. Is 2:15.

The wealth of the rich in his own conceit. Pr 18:11.

The wicked under judgments (bowing or tottering). Ps 62:3. Is 30:12.

MENTIONED IN SCRIPTURE

Of cities. Nu 13:28.

Of houses. 1 S 18:11.

Of temples. 1 Ch 29:4. Is 56:5.

Of vineyards. Nu 22:24. Pr 24:31.

MIRACLES CONNECTED WITH

Falling of the walls of Jericho. Jsh 6:20.

Handwriting on Belshazzar's palace. Dn 5:5, 25–28.

OF CITIES

Adroitness of soldiers in scaling, alluded to. Jl 2:7–9.

Battered by besieging armies. 2 S 20:15. Ezk 4:2–3.

Bodies of enemies sometimes fastened on, as a disgrace. 1 S 31:10.

Broad and places of public resort. 2 K 6:26, 30. Ps 55:10.

Custom of dedicating. Ne 12:27.

Danger of approaching too near to, in time of war. 2 S 11:20–21.

Destruction of, a punishment and cause of grief. Dt 28:52. Ne 1:3; 2:12–17.

Falling of, sometimes occasioned great destruction. 1 K 20:30.

Frequently laid in ruins. 2 Ch 25:23; 36:19. Jr 50:15.

Had towers built on them. 2 Ch 26:9; 32:5. Ps 48:12. S S 8:10.

Houses often built on. Jsh 2:15.

Houses sometimes broken down to repair and fortify. Is 22:10.

Idolatrous rites performed on. 2 K 3:27.

Instances of persons let down from. Jsh 2:15. Ac 9:24–25. 2 Co 11:33.

Kept by watchmen night and day. S S 5:7. Is 62:6.

Often very high. Dt 1:28; 3:5.

Sometimes burned. Jr 49:27. Am 1:7.

Strongly fortified. Is 2:15; 25:12.

Strongly manned in war. 2 K 18:26.

OF HOUSES

Easily dug through. Gn 49:6. Ezk 8:7–8; 12:5.

Had nails or pegs fastened into them when built. Ec 12:11. Is 22:23.

Liable to leprosy. Lv 14:37.

Often infested with serpents. Am 5:19.

The seat next, the place of distinction. 1 S 20:25.

Usually plastered. Ezk 13:10, with Dn 5:5.

Probably often strengthened with plates of iron or brass. Jr 15:20. Ezk 4:3.

Small towns and villages were not surrounded by. Lv 25:31. Dt 3:5.

WAR

Antiquity of. Gn 14:2.

Frequently long. 2 S 3:1.

Frequently sore and bloody. 1 S 14:22. 1 Ch 5:22. 2 Ch 14:13; 28:6.

ILLUSTRATIVE OF

The contest between antichrist and the church. Rv 11:7; 13:4, 7.

The contest of saints with the enemies of their salvation. Ro 7:23. 2 Co 10:3. Ep 6:12. 1 Tm 1:18.

The malignity of the wicked. Ps 55:21.

Our contest with death. Ec 8:8.

THE JEWS

Expert in. 1 Ch 12:33, 35–36. S S 3:8.

Frequently engaged in. Jsh 6—11. 1 K 14:30; 15:7–16.

Large armies frequently engaged in. 2 Ch 13:3; 14:9.

OFTEN ATTENDED BY

Cruelty. Jr 18:21. Lm 5:11–14.

Devastation. Is 1:7.

Famine. Is 51:19. Jr 14:15. Lm 5:10.

Pestilence. Jr 27:13; 28:8.

Often sent as a punishment for sin. Jg 5:8.

Originates in the lusts of men. Ja 4:1.

PRECEDED BY

Consultation. Lk 14:31, with Pr 24:6.

Great preparation. Jl 3:9.

Rumors. Jr 4:19. Mt 24:6.

Records often kept of. Nu 21:14.

Weapons used in. Jsh 1:14. Jg 18:11.

WARFARE OF SAINTS

ARMOR FOR

Breastplate of righteousness. Ep 6:14.

Called armor of God. Ep 6:11.

Called armor of light. Ro 13:12.

Called armor of righteousness. 2 Co 6:7.

Girdle of truth. Ep 6:14.

Helmet of salvation. Ep 6:17. 1 Th 5:8.

Mighty through God. 2 Co 10:4–5.

Must be put on. Ro 13:12. Ep 6:11.

Not carnal. 2 Co 10:4.

Preparation of the gospel. Ep 6:15.

Shield of faith. Ep 6:16.
Sword of the Spirit. Ep 6:17.
To be on right hand and left. 2 Co 6:7.
The whole, is required. Ep 6:13.
Called the good fight of faith. 1 Tm 6:12.
Illustrated. Is 9:5. Zc 10:5.
Is
A good warfare. 1 Tm 1:18–19.
Not after the flesh. 2 Co 10:3.
Is Against
Death. 1 Co 15:26, with He 2:14–15.
The devil. Gn 3:15. 2 Co 2:11. Ep 6:12.
Ja 4:7. 1 P 5:8. Rv 12:17.
Enemies. Pss 38:19; 56:2; 59:3.
The flesh. Ro 7:23. 1 Co 9:25–27. 2 Co
12:7. Gl 5:17. 1 P 2:11.
The world. Jn 16:33. 1 Jn 5:4–5.
Mere professors do not maintain. Jr 9:3.
Often arises from the opposition of friends or
relatives. Mi 7:6, with Mt 10:35–36.
Saints
All engaged in. Php 1:30.
Comforted by God in. 2 Co 7:5–6.
Delivered by Christ in. 2 Tm 4:18.
Encouraged in. Is 41:11–12. Is 51:12.
Mi 7:8. 1 Jn 4:4.
Exhorted to diligence in. 1 Tm 6:12. Jde
1:3.
Helped by God in. Ps 118:13. Is
41:13–14.
Must stand firm in. Ep 6:13–14.
Protected by God in. Ps 140:7.
Strengthened by Christ in. 2 Co 12:9. 2
Tm 4:17.
Strengthened by God in. Pss 20:2; 27:14.
Is 41:70.
Thank God for victory in. Ro 7:25. 1 Co
15:57.
They Who Overcome in, Shall
Be clothed in white raiment. Rv 3:5.
Be confessed by Christ before God the Fa-
ther. Rv 3:5.
Be pillars in the temple of God. Rv 3:12.
Be sons of God. Rv 21:7.
Eat of the hidden manna. Rv 2:17.
Eat of the tree of life. Rv 2:7.
Have God as their God. Rv 21:7.
Have the morning star. Rv 2:28.
Have the name of God written upon them
by Christ. Rv 3:12.
Have power over the nations. Rv 2:26.
Have a white stone, and in it a new name
written. Rv 2:17.
Inherit all things. Rv 21:7.

Not be hurt by the second death. Rv 2:11.
Not have their names blotted out of the
book of life. Rv 3:5.
Sit with Christ in his throne. Rv 3:21.
To Be Carried on
Under Christ, as our captain. He 2:10.
Under the Lord's banner. Ps 60:4.
With confidence in God. Ps 27:1–3.
With earnestness. Jde 1:3.
With endurance of hardness. 2 Tm 2:3,
10.
With faith. 1 Tm 1:18–19.
With a good conscience. 1 Tm 1:18–19.
With prayer. Ps 35:1–3. Ep 6:18.
With self-denial. 1 Co 9:25–27.
With sobriety. 1 Th 5:6. 1 P 5:8.
With steadfastness in the faith. 1 Co
16:13. 1 P 5:9, with He 10:23.
With watchfulness. 1 Co 16:13. 1 P 5:8.
Without earthly entanglements. 2 Tm
2:4.
Victory in, Is
By faith. He 11:33–37. 1 Jn 5:4–5.
From God. 1 Co 15:57. 2 Co 2:14.
Over all that exalts itself. 2 Co 10:5.
Over death and the grave. Is 25:8; 26:19.
Ho 13:14. 1 Co 15:54–55.
Over the devil. Ro 16:20. 1 Jn 2:14.
Over the flesh. Ro 7:24–25. Gl 5:24.
Over the world. 1 Jn 5:4–5.
Through Christ. Ro 7:25. 1 Co 15:27. 2
Co 12:9. Rv 12:11.
Triumphant. Ro 8:37. 2 Co 10:5.

WATCHFULNESS

Blessedness of. Lk 12:37. Rv 16:15.
Christ an example of. Mt 26:38, 40. Lk
6:12.
Commanded. Mk 13:37. Rv 3:2.
Danger of remissness in. Mt 24:48–51; 25:5,
8, 12. Rv 3:3.
Exhortations to. 1 Th 5:6. 1 P 4:7.
Faithful ministers approved by. Mt
24:45–46. Lk 12:41–44.
Faithful ministers exercise. He 13:17.
God especially requires in ministers. Ezk
3:17, with Is 62:6. Mk 13:34.
Ministers exhorted to. Ac 20:31. 2 Tm 4:5.
Motives to
Expected direction from God. Hk 2:1.
Incessant assaults of the devil. 1 P 5:8.
Liability to temptation. Mt 26:41.
Uncertain time of the coming of Christ
Mt 24:42; 25:13. Mk 13:35–36.

Saints pray to be kept in a state of. Ps 141:3.

SHOULD BE

At all times. Pr 8:34.
In all things. 2 Tm 4:5.
With heedfulness. Mk 13:33.
With prayer. Lk 21:36. Ep 6:18.
With sobriety. 1 Th 5:6. 1 P 4:7.
With steadfastness in the faith. 1 Co 16:13.
With thanksgiving. Cl 4:2.

Unfaithful ministers devoid of. Is 56:10.
The wicked averse to. 1 Th 5:7.

WATCHMEN

Citizens sometimes acted as. Ne 7:3.
Danger of sleeping on their posts referred to. Mt 28:13–14.

ILLUSTRATIVE OF

Anxious waiting for God (when looking for the morning). Ps 130:5–6.
Careless ministers (when blind). Is 56:10.
Ministers. Is 52:8; 62:6. Ezk 3:17. He 13:17.

IN TIME OF DANGER

Increased in number. Jr 51:12.
Reported the approach of all strangers. 2 S 18:24–27. 2 K 9:18–20. Is 21:6–7, 9.
Sounded an alarm at the approach of enemies. Ezk 33:2–3.
Vigilant night and day. Ne 4:9. Is 21:8.

Neglecting to give warning punished with death. Ezk 33:6.
Often interrogated by passengers. Is 21:11.
Paraded the streets at night to preserve order. S S 3:3; 5:7.
Relieved by turns. Ne 7:3.
Soldiers generally acted as. Mt 27:65–66.

STATIONED

Around the temple in Jerusalem on special occasions. 2 K 11:6.
In the streets of cities. Ps 127:1.
On watchtowers. 2 K 9:17. Is 21:5.
On the walls of cities. Is 62:6.

Vigilance of, vain without God's protection. Ps 127:1.

WATER

Artificial mode of conveying into large cities. 2 K 20:20.
Carried in vessels. Gn 21:14. 1 S 26:11. Mk 14:13.

COLLECTED IN

Brooks. 2 S 17:20. 1 K 18:5.
Clouds. Gn 1:7. Jb 26:8–9.

Fountains. 1 K 18:5. 2 Ch 32:3.
Ponds. Ex 7:19. Is 19:10.
Pools. 1 K 22:38. Ne 2:14.
Rivers. Is 8:7. Jr 2:18.
The sea. Gn 1:9–10. Is 11:9.
Springs. Jsh 15:19.
Streams. Ps 78:16. Is 35:6.
Wells. Gn 21:19.

Congealed by cold. Jb 38:29. Ps 147:16–17.

DESCRIBED AS

Cleansing. Ezk 36:25. Ep 5:26.
Fluid. Ps 78:16. Pr 30:4.
Penetrating. Ps 109:18.
Reflecting images. Pr 27:9.
Refreshing. Jb 22:7. Pr 25:25.
Unstable. Gn 49:4.
Wearing the hardest substances. Jb 14:19.

Drops from the clouds in rain. Dt 11:11. 2 S 21:10.
An element of the world. Gn 1:2.
Frequently brackish and unfit for use. Ex 15:23. 2 K 2:19.

GOD ORIGINALLY

Collected into one place. Gn 1:9.
Created the firmament to divide. Gn 1:6–7.
Created fowls and fishes from. Gn 1:20–21.

ILLUSTRATIVE OF

The career of the wicked (when rapidly flowing away). Jb 24:18. Ps 58:7.
Counsel in the heart (when deep). Pr 20:5.
Death (when spilled on the ground). 2 S 14:14.
Different nations and people (when many). Rv 17:1, 15. Jr 51:13.
Faintness and cowardness (in its weakness). Jsh 7:5. Ezk 7:17.
Faintness by terror (when poured out). Ps 22:14.
General diffusion of the knowledge of God (when covering the sea). Is 11:9. Hk 2:14.
Gifts and graces of the Holy Spirit. Is 41:17–18; 44:3. Ezk 36:25. Jn 7:38–39.
Hostile armies. Is 8:7; 17:13.
Numerous progeny (when poured out of buckets). Nu 24:7.
The ordinances of the gospel (when still). Ps 23:2.
Persecutions. Ps 88:17.
Persecutors. Ps 124:4–5.

Severe affliction (when deep). Pss 66:12; 69:1. Is 30:20; 43:2.

Strife and contention (when difficult to stop). Pr 17:14.

Support of God. Is 8:6.

A variety of afflictions (when many). 2 S 22:17.

A wavering disposition (in its instability). Gn 49:4.

The word of Christ (when many and noisy). Rv 1:15.

The words of the wise (when deep). Pr 18:4.

The wrath of God (when poured out). Ho 5:10.

Kept for purification in large pots. Jn 2:6.

MIRACLES CONNECTED WITH

Brought from the jawbone of an ass. Jg 15:19.

Brought from the rock. Ex 17:6. Nu 20:11.

Consumed by fire from heaven. 1 K 18:38.

Divided and made to stand on heap. Ex 14:21–22.

Healing powers communicated to. 2 K 5:14. Jn 5:4; 9:7.

Iron made to swim in. 2 K 6:5–6.

Our Lord, etc., walked on. Mt 14:26–29.

Trenches filled with. 2 K 3:17–22.

Turned into blood. Ex 7:17, 20.

Turned into wine. Jn 2:7–9.

Necessary to the comfort and happiness of man. Is 41:17, with Zc 9:11.

Necessary to vegetation. Gn 2:5–6. Jb 14:9. Is 1:30.

Rises in vapor to the clouds. Ec 1:7, with Ps 104:8.

Some plants particularly require. Jb 8:11.

USED BY THE JEWS

As their principal beverage. Gn 24:43. 1 K 13:19, 22; 18:4. Ho 2:5.

For culinary purposes. Ex 12:9.

For legal purification. Ex 29:4. He 9:10, 19.

For washing the person. Gn 18:4; 24:32.

Want of, a great calamity. Ex 17:1–3. Nu 20:2. 2 K 3:9–10. Is 3:1.

When scarce, sold at an enormous price. Lm 5:4.

The world and its inhabitants once destroyed by. Gn 7:20–23, with 2 P 3:6.

The world not to be again destroyed by. Gn 9:8–15. 2 P 3:7.

WAVE OFFERING

CONSISTED OF

Breast of all peace offerings. Lv 7:30; 9:18, 21. Nu 6:17, 20.

Breast of the priest's consecration ram. Ex 29:26. Lv 8:29.

Fat, right shoulder, etc., of the priest's consecration ram. Ex 29:22–23. Lv 8:25–26.

First fruits of barley harvest. Lv 23:10–11.

First fruits of wheaten bread. Lv 23:20.

Jealousy offering. Nu 5:25.

Left shoulder of Nazarite's peace offering. Nu 6:17, 19.

Leper's trespass offering. Lv 14:12, 24.

Fat, etc., of the consecration ram burnt on the altar. Ex 29:25. Lv 8:28.

Given to the priest as his due. Ex 29:26–28. Lv 7:31, 34; 8:29; 10:15; 23:20. Nu 18:11.

Placed in the hand of the priest and waved before the Lord. Ex 29:24. Lv 8:27.

To be eaten in a holy place by the priest's family. Lv 10:14.

WEALTH

See Prosperity; Riches.

WEEKS

The Feast of Pentecost called the Feast of. Ex 34:22, with Ac 2:1.

Origin of computing time by. Gn 2:2.

A period of time consisting of seven days. Lv 23:15–16. Lk 18:12.

A space of seven years sometimes so called. Gn 29:27–28. Dn 9:24–25, 27.

WEIGHTS

All metals given by. Ex 37:24. 1 Ch 28:14.

Frequently used in scales or balances. Jb 31:6. Is 40:12.

Generally regulated by the standard of the sanctuary. Ex 30:24.

ILLUSTRATED

The exceeding glory reserved for saints (when heavy). 2 Co 4:17.

Restraints put on the elements. Jb 28:25.

Sins. He 12:1.

THE JEWS

Forbidden to have divers. Dt 25:13–14.

Forbidden to have unjust. Lv 19:35–36.

Frequently used unjust. Mi 6:11.

MENTIONED IN SCRIPTURE

Bekah or half shekel. Gn 24:22.

Dram. Ne 7:70–71.

Gerah.   Ex 30:13. Ezk 45:12.
Maneh or pound.   Ne 7:71. Ezk 45:12.
Shekel.   Ex 30:13. Ezk 45:12.
Talent.   2 S 12:30. Rv 16:21.
Provisions sold by, in times of scarcity.   Lv
  26:26. Ezk 4:10, 16.
Sometimes regulated by the king's standard.
  2 S 14:26.
Value of money estimated according to.   Gn
  23:16; 43:21. Jr 32:9.

WELLS
Canaan abounded with.   Dt 6:11.
First mention of.   Gn 16:14.
A frequent cause of strife.   Gn 21:25;
  26:21–22. Ex 2:16–17.
FREQUENTED BY
  Travelers.   Gn 24:11, 13, 42. Jn 4:6.
  Women who came to draw water.   Gn
    24:13–14. Jn 4:7.
FREQUENTLY DUG
  In the courts of houses.   2 S 17:18.
  In the desert.   2 Ch 26:10.
  Near encampments.   Gn 21:30; 26:18.
  Outside cities.   Gn 24:11. Jn 4:6, 8.
Had troughs placed near for watering cattle.
  Gn 24:19–20. Ex 2:16.
ILLUSTRATIVE OF
  Enjoyment of domestic happiness (when
    drinking from one's own).   Pr 5:15.
  The Holy Spirit in saints.   S S 4:15, with Jn
    4:14.
  Hypocrites (when without water).   2 P
    2:17.
  The mouth of the righteous.   Pr 10:11.
  The ordinances of the church.   Is 12:3.
  Understanding and wisdom in man.   Pr
    16:22; 18:4.
Many supplied from Lebanon.   S S 4:15.
MENTIONED IN SCRIPTURE
  Beer (east of Jordon).   Nu 21:16–18.
  Beer-lahai-roi.   Gn 16:14.
  Beer-sheba.   Gn 21:30–31.
  Bethlehem.   2 S 23:15. 1 Ch 11:17–18.
  Elim.   Ex 15:27.
  Esek.   Gn 26:20.
  Hagar.   Gn 21:19.
  Haran.   Gn 29:3–4.
  Jacob.   Jn 4:6.
  Rehoboth.   Gn 26:22.
  Sitnah.   Gn 26:21.
Names often given to.   Gn 16:14; 21:31.
Often afforded no water.   Jr 14:3. Zc 9:11.

Often covered to prevent their being filled
  with sand.   Gn 29:2–3.
Often deep and difficult to draw from.   Jn
  4:11.
Often stopped up by enemies.   Gn 26:15, 18.
  2 K 3:19, 25.
Strangers not to draw from, without permis-
  sion.   Nu 20:17.
Supplied by springs.   Pr 16:22.
Supplied by the rain.   Ps 84:6.
Surrounded by trees.   Gn 49:22. Ex 15:27.
Water of, frequently sold.   Nu 20:19.

WHIRLWIND
Arose from the earth.   Jr 25:32.
Called the whirlwind of the Lord.   Jr 23:19;
  30:23.
Destructive nature of.   Pr 1:27.
Frequently continued for a long time.   Jr
  30:23.
Generally came from the south.   Jb 37:9. Is
  21:1. Zc 9:14.
ILLUSTRATIVE OF THE
  Fury of God's judgments.   Jr 25:32; 30:23.
  Speed with which God executes his pur-
    poses.   Na 1:3.
  Sudden destruction of the wicked.   Ps
    58:9. Pr 1:27. Is 17:13; 40:24; 41:16. Jr
    30:23.
  Unavoidable fruit of a life of sin and vanity.
    Ho 8:7.
  Velocity of the chariots in hostile armies.
    Is 5:28. Jr 4:13.
  Velocity of Christ's second coming.   Is
    66:15.
MIRACLES CONNECTED WITH
  Elijah taken to heaven in.   2 K 2:1, 11.
  God spoke to Job from.   Jb 38:1; 40:6.
Sometimes came from the north.   Ezk 1:4.

WICKED
CHARACTER OF
  Abominable.   Rv 21:8.
  Alienated from God.   Ep 4:18. Cl 1:21.
  Blasphemous.   Lk 22:65. Rv 16:9.
  Blinded.   2 Co 4:4. Ep 4:18.
  Boastful.   Pss 10:3; 49:6.
  Conspiring against God's people.   Ne 4:8;
    6:2. Ps 38:12.
  Covetous.   Mi 2:2. Ro 1:29.
  Deceitful.   Ps 5:6. Ro 3:13.
  Delighting in the iniquity of others.   Pr
    2:14. Ro 1:32.

Despising the works of the faithful. Ne
2:19; 4:2. 2 Tm 3:3–4.

Destructive. Is 59:7.

Disobedient. Ne 9:26. Ti 3:3. 1 P 2:7.

Enticing to evil. Pr 1:10–14. 2 Tm 3:6.

Envious. Ne 2:10. Ti 3:3.

Fearful. Pr 28:1. Rv 21:8.

Fierce. Pr 16:29. 2 Tm 3:3.

Foolish. Dt 32:6. Ps 5:5.

Forgetting God. Jb 8:13.

Fraudulent. Ps 37:21. Mi 6:11.

Froward. Pr 21:8. Is 57:17.

Glorying in their shame. Php 3:19.

Hardhearted. Ezk 3:7.

Hating the light. Jb 24:13. Jn 3:20.

Heady and high-minded. 2 Tm 3:4.

Hostile to God. Ro 8:7. Cl 1:21.

Hypocritical. Is 29:13. 2 Tm 3:5.

Ignorant of God. Ho 4:1. 2 Th 1:8.

Impudent. Ezk 2:4.

Incontinent. 2 Tm 3:3.

Infidel. Pss 10:4; 14:1.

Loathsome. Pr 13:5.

Lovers of pleasure more than of God. 2
Tm 3:4.

Lying. Pss 58:3; 64:4. Is 59:4.

Mischievous. Pr 24:8. Mi 7:3.

Murderous. Pss 10:8; 94:6. Ro 1:29.

Prayerless. Jb 21:15. Ps 53:4.

Persecuting. Pss 69:26; 109:16.

Perverse. Dt 32:5.

Proud. Ps 59:12. Ob 1:3. 2 Tm 3:2.

Rejoicing in the affliction of saints. Ps
35:15.

Reprobate. 2 Co 13:5. 2 Tm 3:8. Ti
1:16.

Selfish. 2 Tm 3:2.

Sensual. Php 3:19. Jde 1:19.

Sold under sin. 1 K 21:20. 2 K 17:17.

Stiff-hearted. Ezk 2:4.

Stiff-necked. Ex 33:5. Ac 7:51.

Uncircumcised in heart. Jr 9:26. Ac 7:51.

Ungodly. Pr 16:27.

Unholy. 2 Tm 3:2.

Unjust. Pr 11:7. Is 26:10.

Unmerciful. Ro 1:31.

Unprofitable. Mt 25:30. Ro 3:12.

Unruly. Ti 1:10.

Unthankful. Lk 6:35. 2 Tm 3:2.

Untoward. Ac 2:40.

Unwise. Dt 32:6.

COMPARED TO

Abominable branches. Is 14:19.

Ashes under the feet. Ml 4:3.

Bad fishes. Mt 13:48.

Beasts. Ps 49:12. 2 P 2:12.

Blind men. Zp 1:17. Mt 15:14.

Brass and iron, etc. Jr 6:28. Ezk 22:18.

Briars and thorns. Is 55:13. Ezk 2:6.

Bulls of Bashan. Ps 22:12.

Carcasses trodden under feet. Is 14:19.

Chaff. Jb 21:18. Ps 1:4. Mt 3:12.

Clouds without water. Jde 1:12.

Corn blasted. 2 K 19:26.

Corrupt trees. Lk 6:43.

Deaf adders. Ps 58:4.

Dogs. Pr 26:11. Mt 7:6. 2 P 2:22.

Dross. Ps 119:119. Ezk 22:18–19.

Early dew. Ho 13:3.

Evil figs. Jr 24:8.

Fading oaks. Is 1:30.

Fiery oven. Ps 21:9. Ho 7:4.

Fire of thorns. Ps 118:12.

Fools building upon sand. Mt 7:26.

Fuel of fire. Is 9:19.

Garden without water. Is 1:30.

Goats. Mt 25:32.

Grass. Pss 37:2; 92:7.

Grass on the housetop. 2 K 19:26.

Green bay trees. Ps 37:35.

Green herbs. Ps 37:2.

Heath in the desert. Jr 17:6.

Horses rushing into the battle. Jr 8:6.

Idols. Ps 115:8.

Lions greedy of prey. Ps 17:12.

Melting wax. Ps 68:2.

Morning clouds. Ho 13:3.

Moth-eaten garments. Is 50:9; 51:8.

Passing whirlwinds. Pr 10:25.

Potsherds. Pr 26:23.

Raging waves of the sea. Jde 1:13.

Reprobate silver. Jr 6:30.

Scorpions. Ezk 2:6.

Serpents. Ps 58:4. Mt 23:33.

Smoke. Ho 13:3.

Stony ground. Mt 13:5.

Stubble. Jb 21:18. Ml 4:1.

Swine. Mt 7:6. 2 P 2:22.

Tares. Mt 13:38.

Troubled sea. Is 57:20.

Visions of the night. Jb 20:8.

Wandering stars. Jde 1:13.

Wayward children. Mt 11:16.

Wells without water. 2 P 2:17.

Wheels. Ps 83:13.

Whited sepulchres. Mt 23:27.

Wild ass's colts. Jb 11:12.

WIDOWS

Allowed to marry again. Ro 7:3.
Blessings on those who relieve. Dt 14:29.
Character of true. Lk 2:37. 1 Tm 5:5, 10.
Clothed in mourning after the death of husbands. Gn 38:14, 19. 2 S 14:2, 5.
Curse for perverting judgment of. Dt 27:19.
Exhorted to trust in God. Jr 49:11.
Frequently oppressed and persecuted. Jb 24:3. Ezk 22:7.

GOD

Establishes the border of. Pr 15:25.
Judges for. Dt 10:18. Ps 68:5.
Relieves. Ps 146:9.
Surely hears the cry of. Ex 22:23.
Will witness against oppressors of. Mt 3:5.

ILLUSTRATIVE OF

A desolate condition. Is 47:8–9.
Zion in captivity. Lm 1:1.
Increase of, threatened as a punishment. Ex 22:24. Jr 15:8; 18:21.
Instances of great liberality in. 1 K 17:9–15. Mk 12:42–43.
Intermarrying with by kings, considered treason. 1 K 2:21–24.

LAWS RESPECTING

Allowed to glean in fields and vineyards. Dt 24:19.
Bound to perform their vows. Nu 30:9.
Not to be oppressed. Ex 22:22. Dt 27:19.
Not to intermarry with priests. Lv 21:14.
Raiment not to be taken in pledge by creditors. Dt 24:17.
Share in public rejoicings. Dt 16:11, 14.
Share in the triennial tithe. Dt 14:28–29; 26:12–13.
When daughters of priests and childless, to partake of the holy things. Lv 22:13.
When left without children, to be married by their husband's nearest of kin. Dt 25:5–6. Ru 3:10–13, with 4:4–5. Mt 22:24–26.
Often devoted themselves entirely to God's service. Lk 2:37. 1 Tm 5:10.
Released from all obligation to former husbands. Ro 7:3.
Reproach connected with. Is 54:4.

SAINTS

Cause joy to. Jb 29:13.
Disappoint not. Jb 31:16.
Relieve. Ac 9:39.

SHOULD BE

Allowed to share in our blessings. Dt 14:29; 16:11, 14; 24:19–21.
Honored, if widows indeed. 1 Tm 5:3.
Pleaded for. Is 1:17.
Relieved by the church. Ac 6:1. 1 Tm 5:9.
Relieved by their friends. 1 Tm 5:4, 16.
Visited in affliction. Ja 1:27.

SHOULD NOT BE

Afflicted. Ex 22:22.
Deprived of raiment in pledge. Dt 24:17.
Oppressed. Jr 6:6. Zc 7:10.
Treated with violence. Jr 22:3.
Specially taken care of by the primitive church. Ac 6:1. 1 Tm 5:9.
Though poor, may be liberal. Mk 12:42–43.
A type of Zion in affliction. Lm 5:3.
Under the special protection of God. Dt 10:18. Ps 68:5.
When young, exposed to many temptations. 1 Tm 5:11–14.

THE WICKED

Do no good to. Jb 24:21.
Make a prey of. Is 10:2. Mt 23:14.
Reject the cause of. Is 1:23.
Send away empty. Jb 22:9.
Slay. Ps 94:6.
Take pledges from. Jb 24:3.
Vex. Ezk 22:7.
Woe to those who oppress. Is 10:1–2.

WIND

Accomplishes the purposes of God. Ps 148:8.
Drying nature of. Gn 8:1. Is 11:15.
Frequently brings rain. 1 K 18:44–45. (See also 2 K 3:17.)
From the north, drives away rain. Pr 25:23.

GOD

Assuages. Mt 8:26; 14:32.
Brings forth, out of his treasuries. Ps 135:7. Jr 10:13.
Changes. Ps 78:26.
Created. Am 4:14.
Gathers in his hand. Pr 30:4.
Raises. Ps 107:25. Jnh 4:8.
Restrains. Jb 28:25. Ps 107:29.

ILLUSTRATIVE OF

A course of sin (sowing). Ho 8:7.
Disappointed expectations (bringing forth). Is 26:18.
False doctrines Ep 4:14.
Iniquity which leads to destruction. Is 64:6.
The judgments of God (when destructive). Is 27:8; 29:6; 41:16.
The life of man. Jb 7:7.
Molten images. Is 41:29.

One who boasts of a false gift (when without rain). Pr 25:14.

The operations of the Holy Spirit. Ezk 37:9. Jn 3:8. Ac 2:2.

The speeches of the desperate. Jb 6:26.

Terrors which pursue the soul. Jb 30:15.

Vain hopes (feeding upon). Ho 12:1.

The wicked (as chaff or stubble before). Jb 21:18. Ps 1:4.

Its movement of the leaves noticed. Is 7:2. Mt 11:7. Rv 6:13.

MENTIONED IN SCRIPTURE

East. Jb 27:21. Ezk 17:10. Ho 13:15.

Euroclydon. Ac 27:14.

North. Pr 25:23. S S 4:16.

Simoon or pestilential wind. 2 S 19:7, with 35. Jr 4:11.

South. Jb 37:17. Lk 12:55.

West. Ex 10:19.

Whirlwind. Jb 37:9.

MIRACLES CONNECTED WITH

Calmed by casting out Jonah. Jnh 1:15.

Calmed by Christ. Mt 8:26; 14:32.

Locusts brought by. Ex 10:13.

Locusts removed by. Ex 10:19.

Quails brought by. Nu 11:31.

Raised on account of Jonah. Jnh 1:4.

Red Sea divided by. Ex 14:21.

Rocks and mountains rent by. 1 K 19:11.

Often blighting. Ps 103:16. Is 40:7.

Purifying nature of. Jb 37:21. Jr 4:11.

TEMPESTUOUS

Destroys houses. Jb 1:19. Mt 7:27.

Drives about the largest ships. Mt 14:24. Ac 27:18. Ja 3:4.

Raises the sea in waves. Ps 107:25. Jn 6:18.

Theory of, above man's comprehension. Jn 3:8.

Variable nature of. Ec 1:6.

WHEN VIOLENT, CALLED

Fierce. Ja 3:4.

Great and strong. 1 K 19:11.

Mighty. Ac 2:2. Rv 6:13.

Rough. Is 27:8.

Storm. Jb 21:18. Ps 83:15.

Stormy. Pss 55:8; 148:8. Ezk 13:11, 13.

Tempest. Jb 9:17; 27:20. Jnh 1:4.

WINE

An article of extensive commerce. Ezk 27:18.

CHARACTERIZED AS

Cheering God and man. Jg 9:13. Zc 9:17.

Gladdening the heart. Ps 104:15.

Making mirthful. Es 1:10. Ec 10:19.

Strengthening. 2 S 16:2. S S 2:5.

Consequence of putting (when new) into old bottles. Mk 2:22.

Custom of giving to persons in pain or suffering, mixed with drugs. Pr 31:6. Mk 15:23.

Custom of presenting to travelers. Gn 14:18. 1 S 25:18.

First fruits of, to be offered to God. Dt 18:4. 2 Ch 31:5.

First mention of. Gn 9:20–21.

First mode of making, noticed. Gn 40:11.

Forbidden to Nazarites during their separation. Nu 6:3.

Forbidden to the priests while engaged in the tabernacle. Lv 10:9.

Generally made by treading the grapes in a press. Ne 13:15. Is 63:2–3.

Given in abundance to the Jews when obedient. Ho 2:22. Jl 2:19, 24. Zc 9:17.

ILLUSTRATIVE OF

The abominations of the apostasy. Rv 17:2; 18:3.

The blessings of the gospel. Pr 9:2, 5. Is 25:6; 55:1.

The blood of Christ. Mt 26:27–29.

Violence and rapine. Pr 4:17.

The wrath and judgments of God. Pss 60:3; 75:8. Jr 13:12–14; 25:15–18.

Improved by age. Lk 5:39.

IN EXCESS

Forbidden. Ep 5:18.

Impairs the health. 1 S 25:37. Ho 4:11.

Impairs the judgment and memory. Pr 31:4–5. Is 28:7.

Inflames the passions. Is 5:11.

Infuriates the temper. Pr 20:1.

Leads to remorse. Pr 29:32.

Leads to sorrow and contention. Pr 23:29–30.

In times of scarcity, mixed with water. Is 1:22.

The Jews freqently deprived of, as a punishment. Is 24:7, 11. Ho 2:9. Jl 1:10. Hg 1:11; 2:16.

The Jews frequently drank to excess. Is 5:11. Jl 3:3. Am 6:6.

Kept in bottles. 1 S 25:18. Hk 2:15.

Love of Christ to be preferred to. S S 1:2, 4.

MADE OF

Juice of the grape. Gn 49:11.

Juice of the pomegranate. S S 8:2.

Many kinds of. Ne 5:18.

Never drunk by Rechabites. Jr 35:5–6.

Often spiced to increase its strength, etc. Pr 9:2, 5; 23:30.

PLACES CELEBRATED FOR
Assyria. 2 K 18:32. Is 36:17.
Canaan in general. Dt 33:28.
Helbon. Ezk 27:18.
Lebanon. Ho 14:17.
Moab. Is 16:8–10. Jr 48:32–33.
Possessions of Judah. Gn 49:8, 11–12.
Red, most esteemed. Pr 23:31. Is 27:2.
Refining of, alluded to. Is 25:6.
Sometimes mixed with milk as a beverage. S S 5:1.
Stored in cellars. 1 Ch 27:27.
Sweet, esteemed for flavor and strength. Is 49:26. Am 9:13. Mi 6:15.

USED
As a beverage from the earliest age. Gn 9:21; 27:25.
As a medicine. Lk 10:34. 1 Tm 5:23.
At all feasts and entertainments. Es 1:7; 5:6. Is 5:12. Dn 5:1–4. Jn 2:3.
For drink offerings in idolatrous worship. Dt 32:37–38.
For drink offerings in the worship of God. Ex 29:40. Nu 15:4–10.
Water miraculously turned into. Jn 2:9.
With corn and oil, denoted all temporal blessings. Gn 27:28, 37. Ps 4:7, Ho 2:8. Jl 2:19.

WINTER
God makes. Ps 74:17.
Illustrative of seasons of spiritual adversity. S S 2:11.
The Jews frequently had special houses for. Jr 36:22. Am 3:15.
Ships laid up in port during. Ac 27:9; 27:12; 28:11.
Unsuited for traveling. Mt 24:20. 2 Tm 4:21.
Yearly return of, secured by covenant. Gn 8:22.

WISDOM
NATURAL
Foolishness with God. 1 Co 3:19.
Not to be trusted. 1 Co 2:5.
SPIRITUAL
Begins with the fear of the Lord. Ps 111:10.
Granted those who ask. Ja 1:5.
Priceless. Pr 8:11.
Unknown by worldly leaders. 1 Co 2:7–8.

THAT OF CHRIST
Amazed men during his ministry. Lk 4:36.
Astonished men during his youth. Lk 2:47.
Increased with his years. Lk 2:52.
Should guide Christians. 1 Co 2:16. Php 2:5.

WISDOM OF GOD
All human wisdom derived from. Ezr 7:25.
DESCRIBED AS
Beyond human comprehension. Ps 139:6.
Incomparable. Is 44:7. Jr 10:7.
Infinite. Ps 147:5. Ro 11:33.
Mighty. Jb 36:5.
Perfect. Jb 36:4; 37:16.
Underived. Jb 21:22. Is 40:44.
Universal. Jb 28:24. Dn 2:22. Ac 15:18.
Unsearchable. Is 40:28. Ro 11:33.
Wonderful. Ps 139:6.
EXHIBITED IN
His counsels. Is 28:29. Jr 32:19.
His foreshowing events. Is 42:9; 46:10.
His works. Jb 37:16. Pss 104:24; 136:5. Pr 3:19. Jr 10:12.
Redemption. 1 Co 1:24. Ep 1:8; 3:10.
Searching the heart. 1 Ch 28:9. Rv 2:23.
Understanding the thoughts. 1 Ch 28:9. Ps 139:2.
EXHIBITED IN KNOWING
His saints. 2 S 7:20. 2 Tm 2:19.
The actions. Jb 34:21. Ps 139:2–3.
The afflictions of saints. Ex 3:7. Ps 142:3.
The heart. Ps 44:21. Pr 15:11. Lk 16:15.
The infirmities of saints. Ps 103:14.
The minutest matters. Mt 10:29–30.
The most secret things. Mt 6:18.
The time of judgment. Mt 24:36.
The wants of saints. Dt 2:7. Mt 6:8.
The way of saints. Jb 23:10. Ps 1:6.
The wicked. Ne 9:10. Jb 11:11.
The words. Ps 139:4.
The works of the wicked. Is 66:18.
The gospel contains treasures of. 1 Co 2:7.
Nothing concealed from. Ps 139:12.
One of his attributes. 1 S 2:3. Jb 9:4.
Saints ascribe to him. Dn 2.20.
Should be magnified. Ro 16:27. Jde 1:25.
The wicked question. Ps 73:11. Is 47:10.
Wisdom of saints derived from. Ezr 7:25.

WITNESS OF THE HOLY SPIRIT
Borne against all unbelievers. Ne 9:30. Ac 28:25–27.

BORNE TO CHRIST

As coming to redeem and sanctify. 1 Jn 5:6.

As exalted to be Prince and Savior to give repentance. Ac 5:31–32.

As foretold by himself. Jn 15:26.

As Messiah. Lk 3:22, with Jn 1:32–33.

As perfecting saints. He 10:14–15.

In heaven. 1 Jn 5:7, 11.

On earth. 1 Jn 5:8.

Faithful preaching of the apostles accompanied by. 1 Co 2:4. 1 Th 1:5.

First preaching of the gospel confirmed by. Ac 14:3, with He 2:4.

Is truth. 1 Jn 5:6.

GIVEN TO SAINTS

As an evidence of adoption. Ro 8:16.

As an evidence of Christ in them. 1 Jn 3:24.

As an evidence of God in them. 1 Jn 4:13.

On believing. Ac 15:8. 1 Jn 5:10.

To testify to them of Christ. Jn 15:26.

To be implicitly received. 1 Jn 5:6, 9.

WITNESSING
For Christ. Ac 1:8.

For God. Is 43:10.

In our worship. 1 Co 14:25.

We must always be ready for. 1 P 5:12.

WIVES
DUTIES OF, TO THEIR HUSBANDS

To be faithful to them. 1 Co 7:3–5, 10.

To be subject to them. Gn 3:16. Ep 5:22, 24. 1 P 3:1.

To love them. Ti 2:4.

To obey them. 1 Co 14:34. Ti 2:5.

To remain with them for life. Ro 7:2–3.

To reverence them. Ep 5:33.

GOOD

Are benevolent to the poor. Pr 31:20.

Are a blessing to husbands. Pr 12:4; 31:10, 12.

Are diligent and prudent. Pr 31:13–27.

Are from the Lord. Pr 19:14.

Are praised by husbands. Pr 31:28.

Are a token of the favor of God. Pr 18:22.

Bring honor on husbands. Pr 31:23.

Duty of, to unbelieving husbands. 1 Co 7:13–14, 16. 1 P 3:1–2.

Secure confidence of husbands. Pr 31:11.

Should be silent in the churches. 1 Co 14:34.

Not to be selected from among the ungodly. Gn 24:3; 26:34–35; 28:1.

Of ministers, should be exemplary. 1 Tm 3:11.

SHOULD BE ADORNED

Not with ornaments. 1 Tm 2:9. 1 P 3:3.

With good works. 1 Tm 2:10; 5:10.

With a meek and quiet spirit. 1 P 3:4–5.

With modesty and sobriety. 1 Tm 2:9.

Should seek religious instruction from their husbands. 1 Co 14:35.

WOLF
Destructive to flocks of sheep. Jn 10:12

ILLUSTRATIVE OF

The change effected by conversion (taming of). Is 11:6; 65:25.

The devil. Jn 10:12.

False teachers. Mt 7:15. Ac 20:29.

Fierce enemies. Jr 5:6. Hk 1:8.

The tribe of Benjamin. Gn 49:27.

The wicked. Mt 10:16. Lk 10:3.

Wicked rulers. Ezk 22:27. Zp 3:3.

Particularly fierce in the evening when it seeks its prey. Jr 5:6. Hk 1:8.

Rapacious nature of. Gn 49:27.

WOMAN
Allowed to join in the temple music from the time of David. 1 Ch 25:5–6. Ezr 2:65. Ne 7:67.

CHARACTERIZED AS

Loving and affectionate. 2 S 1:26.

Tender and constant to her offspring. Is 49:15. Lm 4:10.

Timid. Is 19:16. Jr 50:37; 51:30. Na 3:13.

Weaker than man. 1 P 3:7.

Considered a valuable booty in war. Dt 20:14. 1 S 30:2.

Curse pronounced on. Gn 3:16.

Deceived by Satan. Gn 3:1–6. 2 Co 11:3. 1 Tm 2:14.

Generally wore a veil in the presence of the other sex. Gn 24:65.

Good and virtuous, described, Pr 31:10–28.

Had a court of the tabernacle assigned to them. Ex 38:8. 1 S 2:22.

ILLUSTRATIVE OF

Apostasy (when lewd). Rv 17:4, 18.

Backsliding Israel (when delicate). Jr 6:2.

The church of Christ (when gloriously ar-

·rayed). Ps 45:13. Gl 4:26, with Rv 12:1.

The church of Israel in her captivity (when forsaken). Is 54:6.

Mere professors (when foolish). Mt 25:1–3.

Saints (when chaste and holy). S S 1:3. 2 Co 11:2. Rv 14:4.

Saints (when wise). Mt 25:1–2, 4.

A state of carnal security (when at ease and careless). Is 32:9, 11.

Led man to disobey God. Gn 3:6, 11–12.

OF DISTINCTION

Fair and graceful. Gn 12:11; 24:16. S S 1:8. Am 8:13.

Fond of dress and ornaments. Is 3:17–23.

Haughty in their deportment. Is 3:16.

Wore their hair plaited and adorned with gold and pearls. Is 3:24, with 1 Tm 2:9.

Of the poorer classes, swarthy from exposure to the sun. S S 1:5–6.

OFTEN ENGAGED IN

Agriculture. Ru 2:8. S S 1:6.

Attending funerals as mourners. Jr 9:17, 20.

Celebrating the victories of the nation. Ex 15:20–21. Jg 11:34. 1 S 18:6–7.

Domestic employments. Gn 18:6. Pr 31:15.

Drawing and carrying water. Gn 24:11, 13, 15–16. 1 S 9:11. Jn 4:7.

Embroidery. Pr 31:22.

Grinding corn. Mt 24:41. Lk 17:35.

Spinning. Pr 31:13–14.

Tending sheep. Gn 29:9. Ex 2:16.

Origin of name. Gn 2:23.

ORIGINALLY MADE

By God in his own image. Gn 1:27.

For man. 1 Co 11:9.

From one of Adam's ribs. Gn 2:21–22.

Subordinate to man. 1 Co 11:3.

To be the glory of man. 1 Co 11:7.

To be a helpmeet for man. Gn 2:18, 20.

Punishment for injuring, when with child. Ex 21:22–25.

Required to hear and obey the law. Jsh 8:35.

Safety in childbirth promised to the faithful and holy. 1 Tm 2:15.

SOMETIMES

Active in instigating to iniquity. Nu 31:15–16. 1 K 21:25. Ne 13:26.

Fond of self-indulgence. Is 32:9–11.

Lived in a separate apartment or tent. Gn 18:9; 24:67. Es 2:9, 11.

Silly and easily led into error. 2 Tm 3:6.

Subtle and deceitful. Pr 7:10. Ec 7:26.

Zealous in promoting superstition and idolatry. Jr 7:18. Ezk 13:17, 23.

Submissive and respectful to husband. 1 P 3:6, with Gn 18:12

To be governed by, considered a calamity by the Jews. Is 3:12.

To be slain by, considered a great disgrace. Jg 9:54.

To wear her hair long as a covering. 1 Co 11:15.

Unfaithfulness of, when married, found out by the waters of jealousy. Nu 5:14–28.

Virtuous, held in high estimation. Ru 3:11.

Vows of, when married, not binding upon the husband. Nu 30:6–8.

YOUNG

Called damsels. Gn 24:55. Mk 5:39.

Called maids. Ex 2:8. Lk 8:51–52.

Called virgins. Gn 24:16. Lm 1:4.

Could not marry without consent of parents. Gn 24:3–4; 34:6. Ex 22:17.

Fond of ornaments. Jr 2:32.

Gay and mirthsome. Jg 11:34; 21:21. Jr 31:13. Zc 9:17.

Inherited parents' property when there was no male heir. Nu 27:8.

Kind and courteous to strangers. Gn 24:17.

Not to be given in marriage, considered a calamity. Jg 11:37. Ps 78:63. Is 4:1.

Of distinction, dressed in robes of various colors. 2 S 13:18. Ps 45:14.

Often taken captive. Lm 1:18. Ezk 30:17–18.

Often treated with great cruelty in war. Dt 32:25. Lm 2:21; 5:11.

Punishment for seducing when betrothed. Dt 22:23–27.

Punishment for seducing when not betrothed. Ex 22:16–17. Dt 22:28–29.

Required to learn from and imitate their elders. Ti 2:4.

WORKS, GOOD

A blessing attends. Ja 1:25.

By Jesus Christ to the glory and praise of God. Php 1:11.

CALLED

Fruits meet for repentance. Mt 3:8.

Fruits of righteousness. Php 1:11.

Good fruits. Ja 3:17.

Works and labors of love. He 6:10.

Christ as an example of. Jn 10:32. Ac 10:38.
Designed to lead others to glorify God. Mt 5:16. 1 P 2:12.
God glorified by. Jn 15:8.
God remembers. Ne 13:14, with He 6:9–10.
Heavenly wisdom full of. Ja 3:17.
Holy women should manifest. 1 Tm 2:10; 5:10.
Illustrated. Jn 15:5.
In the judgment, will be an evidence of faith. Mt 25:34–40, Ja 2:14–20.
Justification unattainable by. Ro 3:20. Gl 2:16.

MINISTERS SHOULD
Be patterns of. Ti 2:7.
Exhort to. 1 Tm 6:17–18. Ti 3:1, 8, 14.

SAINTS
Are full of. Ac 9:36
Are zealous of. Ti 2:14.
Bring to the light their. Jn 3:21.
Created in Christ unto. Ep 2:10.
Exhorted to put on. Cl 3:12–14.
Followed into rest by their. Rv 14:13.
Should abound to all. 2 Co 9:8.
Should avoid ostentation in. Mt 6:1–18.
Should be careful to maintain. Ti 3:8, 14.
Should be established in. 2 Th 2:17
Should be fruitful in. Cl 1:10.
Should be furnished unto all. 2 Tm 3:17.
Should be perfect in. He 13:21.
Should be prepared unto all. 2 Tm 2:21.
Should be ready to all. Ti 3:1.
Should be rich in. 1 Tm 6:18.
Should be manifest, with meekness. Ja 3:13.
Should provoke each other to. He 10:24.

Salvation unattainable by. Ep 2:8–9. 2 Tm 1:9. Ti 3:5.
The scripture designed to lead us to. 2 Tm 3:16–17. Ja 1:25.
Shall be brought into the judgment. Ec 12:14, with 2 Co 5:10.
They alone who abide in Christ can perform. Jn 15:4–5.
To be performed in Christ's name. Cl 3:17.
The wicked reprobate unto. Ti 1:16.
Wrought by God in us. Is 26:12. Php 2:13.

WORSHIP
Commanded. Ex 34:14. Pss 95:6; 147:7–11.
EXAMPLES OF
All people. Ps 148:11–13.
All things. Ps 148:1–10.
Angels. Is 6:1–6. Lk 2:13. Rv 7:11–12.
Athenians. Ac 17:15–34.
Cain and Abel. Gn 4:1–16.
Heavenly beings. Rv 4:1–11.
Moses. Ex 3:5.
Multitudes. Rv 19:1–18.
The redeemed. Rv 15:3–4.
Solomon. 2 Ch 6:1–42.
Young and old. Ps 148:12–13.
Prophesied. Is 66:23.
TRUE
In spirit and in truth. Jn 4:24.
More than sacrifice desired. Ho 6:6.
What God wants. Mi 6:6–8.
VALUE OF
Convinces unbelievers. 1 Co 14:22–25.
Glorifies God. Ps 50:23.
Strengthens fellowship. Ac 2:42–47.

YZ ❧

YEARS

Commencement of, changed after the exodus. Ex 12:2.

DIVIDED INTO
Days. Gn 25:7. Es 9:27.
Months. Gn 7:11. 1 Ch 27:1.
Seasons. Gn 8:22.
Weeks. Dn 7:27. Lk 18:12.
Early computation of time by. Gn 5:3.

ILLUSTRATIVE OF
The dispensation of the gospel (acceptable). Is 61:2. Lk 4:19.
Judgments (of recompenses). Is 34:8.
Manhood (coming to). He 11:24.
Old age (being full of). Gn 25:8.
Old age (well stricken in). Lk 1:7.
Prosperity (of the right hand of the Most High). Ps 77:10.
Redemption by Christ (of the redeemed). Is 63:4.
Severe judgments (of visitation). Jr 11:23;23:12.
In prophetic computation, days reckoned as. Dn 12:11–12.
Length of, during the patriarchal age. Gn 7:11; 8:13, with Gn 7:24; 8:3.

REMARKABLE
Jubilee. Lv 25:11.
Sabbatical. Lv 25:4.
Sun and moon appointed to mark out. Gn 1:14.

YOUTH

Cleansing of. Ps 119:9.
Glory of. Pr 20:29.
Must be sober-minded. Ti 2:6.
No one should despise. 1 Tm 4:12.
Power of. 1 Jn 2:13.
Rejoice in. Ec 11:9
Renewed. Ps 103:5.
Shall see visions. Ac 2:17.
A time to remember the Creator. Ec 12:1.

ZEAL

Christ an example of. Ps 69:9. Jn 2:17.
Exhortation to. Ro 12:11. Rv 3:19.
Godly sorrow leads to. 2 Co 7:10–11.
Of saints. Ps 119:139.
Provokes others to do good. 2 Co 9:2.

SHOULD BE EXHIBITED
Against idolatry. 2 K 23:4–14.
For the glory of God. Nu 25:11, 13
For the welfare of saints. Cl 4:13.
In contending for the faith. Jde 1:3.
In desiring the salvation of others. Ac 26:29. Ro 10:1.
In missionary labors. Ro 15:19, 23.
In spirit. Ro 12:11.
In well-doing. Gl 4:18. Ti 2:14.
Sometimes not according to knowledge. Ro 10:2. Gl 1:14. Ac 21:20.
Sometimes wrongly directed. 2 S 21:2. Ac 22:3–4. Php 3:6.
Ungodly men sometimes pretend to. 2 K 10:16. Mt 23:15.